Critical Issues in Education

Dialogues and Dialectics

Critical Issues in Education

Dialogues and Dialectics

EIGHTH EDITION

Jack L. Nelson
Rutgers University

Stuart B. Palonsky
University of Missouri

Mary Rose McCarthy
Pace University

FOREWORD BY

Nel Noddings
Stanford University; Teachers College, Columbia University

The McGraw·Hill Companies

Connect
Learn
Succeed™

CRITICAL ISSUES IN EDUCATION, EIGHTH EDITION

Published by McGraw-Hill, a business unit of The McGraw-Hill Companies, Inc., 1221 Avenue of the Americas, New York, NY 10020. Copyright © 2013 by The McGraw-Hill Companies, Inc. All rights reserved. Printed in the United States of America. Previous editions © 2012, 2010, and 2007. No part of this publication may be reproduced or distributed in any form or by any means, or stored in a database or retrieval system, without the prior written consent of The McGraw-Hill Companies, Inc., including, but not limited to, in any network or other electronic storage or transmission, or broadcast for distance learning.

Some ancillaries, including electronic and print components, may not be available to customers outside the United States.

This book is printed on acid-free paper containing 10% postconsumer waste.

1 2 3 4 5 6 7 8 9 0 DOC/DOC 1 0 9 8 7 6 5 4 3 2

ISBN 978–0–07–802437–5
MHID 0–07–802437–4

Vice President & Editor-in-Chief: *Michael Ryan*
Publisher: *Michael Sugarman*
Senior Sponsoring Editor: *Debra B. Hash*
Marketing Coordinator: *Angela FitzPatrick*
Senior Project Manager: *Lisa A. Bruflodt*
Buyer: *Nicole Baumgartner*
Cover Designer: *Studio Montage, St. Louis, MO*
Cover Credit: *Nick Clements/Getty Images*
Typeface: *10/12 Palatino*
Compositor: *S4Carlisle Publishing Services*
Printer: *R. R. Donnelley*

All credits appearing on page or at the end of the book are considered to be an extension of the copyright page.

Library of Congress Cataloging-in-Publication Data

Nelson, Jack L.
Critical issues in education: dialogues and dialectics / Jack L. Nelson, Stuart B. Palonsky, Mary Rose McCarthy; foreword by Nel Noddings.—8th ed.
    p. cm.
    ISBN 978–0–07–802437–5 (pbk.)—ISBN 0–07–802437–4   1. Education—United States.
2. Teaching—United States.   3. Educational evaluation—United States.   4. Critical thinking—United States. I. Palonsky, Stuart B. II. McCarthy, Mary Rose, Ph. D. III. Title.

LA217.2.N45   2012
370.973—dc23

                                                    2012017615

www.mhhe.com

About the Authors

JACK L. NELSON is Professor Emeritus, Rutgers University Graduate School of Education. His teaching career includes experience at elementary and secondary school levels and tenured faculty positions at California State University, Los Angeles, and the State University of New York, Buffalo, before his thirty years at Rutgers. In the United States, he was a visiting scholar at the University of California, Berkeley; Stanford University; the University of Colorado; Colgate University; the City University of New York; and the University of Washington. In Great Britain, he was a visiting scholar for several years at Cambridge University and at Jordanhill College in Scotland. In Australia, he was a visiting scholar at the University of Sydney, Curtin University, Edith Cowan University, and the University of Queensland. His BA is from the University of Denver; MA from California State University, Los Angeles; and doctorate from the University of Southern California. *Critical Issues in Education* is his seventeenth book, and he has published almost 200 articles, chapters, and reviews in a variety of journals. His awards include citations from the American Association of University Professors and the National Council for the Social Studies. He is listed in *Contemporary Authors* and *Who's Who in America*.

STUART B. PALONSKY is professor of education and a member of the Honors College humanities faculty at the University of Missouri. He was graduated from the State University of New York, Oneonta, and Michigan State University. A former high school social studies teacher in New York and New Jersey, Palonsky taught reading and English to speakers of other languages while serving in the U.S. Army. His publications include the book *900 Shows a Year: A Look at Teaching from the Teacher's Side of the Desk*, an ethnographic account of high school teaching. Between 1991 and 2011, Palonsky was the director of MU's Honors College. Palonsky and Nelson were colleagues at Rutgers University and played tennis regularly, if not well.

MARY ROSE McCARTHY received her PhD from the State University of New York, Buffalo, in the social foundations of education with a concentration in the history of education. While at Buffalo, she was a presidential fellow and a member of the Buffalo Research Institute on Teacher Education. She is an associate professor in the School of Education at Pace University. Her research has provided the opportunity to develop historical perspectives from which to view current educational reforms. She finds the Depression-era dialectic particularly instructive in that effort. And she finds the absence of contemporary reformers who stress the possibility that education can change the world and not just the life chances of individuals particularly disturbing but not surprising. Among her experiences are periods as a secondary school teacher and administrator, director of a work cooperative for guests at a Catholic Worker House of Hospitality, and a family life educator for parents of at-risk children. Her publications include works on women's education, history of teacher education, students with disabilities, inclusive education, and desegregation of schools. Her current research interests include educational reform and progressive teacher education.

Brief Contents

Part Two
WHAT SHOULD BE TAUGHT?
KNOWLEDGE AND LITERACY

Part Three
THE SCHOOL COMMUNITY
INDIVIDUALS AND ENVIRONMENTS

Contents

Part Two
WHAT SHOULD BE TAUGHT?
KNOWLEDGE AND LITERACY

Part Three
THE SCHOOL COMMUNITY
INDIVIDUALS AND ENVIRONMENTS

Foreword

Can we teach students to think critically? Critical thinking is a goal much touted today. We live an age of ideology and uncritically held loyalties. Such an attitude is acceptable in, say, sports where we cheer for our favorite team through thick and thin. But it is an unhealthy way to approach politics, education, or religion. *Critical Issues in Education* provides some much-needed help with this task.

In this very welcome eighth edition, the authors tackle issues such as school finance, gender equity, multiculturalism, school reform, and a host of other controversial topics in education. They believe, as I do, that people learn to be critical thinkers by grappling with critical issues in public debate (Noddings, 2006). It is not enough to learn the formal rules of logic and argument; these must be put to use on genuine problems. Indeed, struggling with critical issues under the guidance of a good teacher may be the best way to learn the formal rules. That comment suggests a critical issue to think about in pedagogy: Should students be required to learn the basic rules, details of information, and algorithms before attempting to solve problems, or should they learn the rules in the process of problem solving? Should our answer differ, depending on the subject matter or age of students? Does it inevitably depend on the knowledge and skills of the teacher?

This edition also presents new material on the evaluation of teachers, cyberbullying, and lesbian, gay, and transgender issues. The authors have also extended their discussion of values and character education. These topics are loaded with critical issues.

Their new treatment of school privatization and commercialization is especially important today. Most citizens react with appreciation when business organizations take an interest in our public schools. But when is that interest educationally appropriate? How much influence should the Business Round-table and other corporate organizations have on public education? Perhaps criticisms and recommendations from these groups are too often accepted uncritically (Emery and Ohanian, 2004). We need to ask, Is the criticism well founded? Who profits from the recommendation? Where, if at all, do the aims of education and of business overlap?

Discipline is a topic of major interest to every teacher. We need to discuss methods and tactics critically. Educators are—or should be—accountable for means as well as ends. If, for example, a teacher maintains an orderly classroom, does it matter how she does it? Put so starkly, most of us would respond that of course it matters. What methods are ethically justified? What tactics contribute to the growth of democratic character? How far should schools go in monitoring students' behavior outside of school? Cyberbullying is a growing problem educators must face.

These matters require critical thought. When we encounter discipline problems, there is a temptation to seize any tactic that promises a solution. We sometimes forget to ask, Why are we having this problem? Too often, a faculty leaps to the conclusion that there is "something wrong with these kids"—and sometimes that conclusion is right, but often it is not.

When I was a high school mathematics teacher (more than thirty years ago), kids did not swear in class (and never at the teacher), listened in class (or pretended to), and usually did their homework. Were kids better then? Do students now need character education—perhaps uniforms, ceremonies, and consistent patterns of reward and punishment? Maybe. But consider. At that time, there were no security guards in most schools, no locked exits, no metal detectors. A little earlier—when I was myself a high school student—we had a full hour for lunch and could go where we wished; we had the same teachers for four years in many of our subjects; we knew instantly, in our small school, when a stranger was on campus. Perhaps it is *conditions* and not kids that have changed. If that is the case, how should we proceed to analyze our discipline problems?

I am not suggesting that character education should be rejected out of hand. There is much of value in it. But exactly *what* should we borrow from it? Why should we engage in it? What outcomes can we reasonably expect? And how should we try to reach them? George Orwell (1981) said of his own school days (crammed with character education of a highly questionable sort), "I was in a world where it was *not possible* for me to be good. . . . Life was more terrible, and I was more wicked, than I had imagined" (p. 5). Educators must make it both desirable and possible for students to be good. How might the conditions of schooling be changed to support this goal?

The updated chapter on immigration and education is timely. Immigration has, once again, become a hot-button issue in politics and social life. We are conflicted about how to handle legal and illegal immigration with justice and fairness while protecting our borders and continuing our tradition as a nation of immigrants. The topic is crucial in today's schools. How can schools welcome children and help them to learn when some state governments are frightening families away?

The discussion of critical issues is difficult—an enterprise littered with opportunities to attack persons instead of arguments. We human beings have not yet learned how to conduct these discussions effectively. In private social life, we generally avoid topics that might trigger passionate disagreement. It is not considered polite to talk critically about religion or politics. In schools, too, we usually avoid controversial issues (Noddings, 2012), and this avoidance is supported by the careful vetting (censoring?) of school textbooks.

Rejecting the "war model" of debate, we have to learn how to participate intelligently and respectfully in critical discussions. *Critical Issues in Education* makes a significant contribution to the achievement of this goal.

Finally, it is worth repeating something I've said in my forewords to earlier editions: as you read this book, be ready to think and speak up but be gentle with your opponents.

Nel Noddings
Stanford University

References

EMERY, K., AND OHANIAN, S. (2004). *Why Is Corporate America Bashing Our Public Schools?* Portsmouth, NH: Heinemann.

NODDINGS, N. (2006). *Critical Lessons: What Our Schools Might Teach but Do Not.* Cambridge: Cambridge University Press.

————. (2012). *Peace Education: How We Come to Love and Hate War.* Cambridge: Cambridge University Press.

ORWELL, G. (1981). *A Collection of Essays.* San Diego: Harcourt Brace.

Preface

Greetings

Welcome to the eighth edition of *Critical Issues in Education*, a complete revision with updating and rewriting. Each chapter offers two original, competing sides of pervasive controversies about schooling. Evidence, expert opinion, and arguments are provided for each side to stimulate critical thinking about school in contemporary society. We encourage your exploration and critical engagement.

School is controversial. You might think that sex, politics, and religion are the only hot topics for debate, while school may be seen as tranquil and bland—but education ranks up high on the list of strongly held beliefs and equally strong contrary views. Just ask an assortment of relatives and friends what they think of American schools and be ready to hear arguments. Actually, school issues incorporate the hotter topics of sex, politics and religion:

- Sex education, gender bias, and gay/lesbian treatment are examples of in-school issues.
- Politics in and over education include power plays for influence, battles about economics and finance, and combat over school reform efforts.
- The role of religion in education has been a controversy for more than a century.

School and Controversies

Persistent school issues reflect ideological disagreements in areas like politics, economics, and social values. Newspapers and magazines report educational information like student test scores, school finance decisions, and various school activities. But mass media often ignore or gloss over basic social or ideological conflicts that lie below the surface of the news. And news media can sterilize issues by presenting only one view. Few media provide alternative views of an issue. This implies that there is only one correct view on a topic, and it obscures important distinctions surrounding school controversies.

For over 300 years, people on this continent have agreed on the importance of education but have disagreed over how it should be controlled, financed, organized, conducted, and evaluated. Over two centuries ago, a very young United States was debating whether to establish free and compulsory education, arguing over who should be educated, who should pay, and what should be taught. We have mass public education now, but some of these same arguments continue about schools.

Some say that American schools are in deep trouble and getting worse, with poor teachers and weak programs of study. Others view their schools as remarkably good, with excellent teachers and high-quality programs. New views emerge as debates over education stimulate us to rethink our positions. The terrain of education is rugged and rocky, with few clear paths and many conflicting road signs. It is controversial.

Organization of the Book

An introductory chapter presents background and a process for examining debates in education and reform efforts.

The three following sections are each devoted to a major question about schooling and provide a thematic context:

Part One: Whose Interests Should Schools Serve? Theme: Justice and Equity

Part Two: What Should Be Taught? Theme: Knowledge and Literacy

Part Three: The School Community. Theme: Individuals and Environments

Each part contains chapters on specific critical issues, and each chapter contains two essays expressing divergent positions on that issue. Obviously, these do not exhaust all the possible positions; they do provide at least two views on the issue. References are provided in each chapter to encourage further exploration. At the end of each chapter are a few questions to consider and discuss.

The three coauthors each took primary responsibility for writing different parts of this volume. For Jack Nelson, this includes the Introductions to Part One and Part Two and Chapters 1, 4, 10, 12, 15, and 17. For Stuart Palonsky, it includes the Introduction to Part Three and Chapters 8, 11, 14, and 16. And for Mary Rose McCarthy, it includes Chapters 5, 6, 9, and 13. Stu and Jack jointly prepared Chapter 7, with assistance from Valerie Pang.

Acknowledgments

We thank Nel Noddings of Stanford University and Teachers College, Columbia University, for her stimulating foreword.

We thank colleagues and reviewers who made many suggestions for this revision. We received particularly valuable suggestions from a variety of faculty members and students who have used this book in one or more of its seven previous editions. Thanks to them for their important contributions.

We owe great intellectual debts to a long list of scholars, writers, teachers, and others who examine education and society and who express divergent ideas in the extensive literature available. This includes a variety of educational and social theorists and critics as well as a corps of school practitioners who live the life of schools. We also are indebted to students, colleagues, and others who provided specific criticism and assistance as we worked through the various topics. In particular, we express appreciation to Allison McNamara, our primary editor at McGraw-Hill, and the McGraw-Hill education editor.

We owe special thanks to Gwen, Nancy, and Ken for their support, enthusiasm, and criticism when needed.

Many colleagues have reviewed the manuscript of this edition, given us good criticism as the work progressed, or provided provocative ideas to challenge us along the way. We thank them for their help and suggestions. Among these are John B. Aston, Southwest Texas State University; Paul Bash, Oceanside/Vinaka Debates; Pat Benne, Wittenberg University; Richard Berkau, Vinaka Debates; David Blacker, University of Delaware; Deron R. Boyles, Georgia State University; General David Brahms, Vinaka Debates; Wade A. Carpenter, Berry College; Mark Caruana, attorney, Carlsbad, California; David Cauble, Western Nebraska Community College; Cathryn A. Chappell, University of Akron; John Cline, Carlsbad–Vinaka Debates; Linda T. Coats, Mississippi State University; Jorge Correa, Mount Berry College; Diane Crews, Binghamton University; Frances P. Crocker, Lenoir Rhyne College; Warren Crown, Rutgers University; James Daly, Seton Hall University; Emily de la Cruz, Portland State University; Russell Dennis, Bucknell University; Xu Di, University of West Florida; Annette Digby, University of Arkansas; Kathleen A. Dolgos, Kutztown University; Beverly Durham, school reform advocate, Fishers, Indiana; Gloria Earl, Indiana Wesleyan University; Herbert Edwards, attorney, Harbor Springs, Michigan; Paul Edwards, attorney, Colorado Springs, Colorado; William and Sheila Fernekes, Hunterdon, New Jersey, Central High School; Albert Finocchio, Emeritus, St. Bonaventure University; Mark Garrison, D'Youville College; William Gaudelli III, Teachers College, Columbia University; Karen Graves, Denison University; Harry D. Hall, Indiana Wesleyan University; Julia O. Harper, Azusa Pacific University; Warren R. Heydenberk, Lehigh University; Robert Higgins, Curator Emeritus, Smithsonian Institution and University of North Carolina, Asheville; Sharon Hobbs, Montana State University; Michael Imber, University of Kansas; Mary Ann Isberg, artist-in-residence, Denver, Colorado; Evelyn Jirgal, Vinaka Debates; Chris Johnson, University of Arizona; Tony W. Johnson, West Chester University; Jean Ketter, Grinnell College; Ramon Khalona, engineer and technological consultant, Carlsbad, California; Nancy Knipping, University of Missouri; Robert Lawrence, musical theorist, Vinaka/Carlsbad Debates, Joslen Letscher, University of Detroit–Mercy; Becky Lewis, State University College at Geneseo; Charles Love, University of South Carolina–Upstate; Stephen Earl Lucas, University of Illinois, Urbana-Champaign; Chogallah Maroufi, California State University at Los Angeles; Gary E. Martin, Northern Arizona University; Cornelia McCarthy, State University of New York Maritime College; Joseph McCarthy, Suffolk University;

Barbara Bredefeld Meyer, Illinois State University; David Michels, Carlsbad–Vinaka Debates; Wally Moroz, Edith Cowan University, Perth, Australia; Maxine G. Morris, Missouri Southern State University; John D. Napier, University of Georgia; Nel Noddings, Stanford University; Julie R. Palmour, Piedmont College; Valerie Pang, San Diego State University; Nancy Patterson, Bowling Green State University; Maike Philipsen, Virginia Commonwealth University; Kel Phillipson, website designer and technical director, London, England; Yasmeen Qadri, University of Central Florida; Adah Ward Randolph, Ohio University; Christopher Roellke, Vassar College; Bonnie Rose, Riverside City Schools, California; Betty Sauer, Palo Alto Schools; Dawn Shinew, Washington State University; Barbara R. Sjostrom, Rowan University; Leslie Soodak, Pace University; William Stanley, Monmouth University; Colonel Robert Stoffey, Vinaka Debates; Susan Talburt, Georgia State University; Ronald K. Templeton, The Citadel; Doris Terr, City Schools of New York; Daniel Tierney, actor and moderator, Vinaka/Carlsbad Debates; Atilano Valencia, California State University, Fresno; John Vernon, engineering craftsman, Del Mar, California; Mark Vollmer, Senior Consultant, Conexus, Brisbane, Australia; Burt Weltman, William Paterson College; and David and Janelle Wiedemann, political analysis consultants, Centennial, Colorado.

We dedicate this effort to Meg, Kel, Jordan, Warwick, Jonathan, Skyler, Olwyn, Megan, Jasmyn, Conall Barbara, Mark, Steven, Kim, Robert, Mary Catherine, and others of the generations of students and teachers who are at the center of critical education issues in this twenty-first century.

Jack L. Nelson

Stuart B. Palonsky

Mary Rose McCarthy

CHAPTER 1

Introduction: Critical Issues and Critical Thinking

About This Book: Significant controversies deserve critical thinking. Schools are controversial because they are so important. This book presents debates over sixteen pervasive educational issues, in Chapters 2 through 17, organized under three thematic sections:

Part One: Whose Interests Should Schools Serve?

Theme: Justice and Equity

Part Two: What Should Be Taught?

Theme: Knowledge and Literacy

Part Three: The School Community

Theme: Individuals and Environments

Each chapter contains two original essays presenting divergent positions on that topic. These position essays include data, research, and arguments that support that view of the issue. We advocate critical thinking about these topics, thinking that includes reasoned consideration of divergent views (Ennis, 2011; Hess, 2011, 2012; Brookfield, 2012).

About This Chapter: Chapter 1 introduces ideas about critical thinking using dialogue and dialectic reasoning; and the chapter includes information about some of the historic, philosophic, political, and social contexts that surround current school controversies. Since school criticism and reform efforts flow from these issues, we offer some examples. Issues do not arise in a vacuum, nor are all criticisms and reforms equally valid or positive. Welcome to this exchange of ideas.

EDUCATION AS CONTROVERSY

It [education] is also, like democracy itself, loose, shaggy, and inefficient, full of redundancies and conflicting goals. . . . But by the fundamental test of attractiveness to students and their families, the system—which is one of the world's most ethnically diverse and decentralized—is, as a whole, succeeding.

—Lemann (2010, p. 1)

What would it take to generate significant improvement in American schooling? The current path forward is not going to take us there. Expectations far outstrip performance.

—Mehta (2011, p. 1)

If you like arguments, you will love the study of education. Few topics elicit more disagreement or have as much at stake for our future. Even if you don't like arguments, your life and our society are influenced by the debates and the resulting decisions. Arguments over education seldom challenge a broad agreement on its value. There is strong support for education. We disagree over the purposes, nature, form, and process but not on its fundamental virtues. That still provides plenty of opportunities for bitter fights.

Current controversies about schools and schooling include the increasing role of the federal government in school policy, how to measure school and teacher quality, the relative value of charter schools and public versus private education, teacher unions and contracts, student bullies and discipline, school funding, what is taught and how, and a host of local and state issues that arise on an almost daily basis.

For one example, federal legislation, like the No Child Left Behind Act of 2002 and the Race to the Top funds provided in the American Recovery and Reinvestment Act of 2009 expand the federal role and funding in what has been a state and local activity. These laws offer carrots of funds and sticks of penalties to prod school districts and states to change school policies and operations. They set national standards and accountability, increase testing, and challenge traditional ways of schools. Critics contend that these laws have not produced remarkable improvements in schools or student achievement and that they do the following:

- Grossly underfund mandates and impose unreimbursed costs on schools
- Misevaluate education by excessive reliance on testing
- Limit curriculum and local decision making
- Unnecessarily punish schools for social problems, like poverty
- Force teachers and students into conformity
- Restrict critical thinking
- Expand federal intervention into a state responsibility

(See Meier and Wood, 2004; American Federation of Teachers, 2005; McKenzie, 2006, 2007; National Education Association, 2006; Sunderman, 2006; Ravitch, 2007, 2010; Nichols and Berliner, 2008; Science News, 2008; Spring, 2008).

Another example of school arguments involves the teaching of evolution and creationism (Johnson, 2006; Rudoren, 2006; Scott, 2009; Hallowell, 2011), a school and social issue since Darwin. The Scopes trial illustrated this over eighty years ago, and the effort to place intelligent design in the science curriculum carries the controversy forward into the twenty-first century. Intelligent design, a variation of the creationist position, challenges Darwinian theories on natural selection and evolution (see www.intelligentdesignnetwork.org). Evolutionists find there is no credible scientific evidence that is better than evolutionary theory and that religious beliefs should not overwhelm science.

The intelligent design position is expressed in publications (Behe, Dembski, and Meyer, 2000; Dembski, 2004; Strobel, 2004; House, 2008; www.uncommon descent.com). The opposition appears in other sources (Perakh, 2003; Forrest and Gross, 2004; Young and Edis, 2004; Hitchens, 2007; Coyne, 2009; Dawkins, 2009; Scott, 2009).

Jacoby (2008) states,

> Americans are alone in the developed world in their view of evolution by means of natural selection as "controversial" rather than as settled mainstream science. The continuing strength of religious fundamentalism in America (again, unique in the developed world) is generally cited as the sole reason for the bizarre persistence of anti-evolutionism. . . . The real and more complex explanation may lie not in America's brand of faith but in the public's ignorance about science in general as well as evolution in particular. (p. xvii)

Recent national research shows that a majority of U.S. high school biology teachers avoid or limit teaching about evolution, presumably because it is so controversial (Berkman and Plutzer, 2010). The Texas State Board of Education still devotes interest to an effort to add creationism to the science curriculum (Hallowell, 2011).

Obviously, what we teach in schools is a reflection of what we consider true, accurate, consistent, and reasoned. This controversy is larger than a minor question of specific information taught in some science classes; it reflects deeper social conflicts between religion and science and church and state, among divergent social values, about academic freedom for teachers and students, and regarding the nature of knowledge and the core purposes of education. Sloan-Lynch (2010), in a philosophical treatise, states, "Democratic schools should teach those beliefs most likely to be true and impart the guiding principles of scientific investigation" (p. 119).

Disputes over federal laws and evolution/creationism illustrate strident school debates involving deeply held views from politics to religion. If school was inconsequential, it would not be worthy of intense, long-lived disputes. Education is not a trivial pursuit. It is necessary for the survival and development of each person and society. Strong opinions define many controversial topics, but schooling is unusual because few controversial topics have so many personally experienced experts. School is one social institution that virtually all people have experienced for long periods, and most have an opinion about it. So we argue about education and the formal agency we use for education—the schools.

Education and Schooling

Education, of course, is far more than just what goes on in school. But schools are usually at the center of public arguments about education because schools are the social organizations that take on the formalized task of educating. In colonial America, most people received their education outside of schools (Bailyn, 1960). Some of today's reluctant students might prefer that alternative to their life in school, but that is not an option available to many. For these students, school may even be an impediment to education—it interferes with their learning about life. They become educated despite school.

For the vast majority, however, much of the most important learning—and certainly most of the formal learning—occurs in school. Book and computer learning are hallmarks of schools, and society expects schools to remain that central learning location for academic knowledge. In addition to academics, there is an expectation that school also will be a place of intellectual development. Intellectual learning differs from academic learning in its development of skeptical and questioning attitudes and its focus on ideas rather than on information (Gella, 1976; Gouldner, 1979; Barber, 1998; Schneider, 2004; Jacoby, 2008). Academic learning includes formal study of typical subjects: English, science, history, arts, math, social sciences, languages, and so on. Intellectual learning includes raising questions, critical thinking, creative interpretation, and being unlimited by subject-field discipline boundaries in the examination of ideas. Some people become concerned when schools heavily engage in intellectual learning; open examination of ideas and skepticism can lead to controversial topics—a threat to some.

In addition to academic and intellectual responsibilities of schools, there are also social expectations for schools to take on responsibility for the ethical, physical, and emotional development of children as well as for their safety, health, and civility. Academic, intellectual, practical, moral, and behavioral responsibilities have long been multiple foci of schools. Schools have accepted some responsibility for addressing such social problems as drugs, sexual mores, incivility, bullying, and crime. For several decades, we have had proposals for making schools even more the centers of their communities, open all year, seven days a week, early morning to late night, and taking on more social responsibilities (Dryfoos, 2002; Strike, 2004).

The significance of these responsibilities is suggested in the strength and intensity of the great debates over schools. In today's world, those who can't read, write, or calculate adequately bear a heavy burden in daily existence. Those lacking fundamental knowledge and skills suffer social, economic, political, and personal difficulty. The society that does not pay enough attention to schooling also suffers; it is on a downhill slope (Fuentes, 2005).

Nolan (1996) notes,

> Of all the issues that are likely to generate controversy, no issue hits closer to home than the education and care of children. A cursory glance at many of the most heated issues in the culture wars reveals just how pivotal education is.

Multiculturalism, sex education, condom distribution, guns in school, textbook selection, creationism, values clarification—controversies over these issues demonstrate how educational institutions have become a primary focus of the culture wars . . . the battle over the schools then is nothing less than a struggle for the future of America. (p. 37)

Some of the continuing questions about education, schools, and society:

- How should we evaluate schools, teachers, curricula, and society's support of schools?
- How should we address problems of inequality, racism, sexual discrimination, and violence in schools?
- Who should be going to school, for how long, to study what, and for what purposes?
- How should schools be financed, and how well?
- What is the best approach to religion, values, character, and academic subjects for schools?
- How should schools be organized and operated?
- Why do we seem clueless about the best education when there are plenty of clues and firm opinions about it?

Cycles of criticism and reform in education are not new (Cuban, 2003). We have had educational reform advocates for so long that it is impossible to identify their beginnings. Perhaps the first educational reformer, a member of some prehistoric group, rose up to protest that children were not learning the basic skills as he had. Another member may have proposed a radical new plan to improve children's hunting-and-gathering skills. Some of the bashed skulls lying about prehistoric sites are probably the results of arguments over education.

Critical Thinking, Dialogue, and Dialectics

Questions about schooling stimulate a variety of potential and often competing answers, but there is no single set of clear and uncontested resolutions. Life would be easier (although less interesting) if we had single and simple answers to all our problems. But critical social issues are usually too complex to be adequately resolved by easy or absolute solutions. In fact, simple answers often create new problems or merely cause the problems they were supposed to solve to rise again. Research shows that problem-based learning is a rich and comprehensive way to gain understanding, whether or not clear answers emerge. For many, it is far better than lecture-based education (Wirkala and Kuhn, 2011; Brookfield, 2012).

Quick, easy, and absolute resolutions are readily available in contemporary society—radio talk shows, newspaper editorials and responses, websites and chat rooms, and coffee shops are among the places where we can find clear and forceful answers to most of our problems, including educational issues. These answers may be simple, clear, and forceful—but often will be contradictory, competing, or inconsistent. Significant debates over complicated human issues such as sex, politics, and religion are engaging partly because they usually are not subject to quick and easy resolution.

A proper skepticism and critical thinking are the friends of wisdom. Critical thinking, the main process and goal of education, involves at least the following:

- Recognition that an important issue deserves considered judgment
- Thoughtful formulation of good questions
- A search for possible answers and evaluating pertinent evidence
- Consideration of alternative views and competing evidence
- Drawing of tentative conclusions that are acceptable until another question or a better answer arises

Critical thinking is far more difficult—and significantly more important—than just finding answers (Emerson, Boes, and Mosteller, 2002; Kincheloe and Weil, 2004; Shermer, 2011). The search for knowledge goes well beyond puzzle pages with answers printed upside down at the bottom or reporting back to a teacher what an encyclopedia says. Dialogue and dialectics can help.

Dialogue and the Case for Dialectic Reasoning

Arguments easily can dissolve into shouting matches or even fistfights. Whether arguments are trivial or significant, they can be heated and unthinking. It is easy to recognize the merits of our own position, and we are not always eager to admit the virtues of others. Arguments about important topics, however, should not devolve into shouting or personal attack. Knowledge and social improvement depend on rational and civil argument: "Disagreement is a key element of communal deliberations" (Makau and Marty, 2001, p. 7). Active democracy requires it (Gutmann and Thompson, 1996, 2004; Hess, 2002; Zurn, 2007). Good arguments can be thoughtful and reasoned, a dialogue between two different points of view—or dialectic reasoning with opposing views.

Dialogue calls for two persons or two ideas—we can have dialogue with ourselves, but we need at least two ideas. Monologues, to others or ourselves, can be valuable for gaining ideas; most textbooks operate as monologues, presenting one view. But dialogue is more dynamic and more challenging. Not all dialogue, however, is civil and productive. It can operate at the lowest level, used to browbeat others into agreement, as in a kind of Socratic attack. Noddings (1995b) notes, "Socrates himself taught by engaging others in dialogue . . . he dominates the dialogue and leads the listeners . . . forcing his listeners gently and not so gently to see the errors in their thinking" (pp. 6, 7). But reasoned dialogue involves active consideration of a different view and interest in interaction (Mercer, 2008; National Coalition for Dialogue and Deliberation, 2008). We advocate informed skepticism, using reasoned dialogue in examining educational issues—but we go further, encouraging development of a dialectic approach for some issues in the search for improvement in education.

Reasoned dialogue calls for listening, understanding evidence, and assessing the quality of sources and persuasiveness of the arguments (Audi, 2001; McCabe, 2000). Dialectic reasoning, the examination of opposing ideas to develop a creative and superior idea, is a level beyond dialogue (Sim, 1999; Farrar, 2000; Sciabarra, 2000). Both are practices of critical thinking.

Dialogue and dialectic are dynamic, interactive, and optimistic. They are optimistic since they take the stance that things can and should be improved. Arguments are not the only way to reason. Intuition, for example, is perfectly suitable, as is reading and contemplation.

Dialogue does not expect much beyond civil discussion to gain understanding. Dialectic reasoning uses disputes and divergent opinions to arrive at a better idea. The dialectic occurs when you pit one argument (thesis) against another (antithesis) in an effort to develop a synthesis superior to either (see Figure 1.1). It is an inquiry into important issues that identifies the main points, important evidence, and logical arguments used by each of at least two divergent views on an issue. This requires critical examination of the evidence and arguments on each side of a dispute, granting each side some credibility. A dialectic approach is dynamic. A synthesis from one level of dialectic reasoning can become a new thesis at a more sophisticated level, and the process of inquiry continues to spiral (Adler, 1927; Cooper, 1967; Rychlak, 1976; Noddings, 1995b; Blumenfeld-Jones, 2004). True inquiry is lifelong.

The purpose for dialectic reasoning between competing ideas is not to defeat one and accept the other but rather to search for an improved idea. Dialectic reasoning is not merely the search to certify one side as a winner or to find a political compromise, especially a compromise that pleases neither side very well. It is a search for a higher level of idea that accommodates or incorporates

FIGURE 1.1 Dialectic Reasoning: A Simplified Diagram

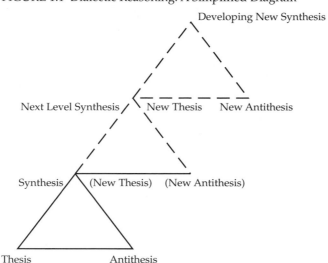

the most important points in the thesis and antithesis. Sciabarra (2000) describes the dialectic process as follows:

> Dialectical method is neither dualistic nor monistic. A thinker who employs a dialectic method embraces neither a pole nor the middle of a duality of extremes. Rather, the dialectical method anchors the thinker to both camps.
>
> The dialectic thinker refuses to recognize these camps as mutually exclusive or apparent opposites. . . . He or she strives to uncover the common roots of apparent opposites . . . [and] presents an integrated alternative. (p. 16)

For a simple example on a complicated topic, many early philosophers considered individual freedom and social freedom as opposites (Marcuse, 1960). One could enjoy individual freedom only by trampling on social freedoms, and a society could exert its freedom only by limiting the freedom of individuals. One was a thesis, the other its antithesis—apparently opposite views. A synthesis develops as both freedoms are considered necessary to modern civilization and to individuals, using the view that individual freedoms are best maintained in a free society. Without society, humans have no freedom in practice; there is no freedom in mere survival. Without individual freedoms, society cannot be free in practice; the range of individual freedom depends on agreement with other individuals in a social contract requiring essential equality, a system of laws, and rational thinking.

Philosophers have used the idea of dialectics in many different ways; it has justified opposite radical conclusions like absolute social control, as in forms of Marxism, or absolute individualism and against society, as in some of the libertarian ideas of Ayn Rand (Sciabarra, 1999). But Aristotle, the moderate philosopher who initiated Western political philosophy, could be considered the father of dialectic reasoning. He saw dialectic and rhetoric as mutually supportive arts, with dialectic the logical means for developing arguments and rhetoric the means of persuasion, speaking or writing, that uses the results of dialectic reasoning. Aristotle favored the dialectic because it required examining serious questions from many different positions.

The dialectic approach is fundamentally optimistic: it assumes that there are better ideas for improving society and that examining diverse ideas is a productive way to develop them. Many issues can't resolve well into a synthesis at any given time, but that does not denigrate the dialectic approach as a good way to comprehend and critically examine opposing positions. Dialectic reasoning may require more energy than you think necessary for some of the educational issues in this book, and dialogue will be perfectly satisfactory. The dialectic process, though, is a valuable tool for considering knotty social problems. It offers a means for depersonalizing various strongly held opinions to strive for a common good in improving schools (Van Emeren and GootenHorst, 2003; Caranfa, 2004). As with most educative practices, it is not the finding of predetermined right answers but rather the process of thinking that is most important. A right answer is good for solving a single problem, but a good process is useful for many problems.

Dialogues and dialectics don't necessarily lead to truth; they can merely repeat errors and bias. Thus, we advocate a healthy, informed skepticism in examining these disputes. In the ancient Greek tradition, skepticism meant to raising questions about reasons, evidence, and arguments (Sim, 1999; Wright, 2001; Shermer, 2011). Skepticism is not simply doubt, despair, or cynicism; it is intelligent inquiry. Without skepticism, we easily can fall into "complacent self-deception and dogmatism"; with it, we can "effectively advance the frontiers of inquiry and knowledge," applying this knowledge to "practical life, ethics, and politics" (Kurtz, 1992, p. 9). Dialogues and dialectics on educational issues, with prudent skepticism, are thoughtful forms of inquiry (McLaren and Houston, 2004; Van Luchene, 2004).

A TRADITION OF SCHOOL CRITICISM AND REFORM

From the intensity and vigor of public debate over schooling, a debate in Western society at least since the time of Socrates, one would expect either dramatic changes in schools or their abolition in favor of an alternative structure. One of the two accusations leveled against Socrates in the indictment that brought him to trial and brought on his suicide was "corruption of the young." Socrates may have paid the ultimate price for being an educational reformer in a political setting that was not ready for his reforms. At least one critic has argued to abolish schools (Illich, 1971), and some have proposed revolutionary changes in schooling (Sinclair, 1924; Rafferty, 1968; Apple, 1990). Most changes have been moderate, however, and no radical attempts have succeeded.

Some school purposes are commonly accepted, such as distributing knowledge and providing opportunity, but controversies arise over what knowledge we should distribute, which children should get which opportunities, and who should be making these decisions. For more than 3,000 years, human societies have recognized the value of education—and argued about what the goal of schooling should be and how to achieve it (Ulich, 1954).

Shifts in criticism and efforts at reform are common in U.S. educational history (Cremin, 1961; Welter, 1962; Karier, 1967; Tyack, 1967; Katz, 1971; Ravitch, 2000, 2010; Cuban, 2003; Ross and Gibson, 2006), but schools actually change only modestly. Some critics change views as things develop. David Mamet, a controversial playwright who espoused generally liberal ideas in his early works, has become highly critical of liberalism and the "liberal media." And he thinks education goes too far in teaching multiculturalism, diversity, social justice, and sex education—which, he claims, are topics that are "simply none of their business." His view is that schools should only teach to read and write and expose students to "documents and principles which *unite* us as a nation" (Mamet, 2011, p. 201). Controversial social topics and critical thinking are not on his newest agenda for schools.

Diane Ravitch, on the other hand, was notable as a critic of progressive ideas and as a traditionalist activist in a high level position in the U.S. Department of Education over a decade ago. But she now publicly and actively opposes much of the traditionalist reform of the recent past and its unfortunate results in schools (Ravitch, 2000, 2010). Her schooling agenda now, presumably, would include, even require, social issues and critical thinking. Traditional and progressive agendas differ; schools respond by moving very gradually in one direction with a few widely publicized examples of reform and then await the next movement. Kaestle (1985) notes that the "real school system is more like a huge tanker going down the middle of a channel, rocking a bit from side to side as it attends to one slight current and then to another" (p. 423).

School Reform in Early Twentieth-Century America

The United States has a long tradition of innovation in education, stemming from its pioneer role in providing mass education at public expense. There are some major failures in this history, most notably the lack of equal educational opportunities for African Americans, Native Americans, women, immigrants, and those of lower income. We have, however, expanded education as a means for developing democracy and offering some social mobility. We may not realize these ambitions, and our real intentions may be less altruistic (Katz, 1968). But idealization of democratic reform through education is an American tradition.

American schools, from the nineteenth century, were expected to blend immigrants into the American mainstream through compulsory education on such subjects as English, American history, and civics. A history of racism, sexism, and ethnic prejudice was commonly ignored in American social life and schools while we labored under the myth that everyone shared a happy society who should all talk, think, and form values the same way. Schools were a primary social agency to meld students from divergent cultural backgrounds into the American ideal, which, unsurprisingly, exhibited European, white, male characteristics and values. English language and belief in the superiority of Western literature, history, politics, and economics dominated the schools. Schools were key institutions in "Americanizing" generations of immigrants.

In the early twentieth century, urbanization and industrialization created the need for different forms of school services. Large numbers of children from the working classes were in schools in urban areas, and the traditional classical curriculum, teaching methods, and leisure-class approach stumbled. Extensive development of vocational and technical courses was the most dominant change in schooling before World War I, as school activities broadened to include medical exams, health instruction, free lunch programs, schools open during vacation periods for working parents, and other community services. These reforms fit the evolving sense of social progressivism (Jacoby, 2008). The progressive education movement, from about 1920 to World War II, incorporated severe criticisms of traditional schooling ideas and such practices as corporal punishment, rigid discipline, rote memorization and drill, stress on the classics, and high failure rates.

Progressives advocated engaging in practical experiences and projects, community activities, study of controversial topics, practicing democracy in the schools, and study of social problems. Schools became more open to students of all classes, and the curriculum moved from more esoteric studies to courses with social applications, such as home economics, business and vocational education, current events, health, sociology, sex education, and consumer math. Sporadic criticisms of progressive thought cropped up throughout that time, but a reform movement from traditionalists gained public interest near the end of the Depression and again following World War II. Graham (1967), summarizing the shift, states,

> Sometime between 1919 and 1955 the phrase "progressive education" shifted from a term of praise to one of opprobrium. To the American public of 1919, progressive education meant all that was good in education; thirty-five years later nearly all the ills in American education were blamed on it. (p. 145)

Gurney Chambers (1948) notes that after the 1929 stock market crash, education came under attack: "Teachers were rebuked for their complacency and inertia, and progressive schools, surprisingly enough, were blamed for the increasing crime and divorce rates and political corruption" (pp. 142–143).

Jacoby (2008), writing about the history of anti-intellectualism in America, states, "Ironically, the denigration of professional educators did not really take hold until the middle of the twentieth century . . . in the eighteenth and nineteenth centuries . . . the hiring of a schoolmaster was one of the two fundamental markers of civilization in frontier communities (the other being the presence of a minister)" (p. xvi).

Cycles of Educational Reform after World War II

Attacks on schools increased in intensity and frequency during the late 1940s and 1950s. The great school debates of this time involved many issues that extend into the twenty-first century. Church-state issues, including school prayer and use of public funds for religious education and other school services, gained significance. Racial issues, with the landmark Supreme Court decision in *Brown v. Board of Education of Topeka* (1954) and forced busing, became another focus of school controversy. Rapidly increasing tax burdens to pay for new schools and teachers required by the baby boom aroused protests from many school critics. Rising expectations for education were driven by the thousands of "non-college-prep" veterans who went to college on the GI Bill. Curricular issues, including disputes over the most effective way to teach reading and over test scores showing students did not know enough history or math or science or English, filled the popular press.

Politically, the McCarthy period "Red Scare" produced rampant public fear of a creeping communistic influence in American life and created suspicions that schools were breeding grounds for "communal" and progressive thought. These and other factors led to renewed criticism of schools. For many, there was simply a lingering sense that schools were not doing their job. Two books illustrate the criticisms of this period: Albert Lynd's (1950) *Quackery in the Public Schools* and Arthur Bestor's (1953) *Educational Wastelands*. Each attacked progressive education and the "educationists" who advocated it for turning schools from traditional discipline and subject knowledge toward the "felt needs" of children. As historian Clarence Karier (1985) notes, "The educationist who spoke out for 'progressive education' and 'life adjustment education' appeared increasingly out of place in the postwar, cold war period" (p. 238).

Major foundations examined America's schools. The Ford Foundation made education a focal point. Grants were made to the Educational Testing Service to improve measures of student performance. The Carnegie Foundation asked James Bryant Conant, former president of Harvard and U.S. ambassador to West Germany, to conduct a series of studies of public education. There was much public criticism of the academic failures of American schools. The Soviet launch of *Sputnik* in 1957, ahead of the United States, gave a new focus for educational reform. *Sputnik* was a highly visible catalyst for conservative critics, illustrating a lack of American competitiveness that they attributed to progressive reforms in schools during the pre–World War II period. Critics blamed the "permissive" atmosphere in schools for this deficiency.

Excellence and Its Discontents: Post-**Sputnik**

Post-*Sputnik* reform included a reinstitution of rigor, discipline, traditional subject teaching, and standards. They added up to the theme, to be repeated in the 1980s, of "excellence." There are remarkable similarities in the language and rationales used in the earlier reform movement and those used in the 1980s efforts to return schools to traditional work. International competition, advancing technology, and the needs of business are rationales cited in the literature of both periods.

Excellence, ill defined and excessively used, is a cue word that shows up in many reports and statements from both periods. Gardner's (1958) *The Pursuit of Excellence: Education and the Future of America*, is one illustration. Another term common to both periods is *mediocrity*, a threat suggested in the title of Mortimer Smith's (1954) book *The Diminished Mind: A Study of Planned Mediocrity in Our Public Schools*.

Conant's (1958) report, *The American High School Today*, was a moderate book that proposed a standard secondary school curriculum, tracking by ability group, special courses for gifted students, improvements in English composition, better counseling, and other recommendations. Federal funds for reform were increased in the late 1950s and early 1960s. The National Defense Education Act responded to pleas that schools were key to providing "national defense" and that *Sputnik* showed that the United States was militarily vulnerable. Funds to improve teaching in science and math, foreign languages, social studies, and English encouraged university scholars in each field to determine better ways to convey the subject matter; many projects attempted to make the curriculum "teacherproof" (as in foolproof) to prevent classroom teachers from teaching it incorrectly. Teacher education came in for its share of criticism, with blasts at teachers' colleges, the progressive techniques they advocated, and the quality of students going into teaching. This all sounds hauntingly familiar to those who read current educational criticism.

As the trend toward conservative educational ideas gained support and school practice turned back to standards and "rigor," criticism from the left began to emerge. This liberal criticism was a response to the rote memorization, excessive testing, lockstep schooling, and increased school dropout and failure rates that began to characterize schools. Paul Goodman, George Dennison, Edgar Z. Friedenberg, A. S. Neill in England, Nat Hentoff, John Holt, Herbert Kohl, and Jonathan Kozol attacked schools for their sterility, bureaucracy, boredom, lack of creativity, rigidity, powerlessness of students and teachers, and inadequacy in educating disadvantaged youth. Holt (1964) stated,

> Most children in school fail. . . . They fail because they are afraid, bored, and confused . . . bored because the things they are given and told to do in school are so trivial, so dull, and make such limited and narrow demands on the wide spectrum of their intelligence, capabilities, and talents. . . . Schools should be a place where children learn what they want to know, instead of what we think they ought to know. (pp. xiii, xiv, 174)

This 1960s liberal reform rebelled against conservative authoritarianism and the dehumanization of schools. Reforms included open education, nongraded schools, more student freedom, more electives, less reliance on standardized tests, abolition of dress codes and rigid rules, and more teacher-student equality. The Vietnam War and demonstrations spurred the politics that stimulated much of the late 1960s educational reform literature.

Multicultural education was not on the educational agenda in early America because mass schooling was supposed to produce a melting pot where various cultural strands were blended into the "new American." The civil rights movement in the 1950s and 1960s showed that the melting pot thesis about American society was a myth. This led to other approaches to diversity and unity. One was separatism, where each major subcultural group would go its own way with separate social and school structures. Another was an effort to reconstitute a form of the melting pot by enforcing integration in such institutions as housing, restaurants, and schools. Integration often led to resegregation by white flight and establishment of private all-white academies. Multicultural education, which aimed to recognize positive contributions of a variety of national, racial, ethnic, gender, and other groups to American life, developed as a way to recognize both diversity and unity.

The multicultural effort intended to correct a century of schooling that featured white male American or European heroes from the middle and upper social classes. African American, Latino, and women authors now showed up on lists of standard readings in English classes. The societal contributions of Native Americans, blacks, Chicanos, and females were added to history and civics books. Equal physical education opportunities for boys and girls, compensatory education for the disadvantaged, and programs featuring minority and women role models were developed.

Traditionalism Revisited: The 1980s and Beyond

In the early 1980s, reports of falling SAT and ACT scores, drug abuse, vandalism, and chaos in schools increased public receptivity to traditionalist reform. Nervousness about international competition, resurgence of business and technology as dominant features of society, and questions about shifting morality and values provided a political setting that blamed schools for inadequacies. The presidentially appointed National Commission on Excellence in Education (1983) published a highly political document, *A Nation at Risk*, which claimed that there was a "rising tide of mediocrity" in schools. Ensuing public debate produced a flurry of legislation to develop "excellence" by increasing the competitive nature of schooling and testable standards.

Student protests of the 1960s died, and a negative reaction set in. "Yuppies" (young upwardly mobile professionals) emerged as role models for student style in the 1980s, embracing careerism and corporate fashion. There was an increasing perception of disarray in the American family and a return to religion for many. Open confrontation with communism subsided as the Iron Curtain collapsed in the late 1980s. Anticommunism, a major influence on conservative educational reform since the 1920s, was replaced by the War on Drugs and character education. Schools were blamed for social ills and challenges to traditional values, and they were expected to respond to these strains by suddenly becoming academically excellent and moralistic.

Foundations and individual critics again undertook the study of schools. These include generally conservative reports from the Twentieth Century Fund (1983), the College Entrance Examination Board (1983), and the National Science Foundation (1983) as well as Mortimer Adler's (1982) *The Paideia Proposal*. The more liberal works included John Goodlad's (1983) *A Place Called School* and Theodore Sizer's (1984) *Horace's Compromise*. Ernest Boyer's (1983) moderate *High School* for the Carnegie Foundation also was popular.

States pumped up school financing until the 1990s recession, and state officials, having enacted myriad new regulations governing school matters, began claiming some credit for educational change (*Results in Education*, 1990; *The Education Reform Decade*, 1990; Webster and McMillin, 1991). In the main, jawboning by the federal government and increased regulatory activity in the states produced little in the way of dramatic change, but many adjustments were undertaken. Most underlying social problems—for example, poverty, family disruption, discrimination, and economic imbalance—worsened during the 1980s, and schools suffer the continuing effects. In the 1990s, the focus of educational criticism and reform shifted from state regulation and test score worries to more diverse views of the national influence on local schools, school choice, curriculum control, at-risk students, restructuring schools for school-based management, teacher empowerment, parental involvement, and shared decision making. These ideas are potentially conflicting, some leading to increased centralization and others leading to increased decentralization.

Into the twenty-first century, the idea of replacing the traditional canons of literature and social thought with modern multicultural material engendered other battles framed within the "culture wars." Finn (1990b) and Ravitch (1990), former high officials of the U.S. Department of Education, argue for teaching traditional content emphasizing unified American views rather than diverse views from segments of society. The Organization of American Historians, however, supports the teaching of non-Western culture and diversity in schools (Winkler, 1991). Camille Paglia (1990), arguing against feminist positions, says that her work "accepts the canonical Western tradition and rejects the modernist idea that culture has collapsed into meaningless fragments" (p. xii). This battle also emerged when Stanford University's faculty debated whether to substitute modern literature for traditional in its basic course, when New York State social studies curriculum revision for multicultural content aroused a firestorm, and when English-only resolutions were adopted by state legislatures.

Other arguments over multicultural education linked it with politically correct speech in schools (*National Review*, 1990; D'Souza, 1991; *The Progressive*, 1991; Winkler, 1991; Banks, 1995). "Politically correct" speech, defined as speech that does not denigrate any minority group, gender, or sexual preference, attracts protest because it is equivalent to censorship, stifling free expression. Protecting civil rights to free speech appeared to be at odds with protecting the civility of schools and protecting the "multiculturally diverse" from enduring negative comments. The argument against politically correct speech is that the free marketplace of ideas requires free speech, not courteous speech, and the best response to epithets and slurs is reasoned argument and public disapproval. Although few are open advocates of politically correct regulations in schools, many would like to find a way to limit racist and sexist comments and graffiti. School is an obvious battleground for this issue.

Another continuing issue is the use and abuse of technology in schools (Oppenheimer, 2003). Through the search for knowledge, we develop faster and more comprehensive systems of communication, travel, and research—which then require faster and more comprehensive systems of education to comprehend and extend that knowledge. Doheny-Farina (1996), discussing the coming of virtual society and virtual schools, cites the argument that "distance education will become the norm, the least expensive way to deliver the educational product, while face-to-face teaching will be only for the well-to-do"(p. 108). He concludes, however, that "most of those [distance learning] materials will be in the form of prescribed packages, which over time will tend to centralize expertise" and that "the virtualization of school removes it from the fabric of the local community" (pp. 110, 116, 117). Educational theorist Michael Apple (1994; Bromley and Apple, 2002) claims that distance learning de-skills teachers, making them switch-turners and simple conduits for other people's ideas and procedures. That will destroy the central characteristic of democratic education: the freedom to learn and to teach.

In the United States, we are reform minded about all aspects of society, and, as in our views on schools, we hold widely disparate views on what societal changes we need to make. Historian David Tyack (1991), discussing the intertwining of school reform with social reform, says, "For over a century and a half, Americans have translated their cultural anxieties and hopes into demands for educational reform" (p. 1).

Evaluation of 1980s Reforms

There is general agreement that results of reform efforts have been mixed. No clear evidence indicates that the reforms have significantly changed education. Analyses of the 1980s school reform show great diversity (Giroux, 1989; Finn, 1990a; *U.S. News and World Report*, 1990; Darling-Hammond, 1991; Fiske, 1991; Moynihan, 1991; Safire, 1991; *New York Times*, 1992). Ideological chasms appear among the analysts as they try to explain why the reforms did not seem to work and what should be done now. Stories about drugs, shootings, and gang violence around schools compete with news articles stating that American students can't read, are ignorant in math and science, and fail tests of common knowledge in history and geography (Holt, 1964; *Newsweek*, 1989; Hawley, 1990; Novak, 1990).

Critics (Bastian et al., 1985; Presseisen, 1985; Giroux, 1988a) charge that the 1980s school reform movement was dominated by mainstream conservative thought. This conservative agenda includes standardization, more testing, a return to basics, implanting patriotic values, increased regulation, more homework for students, less student freedom, renewed emphasis on dress codes and socially acceptable behavior for students and teachers, stricter discipline, and teacher accountability.

From a liberal/progressive view, schools are defective because they are too standardized, excessively competitive, and too factory-like. Students are measured and sorted in an assembly-line atmosphere where social class, gender, and race determine which students get which treatments. Teachers are deprofessionalized and treated as servile workers. Critical thinking is punished; one kind of curriculum or classroom instruction fits all. Creativity and joy are excluded from the school lexicon because education is supposed to be hard, dreary, boring work (McLaren, 1989; Purpel, 1989; Fisher, 1991; Nathan, 1991; Sacks, 1999; Wraga, 2001; Schoenfeld, 2002). Making schools active, pleasant, student oriented, critical, and sensitive to social problems is the reform they advocate.

Educational researchers David Berliner and Bruce Biddle (1995) present test scores, international school finance data, and various other indicators of achievement and support, and they conclude that school critics are mistaken or uninformed. They discount critics' assertions that student achievement and teacher quality have declined and that schools are failing society. Berliner and Biddle summarize their analysis with the response that "these assertions are errant nonsense" (p. 13), and they conclude that "American education has recently been subjected to an unwarranted, vigorous, and damaging attack—a

Manufactured Crisis . . . the major claims of the attack turn out to have been myths; the Manufactured Crisis was revealed as a Big Lie" (p. 343).

Conservative school reform was, however, the main influence on schooling in the United States at the end of the twentieth century. Proposals and action for school change include academically tougher schools, vouchers, charter schools, rigorous standards and more testing, more discipline, privatized management, and training in moral behavior.

Liberal and radical ideas for schools did not disappear (Fullen, 2000; Bracey, 2002b; Giroux, 2004). Teacher empowerment, academic freedom, student rights, limiting testing, providing student choice, and active social criticism and participation are ideas percolating in school reform to come. Reconstructionist ideas placing schools at the center of social change have not been entirely forgotten in the current surge of literature on schools and reform. William Stanley (1992, 2001) rethinks social reconstructionism and examines key ideas from the critical pedagogy movement to offer educational possibilities for the twenty-first century. His focus on practical reasoning provides critical examination of social issues and stimulates positive social action.

Continuing Debates over Schooling

Humans have long argued about what knowledge children should learn, how they should behave, and who should teach them. Basic subjects like reading and mathematics instruction are often at the eye of the hurricane because of their importance in the ongoing lives of students and their future prospects. Reading has long been the focus of debates over phonics and whole-language instruction, though often it is a more ideological and political issue than merely finding the best way to teach (Coles, 2003; *Kappan*, 2001). Arguments over the best approaches to mathematical literacy have included "civil rights" questions (Moses and Cobb, 2001) as well as competing ideologies in curricular reform that Schoenfeld (2002) claims "gave rise to the math wars and catalyzed the existence of what is in essence a neo-conservative back-to-basics movement. This way lies madness" (p. 22). Nearly all subject fields have experienced the same problems in finding stability in seas of change dependent on ideological and political contexts. They present a bewildering array of educational ideas, from left-wing, right-wing, moderate, and radical positions.

The Changing Focus of Debates

In the early twenty-first century, public debate over education changed from a primary focus on crisis, hand-wringing, and derisive blame to arguments over which political candidate offers more financial support, smaller classes, and better facilities and teachers to schools. The 1980s competition to bash schools and teachers has been partially replaced by a public affirmation that the future of schools and of society are intertwined. Serious disagreements, of course, continue on most school topics, and we still get teacher bashing on occasion. The general tenor of the debates, however, has shifted from castigation and condemnation to diverse proposals for funding, accountability, standards, and specific corrective action. Finance problems may derail most reforms. There are still sharply negative criticisms of the current state of schooling, but more moderate voices are more common in the schooling debates of 2010–2020.

The 1983 claim that schools were floating on a "rising tide of mediocrity," had put the nation at risk, and were responsible for declining American values and economic competitiveness was followed by different analyses of the same kinds of data from 1980 to 2010 indicating that schools were not as bad as this (Bracey, 1992, 1994, 1995, 1997, 1998, 2002a; Berliner, 1993; Berliner and Biddle, 1995; Lemann, 2010). The politics of bashing schools and teachers, however, benefits politicians seeking an issue. The politics of school critique and governmental or privatization intervention for reform are attention getting, and politicians find schools an excellent target. This means more attention paid to school failures than to school successes.

Nocera (2011), who normally discusses politics and economics in the *New York Times*, presented an essay on education and school reform that summarizes the situation: "Demonizing teachers for the failures of poor students, and pretending that reforming the schools is all that is needed, as the reformers tend to do, is both misguided and counterproductive" (p. A25).

Public Ratings of Schools

One of the most surprising things about the extremely negative school criticism between 1980 and now is that public rating of public schools has remained consistently high. Even with negative publicity about schools, survey evidence shows that public rating of *local* public schools actually has been positive (and often increasingly so) for over a quarter of a century. The annual Phi Delta Kappa/Gallup Poll has surveyed the public since 1974. In 1992, the poll showed the largest one-year increase in the grades people give their local public schools in almost two decades, from 40 percent grading their schools A or B in 1992 to 47 percent rating them that high in 1993 (Elam et al., 1993). In 1998, the annual poll showed that 46 percent of all respondents gave their local schools an A or B, and 52 percent of public school parents gave their children's schools an A or B grade (Rose and Gallup, 1998). The poll of 2001 found that a majority (51 percent) of the public gives public schools an A or B rating, and 62 percent of parents with children in public schools rate them A or B (Rose and Gallup, 2001, 2007). Those closest to the schools rate them much better than media reports would suggest (Rose and Gallup, 2005, 2007; Gallup, 2011).

Ironically, people rate their own local schools significantly higher than they rate schools across the nation (only 20 percent in 1998 and 23 percent in 2001 give the nation's schools an A or B). For the school their oldest children attended, the rating is very high (about 80 percent rating them A or B). Gallup interpreted these data to suggest that the more the public knows about actual practices in schools, the better they rate them. The data also indicate that negative publicity from political and media treatment of schooling influences the way people grade other schools they know the least.

Decreasing negative criticism of schools might suggest that school reforms in the past fifteen years have been successful, but that would be a misreading. No clear evidence exists about each set of reforms and their consequences; outcomes are still in dispute. Although many claims surround specific reforms, few comprehensive studies show that any school is significantly better or worse now as a result of reforms. Since recent evidence shows schools were never as bad as government and media reported, one could make the case that some reforms actually hindered school progress by improperly blaming and alienating teachers and by forcing more testing and governmental intervention in school requirements and operations. The current concept of school accountability leads to more testing and probably more hand-wringing, as test scores do not satisfy the critics.

Public schools get good ratings from their closest observers, and schools in the United States are rated by the public higher than many other institutions of American society. Even though local schools are well received, schooling remains one of the most controversial topics in society. Schools benefit from good criticism, but the evidence should suggest that we maintain a level of skepticism about some negative media reports and political statements about schools.

Although polls continue to show general public support of local schools, most of us can identify one or more areas needing correction. Impatient or burned-out teachers, cloddish administrators, frazzled counselors, and outdated textbooks and curricula are examples. Most of us know the virtues as well as the warts and blemishes of schools from our direct personal experience. Some critics propose quick and simplistic reforms to improve schools. Fortunately, most people understand that change in schooling is more complex and that potential consequences of change need more thought.

Reformers see schools as either the cause of some problem or part of the cure. We are led to believe that schools can solve major social problems, such as racism, sexism, automobile accidents, AIDS, teenage pregnancy, and drugs. Reform has not been especially productive in student achievement, curing social ills, intellectual development, or student and public happiness about schools. Yet the arguments over reform have helped air ideological and political baggage that weighs on the reforms. Perhaps there is a better word than *reform* to use in discussing school improvement. Reform school was the institution where young social deviants and juvenile criminals were sent; "reform schools" seems a strange phrasing in that context.

Ravitch (2010) apparently has recognized that much of the current reform movement has gone in the wrong direction, but there are a complex of forces that continue to claim that there is a crisis in education and often blame teachers and, more particularly, teacher unions with or without evidence. Rothstein (2011), in a critical essay review, describes some of that effort.

THE POLITICAL CONTEXT OF SCHOOLING

Education has emerged again as one of the most highly charged areas in political contests. Candidates offer clean, neat, and simple answers to long-term school problems with often inconsistent messages about schools:

- Improve test scores but also cut school expenses.
- Repair buildings but also lower taxes.
- Allow more local control but impose more national standards and support.
- Educate against violence and drug abuse but also teach only the basics.
- Improve sex education but do not teach values in school.
- Make teachers more accountable but give teachers more freedom and responsibility.
- Increase distance learning by computers but also increase daily school time and the school year.
- Increase school competition for grades and awards but make schools more collaborative, inclusive, and supportive.

School debates can be schizophrenic. Theodore Sizer said, "Everybody is for high test scores till their kids get low test scores" (Bronner, 1998). It is easy to claim that our own education was vastly superior to what students now get in school and to advocate a return to the good old days. But how many would actually want their children to return to the reality and limitations of yesterday's schools?

The political nature of educational debates is illustrated by actions surrounding the Sandia Report on schools just a decade ago. The government suppressed for two years a major government-sponsored study showing that U.S. schools were better than the first Bush administration wanted to divulge. The Sandia Report showed that U.S. schools were far better than government and influential media were reporting. "Much of the 'crisis' commentary today claims total system-wide failure in education. Our research shows that this is simply not true" (Carson, Huelskamp, and Woodall, 1992, p. 99).

Schools are both political agencies and handy targets from every side of party politics. Schools consume more local budget money than any other social agency and are among the top consumers of state funds. Schools are a major responsibility under state legislation and local control, subjecting them to political pressures both from those in office and those vying to be.

EDUCATIONAL CRITICISM
AND DEMOCRATIC VITALITY

Critics of schools are easy to find. People are not bashful about noting school problems but disagree over what is wrong, who is responsible, and what should be done to change schools. Of all social institutions in a democracy, the school should be the most ready for examination; education rests on critical assessment and reassessment. That does not mean that all criticism is justified or even useful. Some of it is simplistic, mean-spirited, or wrongheadedly arrogant. But much of it is thoughtful and cogent. Although some unjustified criticism can be detrimental to education in a democracy, open debate can permit the best ideas to percolate, to be developed and revised, and to be evaluated (DeWiel, 2000; Hess, 2012).

Over the long haul, schooling has improved, and civilization has been served by the debates over education. More people get more education of a better quality across the world now than in previous generations. Despite periodic lapses and declines, the global movement toward increased and improved schooling for more students continues. The debates force us to reconsider ideas about schooling and increase our sophistication about schools and society.

Democratic vitality and educational criticism are good companions. Democracy, as Thomas Jefferson so wisely noted, requires an enlightened public and free dissent. Education is the primary means to enlightenment and to thoughtful dissent. It follows that schools would be among those fundamental social institutions under continuing public criticism in a society striving to improve its democracy:

- Alexis de Tocqueville (1848/1969) introduced his classic study of democracy in the very young United States by stating,

    The first duty imposed on those who now direct society is to educate democracy; to put, if possible, new life into its beliefs. (p. 12)

- Bertrand Russell (1928) noted that education is basic to democracy:

    It is in itself desirable to be able to read and write . . . an ignorant population is a disgrace to a civilized country, and . . . democracy is impossible without education. (p. 128)

- John Dewey (1916) put schools at the center of democracy:

    The devotion of democracy to education is a familiar fact . . . a democratic society repudiates the principle of external authority, it must find a substitute in voluntary disposition and interest; these can only be created by education. (p. 87)

Both democratic vitality and educational criticism require open expression of diverse ideas, yet both are based on an optimistic sense of unity of purpose. Diverse ideas and criticism provide necessary tests of our ideas. Criticism easily can appear to be negative, pessimistic, or cynical, but these are not its only forms. Informed skepticism, the purpose for this book, offers a more optimistic view without becoming like Pollyanna. Diverse ideas are sought because we think, optimistically, that education can be improved. Unity of purpose suggests that there is a bedrock of agreement on basic values, the criteria against which to judge diverse ideas. Without diverse ideas, there is no vitality and opportunity for progress; without unity of purpose, diverse ideas can be chaotic and irrational.

Global Democratization and Purposes of Education

In these first two decades of the twenty-first century, school remains the most common approach to education around the world. Schools for children of the elite classes have existed since ancient times, but mass education in schools is a relatively recent global phenomenon. Although it is essentially a twentieth-century development, mass schooling has become dominant worldwide as democracy has become the dominant global trend in governments. But democratization is not always positive and progressive. Shapiro and Macedo (2000) pose the kind of problems that confront societies and their schools in developing democratic life:

> The principles and practices of democracy continue to spread even more widely, and it is hard to imagine that there is a corner of the globe into which they will not penetrate. But the euphoria of democratic revolutions is typically short-lived, and its attainment seems typically to be followed by disgruntlement and even cynicism about the actual operation of democratic institutions. . . . Of course, it is far easier to perceive the need for reform than to prescribe specific proposals. (p. 1)

Garforth (1980) points out, "Undoubtedly, democracy at its best is a great educative force, but . . . it is not immune from dishonesty, corruption, and the betrayal of truth" (p. 20). Democratization brings the need for mass schooling and critical literacy (Torres, 2002). Dictatorship seems to work better with less education for the general public, but miseducation of the public in a democracy is dysfunctional. A strong democracy requires a critical citizenry, a public capable of engaging in critical thinking. Critical citizens depend on critical education (Norris, 1999; Winthrop, 2000; Giroux, 2004; Schweber, 2012). This is a significant concern for the United States, where democracy and mass education are well developed and supported; it is even more significant for nations where these traditions are weaker.

Global Dimensions of Education

Public and private schools are the social institutions organized to provide formal education in modern nations, involving nearly all the student-age populations. Wealthier nations provide and require schooling for the largest proportion of children for the longest period, but less wealthy nations have rapidly increased primary school education and are moving to expand secondary and higher education opportunities for more students. In 1950, only 16 percent of the world's students of high school age were in secondary schools, and 3 percent of age-related students were in colleges. By 2000, over 34 percent of high school–age students around the world were in secondary schools and 8 percent of the age-related students were in college. Figure 1.2 shows the global effort to educate (UNESCO, 2005; U.S. Census Bureau, 2008, 2010).

The schools of the world now employ about 80 million teachers, making up the world's largest professional occupation. Finding adequate resources to support these teachers and operate schools is a major global issue. The United Nations has undertaken a significant role in improving education and treatment of children. International treaties and conventions on education indicate the

FIGURE 1.2 World Population, School Enrollments, Teachers, and Expenditures, 1980–2010

	1980	1990	2000	2010 est.
Population	4.4 billion	5.3 billion	6.2 billion	6.8 billion
Enrollment	856 million	1.1 billion	1.2 billion	1.4 billion
Teachers	38 million	47 million	60 million	80 million
School Expenditures in U.S. Dollars	$516 billion	$986 billion	$1.8 trillion	$3 trillion

importance of schooling worldwide. Still, schools in the poorest nations face serious shortages of basic requirements, including adequate buildings and textbooks. Some schools in all parts of the world are in poor physical condition and are getting worse, but poorer nations suffer more in lack of school facilities and support. This will further increase separation between rich and poor nations since schooling is future oriented (UNESCO, 2000, 2010).

The world's population is almost 7 billion, doubling since 1960. Developing nations have about 80 percent of the people, up from 70 percent in 1960. The growth rate has slowed to about 1.2 percent annually, which, along with better education and health, means that the population is aging. The median age in developing nations is now about twenty-four years old, up from about nineteen years a quarter of a century ago. The median age in more developed nations is thirty-seven, up from twenty-nine years in 1975. Illiteracy not addressed when many of these people were younger is an increasing problem, along with the extensive current global effort to provide literacy to youth. That suggests global needs for educational programs for older citizens in addition to the well-known needs for schooling for those under eighteen years old.

Global democratization, population growth and distribution in the world, globalization of trade and industry, economic disparities among nations, and increasing age medians are reasons for an increasing interest in education as a primary means for national development and international interchange (Stockmeyer, 2011). Burns et al. (2003) note,

> Education is one of the most powerful instruments known for reducing poverty and inequality and for laying the basis for sustained economic growth. It is fundamental for the construction of democratic societies and dynamic, globally competitive economies. (p. 26)

The recent worldwide economic slowdown and financial crisis can, however, dim prospects for education, especially among poorer nations, as UNESCO (2011) shows:

> Depriving children and youth of opportunities for learning has damaging implications for progress in other areas, including economic growth, poverty reduction, employment creation, health and democracy. (p. 19)

The relationship among education, democracy, economic growth, and social well-being has become a significant global concern, and UNESCO is sounding an alarm. The long-term effects of serious budget cuts in education in the United States can hinder national development and international leadership as well.

The UNESCO Council (2000) states,

> Education opens doors and facilitates social and economic mobility. . . . Education has assumed a central role in the life of societies, and their general progress has become intimately bound up with the vitality and reach of the educational enterprise. . . . At the global level, it has become the biggest industry, absorbing 5% of the world GDP and generating or helping to generate much more. (p. 16)

In the United States, schooling involves large numbers—of people, dollars, and locations. The number of U.S. school districts approaches 15,000, and the number of teachers is about 3.5 million, with school expenditures about $500 billion annually. Table 1.1 summarizes U.S. school enrollments for public and private schools and public school expenditures. Schooling involves significant numbers of people and costs, but school has many payoffs. Unemployment rates are highest for people with less than a high school education and lowest for those with at least a bachelor's degree; the median income of people eighteen years and older increases, consistent with education level attained.

Schools are a focus of criticism and reform efforts because schools are among the most public of institutions, are one of the most common experiences

Table 1.1 Enrollment and Expenditures in Public and Private Schools, United States 1900–2010 (Projected; in thousands)

	Elementary and Secondary School Enrollees				Expenditures (in millions of dollars)	
	Public	%	Private	%	Public	Private
1900	15,500	92	1,350	8	215	n/a
1910	17,800	92	1,550	8	426	n/a
1920	21,500	93	1,690	7	1,036	n/a
1930	25,600	91	2,650	9	2,317	n/a
1940	25,400	91	2,611	9	2,344	n/a
1950	25,111	88	3,380	12	5,838	411
1960	35,150	86	6,300	14	16,700	1,100
1970	45,850	89	5,360	11	43,183	2,500
1980	40,850	88	5,300	12	103,162	7,200
1990	41,200	89	5,230	11	248,900	19,500
2000	47,000	89	5,950	11	389,000	28,400
2010	49,350	89	5,960	11	596,000	48,000

Note: Data for private education are estimated. Private schools include religion-affiliated institutions, some of which include teachers and other staff who are not paid salaries.
n/a = not available.
Source: *Digest of Education Statistics* (2010).

people have, and are immensely important to the lifeblood and future of societies. Virtually every person spends long periods of life in schools; teachers may spend a lifetime. Schools carry significant social trust for transmitting cultural heritage, developing economic and political competence, and providing inspiration and knowledge to improve the future society. The nature and form of that heritage, competence, and knowledge form constant battlegrounds for different views of what schools ought to be and ought to be doing.

The public has lofty expectations for education, giving schools the responsibility for much of their children's welfare, values, skills, and knowledge. Schools are also expected to correct such social ills as crime, teenage pregnancy, and adolescent rudeness and to provide self-fulfillment education, ranging from employment skills to personal happiness. Schools, then, are seen as a source of both problems and solutions.

Unity and Diversity: A Dialectic in Society and Education

Among the conditions of human civilization is the tension between unifying and diverse ideas. We share a vision of the good life with others yet recognize that human improvement depends on new ideas that may conflict with that vision. Unity provides a focus but also complacency, and diversity provides stimulation but also dissension. Both comfort and discontent thus reside in unity and diversity. This tension occurs in life and is most evident in important matters such as schooling. It is also at the center of the culture wars; do we advocate unity or diversity? One is a thesis, the other antithesis.

Diversity and unity commonly are seen as contradictory. Some diverse ideas are too radical, too preposterous, or too challenging to deeply held beliefs for some people. Fundamental religions expect unity and do not accept diversity; criticism of religious dogma is considered heretical and sacrilegious. For those religions, just as for some people who believe they have the only truth, unity of belief is sacrosanct.

On the other hand, some question unity. One argument is that unity of purpose or values is a myth perpetuated by those in power to stay in power. Hard work, frugality, and acceptance of authority are seen as fictional values that are part of an effort by the powerful class to hide their oppressive actions, maintain the social order, and enslave docile workers.

Thus, diversity and unity can be seen as adversarial positions, bound in opposition. Those on the side of unity believe that diverse ideas can be censored, ignored, or disdained; those arguing for diversity consider unity to be a facade hiding the basic conflicts in society.

It also is possible to understand diversity and unity as collateral positions, supporting and energizing. This tension between diversity and unity, multiple views and common principles, informs this book about schools. Among current critical issues in education, debates about purposes and practices of schooling, are such matters as school choice, finance, racism, sexism, child welfare, privatization, curriculum, business orientations, academic freedom, unionism, and testing. These issues reflect deeper social and political tensions between unity and diversity, including tensions between liberty and equality, rights and responsibilities, consensus and conflict, and individual and social development. Diverse ideas combined in a unified purpose is an ideal, not easily and perhaps not ever attained. It is a possible synthesis, drawing on two opposing strands as in dialectic reasoning. But what would it look like in practice? How would we define the kind of diversity and unity expressed?

This book presents two differing views on each topic in each chapter. The views expressed aren't always exactly opposing, but they represent publicly expressed ideas about how schooling could be improved. Contrasting these views in terms of evidence presented and logic of each argument can stimulate a realistic dialogue, offering an opportunity to examine issues as they occur in human discourse. Divergent essays sometimes will use the same data or same published works to make opposite cases, but they usually will offer evidence from widely separate literatures. The search for improvement in society and in schooling is a unifying purpose; dialogues and dialectics require diversity.

School is not only the subject of disputes; it is also the logical place for the thoughtful study of disputes. Schools should be settings where reasoned thought and open inquiry are practiced. They are a suitable location for examining disputes about important issues—those characterized by diverse opinions. Critical issues, those of the greatest significance, often stimulate the most intense disputes.

The next decades of the twenty-first century may be placid or turbulent for schools, a period of recuperation from the latest round of reforms or a new set of attacks. Even in placidity, however, educational issues are sure to arise, cause alarm, and inflame passions. Some of the issues raised will spawn elements of new school reforms, and some will lead to school improvement; nearly all will be disputed.

References

ADLER, M. (1927). *Dialectic.* New York: Harcourt Brace.

———. (1982). *The Paideia Proposal.* New York: Macmillan.

American Federation of Teachers. (2005). "NCLB—Let's Get It Right." May 19. www .AFT.com.

APPLE, M. (1990). *Ideology and Curriculum.* 2nd Ed. London: Routledge.

———. (1994). "Computers and the Deskilling of Teachers." *CPSR Newsletter* 12(2):3.

AUDI, R. (2001). *The Architecture of Reason.* Oxford: Oxford University Press.

BAILYN, B. (1960). *Education in the Forming of American Society.* Chapel Hill: University of North Carolina Press.

BANKS, J. A. (1995). "The Historical Reconstruction of Knowledge about Race: Implications for Transformative Teaching." *Educational Researcher* 24:15–25.

BARBER, B. (1998). *Intellectual Pursuits.* Lanham, MD: Rowman & Littlefield.

BASTIAN, A., ET AL. (1985). *Choosing Equality: The Case for Democratic Schooling.* San Francisco: New World Foundation.

BEHE, M., DEMBSKI, W., AND MEYER, S. (2000). *Science and Evidence for Design in the Universe.* San Francisco: Ignatius Press.

BERKMAN, M., AND PLUTZER, E. (2010). *Evolution, Creationism and the Battle to Control America's Classrooms.* New York: Cambridge University Press.

BERLINER, D. (1993). "Mythology and the American System of Education." *Kappan* 74:632–640.

BERLINER, D., AND BIDDLE, B. J. (1995). *The Manufactured Crisis: Myths, Fraud, and the Attack on America's Public Schools.* Reading, MA: Addison-Wesley.

BESTOR, A. (1953). *Educational Wastelands.* Urbana: University of Illinois Press. (2nd Ed., 1985).

BLUMENFELD-JONES, D. (2004). "The Hope of a Critical Ethics." *Educational Theory* 54(3):263–279.

BOYER, E. (1983). *High School.* New York: Harper and Row.

BRACEY, G. (1992). "The Second Bracey Report on the Condition of Public Education." *Kappan* 74:104–108.

———. (1994). "The Fourth Bracey Report on the Condition of Public Education." *Kappan* 76:115–127.

———. (1995). "Stedman's Myths Miss the Mark." *Educational Leadership* 52:75–78.

———. (1997). *The Truth about America's Schools: The Bracey Reports, 1991–1997.* Bloomington, IN: Phi Delta Kappa.

———. (1998). "The Eighth Bracey Report on the Condition of Public Education." *Kappan* 80(2):112–131.

———. (2002a). "The Twelfth Bracey Report on the Condition of Public Education." *Kappan* 84(2):135–150.

———. (2002b). *The War Against America's Public Schools.* Boston: Allyn and Bacon/ Longmans.

BROMLEY, H., AND APPLE, M., eds. (2002). *Education/Technology/Power.* Albany: State University of New York Press.

BRONNER, E. (1998). "Candidates Latch onto Education Issue." *San Diego Union-Tribune.* September 20.

BROOKFIELD, S. D. (2012). *Teaching for Critical Thinking.* San Francisco: Jossey-Bass.

Brown v. Board of Education of Topeka, Shawnee County, Kansas, et al. (1954). 74 Sup. Ct. 686.

BURNS, B., ET AL. (2003). *Achieving Universal Primary Education by 2015.* Washington, DC: World Bank.

CARANFA, A. (2004). "Silence as the Foundation of Learning." *Educational Theory* 54(2):211–230.

CARSON, C. C., HUELSKAMP, R. M., AND WOODALL, T. D. (1992). "Perspectives on Education in America." Final Draft, April. Albuquerque, NM: Sandia National Laboratories.

CHAMBERS, G. (1948). "Educational Essentialism Thirty Years After." In *Secondary Education: Origins and Directions,* ed. R. Hahn and D. Bidna. New York: Macmillan, 1970.

COLES, G. (2003). *Reading the Naked Truth.* Portsmouth, NH: Heinemann.

College Entrance Examination Board. (1983). *Academic Preparation for College.* New York: College Board.

CONANT, J. B. (1958). *The American High School Today.* New York: McGraw-Hill.

COOPER, D., ed. (1967). *To Free a Generation: The Dialectics of Liberalism.* New York: Collier.

COYNE, J. A. (2009). *Why Evolution Is True.* New York: Viking.

CREMIN, L. (1961). *The Transformation of the School.* New York: Random House.

———. (1965). *The Genius of American Education.* New York: Random House.

CUBAN, L. (2003). "The Great Reappraisal of Public Education." *American Journal of Education* 110(November):3–31.

DARLING-HAMMOND, L. (1991). "Achieving Our Goals: Superficial or Structural Reforms?" *Kappan* 72:286–295.

DAWKINS, R. (2009). *The Greatest Show on Earth*. New York: Free Press.

DEMBSKI, W. (2004). *The Design Revolution*. Downer's Grove, IL: InterVarsity Press.

DE TOCQUEVILLE, A. (1848/1969). *Democracy in America*. Edited by J. P. Mayer. Garden City, NY: Doubleday.

DEWEY, J. (1916). *Democracy and Education*. New York: Macmillan.

DEWIEL, B. (2000). *Democracy: A History of Ideas*. Vancouver: UBC Press.

Digest of Educational Statistics. (2010). www.nces.edu.gov.

DOHENY-FARINA, S. (1996). *The Wired Neighborhood*. New Haven, CT: Yale University Press.

DRYFOOS, J. (2002). "Full-Service Community Schools." *Kappan* 83:393–399.

D'SOUZA, D. (1991). *Illiberal Education: The Politics of Race and Sex on Campus*. New York: Free Press.

ELAM, S., ET AL. (1993). "25th Annual PDK/Gallup Poll." *Kappan* 75(September).

EMERSON, J. D., BOES, L., AND MOSTELLER, F. (2002). "Critical Thinking in College Students." In *Educational Media and Technology Yearbook*, ed. M. A. Fitzgerald et al. Englewood, CO: Libraries Unlimited.

ENNIS, R. H. (2011). "Critical Thinking" *Inquiry* 26(1):4–18.

FARRAR, R. C. (2000). *Sartrean Dialectics*. Lanham, MD: Lexington Books.

FINN, C. (1990a). "The Biggest Reform of All." *Kappan* 71:584–593.

———. (1990b). "Why Can't Our Colleges Convey Our Diverse Culture's Unifying Themes?" *Chronicle of Higher Education* 36, 40, 41.

FISHER, E. (1991). "What Really Counts in Schools?" *Educational Leadership* 48:10–15.

FISKE, E. B. (1991). *Smart Schools, Smart Kids*. New York: Simon and Schuster.

FORREST, B. C., AND GROSS, P. R. (2004). *Creationism's Trojan Horse: The Wedge of Intelligent Design*. New York: Oxford University Press.

FUENTES, C. (2005). *This I Believe*. New York: Random House.

FULLEN, M. (2000). "Three Stories of Education Reform." *Kappan* 83:581–584.

Gallup. (2011). "Education." August 1. www.gallup.com.

GARDNER, J. (1958). *The Pursuit of Excellence: Education and the Future of America*. New York: Rockefeller Brothers Fund.

GARFORTH, F. W. (1980). *Educative Democracy: John Stuart Mill on Education in Society*. Oxford: Oxford University Press.

GELLA, A. (1976). *The Intelligentsia and the Intellectuals*. London: Sage.

GIROUX, H. (1988a). *Schooling and the Struggle for Public Life*. Granby, MA: Bergin and Garvey.

———. (1989). "Rethinking Educational Reform in the Age of George Bush." *Kappan* 70:728–730.

———. (2004). "Critical Pedagogy and the Postmodern/Modern Divide." *Teacher Education Quarterly* 37(1):31–47.

GOODLAD, J. I. (1983). *A Place Called School: Prospects for the Future*. New York: McGraw-Hill.

GOULDNER, A. (1979). *The Future of Intellectuals and the Rise of the New Class*. New York: Seabury Press.

GRAHAM, P. A. (1967). *Progressive Education: From Arcady to Academe*. New York: Teachers College Press.

GUTMANN, A., AND THOMPSON, D. (1996). *Democracy and Disagreement*. Cambridge, MA: Harvard University Press.

———. (2004). *Why Deliberative Democracy?* Princeton, NJ: Princeton University Press.

HALLOWELL, B. (2011). "Evolution vs. Creationism." *The Blaze*. July 21. www.theblaze.com.

HAWLEY, R. A. (1990). "The Bumpy Road to Drug-Free Schools" *Kappan* 72:310–314.

HESS, D. G. (2002). "Discussing Controversial Public Issues in Secondary Social Studies Classrooms." *Theory and Research in Social Education* 30(1):10–41.

————. (2011). "Discussions That Drive Democracy." *Educational Leadership* 69(1):69–73.

————. (2012). *Scheduled publication. Courting Democracy.* New York: Routledge.

HITCHENS, C. (2007). *God Is Not Great.* New York: Hatchette Book Group.

HOLT, J. (1964). *How Children Fail.* New York: Pitman.

HOUSE, H. W. (2008). *Intelligent Design 101.* Grand Rapids, MI: Kregel Publications.

ILLICH, I. (1971). *Deschooling Society.* New York: Harper and Row.

JACOBY, S. (2008). *The Age of American Unreason.* New York: Pantheon.

JOHNSON, K. (2006). "Anti-Darwinism Bill Fails in Utah." *New York Times.* February 28. www.nytimes.com.

KAESTLE, C. F. (1985). "Education Reform and the Swinging Pendulum." *Kappan* 66:410–415.

————. (2001). "No Quick and Dirty." *Kappan* 83:278.

KARIER, C. (1967). *Man, Society, and Education.* Chicago: Scott, Foresman.

————. (1985). "Retrospective One." In *Educational Wastelands,* 2nd Ed., by A. Bestor. Urbana: University of Illinois Press.

KATZ, M. (1968). *The Irony of Early School Reform.* Cambridge, MA: Harvard University Press.

————. (1971). *Class, Bureaucracy, and Schools: The Illusion of Educational Change in America.* New York: Praeger.

KINCHELOE, J. L., AND WEIL, D., eds. (2004) *Critical Thinking and Learning.* Westport, CT: Greenwood Press.

KURTZ, P. (1992). *The New Skepticism.* Buffalo, NY: Prometheus Books.

LEMANN, N. (2010). "Comment: Schoolwork." *The New Yorker.* September 27. www.newyorker.com.

LYND, A. (1950). *Quackery in the Public Schools.* Boston: Little, Brown.

MAKAU, J. M., AND MARTY, D. L. (2001). *Cooperative Argumentation: A Model for a Deliberative Community.* Prospect Heights, IL: Waveland Press.

MAMET, D. (2011). *The Secret Knowledge.* New York: Sentinel.

MARCUSE, H. (1960). *Reason and Revolution.* Boston: Beacon Press.

McCABE, M. M. (2000). *Plato and His Predecessors.* Cambridge: Cambridge University Press.

McKENZIE, J. (2006). "The Harsh Bigotry of Bad Policy." *No Child Left* 4(3). www.nochildleft.com.

————. (2007). "The Last Word." *No Child Left* 5(5, May).

————. (2008). "After NCLB: Back to the Basics of Inquiry and Comprehension." *From Now On* 17(5, May):1.

McLAREN, P. (1989). *Life in Schools.* New York: Longman.

McLAREN, P., AND HOUSTON, D. (2004). "Revolutionary Ecologies." *Educational Studies* 36(1):27–45.

MEHTA, J. (2011). "The Future of School Reform." *Education Week.* June 6. www.edweek.com, 1.

MEIER, D., AND WOOD, G., eds. (2004). *Many Children Left Behind.* Bellingham, WA: FNO Press.

MERCER, N. (2008). "The Seeds of Time: Why Classroom Dialogue Needs a Temporal Analysis." *Journal of the Learning Sciences* 17(1):33–59.

MOSES, R., AND COBB, C. E. (2001). *Radical Equations: Math Literacy and Civil Rights.* Boston: Beacon Press.

MOYNIHAN, D. P. (1991). "Educational Goals and Political Plans." *The Public Interest,* Winter, 32–49.

NATHAN, J. (1991). "Toward Educational Change and Economic Justice: An Interview with Herbert Kohl." *Kappan* 72:678–681.

National Coalition for Dialogue and Deliberation. (2008). National Coalition for Dialogue and Deliberation Online Newsletter. www.thataway.org.

National Commission on Excellence in Education. (1983). *A Nation at Risk.* Washington, DC: U.S. Government Printing Office.

National Education Association. (2006). "Independent Commission on NCLB." News release. February. www.NEA.org.

National Review. (1990). "Academic Watch." 42, 18.

National Science Foundation. (1983). *Educating Americans for the 21st Century.* Washington, DC: National Science Foundation.

Newsweek. (1989). "Kids: Deadly Force." 111:18–20.

New York Times. (1992). "Education Life." Special supplement. January 5.

———. (2005)."Stand Firm for Educational Fairness." April 22.

Nichols, S. L., and Berliner, D. C. (2008). "Testing the Joy Out of Learning," *Educational Leadership* 65(6):14–18.

Nocera, J. (2011). "The Limits of School Reform." *New York Times.* April 26.

Noddings, N. (1995). *Philosophy of Education.* Boulder, CO: Westview Press.

Nolan, J. L. (1996). *The American Culture Wars.* Charlottesville: University of Virginia Press.

Norris, P., ed. (1999). *Critical Citizens.* New York: Oxford University Press.

Novak, M. (1990). "Scaring Our Children." *Forbes* 144:167.

Oppenheimer, T. (2003). *The Flickering Mind.* New York: Random House.

Paglia, C. (1990). *Sexual Personae.* New Haven, CT: Yale University Press.

Perakh, M. (2003). *Unintelligent Design.* Buffalo, NY: Prometheus Books.

Presseisen, B. (1985). *Unlearned Lessons.* Philadelphia: Falmer Press.

Purpel, D. (1989). *The Moral and Spiritual Crisis in Education: A Curriculum for Justice and Compassion in Education.* Granby, MA: Bergin and Garvey.

Rafferty, M. (1968). *Max Rafferty on Education.* New York: Devon Adair.

Ravitch, D. (1990). "Multiculturalism: E Pluribus Plures." *American Scholar* 59:337–354.

———. (2000). *Left Back: A Century of Battles over School Reform.* New York: Simon and Schuster.

———. (2007). "Get Congress Out of the Classroom." *New York Times*, October 3. www.nytimes.com.

———. (2010). *The Death and Life of the Great American School System.* New York: Basic Books.

Results in Education: 1990. (1990). The Governors' 1991 Report on Education. Washington, DC: National Governors' Association.

Rose, L. C., and Gallup, A. M. (1998). "The 30th Phi Delta Kappa/Gallup Poll of the Public's Attitudes toward the Public Schools." *Kappan* 80(1):41–56.

———. (2001). "The 33rd Annual Phi Delta Kappa/Gallup Poll." *Kappan* 83:41–47.

———. (2005). "The 37th Annual Phi Delta Kappa/Gallup Poll." *Kappan* 87(1):41–57.

———. (2007). "The 39th Annual Phi Delta Kappa/Gallup Poll." *Kappan* 89(1):41–47.

Ross, E. W., and Gibson, R. eds. (2006). *Neoliberalism and Educational Reform.* Cresskill, NJ: Hampton Press.

Rothstein, R. (2011). "Grading the Education Reformers." *Education Review* 14(8). www.edrev.info.

Rudroren, J. (2006). "Ohio Board Undoes Stand on Evolution." *New York Times.* February 15. www.nytimes.com.

Russell, B. (1928). *Sceptical Essays.* London: George Allen and Unwin.

Rychlak, J. F., ed. (1976). *Dialectic.* Basel: Karger.

Sacks, P. (1999). *Standardized Minds.* Cambridge, MA: Perseus Books.

Safire, W. (1991). "Abandon the Pony Express." *New York Times.* April 25.

Schneider, C. G. (2004). "Practicing Liberal Education." *Liberal Education* 9(2):8–10.

SCHOENFELD, A. H. (2002). "Making Mathematics Work for All Children." *Educational Researcher* 31:13–25.

SCHWEBER, H. H. (2012). *Democracy and Authenticity*. New York: Cambridge University Press.

SCIABARRA, C. M. (1999). *Ayn Rand: The Russian Radical*. University Park: Pennsylvania State University Press.

———. (2000). *Total Freedom: Toward Dialectical Libertarianism*. University Park: Pennsylvania State University Press.

Science News. (2008). "Negative Implications of No Child Left Behind." February 16. www.sciencedaily.com.

SCOTT, E. (2009). *Evolution versus Creationism*. Berkeley: University of California Press.

SHAPIRO, I., AND MACEDO, S. (2000). *Designing Democratic Institutions, Nomos 42*. New York: New York University Press.

SHERMER, M. (2011). *The Believing Brain*. New York: Times Books, Henry Holt.

SIM, M. (1999). *From Puzzles to Principles*. Lanham, MD: Lexington Books.

SINCLAIR, U. (1924). *The Goslings*. Pasadena, CA: Sinclair.

SIZER, T. (1984). *Horace's Compromise: The Dilemma of the American High School*. Boston: Houghton Mifflin.

SLOAN-LYNCH, J. (2010). "Philosophers to the Rescue? The Failed Attempt to Defend the Inclusion of Intelligent Design in Public Schools." *Philosophy and Public Policy Quarterly* 30(1/2):18–23.

SMITH, M. (1954). *The Diminished Mind: A Study of Planned Mediocrity in Our Public Schools*. New York: Regnery.

SPRING, J. (2008). No Child Left Behind as Political Fraud." In *What Is Authentic Educational Reform?*, ed. H. L. Johnson and A. Salz. New York: Lawrence Erlbaum Associates.

STANLEY, W. B. (1992). *Education for Utopia: Social Reconstructionism and Critical Pedagogy in the Postmodern Era*. Albany: State University of New York Press.

———, ed. (2001). *Social Studies Research for the 21st Century*. Greenwich, CT: Information Age Publishers.

STOCKMEYER, D. (2011). *Democratization around the World*. Lewiston, NY: Edwin Mellen Press.

STRIKE, K. A. (2004). "Community, the Missing Element of School Reform." *American Journal of Education* 110(May):215–232.

STROBEL, L. (2004). *The Case for a Creator*. Grand Rapids, MI: Zondervan.

SUNDERMAN, G. L. (2006). "The Unraveling of No Child Left Behind." Report. Civil Rights Project of Harvard University. February www.civilrightsproject.harvard.edu.

The Education Reform Decade. (1990). Policy Information Report. Princeton, NJ: Educational Testing Service.

The Progressive. (1991). "The PC Monster." 55, 9.

TORRES, C. A. (2002). "Globalization, Education, and Citizenship." *American Educational Research Journal* 39(2):363–378.

Twentieth-Century Fund. (1983). *Making the Grade*. New York: Twentieth-Century Fund.

TYACK, D. (1967). *Turning Points in American Educational History*. Waltham, MA: Blaisdell.

———. (1991). "Public School Reform: Policy Talk and Institutional Practice." *American Journal of Education* 100:1–19.

ULICH, R. (1954). *Three Thousand Years of Educational Wisdom*. 2nd Ed. Cambridge, MA: Harvard University Press.

UNESCO. (2003). *Financing Education*. Paris: UNESCO.

UNESCO. (2005). *Education for All*. Paris: UNESCO Publishing.

————. (2010, 2011). *Global Education Digest 2010.* (2010). Paris: UNESCO Publishing.

UNESCO Council. (2000). *Report on the World Social Condition, 2000.* New York: United Nations.

UNESCO World Education Report, 2000. (2000). "The Right to Education: Towards Education for All throughout Life." Paris: UNESCO Publishing.

U.S. Census Bureau. (2008). International Data Base. March 27. www.census.gov.

————. (2010). International Data Base. April. www.census.gov.

U.S. News and World Report. (1990). "The Keys to School Reform." February 26, 108, 50–53.

VAN EMEREN, F. H., AND GOOTENHORST, R. (2003). "A Pragma-Dialectic Procedure for a Critical Discussion." *Argumentation* 17(4):365–386.

Van LUCHENE, S. R. (2004). "Rekindling the Dialogue: Education according to Plato and Dewey." *Academe* 90(3):54–57.

WEBSTER, W. E., AND McMILLIN, J. D. (1991). "A Report on Calls for Secondary School Reform in the United States." *NASSP Bulletin* 75:77–83.

WELTER, R. (1962). *Popular Education and Democratic Thought in America.* New York: Columbia University Press.

WINKLER, K. (1991). "Organization of American Historians Backs Teaching of Non-Western Culture and Diversity in Schools." *Chronicle of Higher Education* 37:5–8.

WINTHROP, N. (2000). *Democratic Theory as Public Philosophy.* Sydney: Ashgate.

WIRKALA, C., AND KUHN, D. (2011). "Problem-Based Learning in K-12 Education: Is It Effective and How Does It Achieve Its Effects?" *American Educational Research Journal* 48(5):1157–1186.

WRAGA, W. (2001). "Left Out: The Villainization of Progressive Education in the United States." *Educational Researcher* 30:7.

WRIGHT, L. (2001). *Critical Thinking.* New York: Oxford University Press.

YOUNG, M., AND EDIS, T. (2004). *Why Intelligent Design Fails.* New Brunswick, NJ: Rutgers University Press.

ZURN, C. F. (2007). *Deliberative Democracy and the Institutions of Judicial Review.* Cambridge: Cambridge University Press.

Whose Interests Should Schools Serve?

Justice and Equity

About **Part One:** Chapters in Part One cover competing ideological interests in regard to schools. Chapters 2 through 7 include divergent views on charter schools and vouchers, school financing, gender equity, standards and school accountability, church/state interests in schooling, privatization and corporate interests, and immigration issues.

Each topic involves basic questions about justice and equity in American society, often filtered through political terms like *liberalism* and *conservatism* as well as through personal and ethical principles. Some practices and policies as are labeled "conservative" and others as "liberal," with a few "radical." Personal or ethical connotations of "good," "right," "proper," "just," and "equitable" support them (Monroe, 2012; Winter, 2012). These political and personal filters may not be accurate labels or precise indicators of ideologies or personal positions, but they are widely used (Pew Research Center, 2011; Marietta, 2012). Schooling battles often fall within the themes of justice and equity.

PART ONE: COMPETING INTERESTS

Schools serve many masters: students, parents, teachers, administrators, government, commerce, media, special interest groups, and varying educational philosophies and laws. These are usually competitive interests with divergent agendas, the realm of politics, economics, social conscience, and ideology (Mauro, 2008). Politics is concerned with the distribution of power among interests, economics with the distribution of wealth, and social conscience and ideology with rationales that people use to justify practices and policies.

Justice and equity are basic to a consideration of which interests should be emphasized in schooling. But we have differing views of what constitutes a just or equitable system (Kitching, 2001; Little, 2002; Mitzman, 2003; Barry, 2005; Fuentes, 2005; Kolm, 2005; Sandel, 2010). Evaluating the quality of equity and justice in society and schools involves interests as a major concern (Rawls, 1971, 1999, 2001, 2005; Bowles, Gintis, and Gross, 2005).

We all have interests, and we are members of groups that have interests. We want good things for ourselves, our families, our friends, our associations, and our society. We may also want negative consequences for our enemies, our competitors, and others who oppose our interests. We like to hear that our nation's writers, scientists, athletes, actors, students, or workers have won awards in international competitions. We are dismayed by reports that our children's test scores are lower than scores in other neighborhoods or nations. We compete with a family down the street or some obnoxious cousin, and we want our interests to be successful. There are, of course, times when our personal interests and family or group interests are in opposition, as in family arguments over who should get the family car, what kind of career to pursue, or whether to support a war.

Self-Interest

Enlightened self-interest is a pleasant way of describing why we do things that benefit ourselves without hurting others. Novelist and philosopher Ayn Rand (1943, 1997) is a strong advocate of self-interest, though she incorporates an enlightened provision that individuals should respect others' rights. She considers selfishness a virtue and argues against altruism and its idea that others are more important than oneself. Rand's views provide excellent examples of rugged individualism and "titanic self-assertion" (Gladstein, 1999, p. 1). Anthony Downs (1957, 1997) provides similar support for enlightened self-interest in the marketplace. Enlightened self-interest, where no damage is intended for others and there is a sense of social responsibility, can still create serious conflicts as individual or group interests compete for scarce resources. Who gets to decide whose self-interests are enlightened and on what criteria?

Unenlightened self-interest, where selfishness without social conscience is the pattern, is just greed. Recent examples at Enron, banks, financial institutions, and other corporations illustrate this point. Major executives make millions of dollars in salary, perks, and stock options while workers are underpaid, misinformed, and lose retirement and medical benefits— even when the executives know how badly the company was doing. Greed, corruption, and fraud occur in politics, in schools, in corporate life, and even in religious institutions.

Certainly, individual interests need not be so ruthless and irresponsible. Altruism can be seen as one form of socially beneficial self-interest. "Do unto others as you would have them do unto you" is the Golden Rule, a principle that is shared by virtually every culture in the world. Self-interest provides a rationale for the Golden Rule; we want to have a good life, and that depends on others also having a good life. Teachers often recognize that their self-interest is served by having happy and successful students. There are, of course, many selfless people who devote their lives to helping others; Mother Teresa and Martin Luther King come to mind. They have interests but are not absorbed with their own welfare.

Social Interests

Beyond individual interests are group interests, and these can be very competitive. Special interests have become a term of derision in politics—we label the opposition candidate in an election campaign as being in the clutches of special interest groups. Yet we all belong to various special interest groups by our own or our family's occupations, geographic area, hobbies, charities, travel, religion, shopping, educational pursuits, and nearly all other endeavors.

Obviously, these interests do not always coincide. We would like lower taxes but appreciate public benefits such as roads, police, clean parks, and schools. We prefer a healthy environment but like products that come from chemicals, plastics, and other pollution-producing manufacturers. We join or support groups that advocate those ideas we share, even if at times we act in a manner that is not internally consistent.

Then there are our societal and national interests. Our stated policy, whether under a Democratic or Republican administration, is to defend national interests in international affairs—trade, borders, war, terrorism, and so on. Not remarkably, each nation places national interest as foremost, though clearly the definition and delineation

of national interest differs. National interest has been one of the fuels of war, genocide, militarism, border vigilantism, isolation, denial of human rights, trade restriction, and international posturing (Herbert, 2005; Bandy and Smith, 2005; Pavola and Lowe, 2005). It also has been a fuel for peace, international understanding, freedom, trade agreements, charity, economic development, and the protection of human rights (Nelson and Green, 1980; Hahnel, 2005). Our use of language shows interests at work: the "Axis of Evil" identifies nations and groups our government considers threatening, "Manifest Destiny" was invoked to cover the invasion of Native American territory in the West, and the "war on terrorism" is used as grounds for changing accepted patterns of civil rights and civil liberties.

Societal interests involve such matters as general safety and welfare, the environment, health, education, security, transportation, communication, freedom, and order. These topics concern people across such political boundaries as cities, states, and nations. Residents of cities, suburbs, and rural areas are interested in safe highways and airports and good hospitals and schools—these are public interests, whether the social institutions are privately or publicly operated. The public also has a stake in how these quality-of-life areas are handled; many are government controlled and operated, some are government regulated but privately operated, and some are privately controlled and operated with little governmental oversight.

Schooling is one of the most important of those broad public concerns in the

United States. Laws govern nearly all forms of schooling to include required attendance, financing, staff credentials, curriculum, and operational requirements. Most school-age students in the United States attend public schools, controlled and operated by government. But about 15 percent of all students are enrolled in some form of private schooling, including independent schools, religiously affiliated schools, trade schools, and homeschooling. In addition, there are efforts to provide vouchers for funding to parents who want to take their children from public schools to private schools, efforts to establish charter schools in the public districts for relief from some governmental regulation, and efforts to privatize public school operation by contracting with corporations.

Ideas of justice and equity provide rationales for mediating, adjudicating, mitigating, criticizing, and evaluating the various conflicts among interests, but justice and equity are not without debate themselves.

Justice and Equity: Sounds Good to Me

Justice sounds simple enough and is certainly above dispute as a fundamental element in a well-ordered society—or family, organization, school, or relationship with others. We want to live in a society, family, school, or relationship that is just. We rail against situations we consider unjust. The difficulty, of course, is that justice depends on many factors: a set of socially agreed on values and principles, legal and moral traditions, the political and economic situation, technical and practical definitions of terms used, the time period and geographic location, social and individual conditions, and the eye of the beholder. Justice, then, is dependent on such things as where you happen to be, when, who you are, how you are represented, and what you think of it.

This is not to suggest that justice is just a fuzzy idea that can never be defined and is too nebulous to have much impact on your life. Indeed, justice is the forming idea for nearly all political theory, law, ethics, and human relations. It has a history of very specific definitions in particular situations yet is still under constant redefinition by a variety of people from parents to legislators. Burning witches at the stake was considered justice at one time; using the rod to physically punish misbehaving students was an accepted schoolmarm's role in the school justice system of the past. The ultimate punishment, death, is considered too uncivilized to be justice in some nations; others use it routinely.

The existing concept of justice has an impact on your life in virtually all settings and can easily be the most important of influences. Consider being accused of a serious crime; consider being the victim. Think of the times you got a grade you think you did not deserve; think of the teacher's view of the same grade. Put yourself into the shoes of someone who suffers from a severe physical or mental disorder, lives in a dictatorship, or is audited by the Internal Revenue Service. Each of these has a justice component. Everyday complaints about restaurant food or a department store purchase pose questions of justice, albeit more trivial. Waiters and store clerks usually employ a sense of justice in dealing with or ignoring complaining customers. Justice is both an ideal and a practical matter of significance for individuals and society, but it is a concept fraught with difficulties in definition and interpretation.

Justice incorporates ideas of impartiality and fairness, two concepts as difficult to discern as justice. Was Solomon impartial? Could his decision be fair to all? How do we know that any judge is impartial and fair? Was the Supreme Court impartial and fair in their differing historic decisions on slavery, women's suffrage, segregated schools, abortion, or Bush versus Gore? Were those stock market analysts impartial when they recommended buying subprime mortgage bundles as they collapsed? Was your teacher fair and impartial when you got the grade you think you did not deserve? Is school a good place to learn about justice, fairness, and impartiality— and do schools provide good models for how justice, fairness, and impartiality should work?

Stuart Hampshire (2000), arguing that the basis of justice lies in human conflicts, states that "fairness in procedures for resolving conflicts is the fundamental kind of fairness" (p. 4).

Conflicts are a continuing and engaging human condition. Dialogue and dialectics can assist in examining conflicting views, but our sense of justice requires a belief in fair procedures for dealing with them (Fishkin, 1992). The procedural fairness that Hampshire advocates may result in unequal conditions. Divorcing parents who fight over child custody are unlikely to achieve equal condition. Selecting the Teachers of the Year in a school district may incorporate a fair procedure with impartial judging, but results are unequal. But when we think the procedures were generally fair, unequal results can be better tolerated.

The concept of fairness is essential to our ideas of justice—and fair procedures are a basic condition for justice in a legitimate democracy. Legitimacy, in a democracy, is the granting of authority to government by the people—a form of social contract. This is the idea of the consent of the governed, a concept disputed by some political theorists, but it continues to be widely held (Rawls, 1999, 2005). We accept decisions, even if we don't like them, when we feel that the procedure is fair. If there is widespread concern that basic procedures are unfair, we have social unrest and the seeds of revolution.

Equity and Equality

Equity is a concept directly related to justice and includes the idea of equal treatment under natural law or rights without bias or favoritism. Equity and equality are concepts that can differ significantly. Equality can be measured by condition—each person has exactly the same. Or it can be equality of treatment—each one is treated the same based on some principle, such as "All men are created equal." But often we think that some seem to be more equal than others; we can suspect gender inequality at work in the preceding quote on the equality of men. These are issues of equity and justice. Is it possible to distribute things in a truly equal manner? Political scientist

David Spitz (1982) notes, "Equality drives us into an insoluble moral dilemma, and therefore into practices that contradict what we preach. . . . To impose equality of results . . . is to limit equality of opportunity. We cannot have both equalities simultaneously" (p. 105).

Equity does not require equality, but it does expect a process deemed fair. Most of our notions of equality in the United States are procedural—equal treatment under the law, which is similar to the idea of procedural fairness. These ideas provide for opportunity but do not specify equal results or conditions. The idea of equity provides a concept for judging the procedure of equal treatment. Under equity, exactly equal conditions or results are not required; there is no mandate that good things are distributed to all in an equal manner. Instead, there is an expectation for justice—any unequal distribution must be justified by some significant social or ethical principle (Rawls, 1971, 1999, 2001).

For example, we could justify providing special funds and separate programs for gifted and talented students in school because those students are meritorious and have the potential to give back more to the school and, later, to society. But not everyone would agree that this is a democratic or equitable justification or that these students deserve special treatment or make more community contributions. Using Rawlsian theory on distributive justice, McKenzie (1984) studied school programs for gifted and talented students and concluded that such programs were undemocratic and unfair in selection and special treatment and did not provide for

having those specially treated students give something back to the school and society. Tracking students into separate curriculums for college preparation, vocational training, general studies, and special education brings up similar issues of justice and equity. Are inclusion or mainstreaming programs more equitable and just?

In the last quarter of the twentieth century, we decided that justice is served when we provide special access to public buildings for people who require a wheelchair. That is based on a principle of equity turned into law that equal access requires special treatment for one group. Equity, then, can include inequality if the basic premise is that of justice. Affirmative action programs are predicated on this idea, making up for previous unjust discrimination. Improved funding for programs such as special education, Head Start, and school lunches for poor families is an equity topic. Special school treatment of the children of minority or immigrant families, whether by ethnic group, nationality, or income, represents another example.

Programs to redress previous inequalities and discrimination based on gender, race, class, or sexual orientation also are equity issues. Inequalities in public financing among local school districts are the subject of several different state supreme court decisions based on equal treatment. Children, their parents, taxpayers, constitutional lawyers, citizens in neighboring school districts, and most of the rest of society have interests in such equity issues. Should new national standards in various subject fields be imposed on all children in every school? Should some public schools be operated by private corporations? Should private schools have access to public money? Should religion be part of public education, and should it be supported by public funds? Each of these examples, of course, has been and continues to be hotly contested social and educational policy and practice. As in political discourse, these issues have ideological dimensions.

Interests, Politics, and Ideologies

Our interests are incorporated in and modified by ideas—liberal, conservative, radical, and reactionary. Although these labels may not identify each of us or our views on various topics, they represent broad, divergent views, and they can be used to examine social and educational issues. Ideologies enable people to explain and justify the society they would prefer (Jacoby, 2005). An ideology includes assumptions about the nature and purpose of society and related nature of individuals (Shils, 1968), it provides criteria against which one can judge human life and society (Lane, 1962), and it provides a means for self-identification (Erikson, 1960). Ideologies are broadly coherent structures of attitudes, values, and beliefs that influence individual perceptions and social policy (Piper, 1997).

Political ideologies are widely known, from radical right to radical left with conservatives and liberals somewhere near the center (Freeden, 1998; White, 2011; see also the *Journal of Political Ideologies*). The right and left political conflict is often starkly presented.

Ideological debates can be fiery and passionate, if not always reasonable, realistic, or precise.

LIBERALISM, LIBERALS, CONSERVATIVES, AND RADICALS: CONFUSION

Continuing disputes about justice and equity as they apply to individual and social rights are among the grand debates in democratic history and philosophy (Nozick, 1974; Sandel, 1998; Valentyne, 2003; Barry, 2005; Hahnel, 2005; Rawls, 2005; Charen, 2012). These disputes revolve around disparate opinions about the relative rights of individuals and of society and how equity among those rights should be determined. Although it is a bit confusing to use a similar term to mean different things, the current models of *conservatives* and *liberals* follow a Western tradition of liberalism.

Liberalism, a belief in freedom and equality, is the dominant political philosophy among Western democracies (de Ruggiero, 1927; Noddings, 1995; Klosko, 2000; Richardson, 2001; Kolm, 2005). Shapiro (1958), who traces the history of liberalism through major political literature, states, "What has characterized liberalism at all times is its unshaken belief in the necessity of freedom to achieve every desirable aim.... Equality is another fundamental liberal principle" (pp. 10, 11). This dual belief separates the philosophy of modern Western nations from some other political ideas, such as divine right of kings, aristocracy by birth and social class, or theocratic rule. In the United States and other Western democracies, we don't argue seriously for a return to colonial-period theocratic governments, European feudal dictatorships, or politically powerful monarchies. We do argue about the relative weight that should be given to individual freedoms and social constraints (Dahl, 1999; Kramer and Kimball, 1999; Reisman, 1999; Geuss, 2001; Henderson, 2001; Newey, 2001; Fuentes, 2005). Berlin (1969), points out that

> Liberty is not the only goal . . . if others are deprived of it . . . then I do not want it for myself. . . . To avoid glaring inequality or widespread misery I am ready to sacrifice some, or all, of my freedom; I may do so willingly and freely: but it is freedom that I am giving up for the sake of justice or equality. (p. 125)

In the main, both conservatives and liberals in the United States support the basic ideas of democratic freedoms and equality—tenets of traditional liberalism (Dewey, 1930; Lippman, 1934; Russell, 1955; Spitz, 1982; Bellah et al., 1985; Gutman, 1999; Spragens, 1999; Gill, 2001; Tomasi, 2001; Rawls, 2005). The major differences between conservatives and liberals revolve around what are the best definitions or criteria for freedom and equality, what is the best balance between them, how that balance can best be achieved, and how each is served in a specific situation.

In addition to possible confusion with the use of the term *liberalism*, another of the intriguing and often confusing trends in contemporary politics and educational politics is the shifting of ideas between conservatives and liberals as they attempt to influence the public's interests and plot potentially successful political positions. Political parties move toward the center to capture votes to get their candidates elected, resulting in some blurring of the conservative and liberal markers we are accustomed to using. Basic ideological differences may remain for the Republican and Democratic parties, but individual candidates don't easily fit on all issues in public life. Each party has a conservative and a liberal wing, and there is a large group of people inside and out of the parties who prefer to be considered independent (Pew Research Center, 2011).

New Democrats, like Bill Clinton and Barack Obama, work to cut the deficit, stimulate the economy and increase corporate wealth, and actively support imposing national standards on schools. These had been Republican and conservative views. New Republicans, like George W. Bush, increase public spending and the deficit, support the U.S. Department of Education, and give illegal immigrants opportunities— previously Democratic and liberal views. Specific political party positions and the views of individual candidates may not correlate well with divergent underlying political ideologies. But within each party there is often a contest among candidates to be identified as more conservative, if Republican, or more liberal, if Democrat, as a way of attracting core party voters. This suggests the basic ideological orientation of each of the parties, but conservative and liberal labels don't stick on individuals as well as some might like.

We continue, despite the confusions, to use conservative and liberal labels to identify ideas and issues and to mark various people. The labels still have meaning, despite the confusions and shifting, in politics and education.

Contemporary political disputes between "conservatives" and "liberals" occur over questions of balance and process, and they spill over into our debates on lawmaking, court proceedings, and schooling. Current conservatives, in general, want to limit governmental interference in individual freedom; current liberals generally want to ensure individual rights by governmental regulation. Conservatives argue for unregulated rights of individuals to own guns, liberals for governmental regulation of gun ownership. There are many areas of muddiness in this separation, giving pause to gross labeling.

One of these muddy areas is abortion, where liberals tend to support women's right to choose and conservatives tend to want government to restrict abortions. Another is free speech, where liberals tend to support more individual freedom and conservatives tend to want limits imposed on opposing views of sexuality, patriotism, politics, and economics. A third example includes some school topics, where liberals tend to support more individual freedom for students and teachers to examine controversial topics, to protest, and to criticize, and conservatives tend to support government-imposed standards, school and teacher accountability, socially acceptable student behavior, and restrictions on what topics can be studied.

Definitions of conservative and liberal may be slippery, but these terms are commonly applied and widely understood to refer to two distinct groups of ideas and people in any time period. Liberal ideas in one period may be considered conservative in another and vice versa. Neoconservative and neoliberal views are a rethinking of conservative or liberal ideas (Steinfels, 1979; Rothenberg, 1984; DeMuth and Kristol, 1995; Piper, 1997; Dahl, 1999; Newey, 2001; Richardson, 2001).

More deeply discordant ideological roots, including a variety of radical positions on what a society and its schools should be, run beyond the mainstream liberal and conservative dialogue. Radical critiques influence the general debate by providing extreme positions, allowing liberals and conservatives to take more popular positions in the center. Radical ideas tend to have limited credibility in mainstream discussions, but liberals and conservatives draw from those ideas in proposing reforms (Dahl, 1999). Critical positions often appear first in the radical literature, then filter into the liberal and conservative rhetoric (Braun and Scheinberg, 1997; Nelson, Carlson, and Linton, 1972; Dahl, 1999; Simhony and Weinstein, 2001).

Mainstream views sound more reasonable as bases for reform, but radical ideas contain the seeds for longer-term and more significant change. In the age when kings and queens were presumed to rule by divine right, democracy was a radical view. In a dictatorship, individual freedom is radical.

INDIVIDUAL AND SOCIAL RIGHTS

One of the major struggles in determining justice in a democracy lies in finding a suitable balance between the interests of individuals and communities. This struggle has many titles but often is described as an ideological battle between individualism and communitarianism. These ideologies compete in their emphases, and in their more extreme versions offer a dialectic.

The radical right wing, known as reactionaries or libertarians, advocates individual freedoms with the least restraint possible. As Nozick (1974) phrases it,

> Individuals have rights, and there are things no person or group may do to them (without violating their rights). So strong and far-reaching are these rights that they raise the question of what, if anything, the state and its officials may do. How much room do individual rights leave for the state? . . . Our main conclusions about the state are that a minimal state, limited to the narrow functions of protection against force, theft, fraud, enforcement of contracts, and so on, is justified; that any more extensive state will violate person's rights not to be forced to do certain things, and is unjustified. (p. ix)

In addition to an antistate position, libertarians convey a strong procapitalism view, relatively unfettered entrepreneurship, and private enterprise. Excessive governmental control is assumed to kill individual initiative. Government, to libertarians, is an unfortunate development that has grown too large and too encompassing—stifling individual freedoms (Jonescu, 2012).

Libertarians want to dismantle the government, abolishing regulation, taxation, and public financing. They would eliminate Social Security, Medicare, welfare, public education, and the right of government to take property under eminent domain; libertarians aim at "nothing short of the privatization of social existence" (Newman, 1984, p. 162). As Thomas Sowell (1999) says, "The welfare state, however, has made many of the respectable, self-supporting poor look like chumps, as the government has lavished innumerable programs on those who violate all rules and refuse to take responsibility for themselves" (p. 89). Not all libertarians share the view that all government is harmful; some recognize a need for some governmental role in mediating disputes, regulating commerce in basic human needs, and protecting society. Many Tea Party members share this concept of a very limited government.

On the other side are communitarians of various stripes. Their major critique involves greed and social corruption of unregulated capitalism and the selfishness and self-centeredness that accompanies individualism. They believe that community, our social glue, is in serious jeopardy from excessive individualism. Some of these critiques take great pains to separate individualism—a belief in oneself above others—from individuality—an expression of the value of recognizing each person's worth. John Dewey's (1933) treatise on that separation is significant. He develops in other writings on democracy and schooling his concept that individual differences and individual learning are consistent with his concept of education as a social process (Dewey, 1916, 1930). Dewey also writes of a broader set of conflicts:

> There can be no conflict between the individual and the social. For both of these terms refer to pure abstractions. What do exist are conflicts between some individuals and some arrangements in social life; between groups and classes of individuals; between nations and races; between old traditions embedded in institutions and new ways of thinking and acting which spring from those few individuals who attack what is socially accepted. (Dewey, in Ratner, 1939, p. 435)

Communitarians don't always ignore or denigrate the value of individuals; they advocate a balance between individual liberty and social needs for common purposes—balancing rights and order (Sandel, 1998, 2010). Amitai Etzioni (1996) notes a major shift from "traditional" social order by edict, authoritarian rule, and rigid control to increasing individual rights. He argues,

> Some societies have lost their equilibrium, and are heavily burdened with the antisocial consequences of excessive liberty (not a concept libertarians or liberals often use). (p. xvii)

More radical communitarians argue for egalitarian answers to the excesses of individualism. They see a breakdown of social values, family structures, social responsibilities, shared interests, and collective purposes that constitute a decent society.

Among their concerns is the greedy continuation of "me" generation mentality and expansion of "yuppiness," antigovernment attacks that can undermine public confidence and lead to debilitating and discriminatory competitiveness, destruction of environmental protections and other regulatory needs, increased private territoriality, and suspicion of others. Unbridled individualism poses, they contend, clear and negative repercussions in charitable works, public welfare, public services, and public education—those major contributions to our civilization. Excessive individualism also appears in efforts to deregulate utilities and corporations, privatize public services, and maintain a social hierarchy based on birth, wealth, and historical status. Individualism is not usually advocated by members of the social class at the bottom. A premise of individualists is that those who have should continue to have. Egalitarian answers, in opposition, include expansion and guarantees of equal opportunities, forms of affirmative action, progressive taxation and redistribution of wealth, and such programs as national health care, Head Start, and safety net welfare. These intend to correct or mitigate inequalities among groups.

Failures in corporate and accounting self-regulation prompt an upsurge of interest in increasing public regulation and accountability. As in the antitrust period in the early twentieth century, this has ignited public concern about patterns of deregulation, privatization, and rampant individualism.

Ideological Roots of School Disputes

Competing ideas with differing expectations for schools include freedom and equality, public and private, individual and society, the masses and the elites, unity and diversity, and the religious and the secular.

Dualisms are false in that they don't exist in complete isolation from each other and don't usually require a pristine choice. We can't have mind without body, and body without mind may be possible, but we have no certain knowledge of that. So we can't choose either body or mind. But we are faced continuously with situations where we must exercise choice among competing interests. Those choices often are between two political ideologies, two opposing sets of interests, or two parts of a dialectic—each side of which entails some potentially good and bad consequences. Dualisms are useful as mental constructions to assist in making that choice or finding a new synthesis; they can assist in reasoned dialogue about competing interests and ideologies. Schooling is one very public activity where such dualisms occur with frequency.

Schools are directly engaged in developing the individuals and society of the future, and people care a

great deal about what kind of individuals and society will develop. As Apple (1990) states, "The conflicts over what should be taught are sharp and deep. It is not only an educational issue, but one that is inherently ideological and political" (p. vii). Traditionalists share a view that schools ought to follow time-honored ideas, practices, and authorities from a previous golden age of education. Progressivists share a different view that schools must be flexible, child centered, and future oriented.

Each ideology provides different views of schooling, from advocating abolition of public schools to using public schools for social criticism and the overthrow of oppression. Divergent views of schooling and politics can be understood in terms of an ideological continuum: from elitist positions on the extreme right to egalitarian positions on the extreme left, with mainstream conservative and liberal positions in the center (see Figure 1).

Radical right-wing ideas about schooling are not uniform; they come from different special interest groups. Some

FIGURE 1 A Spectrum of Political and Educational Views

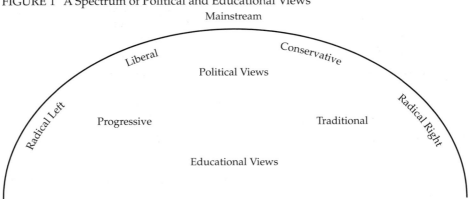

promote teaching fundamentalist religious dogma. Some seek to censor teaching materials dealing with sex, socialism, atheism, or anything they think is anti-American. And some want to undercut publicly supported schools in favor of elite schooling for a select group of students. Right-wing groups have attacked secular humanism, feminism, abortion rights, sex education, global education, and values education in schools.

Radical educational ideologies from the right include the views of the following:

> Libertarians: "Get government off our backs and out of our schools."
>
> Abolitionists: "Abolish public schooling."
>
> Extreme elitists: "Schooling for the best only; the rest into the work pool."

The radical left wing also offers a critical view of schools. Some see education as the way for the masses to uncover the evils of capitalism and the corporate state. Some propose education as the means for revolution, opening all the institutions of society to criticism. Left-wing groups have attacked business-sponsored teaching materials, religious dogma in public schools, tracking, discrimination, social control, and education for patriotic obedience.

Radical left-wing views include those of the following:

> Liberationists: "Liberate students from oppressive forces in school and society."

> Reconstructionists: "Use schools to criticize and remake society."
>
> Extreme egalitarians: "Abolish all privilege or distinction."

Conservative, liberal, and radical views of society and education provide different rationales for criticism of schools and different proposals for reform. They are general frameworks that underlie individual and group discontent with schools. Radical views are important because they present stark and clearly defined differences between egalitarian and elitist ideologies. However, mainstream conservative and liberal ideas govern most reform movements because of their general popularity and immense influence over media and government. Liberals, conservatives, and radicals differ in their views of which mainstream position has the schools in its grip (Aronowitz and Giroux, 1993).

The importance of education in society is reflected in controversies surrounding divergent ideological positions and the interests they represent.

In education, these fundamental goals and general practices have varied during different times and in different locations. Primitive education was dedicated to survival and continuing rituals and life patterns established by elders. Ancient schooling was devoted largely to inculcation of religious learnings. In Athens, philosophic and contemplative schooling supplanted religious, while Spartan education was heavily committed to the military life. Roman schooling was more practical than philosophic and intended for developing strong loyalty and citizenship. Spiritual ideas predominated in schools of the Middle Ages, a preparation for the afterlife. The Renaissance brought different goals for schools—enlightenment, development of human capacities, and individual creativity. For most of this time, formal schooling was for the elites, usually for families of religious, social, and political leaders. The main schooling arguments concerned how society's leaders should be prepared: strict learning of traditional roles, rituals, and concepts of knowledge—or contemplation of the good—or enlightenment and more flexible learnings.

Mass education arose as democracy developed, fostered especially in schooling in the United States from the mid-nineteenth century, and now spread throughout the industrialized world. Schooling for all developed some different educational goals under differing ideologies: basic literacy and numeracy, social control, civic responsibility, loyalty and patriotism, vocational and home training, character and values development, health and safety knowledge, human relationships, self-reliance and realization, and solving problems. Schooling also shifted toward more secular, scientific, and technological goals. Consistent with the evolution in democratic political concepts, ideas about schooling shifted from a focus on basic literacy and social control to broader intellectual development and increasing interest in individuality.

Newer developments in educational ideas challenged established purposes and practices in schools and posed interesting questions on the relation of individuals to their societies and important issues of justice and equity.

What dimensions of justice and equity should be expected in schools and classrooms? How should schools address justice and equity regarding individual choice, racism, gender, class, wealth, and religion? What interests are at stake? Competing answers to these questions show disparate interests. Chapters 2 through 9 involve schooling issues that raise questions of justice, fairness, and impartiality.

We would like to include in this volume all viewpoints on each educational issue, but that is an obvious impossibility. We have, therefore, limited each chapter to two distinct positions about the topic covered to stress the dialogue or dialectic quality of the issue. These positions draw from liberal-progressive ideas, from conservative-traditional, and from radical critiques from the left or right. Additional references to conservative, liberal, and radical literature are included, and we encourage exploration of these highly divergent views.

References

APPLE, M. (1990). *Ideology and Curriculum.* 2nd Ed. London: Routledge.

ARONOWITZ, S., AND GIROUX, H. (1983). *Education Under Siege.* South Hadley, MA: Bergin and Garvey.

BANDY, J., AND SMITH, J. (2005). *Coalitions across Borders.* Lanham, MD: Rowman & Littlefield.

BARRY, B. (2005). *Why Social Justice Matters.* Cambridge: Polity.

BELLAH, R. N., ET AL. (1985). *Habits of the Heart: Individualism and Commitment in American Life.* Berkeley: University of California Press.

BERLIN, I. (1969). *Four Essays on Liberty.* Oxford: Oxford University Press.

BOWLES, S., GINTIS, H., and GROSS, M. O. (2005). *Unequal Chances.* Princeton, NJ: Princeton University Press.

BRAUN, A., AND SCHEINBERG, S. (1997). *The Extreme Right.* Boulder, CO: Westview Press.

CHAREN. M. (2012). "Is Liberalism Immoral?" National Review Online. nationalreview.com. Mar. 16.

DAHL, G. (1999). *Radical Conservatism and the Future of Politics.* London: Sage.

DeMUTH, C., AND KRISTOL, W. (1995). *The Neoconservative Imagination.* Washington, DC: AEI Press.

DE RUGGERIO, G. (1927). *The History of European Liberalism.* Translated by R. G. Collingwood. Boston: Beacon Press.

DEWEY, J. (1916). *Democracy and Education.* New York: Macmillan.

———. (1930). *Individualism Old and New.* New York: Minton, Balch, and Co.

———. (1933). *How We Think.* Boston: D. C. Heath.

DOWNS, A. (1957). *An Economic Theory of Democracy.* New York: Harper/Addison Wesley.

ERIKSON, E. H. (1960). *Childhood and Society.* New York: W. W. Norton.

ETZIONI, A. (1996). *The New Golden Rule.* New York: Basic Books.

FISHKIN, J. S. (1992). *The Dialogue of Justice.* New Haven, CT: Yale University Press.

FREEDEN, M. (1998). *Ideologies and Political Theory.* Oxford: Oxford University Press.

FUENTES, C. (2005). *This I Believe.* New York: Random House.

GEUSS, R. (2001). *History and Illusion in Politics.* Cambridge: Cambridge University Press.

GILL, E. R. (2001). *Becoming Free: Autonomy and Diversity in the Liberal Polity.* Lawrence: University Press of Kansas.

GLADSTEIN, M. R. (1999). *The New Ayn Rand Companion.* Westport, CT: Greenwood.

GUTMAN, A. (1999). *Democratic Education.* Princeton, NJ: Princeton University Press.

HAHNEL, R. (2005). *Economic Justice and Democracy.* New York: Routledge.

HAMPSHIRE, S. (2000). *Justice Is Conflict.* Princeton, NJ: Princeton University Press.

HENDERSON, D. (2001). *Anti-Liberalism 2000.* London: Institute of Economic Affairs.

HERBERT, B. (2005). *Promises Betrayed.* New York: New York Times Books.

JACOBY, R. (2005). *Picture Imperfect: Utopian Thought for an Anti-Utopian Age.* New York: Columbia University Press.

JONESCU, D. (2012). "On Restoring American Individualism." American Thinker. americanthinker.com. Mar. 30.

Journal of Political Ideologies. London: Routledge.

KITCHING, G. (2001). *Seeking Social Justice through Globalization.* University Park: Pennsylvania State University Press.

KLOSKO, G. (2000). *Democratic Procedures and Liberal Consensus.* New York: Oxford University Press.

KOLM, S-C. (2005). *Macrojustice: The Political Economy of Fairness.* Cambridge: Cambridge University Press.

KRAMER, H., AND KIMBALL, R. (1999). *The Betrayal of Liberalism.* Chicago: Ivan R. Dee.

LANE, R. E. (1962). *Political Ideology.* New York: The Free Press of Glencoe.

LIPPMAN, W. (1934). *The Method of Freedom.* New York: Macmillan.

LITTLE, I. M. D. (2002). *Ethics, Economics, and Politics.* Oxford: Oxford University Press.

MARIETTA, M. (2012). *A Citizen's Guide to American Ideology: Conservatism and Liberalism in Contemporary Politics.* New York: Routledge.

MAURO, R. M. (2008). "Political Science Education and the Conceptual Analysis of Ideology." *Journal of Political Ideologies* 13(1):55–72.

McKENZIE, J. (1984). *A Study of the Relative Democratic Nature of Gifted Education Programs in New Jersey.* Unpublished dissertation, Rutgers University.

MITZMAN, A. (2003). *Prometheus Revisited: The Quest for Global Justice in the Twenty-First Century.* Amherst, MA: University of Massachusetts Press.

MONROE, K. R. (2012). *Ethics in an Age of Terrorism and Genocide.* Princeton: Princeton University Press.

NELSON, J., CARLSON, K., AND LINTON, T. 1972). *Radical Ideas and the Schools.* New York: Holt, Rinehart and Winston.

NELSON, J., AND GREEN, V. (1980). *International Human Rights.* Stanfordville, NY: Coleman Publishers.

NEWEY, G. (2001). *After Politics.* New York: Palgrave.

NEWMAN, S. L. (1984). *Liberalism at Wit's End.* Ithaca, NY: Cornell University Press.

NODDINGS, N. (1995). *Philosophy of Education.* Boulder, CO: Westview Press.

NOZICK, R. (1974). *Anarchy, State, and Utopia.* New York: Basic Books.

PAVOLA, J., AND LOWE, I., eds. (2005). *Environmental Values in a Globalizing World.* New York: Routledge.

Pew Research Center. (2011). "Report: Beyond Red and Blue." May 4. www .people-press.org.

PIPER, J. R. (1997). *Ideologies and Institutions.* New York: Rowman & Littlefield.

RAND, A. (1943). *The Fountainhead.* New York: New American Library.

———. (1997). *The Journals of Ayn Rand.* Edited by D. Harriman. New York: Dutton.

RATNER, J. (1939). *Intelligence in the Modern World: John Dewey's Philosophy.* New York: Random House.

RAWLS, J. (1971). *A Theory of Justice.* Cambridge, MA: Harvard University Press.

———. (1999). *The Law of Peoples.* Cambridge, MA: Harvard University Press.

———. (2001). *Justice as Fairness.* Edited by E. Kelly. Cambridge, MA: Harvard University Press.

———. (2005). *Political Liberalism.* Expanded Ed. New York: Columbia University Press.

REISMAN, D. (1999). *Conservative Capitalism.* New York: St. Martin's Press.

RICHARDSON, J. L. (2001). *Contending Liberalisms in World Politics.* Boulder, CO: Lynne Rienner.

ROTHENBERG, R. (1984). *The Neoliberals.* New York: Simon and Schuster.

RUSSELL, B. (1955). *Authority and the Individual.* London: Allen and Unwin.

SANDEL M. (1998). *Liberalism and the Limits of Justice.* 2d Ed. Cambridge: Cambridge University Press.

———. (2010). *Justice: What Is the Right Thing to Do?* New York: Farrar, Straus and Giroux.

SHAPIRO, J. S. (1958). *Liberalism: Its Meaning and History.* New York: D. Van Nostrand.

SHILS, E. (1968). "The Concept of Ideology." In *The International Encyclopedia of the Social Sciences*, ed. D. Sills. New York: Macmillan.

SIMHONY, A., and WEINSTEIN, D. (2001). *The New Liberalism.* Cambridge: Cambridge University Press.

SOWELL, T. (1999). *The Quest for Cosmic Justice.* New York: Free Press.

SPITZ, D. (1982). *The Real World of Liberalism.* Chicago: University of Chicago Press.

SPRAGENS, T. A. (1999). *Civic Liberalism.* Lanham, MD: Rowman & Littlefield.

STEINFELS, P. (1979). *The Neoconservatives.* New York: Simon and Schuster.

TOMASI, J. (2001). *Liberalism Beyond Justice.* Princeton, NJ: Princeton University Press.

VALENTYNE, P., ed., (2003). *Equality and Justice.* Vols. 1–6. New York: Routledge.

WHITE, J. (2011). "Left and Right as Political Resources." *Journal of Political Ideologies* 16(2):123–144.

WINTER, M. (2012). *Rethinking Virtue Ethics.* New York: Springer.

CHAPTER 2

Family Choice in Education: Public Interest or Private Good

Is family choice of schools in the public interest?

POSITION 1: CHOICE CREATES COMPETITION THAT IMPROVES OUTCOMES FOR INDIVIDUAL STUDENTS

We believe that parents should have a range of options, including great public schools, public charter schools, and access to high-quality private schools through school vouchers and scholarship tax credit programs. Educational excellence has nothing to do with the label on the front of the school. That's why it is about a fundamental right for parents to have access to whichever quality schools serve their kids best.

—American Federation for Children (2011)

Why Educational Choice Is Needed

If your children attended a school in which most students scored below the state average on standardized tests, what could you do? What if they were enrolled in a school with few certified teachers, overcrowded classrooms, few computers, little lab equipment, and not enough books or other supplies? Could you find a way to get them the education they need? If you were unhappy with your child's school because the curriculum was not rigorous enough or because it violated your beliefs and values, how could you remedy the situation? Depending on a family's income, those choices become even more limited.

Dissatisfied families can work to correct problems in their children's public schools. Doing so, however, often involves a long, cumbersome process of political action—meeting with teachers and principals, attending school board meetings, working on committees, and being an active presence in a school. Time and energy commitments usually are more than most parents can make, and risk of failure and frustration is high. Even when these efforts are successful, the resulting changes may come too late for the students whose parents initially tried to make them. Students are in a particular grade for only one year. Schools often cannot modify programs or policies that quickly. Although working for long-term change is an option, it is a choice that doesn't meet the most immediate needs of parents and children.

Families with enough money can decide to send their children to expensive, nonsectarian private schools. Their budget can absorb the cost of this decision even as the parents continue paying taxes to support public schools. Additionally, because there are only a limited number of such schools, attending them may mean that students must live away from their families for long periods. This disruption of family life for the sake of a child's education is not often an attractive option for parents or young people, even when the family can afford it. Instead of increasing parental influence in children's lives, this choice weakens it. Private schools remain options only for the wealthiest families since the tuition costs run into the tens of thousands of dollars per child.

Parents with more limited financial resources can choose to send their children to less expensive and more accessible private schools affiliated with religious organizations (McDonald, 2012). In fact, of the almost 34,000 private schools in the United States, close to 68 percent have connections to a religious group (Broughman, Swaim, and Hryczaniuk, 2011). However, this choice is still of limited help. Many families are not comfortable with the differences between their religious beliefs and those of the organization sponsoring the school. In times of economic distress, tuition may become too much of a burden for the family budget to bear.

Indeed, if a family has no surplus funds in its budget, the option of any kind of private school is not available. Most poor children attend urban or rural public schools, where achievement lags behind their peers in suburban schools, particularly for children of color and English language learners (Aud, Fox, and KewalRamani, 2010). Many African American and Latino parents are deeply concerned about the quality of their children's education; however, without viable family choice programs, they cannot translate their concerns into action (Black Alliance for Educational Options, 2011; Hispanic Council for Reform and Educational Options, 2011). However, the organization of public education hinders families in their efforts to provide their children with the advantages of a good education.

Because Americans wanted to maintain a high level of local control over schools, districts were established on the basis of geography—meaning that cities, towns, villages, or any part of those municipalities can become school districts. That way, local branches of government, most often school boards, can be elected by and held responsible to residents of the areas the schools serve. In practice, however, these forms of governance have become less responsive to dissatisfied parents. Many critics believe that public school bureaucracy has, over time, become elaborate and self-protective (Klein, 2011; Turque, 2011).

For example, once a district is established, students are assigned to schools on the basis of where they live within and among those districts. The dividing lines are firmly maintained. Moving from school to school within a district often is difficult; moving from district to district (unless the family changes its residence) is almost impossible. Assigning students to schools on the basis of their residence minimizes parents' choice about the school their children can attend. Families' financial situations, not their commitments to their children, determine the amount of educational choice they have. If a family can afford to live where a school matches their hopes and ambitions, then all is well. If a family lives where that match does not exist and they cannot afford to move to a better district, then their relative poverty deprives them of the freedom to choose their children's school.

Others besides parents are concerned about education and have expertise to contribute in deciding what kind of schools and programs will best serve children and our society. Educators have access to research about academic programs that ensure success for children having difficulties with traditional ways of teaching and learning. Health professionals have suggestions about issues affecting children's physical and emotional well-being and how those concerns can be addressed in schools. Businesspeople can offer advice and support to schools in preparing young people for their future in an ever more demanding job market. However, despite the goodwill and knowledge these people bring to questions about education, none of them is as concerned about the welfare of an individual child as his or her loving and committed parents. While parental authority with regard to children is not unlimited in this country, we Americans believe that generally it should be the most significant factor in determining most aspects of a child's life. Of those concerned about a child's education, parents have the most long-term relationship with children, giving them insights into what is right for their child that not even the most famous educational expert could ever hope to have. Ultimately, parents should be the final decision makers about *their* child's education. As Americans, we should work to ensure that all parents have this right, not just those who have achieved a certain level of economic success. In the last twenty years, we have come to recognize that state-sponsored schools historically put a stranglehold on parental choice, which Americans increasingly support. In a recent Gallup Poll, 74 percent favored allowing parents to choose which public school their children attended regardless of where they live, 70 percent favored charter schools, and 34 percent favored allowing children to attend private schools at public expense (Bushaw and Lopez, 2011). Public policy has responded to the need for a marketplace of school choices for families by creating several options. Among them are choices within the public school system, on its "borders," and in private schools. In each case, public monies provide the necessary funding.

Options for Parents and Children

Open Enrollment and Magnet Schools

Within the public school system, districts have adopted "open enrollment" or "choice" policies that allow families to research, visit, and apply to a number of schools they believe will best serve their children. Geography is no longer a barrier to educational options; districts provide transportation to whatever school the child attends. When they look over the landscape of schools from which they can choose, parents find large, comprehensive schools; schools linked and responsive to neighborhoods; small schools that provide individualized attention; and magnet schools with specialized curricula, designed to attract and serve particular groups of students. In addition, some states and the District of Columbia have created options that allow taxpayer monies to be turned over to private schools in the form of vouchers. Other states provide substantial tax credits for corporations that provide students in low-performing districts with scholarships to private schools. Charter schools are other publicly funded choices. They operate on the edges of public school district—within the borders and under the jurisdiction of some regulations but freed from rules that prevent public schools from serving all children well.

The first option has been tried with limited success. The 2001 No Child Left Behind legislation provided some choice by allowing parents to transfer their children from failing schools to more successful ones. Effective open enrollment policies allow students to cross invisible boundaries created by school attendance zones. The integration of high- and low-achieving, rich and poor, African American, White, and Latino students has benefits for all of them. Young people from less privileged backgrounds attend schools that are high performing with teachers who are highly effective. They learn the habits of mind and the etiquette of the middle- and upper-class peers. Students from wealthier families gain experiences with people whose backgrounds are different from their own, in the process becoming better prepared for the diverse world they will enter. Except for Alabama, Maryland, North Carolina, and Virginia, all states have enacted some type of "open enrollment" policy. However, very few of the states' policies require schools within districts or districts within states to participate in open enrollment. There is little or no incentive for successful schools or districts to accept students from failing ones (U.S. Department of Education, 2011b).

Other forms of open enrollment allow students to choose among many options within a district—in New York City, for example, a student can list up to twelve high schools that he or she would like to attend. Students are accepted into one school, and up to 48 percent receive their first choice. Students who are not accepted into any of their choices—about 45 percent begin the process again by visiting "school fairs" where underenrolled schools (often newly created ones) explain their programs and the advantages a student will gain by attending (Jennings, 2010; Robbins, 2011a, 2011b). The prestige attached to various schools benefits the students who attend them. Like elite colleges, such schools incorporate students into networks of highly successful alumni and families of other students. In applying to multiple schools and finding themselves evaluated against other students who are competing for the same spots, students get a taste of the process of advancement in this society. The pride that they feel in being accepted appears to be a motivating force in their commitment to academic tasks and, ultimately, to achievement (Rosenbloom, 2010). New York City has been rated first in the nation with regard to providing meaningful school choice for parents (Whitehurst, 2011). However, nationwide, other districts are providing choice for families, and in the process they are addressing issues of concern such as transportation, parents' access to information, and funding that can limit the success of open enrollment.

In the 1970s, some districts used "magnet schools" to draw students from all across a district as part of their efforts to desegregate. They remain vibrant learning centers in many cities. "Magnet schools offer a wide range of distinctive education programs. Some emphasize academic subjects such as math, science, technology, language immersion, visual and performing arts, or humanities. Others use specific instructional approaches, such as Montessori methods, or approaches found in international baccalaureate programs or early college programs" (U.S. Department of Education, 2011a). The magnet school approach to choice enables families to match school specialties with students' interests. When students find schools that meet their goals and fit their particular skills and passions, they are more likely to take on academic tasks that might otherwise be too burdensome—or boring (Alvarez, Edwards, and Harris, 2010). More than 2,200 magnets operate in the United States and serve approximately 1.5 million students, most of them in high schools (Chen, 2011). Studies have shown that young people who attend magnet schools experience less segregated environments and achieve more academic success than do their counterparts in traditional public schools in the same cities (Frahm, 2010). Magnet schools are an increasingly popular choice for urban parents who want their children to have the advantages provided by a diverse student body in which there are high expectations for academic success (Haynes, Phillips, and Goldring, 2010). Students who attend magnet schools perceive them as providing better preparation for college and careers, increasing their chances for academic and economic success (Williams, 2010).

Vouchers

Vouchers transfer taxpayer dollars directly to families to allow them to pay for the educational program they believe will be most beneficial for their child. Milton Friedman, an economist who first proposed vouchers fifty years ago, believed that the idea would work best if each family received an amount of money equal to their school district's per-pupil expenditure (Hendrie, 2004). Additional subsidies would be provided for children with special needs. Ideally, there would be no restriction against parents' adding their own money to what they received from the government to pay for more expensive schools— and there would be no restriction on what type of school a family could choose.

In the early 1990s, experiments with vouchers began with privately funding programs. The largest, the Children's Scholarship Fund, sponsors nearly

26,000 children across the country. However, these programs cannot keep pace with the applications from parents who want to provide their children with the benefits of a private school education (Children's Scholarship Fund, 2011). Seven states—Florida, Utah, Main, Ohio, Vermont, Wisconsin, and Indiana—and the District of Columbia have voucher programs (Sutton & King, 2011; Zehr, 2011). Milwaukee and Cleveland have the largest publicly funded programs in the country. Approximately 50,000 children in those cities attend private schools, mostly affiliated with religious institutions (Alliance for School Choice, 2011). The schools meet state health and safety standards and regulations and agree to use random selection processes in admitting voucher students. Families that have used vouchers in Milwaukee, Cleveland, and Washington report greater satisfaction with their schools than do parents who children attend traditional public schools (Witte, Wolf, Cowen, Fleming, and Lucas-McLean, 2008).

Proponents of vouchers argue that one advantage they have over other choice programs is that they allow parents to select schools that not only match their children's academic interests but also conform to the family's values. It is difficult, for example, for young Muslims to find space within their schools where they can meet their obligation to pray; they cannot leave school on Fridays, their holy day, to attend services at their mosques (MacFarquhar, 2008). Both Muslims and Jews sometimes find it difficult to obtain food in public school cafeterias that meets their dietary laws. The coeducational nature of public schools also violates the religious beliefs of some students and their families (MacFarquhar, 2008; Zine, 2007). Voucher programs allow parents to remove their children from schools they find offensive and place them in schools that match their religious beliefs.

Critics of vouchers question the use of taxpayer dollars to educate children in schools affiliated with religious groups. Some of their concern is rooted in their understanding of the First Amendment's prohibition against governmental support of religion. Beginning in the 1940s, the Supreme Court began to enforce the ban by creating standards that limited states and municipalities' relationships to religious institutions, establishing a greater distance between church and state than had previously existed. However, the Court has also held that many government policies benefiting religious groups *are* constitutional. For example, tax exemption for churches and religious schools, tax deductions of contributions to religious charities, tax credits for tuition paid to religious schools, transportation for children in those schools, and police or fire protection of religious institutions have all been declared legal. Even more closely related to the question of school choice, the GI Bill, Pell grants, federally subsidized student loans, and state tuition assistance programs for college students have not been declared unconstitutional even though some money from those programs has gone to schools directly affiliated with religious groups. The Court has established a policy of "neutrality" with regard to such funding. If a program provides benefits to individuals according to neutral guidelines and the individuals use those benefits for a service provided by a religious group, the wall between church and state has not been violated. The government is not supporting a religious institution; individuals are doing so through private decisions (*Mueller v. Allen*, 1983; *Witters v. Washington Department of Services for the Blind*, 1986; *Zobrest v. Catalina Foothills School District*, 1993; *Agostini v. Felton*, 1997). Using that reasoning, the justices ruled that the Cleveland voucher program was legal.

Another concern about using taxpayer dollars to provide funds for private education is the potential for discriminatory admissions policies in nonpublic schools. Opponents suggest that religious schools, for example, will be able to refuse admission to young people who are not members of the religious organizations with which the schools are affiliated. They also argue that private schools will be able to refuse students with conditions that create special educational needs. While it is certainly justified to worry about unfair admissions practices, current laws already protect young people from arbitrary discrimination. In fact, these laws were used to correct just such problems in the admissions policies of several high schools participating in the Milwaukee voucher program (Garn and Cobb, 2008). However, the Supreme Court has also ruled that private organizations, even those that benefit from indirect taxpayer support, can refuse to admit members who inclusion would significantly violate the organization's beliefs (*Roberts v. United States Jaycees*, 1984; *Hurley v. Irish American Gay, Lesbian, Bisexual Group of Boston*, 1995; *Boy Scouts of America v. Dale*, 2000). The Court has not yet established whether these rulings apply to church-affiliated schools, but it seems likely that they would.

Voucher opponents also raise objections based on their fear that parents could use taxpayer funds to send children to schools affiliated with organizations whose beliefs violate American values. At times, their concerns seem exaggerated and based more on opposition to the principle of choice than on any real danger that groups such as the Ku Klux Klan or Muslim extremists would found voucher-funded schools. Laws already exist to prevent anyone in the United States, including school teachers and administrators, from advocating illegal activities.

Just because government would not be running schools funded through voucher payments, it does not necessary follow that there could be no oversight of such schools. Student progress could be monitored. Many private schools already participate in state accountability systems. These oversight systems could be modeled on European "inspectorates" and modified to America's needs to ensure that a return to the monopoly of government-run schools was unnecessary (Betts et al., 2006).

Charter Schools

Charter schools are another option that is increasingly available to parents who want to ensure that their children receive an education designed to help them achieve academic and economic success. Charter schools are relatively autonomous of local school district control—they are able to choose their own governing boards, hire and terminate teachers without meeting union contracts or state certification requirements, design and deliver innovative curricula, and use instructional techniques that meet individual students' needs. In exchange for the increased autonomy, charter schools are held accountable for student performance and are subject to closure if they are found to be unsuccessful. The first charter school opened in 1992; twenty years later, there are almost 5,000, serving 1.6 million children—approximately 3 percent of all public school students (Dynarski, Hoxby, Loveless, Schneider, Whitehurst, and Witte, 2010; Miron, 2011).

In order for charters to provide the best opportunities to individual students, nonprofit charter management organizations (CMOs) or networks have been developed. Among the most successful are KIPP (Knowledge Is Power Program) and Uncommon Schools. The schools operated by these CMOs are college preparatory and serve students in low-income urban neighborhoods. KIPP schools describe themselves as "free, open-enrollment, college-preparatory public schools where underserved students develop the knowledge, skills, and character traits needed to succeed in top quality high schools, colleges, and the competitive world beyond." They are built on five principles known as the five "pillars"—high expectations, choice and commitment, more time, power to lead, and focus on results (KIPP, 2011). Uncommon Schools identify themselves as "a community of educators, families, and students united by the fierce belief that every student can graduate from college." Like KIPP schools, they focus on preparing their students to be college ready. They hold high expectations, provide consistent and constructive feedback, and use data extensively to "drive" instruction and ensure student success (Uncommon Schools, 2011). While not all CMOs are alike in every respect, they do share the core vision of KIPP and Uncommon Schools—that economic hardship should not prevent young people from obtaining an education that will help them achieve personal success. Most CMOs are concerned about the behavioral climate in their schools. Students and their parents can be assured that schoolmates will be focused on their education and refrain from disrespectful or hurtful actions—or they will be dismissed. In charter schools, the belief that hard work is the only path to success is emphasized as well. Students and parents often are required to sign "contracts" that express their commitment to "work hard and be nice" (KIPP, 2011). Teachers are also expected to take their responsibility for student achievement seriously; they are evaluated and rewarded or penalized on those terms (Lake, Dusseault, Bowen, Demeritt, and Hill, 2010). Charter schools are sites where individual commitment and effort are expected and rewarded. In those ways, they mirror and prepare students for our free-market society.

Charter schools receive per-pupil funding from the state and/or local school district, but for a variety of reasons, on average, they receive approximately 20 percent less money than traditional public schools (Dynarski et al., 2010; Miron, 2011). Many are required to pay rent or buy buildings in which to house their students. Fortunately, charter schools are able to raise additional funds through donations from individuals or corporations. In fact, many large corporations have given millions of dollars to charter schools. For example, Doris and Donald Fisher, founders of the Gap clothing store chain, have given $60 million to KIPP. The Walton family, owners of Walmart, has contributed over $25 million to KIPP schools and over $157 million to charter schools and other programs that support choice. These extra funds make it possible for charters to offer longer days than traditional public schools do, to provide students with extra academic support, and to offer activities that make them competitive with more privileged peers.

Studies of student achievement in charter schools taken as a whole do not provide evidence that they are all helping young people make more progress than their counterparts in traditional public schools. They demonstrate great variability in the impact that charters have on student progress (Dynarski et al., 2010; Miron, 2011). When the studies are disaggregated, they reveal that some charters are much more successful than the traditional public schools that students would have attended (Hoxby, Murarka, and Kang, 2009). However, students and parents express high satisfaction with their choice of a charter school (Gleason, Clark, Tuttle, and Dwoyer, 2010). They welcome their children's academic and social development and believe that the schools are superior to those they previously attended.

The founders of the modern American educational system believed that it was innovative and necessary to have government provide schools for the country's children, organize their curriculum, certify that teachers were qualified, and deliver services like career counseling and extracurricular activities. However, we have come to understand that governmental structures can, over time, become ineffective and overly costly. A greater reliance on a marketlike structure that allows choice can promote freedom and improve education. When there is a monopoly and only governments run publicly funded schools, families are forced to choose them—if only because the other options are so costly. Allowing—and funding—choices other than traditional schools provides more Americans with freedom to seek out the kind of education they believe is right for their children and to share in the competitive advantages enjoyed by people whose wealth has made those choices possible in the past. Choice improves education because when public schools are no longer guaranteed "customers," they face competition, and that competition serves as an incentive to improve. Schools' survival would be dependent on parents' decisions about their effectiveness, efficiency, responsiveness, and innovation. They would have a much greater motivation to ensure high levels of customer satisfaction than they do under the current system (Moe, 2008).

Every American deserves to achieve as much as they are willing to work for. Family choice of schools releases the power of the market to help ensure that they do.

POSITION 2: CHOICE LIMITS PUBLIC SCHOOLS' ABILITY TO ACHIEVE SOCIAL GOALS

It is unlikely that the United States would have emerged as a world leader had it left the development of education to the whim and will of the free market. But the market, with its great strengths, is not the appropriate mechanism to supply services that should be distributed equally to people in every neighborhood in every city and town in the nation without regard to their ability or political power. The market is not the right mechanism to supply police protection or fire protection, nor is it the right mechanism to supply public education.

—Ravitch (2010, p. 116)

Americans accepted the idea of the "common school" in the mid-nineteenth century and saw it as a way to prepare citizens who had the knowledge and habits needed for self-governance of the new nation. The idea was that, through public education, young people from all socioeconomic backgrounds would be prepared to vote and serve on juries; to behave responsibly toward government, property, and the rights of others; and to be honest and productive workers. They would learn tolerance and respect for the diverse people and different points of view in the country (Good and Braden, 2000). Americans were willing to hand over hard-earned money to the government in the form of school taxes because they believed that public education would return "profits" to every member of society, not just to schoolchildren and their families. Americans also decided that choices about education— funding, teachers, and curricula—should be made through the electoral and representative processes characteristic of our public life. For more than 150 years, elected school boards or other forms of local governments have managed schools. If people disagreed with decisions by these elected officials, they elected others. Taxpayers had the right to make choices about schools they supported financially and thus continued to support a system that was unique and served as a beacon for immigrants who wanted their children to have better lives.

After World War II, however, some Americans began to question the role of government in society. In order to respond to the Great Depression and World War II, governmental programs and regulation increased in the 1930s and 1940s. In the 1950s, there was a political and social backlash. As Americans began to understand the loss of freedom that people living under communism had suffered, some people became increasingly concerned that any form of collectivism could have similar results. They saw governmental involvement in daily life as a movement in that direction. They believed that individual liberty could be protected in a society only when individual property rights, the rule of law, free markets, and free trade were respected. They argued that most industries should be run exclusively by private companies, that competition within an industry should be encouraged, and that government should not regulate how business could be conducted. To them, if competition, privatization, and deregulation existed, then efficiency and productivity would improve, the quality of goods and services would increase, costs would decrease, and the tax burden would be lessened. Such a world would be an environment where all social institutions, including education, would operate with maximum efficiency (Fiala and Owens, 2010). This emerging distrust of government's influence was coupled with a critique of American public schools. After the Soviet Union launched a satellite into space in 1957, there was growing concern that the education system was inadequate to protect the U.S. economy from the threat of communist competition. Critics argued that schools of education inadequately prepared teachers, that unions protected incompetent school professionals, and that public school curricula had been "dumbed" down. They believed that because public schools faced no meaningful competition from private schools, they were inefficient and inadequate.

In the 1960s, the argument to allow free-market principles, including competition, to improve schooling and promote individual rights became entwined with court-ordered desegregation. Some critics of governmental interference in daily life saw the *Brown v. Board of Education* (1954) decision as an example of the harm that too much large government could cause. They believed that private individuals and businesses, through local governments, had the right to create a way of life that privileged one race over another and established laws that protected those privileges (Fiala and Duncan, 2010). Milton Friedman, often cited as the "father" of the school choice movement, argued that providing families with school funding directly would eliminate the need for enforced desegregation. Courts would not have to impose a particular idea of justice or require that young children be bused to schools across town from their homes. Families could choose all-white, all-black, or mixed schools as they saw fit, and the forces of the market would ensure the success of the schools that most people preferred as they "voted with their feet." Drawing on Friedman's ideas of vouchers, southern states, including Mississippi, Alabama, Arkansas, Georgia, Louisiana, North Carolina, South Carolina, and Virginia, issued them to white students attending segregated private schools (Fiala and Duncan, 2010; Sutton and King, 2011). The Supreme Court ruled that the use of vouchers to sidestep the law requiring an end to segregated schools was illegal, and the practice ceased. However, the idea of vouchers to provide families with school choice remained.

By contrast, in the 1970s, school choice within the public school system was used to integrate public urban schools. Magnet schools, with rigorous and appealing academic programs, were established to attract white and black families to send their children to school together. In the 1980s, the movement for school choice remained vocal, with calls for vouchers for religious schools. Later that decade, a new form of choice emerged. Albert Shanker, leader of the American Federation of Teachers, advocated that teachers be allowed to create "charter schools," in which innovative instructional techniques could be piloted (Shanker, 1988). His support for the concept decreased as he saw how it was taken over by noneducators and people committed to dismantling the public school systems. However, charter schools continued to gain supporters and received backing in the Bush, Clinton, and Obama administrations.

Over time, the idea of a public school system that deserved funding because it prepared citizens has been replaced by the idea that tax dollars should be used to improve the chances of individual children to obtain an education that will make them economically successful. Schooling was no longer seen as a way to achieve the "common good." Instead, its purpose was the "private good" of individual children. Once education was seen as a commodity to be obtained rather than a service to be provided, support for a "marketplace" where competing providers would offer that "product" was inevitable among those who see the forces of the free market as the best way to guarantee individual freedom. Their support has proven powerfully persuasive; however, the market model of publicly funded education has serious flaws that limit the ability of the electorate to direct school policy, to oversee the use of funding, and to ensure equal access to schools. Long-standing social problems are not addressed by family choice: schools remain segregated, and differences in achievement among rich and poor; white, black, and Latino; and male and female are not corrected. In fact, the educational marketplace acts pretty much the way most free markets do—people with money; information; the "right" social class, ethnicity, or gender; and powerful personal connections have access to "better" goods. A hierarchy among products emerges, and existing social injustices are perpetuated. Most important, the needs of the national community are sacrificed to the desires of the lucky few.

Choice and Integration

Family choice policies have been used by racial isolationists (vouchers for all-white private schools in the post-*Brown* South) and by integrationists (urban magnet schools). Since the courts ruled against the use of choice to support segregated schools, choice proponents have argued that creating attractive options for parents will help integrate American education. For example, voucher supporters have suggested that because private schools, especially urban Catholic schools, draw from larger geographic areas than public schools, they will be able to attract more diverse student populations. Vouchers will make it possible for more minority parents, disproportionately represented among the poor, to choose private schools, resulting in greater integration in K–12 settings. In Milwaukee, in the early days of the voucher program, supporters claimed that it had resulted in greater diversity in participating private schools. However, the greater racial balance may actually have been the result of white flight. The number of minority students did increase; however, the number of white students decreased even more. So, the demographic changes could represent a trend toward increasing segregation in schools that previously were more integrated than public schools (Wolf, 2008).

Charter schools also appear to do little to remedy racial and ethnic segregation in publicly funded schools. The research indicates that charters are more racially segregated than the districts from which students come in every state and metropolitan area (Frankenburg, Siegel-Hawley, and Wang, 2011). In one study of almost 1,000 charter schools across the country, only 25 percent had student populations similar to that of the district from which students came (Miron, Uschel, Mathis, and Tornquist, 2010). In New York City charter schools, students are much more likely to be African American and much less likely to be white or Asian than the average student in traditional public schools in the City (Hoxby et al., 2009).

Even magnet schools appear to have lost their ability to lessen racial isolation. As more and more school districts are released from court-ordered school desegregation plans, fewer white parents are choosing to send their children to those schools (Smrekar, 2009; Haynes et al., 2010).

Supporters of family choice seem able to ignore how race and class prejudice affect the marketplace they are trying to create. First, the ability to take part in choice programs is dependent on whether families have access to information about their options and whether the need for transportation to schools is met. If school districts do not provide outreach and transportation to all families, children attending "schools of choice" are in more segregated environments than they would have been if they had stayed in schools in their geographically based attendance zones (Bifulco, Ladd, and Ross, 2009). White parents often measure school quality by the "qualities" of the students and believe that the classmates who are white and middle class make the best companions for their children (O'Shaunessy, 2007). Research and experience has shown that there is a "tipping point"—a demographic profile at which white parents leave a school or district. Most studies indicate that once the black enrollment in a school or district reaches approximately 30 percent, white enrollment decreases (Gulosino and d'Entremont, 2011). Most schools of choice do not attempt to balance racial enrollments, and there has been disincentive from the federal government to do so. Consequently, market forces take over, and schools of choice reflect the racial prejudices of the society. Nothing in choice plans diminishes these social realities.

In addition to segregation by race, school choice encourages other forms of isolation. Data indicate that there are fewer English language learners or students with disabilities in charter schools (Miron et al., 2010; Frankenberg et al., 2011). Furthermore, the religious affiliation of many schools participating in voucher programs and the conversion of some religious schools to charters also pose problems. They protect families' desires that children participate in their traditions at the expense of the social goal of broadening young peoples' horizons and helping them take their place in an increasingly diverse society (Crowson and Goldring, 2009). Sectarian schools do not prepare young people adequately enough to meet society's goals and, therefore, are not worthy of public funding.

Choice and Academic Achievement

Proponents of family choice in education argue that public schools, especially those that serve poor children, no longer enable their students to learn and excel academically to a level that will prepare them for college and the labor force. They believe that the competition created by an array of educational choices will result in improved outcomes not only in schools of choice but also in the traditional public schools that are challenged by them. However, the promise seems to be unfulfilled.

The outcomes of voucher programs that allow children to attend private schools at public expense have been studied for many years. Previous research on the differences between private and public schools demonstrated that private school students do have slightly higher academic achievement than their public school counterparts. However, that same research indicates that most differences between students can be attributed to factors beyond schools' control, including parents' educational attainment and their income. In the past, researchers showed that the "private school effect"—the amount of the difference in achievement between public and private school students that can be attributed to attending private school—is very small indeed (Coleman, Hoffer, and Kilgore, 1982; Alexander and Pallas, 1985; Hoffer, 2000).

Research on the largest voucher programs—Milwaukee, Cleveland, and Washington, D.C.—have demonstrated that attending a private school does not in and of itself guarantee higher academic achievement. Evaluations have found little or no difference in voucher public school students' performances. In Washington, although students attending private schools using vouchers did have marginally higher reading scores, the most disadvantaged students have not shown test score gains statistically different from their peers in traditional public schools (Wolf, 2010). In Milwaukee, researchers have found no significant effects of the voucher program on the rates of student gains in reading and math achievement (Wolf, 2011). In Cleveland and throughout Ohio, into which vouchers have expanded, students in traditional public schools outperform voucher students on state-mandated standardized tests (Ott, 2011).

Findings about student achievement in charter schools are less consistent. One of the largest projects included approximately 65 percent of charters across the country. The study found that of charter school students, 17 percent had higher results than comparable traditional public schools (TPS) students, 37 percent had significantly worse results, and 46 percent had average growth no different from students in traditional public schools (Center for Research on Education Outcomes, 2009; Miron, 2011). Another project examined the results for students attending charter middle schools for which there was so much demand that the schools had to hold lotteries to choose students. This study found that charters were neither more nor less successful than traditional public schools in improving students' academic achievement, their behavior, or their progress through school (Gleason et al., 2010). There are over sixty studies that provide evidence of charter schools' impact on student achievement. The conclusions that can be drawn from them are that, in general, charter schools perform at levels similar to those of traditional charter schools but that that performance differs widely among charter schools. When charters are viewed nationally or at the state level, they appear to have less impact than traditional public schools; when a small number of schools are studied, the results tend to be more positive in charter schools (Miron, 2011). For example, two studies of New York City charter school students did find that they outperformed traditional public school students on standardized tests. However, many charters in those studies had the financial resources to provide longer school days and school years, multiple instances of testing students, and additional pay for high-performing teachers, all of which at least one study acknowledged as being correlated with the schools' positive results (Center for Research on Education Outcomes, 2010; Hoxby et al., 2010).

Charter school advocates argue that they receive less state and federal funding than traditional public schools—by as much as 20 percent—and that they "do more with less." However, the differences in resources among schools of choice and between those schools and traditional public schools have several sources. State funding formulae are very complicated, but, in general, schools with needier students receive a larger share of state and federal educational dollars. One reason why charters receive less money is that they serve fewer of the neediest students, particularly students with disabilities (Miron and Urschel, 2010). In addition, charter schools are not required to provide transportation or food (although some do). Those schools that do not provide those services do not receive the subsidies that public schools, which are mandated to provide them, do. They are able, however, to supplement their public dollars with private ones—and they do. One study found that some charters receive private funds exceeding $10,000 per pupil more than traditional public schools receive and $10,000 more than the less philanthropically "popular" charter schools (Baker and Ferris, 2011). For example, in 2008, the New Schools Venture Fund provided $1.3 million to the Achievement First network and $650,000 to the parent organization of Excellence of Bedford Stuyvesant, Kings Collegiate, and Williamsburg Collegiate. The Walton Family Foundation provided an additional $460,000 to Achievement First. Walton provided $5.2 million to the national KIPP organization, and the Gates Foundation provided $2 million. In addition, Walton provided smaller grants directly to schools such as Harlem Link Academy ($50,000) and Girls Preparatory ($50,000). The success academies (Harlem Success Academy) received $510,000 from Walton and $250,000 from New Schools Venture Fund to support three new schools (Baker and Ferris, 2011). The ability of those charters to obtain substantial private donations are linked to the socioeconomic status of the students and to the contacts that some charters' founders and leaders have through family and other social networks (Miron and Urschel, 2010). It appears that rather than creating greater equity in the resources available to all children's education, the charter school movement is re-creating the hierarchy of schools in the traditional public sector, establishing a system of "have" and "have-not" schools. And they are doing so while not providing the academic gains they promised.

Choice and Public Accountability

Choice proponents want to sidestep the democratic decision-making process when it comes to schooling. They dislike the compromises it demands with regard to policies and curricula, perhaps because compromises require everyone to "give in and give up" on some issues. Advocates of family choice argue that allowing free market forces to operate with regard to education will safeguard families from unwanted loss of their freedom to educate their children as they see fit. In actuality, it allows them to avoid participation in dialogues with other citizens that enable the creation of shared societal values, which are vital for maintaining a viable democracy.

For example, most charter school laws and voucher programs do not require that those schools be responsible for the protection of all students' rights, including those of students with disabilities. Schools in choice programs can operate with what would be for traditional public schools discriminatory admissions policies. Religious schools, those for which students most often receive vouchers, can use the religious commitments of parents as admissions criteria, adopt textbooks in all subjects that support the beliefs of their denomination, require all students to participate in religious instruction, and hire and fire teachers on the basis of their commitments to the faith communities' beliefs. Disciplinary practices in voucher and charter schools are subject to less public scrutiny than in traditional public schools.

Voucher and charter schools' fiscal accountability is less rigorous as well. It is increasingly common for charter schools to create independent nonprofit organizations to accept and spend private gifts to the schools. "It can be argued that while charters may be accountable to their private contributors, as public charter schools they are also expected to be accountable to public authorities for use of these private monies—but in practice are not" (Miron and Urschel, 2010, p. 16). Research has also indicated that the lack of accountability in charter schools allows them to spend more on administration than do traditional public school districts. "This is surprising, given that advocates of privatization and charter schools commonly complain that inefficient and wasteful bureaucracies in traditional public schools make them ineffective" (Miron and Urschel, 2010, p. 30).

The limitations of current accountability systems for family choice programs are serious. Current accountability systems focus on test scores and relieve choice schools of the need to be answerable for their fiscal, admissions, discipline, and curricular policies. Of even more consequence is the fact that they are not held responsible for their contribution to societal goals even though they operate with public funds. Schools that answer only to the degree that its "consumers"—families and students—are satisfied are called "private" because they provide private goods and use only private funds. When Americans began to use public funds to pay for schooling, they called those schools "common" because they served the common good. It is time to return to that concept.

For Discussion

1. The Supreme Court has ruled that providing parents with governmental funds to pay for their children's education is constitutional even if they use the money to pay for tuition at a school sponsored by a religious organization. How can you reconcile that ruling with the constitutional guarantee of the separation of church and state?

2. Sponsors of family choice have argued that allowing schools to become part of the "free market" competition is the only way to improve the quality of public education in the United States. Do you agree with the idea of allowing market forces to operate on schools? Are there any characteristics of the free market system that would prevent competition among schools from achieving the goal of equality?

Does freedom of choice alone guarantee that all consumers have an equal chance in the marketplace? Do other protections need to be in place?

3. Imagine that a voucher program has been created in your state and that you have been asked to create the "accountability" regulations for private schools receiving such payments. Create a set of rules and develop a "white paper" explaining your rationale.

4. Design a proposal for a charter school you'd like to create. Explain the mission of the school, its organizational structure, and the ways it would differ from a traditional public school. Investigate your state and local school district's regulations concerning charter schools and be sure your proposal complies with those rules.

References

Agostini v. Felton. (1997). 522 U.S. 803.

ALEXANDER, K. L., AND PALLAS, A. M. (1985). "School Sector and Cognitive Performance: When Is a Little a Little?" *Sociology of Education*, April, 115–128.

Alliance for School Choice. (2011). "School Choice Options." www.allianceforschool choice.org/school-choice-options.

ALVAREZ, C., EDWARDS, D., AND HARRIS, B. (2010). "STEM Specialty Programs: A Pathway for Under-Represented Students into STEM Fields." *NCSSSMST Journal* 16(1):27–29.

American Federation for Children. (2011). "Why School Choice?" www.federationfor children.org/why-school-choice.

AUD, S., FOX, M., AND KEWALRAMANI, A. (2010). *Status and Trends in the Education of Racial and Ethnic Groups* (NCES 2010-015). Washington, DC: U.S. Department of Education, National Center for Education Statistics.

BAKER, B. D., AND FERRIS, R. (2011). *Adding Up the Spending: Fiscal Disparities and Philanthropy among New York City Charter Schools.* Boulder, CO: National Education Policy Center. http://nepc.colorado.edu/publication/NYC-charter-disparities.

BETTS, J., ET AL. (2006). *Does School Choice Work? Effects on Student Integration and Achievement.* San Francisco: Public Policy Institute of California.

BIFULCO, R., LADD, H. F., AND ROSS, S. (2009). "The Effects of Public School Choice on Those Left Behind: Evidence from Durham, North Carolina." *Peabody Journal of Education: Issues of Leadership, Policy, and Organizations* 84(2):130–149.

Black Alliance for Educational Options. (2011). "Homepage." www.baeo.org.

Boy Scouts of America v. Dale. (2000). 530 U.S. 640.

BROUGHMAN, S., SWAIM, N., & HRYCZANIUK, C, (2011). *Characteristics of Private Schools in the United States: Results from the 2009–2010 Private School Universe Survey* (NCES 2011–339). Washington, DC: U.S. Department of Education, National Center for Education Statistics.

BUSHAW, W., AND LOPEZ, S. (2011). "The 43rd Annual Phi Delta Kappan/Gallup Poll of the Public's Attitudes toward the Public Schools." *Phi Delta Kappan* 93(1):9–26.

Center for Research on Education Outcomes. (2009). *Multiple Choice: Charter School Performance in 16 States.* Palo Alto, CA: Center for Research on Education Outcomes, Stanford University.

———. (2010). *Charter School Performance in New York City.* Palo Alto, CA: Center for Research on Education Outcomes, Stanford University.

CHEN, C. (2011). *Numbers and Types of Public Elementary and Secondary Schools from the Common Core of Data: School Year 2009–10* (NCES 2011-345). Washington, DC: U.S. Department of Education, National Center for Education Statistics. http://nces .ed.gov/pubsearch.

Children's Scholarship Fund. (2011). "Why CSF: A Brief Overview." www.scholarshipfund
.org/drupal1/?q=why-csf.

COLEMAN, J., HOFFER, T., AND KILGORE, S. (1982). *High School Achievement*. New York:
Basic Books.

CROWSON, R. L., AND GOLDRING, E. (2009). "The New Localism: Re-Examining Issues of
Neighborhood and Community in Public Education." *Yearbook of the National Society
for the Study of Education* 108(1):1–24.

DYNARSKI, S., HOXBY, C., LOVELESS, T., SCHNEIDER, M., WHITEHURST, G., AND WITTE, J.
(2010). *Charter Schools: A Report on Rethinking the Federal Role in Education*. Washington,
DC: Brown Center on Education Policy at the Brookings Institution.

FIALA, T., & OWENS, D. (2010). "Education Policy and *Friedmanomics*: Free Market Ideology and Its Impact on School Reform." Paper presented at the 68th annual national
conference of the Midwest Political Science Association, Chicago, April 23. ERIC Document ED510611.

FRAHM, R. (2010). "$2 Billion Later: Do Magnet Schools Help Kids Learn?" *The Connecti-
cut Mirror*. January 25.

FRANKENBERG, E., SIEGEL-HAWLEY, G., AND WANG, J. (2011). "Choice without Equity:
Charter School Segregation." *Education Policy Analysis Archives* 19(1):1–96.

GARN, G., AND COBB, C. (2008). "School Choice and Accountability." East Lansing, MI:
Great Lakes Center for Education Research and Practice. www.greatlakescenter.org/
docs/Research/2008charter/policy_briefs/04.pdf.

GLEASON, P., CLARK, M., TUTTLE, C., AND DWOYER, E. (2010). *The Evaluation of Charter
School Impacts: Final Report* (NCEE 2010-4029). Washington, DC: U.S. Department of
Education, National Center for Education Evaluation and Regional Assistance, Insti-
tute of Education Sciences.

GOOD, T., AND BRADEN, J. (2000). *The Great School Debate: Choice, Vouchers and Charters*.
Mahwah, NJ: Lawrence Erlbaum.

GULOSINO, C., AND d'ENTREMONT, C. (2011). "Circles of Influence: An Analysis of Charter School Location and Racial Patterns at Varying Geographic Scales." *Education
Policy Analysis Archives* 19(3):1–28.

HAYNES, K., PHILLIPS, K., AND GOLDRING, E. (2010). "Latino Parents' Choice of Magnet
Schools: How School Choice Differs across Racial and Ethnic Boundaries." *Education
and Urban Society* 42(6):758–789.

HENDRIE, C. (2004). "*Friedmans'* Foundation Rates Voucher Plans." *Education Week* 23(27):5.

Hispanic Council for Reform and Educational Options. (2011). "Homepage." www.hcreo.com.

HOFFER, T. (2000). "Catholic School Attendance and Student Achievement: A Review
and Extension of the Research." In *Catholic Schools at the Crossroads*, ed. J. Youniss, and
J. Convey (New York: Teachers College Press).

HOXBY, C., MURARKA, S., AND KANG, J. (2009). *How New York City's Charter Schools Affect
Achievement, August 2009 Report*. Cambridge, MA: New York City Charter Schools
Evaluation Project.

Hurley v. Irish American Gay, Lesbian, Bisexual Group of Boston. (1995). 515 U.S. 557.

JENNINGS, J. (2010). "School Choice or Schools' Choice: Managing in an Era of Accountability." *Sociology of Education* 83(3):227–247.

KIPP Foundation. (2011). "Schools." www.kipp.org/schools.

KLEIN, J. (2011). "The Failure of American Schools." *The Atlantic*. June. www.theatlantic
.com/magazine/archive/2011/06/the-failure-of-american-schools/8497/

LAKE, R., DUSSEAULT, B., BOWEN, M., DEMERITT, A., AND HILL, P. (2010). *The National
Study of Charter Management Organization (CMO) Effectiveness Report on Interim Find-
ings*. Seattle: Mathematica Policy Research and the Center on Reinventing Public
Education.

MacFarquhar, N. (2008). "Many Muslims Turn to Home Schooling." *New York Times*. March 26.

McDonald, D. (2012). "United States Catholic Elementary and Secondary Schools 2010–2012: The Annual Satistical Report on Schools, Enrollment, and Staffing." Washington, D.C.: National Catholic Education Association. http://www.ncea.org/news/annualdatareport.asp

Miron, G. (2011). "Review of 'Charter Schools: A Report on Rethinking the Federal Role in Education.'" Boulder, CO: National Education Policy Center. http://nepc.colorado.edu/thinktank/review-charter-federal.

Miron, G., and Urschel, J. (2010). *Equal or Fair? A Study of Revenues and Expenditure in American Charter Schools*. Boulder, CO: Education and the Public Interest Center and Education Policy Research Unit. http://epicpolicy.org/publication/charter-school-finance.

Miron, G., Urschel, J. L., Mathis, W. J., and Tornquist, E. (2010). *Schools without Diversity: Education Management Organizations, Charter Schools and the Demographic Stratification of the American School System*. Boulder, CO: Education and the Public Interest Center and Education Policy Research Unit. http://epicpolicy.org/publication/schools-without-diversity.

Moe, T. (2008). "Beyond the Free Market: The Structure of School Choice." *Brigham Young Law Review* 1:557–592.

Mueller v. Allen. (1983). 463 U.S. 388.

O'Shaunessy, T. (2007). "Parental Choice and School Quality When Peer and Scale Effects Matter." *Economics of Education Review* 26(4):501–515.

Ott, T. (2011). "Cleveland Students Hold Their Own with Voucher Students on State Tests." *Cleveland Plaini Dealer*. February, 22. http://blog.cleveland.com/metro/2011/02/cleveland_students_hold_own_wi.html

Ravitch, D. (2010). *The Death and Life of the Great American School System: How Testing and Choice Are Undermining Education*. New York: Basic Books.

Robbins, L. (2011a). "For Some Eighth Graders, Belated Good News." *New York Times*. May 29.

———. (2011b). "Lost in the School Choice Maze." *New York Times*. May 8.

Roberts v. United States Jaycees. (1984). 468 U.S. 609.

Rosenbloom, S. (2010). "My So-Called Choice." *Urban Review* 42(1):1–21.

Shanker, A. (1988). "Restructuring Our Schools." *Peabody Journal of Education* 65(3):88–100.

Smrekar, C. (2009). "Beyond the Tipping Point: Issues of Racial Diversity in Magnet Schools Following Unitary Status." *Peabody Journal of Education* 84(2):209–226.

Sutton, R., and King. L. (2011). "School Vouchers in a Climate of Political Change." *Journal of Education Finance* 36(3):244–267.

Turque, B. (2011). "Rhee: D.C. School Bureaucracy Makes No Sense." *Washington Post*. March 3.

Uncommon Schools. (2011). "We Are Uncommon." www.uncommonschools.org/our-approach/who-we-are.

U.S. Department of Education. (2011a). "Magnet School Assistance Program." www2.ed.gov/programs/magnet/index.html.

———. (2011b). "State Education Reforms (SER), Table 4.2." http://nces.ed.gov/programs/statereform/tab4_2.asp.

Whitehurst, G. (2011). *The Education Choice and Competition Index: Background and Results 2011*. Washington, DC: Brookings Institution.

Williams, S. (2010). "Through the Eyes of Friends: An Investigation of School Context and Cross-Racial Friendships in Racially Mixed Schools." *Urban Education* 45(4):480–505.

WITTE, J., WOLF, P., COWEN, J., FLEMING, D., AND LUCAS-MCLEAN, J. (2008). *MPCP Longitudinal Growth Study: Baseline Report.* Fayetteville: School Choice Demonstration Project, University of Arkansas.

Witters v. Washington Department of Services for the Blind. (1986). 474 U.S. 481.

WOLF, P. (2008). *The Comprehensive Longitudinal Evaluation of the Milwaukee Parental Choice Program: Summary of Baseline Reports.* Fayetteville: School Choice Demonstration Project, University of Arkansas.

———. (2010). "School Vouchers in Washington, DC: Achievement Impacts and Their Implications for Social Justice." *Educational Research and Evaluation* 16(10):131–150.

———. (2011). "The Comprehensive Longitudinal Evaluation of the Milwaukee Parental Choice Program: Summary of Fourth Year Reports." www.uark.edu/ua/der/SCDP/Milwaukee_Research.html.

ZEHR, M. (2011). "Capacity Issue Looms for Vouchers." *Education Week.* June 15.

ZINE, J. (2007). "Safe Havens or Religious Ghettos? Narratives of Islamic Schooling in Canada." *Race, Ethnicity, and Education* 10(1):71–92.

Zobrest v. Catalina Foothills School District. (1993). 509 U.S. 1.

CHAPTER 3

Financing Schools: Equity or Privilege

Should government make educational spending equitable within and among school districts?

POSITION 1: EQUITABLE EDUCATIONAL SPENDING IS A MATTER OF JUSTICE

No matter which fiscal equity measure is used, it is clear that districts with a high percentage of low-income children are not receiving their fair share of state and local education funding in many states.

—Epstein (2011, p. 17)

Some Consequences of Inequitable School Funding

In 1991, Jonathan Kozol described the "savage inequalities" American children faced in public school. Ten years later, activists around the country were still uncovering similar conditions (Oakes, 2002; Campaign for Fiscal Equity, 2001). Almost twenty years later, differences among schools within a state or among schools within a district remain because of how we finance public education and allocate those funds. The shocking disparities among school facilities and resources constitute unequal educational opportunities for our young people. The differences among schools within a state or even a district result from the way we finance public education in the United States since a fundamental injustice is built in to that system (Baker, Sciarra, and Farrie, 2010; Hall and Ushomirsky, 2010).

The conditions of underfunded schools make the best argument for why changes in school financing were and remain necessary. For the most part, those children in the United States whom fate has placed in middle- or upper-class families attend schools that are well equipped, safe, and clean. They have science labs and the necessary supplies for conducting experiments. They have access to up-to-date technology, which often is housed in libraries stocked with reference materials. Their textbooks are relatively new, and, more important, each student has one. The schools of the "lucky" have art rooms and gyms, pools and playing fields, and auditoriums and music rooms. When these districts spend money to improve facilities, the funds go to improvements—such as new science labs or computer equipment—intended to enhance learning directly (Epstein, 2011).

In the urban schools that are attended by children from the poorest families, conditions are dramatically different. The buildings are overcrowded; almost half hold classes in temporary buildings (U.S. Department of Education, 2011). They need to build new schools to replace out-of-date facilities, create additions to current buildings to house science and computer labs, upgrade heating and cooling facilities, repair plumbing and roofs, paint classrooms, replace lockers and boilers, and update security and technology systems (Casserly, Lachlan-Haché, and Naik, 2011). The quality of school facilities affects teacher and student attendance negatively. Teachers report missing up to four days per year because of health issues caused by school conditions; students attend school less frequently when facilities are inadequate and have lower academic achievement, conceivably as a result of their absences (BEST, 2011).

These differences in facilities are attributable to funding spent on each child (Epstein, 2011). In most other nations, the national government—not the state, province, city, or town—provides most school funding. In the United States, the federal government provides less than 10 percent. As a result, students depend on state and local governments to pay for their schools. States contribute about 40 percent of monies spent on schools. Even when adjusted for differences in the cost of living among the states, real disparities among available funds for schools remain. States like New Jersey, New York, Connecticut, and Rhode Island spend two or three times as much per student as Utah, Mississippi, Louisiana, and Tennessee do (Hightower, 2011). Intrastate differences also account for differences in the type of education students receive. For example, in New York State, combined state and local funding is almost 20 percent less for children in districts where at least 30 percent live in poverty than in the state as a whole. "Understanding the fairness of the 50 state finance systems is crucial to the national effort to ensure access to high-quality education and to close opportunity and achievement gaps among subgroups of students, particularly low-income students" (Baker et al., 2010, p. 8).

Causes of Inequitable School Funding

American public schools have long been a beacon of hope for the residents of this country. From the early 1800s, education offered the promise of social mobility. Schooling would help to equalize opportunities for all young people to better their lot in life. When reformers encouraged taxpayers to accept the responsibility of paying for schools, they promised that by doing so, they would be providing young people with the chance to increase their own wealth and that of the nation as a whole. Tax dollars spent on schools would help to eliminate the potential for conflict between rich and poor by decreasing the numbers of the poor. Horace Mann expressed the belief this way: "Education, then, beyond all other devices of human origin, is the great equalizer of the conditions of men—the balance-wheel of the social machinery" (quoted in Cremin, 1957, p. 87).

Although many Americans came to believe that education should not be a luxury that only the wealthy could afford, they worried about how publicly funded schools would be controlled. As compromises built in to the Constitution suggest, having secured their independence from England, Americans in the early republican period wanted to limit the power of centralized governments. In establishing public schools, they did not want local communities to lose control over what children would learn and who would teach them. States authorized local governments to impose property taxes on their citizens and to use those funds for the support of schools. Because these revenues came from local communities rather than state or federal governments, primary control of schools remained with municipalities themselves. Through elected boards of education, the community maintained control of curriculum, hiring of teachers, and allocation of funding. Despite the growing oversight of schools by state agencies and centralization of teacher preparation and, sometimes, curricula, nineteenth-century Americans were reassured local funding guaranteed that ultimate control of their schools would remain in their hands (Tyack, 1974; Katz, 1975; Urban and Wagoner, 2000).

The system remained in place, essentially unchanged, until the 1930s. When a local school district ran out of money, it had nowhere to turn for help. Most often, the district closed its doors until additional revenues were available. During the Depression, cities, towns, and villages faced tremendous financial difficulties. School districts across the country had trouble meeting payrolls and maintaining their buildings. Many states were able to provide assistance through their income and sales tax collections (Mackey, 1998). State-level financial contributions more than doubled for public education between 1930 and 1950, finally averaging approximately 40 percent of school budgets (Mackey, 1998). That percentage has continued to increase slowly. Nationally, states contribute almost half of school districts' revenue. Local funding is slightly less than half. A small contribution from federal tax dollars (roughly 7 percent) makes up the remainder (Zhou, 2008).

So, if states are providing almost half of school districts' resources, why do disparities among districts still exist? Can't states provide enough money to equalize the resources available to each child regardless of his or her parents' income? To a certain extent, states' contribution to school funding has helped lessen the differences among schools (Glenn and Picus, 2007; Arroyo, 2008; Epstein, 2011). However, continued reliance on local property taxes to fund almost half of a district's budget still leads to large disparities in the amount of money available to educate students. Here's how it happens.

A local school district is authorized to levy property taxes and, through their votes, citizens have some voice in the rate at which they will be taxed.

Let's imagine two districts—one urban and one suburban—that adopt the same property tax rate of 2 percent. In the suburban community, District A, the total value of property that can be taxed averages out to be $250,000 per child enrolled in the district's schools. In the inner-city community, District B, the property tax base is $50,000 per pupil. When taxpayers in each community pay the same rate, 2 percent, District A raises $5,000 to spend on each student in its schools. District B raises only $1,000. To achieve equality with District A in the amount they could spend on their children's education, taxpayers in District B would have to agree to a tax rate of 10 percent. When you consider that most taxpayers in District B have dramatically lower incomes than those in District A, you can see how much of a hardship such a high tax rate would be. People who already are poor would be forced to pay a much higher percentage of their income to fund their schools than their wealthier neighbors do. The higher rates of taxes in District B would make it less attractive to home owners and business owners.

Despite the sacrifices involved in creating such higher tax rates, that is what many urban and rural school districts have been forced to do. However, political and economic realities put a ceiling on how much they could raise the tax rate and how much of the funds could be allocated to school expenses. As a result, even though residents of those communities pay a higher share of their income to fund their schools, they never raise enough money to equal resources available to schools in wealthier communities (Noguera, 2004). This pattern creates fundamental inequalities of educational opportunity in the United States, and in those states that rely most heavily on property taxes for educational funding, the disparity between revenues available for students in high- and low-poverty schools is the greatest (Baker et al., 2010; Epstein, 2011).

Legal Challenges to Inequitable School Financing

Since 2000, court cases in at least thirty-six states challenged school funding inequities. These changes, however, did not come easily. In some states, there was vociferous and politically powerful opposition to them.

In New Jersey, for example, the state fought the court's decision for more than twenty years. Parents, school staff, and elected officials from wealthier districts mounted vigorous campaigns against implementation of the court's order to equalize spending in public schools:

> [There was] stubborn, hard-bitten opposition to distributing public resources equitably. Many individuals and groups fought publicly and zealously to continue to use the public schools and the public purse to maintain advantages for wealthy white communities, families and children at the expense of poor nonwhite communities, families and children. . . . Many of the participants felt no sense of shame as they argued to maintain an inherently unequal system of public education in which public money was used to confer private privilege to students in their well-appointed suburban schools while basic health and safety standards were routinely violated in their underfinanced urban counterparts. (Firestone, Goertz, and Natriello, 1997, p. 159)

This opposition should not have been unexpected. The authors of a comprehensive report on financing American schools found that conflicts involved in providing equity in school financing are rooted in competing values:

> Most Americans believe in equality of opportunity, but they also believe in the right of parents to choose to spend their money for the benefit of their own children. Most Americans believe that every child has a right to a good education in a publicly funded common school but they also believe in freedom of mobility in a way that allows affluent Americans to live together in locales able to easily support good schools and that tends to concentrate poverty and disadvantage, often in urban areas. . . . None of these commitments is unworthy and each has a claim for attention. But given these conflicting values, no model of either the finance system or of the education system as a whole could ever be consistent with all of them. (Ladd and Hansen, 1999, p. 264)

This opposition did not take place in political isolation. In the last thirty years in their unyielding pursuit of less governmental involvement in our lives, conservative politicians and their supporters have shifted the balance of power in such conflicts in favor of the rights of individuals and away from the common good. For example, in the last three decades, many Americans came to resent efforts made by the government to achieve equality of opportunity for all citizens. They believed these efforts unfairly penalized hardworking people who have achieved a measure of success through their own labor and sacrifice. They believed these governmental attempts to create a just society were fundamentally unfair and rewarded those who had not worked as hard as they did and who had come to expect handouts. They believed their tax dollars were "theirs" and did not belong to the community at large. They expected returns on those payments that directly benefited them and their families.

This attitude played out in a special way with regard to property taxes. Connected as they are to the value of the homes they have struggled to provide for their families, property taxes represent, for many people, an investment in their children's future. They believe they should be used for their own school districts and not applied to those of children whose parents are unwilling to support education in their locality.

Those who adopt the "me-first" attitude justify it by making claims about their own success that are not completely accurate. They attribute their achievements only to hard work and ignore advantages race and socioeconomic status of their own parents may have given them. Consciously or unconsciously, they appear to want to maintain advantages with which their children come into the world, even if doing so means other children are seriously disadvantaged. Correct or not, however, these attitudes are translated into powerful political forces when citizens who hold them exercise their right to vote. They result in opposition to proposals that school funding be centralized at the state or federal level.

The genius of the American system of government, however, helps us work through these conflicts of values in unique ways. The system of checks and balances built in to our political system protects us from impulses to sacrifice our commitment to equality in the name of individual freedom. In the case of school financing, the courts have provided the much-needed check to legislative and executive policies that unfairly limit the educational opportunity and achievement of poor and/or minority students. By holding states accountable to their constitutional obligations to provide adequate schooling for all their children, the courts ensure that the Fourteenth Amendment, providing equal protection under the law for all citizens, is safeguarded even from understandable desires of loving parents to care first and foremost for their own children.

"Adequacy" and School Funding

The earliest school funding equity case established *fiscal neutrality* as the litmus test for the constitutionality of school financing in various states (*Serrano v. Priest*, 1971). States were ordered to reduce disparities among districts by providing low-wealth communities with additional funds or tax relief as long as the municipality made a good-faith effort to contribute to schools. It was a fairly straightforward, dollar-for-dollar equality; it was easily measured, if not so easily achieved. However, other court decisions have pointed us toward more complex and, ultimately, more just definitions of equity when the term is applied to school funding.

Later cases changed the criteria from *fiscal neutrality* to *adequacy*. State constitutions guarantee the right to "thorough and efficient," "sound, basic," or "suitable" public education systems (Campaign for Fiscal Equity, 2001; Imber, 2004). "When a service is constitutionally mandated, it becomes the duty, not the prerogative of the legislature to provide that service and the job of the judiciary to ensure that the service is being provided in a constitutionally acceptable manner" (Imber, 2004, p. 46). Lawsuits that challenge the way schools are financed have been filed in forty-five states (Access Quality Education, 2008). Courts are ruling that states are required to provide enough resources to their school districts to ensure that the children under their care receive an education "adequate" to fulfill their constitutional mandate.

The shift from fiscal equity to adequacy has gotten a push from the national movement to raise educational standards. The No Child Left Behind Act of 2001 laid out ambitious goals and held states and districts accountable for meeting them. As a result, thirty states have had adequacy studies conducted to define what constitutes an acceptable level of academic achievement for their students, determine what resources are needed to see that each child meets those standards, and then to create funding formulas providing those resources to every student in the state (Rebell, 2007).

A consensus definition of what constitutes an "adequate" education has emerged from state court rulings: "The preparation of students to function productively as capable voters, jurors, and citizens of a democratic society and to be able to compete effectively in the economy" (Rebell, 2008b, p. 432). To be effective citizens and workers, students need literacy and oral fluency in English; mathematical and scientific knowledge; fundamental understanding of geography, history, and political and economic systems; critical thinking skills; social and communication skills; and sufficient intellectual or vocational skills to move forward in educational or employment settings. To develop such knowledge and skills, schools need teachers and administrators qualified to provide academic instruction and to create a safe and orderly learning environment; adequate school facilities; appropriate class sizes; supplemental and remedial programs for students from high-poverty backgrounds, students with disabilities, and English language learners; and resources such as textbooks, libraries, laboratories, and computers (Rebell, 2008b). However, the cost of providing an "adequate" education varies, depending on the needs of students and the historic, social, and political contexts that have shaped their schools. Schools and districts whose populations include more poor, disabled, or non–English-speaking students require more financial resources to achieve the same results as their wealthier, nondisabled, and English-speaking peers. Translating those differences in need into funding formulas is called "costing out."

A variety of costing-out methods have been used around the country. Some states have relied on the judgment of experienced educators, some on educational researchers. Others have built on the analysis of the resources that successful school districts have and determine how much it would cost to replicate those resources in less successful schools. The most successful processes of determining adequacy in school funding—those that are approved by the courts—appear to share some characteristics regardless of the specific method they use. These characteristics are carefully articulated outcomes or goals; rigorous attention to the needs of poor, disabled, and non–English-speaking students; minimizing the political manipulation of the process; and a high degree of openness and public engagement in the process (Rebell, 2007). Whatever process is used, once a state has determined the basic cost of providing a sound education, it can guarantee every student that amount of funding and then provide additional resources to those districts that serve large numbers of poor, disabled, or non–English-speaking students.

Adequacy litigation has had some success in reducing inequity in school financing. However, inequity remains. Only fourteen states provide greater funding to high-poverty districts than to low-poverty ones. Twenty states give more revenue to wealthier districts than to poorer ones. Fourteen states have systems that provide the same amount of funding to school districts regardless of the needs of students (Baker et al., 2010).

Centralizing School Funding

Money does matter when it comes to education. Despite early studies emphasizing the influence of nonschool factors, such as family background and neighborhood environment (Coleman, 1966; Hanushek, 1996), growing evidence shows that student achievement is affected by the amount of money schools spend on their education (Glenn, 2009). If schools have enough financial resources to create small classes, employ experienced and well-educated teachers, provide ongoing professional development for those teachers, buy enough textbooks and other curricular materials, and repair and maintain their buildings, then student achievement is positively affected (Barth and Nitta, 2008; Rebell, 2008a; Glenn, 2009).

A commitment to providing high-standard adequacy in education means that all schools have those resources. It is clear that differences in local communities' abilities to raise revenue through property taxes means that overreliance on mixed funding streams for schools will always result in unfair disparities among schools. The courts have attempted to remedy the injustice by creating new obligations for the states to ensure that all districts within their borders have the income to provide adequate education for all. However, these remedies cannot fully correct the problem. What is needed instead is a radical rethinking of school funding.

Instead of dividing the fiscal responsibility for schools between the state and local governments, equality would be better served if the states had access to all tax dollars collected to support education and could distribute them "unequally." That is, if the amount of money currently being collected through property taxes could go to the state instead of to local governments, then each district—and each school—could receive the amount of money that it had been determined was needed to provide "adequate" education for its children. Districts with more educationally needy students—English language learners, young people with disabilities, or children living in poverty—would receive higher per-pupil allotments. Providing schools with resources that were matched to the needs of their students would, for the first time in American history, really ensure that the conditions of a child's birth did not determine his or her opportunities.

Of course, adequate oversight by federal, state, and local government is needed to ensure that resources are being spent appropriately and honestly; such accountability is difficult but not impossible to achieve, and the requirements of No Child Left Behind are pressuring states to create such systems. Convincing residents of affluent communities to support state-based systems of school funding will not be easy. Their resistance could be overcome, however, if states collected revenue for schools in ways that could be perceived as equitable—such as sales, use, or income taxes or revenue from recreational activities, such as lotteries or casinos.

When states and municipalities share the cost of schools, one party may back out of an agreement, claiming that their revenue did not match projections on which the settlement was based. When that happens, as it has recently in New York State, students lose resources they need to learn while a long, intractable political argument takes place. If there were only one government body responsible for school funding, voters would be better able to hold their leaders accountable and ensure that all students were adequately and justly served. Equity in school finance is a matter of justice. The courts have ruled that all children in this country have constitutionally guaranteed rights to equal treatment. Clearly, they are currently not receiving that protection under the present system of paying for schools. Issues of individual freedom, local control, and overinvolvement by government in our daily lives certainly deserve consideration. They do not, however, automatically outweigh the rights of all children to receive an education that will empower them to be competent to take up their duties as citizens, members of society, and workers. Centralizing the funding for public schools will ensure that all children in a state have the resources they need to meet its learning standards regardless of where they live or their families' socioeconomic status. Every other educational funding formula is designed to maintain the privilege of wealthier families at the expense of the rights of less affluent ones.

POSITION 2: PRIVILEGED EDUCATIONAL SPENDING IS NECESSARY IN A FREE MARKET ECONOMY

There can be unfortunate, if often unacknowledged, consequences when we seek to universalize excellence. Such efforts can dilute instructional quality, make it tougher for teachers to go as deep or as fast as they otherwise might, and distract attention from advanced students.

—Hess (2011)

Those suggesting that we provide equitable funding for American public schools in an attempt to ensure equal opportunity for children are well meaning but misguided. They demonstrate a concern for justice for some but almost completely ignore the rights of others. In the concern to provide what they call equal educational opportunity for children, they forget to consider taxpayers' freedom to exercise the maximum possible control over the use of their money. They deny those footing the bill the opportunity to see that their funds are spent efficiently, wisely, and honestly; they ignore strong reasons for allowing parents and other taxpayers to support their own children's schools to the full extent of their ability; and they dismiss strong arguments in favor of supporting academic achievement for more able students who will be able to make significant returns on public funds spent on their education.

The Missing Connection between School Finances and Academic Achievement

Those who support equitable educational funding schemes believe that we should allow federal or state governments to collect taxes and distribute them unequally among all school districts. In doing so, they say, we will provide schools in poorer districts with needed resources to help students improve their academic performance. That is, they believe that in order to compensate for what parents are unable or unwilling to provide for their children, taxpayers should provide greater funding for poor children, those who are English language learners, and those who are disabled. They argue that these students need and deserve more of the public resources than those students whose backgrounds better prepared them for school success. It sounds as if the plan has possibilities for addressing the persistent problem of underachievement by students from low socioeconomic backgrounds. It would if a link could be made between a school's material resources and its students' academic achievement.

However, in over four decades, scholars have been unable to demonstrate conclusively that such a link exists.

The first of these research efforts, the famous "Coleman study," took place in the mid-1960s. It was the era of President Johnson's War on Poverty, and many Americans were convinced that schools could be a primary tool in winning that battle. James Coleman and his colleagues conducted a large-scale national survey of thousands of schools. They calculated the resources that they assumed would be connected to student achievement—teacher education and experience, number of books in the library, laboratory equipment, and so on. In other words, they counted the things that money can buy. The results were surprising, even to them. They concluded that a school's material resources had little effect on student achievement. Instead, they found that "family background differences account for much more variance in achievements than do school differences" (Coleman, 1966, p. 73). Other researchers reached the same conclusion: "There is no strong system relationship between school expenditures and student performance" (Hanushek, 1989, p. 46). Those researchers who claimed that their studies indicated that a few factors related to funding do affect school performance could not definitively show that providing more resources to schools serving children from poor or uncaring family backgrounds improved those children's academic achievement (Hedges, Laine, and Greenwald, 1994). Even recent experiments in increased school funding have not conclusively defined the relationship between money and student success (Costrell, Hanushek, and Loeb, 2008; Hanushek and Lindseth, 2009). "Decades of social science research have demonstrated that differences in the quality of schools can explain about one-third of the variation in student achievement. But the other two-thirds is attributable to non-school factors" (Rothstein, 2010).

For example, poverty increases the likelihood that families will become more mobile and children will have to change schools. Homes may be crowded with few quiet spaces for study or homework. Poor children are more likely to come to school hungry or malnourished, to be in poor health, and to live with adults who are under emotional stress (Rothstein, 2010; Mishel and Shierholz, 2011). Mothers and fathers living in poverty are not able to prepare young people for challenges they will face in schools. They do not have money to buy books or computers; they cannot take them to concerts. They have so many other problems and demands on their time that they cannot give children the attention they need to grow and develop. No matter how much money is spent on education, it cannot make up completely for all that poverty denies children (Rothstein, 2010).

Let's face it—if more money led to better academic performance, we would have it by now. In the last three decades of the twentieth century, we spent more money for each child's education than any other industrialized nation (Organization for Economic Cooperation and Development, 2011). In the last ten years alone, spending on education has risen 29 percent nationally (in constant dollars) and by 35 percent in high poverty schools (Aud et al., 2010). However, some children are still less successful than others. It may simply be that family situations cannot be overcome by spending more money in schools. Taxpayers have a right to insist that their hard-earned money be spend in the most efficient way possible. Instead of diverting other people's money to schools with large numbers of failing students, it would be a wiser use of public funds to provide poor children and their families with social services they need to create better lives.

We need to change the realities of their homes and neighborhoods if children are going to be able to take advantage of what schools have to offer. We should channel tax dollars to fight crime, provide recreational facilities, and create jobs, rather than waste money on schools, and we should ensure that every child has adequate health care—both physical and mental—and lives in a safe home and neighborhood. Only then will they come to school ready to learn. Spending money to solve their economic and social problems directly will be a better choice than putting more money into school districts that are often corrupt and mismanaged (Rothstein, 2010).

Historical Misuse of Public Funds in Urban School Districts

Urban schools have long been used to better the lives of some city residents at the expense of children's education. Urban school districts historically have been a source of patronage jobs that politicians could hand out in exchange for votes. Members of various ethnic communities have, in their turn, assumed control of the districts and provided salaries to members of their constituencies— sometimes without requiring work in return (Connors, 1971). "The history of patronage is a method by which city residents without access to other political and economic resources have taken care of themselves and their friends" (Anyon, 1997, p. 159). In the 1980s, one critic charged that in a city in the Northeast, "the political patronage has been so widespread that those filling district positions of responsibility have no idea of their actual duties. Positions were created to be filled by cronies. Routine hiring, evaluating and record keeping were not only bypassed but not even expected" (Morris, 1989, p. 18). The situation has not dramatically improved. "The patronage system in large cities has been responsible for the appointment of many unskilled, educationally marginal school administrators. The history of patronage has also been partly responsible for those inner-city teachers who are ineffective" (Anyon, 1997, p. 158).

In many school districts, patronage jobs have resulted in bureaucracies that hamper teachers' abilities to meet students' needs. Employees within these bureaucracies are sometimes involved in corrupt and illegal activities. Administrators and employees in large urban districts are routinely arrested for taking bribes and diverting public funds for their private use (Editor, 2011b; Gonzalez, 2011; Heller, 2011). Any scheme to increase funding to these districts would have to ensure that new monies did not create more ineffective administrative positions. In addition, oversight procedures would need to be in place to prevent misappropriation of new funds.

As part of their legacy of providing patronage jobs, urban schools also employ a large number of paraprofessionals. These jobs are an excellent source of income for local community members. Cafeteria workers, teachers' aides, attendance assistants, special education aides, bus drivers, transportation aides, and sentries are all positions that ordinarily require no education beyond high school. They are jobs that members of the neighborhoods around the schools seek out. Getting one's name on "the list" is often a matter of *who*, not *what*, you know. In many cities, these paraprofessionals have unionized and command far higher wages in the school system than they would be able to earn in similar private sector jobs.

In the past, teachers who were hired in urban schools were often better "connected" than "prepared." Union contracts protect underqualified teachers who entered the system under preexisting patronage arrangements under the guise of "seniority" privileges and often prevent principals from hiring less experienced but more committed teachers. The problem is magnified when money becomes tight and layoffs are required. Less effective teachers maintain their jobs, while more effective, newly hired ones lose theirs (Editor, 2011a; Ghatt, 2011).

Those who demand, in the name of justice, that hardworking taxpayers provide more funds to these mismanaged districts need to rethink their priorities. No such increases in funding should take place until appropriate personnel, accounting, and management policies and practices are in place. Fairness to those paying the bills demands no less. No taxpayer should be asked to sacrifice to provide opportunities for "fat cats" to get richer by skimming money from school budgets or providing jobs for those who keep them in power. School finance equalization plans would do just that.

The Consequences of Equalizing School Finance

Lower Student Achievement

Those who propose we equalize funding at the state or federal level seem oblivious to what happens when such attempts are made. The "equalizers" have been successful in some states, often with disastrous results. There are two options for creating equalization plans for school spending. The financing can be "leveled up" or "leveled down." In leveling up, the state funds all schools at the same per-pupil rate as the wealthiest districts. In leveling down, all schools receive a per-pupil amount equivalent to that being spent in middle-class or poorer districts in the state. In most leveling-down schemes, a limit is placed on what a district can spend above the state subsidy. Leveling up is an expensive proposition. It requires an increase in taxes across a state; people pay higher taxes, but only a few of them see increased services to their communities as a result of those rate hikes. As a result, leveling-up schemes are unpopular and rarely are implemented fully.

In 1971, the California Supreme Court heard the first legal challenge to differences in school financing. In that case, *Serrano v. Priest*, the court held that inequalities in district per-pupil funding violated the equal protection clauses of the state and federal constitution. Those who supported equalization of school spending believed they had won a victory. They assumed that the changes resulting from the court order would improve education for all California's students. They were wrong. Taxpayers revolted against any plan to increase state taxes in order to equalize school spending (Fischel, 1989, 1996). They passed Proposition 13, which placed a "cap" on taxes and effectively limited funds for all California districts. The result is the schools that educate high-poverty students receive only $13 more per student than do their counterparts serving wealthier students (Timar and Roza, 2008). Despite claims that centralizing the funding of their schools would improve their academic chances, California's students are performing below national averages on the National Assessment of Educational Progress in mathematics and reading (U.S. Department of Education, 2006, 2007) Five states—Oklahoma, South Carolina, Hawaii, Michigan, and Kansas—provide more than 90 percent of public schools' funding, a greater centralization of funding than in California (Hoxby, 2003). In two of those states, Kansas and Michigan, the average test scores were higher than the national average; in the other these three, they were somewhat lower (U.S. Department of Education, 2011b). In other words, funding schools almost exclusively at the state level is no guarantee that academic achievement will improve.

Decreases in Local Support

Research into other instances of equalization attempts shows that court-ordered increases in state financial support for schools often were accompanied by decreases in local support. In other words, schools did not experience a real increase in resources. Municipalities sometimes saw the increased state aid as an opportunity to reduce the local tax burden on residents instead of a chance to provide better schools for their children (Driscoll and Salmon, 2008). These decisions made sense politically and economically for those cities and towns. They also reflected the antagonism often generated by decisions imposed on people by judges. It is not only local financial support for schools that suffers as a result of centralizing finance. When the state exercises a high degree of control over schools' fundings, it necessarily means that local parents and residents have less control. Parents and neighbors can find this alienating. They are less likely to be involved in schools if they feel they have no real power over educational decisions. They are also less likely to make the additional contributions of time and material resources if they have little say in how those commodities are used (Hoxby, 2003). No school district can afford to lose the parents who are most interested in their children's school success.

Loss of Local Control

One of the most unique aspects of the U.S. school system is the fact that schools historically have been designed to meet the needs of individual areas. In the late nineteenth and early twentieth centuries, for example, different courses of study were taught in rural schools than in urban ones. Each local school district, working with concerned members of the community, was able to create schools that met its children's needs (Cremin, 1961). Schools were able to hire and fire teachers and could do so on the basis of criteria established locally. A teacher needed to live up to an individual community's standards, not just ones created by some state bureaucrats with little or no sense of the municipality's needs or values.

Even in the late twentieth century, local control of schools remained an important aspect of their governance. Taxpayers could accept or reject school boards' proposed budgets. They could elect or throw out of office school board members. In doing so, they ensured that their ideas for their children's education would be carried out in the schools. In addition, taxpayers could select those elected officials who set property tax rates for funding schools and thus could work to see that their tax burden would not be unduly high. Because most people in a town, city, or village had attended a local school or had children who did, interest in a local school district was high. The added dimension of locally controlling school funding increased taxpayers' involvement in the schools. People are willing to pay if they can see that their money is being spent on something of value and that they have something to say about what constitutes that value.

When school funding is substantially centralized—when states take over most of the task of paying for education—taxpayers lose a substantial amount of the control over the schools for which they are paying. When local control is lost, administrators' flexibility is also sacrificed. Local school and civic leaders can no longer respond effectively to the needs of their community and their students. For example, some schools may want after-school programs, others may want to provide very small classes, and still others may want to create accelerated programs. When funding is centralized and its distribution mandated by the state, programmatic decisions are no longer theirs to make (Hess, 2011).

Good Schools Are a Reward for Hard Work

Whether proponents of centralized educational funding like it or not, we live in a capitalist society. We have an economic system that thrives on full and fair competition among businesses and workers. If you produce a product or provide a service that members of society value, you are more highly rewarded than those who do not. It is a system that has created a standard of living in the United States that is the envy of the rest of the world. We provide safety nets for those who cannot participate in the free market; we do so even for the children of those who will not take part.

However, one reason this economy works so well is because people can enjoy the fruits of their labor. Those who "crack the system" and figure out what the public will buy can reap monetary rewards that they then can translate into assets, one of the most cherished of which is a home. One of the factors that most influence those home buyers is the opportunity to provide better schools and safer neighborhoods for their children. In turn, the quality of schools is an important factor in determining the market value of a home. Equalizing funding for schools and ensuring that all students receive the same advantages will remove one of the primary reasons why one house is worth more than another.

The American economic system is based on competition and on the idea that some things are "better" than others. These perceived advantages provide an incentive for most Americans to work hard, save, and spend their money. If we centralize school spending and equalize the education children receive, we remove one of the greatest incentives for adults to make sacrifices of time and money that this economy requires. It may not seem "fair," but, in general, the system works, and it is foolish to think about making dramatic changes to it.

Kozol (2006) laments the fact that children in poorer school districts perceive the differences between their schools and those in wealthier districts. He suggests that this awareness makes young people bitter and that as a result they eventually drop out of the competition that is at the heart of the American economic system. There is, however, another way of looking at the children's awareness. We can see it as the same kind of knowledge that has propelled so many others in this country to work harder than they ever imagined possible. We can see it as providing the same kind of motivation possessed by the pioneers who crossed this country in search of a better life. Some who currently live in municipalities that provide more resources for their schools started out in neighborhoods such as those that Kozol and others describe. Their hard work, determination, and perseverance enabled them to provide a better life for their children. We should not assume that today's young people are incapable of the same kind of effort and success. We need to hold out the promise of rewards for the kind of behavior that most benefits this society. Equalizing school funding takes away one of the primary reasons people choose to act in ways that will build up this great country. We cannot risk the consequences of removing that motivation.

For Discussion

1. Research your own state. Have there been lawsuits pursuing equity in educational funding? What were the arguments, pro and con? What were the courts' decisions? Have they been implemented? What have been the results?
2. Some proposals for reducing school financial inequity rely on a shift from property tax revenue to sales tax revenue. Discuss the pros and cons of such a shift. Remember to consider questions such as the reliability of each revenue source in times of economic difficulty.
3. Consider how increased state contributions to school districts may affect local control of schools. Research your own state's policies with regard to the level of independence that school districts have in the areas of curriculum, testing, personnel, and length of the school year.
4. For a moment, turn the whole question of school financing on its head and consider whether governments have the right to tax citizens to pay for schools. Discuss whether such taxation violates individual rights of those citizens who do not have children in public schools. In doing so, you might try to support the arguments that only parents have the right and obligation to provide their children with education they deem appropriate and that government has no right to interfere in their decisions. What might be some effects on the country of implementing such a school financing policy?

References

Access Quality Education. (2008). "Litigation." www.schoolfunding.info/litigation/litigation.php3.

ANYON, J. (1997). *Ghetto Schooling.* New York: Teachers College Press.

ARROYO, C. (2008). "The Funding Gap." Washington, DC: The Education Trust. www2 .edtrust.org/NR/rdonlyres/5AF8F288-949D-4677-82CF-5A867A8E9153/0/ FundingGap2007.pdf.

AUD, S., ET AL. (2010). *The Condition of Education 2010* (NCES 2010-028). Washington, DC: U.S. Department of Education, National Center for Education Statistics, Institute of Education Sciences.

BAKER, B., SCIARRA, D., AND FARRIE, D. (2010). *Is School Funding Fair? A National Report Card.* Newark, NJ: Education Law Center.

BARTH, J., AND NITTA, K. (2008). *Education in the Post Lakeview Era.* Little Rock: Arkansas Advocates for Children and Families. www.schoolfunding.info/states/ar/ARAdvocates-AchievementGap08.pdf.

BEST (Building Educational Success Together). (2011). *PK-12 Public School Facility Infrastructure Fact Sheet.* Washington, DC: 21st Century School Fund. www.21CSF.org.

Campaign for Fiscal Equity. (2001). "In Evidence: Policy Reports from the CFE Trial. Special Report: The Trial Court's Decision." New York: Campaign for Fiscal Equity. http://www.cfequity.org/static_pages/pdfs/3decn25.pdf

CASSERLY, M., LACHLAN-HACHÉ, J., AND NAIK, M. (2011). *Facility Needs and Costs in America's Great City Schools.* Washington, DC: Council of Great City Schools.

COLEMAN, J. (1966). *Equality of Educational Opportunity.* Washington, DC: U.S. Department of Health, Education, and Welfare, Office of Education.

CONNORS, R. (1971). *A Cycle of Power: The Career of Jersey City Mayor Frank Hague.* Metuchen, NJ: Scarecrow Press.

COSTRELL, R., HANUSHEK, E., AND LOEB, S. (2008). "What Do Cost Functions Tell Us About the Cost of an Adequate Education?" *Peabody Journal of Education* 83(2): 198–223.

CREMIN, L., ED. (1957). *The Republic and the School: Horace Mann on the Education of Free Men.* New York: Teachers College Press.

———. (1961). *The Transformation of the School: Progressivism in American Education 1876–1957.* New York: Random House.

DRISCOLL, L., AND SALMON, R. (2008). "How Increased State Equalization Aid Resulted in Greater Disparities: An Unexpected Consequence for the Commonwealth of Virginia." *Journal of Educational Finance* 33(3):238–261.

Editor (2011a). "Fairness in Firing Teachers." *New York Times.* March 6.

———. (2011b). "Fraud at School: The U.S. Attorney Is Right to Look at Education Funds." *Pittsburgh Post Gazette.* November 14.

EPSTEIN, D. (2011). *Measuring Inequity in School Funding.* Washington, DC: Center for American Progress.

FIRESTONE, W., GOERTZ, M., AND NATRIELLO, G. (1997). *From Cashbox to Classroom: The Struggle for Fiscal Reform and Educational Change in New Jersey.* New York: Teachers College Press.

FISCHEL, W. (1989). "Did Serrano Cause Proposition 13?" *National Tax Journal,* December, 465–474.

———. (1996). "How Serrano Caused Proposition 13." *Journal of Law and Politics* 12:607–645.

FORDHAM, S., AND OGBU, J. (1986). "Black Students' School Success: Coping with the 'Burden of Acting White.'" *The Urban Review* 18(1):176–206.

GHATT, J. (2011). "School Unions' Last Hired/First Fired Policies Punish Great Teachers, Hurt Students." *Washington Times*. May 12.

GLENN, W. (2009). "School Finance Adequacy Litigation and Student Achievement: A Longitudinal Analysis." *Journal of Education Finance* 34(3):247–366.

GLENN, W., AND PICUS, L. (2007). "The *Williams* Settlement and the for Future School Finance Adequacy Litigation in California." *Journal of Education Finance* 32(3):382–394.

GONZALEZ, J. (2011). "More $Cheming: Yet Another High-Paid Consultant Charged with Bilking Millions." *New York Daily News*. April 29.

HALL, D., AND USHOMIRSKY, N. (2010). *Closing the Hidden Funding Gaps in Our Schools.* Washington, DC: The Education Trust.

HANUSHEK, E. (1989). "The Impact of Differential Expenditures on School Performance." *Educational Researcher*, May, 45–51.

———. (1996). "School Resources and Student Performances." In *Does Money Matter? The Effect of School Resources on Student Achievement and Adult Success*, ed. G. Burtless. Washington, DC: Brookings Institution.

HANUSHEK, E., AND LINDSETH, A. (2009). "The Effectiveness of Court-Ordered Funding of Schools." *Education Outlook* 6:1–9.

HEDGES, L., LAINE, R., AND GREENWALD, R. (1994). "Does Money Matter? A Meta-Analysis of Studies of the Effects of Differential School Inputs on Student Outcomes." *Educational Researcher* 23(3):5–14.

HELLER, K. (2011). "A Moment of Corrupt Clarity in Philadelphia Politics." *Philadelphia Inquirer*. September 28.

HESS, F. (2011). "Our Achievement Gap Mania." *National Affairs* 9(Fall). www.national affairs.com/publications/detail/our-achievement-gap-mania.

HIGHTOWER, A. (2011). "Weighing States' School Performance, Policymaking." *Education Week*. January 5. www.edweek.org/ew/articles/2011/01/13/16stateofthestates .h30.html.

HOXBY, C. (2003). "Achievement, Efficiency and Centralization in California Public Schools." Prepared for *Williams v. California*. www.decentschools.org.

IMBER, M. (2004). "Adequacy in School Funding." *American School Board Journal*, November, 46–47.

KATZ, M. (1975). *Class, Bureaucracy and Schools: The Illusion of Educational Change in America.* New York: Praeger.

KOZOL, J. (2006). "Jonathan Kozol Takes on the World." *District Administration*. January. www.districtadministration.com/viewarticle.aspx?articleid=37&p=1#0.

LADD, H., AND HANSEN, J., EDS. (1999). *Making Money Matter: Financing America's Schools.* Washington, DC: National Academy Press.

MACKEY, S. (1998). "The School Money Puzzle." *Government Finance Review* 2:39–42.

MISHEL, L., AND SHIERHOLZ, H. (2011). "Sustained, High Joblessness, Causes Lasting Damage to Wages, Benefits, Income, and Wealth." Economic Policy Institute Issue Brief 324. Washington, DC: Economic Policy Institute.

MORRIS, G. (1989). "The Blackboard Jungle Revisited." *National Review* 41(8):18–19.

NOGUERA, P. (2004). "Racial Isolation, Poverty, and the Limits of Local Control in Oakland." *Teachers College Record* 106(11): 2146–2170.

OAKES, J. (2002). "Education Inadequacy, Inequality, and Failed State Policy: A Synthesis of Expert Reports Prepared for *Williams v. State of California*. www.decentschools.org/ experts.php.

Organization for Economic Cooperation and Development. (2011). *Education at a Glance 2011: OECD Indicators.* Paris: OECD Publishing. http://www.oecd.org/document/ 2/0,3746,en_2649_39263238_48634114_1_1_1_1,00.html

————. (2007). "Professional Rigor, Public Engagement and Judicial Review: A Proposal for Enhancy the Validity of Education Adequacy Studies." *Teachers College Record* 109(6): 1303–1373.

REBELL, M. (2008a). "Equal Opportunity and the Courts." *Phi Delta Kappan* 89(6):432–439. www.pdkintl.org/kappan/k_v89/k0802reb.htm.

————. (2008b). "Sleepless in Seattle: There's Still Hope for Equal Educational Opportunity." *Education Week*, February 13, 32–33.

ROTHSTEIN, R. (2010). "How to Fix our Schools." Economic Policy Institute Issue Brief 286. Washington, DC: Economic Policy Institute.

Serrano v. Priest. (1971). 5 Cal.3d 584.

TIMAR, T., AND ROZA, M. (2008). "A False Dilemma: Should Decisions about Education Resource Use Be Made at the State or Local Level?" Paper presented at the University of California, Davis Center for Applied Policy in Education Symposium, Davis, CA. April 18.

TYACK, D. (1974). *The One Best System: A History of American Urban Education.* Cambridge, MA: Harvard University Press.

U.S. Department of Education. (2006). *The Condition of Education 2006* (NCES 2006-071). Washington, DC: U.S. Government Printing Office.

————. (2007). *The Condition of Education 2007* (NCES 2007-064). Washington, DC: National Center for Educational Statistics.

————. (2011). *The Digest of Educational Statistics 2010.* Table 106. Washington, DC: National Center for Educational Statistics.

URBAN, W., AND WAGONER, J. (2000). *American Education: A History.* 2nd Ed. New York: McGraw-Hill.

ZHOU, L. (2008). *Revenues and Expenditures for Public Elementary and Secondary Education: School Year 2005–06 (Fiscal Year 2006)* (NCES 2008-328). Washington, DC: U.S. Department of Education, National Center for Education Statistics, Institute of Education Sciences. http://nces.ed.gov/pubsearch/pubsinfo.asp?pubid=2008328.

CHAPTER 4

Privatization, Commercialization, and the Business of School: Complementing or Competing Interests

Should schools be more like business?

POSITION 1: PRIVATIZING AND/OR CORPORATE SUPPORT CAN IMPROVE EDUCATION

The United States cannot succeed in the international economy without a well-educated, well-trained workforce. The United States needs a strong education system to prepare the next generation of workers for the ever-changing economy.

—Business Roundtable (2008, p. 2)

The only way for Americans to get rid of their public schools is to privatize them.

—Blumenfeld (2011)

Privatization and Direct Corporate Engagement Needed

Schools, students, parents, and taxpayers gain when business ideas and competition are encouraged in education. Privatizing schools (or many of their services) and engaging corporations directly in school matters are two good ways to improve American education (Snell, 2011; Gilroy, 2012; see www.reason.org).

Privatization can benefit schools by bringing the efficiency and effectiveness of private enterprise to bear on school organization and operation. Corporations and local businesses can also benefit schools by providing funds and political support for needed facilities and services. Corporations are often eager to help by purchasing the rights to name buildings, events, or school programs. This provides competitive incentive for schools as businesses make offers and provides a source of funds. Business interests go far beyond simply financial sponsorship or privatizing some activities of public schools. The U.S. Chamber of Commerce, through its Institute for a Competitive Workforce (2011), notes, "If business leaders are serious about school improvement, they must play a more forceful role and drive harder bargains with state officials and school district administrators." Privatization offers a direct way to improve schools.

The health and vitality of our economy and our society depend on schools. Businesspeople understand this principle. For many years, corporations and local businesses have been among the strongest supporters of education. Business enterprises provide substantial financial contributions, internships and scholarships, guest speakers and teaching materials, advisers and consultants, fund-raising assistance, and employment for parents, students, and other taxpayers. Leaders of the business community recognize the significant benefits that good schools offer, and they are active advocates of improvements in education.

Public schools are prime candidates for privatization. Privatization involves changing services once operated by governmental agencies to private ownership or operation. This cuts the high cost to taxpayers, government bloat, and the typical inefficiencies of governmental activities and monopolies. Public education is one of the most tax-costly, bloated, and inefficient enterprises of government. It is also largely monopolistic but has not consistently produced sound education (*The Economist*, 2005). For these and other reasons, public education has not fulfilled its social purpose of providing high-quality education at reasonable cost. With no competition and a tradition of inefficiency, public schools have become the major burden on and frustration for the local taxpayer. Privatization offers market efficiency, accountability, professional design, and choice (Lipana, 2011).

Reasons for the Privatization of American Public Schools

Improving Schools for Our Children

The most important reason to involve private enterprise in schools is to benefit our children. They deserve the best schools we can provide. The bureaucracy created for government-operated schools overwhelms local budgets and does not respond to complaints. Privatization increases accountability, making school staffs responsible for meeting performance standards for the benefit of children. Accountability, a keystone of private enterprise, offers a way to clearly identify problems and reward good performance in schools. Instead of weak, vague educational jargon that hides poor school practices, private enterprise sets specific goals and measures how well schools meet them. Schools that work will be rewarded; those that don't will be changed or closed.

The Edison Schools, an innovative approach to school privatization, contracts with public schools to operate them with no increase in costs but with better results. In addition, Edison offers opportunity for stockholders to participate while providing a public good. The improving quality of schooling in Edison-related schools is documented (Chubb, 1998; Edison Learning, 2012; see www .edisonlearning.com); academic scores of students are improving under Edison leadership. Private contractors put performance conditions in their contracts. What public school operation gives the public the same guarantee?

Providing Democratic Choice—Breaking the Public School Monopoly

Privatizing schools offers choices to parents concerned about their children's education. School choice is certainly in the best interest of children and their parents, but it also forces schools to compete to attract students and financial support.

The public schools have had a monopoly for far too long and suffer from lack of competition. Privatization can bring customer satisfaction and state-of-the-art efficiency to such schools. Studies show k12 private programs work. (k12 inc., 2012). Of course, public schools do not welcome privatization, and their unions continue to fight it (Murphy, 2004; Snell, 2005; *The Economist*, 2005).

Increasing Productivity in Education

Privatizing increases productivity in public schools, a place where productivity has not changed for a century. Most public school districts operate in much the same manner as when our grandparents were students. Expensive, labor-intensive public schools sap local and state finances. Improvements in technology and communications have revolutionized U.S. business and provided manifold increases in productivity but have virtually not changed public schools. Most school administrators come through the ranks of education and lack the business background and discipline needed to develop and implement sound strategic planning, efficient resource allocations, monitoring and accountability control, and effective management in schools. That may explain their lack of interest in improving productivity (Hentschke et al., 2004).

Meeting Global Competition

International competition requires the United States to remain on the cutting edge of innovation or else suffer future decline. If public schools are not up to the task, we need to find other approaches. Privatization of schools is an idea whose time has come.

As democracy and capitalism increase across the globe, privatization will continue to be a strong movement in public life during the twenty-first century. Government-run operations show weaknesses that private enterprise can overcome. Worldwide, leaders recognize private enterprise as the key vehicle for improving citizens' lives while making government more efficient with available funds and resources. Nations from differing economic traditions are moving toward private operation of a variety of public services. Schools are among the social institutions increasingly undergoing privatization in many nations. England and New Zealand provide excellent examples of this process; the public in each of these nations recognizes the value of private enterprise in more effectively and efficiently operating schools. The United States is actually lagging behind other nations in this global movement.

A Variety of Approaches to School Privatization: Charter Schools to Food Operations

Complete privatization offers some distinct advantages, such as allowing districts to hold private managers accountable for student learning, but it is also possible to identify limited segments of current school operations that private contractors could handle to the benefit of students and taxpayers. In public-private partnerships, the school board hires private managers to run the public schools under a multiyear contract that specifies performance standards and allows the board to fire the managers with ninety days' notice.

Educational management organizations, similar to health maintenance organizations for medical care, are emerging to improve schools. Sylvan Learning Systems, Nobel Learning Communities, Edison Learning, and Knowledge Universe are examples of private management of education. The twenty-first century should see expansion of school privatization from 13 percent in 2000 to 25 percent by 2020 (Hentschke et al., 2004). Edison is involved with about 400 schools, educating 450,000 students (www.edisonlearning.com).

Under complete privatization, rigorous contracts with the local board of education guarantee performance. Included in complete privatization would be all activities, including managing the school(s), hiring and evaluating staff, developing the curriculum, evaluating student learning, communicating with parents and the community, and providing custodial and ancillary maintenance. These individual items also are excellent candidates for partial privatization of school operations.

Public schools now contract for selected management services that are too costly or too cumbersome to handle under public control. Districts contract payroll and accounting services. Others find that contracting with popular fast-food companies, such as McDonald's and Pizza Hut, to provide school lunch service is more cost effective, more acceptable to students, and sometimes more nutritious than the standard school cafeteria food. Private contracts for specific services, from the provision of food to managing all school operations, have proved their value to students, school officials, and taxpayers. Piecemeal privatization of school services has been working well for years in many schools. Now private operation of individual schools—and even entire city school districts—is developing.

Obstacles to Privatization of Schools

When people understand that, for less cost, they can have better service and more accountability, they quickly become supporters of the shift to private operation. Other, more difficult obstacles remain.

Public employee labor unions lobby against privatization of public services— obvious self-interest. Teacher unions have been particularly active opposing school privatization and are among the largest, best-financed, and most active organizations in state legislatures. Many state legislators fear their power. Teacher unions filed suit against school vouchers in Milwaukee and against school management contracts in Baltimore; Hartford, Connecticut; and Wilkins- burg, Pennsylvania, and against school janitorial contracts in California (Eggers and O'Leary, 1996). The teachers union actively but unsuccessfully opposed the shift to privatization of schools in Philadelphia (Steinberg, 2002; Snell, 2005).

Government bureaucracies also present obstacles to private enterprise since bureaucracies may lose some of their power. Charter schools are not subject to some of the bureaucratic regulations that have kept the public school establish- ment so entrenched. They may establish teacher accountability without tenure requirements, develop a curriculum without contending with state mandates, and organize classes and provide instruction without meeting some of the trivial specifications that have petrified public education. The public education bureaucracy built a massive fortress of regulations. It is the Internal Revenue Service of the school business.

Businesspeople know that there may be no more important work in Ameri- can society than the improvement of schools. Good schools are simply good business.

Corporate Involvement in Schools

The strength of U.S. society lies in the fortuitous combination of democracy and capitalism. Free enterprise is a basic condition for releasing the entrepreneurial spirit in humans, and entrepreneurs built and developed this great nation. The free marketplace for which the United States has become respected globally requires continual improvement—that directly incorporates education. Schools are key to the future development of the American economy (Business Round- table, 2008).

Our success causes many other nations to emulate American entrepreneur- ship. That is complimentary, but it is also a challenge. The breakdown of most communist countries at the end of the 1980s illustrates the flawed nature of socialism. The death of communism finds the twenty-first century a world of competing capitalist nations. This new scenario requires even more U.S. com- mitment to an education-business partnership. Schooling that will maintain our leadership in international business competition is a top priority. With or with- out privatization, business must enter into new and more intertwined partner- ships with schools to ensure that the United States keeps its competitive edge in global markets.

Business Interest in Partnerships with Schools

It is this competition for school completion and school quality that demands the joint interests of businesspeople, corporations, and school people. Consistent with these beliefs, business leaders are in the forefront of efforts to reform schools (Ramsey, 1993; Aaron et al., 2003; Business Roundtable, 2010). The Business Roundtable, an organization of the chief executive officers (CEOs) of the 200 most prominent U.S. corporations, was an early and strong supporter of the No Child Left Behind (NCLB) Act of 2002. The Roundtable website (www.busi nessroundtable.org) contains links to various Roundtable school reform activities and forums that follow up on the implementation of NCLB legislation. The companies with membership in the Roundtable employ about 34 million people. That constitutes a very sizable and influential group of corporate people with educational interests.

Corporate support for school improvement goes far beyond that in earlier days and now includes leading businesses in virtually all segments of the economy (Koebler, 2011; *Philanthropy News Digest*, 2011). These corporate-sponsored school activities focus on such diverse areas as academic instructional improvement, career awareness, civic and character education, drug abuse prevention, dropout prevention, and programs for the disadvantaged.

School-Business Partnerships

The president of the National Education Association, in announcing a new form of responsible unionism, stated, "Despite the political rhetoric, public schools and business are natural allies" (Chase, 1998). This allied position bodes well for dramatic improvements in schooling and offers opportunities for school-business partnerships to provide leadership and support.

Almost all the member corporations of the Business Roundtable belong to school partnerships for educational improvement. The Council for Corporate and School Partnerships, established by Coca-Cola in 2001 (www.corpschool partners.org), offers support and rewards for schools engaged in partnership activities. The purpose for the council is to encourage school-business partnerships that improve the academic, social, or physical well-being of students. The council presents large awards per year to model school-business partnerships. There are now several hundred such partnerships, representing nearly every state, competing for the awards.

The Boston Compact established a partnership between Boston's schools and the Boston Private Industry Council. Businesses promised students jobs if the schools were able to raise test scores and decrease dropout rates. This alliance has provided jobs for over 1,000 graduates, and reading and math scores have improved (www.bostonpic.org).

Through such partnerships, business leaders can come into the schools to teach, to talk with students, and to help teachers and guidance counselors develop programs to improve student skills and attitudes. Students can visit places of employment and gain understanding of the economy and business interests and concerns. Partnerships can establish work-study arrangements for students, produce teaching materials, and provide financial support for all aspects of schooling from teacher seminars to improving school technology and career guidance. Many businesses participate in "Adopt-a-School" programs that enrich the school's ability to prepare students for employment. Other businesses invite teachers to visit, provide summer employment and other opportunities for teachers to learn about their operations, and prepare free teaching materials. Business-to-school financial support by direct grants, special project sponsorship, advertising in school media, discounted purchase arrangements, equipment and resource acquisition, and a variety of other avenues provides much-needed money for school uses.

Corporations help schools in these key areas because they recognize the value of helping students reach their full potential. This is not a new role for business leadership in U.S. schools; business-education relations have a long and positive history (Mann, 1987). These contributions include cash, services, sympathy, and assistance in political and economic coalitions. There are many varieties of school-business partnerships; the most effective ones provide for mutual respect and participation, with each partner satisfied with the results (Daniels Fund, 2008; Hann, 2008).

Education and the Changing Nature of Employment in the United States

Prominent changes in the nature of employment in American society have had major implications for schools. Historically, the shift was from agricultural to manufacturing jobs; now the shift is from manufacturing to service and information. In the short space of the last fifty years, the proportion of farmers and farmworkers has declined from almost 20 percent of the workforce to only 3 percent; manufacturing jobs have declined from about 32 to 27 percent of total employment, whereas service jobs have increased from about 53 to 69 percent. The service sector has grown primarily in social and producer services (e.g., health and medical technology) rather than in personal services (e.g., hairdressing or domestic work) or distributive services (e.g., sales and delivery). The most prominent change has been in the kinds of jobs available. White-collar jobs rose from about 45 percent of the labor force in 1940 to over 70 percent by the mid-1980s and about 80 percent by 2010. Blue-collar jobs declined from about 42 percent to about 20 percent over the same period (U.S. Census Bureau 2007, 2011).

In educational terms, this means that students need more and better schooling. Many agricultural jobs no longer demand just sheer physical labor but involve technical work that requires strong academic skills. White-collar jobs typically require increased education. Data show how the level of education relates to income (see figure 4.1). Women, although experiencing a history of lower average earnings, are increasingly using education to improve their incomes.

In earlier times, basic literacy could be recommended purely for its inherent values; it had no special relation to people' work requirements. In a period when most citizens lived rural, agricultural lives, reading, writing, and calculating

FIGURE 4.1 Education, Earning Power, and Gender

Educational Attainment	Average Annual Earnings		Expected Lifetime	
	Male	Female	Male	Female
Less than High School	$28,000	$22,000	$1,300,000	$1,000,000
High School Graduate	43,000	32,000	2,000,000	1,500,000
Some College	50,000	36,000	2,350,000	1,700,000
Associate Degree	54,000	39,000	2,500,000	1,800,000
Bachelor's and Higher	94,000	60,000	4,400,000	2,800,000

Note: Annual earnings based on 2009 income data (U.S. Census Bureau), rounded. Lifetime earnings extrapolated to age 65.

Source: U.S. Census Bureau (2005, 2007, 2011).

were nice to know but not necessary for securing and keeping employment. Even in those times, however, obvious links existed between education and employment. A study conducted in 1867 by the Commonwealth of Pennsylvania, for example, showed that income was related directly to literacy: those who could not read earned an average of $36 per month, those who could read but were otherwise poorly educated earned an average of $52 a month, and those who were well educated earned an average of $90 a month (Soltow and Stevens, 1981). But literacy for business purposes does not mean just proficiency in reading and writing. It means a set of values related to work.

There is a correlation between education and income, between education and national development, and between education and "the good life." Nations with the highest levels of education also have the highest levels of wealth, innovation, and achievement (Isaak, 2005). Social class and occupational experience are also influential in employment status, but education had the greatest effect.

Consumers and Schools

In addition to the business interest in education for developing the economy and preparing good employees, there is an obvious interest in the schools as a location of consumers. Consumers, of course, are one of the driving forces of our economy. It is not only the earnings of retail stores that rise and fall according to consumer choices. Manufacturers of electronics, clothing, appliances, and vehicles, as well as their suppliers of raw materials, are also subject to consumer selections. Banks and other financial institutions, gas and oil companies, house construction and repair agencies, food producers and suppliers, entertainment industries, and other consumer-driven corporations exist and change because of what people buy.

Consumer confidence is one of the major indicators of economic activity, one closely examined by Wall Street firms and market watchers worldwide. We are a consumer society. A free market gives us competition that provides choices among quality, prices, and variety. An important part of the economic process in a consumer society is getting information to the consumer about new or improved products and services, places to obtain them, reminders about trade names, and ways to obtain competitive prices or opportunities. This is a place for corporate notices, news releases, advertising, and other uses of media to convey information. Although we may complain at times about some advertising, we recognize that much of the information that ads contain is valuable. Through advertising, we learn of innovations, modifications, and opportunities that make our lives easier or happier. We can find better prices, products, and services for things we want. We can find standards against which we can measure products and services. Advertising provides us with important ideas and information, necessary to our roles as consumers. The marketplace adjusts according to the decisions made by consumers; advertising adjusts according to the market and how consumers respond to ads.

Consumer life does not stop at the school door. After all, students are consumers, and they influence consumer decisions in families. They deserve to know about products and services available. The school setting is an appropriate location for some of that information. Schools employ teachers and administrators to develop curricula and classroom practices designed to help students gain an adequate understanding of life. Student life outside of school involves advertising and commerce. Schools should provide education that reflects the society, and societies depend on commerce. Businesses know that children and adolescents are a very significant segment of buyers, among the most important in many areas of retail purchases. Within this context, the provision of corporate-sponsored school material offers information for students, and it gives financial support for schools. Students can learn from the material, and schools are relieved from the extra burden of paying for it.

Business Approaches to School Operation

Schools could also benefit from the use of business models in school organization and operation. Schools are often inefficient. If U.S. industry had been as stultified as the schools, it would have failed long ago. In fact, those businesses that have not updated and improved their efficiency and productivity have failed; private enterprise cannot survive stagnation. Yet we have protected our schools from this necessary competition.

Improved technology and productivity could increase school efficiency considerably. For example, if innovative technologies come into play, the teacher could present more interesting material to larger groups in less time, individual students could work more extensively on computers under the general guidance of the teacher or a teacher's aide, the school day and curriculum could be more varied, parents could get up-to-date information on their child's progress, early warning systems could limit student failures, and teachers could identify their own and their students' peak performance data. Schools would be organized very differently, but that is what we need. Businesses are constantly reorganizing to achieve better productivity because competition demands it.

Another businesslike approach that could bring great benefits to schools is in the use of incentives and rewards for good performance. Currently, schools pay teachers on the basis of nineteenth-century ideas that all teachers are the same and that only increased experience should provide increased income. This levels down the performance of many teachers and schools to the lowest common denominator. There is no incentive for individual teachers to perform in a superior manner. With teacher pay based on performance, the most talented teachers will get better salaries, and other teachers will have a very good reason to start measuring up. That would make the salaries for the best teachers competitive with salaries for other professionals and would attract more topflight college graduates into teaching.

Another place to bring incentives for performance is in school administration. Often, administrator salaries are limited by job title, and excellent performance is rewarded only by having to change jobs. One idea would be to tie administrator income to accountability standards. When administrators lead their schools forward to better student achievement, they get increased income through bonuses or other rewards.

Business thinking can help education in other areas. School buildings are often large, inefficiently utilized, and costly to build and maintain. In districts where student enrollment has declined, expensive school buildings have been sold, destroyed, or renovated at great public financial loss. Some school buildings are used less than half the year and then for only one-third of the day. The practice of issuing bonds has passed the debt for building these behemoths on to future generations. Many small schools, with separate buildings and school staffs, could be reorganized into less costly regional districts if we applied business concepts. Individual school districts purchase millions of dollars' worth of books, equipment, and teaching materials at high cost when a coordinated effort could decrease such expense considerably.

Businesses have shown that they can train large numbers of employees by using video and computer systems, lectures, programmed materials, self-study, and other devices that do not consume the high levels of precious human resources that schools use. Furthermore, this training occurs in facilities used extensively for the whole of each year.

This is not a time for schools to continue their course—it is a time to change schools, and business-proven techniques can effect the changes. The structure of business based on a competitive marketplace has withstood the most severe tests of war, depression, and dislocation. We need to introduce contemporary business management—management concerned with improved efficiency and productivity—into education. And we need to offer privatization of schools or many of their services as a competitive challenge to a public monopoly.

It is a social and educational necessity that we reorder our schools to give students solid grounding in academic skills and good, positive workplace values. It is an economic necessity that we reorganize school operations to more closely approximate good business practices. All in all, business has much to offer education, much more than just providing money for school projects (Feulner, 1991; Mandel et al., 1995; Oravitz, 1999; Aaron et al., 2003; Weldon, 2011). Financial support alone cannot confront the crisis in education. Developing basic and advanced skills, improving workplace attitudes and values, increasing the productivity of U.S. business, enhancing our competitive stance in international markets, and making schools more efficient are goals that business and the schools share. For the good of our young people and for our future as a nation, we need to encourage privatization and strong alliances with business to reach these shared goals.

POSITION 2: PUBLIC SCHOOLS SHOULD BE PUBLIC

Schools have become integral to the marketing plans of a vast array of corporations as commercial interests—through advertising, sponsorship of curriculum and programs, marketing of consumer products, for-profit privatization, and fund-raising tied to commercial entities—continue to influence public education.

—Molnar (2004, p. 1)

The public is losing its sense of ownership of its schools, which threatens democracy itself.

—Mathews (2008, p. 560)

The idea that private operation of public services is superior is a socially destructive myth (Krugman, 2011, 2012; Nealon, 2012). Schrag (1999) points out that "the pattern in our society is toward withdrawal from community into private, gated enclaves with private security, private recreational facilities, private everything, even as the public facilities deteriorate." Self-serving myths—promoted in the corporate world and corporate-oriented mass media—are that private enterprise offers superior services, efficiency, competition, and management.

Is Privatization Better?

The actual privatization record does not support claims of improving efficiency (Krugman, 2002; Levin, 2006). Typically, private contractors submit low bids to get a contract, then move prices up—or have cost overruns—after government workers have been eliminated and are no threat to the contractor.

There is no solid evidence of superior performance, higher quality, lower costs, or better management in schools by the private sector. Evidence demonstrates the opposite. Edison Schools, the largest of private corporations running schools, can produce no substantial data of improvements in academic performance by students (Miron and Applegate, 2000; Bracey, 2002, 2008; Henriques and Steinberg, 2002a, 2002b; Holloway, 2002; American Federation of Teachers, 2003; Lubienski and Lubienski, 2004; Ratchford, 2005; Molner, Miron, and Urschel, 2010).

Edison was founded in 1992 and was considered the harbinger of the new school privatization trend that would take over, improve schools, eliminate the public monopoly, and make money for investors. Independent research on student achievement showed poor comparative results, and over the course of about ten years, almost thirty public school districts in fourteen states canceled privatization contracts with Edison. In regard to making money for investors by being more efficient and using "business-based" ideas, Edison went public in 1999 and traded stock for four years with only one profitable quarter, and the price fell from $40 per share to 14 cents per share. Additionally, the Securities and Exchange Commission said that Edison failed to disclose that 40 percent ($150 million) of its claimed money was never seen. The corporation went private in 2003, senior management was replaced, the name was changed to Edison Learning Corporation, and its focus changed from managing schools to "partnering" with schools to provide some services like tutoring and testing (Henriques and Steinberg, 2002b; Mathews, 2003; Quart, 2003; Moberg, 2004; Saltman, 2005, 2012; Parents Advocating School Accountability, 2009).

Henry Levin (2006), an economist who directs the Center for the Study of Privatization in Education at Columbia University, summarizes research on claims about private operation of public schools:

> Studies of EMOs [for-profit educational management organizations, like Edison Schools] have found greater administration costs than comparable public schools. EMO contracts have also been more costly than funding received by similar public school sites. Moreover, there is little evidence that EMO-run schools outperform public schools with similar students. (pp. 11, 12)

Uncritical reporting by mass media on charter schools describes them as innovations to improve education but hides their lack of academic performance and cost. Not all charter schools are private, but many are, and there is a false presumption that they are somehow better than public education. A vast, two-and-a-half-year study by researchers at the University of California, Los Angeles, finds that charter schools neither fulfill their promises nor improve student achievement (Magee and Leopold, 1998). A Stanford University (2009) research study released in 2009 found that while 17 percent of charters had student achievement scores better than comparable public schools, 40 percent of the charters showed no improvement, and 37 percent had significantly worse scores than traditional public schools. Teacher satisfaction also suffers; recent studies show that teachers in charter schools are 132 percent more likely to leave than are teachers in public schools (Stuit and Smith, 2009). Some charter schools, relieved from many state regulations, have serious problems in finances, student achievement, and operations. A Brookings Institute Brown Center (2002) report on American education, examining academic achievement in charter schools in ten states from 1999 to 2001, concludes that "in a nutshell, charter schools performed about one-quarter standard deviation below comparable regular public schools on these three years of state tests" (p. 1). Privatizing schools is not improvement or progress, just another avenue for private wealth to gain more control (Arsen and Ni, 2012; Giroux, 2012; Krugman, 2012; Saltman, 2012; Ward, 2012).

Do corporations do things better than public agencies, or are they just better at public relations? Are Enron, Bank of America, Lehman Brothers, and subprime mortgage bundlers good examples of how privatization might work for education? Should we work out a system for privatizing public schools that would handsomely reward the school CEO and a chosen few insiders, penalize the workers and general stockholders, and allow a failing corporation to walk away from the schools with little responsibility for their failure?

Social Purposes and Private Goals

In a capitalistic democracy, some activities fit private enterprise and some deserve public operation and oversight. Kozol, in *Rethinking Schools* (1998), finds no evidence that "a competitive free market, unrestricted, without a strong counterpoise within the public sector will ever dispense decent medical care, sanitation, transportation, or education to the people" (p. 1).

The fundamental social purposes of public education in a democracy must be the centerpoint of any substantial debate over privatization. We can measure public and private operation of schools against the broad social purposes of schooling. Any debate over privatizing public schools should focus on whether public or private control is more likely to move us toward fulfilling those large social purposes (Giroux, 2012).

The clamor to privatize and a long-term campaign to demonize public schools have stifled the more significant debate on social purposes. Lacking is the necessary long-range social perspective in the pressure to privatize schools (Hunter and Brown, 1995). Shortsighted goals of achieving higher test scores and saving money are simply insufficient reasons for privatizing, even if private schools could ensure these results. Of course, they can't, and short-term test score improvement has been shown to be the result of manipulation, not superior schooling.

Despite a century-long tradition of excellent public service in difficult social and financial conditions, public schools have been subjected to a relentlessly negative campaign during the past two decades. Ironically, the privatization myth protects private enterprise from similar attacks for its many failures and its significant threat to democracy. The history of private enterprise—with its questionable ethics, cavalier treatment of employees and the public, financial manipulation of the political process, and escapes into bankruptcy or tax-payer bailout when in trouble—goes unmentioned in reporting and in public discourse on privatization. Much support for privatization of public schools revolves around shallow advertising that capitalizes on negative images of public schools, unsupported claims of potential cost savings, and a paternalistic aura that corporations know best. The evidence does not support the claims. For-profit schools do not have innovative practices, curriculum, or management programs (Kaplan, 1996; Zollers and Ramanathan, 1998; Pizarro, 2011; Smith, 2011). They make a profit, but don't improve education (Krugman,2012).

In certain situations and under strict and open public regulation and school district supervision, it is reasonable to provide some aspects of public services, such as food service in school lunchrooms, through private contracts. But wholesale privatizing of schools, where a private corporation controls the management, curriculum, and instructional decisions of a whole school or school district, is an extremely hazardous approach to dealing with public services. In areas as important to society's future as education, privatizing may destroy the soul of democratic life (Saltman, 2000; Bracey, 2001; Sudetic, 2001).

Among the most compelling statements for public education in a democratic society is John Dewey's *Democracy and Education* (1916). In recent years, leading political theorists and education scholars have reiterated the significance of public education to democracy (Gutmann, 1999, 2008; Saltman, 2000; Kadlec, 2007; Ravitch, 2010).

The goals of improving justice, equality, and freedom are central to the idea of a public school but not to private enterprise. We have a long way to go in public education to meet these high standards; minorities and women have not had equal opportunities or freedom in schools. But we are improving significantly in this area, and we continue to pursue those goals in public education. Privatizing, with its attendant emphasis on cutting costs and improving test scores, is less likely to expand opportunities for the weakest or most disadvantaged.

Free, critical study of social problems may not be a goal in corporation-operated schools. Open examination of controversial topics, necessary in democratic society, may conflict with corporate agendas. How many corporations encourage criticism, especially public criticism, of their purposes and practices? Saltman (2000, 2005, 2012) condemns the utter commercialization of public education as a major threat to democracy.

Dayton and Glickman (1994) point clearly to one aspect of the threat:

> A fundamental problem with the privatization movement is that it views public education as merely another individual entitlement and ignores the vital public interests served by common public schools. Public education is democratically controlled by the elected representatives of the People. Ultimately it is the People who decide how public education funds are expended. Privatization systems use public funds, but limit public control. Allowing private control of public funds circumvents the democratic control and interests of the People. (p. 82)

Exposing the Myths of Privatization

Myths about privatization include the ideas that privatization is as follows:

- Efficient, so it can save tax money while providing quality services
- Market driven, so it is responsive to the consumer
- Performance based, rewarding the productive and cutting out the incompetent

Myth: Efficiency

Efficiency is a means, not a goal; the mere act of being efficient is inadequate as a rationale for social policy. Effectiveness is more important. Efficient use of resources, human and other, should aim to preserve and improve the physical and social environment.

The superficial type of efficiency used in the private sector, however, is found wanting. The profit motive defines efficiency as a cost-saving way to increase corporate income. Saving time by requiring dangerous shortcuts may appear to be efficient but may simply be foolhardy. "Efficient" manufacturing has created toxic waste, workplace accidents, worker health problems, over-production, and waste. Actual social costs of this type of efficiency are seldom calculated. In addition, the public often subsidizes the private sector through corporation-friendly policies on taxes and use of natural resources.

Large homes, expensive cars, servants, yachts, exclusive clubs, private planes, and legal and financial assistance to take advantage of tax loopholes typify those who gain the most from private enterprise. These are not accoutrements normally found among public school educators, whose lives are devoted to public service. Conspicuous consumption is a characteristic of private enterprise, not of public employment.

Myth: Market Driven and Consumer Responsive

There is no free and open market in the current economy. Price-fixing, monopolistic trusts, special interest legislation, weak regulatory agencies, and other corporation-protective practices skew the market to benefit the biggest corporations and most politically adept businesspeople. Lobbying, graft, buyouts, control of regulating authorities, and an "old boys' network" combine to deny newcomers equal marketplace opportunity and consumer protection. Most corporate strategies aim to gain control of the market to keep others out, not to encourage free competition. When that doesn't work well, corporations appeal to the government for special treatment or subsidies, or undergo bankruptcy, hurting small investors but leaving executives wealthy. The free market does not exist.

Consumer responsiveness is another figment of the imagination. Marketing to increase consumerism is a high priority in the private sector, but the primary purpose is to increase profits, not to please customers. Enticing consumers to buy things they do not need is one of the purposes. Consumer protection and satisfaction is a public, not a private, concern fostered by decades of consumer manipulation by private businesses.

Myths: The Performance-Based Corporation, Rewarding Merit, and Cutting Incompetence

Another myth about private enterprise is that it is rigorous about performance, expecting increased productivity and eliminating incompetence. But performance, in business terms, is merely selling more products at less cost with more profit. This goal has little to do with quality. Business news is filled with stories of CEOs whose corporations underperform but who still receive large salary increases and bonuses. Incompetence occurs regularly and at high levels, office politics is more important than quality of work, and you can't challenge higher-level decisions even when these decisions obviously are wrong.

In a system of democratic capitalism, where the relationship between public and private sectors is delicate, there are many tensions. Private enterprise has some virtues and advocates, but it creates severe economic disparity among people and carries a history of exploitation. Similarly, public enterprise offers virtues and has supporters but creates tax burdens and opens itself to bureaucratic bungling. Each sector serves different needs of individuals and society at large. Increasing the proportion controlled by the private sector comes at a cost to the public. For a democracy, the cost of privatizing public education is too high. Privatization is not the only business-oriented issue for schools. Commercialization continues to overtake public education.

Kids as Commodities, Schools as Agents

The commercialization of education is one of the most unfortunate developments in modern society. Schools and corporations may share some general social interests, but they have incompatible goals. The major purpose of corporations is to make profits for shareholders and executives; corporations are not concerned with social well-being unless that stance happens to suit their profit-seeking purpose. The major purpose for schooling, however, *is* social well-being; schools are social institutions intended to transmit and expand knowledge and to develop critical thinking.

Corporate strategy in regard to schools is to see students as commodities and schools as advertising agents. The pattern of this work is to offer inducements to have schools become partners in endeavors that bear direct or subtle business imprints. These endeavors are not always as obvious as teaching materials and school television programs that display company logos or school stadiums named after corporate sponsors (Lewin, 2006; Weissman, 2007). Some sponsored resources involve "free enterprise" educational programs or corporate speakers on environmental or governmental policies. Others involve efforts to improve the basic work skills and work ethic of students—future employees. Seldom does corporate sponsorship come with no strings or only with a proviso that schools stimulate creative or critical thinking.

Companies are necessarily interested in self-preservation and expansion of market share. Corporation efforts in schools reflect their interest in the pursuit of commercial enterprise (Apple, 2004; Boninger and Molnar, 2007; Saltman, 2012). Schooling, however, is too important to leave to corporations.

But, sadly, as David Korten (2001) states,

> In modern societies, television has arguably become our most important institution of cultural reproduction. Our schools are probably the second most important. Television has already been wholly colonized by corporate interests, which are now laying claim to our schools. The goal is not simply to sell products and strengthen the consumer culture. It is also to create a political culture that equates the corporate interest with the human interest in the public mind. . . . Corporations are now moving aggressively to colonize the second major institution of cultural reproduction, the schools. (pp. 151, 157)

Commercialization exacts many costs in education; among the most educationally dysfunctional is the impact on critical thinking. As Molnar, Boninger, and Fogarty (2011) show in their annual report on commercializing schools, "Advertising first creates or amplifies adolescents' insecurities, and, then, literally sells them a "solution" in the form of a product that cannot solve the problem it created" (p. 2). The report documents the kinds of harms brought to schools when commercialization takes place, including the following:

- An explicit contradiction between what is taught in schools and what is advertised there; for example, eat healthy foods while the school sponsors unhealthy foods in hallway vending machines.
- Educational activities are displaced or skewed by commercial activities; for example, classes are suspended to ensure attendance at assemblies sponsored by a major high-tech corporation.
- Marketing interests overwhelm and suppress critical thinking; for example, students are encouraged not to question or critique but to accept claims of commercial sponsors.

Extensive Evidence of Commercialization

Commercialization of schools is evident in many areas. Commercial Alert (2011), a campaign to stop companies from exploiting "captive audiences of school children for commercial gain," is one of several watchdog groups that identifies many of the avenues used by corporations to impose on those children:

- Channel One, Bus Radio, and CNN Student News
- Naming rights for school buildings and facilities
- Exclusive contracts for vending machines, soft drinks, and snacks
- Field trip sponsorship
- "Free" teaching materials
- Advertisements on school buses, school equipment, and school materials
- Computer programs that track school student website visits for marketers
- Sponsorship of sports and school events
- Seminars, meals, and events for teachers
- Corporate speakers, temporary company-paid teachers, and curricular designs
- Contests and incentive programs (www.commercialfreechildhood.org; Commercialism in Education Research Unit, www.epicpolicy.org; Deardorff, 2007; www.commercialalert.org)

Channel One expects that schools show it to 90 percent of the students on 90 percent of the school days each year, without teacher interruptions. It has about ten minutes of "news" and two minutes of commercials each day. Schools receive loaner "free" television equipment. Such disparate progressive and conservative leaders as Ralph Nader and Phyllis Schlafly agree that Channel One is a wrong way for schools to go. Nader (1999) says that "Channel One corrupts the integrity of public schools and degrades the moral authority of schools and teachers." Schlafly (1999), president of the right-wing Eagle Forum, says, "Channel One is a 12 minute a day television marketing device forced on a captive audience of teenagers."

A Government Accountability Office report also found that some 200 schools had exclusionary contracts with soda bottling companies, contracts that provide funds for schools in return for limiting sales of on-campus soda to one corporation (Hays, 2000; see www.commercialfreechildhood.org). One school in Georgia actually suspended a student who wore a T-shirt with a Pepsi logo on the school's "Coke Day" (Hertz, 2001). Another place for corporate intrusion on schools when school funding is desired is in selling the right to name schools and school facilities. "Naming" of school facilities and events for corporate dollars now includes more than a building. There is advertising on school buses and school rooftops, sponsorship of school proms, and corporate names on principals' offices, science labs, libraries, cafeterias, and parts of athletic fields (Lewin, 2006; Flowers, 2008; see www.edufundingpartners.com).

Corporate-sponsored teaching material is another area where schools are seen as agents of one view. Some teaching materials provided by oil and coal companies suggest that they are environmentally friendly (Hightower, 2011; Korten, 2001). Noreena Hertz (2001) comments that you can "go into any classroom now, and the quantity of products 'donated' by corporations is startling" (p. 173). As Hertz notes, "Money buys action and influence. In exchange for amounts of money that are often quite small from their point of view, they expect a significant return" (p. 94).

Corporate sponsorship means that students are offered material that not only intends to stimulate purchases of certain products but that also supports corporate views of environmental, social, economic, and governmental actions. The corporate message and orientation come across even when the material does not overtly pressure for consumer purchases.

These materials treat students as follows:

1. Consumers who need to buy some product, service, or viewpoint
2. Potential workers required to be punctual, to have good "work habits," to show deference to management, and to refrain from critical thought
3. Citizens whose opinions and future votes should be pro-business

Contemporary evidence corporate materials for classroom use expanding throughout all aspects of the school (Hertz, 2001; Korten, 2001; Hartman, 2002; Court, 2003; Fege, 2008; Commercial Alert, 2011; Ball, 2012).

Field trips are an example of this creeping commercialization. No longer are school field trips to museums, art galleries, botanical gardens, and fire stations for cultural and civic educational purposes. Now students are sent on trips to stores like the Sports Authority, Petco, A&P or Albertsons supermarkets, and automobile agencies for business purposes. San Diego schools, for example, schedule over seventy-five such commercial field trips during the school year (Parmet, 2005). Field Trip Factory in Chicago organizes this commercial service to businesses and offers it to schools (Cullen, 2004). They offer "permission slips" for students; they claim that they help "meet national learning standards" (www.fieldtripfactory.com).

Even report cards get a commercial spin. One district sent out report cards in McDonald's-printed envelopes that recommend a "Happy Meal" to reward good grades (Deardorff, 2007). Weissman (2007) says, "Marketers can't seem to stop thinking about the spectacular marketing opportunity afforded by schools" (p. 1).

Evidence of this commercialization of education can be found in local schools. Check teaching materials in local classrooms and school libraries to see which materials are commercially sponsored. Examine those sponsored materials to find bias and spin, along with commercial logos and slogans. Find out about classroom use of television, computers, schoolbook covers, and other media or materials that include commercial advertising. Inquire about commercial sponsorship of school activities, publications, and extracurricular events. Examine school bulletin boards for students and for teachers and other noticeable campus locations for advertising. Ask about commercial involvement in machine-available snack and food supplies, field trips, sports events, and academic programs or awards. Ask about teacher conventions and conferences that include commercial sponsorship and find out how many teachers and administrators have participated in commercially sponsored in-service activities.

Corporate Language and Human Capital

This hidden curriculum of business has been successful. We are more concerned with efficiency than effectiveness, with capital than with minds, with investment than with progress, with accountability than with intellect, and with management than with creativity. The human capital concept is a good example of this extension of business orientation into education and society. The human capital view of the world sees people as equivalent to property that can be exploited for commercial benefit or profit. One consequence of this business school approach to education is that individuals begin to think as "maximizers of their own expected utility" (Shiller, 2005). This leads to complete selfishness, with people engaged in calculations of ways to turn all situations to their advantage, and little concern for others. Corporate CEO salaries are one example of this. Corporate lobbying of Congress for protection from lawsuits or to provide special government bailouts for poor corporate management or tax and pension relief are other examples (Buffet, 2011).

A related consequence of this human capital orientation is a likely decline in civic involvement and shared concern. Court (2003) describes it: "The individual's growing commercial relationship with the corporation has coincided with the individual's shrinking social relationship to the civic community and to other individuals" (p. 113).

Another consequence of the human capital view is the differentiation between management and worker, where management decides what skills and attitudes are needed and provides them to workers. Thus, education is more like training. Students are perceived as commodities and the school as a processing plant. In that process, schools are expected to weed out those who don't "fit," who cause trouble, who challenge authority, who make critical evaluations, and who are not business oriented. Henwood (2003) finds that "employer surveys reveal that bosses care less about their employees' candle-power than they do about 'character'—by which they mean self-discipline, enthusiasm, and responsibility. Bosses want underlings who are steadfast, dependable, consistent, punctual, tactful, and who identify with their work" (p. 76). Employees who are considered "creative" or "independent" are given low ratings (Henwood, 2003).

School Reform and Business Interests

Reform movements in education often target the underclasses on the pretext of making them "fit for work and for citizenship." Schools tell students to be obedient, punctual, frugal, neat, respectful, patriotic, and content with their lot in life. The work ethic, drawing from Puritan views, is of great value to industrialists who desire uncomplaining and diligent workers. This ethic has become the school ethic in far too many locations. An opposing view is that of social responsibility, where human rights, dignity, and democratic citizenship are more important than profit. Education for democratic participation, in the pursuit of justice and equality, is still in the rhetoric of school literature but is not acted on in all schools—that would be bad for business.

This disparity in the schools' purposes—preparing students to participate as workers versus preparing them to participate as equal citizens in striving for justice in society—is overlooked in much of the reform literature. As historian Barbara Finkelstein (1984) notes,

> The educational visions of contemporary reformers evoke historic specters of public schools as crucibles in which to forge uniform Americans and disci-plined industrial laborers. (pp. 276–277)

She illustrates this with examples from a business-education alliance in Atlanta, where business conducts the daily activities of the school by provid-ing work study in semiskilled jobs in local businesses, making moral pro-nouncements to promote industrial discipline in students, and establishing public rituals, such as "Free Enterprise Day" and "passports to job oppor-tunity." This (and other business intrusions into schools) leads to "an effec-tive transfer of control over education policy from public school authorities to industrial councils. . . . For the first time in the history of school reform, a deeply materialistic consciousness seems to be overwhelming all other con-cerns" (Finkelstein, 1984, p. 280).

The current period shows the truth of Finkelstein's insight (McNeal, 1992; Molnar, 2004; Boutwell, 1997; Court, 2003; Berger, 2004; Saltman, 2004, 2012; Commercial Alert, 2011). Academic students are especially eager to get good grades in order to get into the right colleges and get high-paying jobs. Many seem uninterested in intellectual development unless it pays off in employment and salaries.

Raymond Callahan (1962) conducted a historical study of what most influenced the development of contemporary public education in its formative period in the early twentieth century:

> At the turn of the century, America had reason to be proud of the educational progress it had made. The dream of equality of educational opportunity had been partly realized . . . the basic institutional framework for a noble conception of education had been created. . . . The story of the next quarter-century of American education—a story of opportunity lost and of the acceptance by educational administrators of an inappropriate philosophy—must be seen . . . the most powerful force was industrialism . . . the business ideology was spread continuously into the bloodstream of American life. . . . It was, therefore, quite natural for Americans, when they thought of reforming the schools, to apply business methods to achieve their ends. (pp. 1, 5)

Callahan considered this business influence tragic for education and society because it substituted efficiency for effectiveness: We got cost control at the sacrifice of high-quality schooling for all. The business dominance stuck, and in the first decades of the twenty-first century, schools are still controlled by a corporate value system. This explains the factory mentality of schools. It explains why teachers are so poorly paid and badly treated—they are considered laborers. It explains why students are treated as objects in a manufacturing process on school assembly lines. It explains the conformity and standardization, the excessive testing, and the organization and financing of schools. It also explains the lack of concern for social justice and ethics, issues that the schools were making progress on until business gained influence.

Upton Sinclair's (1938) devastating criticism of the meatpacking industry for ignoring public health and worker safety in *The Jungle* helped spur federal legislation to found the Food and Drug Administration (FDA) and regulate food products. Sinclair also published two books about schools that showed the detrimental effects of business influence. *The Goose Step* (1922) detailed how major industrialists determined educational policies and controlled appointments and promotions to professorships in the most important universities in the United States. Sinclair also spent two years studying the public schools, finding heavy-handed control by business leaders over school policies and practices across the United States. In *The Goslings* (1924), he stated, "The purpose of this book is to show you how the 'invisible government' of Big Business which controls the rest of America has taken over the charge of your children" (p. ix).

There is considerable evidence that things may have gotten much worse in the seventy-five years since Sinclair wrote about schools and business. Schools often teach what business wants them to teach, but they should teach what society needs and justice requires them to teach. We need to return to the civilizing purposes of schooling—justice and ethics. The school should be the place where commercialization and corporatization are critically examined, not merely imposed. Bakan (2011) states that "our current failure to provide stronger protection of children in the face of corporate-caused harm reveals a sickness in our societal soul." Children's welfare, especially in schools, is undermined by corporate interests. The role of business in society and in schools, positive and negative, deserves study and critique.

Schools have enough work to do in trying to educate the young without adding the temptations and dangers of commercialization. Students are not commodities, and schools should not be business agents. Society should have strong doubts about the wisdom of allowing business leaders to influence how students are educated. Corporate altruistic rhetoric about supporting good schools for all children is clouded by their self-interest in profit. Corporations would like the taxpaying public to pay for the kinds of education they want their employees to have, and they would like schools to convey a positive view of business no matter what its defects. Businesses will serve their own interests if they can gain control of the schools. But schools exist for society's benefit; society is not served by having business interests dominate the schools (Marina, 1994; Buchen, 1999; Korten, 2001).

Business has a grasping and greedy history, whereas education serves essentially civilizing purposes. Among the schools' most positive goals is to enable students to improve society by increasing justice and expanding social ethics to incorporate a stronger concern for others. This ensures the future of American democracy and poses a significant challenge to schools to strive continually for social development. And that requires knowledge, critical thinking, cooperative endeavor, and a set of values based on justice.

Critical examination of business values and practices, in terms of social justice and human ethics, are of great import. We need to invert the current situation, in which business controls schools, to one in which education influences business values and practices, encouraging responsibility and enlightenment. This would put education in its proper role, monitoring the improvement of society by examining various social institutions, including business. It would certainly improve education, and it might improve business.

For Discussion

1. Table 4.1 shows categories and examples of government services that are candidates for privatization.
   a. What are the advantages and disadvantages of privatization in regard to each of the examples?
   b. What criteria should be used to determine the advantages and disadvantages?
   c. How do these criteria fit a discussion of privatizing schools?
   d. Who should be empowered to make the decisions about privatization?

Table 4.1 Government Services and Privatization	
Category of Service	Example Activities for Privatization
Defense	Military support, training
Health	Public hospitals, FDA operations
Transportation	Airports, Amtrak, FA, urban mass transit
Recreation	Parks service, public land development
Justice	Crime control, prisons
Communication	Public radio, monitoring airwaves
Taxes	Collection enforcement, Internal Revenue Service audits

2. Dialogue ideas: Even if we find that it costs more to educate children under private operations, this clearly would show the public the need to better finance schools. Either way, it benefits education. What are the implications of this position?

3. Bill Gates delivered the keynote address at the National Summit on High Schools. The conference was sponsored by Achieve Inc., an organization created by state governors and business leaders to improve school standards and achievement so that graduates are prepared for "college, careers, and citizenship" (www.achieve .org). Gates suggested that the American public schools are obsolete and that America is falling behind in developing "knowledge workers."

   Philip Kovacs (2005), in Commons Dreams (www.commondreams.org), argues that the underlying reason for Gates's view is corporatization. He comments that "raising standards" is tied to corporate interests in obedient workers, that information technology outsources for cheaper labor no matter the quality of American schools, and that active citizenship may conflict with corporate interests because citizens may question why corporations have so much influence.

   a. Select one of these positions or propose a different position on this topic and present an argument in its support. Provide school examples to illustrate the position you select. Discuss the results in class.

   b. How would you define "knowledge workers"? Does teaching fit? Does librarianship? Does automobile repair? Does orthopedic surgeon?

   What criteria are useful in making this definition? Is this corporatization in schools?

4. Do you recall examples of commercialization at schools you attended? Were they generally positive, supportive of the school's mission, or generally negative, distracting from the school's mission?

   What school policies would you recommend for use in considering proposals from businesses for sponsorship, partnerships, or other activities in schools?

References

AARON, H., ET AL., EDS. (2003). *Agenda for the Nation.* Washington, DC: Brookings Institution Press.

ARSEN, D., AND NI, Y. (2012). "Is Administration Leaner in Charter Schools?" National Center for Studies of Privatization in Education. www.nscpe.org. March.

American Federation of Teachers. (2003). "AFT Report on Edison Schools Finds Achievement Worse Than Edison Claims." Washington, DC: American Federation of Teachers.

APPLE, M. (2004). *Ideology and Curriculum.* 3rd Ed. New York: Routledge.

BAKAN, J. (2011). "The Kids Are Not All Right." *New York Times.* August 22, A19.

BALL, S. J. (2012). Global Education Inc. New York: Routledge.

BERGER, A. A. (2004). *Ads, Fads, and Consumer Culture.* 2nd Ed. Lanham, MD: Rowman & Littlefield.

BLUMENFELD, S. (2011). "Should the Public Schools Be Privatized?" *The New American.* May 5. www.newamerican.com.

BONINGER, F., AND MOLNAR, A. (2007). *Adrift.* 10th Annual Report on Schoolhouse Commercialism Trends. www.epicpolicy.org.

BOUTWELL, C. E. (1997). *Shell Game: Corporate America's Agenda for Schools .* Bloomington, IN: Phi Delta Kappa.

BRACEY, G. (2001). *The War against America's Public Schools: Privatizing Schools, Commercializing Education.* Boston: Allyn and Bacon.

————. (2002). "The 12th Bracey Report on the Condition of Public Education." *Kappan* 84(2):135–150.

————. (2008). "Who's Out to Get Public Education?" *Huffington Post*. January 30. www .huffingtonpost.com.

Brown Center. (2002). *Annual Report on Education in the United States—Charter Schools*. Washington, DC: Brookings Institution. www.brook.edu/gs/brown/bc.

BUCHEN, I. (1999). "Business Sees Profit in Education." *The Futurist* 33(5):38–44.

BUFFETT, W. (2011). "Stop Coddling the Super-Rich." *New York Times*. August 19, A21.

Business Roundtable. (2008). "Prospering Together." February. www.businessroundtable.org.

————. (2010). "Road Map for Growth." December 8. www.businessroundtable.com.

CALLAHAN, R. (1962). *Education and the Cult of Efficiency*. Chicago: University of Chicago Press.

CHASE, R. (1998). "Changing the Way the Schools Do Business." *Vital Speeches of the Day* 64:444–446.

CHUBB, J. (1998). "Edison Scores and Scores Again in Boston." *Kappan* 80(3):205–213.

Commercial Alert. (2011). Home page. www.commercialalert.org.

COURT, J. (2003). *Corporateering*. New York: Putnam.

CULLEN, L. T. (2004). "Brand Name Field Trips." *Time*. June 28.

Daniels Fund. (2008). "School Business Partnerships." www.danielsfund.org.

DAYTON, J., AND GLICKMAN, C. D. (1994). "American Constitutional Democracy." *Peabody Journal of Education* 69:62–80.

DEARDORFF, J. (2007). "Fast Food Gets Its Greasy Hands on Report Cards." *Chicago Tribune*. December 16.

DEWEY, J. (1916). Democracy and Education. New York: Macmillan.

Edison Learning. (2012). "Turnaround Success in south Carolina", www.edisonlearning .com. April.

EGGERS, W., AND O'LEARY, J. (1996). "Union Confederates." *American Spectator*. March.

FEGE, A. (2008). "Commercialization of Schools." June. www.commercialfreechildhood.org.

FEULNER, E. J. (1991). "What Business Leaders Can Teach the Educators." *Chief Executive*, September, 16–17.

FINKELSTEIN, B. (1984). "Education and the Retreat from Democracy in the United States, 1979–1980." *Teachers College Record* 86:276–282.

FLOWERS, L. F. (2008). "Naming Rights May Provide Districts with Funding." *Morning News* (Northwestern Arkansas). January 26.

GILROY, L. (2012). "Teachable Moment." Reason. reason.org. April 3.

GIROUX, H. A. (2012). *Education and the Crisis of Public Values*. New York: Peter Lang.

GUTMANN, A. (1999). *Democratic Education*. 2nd Ed. Princeton, NJ: Princeton University Press.

————. (2008). "Educating for Individual Freedom and Democratic Citizenship." In *Oxford Handbook of Philosophy of Education*, ed. H. Siegel. Oxford: Oxford University Press.

HANN, L. W. (2008). "Profit and Loss in School Business Partnerships." *District Administration*. April. www.districtadministration.com.

HARTMAN, T. (2002). *Unequal Protection: The Rise of Corporate Dominance and the Theft of Human Rights*. New York: Rodale Press.

HAYS, C. (2000). "Commercialism in U.S. Schools Is Examined in New Report." *New York Times*. September 14.

HENRIQUES, D. B., AND STEINBERG, J. (2002a). "Operator of Public Schools in Settlement with SEC." *New York Times*. May 15. www.nytimes.com.

————. (2002b). "Woes for Company Running Schools," *New York Times*. May 14. www.nytimes.com.

HENTSCHKE, G., ET AL. (2004). "The Rise of Education Management Organizations." *Privatization Watch* 28(7):13.

HENWOOD, D. (2003). *After the New Economy*. New York: New Press.

HERTZ, N. (2001). *The Silent Takeover: Global Capitalism and the Death of Democracy*. New York: Free Press.

HIGHTOWER, J. (2011). "Big Coal Buys Access to 4th Graders." *Hightower Report*. June 16. www.jimhightower.com.

HOLLOWAY, J. H. (2002). "Research Link: For Profit Schools." *Education Leadership* 59(7):84–85.

HUNTER, R. C., AND BROWN, F., EDS. (1995). "Privatization in Public Education." *Education and Urban Society* 27:107–228.

Institute for a Competitive Workforce. (2011). "Partnership Is a Two-Way Street." www.uschamber.com.

ISAAK, R. (2005). *The Globalization Gap*. New York: Prentice Hall.

k12 inc. (2012). "k-12 Produces Results." www.k12.com. April.

KADLEC, A. (2007). *Dewey's Critical Pragmatism*. Lanham, MD: Rowman & Littlefield.

KAPLAN, G. (1996). "Profits R Us." *Kappan* 78:K1–K12.

KOEBLER, J. (2011). "Major Corporations Promote STEM Education." *US News and World Report*. June 1. www.usnews.com.

KORTEN, D. C. (2001). *When Corporations Rule the World*. San Francisco: Berrett-Koehler.

KOVACS, P. (2005). "Bill Gates and the Corporatization of American 'Public' Schools." www.commondreams.org.

KRUGMAN, P. (2002). "Victors and Spoils." *New York Times*. November 19. www.nytimes.com.

————. (2011). "Messing with Medicare." *New York Times*, July 25, A21.

————. (2012). "Lobbyists, Guns and Money." *New York Times*. March 25. www.nytimes.com.

LEVIN, H. (2006). "Why Is Educational Entrepreneur So Difficult?" Unpublished paper, National Center for the Study of Privatization in Education, Teachers College, Columbia University. January.

LEWIN, T. (2006). "In Public Schools, the Name Game as a Donor Lure." *New York Times*. January 26.

LIPANA, J. (2011). "Save Education, Privatize Government Schools." *American Thinker*. June 12. www.americanthinker.com.

LUBIENSKI, C., AND LUBIENSKI, S. J. (2004). *Re-Examining a Primary Premise of Market Theory*. New York: National Center for the Study of Privatization in Education, Teachers College, Columbia University.

MAGEE, M., AND LEOPOLD, L. S. (1998). "Study Finds Charter Schools Succeed No More Than Others." *San Diego Union-Tribune*. December 4.

MANDEL, M., ET AL. (1995). "Will Schools Ever Get Better?" *Business Week*. April 17, 64–68.

MANN, D. (1987). "Business Involvement and Public School Improvement, Part 2." *Kappan* 69:228–232.

MARINA, A. (1994). "Can the Private Sector Save Public Schools?" *NEA Today* 12:10–12.

MATHEWS, D. (2008). "The Public and the Public Schools." *Kappan* 89(8):560–564.

McNEAL, R. U. (1992). *Kids as Customers*. New York: Lexington Books.

————. (2004). "Virtually Everywhere: Marketing to Children in America's Schools. Seventh Annual Report on Schoolhouse Commercializing Trends, 2003." Arizona State University Commercialism in Education Research Unit. www.asu.edu/educ/eps/ceru/htm.

MIRON, G., AND APPLEGATE, B. (2000). *An Evaluation of Student Achievement in Edison Schools Opened in 1995 and 1996*. Kalamazoo: Evaluation Center, Western Michigan University.

MOBERG, D. (2004). "How Edison Survived." *The Nation* 278(10).

MOLNAR, A. (2004). "Virtually Everywhere: Marketing to Children in America's Schools. Seventh Annual Report on Schoolhouse Commercializing Trends, 2003." Arizona State University Commercialism in Education Research Unit. www.asu.edu/eps/ceru/htm.

MOLNAR, A., BONINGER, F., AND FOGARTY, J. (2011). "The Educational Cost of Commercializing." Annual report. National Education Policy Center, University of Colorado Boulder. November. www.nepc.colorado.edu.

MOLNAR, A., MIRON, G., AND URSCHEL, J. (2010). *Profiles of For Profit Education Management Organizations: 2009–2010*. Boulder, CO: National Education Policy Center, University of Colorado. www.nepc.colorado.edu.

MURPHY, R. L. (2004). "What Is the Proper Way to Run a School." May. www.mises.org.

NADER, R. (1999). Testimony, U.S. Senate Committee on Health, Education, Labor, and Pensions Hearing. May 20.

NEALON, J. T. (2012). Post Modernism, or, The Logic of Just-in-time Capitalism. Stanford: Stanford University Press.

ORAVITZ, J. V. (1999). "Why Can't Schools Be Operated the Way Businesses Are?" *Education Digest* 64(6):15–17.

Parents Advocating School Accountability. (2011). "Canceled Contracts," November 2009. www.pasaf.org.

PARMET, S. (2005). "Reading, Writing and Retail Tours." *San Diego Union-Tribune*. May 2.

Philanthropy News Digest. (2011). "Corporations Pledge $118 Million to Improve Education." July 19. www.foundationcenter.org.

PIZARRO, S. (2011). "Plan to Privatize New Jersey's Schools Reveals a Flawed Outcome." June 20. www.newjerseynewsroom.com.

QUART, A. (2003). *Branded: The Buying and Selling of Teenagers*. New York: Basic Books.

RAMSEY, N. (1993). "What Companies Are Doing." *Fortune* 128:142–150.

RATCHFORD, W. (2005). "Going Public with Schools Privatization." *The Abell Report* 18(3, September/October).

RAVITCH, D. (2010). *The Death and Life of the Great American Public Schools*. New York: Basic Books.

Rethinking Schools. (1998). "The Market Is Not the Answer: An Interview with Jonathan Kozol." www.rethinkingschools.org.

SALTMAN, K. J. (2000). *Collateral Damage: Corporatizing Public Schools—A Threat to Democracy*. Lanham, MD: Rowman & Littlefield.

———. (2005). *The Edison Schools: Corporate Schooling and the Assault on Public Education*. New York: Routledge.

———. (2012). *The Failure of Corporate School Reform*. Boulder, CO: Paradigm Publications.

SCHLAFLY, P. (1999). Testimony, U.S. Senate Committee on Health, Education, Labor and Pensions Hearing. May 20.

SCHRAG, P. (1999). "Private Affluence and Public Squalor." *San Diego Union-Tribune*. January 8.

SHILLER, R. J. (2005). "How Wall Street Learns to Look the Other Way." *New York Times*, February 8. www.nytimes.com.

SINCLAIR, U. (1938). *The Jungle*. London: Cobham House.

———. (1922). *The Goose Step*. Pasadena, CA: Sinclair.

———. (1924). *The Goslings*. Pasadena, CA: Sinclair.

Smith, G. (2011). "Privatization Effort for School Buses Cost State More, Study Says." *The State* (South Carolina). May 8. www.thestate.com.

Snell, L. (2005). "Unions Try to Discredit Education Outsourcing." *Privatization Watch* 29(1):12–13.

———. (2011). *Annual Privatization Report 2010: Education*. Los Angeles: Reason Foundation.

Soltow, L., and Stevens, E. (1981). *The Rise of Literacy and the Common School in the United States: A Socioeconomic Analysis to 1870*. Chicago: University of Chicago Press.

Stanford University. (2009). Research on Educational Outcomes. Stanford, CA: Center for Research on Educational Outcomes, Stanford University.

Steinberg, J. (2002). "Private Groups Get 42 Schools in Philadelphia." *New York Times*. April 18. www.nytimes.com.

Stuit, D. A., and Smith, T. (2009). *Teacher Turnover in Charter Schools*. Nashville: National Center on School Choice, Vanderbilt University.

Sudetic, C. (2001). "Reading, Writing, and Revenue," *Mother Jones* 26(3):84–95.

The Economist. (2005). "The Missing Rung in the Ladder." 376(8435):17.

U.S. Census Bureau. (2005). *Current Population Survey, 2005 Annual Social and Economic Supplement*. June 24. Washington, DC: Government Printing Office.

———. (2007). *Employment, Work Experience, and Earnings by Age and Education*. Table 1. Washington, DC: Government Printing Office.

———. (2011). *Statistical Abstract of the United States*. Table 702. Washington, DC: Government Printing Office.

Ward, S. C. (2012). *Neoliberalism and the Global Restructuring of Knowledge and Education*. New York: Routledge.

Weissman, R. (2007). "Revisiting the Commercialization of Public Schools." *Counter Punch*. June. www.counterpunch.org.

Weldon, T. (2011). "Creating Effective Business-Education Partnerships." *Council of State Governments Newsletter*. July 5. www.csg.org.

Zollers, N., and Ramanathan, A. (1998). "For-Profit Charter Schools and Students with Disabilities." *Kappan* 80(4):297–315.

CHAPTER 5

Religion and Public Schools: Free Expression or Separation

How do schools balance freedom of religious expression and the separation of church and state?

POSITION 1: FREEDOM OF RELIGIOUS EXPRESSION MUST BE PROTECTED IN PUBLIC SCHOOLS

Congress shall make no law respecting an establishment of religion or prohibiting the free exercise thereof. . . .

—U.S. Constitution, First Amendment

Take out a dollar bill. Turn it over to the back. What do you see when you look beneath the heading "The United States of America"? Printed on the dollar, as on every other denomination of American paper currency, is the motto "In God We Trust." Will we soon have to add the phrase "Except in Public Schools"? Students, public school teachers, and administrators who attempt to discuss the God on whom Americans supposedly rely face disciplinary action and lawsuits. Court decisions and pressure from special interest groups have whittled away at religious freedom in schools. This situation can be remedied, and full freedom of religious expression can be restored to all citizens in America's public schools without violating the Constitution. Public schools can protect the basic human right of religious liberty and still maintain the separation of church and state.

The First Amendment

The First Amendment to the Constitution was carefully crafted by the founding fathers to protect what they considered "inalienable rights" of American citizens. For example, they wanted to protect their countrymen's right to practice the religion of their choice without fear. Aware of British history, they knew that one of the greatest impediments to religious freedom was state support of one denomination. To these early Americans, breaking away from England meant, among other things, putting an end to religious conflicts. Therefore, they believed prohibiting governmental support for any individual faith was the best policy for their new republic (Tozer, Violas, and Senese, 2002; Holmes, 2006; Meacham, 2007).

To protect religious freedom, the founders included two clauses in the First Amendment. The first, called the Establishment Clause, decrees that religions and the state should be kept separate so that no religion has more rights than any other. The second clause, the Free Exercise Clause, prevents the government from limiting Americans' expressing religious beliefs in ways that seem right to them. Reading these two clauses carefully is important in understanding that current attempts to banish religion from public schools violate the founders' intention.

The Establishment Clause says, "Congress shall make no law respecting *an* establishment of religion." Many people, when referring to the clause, quote it incorrectly as saying, "Congress shall make no law respecting *the* establishment of religion." The difference is crucial. The first—and accurate—reading clearly shows the intent was to prevent any one religious denomination from receiving governmental support or protection not available to all others. In fact, one of James Madison's original drafts of the religious section of the amendment said, "The civil rights of none shall be abridged on account of religious belief or worship, nor shall any national religion be established" (Robb, 1985, p. 7). His purposes, however, were clear. Governmental support of any one religion or domination was prohibited because it would negatively affect individuals' freedom of religious expression. The fact that many states already had done exactly that added a sense of urgency to the task of the Constitutional Convention. Madison and others wanted to prevent a repeat of the religious wars in England that resulted from royal support of different Christian denominations (Holmes, 2006; Meacham, 2007).

The founding fathers had no intention of barring all mention of God from American public life—almost all professed belief in God, although many did not identify themselves as members of any religious denomination. They routinely began assemblies with prayers for guidance and inspiration. They asked God's blessing on themselves and their countrymen in their foundational documents. Their language in such settings went beyond the traditional words used in different denominations. They spoke of a God who had created all and maintained the world, a God who was bigger than the claims of any individual group of believers (Holmes, 2006; Meacham 2007).

For most of American history, the Supreme Court did not interfere in state laws regarding religious practices in schools (Batte, 2008). Any act on the part of government supporting one religious denomination at the expense of others was considered unconstitutional. Any act of the government limiting an individual's right to free expression of his or her religious beliefs was equally illegitimate. Recently, however, the balance between the needs expressed in the two clauses has been reinterpreted.

The Supreme Court and Religion in Public Schools

Contemporary court decisions have emphasized the Establishment Clause to the detriment of the Free Exercise Clause. The trend began in a decision that, on the surface, appeared to support religious freedom. In 1947 in *Everson v. Board of Education*, the Supreme Court ruled that using state funds to reimburse parents for the cost of transporting children to religious schools did not violate the Establishment Clause. However, in writing the majority opinion, Judge Hugo Black interpreted that section of the First Amendment in a way that ignored its text. Black wrote that the Establishment Clause created "a complete separation between the state and religion" (*Everson v. Board of Education*, 1947). This interpretation was based on a letter Jefferson wrote ten years after ratification of the First Amendment in which he made his famous "wall of separation" statement. It reads, in part, "I contemplate with sovereign reverence that act of the whole American people which declared that their legislature should 'make no law respecting an establishment of religion, or prohibiting the free exercise thereof,' thus building a wall of separation between Church and State" (Koch and Peden, 1944, p. 307).

Those using this statement of Jefferson's to limit individual freedom of religious expression would do well to read the rest of the quote. He writes, "Adhering to this expression of the supreme will of the nation in behalf of the *rights of conscience*, I shall see with sincere satisfaction the progress of those sentiments which tend to restore to man all his natural rights, convinced he has no natural right in opposition to his social duties" (Koch and Peden, 1944, p. 307). Clearly, Jefferson's words about the strict separation between church and state were meant not to limit individual rights but rather to argue against the possibility that any one religious sect would become a "national religion" through government efforts. When understood in this light, Jefferson's "wall" should be seen as the protector of freedom of religious expression (Chadsey, 2007; Waldman, 2009). Instead, it has been used to remove religion from public schools in ways that neither he nor the other founders of this nation intended. Other court cases have followed, relying on the interpretation offered by Justice Black in *Everson*. One by one, they have created a legal legacy that violates the intentions of our founders.

In *McCollum v. Board of Education* (1948), the Supreme Court ruled sectarian religious leaders were constitutionally forbidden from conducting voluntary, optional religious instruction in school buildings. Some years later, the Court held in *Engel v. Vitale* (1962) and *Abington Township School District v. Schempp* (1963) that neither classroom prayer nor Bible readings were constitutional even when students had the option of being excused from participation. Building on the misinterpretation of the Establishment Clause as presented by Justice Black in *Engel*, the Court took the serious step of defining governmental acts to accommodate religious freedom that could be deemed constitutional. In doing so, however, the Court created such narrow parameters that, since *Lemon v. Kurtzman* (1971), almost no religious practices in school have been declared constitutional. The "Lemon test," as the policy has come to be known, consists of three standards that must be met if the action of a school district can be established as protecting religious freedom rather than endorsing religious practices. To be constitutional, a policy or activity supported by a school must (1) have a secular purpose, (2) not have the effect of advancing or inhibiting religion, and (3) avoid excessive entanglement between government and religion (*ACLU Legal Bulletin,* 1996). Applying the Lemon test in other cases has resulted in even more limitations on religious practices in schools.

For example, in *Stone v. Graham* (1980), the Court declared that a state law requiring public schools to post the Ten Commandments was unconstitutional. *Wallace v. Jaffree* (1985) struck down a state law requiring a moment of meditation or silent prayer. In *Lee v. Weisman* (1992), the Court ruled that, even when offered by a private individual with no formal connection to the school or government, prayer at public school graduation is unconstitutional. Apparently, asking students to bow their heads, remain silent, and show respect during such a prayer violates the rights of students who do not believe in God. They are, according to the Court, compelled to participate, and in so insisting on their participation, the school is "conveying a message that religion or a particular religious belief is favored or preferred" over unbelief (*County of Allegheny v. American Civil Liberties Union, Greater Pittsburgh Chapter,* 1989).

Finally, in *Santa Fe Independent School District v. Jane Doe* (2000), the Court ruled that student-led prayer at football games was unconstitutional. Even though participation in such games is purely voluntary, the fact that the school district sponsors and pays for the games makes them governmental actions. So, prayers at the games also are government-supported activities that must pass the Lemon test. The Court says that they do not because there is no secular purpose for the prayers, which have the effect of advancing religion because they will be "perceived by adherents . . . as an endorsement, and by nonadherents as a disapproval, of their individual religious choices" (*School District of the City of Grand Rapids v. Ball,* 1985). In 2002, a federal court ruled that the phrase "under God" in the Pledge of Allegiance also fails the Lemon test (*Newdow v. U.S. Congress,* 2002).

Consequently, students are prevented from leading prayers at high school graduation ceremonies even when members of the senior class want to include such devotions. Student athletes are forbidden from praying at sporting events even in their own locker rooms. School board meetings cannot be opened with prayer or a moment of silent meditation. Teachers cannot discuss their own religious experiences with children even if they believe that their religion commands them to do so. They cannot use such expressions as "God Bless You" in communications with students or parents. Children cannot read Bible stories to classmates as part of oral communication lessons, nor can they express religious beliefs during a class presentation. In addition, they should not expect to see drawings they've made of religious figures or symbols hanging on the walls of their classrooms or schools. Bibles may not be distributed in public schools during regular operating hours. Teachers and students may not celebrate the religious aspects of such holidays as Thanksgiving, Christmas, or Easter (Zirkel, 2010–2011).

History of American Education

Banishing religion from all but the most innocuous aspects of U.S. public school life is truly ironic. The very first schools in the English colonies that would become the United States were instituted for religious reasons. The leaders of the Pilgrims, living in the Massachusetts Bay Colony, passed a law establishing schools that would teach children to read their Bibles. Their literacy would protect them from "that old deluder Satan."

In the early days of the Republic, American schools were, for the most part, privately funded, and religious practices considered an essential part of the curriculum. Early public schools taught religion from a perspective shared with others influenced by the Enlightenment. For them, a shared belief in God was necessary to create the moral discipline required for living in a democratic society (McConnell, 2000). The *McGuffey Readers,* the most popular textbooks for most of the nineteenth century, built on a presumption that Americans shared a belief in God to teach children what behavior was expected of them. Concern for the needs and rights of others, honesty, and perseverance despite difficulties were presented as the responsibility of all God's children in America. "It was almost universally accepted that American democracy drew its strength from the general conviction that there was a divine power, the author of the rights of man defined in America's first political document" (McCluskey, 1967, p. 237). Children were taught that each citizen derived his or her rights from their Almighty Father and that no human being had the right to take away those rights. In that era, most Americans believed the majority could, on the basis of their religious beliefs, determine basic community norms, including the place of religion in the public school curriculum and activities (McCarthy, 1983, p. 7). "Nonsectarian did not mean nonreligious. . . . Nondenominational Christianity was assumed to be 'nonsectarian'" (McConnell, 2000, pp. 1263–1264). Protestant Christian beliefs and practices were incorporated into public schools. Teachers led children in daily prayer. The Bible, usually the King James Version, was read in schools. Religious holidays were celebrated (Goodman and Lesnick, 2001). State laws not only permitted such practices but also mandated them (McCarthy, 1983). So what happened?

The loss of balance between protecting both clauses of the First Amendment's statements on religion began in the first half of the nineteenth century. Immigrant children from Ireland, Germany, and, later, Italy and Eastern Europe swelled American public school enrollment, especially between 1840 and 1924. Most of these children were Catholics. Catholic religious leaders objected to what they saw as the Protestant character of religion being taught in public schools. They did not understand that the religious dimensions of public school life actually were designed to help their children become part of American life (Goodman and Lesnick, 2001; Fessenden, 2005). Their leaders protested strenuously and began a campaign to create schools that socialized children to their own religious beliefs (Sanders, 1977; Tozer et al., 2002). To many Protestant Americans, these early immigrants seemed to reject becoming part of the very country to which they had turned as a refuge from political and economic oppression (Fessenden, 2005).

Despite the conflict, several factors made compromise possible. Immigrants perceived that public education would contribute to their social mobility. Native-born citizens believed that schools would Americanize the newcomers. To achieve both ends, schools made reasonable accommodations. Some districts eliminated Bible readings altogether to end the Catholics' objections to using the Protestant version of the scriptures (Wright, 1999; Fessenden, 2005).

A kind of neutrality among religious denominations was maintained in public schools that preserved the freedom of students and teachers to exercise their religious freedom (Goodman and Lesnick, 2001). Prayers were offered in "theistic" rather than "Christian" language, and holidays from both traditions were celebrated. Catholics and Jews who could not make this accommodation sent their children to schools in which their own beliefs could be practiced more freely (Sanders, 1977; Zeldin, 1986). As some historians see it, by the end of the nineteenth century, sectarian religious practices had been eliminated from public schools. However, schools were still faithful to the project of assimilating children, especially immigrant children, into the American way of life.

In the last half of the twentieth century, public schools were faced with new challenges to that Americanization obligation. Immigrant children from nonbiblical faith traditions began to appear in public schools. Among those who believe in God or seek divine assistance, compromises on language and practices have been achievable. For example, many schools have found ways to accommodate Muslim students' religious obligation to pray five times during the day or fast during Ramadan. (Dorrell, 2007; Longman, 2011; Macedo, 2010). In other instances, dress code regulations have been modified to allow students to dress according to the norms of their religious traditions.

However, in the last sixty years, the delicate balance required to enforce both clauses of the First Amendment has been upset by the growth of a more secular belief system. The United States, like many other Western countries, saw an expansion of agnostic, atheistic, and antireligious philosophies. Those who shared these beliefs were concerned about what they perceived to be the vulnerability of children in schools. They worried that schools, by openly supporting free expression of religious beliefs—indeed by mandating them in some cases—were creating situations in which young people were being taught that religious beliefs were normative. They argued that such tacit approval of religious faith would pressure young people to profess such beliefs themselves without being given the opportunity to evaluate them.

Most Americans—approximately 90 percent—believe in God (Gallup Organization, 2011). Only a very small number of Americans totally reject the existence of a divine being. However, that very vocal and powerful minority brought many of the lawsuits that have had such negative effects on the free exercise of religion by students and teachers (*McCollum v. Board of Education*, 1948; *Zorach v. Clauson*, 1952; *Engel v. Vitale*, 1962; *Abington Township School District v. Schempp*, 1963; and *Murray v. Curlett*, 1963). These "nonbelievers" actually have a belief system that is derived from the secularization of liberal political thought. For secularists, investigation rather than religious teachings is the source of answers to important human questions (Council for Secular Humanism, 2011). Even the

Supreme Court has affirmed that secular humanism is a religious belief and that the rights of those who share that belief to practice their religion are protected by the Free Exercise Clause of the First Amendment (*Torcaso v. Watkins,* 1961; *U.S. v. Seeger,* 1965).

Most Americans who believe in God have come to accept that sectarian religious education no longer is possible in American public schools. Nonbelievers, however, want to impose their ideology in schools in ways that closely resemble the sectarian projects of nineteenth-century school reformers. They argue their beliefs actually are neutral regarding religion. In many ways, however, they are hostile to it. They contend that any expression of belief in God is unconstitutional in public settings because, by being exposed to such activities, their children are coerced into accepting the beliefs from which they spring. In most cases, the Supreme Court has accepted their arguments. The result is that the most privileged belief system in public schools is secularism. The rulings against common prayer, moments of silence, and celebrations of religious holidays in schools give privilege to secular beliefs.

Of course, such a policy clearly is unconstitutional. Several Supreme Court justices have explained what neutrality with regard to religion in public schools really means. Writing in *Everson v. Board of Education* (1947), Hugo Black stated, "State power is no more to be used so as to handicap religions than it is to favor them." In *Abington Township School District v. Schempp* (1963), Tom Clark wrote, "The state may not establish a 'religion of secularism' in the sense of affirmatively opposing or showing hostility to religion, thus 'preferring those who believe in no religion over those who do believe'" (p. 225). In *Lynch v. Donnelly* (1984), Sandra Day O'Connor argued, "What is crucial is that the government practice not have the effect of communicating a message of endorsement or disapproval of religion" (p. 692). It would seem that these warnings were ignored. The public school environment has increasingly become hostile to believers, limiting their freedom of expression while allowing secularists and nonbelievers license to incorporate their beliefs into the curricula. In doing so, the role of religious belief in American culture has been overlooked (Gateways for Better Education, 2011).

Religion and American Culture

While U.S. laws have prevented the establishment of a state sect, religious belief has influenced its culture. From its beginnings, America has been a nation that integrated political and religious understandings of the value of human life and the nature of freedom. According to Supreme Court Justice Anton Scalia, the secular model of the relationship between church and state, requiring that religion be strictly excluded from the public forum, "is not, and never was, the model adopted by America" (*McCreary County v. ACLU,* 2005, p. 74).

As Scalia and others argue, religion has contributed and continues to contribute to the culture of the United States in positive ways. For example, a democracy requires moral citizens who are able to practice self-restraint, put the needs of others above their own interests, and sacrifice for the sake of the common good. Americans have seen religion as one of the most significant teachers of that kind of morality (*McCreary County v. ACLU*, 2005). In fact, our history—distant and recent—demonstrates that the government has affirmed society's belief in God to strengthen us in difficulty, to guide us in perplexity, to comfort us in sorrow, and to express gratitude for the benefits of our shared life. "Historical practices thus demonstrate that there is a distance between the acknowledgement of a single Creator and the establishment of religion" (*McCreary County v. ACLU*, 2005, p. 89). A small minority of believers in impersonal gods, polytheists, and atheists may feel excluded when God is called on in public settings. However, as long as they are not coerced into joining in the invocation, their rights to private belief are maintained (Feldman, 2005).

In fact, "public expressions of religion even hold out the possibility of enabling religious minorities to participate fully in the American public sphere." If we allow the public acknowledgment and celebration of religious holidays, we enable Jewish, Hindu, Buddhist, and Muslim traditions to become part of a traditionally Christian culture. In doing so, we validate the "sense of belonging" in a greater number of citizens and may generate more national loyalty from them (Feldman, 2005).

Curricular Consequences

Integrating religion in U.S. public life and culture is an admittedly difficult and delicate process. Chief Justice William Rehnquist has suggested that in doing so, the courts must be like Janus, the Roman god who was depicted with two faces looking in opposite directions. "One face looks toward the strong role played by religion and religious tradition throughout our Nation's history. . . . The other face looks toward the principle that governmental intervention in religious matters can itself endanger religious freedom" (*Van Orden v. Perry*, 2005, p. 11).

Public schools no longer balance these two aspects of the First Amendment. The perspectives of religious believers have almost been eliminated from public school curricula. In general, fear of controversy has led textbook publishers to neglect the study of religious influences on thought or historical events (Tolson, 2007; Rosenbleth and Bailey, 2008; Passe and Wilcox, 2009). In fact, antagonism to religious approaches exists in most subjects. One of the most serious examples of this conflict takes place daily in science classes when students study the origin of life. Any perspective that does not support the Darwinian theory of natural selection is at best ignored and at worst ridiculed. Evolution is presented as fact even though there is convincing evidence that randomness and material forces alone cannot explain the complexity of the world in which we live.

The theory of intelligent design is a scientific approach to the origins of life that presents such a challenge to the theory of evolution (Dembski and Wells, 2007; Gordon and Dembski, 2011). Opponents of intelligent design fail to distinguish intelligent design science from creationism—the belief that the universe was created in six days as described in the book of Genesis in the Hebrew Bible. However, intelligent design is rooted in the principles of science, not religion. For example, biochemist Michael Behe argues that natural selection cannot explain "irreducibly complex systems"—systems composed of a variety of parts that interact with one another to carry out the system's task. In systems like the flagella of bacteria, the flow of proteins in cells, and the mechanisms that cause blood to clot, the removal of any one part causes the whole to stop working (Behe, 2007). The theory of evolution argues that these systems were produced by a series of small changes to prior systems, taking place in succession. However, that is impossible because if an irreducibly complex system were missing any one of its parts, it would simply not work. There would be no system from which the new one could evolve. Similarly, no known scientific "law" can explain the specific sequence of the four nucleotide bases found in DNA. William Dembski has established a reliable scientific method for identifying designed objects or systems from those that result from chance or the laws of nature (Dembski and Wells, 2007). Even theorists who accept evolution have acknowledged that many organisms seem to be the result of an intelligence beyond the organism itself—an intelligence with a purpose. Some of the most honest among them questioned their own theories (Buell, 2007; Gray, Lukes, Archibald, Keeling, and Doolittle, 2010). However, the law prevents teachers from presenting students with opportunities to hear about this alternative to the theory of evolution (*McLean v. Arkansas Board of Education,* 1982; *Edwards v. Aguillard,* 1987; *Webster v. New Lenox School District,* 1990; *LeVake v. Independent School District 656, et al.,* 2000; *Kitzmiller v. Dover,* 2008).

Some school districts have been blocked by federal courts from alerting students to the theoretical nature of evolution. Cobb County, Georgia, was prevented from placing stickers on science books advising students that material about evolution should be studied and considered critically (Selman Injunction, 2005). Although the Cobb County plan represented a good-faith effort to provide quality education without violating the Constitution, those who objected and won in court prevented a compromise that accommodated both believers and nonbelievers. They imposed a solution that favored nonbelief. In fact, Louisiana is the only state to pass a law that allows school districts to help students think critically about evolution by using supplemental materials to do so, and its efforts are under constant attack by secular humanists (Morelli, 2010).

Health classes are also sites where governmental neutrality toward belief and nonbelief has not been maintained. Students, regardless of their religious beliefs, are compelled to hear presentations about abortion, premarital sex, homosexuality, and masturbation. Despite research showing the efficacy of abstinence-only sex education programs, they are being tossed aside in favor of ones that are silent on the rich Western tradition of philosophical and religious thinking about moral issues (Jemmott, Jemmott, and Fong, 2010; Santos and Phillips, 2011).

The First Amendment religious clauses clearly establish two duties for government regarding freedom of religion. Government must not favor one religion over others and must not prevent citizens from expressing their religious beliefs. The founders assumed that religion would have a vital place in the private and public lives of Americans. When courts ignored that fundamental reality and the historic role of religion by requiring governmental neutrality between belief and nonbelief, they created an unsolvable problem. In protecting a minority of students from hearing religious speech that is "offensive" to them, they have provided inadequately for the rights of students who are religious. "In a country of many diverse traditions and perspectives—some religious, some secular—neutrality cannot be achieved by assuming that one set of beliefs is publicly more acceptable than another . . . religious citizens and religious ideas can contribute to the commonweal along with everyone and everything else" (McConnell, 2000, p. 1264). Certain practices, such as prayer in public gatherings or reference to God in discussions of moral issues, are part of a long-standing American tradition and have enjoyed historical acceptance. If administrators, teachers, and students ensure that no one is coerced to participate in such activities or accept the beliefs on which they are based, the First Amendment can be protected in public schools to a greater degree than it currently is.

POSITION 2: THE SEPARATION OF CHURCH AND STATE MUST BE MAINTAINED IN PUBLIC SCHOOLS

The Civil Rights of none shall be abridged on account of religious belief or worship, not shall any national religion be established, nor shall the full and equal rights of conscience be in any manner, or on any pretence, infringed.

—James Madison (original wording of the First Amendment;
Annals of Congress 434, June 8, 1789)

To hear members of the religious right complain, you'd think that all religious expression had been totally banned in American public schools. Actually, teachers and students enjoy a great deal of freedom to engage in religious speech and practices. The No Child Left Behind Act of 2001's "Guidelines on Constitutionally Protected Prayer in Public Schools" reminded school officials that "the First Amendment forbids religious activity that is sponsored by the government but protects religious activity that is initiated by private individuals" (Paige, 2003, p. 2). The document does enumerate teachers and administrators' actions that are prohibited: leading classes in prayer, reading devotionally from the Bible, persuading or compelling students to participate in prayer or other religious activities, and including prayer at school-sponsored events. However, it also contains an impressive list of students' rights, including reading scriptures, saying grace before meals, and discussing religious views in informal settings such as cafeterias and hallways. Students may also speak to and try to persuade other students about religious topics, participate in prayerful gatherings before and after school, and express their religious beliefs in homework, artwork, and other written and oral assignments—as long as their beliefs cannot be attributed to the school. Their prayer groups or religious clubs must be given the same right to use school facilities as is extended to other extracurricular groups. They can be dismissed for off-premise religious instruction and excused briefly from class to enable them to fulfill religious obligations such as prayer (Pew Forum, 2007). A school can limit these expressions of free speech only to the same degree it limits other comparable words or activities. So, for example, students have the right to distribute religious literature, hold prayer gatherings on school grounds, and discuss their religious beliefs to the same extent that they could engage in similar activities on comparable topics—such as politics or social issues. School districts across the country have created policies to ensure that students can meet their personal religious obligations.

Sounds good, doesn't it? It appears that students who want to engage in religious activities or speak about their faith have lots of freedom to do so. It sounds fair and reasonable—an all-American compromise that respects every student's right to religious liberty. So what's the problem?

Some believers want to break down the separation between church and state. They think that schools ought to sponsor religious activities and coerce students to attend those events. For example, they believe that school officials should be able to organize or mandate prayer at graduation ceremonies or, alternatively, to organize religious "baccalaureate" ceremonies for graduates, their friends, and their families. They believe that it should be acceptable for teachers or principals to encourage students to participate in prayer gatherings before or after school, want teachers to be able to speak openly about their own religious beliefs in classroom settings, and advocate celebrating religious aspects of holidays in school. Their demands violate the First Amendment's prohibition against support of religion by the government.

Establishing Religion in Public Schools

Supporters who argue for greater freedom of religious expression in schools argue that they want the same protection for believers as for nonbelievers. There is evidence, however, that their real intent is to reestablish Christianity as a state-sponsored religion. Members of the religious right often suggest that public schools promote amoral values, are antireligious, and threaten the health and well-being for Christian children and youth (Shortt, 2004). Some leaders have gone so far as to suggest that parents remove their children from public schools, establish Christian alternatives, or home school (Turtel, 2005; D'Escoto and D'Escoto, 2010). Others see public schools as "gardens to cultivate" in the effort to promote their religious beliefs. For example, members of the group Gateways to Better Education "envision public schools as learning communities enriched by the appropriate and lawful expression of Christian values and ideas, and educators teaching about the contribution Christians and Christianity have made and continue to make to America and the world." The group calls on educators to become "Campus Partners" in the effort, provides curricular resources for teachers, and offers materials to begin a local campaign to restore celebrations of religious holidays to schools (Gateways to Education, 2011; Boston, 2010).

"Good News Clubs," organized by the Child Evangelism Foundation, are tools that believers hope to use to create these witnesses. At the club meetings, children sing hymns, memorize Scripture verses, and act out Bible stories. Since 2001, with the blessings of the Supreme Court, they have been able to meet in public schools after classes (*Good News Club v. Milford Central School,* 2001). Leaders have also demanded that administrators allow them to use official school communications to advertise their meetings, and, in cases where secular groups have been allowed to advertise sports clubs or child care centers, the courts have ruled that the religious groups be given the same access to "customers." Other evangelical organizations have come to public schools to offer what they bill as motivational speakers, sometimes intentionally omitting the religious content of their presentations until they arrive at schools (Boston, 2010).

Another result of the *Good News Club* decision is that many schools have opened their buildings to churches that are looking for rent-free worship spaces. Since most schools are busy with activities, including sports, except for Sunday, Christian groups are most often the beneficiaries of this policy. For example, over sixty public schools in New York City provide rent-free homes for mostly evangelical Christian congregations (Stewart, 2011). Fortunately, in an appeal of this policy, the federal Second Circuit Court ruled that the *Good News Club* decision did not require the city to continue to do so. The decision affirmed that the Department of Education had a strong basis to believe "that allowing the religious services to be conducted in schools could be seen as the kind of endorsement of religion that violated the First Amendment's establishment clause" (Weiser, 2011).

Not satisfied with these gains, Christian leaders campaign to include Bible study in public school curriculum itself. Groups like the National Council on Bible Curriculum in Public Schools (NCBPCS) distribute course syllabi in school districts around the country, claiming that they "convey the content of the Bible as compared to literature and history" (Ridenour, 2007). However, reviews of the curriculum by scholars find "various editions of this curriculum have been filled with factual errors, fringe scholarship, and plagiarism. With its promotion of a fundamentalist Protestant understanding of the Bible and a revisionist history of the United States as a distinctively (Protestant) Christian nation, the curriculum appears not to pass legal muster" (Chancey, 2007, p. 554). "Students have been taught one religious interpretation of the Bible. That's not only violating the Constitution, it's also giving students a bad education" (People for the American Way, 2008). Despite sustained political pressure—and lawsuits—to remove the curriculum from schools and prevent even more districts from implementing it, the NCBPCS claims that it "has been voted into 593 school districts (2,135 high schools) in thirty-eight states. Over 400,000 students have already taken this course nationwide, on the high school campus, during school hours, for credit" (NCBCPS, 2011). An electronic version of the curriculum has been introduced, making it even easier and less expensive for districts to adopt (NCBCPS, 2011).

Another way that some religious believers have attempted to ensure that public schools endorse their religious beliefs is by regulating sex education. Because their religious beliefs prohibit sexual intercourse outside of marriage, groups like Focus on the Family, Concerned Women for America, and the American Family Association oppose education about birth control or sexually transmitted infections. As a result of heavy lobbying from the Christian right, from 1996 to 2010 the federal government provided funding for sex education programs only to school districts that have "abstinence-only" sex education. The regulations governing these programs ensured that the beliefs of certain religious groups are embodied in the programs. For example, they required that students be taught that a mutually monogamous relationship in the context of marriage is the expected standard for human sexual activity and that sexual activity outside marriage is likely to have harmful physical or psychological effects. Heterosexuality was also considered the norm, and efforts to address sexual orientation were condemned as part of "the homosexual agenda" (Society for Adolescent Medicine, 2006).

These "standards" are rooted in *some* Americans' religious faith. Federal government funding of only those programs that adhered to them constituted a governmental stamp of approval for a particular set of religious beliefs and violated the First Amendment. New regulations were issued to provide funding for programs that go beyond abstinence and allow students to explore the topic in an atmosphere of religious and intellectual freedom. Funding became available for evidence-based programs that "educate adolescents on both abstinence and contraception to prevent pregnancy and sexually transmitted infections" (National Campaign to Prevent Teen and Unwanted Pregnancy, 2011). Despite the change in policy, the impact of the former policy remains and poses a health threat to young Americans. Only twenty-one states and the District of Columbia mandate sex education. Only eighteen states require that the content include information about birth control—ironically, the same number requiring that instruction on the importance of engaging in sexual activity only within marriage be provided. Of the twelve states that require information about sexual orientation, Alabama, South Carolina, and Texas require that the information be negative toward homosexuality (Guttmacher Institute, 2011).

The Creationism/Intelligent Design Debate

Similar efforts to infuse a particular religious perspective into public school curricula have taken place with regard to science courses. The theory of evolution is one of the most important contributions ever made to our understanding of the connections between all living things and is fundamental to genetics, biochemistry, physiology, and ecology. "Biological evolution is one of the most important ideas of modern science. Evolution is supported by abundant evidence from many different fields of scientific investigation. It underlies the modern biological sciences, including the biomedical sciences, and has applications in many other scientific and engineering disciplines" (National Academy of Sciences, 2008, p. 47). An earth science or biology course that does not include evolution shortchanges students. "Science and technology are so pervasive in modern society that students increasingly need a sound education in the core concepts, applications, and implications of science. Because evolution has and will continue to serve as a critical foundation of the biomedical and life sciences, helping students learn about and understand the scientific evidence, mechanisms, and implications of evolution are fundamental to a high-quality science education" (National Academy of Sciences, 2008, p. 47). Yet, after eighty years, the teaching of evolution is being disputed once more in school districts across the country. Some people are convinced that unless the "theory" of evolution is challenged in science classes, then the state is violating their right to religious liberty and perpetuating intellectual fraud. What is going on?

Some people object to the teaching of evolution because they believe that the world was created 6,000 years ago by a divine being acting purposefully. Beginning with the Scopes trial in 1925, creationists have attempted to protect their children from what they see as the evil influences of the teaching of evolution. Consequently, they have lobbied to have textbooks removed from schools if authors do not give "equal time" to creationism and convinced legislators and departments of education to remove evolution from state science standards that strongly influence the curriculum taught in public schools. They have had all mention of evolution removed from statewide tests, thus giving school districts the green light to ignore the topic in their classes without fear that students will suffer.

However, the courts repudiated their efforts (*Edwards v. Aguillard,* 1987). So creationists repackaged their argument and attempted to seize the intellectual high ground. Instead of lobbying for creationism, they now argue for "intelligent design" theory and want schools to present it to students as an alternative to natural selection—despite the lack of scientific evidence to support their ideas. They argue that science teachers should be required to suggest that it is quite possible that the process of evolution is the work of an "intelligent designer." That is, they want students to be taught that the existence of God is supported by scientific evidence. However, the "antievolutionary" forces would have to redefine science in order to justify that claim.

"The formal scientific definition of theory is quite different from the everyday meaning of the word. It refers to a comprehensive explanation of some aspect of nature that is supported by a vast body of evidence" (National Academy of Sciences, 2008, p. 11). In *McLean v. Arkansas Board of Education* (1982), the Supreme Court noted five characteristics of science: "(1) It is guided by natural law; (2) It has to be explanatory by reference to natural law; (3) It is testable against the empirical world; (4) Its conclusions are tentative; (5) It is falsifiable." Neither creationism nor intelligent design meets such criteria. The "scientific" explanation for creationism, that the universe came into being from "nothingness," cannot be explained in reference to natural law, does not establish its own scientific hypotheses, and is neither testable nor falsifiable. Similarly, intelligent design's claim that there is a plan for the universe does not lead to predictions that are testable or to results that can be verified or reproduced. It is not rooted in natural law but explains the origins of life with reference to a supernatural force. Creationism and intelligent design are, in fact, religious beliefs, and their claims don't need to be tested in order to be accepted as *religious* truths. A person can accept on faith any explanation he or she chooses for the origin of the world or the relationships between its living things. People can draw on statements based on revelation or religious authority. They can take great comfort from such faith and can be profoundly inspired by its explanations. They can study different expressions of those beliefs, comparing and contrasting them—sifting among them for the one that is most convincing. But what they can't do is call them "science."

In contrast, evolution is an explanation for the facts that have been collected through the scientific tools of observation and experimentation (Alberts, 2005). It is a prime example of the way scientific knowledge is constructed: "natural explanations, logically derived from confirmable evidence" (Alberts, 2005). The theory of evolution has been built up through facts, such as "the presence and/or absence of particular fossils in particular strata of the geological column. From these confirmed observations we develop an explanation, an inference, that what explains all of these facts is that species have had histories, and that descent with modification has taken place" (Scott, 2001, p. 6). Scientists no longer debate whether evolution has taken place because the data from experimentation and observation are too strong.

Nevertheless, supporters of intelligent design portray themselves as victims of discrimination, unable to exercise their First Amendment free speech rights. They create slogans such as "Teach the controversy" and "Go where the evidence leads" (Thomas, 2008). They argue for fairness, tolerance for diversity, individual choice, and opposition to censorship, which are powerful arguments in a society committed to those core values. The problem is that there is no controversy, at least no scientific controversy. Instead, adherents of one faith tradition are attempting to alter school curriculum and teaching methods because they cannot be reconciled with their religious beliefs. And they are making gains despite the course decisions declaring the teaching of creationism and intelligent design to be violations of the First Amendment. Louisiana has passed a law requiring that evolution be a topic of critical investigation, logical analysis, and open and objective discussion and allowing the use of supplementary materials, including those produced by organizations and authors with a distinctly religious point of view (Morelli, 2010). Texas also allows the use of such materials (Davis, 2009/2010). A study of high school biology teachers has shown that between 12 and 16 percent are creationist in orientation—"one in eight reported that they teach creationism or intelligent design in a positive light" (Berkman, Pacheco, and Plutzer, 2008). In addition, the topic of evolution has become so controversial that it appears that teachers are reluctant to address it scientifically. Students reported that evolution was addressed superficially most often and that a religiously based critique of the theory was frequently part of the instruction (Bandoli, 2008).

Lately, supporters of intelligent design have avoided any mention of religious motivations or intentions in their efforts to limit the teaching of evolution. They have created what some scholars call "mini-intelligent design." They no longer argue that the intelligent designer must be supernatural. They know that the Supreme Court has ruled that mention of a creator in public schools violates the separation of church and state. So they stick with arguments that adaptations in organisms "scientifically" prove the poverty of evolution as an explanatory theory and hope that Americans, whose own science education has often been limited, will be impressed and lobby for "fairness" (Sober, 2007).

What's the Big Deal?

What's wrong with majority rule in regard to curriculum and religious practices in public schools? Ninety percent of Americans support prayer at school-sponsored events, and 51 percent believe that the creation story in Genesis is literally true (Gallup Organization, 2011). What's the harm in bringing those beliefs into public school? Some argue that America is a nation founded by men with Judeo-Christian beliefs and that religion provides a moral compass for individuals and society. Public prayer and other rituals serve "in the only ways reasonably possible, the legitimate secular purposes of solemnizing public occasions, expressing confidence in the future, and encouraging the recognition of what is worthy of appreciation in society" (*Lynch v. Donnelly*, 1984, p. 693). Only a few people object to them, and in schools no one is forced to participate; they can remain silent while others pray. Why should most citizens be denied their preferences because they would offend a minority of non-Christians or nonbelievers?

While it might prove satisfying in the short term, breaking down the barrier between religion and the state in schools—even in the name of majority rule—is in no one's best interests. It hurts individuals by making full acceptance as a member of the school community dependent on sharing the majority's religious beliefs. Further harm is done by minimizing the complexity of American history at the expense of supporting—or establishing—a more sectarian "truth." Finally, taking down the wall between church and state undermines religion because in the effort to make language, symbols, and practices acceptable to all, they become so bland that they lose all spiritual meaning (Warren, 2003).

When the separation of church and state is violated in schools—for example, by a prayer at a graduation ceremony or a football game or by the introduction of creationist arguments in a science class—students receive the message that belief is favored over nonbelief. So, young people who are atheists or members of nonmonotheistic traditions are plunged into crises of conscience by these school practices. They must either risk their acceptance in the school community or take part in religious activities with which they do not agree. The Establishment Clause was meant to prevent the development of such dilemmas in public spheres. Under its protection, religious belief or nonbelief should be irrelevant in one's ability to participate fully in schooling. Even though members of the majority find the practices untroubling, the situation upsets the delicate balance between individual and collective rights that the Constitution preserves.

Violating the separation of religion and state in schools also harms society. Favoring the beliefs of one religious tradition over others or belief over disbelief creates tensions that pose a threat to the cohesiveness of our very pluralistic society. For example, when "nonsectarian" prayers are said at school events, they reflect the Judeo-Christian tradition. Members of nonmajority religious groups get the message that their beliefs are not really "American"—they are both overlooked and excluded (Warren, 2003). The result is a society in which individuals and groups are assigned social status on the basis of how closely their beliefs adhere to the preferred religion. That kind of social stratification can have serious results. Jews, Hindus, Muslims, Sikhs, other non-Christians, and nonbelievers may isolate themselves from public schools if they feel their rights are not protected in them. That separation could exacerbate differences and cause resentments and misunderstandings. We can look into the past—recent and ancient—and discover the harm that such divisiveness has caused. The struggles of Shiite and Sunni Muslims in Iraq and Protestant and Catholic Christians in Ireland are but two recent examples. In each case, one group's religious beliefs and practices were sanctioned by the government; members of that group enjoyed social and economic privileges that members of the other did not. The results were tragic for both societies.

Although believers argue that religion exerts a good influence by encouraging people to act morally, that opinion overlooks historical reality. Religion has been used to justify slavery, war, terrorism, imperialism, and genocide. Systems of belief suggesting that they have answers to every question can threaten fundamental aspects of democracy. When government endorses religious belief, it limits the necessarily critical discourse about the impact of faith on society.

Finally, breaching Jefferson's wall between church and state jeopardizes religion itself. When one chooses freely to believe, religion has the power to provide comfort, guidance, and a sense of community. When spiritual practices are mandated in public schools, the voluntary nature of religious observance is sacrificed. When participation in spiritual practices is mandated in schools, individual conviction in religion may be lost. As a consequence, people's commitment to a religion may be dependent on the social setting rather than on their own belief. When they leave school, they may leave religious practice behind them as well. Rather than strengthening religion, mandating its practice in school may actually weaken it (Traunmuller and Freitag, 2011).

"The text of the First Amendment is only ink on centuries-old paper; its power lies in the people who give it practical meaning throughout this religiously diverse nation. Were this an easy task, the Supreme Court would not have heard over ninety cases on religious liberty since 1815" (Branch, 2007).

For Discussion

1. The National Academy of Sciences (NAS) has argued that creationism does not meet the criteria for a scientific theory. Investigate the NAS definition further and determine whether creation scientists could gather facts that would support their theory regarding the origin of life on earth and what type of evidence they would need. Can you find other definitions of scientific knowledge that might be expansive enough to include creation science?

2. The courts have ruled that teachers may not communicate their own religious beliefs to students. What do you think is the basis for those rulings? Research other legal limitations that have been placed on teachers' individual freedoms. Do they reflect society's attempt to balance the rights of individuals and needs of a democratic society? Do you agree with the way that balance has been achieved? What would you do differently?

3. Read or watch a film or video version of *Inherit the Wind,* the dramatization of the Scopes trial. Research the actual event as well. What role did the historical and geographical setting play in the case? Would the case have been brought to court in a different location—even during the same period? Speculate on whether geographic differences might exist today regarding the question of religious freedom in public schools. What implications might these differences have for those entering the teaching profession? On what grounds would you base your guesses? How could you verify your thesis?

4. The U.S. Department of Education has issued guidelines for religious expression in public schools. Using those guidelines, take the role of a school superintendent and prepare a set of rules for your school district. Assume that they will need to be approved by your school board and create an explanation for each of the regulations you propose.

References

Abington Township School District v. Schempp. (1963). 374 U.S. 203.

ACLU Legal Bulletin. (1996). "The Establishment Clause and Public Schools." www.aclu .org.issues/religion/pr3.html.

ALBERTS, B. (2005). "Intelligent Design." *New York Times.* February 12.

BANDOLI, J. (2008). "Do State Science Standards Matter?" *American Biology Teacher* 70:212–216.

BATTE, S. (2008). "School Prayer Decision." http://members.tripod.com/candst/pray2a .htm.

BEHE, M. (2007). *The Edge of Evolution: The Search for the Limits of Darwinism.* New York: Free Press.

BERKMAN, M., PACHECO, J., AND PLUTZER, E. (2008). "Evolution and Creationism in America's Classrooms: A National Portrait." *PLOS Biology* 6(5):e124, doi:10.1371/ journal.pb10.0060124.

———. (2010). "Stealth Evangelism in Public Schools." *Church and State* 63(July/August): 7–10.

BRANCH, C. (2007). "Unexcused Absence: Why Public Schools in Religiously Plural Society Must Save a Seat for Religion in the Curriculum." *Emory Law Review* 56:1431.

BUELL, J. (2007). "Preface." In *The Design of Life: Discovering Signs of Intelligence in Biological Systems,* ed. W. Dembski and J. Wells. Dallas: Foundation for Thought and Ethics.

CHADSEY, M. (2007). "Thomas Jefferson and the Establishment Clause." *Akron Law Review* 40:623.

CHANCEY, M. (2007). "A Textbook Example of the Christian Right: The National Council on Bible Curriculum in Public Schools." *Journal of the American Academy of Religion* 75(3):554–581.

Council for Secular Humanism (2011). "What Is Secular Humanism?" www.secularhumanism .org/index.php?section=main&page=what_is_.

County of Allegheny v. American Civil Liberties Union, Greater Pittsburgh Chapter. (1989). 492 U.S. 573.

DAVIS, M. (2009/2010). "Religion, Democracy and the Public Schools." *Journal of Law and Religion* 25(1):33–56.

DEMBSKI, W., AND WELLS, J. (2007). *The Design of Life: Discovering Signs of Intelligence in Biological Systems.* Dallas: Foundation for Thought and Ethics.

D'Escoto, D., and D'Escoto, K. (2010). *The Little Book of Big Reasons to Homeschool.* Nashville: B & H Publishing Group.

Dorrell, O. (2007). "Some Say Schools Giving Muslims Special Treatment." *USA Today.* July 25.

Edwards v. Aguillard. (1987). 482 U.S. 578.

Engel v. Vitale. (1962). 370 U.S. 421.

Everson v. Board of Education. (1947). 330 U.S. 855.

Feldman, N. (2005). "A Church State Solution." *New York Times,* July 3, sec. 6, p. 28.

Fessenden, T. (2005). "The 19th Century Bible Wars and the Separation of Church and State." *Church History* 74(5):784–811.

Gallup Organization. (2011) The Gallup Poll. May 5–8.

Good News Club v. Milford Central School. (2001). 533 U.S. 98.

Goodman, J., and Lesnick, H. (2001). *The Moral Stake in Education.* New York: Longman.

Gordon, B., and Dembski, W., eds. (2011). *The Nature of Nature: Examining the Role of Naturalism in Science.* Wilmington, DE: Intercollegiate Studies Institute.

Gray, M., Lukes, J., Archibald, J., Keeling, P., and Doolittle, W. (2010). "Cell Biology. Irremediable Complexity?" *Science* 330(6006):920–921.

Guttmacher Institute. (2011). "State Policies in Brief: Sex and HIV Education." www.guttmacher.org/statecenter/spibs/spib_SE.pdf.

Holmes, D. (2006). *The Faiths of the Founding Fathers.* New York: Oxford University Press.

Jemmott, J., Jemmott, R., and Fong, G. (2010). "Efficacy of a Theory-Based Abstinence-Only Intervention over 24 Months: A Randomized Controlled Trial with Young Adolescents." *Archives of Pediatric and Adolescent Medicine* 164(2):152–159.

Kitzmiller v. Dover. (2005). 400 F. Supp. 2d 707.

Koch, A., and Peden, W. (1944). *The Life and Selected Writings of Thomas Jefferson.* New York: Random House.

Lee v. Weisman. (1992). 505 U.S. 577.

Lemon v. Kurtzman. (1971). 403 U.S. 602.

LeVake v. Independent School District 656 et al. (2000). 625 N.W.2d 502.

Longman, J. (2011). "Tackling by Moonlight." *New York Times.* August 11.

Lynch v. Donnelly. (1984). 465 U.S. 668.

Macedo, D. (2010). "Debate Grows as U.S. Schools Adjust Calendars to Observe Muslim Holidays." www.foxnews.com/us/2010/08/13/debate-grows-schools-closing-muslim-holidays.

McCarthy, M. (1983). *A Delicate Balance: Church, State and the Schools.* Bloomington, IN: Phi Delta Kappan Educational Foundation.

McCluskey, N. (1967). "The New Secularity and the Requirements of Pluralism." In *Religion and Public Education,* ed. T. Sizer. Boston: Houghton Mifflin.

McCollum v. Board of Education. (1948). 333 U.S. 203.

McConnell, M. (2000). "Religion and Constitutional Rights: Why Is Religious Liberty the 'First Freedom'?" *Cardozo Law Review* 21:1243.

McCreary County v. ACLU. (2005). 2005 U.S. Lexis 5211.

McLean v. Arkansas Board of Education. (1982). 529 F. Supp. 1255.

Meacham, J. (2007). *American Gospel: God, the Founding Fathers and the Birth of a Nation.* New York: Random House.

Morelli, R. (2010). "Survival of the Fittest: An Examination of the Louisiana Science Education Act." *St. John's Law Review* 84:797–832.

Murray v. Curlett. (1963). 371 U.S. 944.

National Academy of Sciences. (2008). *Science, Evolution and Creationism: A View from the National Academy of Sciences.* Washington, DC: National Academy Press.

National Campaign to Prevent Teen and Unwanted Pregnancy. (2011). "Personal Responsibility Education Program." www.thenationalcampaign.org/federalfunding/prep.aspx.

NCBCPS. (2011). "The National Council on Bible Curriculum in the Public Schools Introduces Electronic Version of its Curriculum for Public Schools." Greensboro, NC.http://www.bibleinschools.net/About-Us/NCBCPS-Introduces-Electronic-Version-of-Curriculum.

Newdow v. U.S. Congress. (2002). 293 F. 3d. 597; 328 F.3d 466.

PAIGE, R. (2003). "Guidance on Constitutionally Protected Prayer in Public Elementary and Secondary Schools." U.S.Department of Education. www.ed.gov/policy/gen/guid/religionandschools/prayer_guidance.html.

PASSE, J., AND WILCOX, L. (2009). "Teaching Religion in American's Public Schools: A Necessary Disruption." *The Social Studies,* May–June, 102–106.

People for the American Way. (2008). "Texas School Board Agrees to Stop Teaching Unconstitutional Bible Class In Public Schools." www.pfaw.org/pfaw/general/default.aspx?oid=25063.

Pew Forum on Religion and Public Life. (2007). "Religon in the Public Schools." Washington, DC: The Pew Forum. http://www.pewforum.org/Church-State-Law/Religion-in-the-Public-Schools.aspx.

RIDENOUR, E. (2007). "It's Coming Back and It's Our Constitutional Right." www.biblein schools.net.

ROBB, S. (1985). *In Defense of School Prayer.* Santa Ana, CA: Parca Publishing.

ROSENBLETH, S., AND BAILEY, B. (2008). "Cultivating a Religiously Literate Society." *Religious Education* 103(2):145–161.

SANDERS, J. (1977). *Education of an Urban Minority.* New York: Oxford University Press.

Santa Fe Independent School District v. Jane Doe. (2000). 530 U.S. 290.

SANTOS, F., AND PHILLIPS, A. (2011). "Sex Education Again a Must in City Schools." *New York Times,* August 10, A1.

School District of the City of Grand Rapids v. Ball. (1985). 437 U.S. 373.

Selman Injunction. (20005). *Selman v. Cobb County School Dist,* Civ. No 1 02-CV 2325-CC, 005. U.S. Dist LEXIS 432.

SCOTT, E. (2001). "Dealing with Anti-Evolutionism." National Center for Science Education. www.ncseweb.org/resources.

SHORTT, B. (2004). *The Harsh Truth about Public Schools.* Portland, OR: Chalcedon/Ross House Books.

SOBER, E. (2007). "What's Wrong with Intelligent Design." *Quarterly Review of Biology* 82(1):3–8.

Society for Adolescent Medicine. (2006). "Abstinence-Only Education Policies and Programs: A Position Paper of the Society for Adolescent Medicine." *Journal of Adolescent Health* 38:83–87.

STEWART, K. (2011). "Separation of Church and School." *New York Times.* June 12.

Stone v. Graham. (1980). 449 U.S. 39.

THOMAS, D. (2008). "President's Message." www.cesamenm.org/download/beacon/03_2008beacon.pdf.

TOLSON, J. (2007). "In America, an F in Religion." *US News and World Report* 142(12).

Torcaso v. Watkins. (1961). 367 U.S. 488.

TOZER, S., VIOLAS, P., AND SENESE, G. (2002). *School and Society.* New York: McGraw-Hill.

TRAUNMULLER, R., AND FREITAG, M. (2011). "State Support of Religion: Making or Breaking Faith-Based Social Capital." *Comparative Politics* 43(3):253–269.

TURTEL, J. (2005). *Public Schools, Public Menace: How Public Schools Lie to Parents and Betray Our Children.* New York: Liberty Books.

U.S. v. Seeger. (1965). 380 U.S. 163.

Van Orden v. Perry. (2005). 2005 U.S. LEXIS 5215.

WALDMAN, S. (2009). *Founding Faith: How Our Founding Father Forged a Radical New Approach to Religious Liberty.* New York: Random House.

Wallace v. Jaffree. (1985). 472 U.S. 38.

Warren, C. (2003). "No Need to Stand on Ceremony." *Mercer Law Review,* Summer, 54. Mercer L. Rev. 1669.

Webster v. New Lenox School District (1990). 917 F. 2nd 1004.

WEISER, B. (2011). "Court Lets City Restrict Church Use of Schools." *New York Times.* June 3.

WRIGHT, E. (1999). "Religion in American Education: A Historical View." *Phi Delta Kappan* 81(1):17–20.

ZELDIN, M. (1986). "A Century Later and Worlds Apart: American Reform Jews and the Public School-Private School Dilemma, 1870–1970." Paper presented at the annual meeting of the American Educational Research Association, San Francisco.

ZIRKEL, P. (2010–2011). "Celebrating Holiday or Holy Days." *Phi Delta Kappan,* December–January, 76–77.

Zorach v. Clauson. (1952). 343 U.S. 306.

CHAPTER 6

Gender Equity: Eliminating Discrimination or Accommodating Difference

Should schools or classrooms separate students by gender or sexual identities?

POSITION 1: SEPARATE SCHOOLS OR CLASSROOMS PERPETUATE DISCRIMINATION

In recent years, girls have made tremendous gains in math, science, and higher academic attainment, almost exclusively through co-educational schooling. Now the focus is on boys, who some argue must be segregated to protect them from girls' over-achievement; however, most research indicates that boys, if anything, do better in classrooms with more, *not fewer, female classmates. Girls are a good influence on boys' learning, and boys have been a good influence on girls' ambition and athleticism. Just as brothers and sisters learn from each other in families, boys and girls in co-ed schools have much to gain from learning side-by-side.*

—American Council for CoEducational Schooling (2011)

The ongoing struggle for civil rights in the United States has included efforts to end gender discrimination in public schools. The attempt to ensure equal educational access, opportunity, and achievement has focused primarily on the rights of women, whose exclusion from schools and programs have contributed to inequality in career choices and lifetime earnings. While issues regarding educational equity for men and women still remain to be addressed, additional concerns have emerged regarding the treatment of students whose gender and sexual identities challenge traditional categories. Recent attempts to respond to these concerns have resulted in single-sex or otherwise segregated schools and classes. These changes represent sincere efforts to meet young people's needs. However, they result in discriminatory policies and practices that isolate young people from one another. Public schools were created to provide settings where citizens in a diverse democracy could learn the skills they needed to meet their obligations to protect the rights of all people—not only those whose backgrounds or beliefs or physical characteristics placed them in the majority. Segregated educational settings—no matter how well intentioned—can never serve that purpose.

Gender Roles and Education

Debates about gender equity always have been inextricably connected to society's understanding of gender roles—that is, the social roles men and women were assigned shaped Americans' view of appropriate education for boys and girls. Of course, race and social class also have affected equity between males and females in schools. In some ways, however, notions of what men and women are expected to be and do have transcended those other categories. So, ending discrimination in schools has depended on changes in gender roles—especially for women.

In colonial America, gender roles were rooted in a biblical understanding that women were subservient to men. Yet colonial Christianity also required each believer, male or female, to be able to read and interpret the Scriptures and to provide their children with the same skills. As a result, most boys and girls gained limited access to education through education at home or in "dame" schools. Because males were thought to have the responsibility to work in the public sphere, boys with the potential to become leaders in the community were allowed to pursue more education. Girls, however, were provided with the opportunity to learn only enough to perform private religious and domestic duties (Tyack and Hansot, 1992; Spring, 1997; Urban and Wagoner, 2000; Tozer, Violas, and Senese, 2002).

After the American Revolution, gender roles were rooted in a political, not religious, ideology. In the fledgling country, men continued to have public responsibilities. They were expected to be moral neighbors, informed voters, and responsible businessmen. Schooling was designed to help boys develop manly virtues, such as obedience to authority, respect for the rights of others, an appreciation of "fair play," and patriotism, as well as to provide opportunities to develop appropriate skills in literacy, natural science, history, and mathematics (Tozer et al., 2002).

Women's responsibilities in the Republic remained primarily in the private sphere. They were expected to provide homes in which their sons and daughters learned to be responsible citizens and in which their husbands could find respite from the cares of the world (Douglas, 1977; Tyack and Hansot, 1992; Zinn, 1995). Schooling prepared girls for those domestic duties. Believing that both men and women's contributions were vital to the country's well-being, Americans in general supported gender equity in access and, to some degree, in curriculum (Kaestle, 1983; Evans, 1989; Tyack and Hansot, 1992; Zinn, 1995). Coeducational elementary schools became the country's norm (Tyack and Hansot, 1992; Sklar, 1993).

Equality of access and opportunity in secondary education was, at first, more contentious (Tyack and Hansot, 1992). By the early nineteenth century, upper- and middle-class boys increasingly went beyond elementary school, attending "grammar" schools that prepared them for college or for occupations such as business, surveying, and teaching (Tozer et al., 2002). Pioneers such as Catharine Beecher, Emma Willard, and Mary Lyon argued that the country's well-being required women to extend their duties as "Republican mothers" by taking their "natural" aptitude for teaching into schools. As a result of their arguments and their fund-raising, private "academies" for women opened, allowing girls to continue their educations to prepare for careers as teachers and, eventually, nurses. By the early twentieth century, the academies were replaced by public high schools that admitted boys and girls on a relatively equal footing (Rury, 1991; Tyack and Hansot, 1992; Spring, 1997; Urban and Wagoner, 2000). The belief that both men and women had some role in public life resulted in greater equity in schooling.

However, even as equality of access to high schools improved, gender stereotypes once again resulted in discrimination. During the Progressive Era (1870–1930), girls were tracked into programs preparing them to be teachers, nurses, secretaries, receptionists, and clerks. Their participation in academic course, preparing students for college, decreased (Rury, 1991). Gender-based high school programs persisted, with the result that although more women than men completed high school between 1940 and 1965, fewer women than men earned college degrees in that same period (U.S. Census Bureau, 2011).

However, educational opportunity remained rooted in the belief that men and women had distinct gender characteristics, suiting them for different work. Despite the increased availability of secondary schools and the long struggle to grant women access to colleges and universities (Horowitz, 1984; Solomon, 1986), few women had the opportunity to pursue education preparing them for professions. The right to work in the law, business, medicine, and ministry belonged almost exclusively to men (Horowitz, 1984; Solomon, 1986; Tozer et al., 2002).

The 1960s saw a renewed commitment to the position that biological differences should not affect the kind or quality of education men and women received. Many argued that the differences between men and women actually were more social than biological (Miller, 1976; Chodorow, 1978; Gilligan, 1982; Segal, 1990; Connell, 1995). Scholars investigated the policies, practices, curriculum, and student–teacher interactions in schools for explanations for differences in school achievement between boys and girls and reported many gender in equities (U.S. Department of Health, Education and Welfare, 1978; Sadker and Sadker, 1982, 1994; Mac an Ghaill, 1994).

They found that gender-based tracking still continued and that instructional materials ignored women's contributions to areas other than homemaking, nursing, and education. They discovered the preferential treatment boys received with regard to teacher attention, counseling, athletics, extracurricular activities, and financial aid (Frazier and Sadker, 1973; Howe, 1984; Biklen and Pollard, 1993; American Association of University Women (AAUW), 1995; Sadker and Sadker, 1994). Activists linked educational gender discrimination to the larger civil rights movement, which originally addressed racial inequality. Advocates argued that gender discrimination was also a violation of the Fourteenth Amendment, depriving women of the "unalienable rights" named by the Declaration of Independence and guaranteed by the Constitution. In 1972, Title IX of the Educational Amendment Act was passed to ban discrimination on the basis of sex in *any* educational program or activity receiving federal financial assistance. In 1974, the Women's Educational Equity Act (WEEA) began funding programs that promoted gender equity in schools, including education for teachers and other school personnel, sexual harassment prevention programs, support for pregnant and parenting students, and the development of nondiscriminatory curricula, resources, and standardized tests (U.S. Department of Education, 2011c). Title IX provided the framework for ending gender discrimination; WEEA provided the financial assistance that enable schools to do so. Together, they resulted in progress toward equity in academic achievement as identified by standardized test scores, course taking, participation in sports and extracurricular activities, and college degrees. As a result, women have made remarkable progress in completing their studies. The latest census figures show that for workers who were twenty-five years old or older, 37 percent of women had bachelor's degrees or higher, compared with 35 percent of men. Among younger people (ages twenty-five to twenty-nine), 36 percent of women had bachelor's degrees or higher, compared with 28 percent of men (U.S. Census Bureau, 2011) (see Figure 6.1).

These remarkable developments resulted, at least in part, from efforts to end discriminatory practices in elementary and secondary school. Girls adjusted their course-taking patterns making them better prepared to enter college and previously male-dominated professions. Girls and boys now take advanced science and mathematics courses at almost equal rates. Fourteen percent of girls complete a rigorous curriculum that includes precalculus and physics. Their grade-point averages are higher than those of boys (Nord et al., 2011). As they have taken more math courses, girls' scores on the math section of the SATs have increased (Nord et al., 2011), even though their scores on the National Assessment of Educational Progress lag below those of their male counterparts (U.S. Department of Education, 2011a).

The provisions of Title IX legislation have been applied most noticeably to athletics. Although some gender differences remain with regard to resources, females' participation in scholastic programs has dramatically increased. In

FIGURE 6.1 Percentage of Bachelor's
Degrees Conferred on Women
in Selected Fields of Study

	1970	2009
Engineering	0.7	16.5
Agriculture	4.1	47.6
Business	9.0	48.9
Physical Science	13.6	40.8

Source: Aud et al. (2011).

FIGURE 6.2 Percentage of Graduate Degrees Awarded
to Women in Selected Fields

	1970	2009
Law (L.L.B., J.D.)	5.4	45.8
Medicine (M.D.)	8.4	48.9
Dentistry (D.D.S., D.D.M.)	0.9	46.4
Computer Science (Ph.D.)	1.9	22.4
Engineering (Ph.D.)	0.7	21.7
Physical Sciences (Ph.D.)	5.4	32.3
Business (M.B.A.)	1.6	45.4

Sources: Aud et al. (2011); U.S. Department of Education (2005).

1972, approximately 30,000 women participated in college or university sports programs; in 2011, 192,000 did. Prior to Title IX, athletic scholarships for women were virtually nonexistent. Women now receive 45 percent of the funding available for sports (U.S. Department of Education, 2011b). Before 1927, approximately 300,000 girls played high school sports; today, there are more than 3 million (U.S. Department of Education, 2011b). Greater participation in sports and more funding has increased women's college attendance and enabled more of them to enter previously male-dominated professions (Stevenson, 2010). In addition, there are long-term health benefits. Women who take part in the rigorous exercise required by sports are less likely to develop heart diseases, osteoporosis, and breast cancer over the course of their lives (Tucker Center for Research on Girls and Women in Sport, 2007). They are less likely to become obese (Kaestner and Xu, 2010).

Despite gains in creating equality of educational access, opportunity, and achievement, gender discrimination remains an issue in American schools. Men's and women's teams do not always have the same access to practice time, facilities, and faculty support. Schools have played the "blame" game about Title IX. Funding expensive male sports such as football, basketball, and ice hockey can stretch athletic budgets to the breaking point. Then, prevented by Title IX from discriminating against women's athletics, they cut smaller men's teams and point the finger at Title IX and not the costs associated with the marquee sports. Yet nothing in the law requires that men's teams be cut. In fact, under Title IX, men's opportunities to participate in school athletics, the number of them doing so, and the budgets for their sports have all increased (Irick, 2011). Of course, some colleges and universities have managed this feat by "roster management." That is, they "pad" the roster of women's teams by adding names of students who never compete—and never even practice. They are even allowed to count men who practice with women as females for the sake of Title IX compliance. And those charged with enforcing the law, like the federal Office of Civil Rights, say that the practices are legal.

If enforcement is lax at the college and university level, it has been almost nonexistent in K–12 schools. Only persistent efforts to end discrimination have addressed the discrepancy between boys' and girls' teams with regard to practice sites and times, transportation, and revenues. However, that work is well worth continuing. Female high school athletes are three times more likely than other girls to do better in school and get their diploma. They have higher grades and do better in science and math courses. They are less likely to smoke, do drugs, engage in sexual activity, or become pregnant (National Women's Law Center, 2011).

Other Forms of Sexual Discrimination in Schools

Although inequities between men and women's academic achievement and participation in athletics remain, the nation has made progress toward that goal. The laws that have protected women's rights to enter the same colleges and universities, schools, and courses as men have been effective. In other areas, however, gender equality remains a challenge—especially for students whose sexual orientation or gender identity fall outside the traditional categories of male and female heterosexuals.

Although the majority of lesbian, gay, bisexual, transgendered, and questioning (LGBTQ) students develop as healthy teenagers, as a group they experience higher levels of social isolation, bullying, sexual harassment, and assault than do other students (Birkett, Espelage, and Keonig, 2009; Kosciw, Greytak, and Diaz, 2009; Robinson and Espelage, 2011). In a nationwide survey, 85 percent of LGBT students said that they had been verbally harassed, and 40 percent said that they had been sexually assaulted at school in the prior year and that these attacks were the result of and directed at their sexual orientation (Kosciw, Greytak, Diaz, and Bartkiewicz, 2010). Two-thirds said that they heard homophobic and antigay comments from teachers and 99.4 percent from other students. They also report that teachers are less likely to reprimand or correct those remarks than ones that express ethnic or racial prejudices (Kosciw et al., 2009). Transgendered youths reported particular difficulties with school staff who refuse to accept the students' preferred gender identities. For example, teachers insist on using the students' birth names rather than the ones chosen by the students and encourage them to dress and behave in conformity with the gender they were assigned at birth (McGuire, Anderson, Toomey, and Russell, 2010). Male GBTQ students are at greater risk than females. Students also find that their access to information about sexual orientation or gender minorities is blocked on school computers, while access to antihomosexual and transgendered sites is allowed (American Civil Liberties Union, 2011).

White and Latino LGBTQ youth are bullied more often than black students. Younger students are harassed and assaulted more often than older ones. Young people experienced less victimization and had better attendance when they attended large, urban schools with poorer and more racially diverse student bodies than if they attended schools that were small and homogeneous. Southern and midwestern LGBTQ students experienced more harassing language and behavior than their counterparts in the Northeast, and those in rural communities were harassed and assaulted more often than those in urban and suburban areas. In-school victimization of LGBTQ young people has costly consequences. It is linked to absenteeism, disciplinary problems, and health risks, such as drug use, alcoholism, depression, and attempted suicide, which occur at higher rates in the LBGTQ population than among their heterosexual peers (Kosciw et al., 2009; Robinson and Espelage, 2011). Absenteeism and disciplinary problems are predictors that there is a greater likelihood that a student may not complete high school. For many, these risks continue into adulthood (Russell, Ryan, Toomey, Diaz, and Sanchez, 2010). However, research also shows that LGBTQ students who experience their schools as supportive experience fewer of those negative outcomes (Robinson and Espelage, 2011). Eleven states have laws that protect LGBTQ students from harassment based on gender. Los Angeles schools have added an antibullying program to address the needs of gender-minority and gay students. California has even passed a law to add LGBTQ history to the curriculum in California. The secretary of education has even called on schools to ensure that gay-straight alliances and other such student organizations are given space to meet in schools. These are good beginnings. However, clearly much work needs to be done to ensure that these students experience schools as safe and respectful places.

New Challenges to Ending Discrimination

Historically, the struggle for equal educational access, opportunity, and achievement has taken place in public schools that educate all students regardless of their gender or sexual orientation. This process has improved opportunities for female and LGBTQ students. Schools are sites where gender inequality has been recognized and critiqued and where gender justice has been promoted. However, some reformers have given up on integrated settings and promoted single-sex or gender-restricted settings. In 2004, the Department of Education issued new regulations that permitted single-sex schools and classes in publicly funded schools and imposed few limitations on such projects. In 2006, the department invited and encouraged school districts to create single-gender classes and schools (*Federal Register*, 2006). A decade ago, there were only four single-sex public schools in the country; today, there are almost 100 and almost 400 that have single-sex classes, including a number of charter schools (National Association for Single Sex Public Education, 2011).

Arguments supporting single-sex education generally point to particular weaknesses in the academic achievement of one gender or another. In fact, no review of single-sex education has shown that the setting alone improves those outcomes (Halpern et al., 2011). Most studies show that factors other than gender explain whatever academic advantages may occur in single-sex settings. Analysis of outcomes reveal that students entering such settings often were already outperforming their peers academically and that less successful students transfer out before graduation, skewing the data. Single-sex schools tend to be smaller and have more personal relationships among school community members and teaching strategies that allow students to be more active learners. In addition, parents have made a "pro-academic choice" by sending children to single-sex schools (Weil, 2008). When those factors are included, the single-sex advantage disappears. Enthusiasm for gender-segregated settings appears to be predicated not on science but on bias-sampled anecdotal evidence (Halpern et al., 2011).

Since they cannot prove the effectiveness of single-sex education, proponents simply provide reasons why it *should* work—arguments based on a pseudoscience of gender differences (Sax, 2006, 2007; Gurian, 2007a, 2007b; Halpern et al., 2011). Aside from the facts that girls' brains finish growing sooner than boys' brains do and that the volumes of boys' brain are, on average, larger than those of girls, neuroscientists have found very few gender-related differences in children's brains. Neither of these two differences is related to how or how much either gender learns. Even the differences in how gender affects the way brains work—sound sensitivity, memory, and activation—are not significant enough to indicate that children should be educated differently (Halpern et al., 2011).

Policies allowing publicly funded single-sex education appear to run counter to the law. In 1996, the Supreme Court declared that state funding of single-sex schools was unconstitutional (*United States v. Virginia*, 1996). The court's limitation on the segregation of one group of students from another is rooted in *Brown v. Board of Education of Topeka, Kansas* (1954)—the landmark case that declared racial segregation to be unconstitutional because no imposed separateness can ever constitute equality. Segregation based on gender or sexual identity equally carries negative messages to young people. It fosters belief in significant behavioral or ability differences when none or only superficial ones exist. It reinforces gender stereotyping behavior among students and teachers and even limits the range of socially acceptable ways of being male or female (American Council for CoEducational Schooling, 2011). In addition, it appears that, for boys at least, single-sex settings are more likely to produce aggressive behaviors. Cross-gender friendships in a school setting are a predictor that the school will be a safe place for all students (Faris and Felmlee, 2010). Some supporters of LGBTQ students argue for segregated educational settings for them as well. There are two "gay-friendly" in-person high schools in the country: Harvey Milk in New York and Alliance in Milwaukee. Alliance sponsors a middle school as well. The founders argue that although their students' being safe in schools with other students would be the best possible world, it is not likely to come in time for the young people they educate (Alliance High School, 2011; Hetrick-Martin Institute, 2011). The recent opening of an online high school for LGBTQ (GLBTQ Online High School, 2011) youth poses an additional possibility for segregation—and, sadly, isolation—of young people. However, studies show that diverse schools where students and faculty welcome LGBTQ students and respond quickly to harassment or bullying are safe and promote friendships.

There are proven steps that school districts and communities can take to ensure that all students experience equality in education. Differentiating instruction ensures that across the continuum of learners that includes male and female, heterosexual and straight, and gender-majority and minority students, all can be successful. Promoting understanding among students about gender and sexual orientation and enforcing bans against sexually based verbal or physical harassment and assault provides an atmosphere in which all students can thrive.

"Gay-straight alliances (GSAs) and similar student-initiated groups addressing LGBT issues can play an important role in promoting safer schools and creating more welcoming learning environments. Nationwide, students are forming these groups in part to combat bullying and harassment of LGBT students and to promote understanding and respect in the school community. Although the efforts of these groups focus primarily on the needs of LGBT students, students who have LGBT family members and friends, and students who are perceived to be LGBT, messages of respect, tolerance, and inclusion benefit all" (Duncan, 2011). In schools with gay-straight alliances, students and staff report positive environments for all students, and LGBTQ students experience less harassment or assault (Russell, Muraco, Subramaniam, and Laub, 2009). Ironically, some who advocate segregating young people based on gender actually want to reinforce existing gender roles and heterosexism and ignore the violence that has historically supported them. Creating and maintaining educational policies and settings where gender discrimination is not tolerated, that have zero tolerance and serious consequences for sexually based verbal or physical violence, and that are safe spaces where young citizens unlearn the prejudice of the past is the best way to protect all young people and create a safer future.

POSITION 2: SEPARATE SCHOOLS OR CLASSROOMS ARE NECESSARY

It comes as no surprise to anyone who has raised or educated children that boys and girls are different. While environment and culture play a large part in socializing children into gender roles, the very nature of a child—including the gender—requires us to look at boys and girls differently at home as well as in the classroom. Absolutely equal—but different.

—Gurian Institute (2011)

There is no question that the efforts of many Americans to end educational gender discrimination have resulted in some important gains, especially with regard to access to schools. All phases of public education—from kindergarten to graduate school—are open to members of both genders. However, there are real differences between males and females that deserve accommodation in schools. Rigid policies of "sameness," instead of making legitimate distinctions, actually limit opportunities for students. We have ample evidence that boys and girls do not experience school in the same way.

Gendered Experiences in Schools

The recent generation-long effort to eliminate discrimination from schools began with analyses of the way gender affected students' educational experiences. Researchers found that preschool boys played with tools, simple machines, balls, and blocks much more often than girls (AAUW, 1995). Teachers encouraged boys to be assertive and independent, discouraged girls from taking risks, and rewarded them for being "timid, cooperative and quiet" (Tozer et al., 2002, p. 392).

In elementary schools, teachers worked with boys more often and gave them more attention and affection than they provided girls. They prompted boys to think through projects or answer difficult questions on their own and were more likely to give girls the answers or show them how to do a task. When boys answered a question by calling out, teachers paid attention to what they said. When girls did the same thing, teachers more often ignored the content of the comment and scolded them for not following classroom rules (Sadker and Sadker, 1994). Boys were more likely than girls to be regarded as "troublemakers," have their teachers contact parents about behavioral problems, repeat a grade, and be labeled as learning disabled.

By the time they got to middle school, girls were struggling with messages about their academic competency and had become tentative about speaking up in class (Brown and Gilligan, 1993). By high school, many girls were quite good at "doing school"—that is, presenting their work neatly, turning it in on time, and regurgitating information on tests. They did not, however, excel in independent or critical thinking and rarely took risks in choosing courses or assignments (Brown and Gilligan, 1993; AAUW, 1995). Boys were more likely to take higher-level math, science, and computer classes. They were also more likely to drop out. Boys faced peer pressure to take part in sports, and their masculinity was judged on their ability to compete. They encouraged one another to engage in drug and alcohol use and other risky behaviors. Expressions of emotion were mocked (Kindlon et al., 1999; Pollack, 1999). Acting as if they had power through posturing and violence was rewarded. Interest in "feminine" things, such as reading and the arts, was ridiculed (Kimmel, 2000).

Textbooks contributed to sex discrimination in schools by not deeply challenging traditional understandings of gender. Curricular materials did not affirm differences between members of the same gender or integrate the experiences, needs, and interests of both sexes in their material (AAUW, 1995). Vocational education programs reflected and reproduced traditional gender expectations. Females were overwhelmingly directed or allowed to enter.

Four out of five students reported that they had been the victim of sexual harassment. One-quarter said that it happened to them "often" (AAUW, 1993). Sexual harassment took many forms in secondary schools: comments, jokes, gestures, and looks. Students were touched, grabbed, or pinched. They were subjected to mooning, flashing, and genital exposure. Students became targets of sexual rumors or written graffiti, had their clothes pulled at or off, were spied on in locker rooms, were shown or given unwanted sexual pictures or notes, and were blocked or cornered in sexual ways. They were forced to kiss someone when they did not want to and in some cases to do something even more sexual than kissing. It seemed that no school space was entirely safe. Students reported harassment took place in classrooms, hallways, gyms, cafeterias, locker rooms, parking lots, playgrounds, and buses (AAUW, 1993). Advocates railed against the impact of these behaviors. "The consequences can be devastating, as young women struggle to survive in a learning environment they often experience as toxic. When so much of a female student's day is spent fending off diminishing comments, sexual innuendoes and physical pestering, how can she be expected to thrive at school?" (Larkin, 1997, p. 14).

Finally, researchers found schools discriminated against young women who were pregnant or parenting, doing little to accommodate their special needs. Few schedules were adjusted to allow for the extra time mothers might need to transport their babies to child care. Even fewer provided such centers on-site. These young women were more likely to drop out of school than other female students (U.S. Department of Education, 2011c).

The research made a compelling case that boys and girls had different experiences in schools—and that each group was being shortchanged because of gender discrimination. However, the policies and practices developed to address these issues seem disconnected from the reality they described.

One-Size-Fits-All Regulations

During the 1970s, feminists and other civil rights advocates tried to equate racism and sexism. They lobbied for passage of an Equal Rights Amendment (ERA) that would have prohibited all discrimination on the basis of gender. However, the decadelong national debate on the ERA made it clear to most Americans that treating people differently based on their gender was far different from discriminating on the basis of race. They understood that it sometimes was necessary to make legitimate distinctions between the genders in order to serve the best interests of women and their children.

A determined campaign by those who saw the dangers to women inherent in the ERA convinced Americans that the amendment would prevent the courts from allowing legitimate distinctions to be made in public policies, such as child custody, alimony, and workforce accommodations. After 1977, no state legislature could be persuaded to ratify the amendment. By 1982, even the most ardent feminists declared the effort to pass the ERA to be at an end.

However, efforts to use one-size-fits-all policies to address gender discrimination did not end with the death of the ERA. In 1972, Congress passed Title IX, which required more equitable distribution of educational resources and opportunities among males and females. When Title IX has been applied in rational and thoughtful ways, the consequence has been a more just educational system. However, the problems inherent in ruling out all legitimate distinctions between treatment of the sexes has also created situations in which Title IX's consequences have been unjust—and absurd.

The limitations and resulting failures of the attempt to create gender equity by relying solely on ending discrimination are particularly obvious in the application of Title IX regulations to athletics. The legislation originally was intended to end discrimination in school sports programs. Over time, however, it has created a "quota system" in colleges and universities' athletics programs that actually limits opportunity for some students. Through the efforts of feminists and others who support rigid policies of "nondiscrimination," the law has been interpreted as requiring strict "proportionality" between the percentage of women in a school's student body and the percentage of women participating in varsity sports. That is, if 55 percent of the students at a given institution are female, then 55 percent of the athletes also must be female. Schools are considered in violation of the law and face loss of government aid if they fail to comply (Kennedy, 2007).

Despite girls' increased participation in sports, fewer young women than men make the commitment to take part in intercollegiate athletics. Since they ignore the element of individual choice in the creation of gender identities and the influence of those choices on gender equity in educational settings, proponents of rigid nondiscrimination policies blame schools for the differences in student involvement in sports. When colleges cannot entice or coerce enough women to participate in sports, they are forced to achieve proportionality by cutting men's teams. Sports like track, golf, tennis, rowing, swimming, gymnastics, and wrestling have experienced the greatest decline. There are nearly 1,000 more women's than men's teams in the National Collegiate Athletic Association (Irick, 2011). Proponents of absolute "equality" in sports have now turned their attention to high school athletics. There is every reason to expect that the results will be "equally" devastating to male athletes who want, need, and deserve an opportunity to compete (Gavora, 2007). The absurdity of the claim that this policy helps achieve justice is obvious. Committed male athletes are being deprived of their right to participate in sports and to have that choice supported by their schools. The law never authorized discrimination against men through a policy that does not take into account individual freedom. It was meant to ensure equal opportunity for males and females.

School textbooks have also suffered from efforts at social engineering. Diane Ravitch has documented how publishers have responded to Title IX. Quotas have been imposed on examples, test questions, and illustrations; males and females must appear in fifty-fifty ratios. Words like "actress," "heroine," "brotherhood," and "forefathers" are banned. Women cannot be shown doing household tasks or taking care of children. Men cannot be portrayed in traditional jobs like plumbers or carpenters. Boys cannot express anger; girls cannot be frightened (Ravitch, 2003). Sanitizing textbooks does not create equality. In fact, demanding "political correctness" in texts can hurt efforts to make real progress toward justice. Critics find such efforts easy targets of ridicule and dismiss real concerns as "more of the same." Those who proposed changes to textbooks may have begun with the laudable aim of creating an equal playing field for girls and boys by opening their minds to possibilities that transcended traditional gender roles. However, the result is a system that polices the language and images that young people see—hardly the soil in which freedom of choice can grow.

Perhaps the most absurd consequence of efforts to eliminate all discrepancies in treatment of boys and girls in schools is their effect on school dress codes. According to the most rigid interpretation of the law, districts can make no distinctions between males and females with regard to wearing clothing, jewelry, or makeup to school. Surely, creating equality of educational opportunity for male and female students does not require the creation of policies that equate sameness with fairness. The time has come to explore strategies that recognize and respond appropriately to the learning needs of both boys and girls. Policies and practices that do so will, in the long run, result in more equity for men and women.

Real Differences Require Real Accommodations

There is certainly no denying that biological differences between males and females really exist. Women conceive, gestate, give birth, and suckle new members of the human race. Men do not. But reproductive differences are only one way in which men and women are not the same. Male and female brains also differ. Scientists have known for more than a hundred years that men's brains are larger than women's. However, they have recently discovered that females have almost 20 percent more gray matter in their brains than do males. Men's brain structures allow them to perform better than women when attempting visual or spatial tasks. Women's brain structures help them do better than men on verbal- or language-oriented tasks (Burman, Bitan, and Booth, 2008). "The areas of the brain associated with language appear to work harder in girls during language tasks, and boys and girls rely on different parts of the brain when working on these tasks" (*Science Daily*, 2008). We may not understand completely how physical differences between males and females are related to thinking and learning. We know enough, however, to realize that schools and teachers must be responsive to those differences if children are going to have equal educational opportunity. For example, boys need brightly lit classrooms and teachers who speak in loud, enthusiastic tones. They need exercise periods during the day, more confrontational disciplinary practices, and learning activities that engage them in quests for answers. Girls do better in quieter classrooms where cooperation and bonding are encouraged (Sax, 2006, 2007). Obviously, coeducational settings make it impossible to respond adequately to both sets of needs—they are, to a large degree, mutually exclusive. Single-sex classes and schools are not discriminatory—they are necessary accommodations that produce real and significant results.

It may be too early to understand completely how the physical differences between men and women are related to thinking and learning. However, such differences do exist, and schools need the freedom to explore ways to accommodate them.

Single-Sex Settings

For many years, only those children whose families could afford private schools were able to experience the benefits of single-sex schools (Meyer, 2008). Fortunately, recent changes to the No Child Left Behind Act have made it possible for public schools also to meet the real needs of students. The results have been overwhelmingly positive. All across the country, teachers and administrators report fewer discipline problems, higher test scores, and more time on tasks. Parents say that their children are more eager to go to school and more interested in what happens there. Students say that it is easier to learn (Gerwetz, 2007; Holleran, 2007; Jan, 2008; Meyer, 2008; Weil, 2008; Spielhagen, 2011). Research has shown that the benefits to girls of single-sex education include greater academic engagement, higher SAT scores, more interest in graduate education, academic self-confidence (especially in math and engineering), and a stronger predisposition to extracurricular and political engagement (Sax, 2009).

It may be that single-sex settings are successful not only because they accommodate learning differences between boys and girls. They also present students with alternatives to gender stereotypes and, more important, with spaces in which it is safe to challenge them. For example, in single-sex schools, in addition to acquiring knowledge that will result in increased choices about future education and careers, it also is considered within the range of acceptable femininity for a girl to learn how to work hard, discover what kinds of efforts are successful for her, and develop time management and problem-solving skills. Most important, in such a setting, young women can come to believe that they have tremendous control over the course of their lives and still be considered feminine. Teachers and administrators also expand the definition of acceptable gender behavior for girls in most single-sex schools. Students see women teaching subjects such as chemistry, physics, and advanced mathematics that traditionally have not been considered "feminine" (Meyer, 2008; Weil, 2008).

Research on the effects of single-sex settings on boys provides some evidence that in such spaces, traditional gender roles are challenged as well. There is a greater range in the definitions of masculinity in schools for boys than in coeducational ones. So, many boys and young men take part in activities traditionally defined as "feminine," such as the arts and community service (Excellence Charter School, 2008; National Association for Single Sex Public Education, 2011).

In many ways, in single-sex educational settings students no longer have to match their behavior or attitudes to gender stereotypes. It is ironic that advocates of educational equity oppose them. Similarly, the safe spaces created in schools designed to serve LGBTQ youth allow them to realize their full potential. When they no longer have to match their behavior or appearance to gender stereotypes, they are able to explore a whole range of educational and personal options.

The effort to create educational gender equity is laudable and rightly has been pursued throughout U.S. history. Eliminating truly discriminatory policies and practices has been a necessary part of that process. It has not, however, proven to be a sufficient one. Eliminating the possibility of making legitimate distinctions between educational needs of males and females has prevented the struggle for educational equality from being as successful as justice demands it be.

Educational gender inequity remains a fact of life in American schools. It will continue to do so until educators are allowed to create settings addressing the total process by which gender differences in schools are produced.

By ignoring the tendency of coeducational settings to reproduce society's dominant gender prescriptions and refusing to permit educators to create settings that resist those stereotypes, we perpetuate pressures that result in students' choices to conform to them. What is needed is a commitment to make public education better able to meet the needs of all the students it serves. Young people deserve nothing less than having an equal right to education that recognizes the complexity of the problem of gender.

For Discussion

1. Although the positions in this chapter allude to the effects that race, class, and ethnicity might have on an individual's creation of his or her gender identity, they do not discuss those effects in any detail. Consider how the other facets of a person's identity or situation in life might affect the choices they make about how much or how little to conform to various forms of masculinity or femininity. That is, does a person's race, class, or gender affect how free people feel they are to deviate from gender stereotypes? Depending on your answers, what kinds of changes to the proposals in this chapter do you think are necessary to create gender equity in schools that takes race, class, and ethnicity into consideration?

2. Access information about gender differences in test scores from the Educational Testing Services website at www.ets.org/research. In light of the discussions in this chapter, how do you explain such differences? How do you explain the fact that there appears to be little variance among gender differences from one racial/ethnic group to another? What does that suggest to you about ways to remedy gender inequity?

3. Research your college or university's athletic program. Do they seem to be in compliance with Title IX regulations? Have any male teams been cut to achieve "proportionality"? Interview male and female athletes and coaches to get their views on gender issues in the program and to determine for yourself if any discrimination exists.

4. Advantages of single-sex schools are discussed in Position 2. Can you think of any disadvantages of attending such schools? Are they academic or social in nature? Interview friends or classmates who attended single-sex high schools. How do their experiences confirm the arguments made in the chapter? How do their experiences confirm your speculated disadvantages?

References

Alliance High School. (2011). "The Alliance School Milwaukee." http://allianceschoolnet
.bbnow.org.

American Association of University Women. (1993). *Hostile Hallways: The AAUW Survey of Sexual Harassment in America's Schools*. Washington, DC: American Association of University Women.

———. (1995). *How Schools Shortchange Girls*. New York: Marlowe.

American Civil Liberties Union. (2011). "LGBT Youth and Schools." www.aclu.org/lgbt-rights/lgbt-youth-schools.

American Council for CoEducational Schooling. (2011). "Evidence-Based Answers." http://lives.clas.asu.edu/acces/faq_policy.html.

AUD, S., HUSSAR, W., KENA, G., BIANCO, K., FROHLICH, L., KEMP, J., AND TAHAN, K. (2011). *The Condition of Education 2011* (NCES 2011-033). Washington, DC: U.S. Government Printing Office.

BIKLEN, S., AND POLLARD, D., eds. (1993). *Gender and Education.* Yearbook of the National Society for the Study of Education. Chicago: National Society for the Study of Education.

BIRKETT, M., ESPELAGE, D., AND KOENIG, B. (2009). "LGB and Questioning Students in Schools: The Moderating Effects of Homophobic Bullying and School Climate on Negative Outcomes." *Journal of Youth and Adolescence* 38:989–1000.

BROWN, L., AND GILLIGAN, C. (1993). *Meeting at the Crossroads.* Cambridge, MA: Harvard University Press.

Brown v. Board of Education of Topeka, Kansas. (1954). 347 U.S. 483.

BURMAN, D., BITAN, T., AND BOOTH, J. (2008). "Sex Differences in Neural Processing of Language among Children." *Neuropsychologia* 46(5):1349–1362.

CHODOROW, N. (1978). *The Reproduction of Mothering.* Berkley: University of California Press.

CONNELL, R. (1995). *Masculinities*: Berkeley: University of California Press.

DOUGLAS, A. (1977). *The Feminization of American Culture.* New York: Avon Books.

DUNCAN, A. (2011). "Letter to Colleagues Announcing Release of Legal Guidelines regarding the Equal Access Act and the Recognition of Student-Led Noncurricular Groups." www2.ed.gov/policy/elsec/guid/secletter/110607.html.

Excellence Charter School. (2008). "Our Program." www.uncommonschools.org/ecs/aboutUs/programAndValues.html.

FARIS, R., AND FELMLEE, D. (2010). "Status Struggles: Network Centrality and Gender Segregation in Same- and Cross-Gender Aggression." *American Sociological Review* 76(1):48–73.

———. (2006). "Nondiscrimination on the Basis of Sex in Education Programs or Activities Receiving Federal Financial Assistance; Final Rule." October 25, 62529.

FRAZIER, N., AND SADKER, M. (1973). *Sexism in School and Society.* New York: Harper & Row.

GAVORA, J. (2007). "Sex Games: Coming to a High School Near You." *National Review.* June 20. http://article.nationalreview.com/?q=NTgxOTlmZmMzYTgwMWZkZWY1NDA1YjkxZWE5MTU0Yjc=.

GEWERTZ, J. (2007). "Black Boys' Educational Plight Spurs Single-Gender Schools: New Federal Rules Seen as Chance for Innovation." *Education Week* 26(42):1.

GILLIGAN, C. (1982). *In a Different Voice: Psychological Theory and Women's Development.* Cambridge, MA: Harvard University Press.

GLBTQ Online High School. www.glbtqonlinehighschool.com/academics.html.

Gurian Institute. (2011). "Boys and Girls Learn Differently." www.gurianinstitute.com/sessionDescription.php.

GURIAN, M. (2007a). *The Minds of Boys: Saving Our Sons from Falling Behind in School and Life.* New York: Jossey-Bass.

———. (2007b). *Nurture the Nature.* New York: Jossey-Bass.

HALPERN, D., ET AL. (2011). "The Pseudo-Science of Single-Sex Schooling." *Science Magazine* 333:1706–1707.

Hetrick-Martin Institute. (2011). "The Harvey Milk High School." www.hmi.org/page.aspx?pid=230.

HOLLERAN, K. (2007). "Educators Report Benefits from Gender-Segregated Teaching." *Charleston Daily Mail.* November 7.

HOROWITZ, H. (1984). *Alma Mater.* New York: Knopf.

HOWE, F. (1984). *Myths of Coeducation: Selected Essays.* Bloomington: Indiana University Press.

IRICK, E. (2011). "Student Athlete Participation 1982–1983–2010–2011." Indianapolis: National Collegiate Athletic Association.

JAN, T. (2008). "Keeping the Boys Away from the Girls." *Boston Globe.* May 9.

KAESTLE, C. (1983). *Pillars of the Republic: Common Schools and American Society 1780–1860.* New York: Hill & Wang.

KAESTNER, R., AND XU, X. (2010). "Title IX, Girls' Sports Participation, and Adult Female Physical Activity and Weight." *Evaluation Review* 34(1):52–78.

KENNEDY, C. (2007). "The Athletics Directors' Dilemma: $$$ & Women's Sports." *Gender Issues* 24:34–45.

KIMMEL, M. (2000). "What About the Boys?" *WEEA Digest*, November 1, 1–2, 7–8.

KINDLON, D., ET AL. (1999). *Raising Cain: Protecting the Emotional Life of Boys.* New York: Ballantine.

KOSCIW, J., GREYTAK, E., AND DIAZ, E. (2009). "Who, What, When, Where, and Why: Demographic and Ecological Factors Contributing to Hostile School Climate for Lesbian, Gay, Bisexual, and Transgender Youth." *Journal of Youth and Adolescence* 38:976–988.

KOSCIW, J. G., GREYTAK, E. A., DIAZ, E. M., AND BARTKIEWICZ, M. J. (2010). *The 2009 National School Climate Survey: The Experiences of Lesbian, Gay, Bisexual and Transgender Youth in Our Nation's Schools.* New York: GLSEN.

LARKIN, J. (1997). *Sexual Harassment: High School Girls Speak Out.* Toronto: Second Story Press.

MAC AN GHAILL, M. (1994). *The Making of Men: Masculinities, Sexualities and Schooling.* Buckingham: Open University Press.

MCGUIRE, J., ANDERSON, C., TOOMEY, R., AND RUSSELL, S. (2010). "School Climate for Transgendered Youth." *Journal of Youth and Adolescence* 39:1175–1188.

MEYER, P. (2008). "Learning Separately: the Case for Single Sex School." *Education Next* 8(1): 10–21.

MILLER, J. (1976). *Toward a New Psychology of Women.* Boston: Beacon Press.

National Association for Single Sex Public Education. (2011). "Single-Sex Schools/Single-Sex Classes: What's the Difference." www.singlesexschools.org/schools-schools.htm.

National Women's Law Center. (2011). "The Battle for Gender Equity in Athletics in Elementary and Secondary Schools." March. www.nwlc.org/resource/battle-gender-equity-athletics-elementary-and-secondary-schools.

NORD, C., ROEY, S., PERKINS, R., LYONS, M., LEMANSKI, N., BROWN, J., AND SCHUKNECHT, J. (2011). *The Nation's Report Card: America's High School Graduates* (NCES 2011-462). Washington, DC: U.S. Government Printing Office.

POLLACK, W. (1999). *Real Boys.* New York: Dimensions.

RAVITCH, D. (2003). *The Language Police: How Pressure Groups Restrict What Students Learn.* New York: Alfred A. Knopf.

ROBINSON, J., AND ESPELAGE, D. (2011). "Inequities in Educational and Psychological Outcomes between LGBTQ and Straight Students in Middle and High School." *Educational Researcher* 40(7):315–330.

RURY, J. (1991). *Education and Women's Work.* Albany: State University of New York Press.

RUSSELL, S., MURACO, A., SUBRAMANIAM, A., AND LAMB, C. (2009). "Youth Empowerment and High School Gay-Straight Alliances." *Journal of Youth and Adolescence* 38:891–903.

RUSSELL, S., RYAN, C., TOOMEY, R., DIAZ, R., AND SANCHEZ, J. (2010). "Lesbian, Gay, Bisexual, and Transgender Adolescent School Victimization: Implications for Young Adult Health and Adjustment." *Journal of School Health* 81(5):223–230.

SADKER, M., AND SADKER, D. (1982). *Sex Equity Handbook for Schools.* New York: Longman.

———. (1994). *Failing at Fairness: How Schools Cheat Girls.* New York: Touchstone.

SAX, L. (2006). *Why Gender Matters: What Parents and Teachers Need to Know about the Emerging Science of Sex Differences.* New York: Broadway.

———. (2007). *Boys Adrift: The Five Factors Driving the Growing Epidemic of Unmotivated Boys and Underachieving Young Men.* New York: Basic Books.

SAX, L. (2009). *Women Graduates of Single-Sex and Coeducational High Schools: Differences in Their Characteristics and the Transition to College.* Los Angeles: Sudikoff Family Institute for Education and New Media, UCLA Graduate School of Education and Information Studies. www.gseis.ucla.edu/sudikoff.

Science Daily. (2008). "Boys' And Girls' Brains Are Different: Gender Differences in Language Appear Biological." *Science Daily.* March 5.

SEGAL, L. (1990). *Slow Motion: Changing Masculinities, Changing Men.* London: Virago.

SKLAR, K. (1993). "The Schooling of Girls and Changing Community Values in Massachusetts Towns 1750–1820." *History of Education Quarterly* 33(4):511–542.

SOLOMON, B. (1986). *In the Company of Educated Women.* New Haven, CT: Yale University Press.

SPIELHAGEN, F. (2011). "Middle School Boys and Girls Discuss Single-Sex Education." www.education.com/reference/article/Ref_Middle_School_Boys.

SPRING, J. (1997). *The American School 1642–1996.* New York: McGraw-Hill.

STEVENSON, B. (2010). "Beyond the Classroom: Using Title IX to Measure the Return to High School Sports." National Bureau of Economic Research Working Paper 15728. www.nber.org/papers/w15728.

TOZER, S., VIOLAS, P., AND SENESE, G. (2002). *School and Society: Historical and Contemporary Perspectives.* 4th Ed. Boston: McGraw-Hill.

Tucker Center for Research on Girls and Women in Sport. (2007). *The 2007 Tucker Center Research Report, Developing Physically Active Girls: An Evidence-Based Multidisciplinary Approach.* Minneapolis: Tucker Center for Research on Girls and Women in Sport, University of Minnesota.

TYACK, D., AND HANSOT, E. (1992). *Learning Together: A History of Coeducation in American Public Schools.* New York: Russell Sage Foundation.

United States v. Virginia. (1996). 518 U.S. 515, 533.

URBAN, W., AND WAGONER, J. (2000). *American Education: A History.* New York: McGraw-Hill.

U.S. Census Bureau. (2011). "Educational Attainment of the Population 25 Years and Older by Selected Characteristics." www.census.gov/hhes/socdemo/education/data/cps/2010/tables.html.

U.S. Department of Education. (2005). *Trends in Educational Equity of Girls and Women* (NCES 2005-016). Washington, DC: National Center for Education Statistics.

———. (2007). *The Nation's Report Card: America's High School Graduates: Results from the 2005 NAEP High School Transcript Study* (NCES 2007-467). Washington, DC: U.S. National Center for Educational Statistics. http://nces.ed.gov/nationsreportcard/pdf/studies/2007467.pdf.

———. (2008). *The Conditions of Education, 2008.* Washington DC: National Center for Education Statistics. http://nces.ed.gov/pubsearch/pubsinfo.asp?pubid=2008031.

———. (2011a). *Digest of Educational Statistics.* Washington, DC: National Center for Educational Statistics. http://nces.ed.gov/programs/digest/d10/tables/dt10_152.asp.

———. (2011b). *Equity in Athletics Disclosure Act Survey Results.* Washington, DC: Office of Postsecondary Education. http://ope.ed.gov/athletics/Index.aspx.

———. (2011c). "Women's Educational Equity." www.ed.gov/programs/equity/index.html.

U.S. Department of Health, Education and Welfare. (1978). *Taking Sexism Out of Education: The National Project on Women in Education.* Washington, DC: Author.

WEIL, E. (2008). "Teaching Boys and Girls Separately." *New York Times,* March 2.

ZINN, H. (1995). *A People's History of the United States.* New York: Harper.

CHAPTER 7

New Immigrants and the Schools: Unfair Burden or Business as Usual

Should we require schools to teach the flood of new immigrants?

POSITION 1: SCHOOLS HAVE ALWAYS SERVED TO HELP NEW IMMIGRANTS

Many of the first Settlers of these Provinces, were Men who had received a good Education in Europe, and to their Wisdom and good Management we owe much to our present Prosperity. . . . The present Race are not thought to be generally of equal Ability: For though the American Youth are allow'd not to want Capacity; yet the best Capacities require Cultivation, it being truly with them, as with the best Ground, which unless well tilled and sowed with profitable Seed, produces only ranker Weeds.

—Franklin (1749)

In an anonymously written pamphlet, Benjamin Franklin identified deficiencies in the education of the young men of Pennsylvania and proposed remedies for their academic "misfortunes." Franklin recommended a practical education, gained though work and apprenticeships, and an abstract education, learned through reading, writing, and debate. For young men to prosper in their social and political worlds, Franklin urged the cultivation of a sound and thorough command of the English language. English was not the only language spoken in the colony. By Franklin's own estimate, one-third of Pennsylvanians traced their homeland to the German states and spoke German as a first language. Franklin worried about the colony's future without a common language, and he proposed that English serve as the only language of instruction. He advised that the academy hire a teacher, or rector, who was "a man of good Understanding, good Morals, diligent and patient, learn'd in the Languages and Sciences, and a correct Speaker and Writer of the *English* Tongue" (Franklin, 1749).

In Franklin's time, language diversity varied from colony to colony, and the first census in 1790, coincidentally the year of Franklin's death, provides an interesting picture of national diverse origin. Roughly half the population of the United States was of English descent. Another 15 percent were English speakers from Scotland and Ireland. People of Dutch, French, and Spanish origin made up about 14 percent of the population, and 19 percent were of African heritage (Wiley, 2007). A great many people, including many enslaved Africans and Native Americans, uncounted in the first census, did not speak English as their first language. By 1890, immigrants represented 14.8 percent of the total U.S. population, and very few of the new arrivals of that time were from English-speaking counties.

Record-high immigration rates are projected for the year 2050, when one in five people in the United States is expected to be foreign born (Passel and Cohn, 2008). In the late nineteenth and early twentieth centuries, immigrants tended to settle in urban areas, but twenty-first-century immigrants are settling in cities, suburbs, and small towns. Schools everywhere are being directly affected by immigration, and teaching students whose primary language is not English is becoming common (see Figure 7.1).

The children of immigrants[1] are transforming American schools by their unprecedented numbers and sheer diversity. Forty percent of newcomer

FIGURE 7.1 U.S. Immigration, 1960–2050 (in millions)

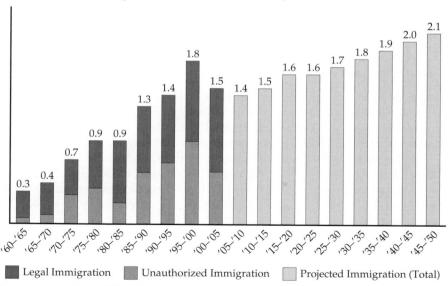

Source: Passel and Cohn (2008, p. 4).

[1]"Children of immigrants" refers to U.S.-born and foreign-born children of recent immigrants who are or will be attending U.S. schools. It includes "first-generation" foreign-born immigrants, U.S.-born "second-generation" immigrants (Suarez-Orozco and Suarez-Orozco, 2001, p. 1), and the so-called 1.5 generation, children arriving in the United States who are not yet of school age (Suarez-Orozco, Suarez-Orozco, and Todorova, 2008, p. 6).

children are from Mexico, the largest sender nation. The remaining 60 percent come from all over the world, with the greatest number arriving from the Caribbean, East Asia, Europe, Canada, and Australia (10 to 11 percent each) and significant populations from Central and South America, Cambodia, Laos, Thailand, and Vietnam (5 to 7 percent each) (Hernandez et al., 2007, p. 2). Immigrant diversity extends beyond numbers and national origins to include the newcomers' level of education and social experience in their home counties. As one team of researchers notes, "On one end of the spectrum, we find children from middle-class urban backgrounds who have been preparing in their countries since early childhood for high-stakes, competitive exams. . . . In sharp contrast are those children from strife-ridden countries with little or no schooling" (Suarez-Orozco and Suarez-Orozco, 2001, p. 128). The children of immigrants have always made good use of the schools to improve themselves and their economic well-being (White and Glick, 2009). Any attempt to deny today's immigrants access to education harms the newcomers and deprives the nation of an educated work-force and important investments in our future.

Language Rights

> Professor Adolphe Cohen of Columbia University, in discussing the teaching of French and German in public schools, said that the attitude of a good many people on that subject was explained to him very aptly by a remark he had once overheard in a streetcar. Two elderly Irish women were talking about their children, when one remarked, "I won't let my children be taught French."
> "Why not?" inquired the other.
> "Sure," replied the first. "If English was good enough for St. Paul to write the Bible in, it's good enough for me" ("Man in the Street," 1905).

American free public education developed in the period between 1830 and 1850, known as the era of the Common School. Schooling at public expense was viewed as broadly beneficial, contributing academic, social, and political value to daily life. Faced with a new and large number of newcomers from Ireland and Germany, advocates of the Common Schools urged the government to provide public-supported education to develop in the new immigrants the language, habits, and values of the old immigrants (Kaestle, 1983). The schools were seen as the most appropriate agency for advancing a common culture. As Joel Spring (2001) notes, in advocating for Common Schools,

> It was argued that if children from a variety of religious, social-class, and ethnic backgrounds were educated in common, there would be a decline in hostility and friction among social groups. In addition, if children educated in common were taught a common social and political ideology, a decrease in conflict and social problems would result. (p. 104)

It was no doubt challenging for nineteenth-century schools to encourage the children of German immigrants to learn English and the children of Irish Catholic immigrants to adopt Protestant values, but today's schools contend with students from everywhere in the world and of every religious belief. Forging a common social and political ideology would be impossible, even if it were desirable. Consider language alone: according to one estimate, within the next several years, over 30 percent of children in public schools will come from homes with limited English proficiency or where English is not the first language. Today, in New York City, more than 100 languages are spoken, and in Rochester, Minnesota, a city of about 86,000 people, there are sixty spoken languages (Bank Street, 2008). Although 82 percent of English language learners (ELLs) in schools come from Spanish-speaking homes, surveys have identified over 350 different first languages spoken among ELLs (National Council of Teachers of English [NCTE] ELL Task Force, 2006, p. 1).

The education of immigrant children has always been a function of public schools, and it is not a responsibility today's schools could shirk, even if they wanted to. Courts in the United States have ruled that the children of immigrants—documented or undocumented—have a right to a free, public education. Take the case of *Plyler v. Doe* (1982), a Supreme Court decision about the constitutionality of a Texas education statute: Texas law allowed local school districts to charge a "tuition fee" for the education of children who were not "legally admitted" into the United States. A class-action lawsuit was brought on behalf of the children of Tyler, Texas, who could not demonstrate that they or their families had been legally admitted to the United States and were required to pay tuition to attend public school. A lower federal court had ruled that the Texas law violated the Equal Protection Clause of the Fourteenth Amendment of the U.S. Constitution, which reads, "Nor shall any State deprive any person of life, liberty, or property, without due process of law; nor deny *to any person within its jurisdiction* the equal protection of the laws." The State of Texas appealed the decision to the Supreme Court.

Justice William Brennan, delivering the majority opinion of the Supreme Court, wrote, "Aliens, even aliens whose presence in this country is unlawful, have long been recognized as 'persons' guaranteed due process of law by the Fifth and Fourteenth Amendments. . . . The American people have always regarded education and [the] acquisition of knowledge as matters of extreme importance. . . . [E]ducation provides the basic tools by which individuals might lead economically productive lives to the benefit of all of us. In sum, education has a fundamental role in maintaining the fabric of our society. . . . Denial of education to some isolated group of children poses an affront to one of the goals of the Equal Protection Clause: the abolition of governmental barriers presenting unreasonable obstacles to advancement based on individual merit. . . . This law imposes a lifetime of hardship on a discrete class of children not accountable for their disabling status" (*Plyler v. Doe*, 1982).

Plyler is still the law of the land, despite attempts by various states and Congress to reverse its effects. The lofty, well-reasoned arguments of the Court notwithstanding, undocumented students are still a vulnerable school population because of their precarious status outside of the school and their struggles with English in the classroom (Rabin, Combs, and Gonzalez, 2008).[2]

Language Matters

"What do you call a person who speaks two languages?"
"Bilingual."
"Okay, and what do you call a person who knows only one?"
"American."

Bilingual speakers outnumber monolingual speakers around the world, and bilingualism is associated with a wide range of cognitive benefits, from better problem-solving skills to improved memory and attention (Adesope et al., 2010). Americans claim to admire bilingualism, a traditional measure of a well-educated person, and typically express envy of anyone who can speak two or more languages. Multilingual job seekers are at an advantage in careers ranging from business to national security, but rarely do American schools encourage English-dominant speakers to become proficient in a second language. Bilingual education has come to mean that all students must learn to speak English no matter how many other languages they speak fluently, and English speakers need not worry about mastering another language (Lopez and Lopez, 2010). The unidirectional approach to second-language instruction penalizes students with limited English proficiency, imposing academic burdens on them not faced by English-dominant speakers. Language instruction of this sort serves to devalue languages other than English, and because language cannot be separated from culture, it denigrates the cultures of speakers of other languages (Salomone, 2010).

The U.S. Congress has been responsive to the role schools play in teaching increasing numbers of ELLs in the classroom. In 1967, Senator Ralph Yarborough of Texas introduced legislation to help school districts create programs for students who did not speak English as a first language at home. Senator Yarborough's bill, aimed at Spanish-speaking students, was designed to teach English as a second language while strengthening the students' heritage language skills and knowledge of their cultural past. Students would be assisted in the development of English, the language essential for their economic security and social integration, and this new learning would not come at the expense of losing their cultural history and original language. The legislation was merged with over thirty other bills and became known as Title VII of

---

[2]Courts in the United States have been sympathetic to the language rights of students who do not speak English as a first language. In 1974, for example, the Supreme Court ruled that the City of San Francisco violated the Civil Rights Act of 1964, which bans discrimination based on "race, color, or national origin," when it had failed to offer appropriate bilingual education to children of Chinese ancestry (*Lau v. Nichols*, 1974). Another case, decided in 1981, found that in order to comply with the *Lau* decision, schools must serve ELLs through programs that follow "sound educational theory" and established principles of good teaching (*Castaneda v. Pickard*, 1981).

the Elementary and Secondary Education Act or the Bilingual Education Act of 1968. Although the legislation did not explicitly require bilingual instruction or teaching in the students' heritage language, it supported innovative multicultural curricula and multilingual instruction (Stewner-Manzanares, 1988).

Adjusting to American schooling is no easy matter for many children of immigrants. Multiple social forces influence the academic success of the children of newcomers, including the difficulties associated with the stress of migration, the separations from long-standing cultural traditions, and, for many immigrants, the complex interplay of poverty, racism, social segregation, and identify formation with new cultural rules (Suarez-Orozco and Todorova, 2003). The education of ELLs has been the center of controversy, and it is not surprising that misconceptions have developed about the programs. You may have heard some or all of the following comments about bilingual education:

- Learning two languages, especially during the early childhood years, confuses children and delays the acquisition of English.
- Total English immersion is the most effective way for ELLs to acquire English.
- Native speakers of English suffer academically if they are enrolled in dual language programs.
- Spanish-speaking Latinos show social and academic delays as early as kindergarten (Espinosa, 2008).

These are all examples of popular myths that do not stand up to academic scrutiny. As Crawford (2007) writes, "A generation of research and practice has shown that developing academic skills and knowledge in students' vernacular supports their acquisition of English" (p. 146). In fact, bilingualism is an asset to all children in a multicultural society, and research reviewed by Espinosa and others demonstrates that young children are capable of learning two languages (NCTE ELL Task Force, 2006; Espinosa, 2008). Researchers have also found that instruction in both English and the heritage language can effectively introduce newcomer children to the success patterns of the dominant culture without denigrating or destroying the home culture, while the loss of home languages has negative consequences for student learning (Adams and Kirova, 2007; Crawford, 2007; Faltis and Coulter, 2008).

Despite these research findings, the federal No Child Left Behind (NCLB) legislation, aimed at promoting accountability, equity, and school reform, neither prohibits nor encourages the development of native language skills and dual language acquisition; bilingualism and biliteracy are not among its goals (National Association for Bilingual Education [NABE], 2007).

ELLs and NCLB

The No Child Left Behind Act of 2001 was designed to hold all learners to high academic standards and ensure that specific subsets of the student population were not ignored or allowed to fall between the cracks of public education. NCLB focuses attention on all categories of student learners, including the historically neglected population of language-minority learners. This is all to the good. Students are generally considered to be advantaged when schools are held accountable for the achievement gains of all learners. Few argue with the spirit of NCLB, but problems abound in this legislation, particularly with the ways in which ELLs are to be assessed (NABE, 2007; Kieffer et al., 2009; Solorzano, 2008).

In 2010, the executive director of Teachers of English to Speakers of Other Languages (TESOL) wrote a letter to the chairman and the ranking member of the Committee on Health, Education, Labor and Pensions of the U.S. Senate expressing her organization's concerns about NCLB tests, noting that "systems built on inappropriate assessment tools or built around the use of a singular test for high-stakes decisions will undermine, rather than promote, the academic success of English language learners." TESOL recommended, among other thing, that all assessments allow the use of multiple measures to assess and report the progress of ELLs, such as curriculum-based rubrics and holistic assessments, and that the native language skills of ELLs should be developed alongside their English language skills (Aronson, 2010, pp. 1–4).

TESOL's objections to NCLB's reliance on single high-stakes exams resonates with the arguments of other antitesting educators, but the well-intentioned goals of NCLB may have especially negative consequences for ELLs. As noted, ELLs are not likely to do well on subject-matter tests in a language that is not the language in which they were introduced to the academic discourse of the subject, that is, the language of instruction. To make matters worse, it is hard if not impossible to determine whether poor student performance is attributable to the student's difficulties with the content or with the language of the exams. In a real sense, every test of content is also a test of language skills (Kieffer et al., 2009).

ELLs, similar to other subgroups labeled under NCLB, must score in the "proficient" range on state exams by 2014, or the schools they attend will face sanctions. The NABE (2007) argues that NCLB will ultimately harm schools and ELL programs: "Virtually all schools with significant ELL enrollments will soon be in the 'failing' category. It is hard to see how such an indiscriminate 'accountability' system . . . has anything to do with improving schools." NCLB threatens the schools attended by ELLs. Referred to by some researchers as its "diversity penalty," the NCLB legislation "requires the largest gains from lower-performing schools, although these schools serve needier students and generally have fewer resources than schools serving wealthier students" (Darling-Hammond, 2008, p. 164).

NABE has joined with more than thirty education and civil rights organizations calling for the overhaul and reorganization of NCLB. Among other elements, NABE (2007) recommends that NCLB legislation allow states and school districts to do the following:

- Develop alternative assessments, in both English and the student's native language, to measure more accurately the student's content knowledge
- Promote the student's native language
- Guarantee that all ELLs, independent of English language proficiency, have access to the full range of school services and educational programs

Cultural Challenges: Teaching More Than Language Skills

Great achievements were the product of [the immigrants'] labors; without their contributions the country could not have taken the form it did. But they paid a heavy price, not only in the painful process of crossing and resettlement but also in the continuous ache of uprootedness. . . . And to the extent that the process succeeded, a widening gulf developed between the immigrants and their children. (Handlin, 1966, pp. xiii, xiv)

Immigration has always been a difficult and stressful experience for newcomer families. Immigrants leave behind friends and familiar ways, and older family members often forfeit esteemed community roles and assume lower social status and lesser-valued employment in the United States. Children of immigrants may struggle in schools as they wrestle with the different culture and unfamiliar language of their new home (Gaytan et al., 2007). Americans have always celebrated the success stories of this nation of immigrants. Today, as in the past, many immigrants do very well in school and life, but many more are at risk of failure. As Suarez-Orozco and Gardner (2003) write, "Our research indicates that while some [children of immigrants] will end up as the beneficiaries of life in the new land, too many others are unable to cope with the global dislocations. As we have come to put it, the life options become Yale or Jail, Princeton or Prison" (p. 3).

Schools can help expand the range of successful options. Schooling is central to the processes by which the children of immigrants are taught to survive and prosper and forge a better life in their new country (Suarez-Orozco, Suarez-Orozco, and Todorova, 2008). In schools, the children of immigrants learn the skills necessary for academic success. Newcomers also experience schools as cultural sites where they are introduced to the social "rules" of American society, and they meet teachers, typically members of the dominant culture, who help them understand their new country and find their way in it. Because of their experience with formal schooling and, typically, their greater language facility, children of immigrants are often asked to play the role of "culture brokers" for their parents and families. These young people, with a foot in each of two worlds, are often called on to mediate the conflicting expectations and experiences of host and heritage cultures while trying to honor both (Adams and Kirova, 2007). Informed teachers, sensitive to immigration issues, can help students navigate between the two worlds.

Schools need to take into account the differences between today's immigrants and the immigrants of earlier periods. It is not uncommon to hear immigrant success stories about someone's grandparents who came to America, learned English in night school, and gave up the ways of the "old country" in order to succeed in America. The old model of assimilation—in which immigrants abandoned heritage languages and cultural identity to become part of the "melting pot" of America—has given way to an understanding that many of today's immigrants want to be bilingual and bicultural and will remain "unmeltable." New immigrants are less willing to follow a path that promises success at the expense of depriving themselves and their children of language diversity and cultural history (Salomone, 2010). They argue that success will follow more comfortably by embracing old and new worlds. Speaking more than one language and being at home in more than one culture can only be of benefit in a multilingual, multicultural world.

Success in schools has always been important to the children of newcomers, but it may be more important today than any time in our history. Given the nature of the American economy, doing well in school is central to economic survival and social integration. In the earlier days of high migration to the United States, schooling certainly figured prominently in individual success, but today, when the U.S. economy has few meaningful jobs for those who do not complete high school, school success matters more than ever (Suarez-Orozco et al., 2008). Schools can help the children of immigrants achieve academically without uprooting them from the traditions of their families. Schools and teachers can help the children of new immigrants preserve their heritage language and culture and maintain their own historical identity while mastering English and the values and skills necessary for economic and social advancement in the United States (Suarez-Orozco and Qin-Hilliard, 2004; Adams and Kirova, 2007; Suarez-Orozco et al., 2008; White and Glick, 2009).

Fearmongering

You may have heard about or read an email claiming that "illegal immigrants" are costing American taxpayers hundreds of billions of dollars a year, more than the financial burden of the wars in Iraq and Afghanistan. This would be shocking if it were true, but an investigation by an independent agency found the claims "rife with errors," generated by groups seeking greater restrictions on immigrants and immigration (FactCheck, 2009). This is an example of fear mongering. What are the reasons for so much anti-immigrant rhetoric? Hard economic times? Foreign terrorism? Simple bias toward new immigrants? It's hard to know, but anti-immigrant sentiment is not unprecedented in the United States, especially when the economy is weak and unemployment is high. During the Great Depression of the 1930s, for example, Americans blamed immigrants for the nation's problems and worried that immigrants would take the jobs of the native-born workers. Two in three Americans believed that "aliens on relief [public assistance] should be sent back to their own countries" (Allen, 2010).

Today, despite a struggling economy, immigrants take low-paying jobs that native-born workers find unattractive, and as workers they pay as much in taxes as government returns to them in the form of services. Immigrants pay social security tax, property tax, sales tax, and income tax. Similar to their native-born counterparts, immigrants lacking a high school diploma impose a net fiscal drain on the economy. That is, immigrants without a high school degree pay less in taxes than the value of the services they receive. The difference drops for immigrants with high school degrees, and immigrants with more than a high school degree generate a fiscal benefit (Camarota, 2009). Immigrants with high skills and/or a high level of education contribute positively to the American economy. Overall, immigrants as a group are not an economic burden. Averaging the contributions and benefits of educated and less-well-educated immigrants, "for the U.S. economy, immigration appears to be more or less awash" (Hanson, 2007, p. 24).

Education has been the traditional key to economic success for all immigrants, past and present, and education can also serve the 11.2 million unauthorized immigrants now living in the United States. Unauthorized immigrants—immigrants who are not legally in the United States—number about 11.2 million, roughly 28 percent of the foreign-born population currently living in the country (Passel and Cohn, 2011). Like everyone else, they need access to schools and school services to enhance their lives, but they are handicapped by their "unauthorized" status. In a review of research, Suarez-Orozco and her colleagues find that millions of immigrant children in the United States are at risk of lower educational performance and limited economic futures because of their unauthorized status. The reviewers conclude "that unauthorized status harms [personal] development, from beginning of life through adolescence and young adulthood, by restricting access to some of the most important pathways to adult well-being and productivity"— beginning with the availability of child care and pre-schools and extending to higher education and subsequent paths to employment (Suarez-Orozco, 2011, p. 462).

Several remedies have been formulated to address the ambiguous status of unauthorized young immigrants, unblocking their potential and bringing economic benefit to them and the nation. The DREAM Act, for example, is one promising piece of federal legislation aimed at undocumented youth fifteen years of age or younger. Although many of these young people have been living in the United States for most of their lives, they currently struggle with the label "illegal immigrants."[3] The DREAM Act, introduced with bipartisan political support, is designed to assist unauthorized immigrants become part of American society. An acronym for Development, Relief, and Education for Alien Minors, DREAM legislation would grant unauthorized youth of good moral character permanent residency status in the United States, and it would open a path to citizenship and economic success not now available. The unauthorized immigrants would have to meet certain conditions, including graduation from high school and completion of a college degree in six years or honorable military service of two years. DREAM legislation has been introduced in both houses of Congress regularly since 2001, but it has not yet become law. When it is passed by Congress and signed by the president, young unauthorized immigrants will be able to contribute to the nation's prosperity and progress and be recognized for what they are: newcomers from other lands who want to be Americans (Dream Act Portal, 2011).

---

[3]"Illegal" and "alien" used as adjectives to modify "immigrant" have an unsavory connotation suggesting something criminal. For children, immigrant status is typically acquired through the decisions and actions taken by their parents or other adults. Negative labels serve only to make the lives of unauthorized newcomers more difficult (Suarez-Orozco, 2011, p. 440).

Summary

The DREAM Act is in harmony with the history of immigration in the United States and the ways in which education helps newly arrived immigrants and serves national ends. Immigrants have always needed the schools, and the nation has always needed the immigrants and prospered from their contributions to the culture and the economy. Schools will adjust to the new immigrants, encourage their aspirations, and help them flourish for the good of the students and the nation as a whole. Helping immigrants find their place in America and equipping them with the tools necessary to succeed have always been the responsibility of schools. It is simply business as usual.

POSITION 2: BAD POLICY OVERBURDENS SCHOOLS

The average immigrant comes to this country much poorer and far less edu-cated than Americans and consumes far more per capita in public services. Economically, immigrants are a net burden on the nation. . . . We are on a treadmill we will never get off if we do not get control of immigration.

—Buchanan (2006, pp. 43, 46)

This cultural struggle over the future of America—and the very definition of America—underlies the immigration fight. The gap between the leftist elites and the rest of America could hardly be broader.

—Gingrich (2008, p. 129)

Education Problems from Immigration, Legal and Illegal

The relation of new immigrants to schools is complex. Historic, political, legal, and cultural issues surround the question of how immigration influences edu-cation. Current massive problems in legal and illegal immigration demonstrate our nation's lack of intelligent control, identification, and law enforcement as well as a lack of adequate funding for the additional social services required. Schools did not create these problems, but they bear much of the brunt of the predicament. Educational problems that stem from weak and ineffective immi-gration policies and practices should be examined within that larger context (Brimelow, 2008).

Long-term problems in immigration policy, implementation, and enforce-ment create unfair and inadequate conditions, especially with regard to those who come into or stay in the United States illegally. Some illegals are smug-gled in, some enter on fraudulent documents, some climb fences or run across fields, and some come legitimately on short-term student or work visas but do not leave when the visa expires. Opportunities for employment and other conditions that make the United States a desirable migration destination, cou-pled with weak national controls and enforcement of laws, have produced a situation of immigration chaos. We have vast numbers of illegals and public outrage that sometimes questions all immigration, legal or not. Human rights, employment, security, economic, taxation, political, and cultural issues arise in this setting. Education is another of the significant issues influenced by and influencing immigration.

Inconsistent policies and disparate practices create special problems and expenses for schools with immigrant populations. Legal immigration is now at record levels in the United States, and illegal immigration produces large but uncharted numbers. The Census Bureau calculates net immigration between 2000 and 2007 at almost 8 million, not accounting for illegal immigrants. In 2010, the official number receiving legal permanent residency (green card) was over 1 million; the Migration Policy Institute (2006) estimates the actual number of legal immigrants to be over 1.8 million annually. Illegal immigration, for obvious reasons, is much more difficult to determine. One source, using U.S. census data, estimates the total number of illegal aliens at over 23 million (Immigration Counters, 2011). Other organizations estimate illegals at between 12 million and 14 million. Uncontrolled future immigration will cause 82 percent of the projected increase in U.S. population between 2005 and 2050, from about 300 million to 438 million. (Pew Research Center, 2008; Passel and Cohn, 2011).

Large-scale legal and illegal immigration presents severe problems for society and schools. The sheer numbers of immigrants, necessary screening and record keeping, expensive special provisions to meet their divergent needs, and potential policing, enforcement, and social welfare requirements to maintain American qualities all impose costs on social services. Buchanan (2006) put the added social costs for schooling, health care, welfare, Social Security, and prisons at about $400 billion per year, far more than the taxes immigrants pay, plus the costs of extra "pressure on land, water, and power resources" (p. 35).

Schooling, alone, is costly: over 5.5 million children of illegal immigrants are in schools in the United States at a total taxpayer cost conservatively estimated at $179 billion since 1996 (Immigration Counters, 2011). According to a study by the Federation for American Immigration Reform (FAIR), education is the largest of taxpayer cost for all services used by illegal immigrants. They estimate the main health and related social services bill at about $113 billion per year, and school spending has now increased to about $52 billion annually. That calculates to more than $1,100 per regular taxpayer household per year just for schooling those here illegally, and it is borne largely by citizens at the state and local levels. States recoup only about 5 percent of this cost through collecting various taxes from illegal immigrants (FAIR, 2011).

Efforts to enact legislation to permit illegal immigrants to attend state-funded colleges and universities at low, subsidized in-state rates can increase taxpayer costs further. In addition, in times when higher-education budgets are being cut and resources strained, institutions are limiting admissions. Illegal students could be displacing qualified students who are legal residents.

Illegal immigration causes higher net costs for schools and other social services than legal immigration. Two-thirds of illegal aliens have not graduated from high school, thus earning less income and contributing less in taxes—while requiring more from U.S. public education and social services. These findings are consistent with a National Research Council study (Smith and Edmonston,

1997) showing that immigrant educational level is the "key determinant of their fiscal impact" (Center for Immigration Studies, 2008, p. 1).

Questions surround American immigration policies in regard to education. Should schools be responsible—and accountable—for the education of all immigrants, legal and illegal? Should this all be taxpayer financed? Should that include taxpayer-subsidized higher education? Should we place no educational barriers on those who want to enter our nation? Should we be concerned about disparities between the levels of schooling of some immigrant groups and others and as compared with levels of regular citizens? Should we require demonstrated fluency in English, knowledge of American history and government, and allegiance to America before immigrants are granted permanent status? These questions are politically thorny.

School Responsibilities, Immigrant Needs, and Who Pays

In 1982, the Supreme Court split five to four in a decision that the Equal Protection Clause of the Constitution required public schools to admit illegal alien children (*Plyler v. Doe*, 1982). The specific conditions that led to that decision could change. The court determined then that admission of illegals would not damage the educational opportunities of citizens' children and that there was no solid evidence that the United States actually intended to deport the illegal parents. If those conditions change or if Congress legislates a school exclusion for these illegal students, there could be a different outcome (FAIR, 2002). For now, that is the law.

Schools are expected to provide basic knowledge, skills, and corrective educational assistance to immigrant children and to help Americanize and integrate them into society. Schools also offer their parents and other immigrant adults avenues to self-improvement and preparation for citizenship. Immigrants from a variety of nations show wide differences in their educational attainment, skills, attitudes toward American traditions and values, English language fluency, and requirements for public assistance.

The gap between regular citizen-student academic achievement and that of immigrants is growing. Data from the Organization for Economic Cooperation and Development show that U.S. immigration caused high school graduation rates in the United States to drop from being the best in the world to being lower than that of sixteen other nations (FAIR, 2002). For a school district, these incoming immigrant educational differences create multiple problems with corollary extra costs. For example, the New York City schools recently identified about 175 different languages among its students. The extra costs and difficulties finding and keeping well-prepared teaching and school staffs to provide appropriate school and other services for this diversity are immense. Table 7.1 shows some characteristics of immigrants by selected states in 2006.

For most states, the current source of the majority of immigrants is Latin America. The percentage of immigrants who have limited English proficiency (LEP) is very high in many of these states; the national average LEP is 52 percent, an increase of 25 percent between 2000 and 2006. The proportion of immigrants

Table 7.1 Selected Characteristics of Immigrants by State, 2006

State	% Population	Source	%	LEP %	No High School Diploma
California	27%	Latin America	53%	59%	37%
New York	21	Latin America	53	46	26
Texas	16	Latin America	74	62	47
Florida	19	Latin America	73	49	25
Illinois	14	Latin America	48	56	31
New Jersey	20	Latin America	46	46	22
Washington	12	Asia	31	49	28
U.S. average	21%			52%	32%

Source: Migration Policy Institute (2008).

who have not completed high school is also high and climbing in these states. The national average is 32 percent, a 50 percent increase in the past ten years. For illegals, the numbers without high school diplomas and with more limited English proficiency are much higher, with higher associated educational costs.

The FAIR report shows that the annual national extra educational cost to taxpayers for illegal immigrant students is more than $7.4 billion (Collins, 2008; FAIR, 2011). Schooling costs from illegal immigration are usually without compensatory funds. Former California Governor Pete Wilson tried to get federal funds to pay, but the case was not adjudicated. Among individual states, California spends about $2.2 billion extra per year. Texas spends over $1 billion annually, Florida about $308 million, Georgia about $231 million, and Illinois about $484 million each year (Collins, 2008).

Birthright-Citizenship

One of the peculiarities of U.S. immigration policy is the provision for birthright citizenship; as the Fourteenth amendment to the Constitution provides, "All persons born or naturalized in the United States, and subject to the jurisdiction thereof, are citizens of the United States and of the state wherein they reside." This amendment, adopted in 1868, was designed primarily to provide citizenship to African Americans at the end of the Civil War, but it is now used by illegal immigrants to obtain U.S. citizenship for the children they bear here. For a fee, smugglers offer to get pregnant women into the United States to have a child. These babies are called "anchor babies" because they provide a legal connection to the United States and offer many benefits to the parents from citizenship application assistance, social welfare, and health to education rights. They also provide a means for sympathy and appeals for leniency when the parents are caught and deportation is likely. Only about 17 percent of the nations of the world have such a birthright-citizenship policy (Lacey, 2011).

The Pew Hispanic Center estimates that about 340,000 of the 4.3 million babies born in the United States in 2008 were to illegals (Pew Research Center, 2010).

Illegal immigrants account for about 4 percent of the total adult U.S. population, but about 8 percent of the population of children; immigrant parents tend to be younger and have higher birthrates than citizens. By 2011, the main reason for high growth rates among Hispanics in the United States was births. Between 2000 and 2010, for example, the Mexican American population grew 7.2 million by birth and 4.2 million by regular immigration (Pew Research Center, 2011).

Political efforts are under way to alter the Fourteenth Amendment by amending it or using legislation and/or court decisions to severely limit birthright-citizenship (*The Economist*, 2011). Surveys find that about 40 percent of citizens favor changing the Constitution to prohibit automatic citizenship for American-born children of illegals. Birthright-citizenship has implications for education, including financing the extra costs, language use, parental fear and invisibility, legal student rights, care for the student if arrest and deportation loom for parents, and others.

A related cost issue for American taxpayers is in the DREAM Act, an act giving a form of permanent residency to children of illegal immigrants for purposes of attending public colleges and universities at low, in-state tuition rates and who could be eligible for full citizenship. This means that taxpayers will be subsidizing the tuition for illegals and that they can jump the line for permanent residency ahead of some who came here legally and are abiding by the rules.

More Than Direct Cost

Poorly controlled immigration gives more than just money problems to schools. Immigrants from highly diverse cultural, tribal, religious, and economic backgrounds, when mixed in the schools, create conditions for significant misunderstandings and potentially explosive environments. Differences stimulate the development of school-disruptive behaviors like gangs, bullying, ethnic slurs, extortion, violence, and threats. They also contribute to student segregation by immigrant group, intimidation, and necessarily restrictive school rules with enforcement officers. This is not consistent with the idea of school as a safe place to gain knowledge and develop positive attitudes toward the nation.

English language fluency is a particular problem with current immigration policies and practices. Not only do many immigrants come with nonexistent or extremely limited English skills, but they often do not want to gain those skills and thus become more estranged from American society and create a further drain on social services. Jarzen (2009) argues that "bilingualism, diversity, and multiculturalisms undermine our national identity . . . the current crop of immigrants have failed at successfully becoming Americans." Akresh and Akresh (2011) point out that proficiency in English is "essential for labor market success" (p. 648). Without English and job skills, they can fall under social welfare protections and need extra costly assistance. They create other problems as well in such areas as getting medical attention or legal assistance (Barclay, 2009; Southern Poverty Law Center, 2009). While over 92 percent of all nations have an official language, we do not. This creates frustrations and public costs in multiple-language documents, ballots, intrepreters, and related social interactions. Over thirty states have enacted laws that stipulate English as the official language, a necessary improvement that should be supported by national legislation and an immigration policy that favors those who are fluent in English (see www.usenglish.org).

A further illustration of this educational problem with immigrants is shown in current school dropout rates among immigrant youth. In New York City, that rate approaches 20 percent for many immigrant groups, while the overall rate in the city is about 9 percent. But for Mexican immigrants the school dropout rate is over 40 percent. Among Mexican immigrants of college age (nineteen to twenty-three), only 6 percent are in higher education, a small fraction of college enrollees from other groups (Semple, 2011). And Mexican immigrants are the fastest growing of all major immigrant groups. These issues are obviously related to language facility, but they also reflect broader questions of immigrant integration and portend future problems, as lesser-educated immigrants are less able to find good jobs and pay appropriate taxes, becoming burdensome on social welfare programs.

The special teaching, curricular, and staff needs created by an influx of immigrants distract schools from their primary purposes for local citizens, requiring additional care and effort. Immigrants are more likely to need other social services, like school nurses and social workers, draining funds from regular school activities.

How did we reach this position where legal and illegal immigration cause such problems for our schools?

Immigration Policies: A Study in Turmoil

Immigration is America's great tradition and glory; it is also its great peril. We are a nation founded by immigrants, and we remain prideful of immigrant contributions to culture, industry, technology, and life. This extraordinary tradition is honored as we eat Italian or Thai or Mexican meals, use computers and televisions invented and enhanced by Irish Americans and Japanese Americans, buy furniture and clothing designed by French Americans and Swedish Americans, and use an imported English language enlarged by contributions from many other languages.

Immigration, if it can be intelligently controlled, balanced, and enforced, helps the United States. But despite periodic public alarm, we have failed to control immigration. Our immigration policies veered from open door to restrictions by nationality and personal history, then to allowing increasing numbers and amnesty for some. Presumably, restrictive laws have not been followed up with serious enforcement and actual control.

The current large-scale immigration wave is the fourth in our history (Leonhardt, 2008). Political reaction to each of the previous great waves—in the 1850s, 1880s, and 1900s—was intense and restrictions ensued. Anti-immigration movements developed as each wave became more threatening to Americans. Laws were passed to limit immigration with modest results in attempts to bring more orderliness to the process. Table 7.2 shows the main waves of immigration per 1,000 American citizens by decade since the early 1820s.

Table 7.2 Average Annual Immigration per 1,000 Citizens							
1.3	12.1	10.5	11.0	4.0	0.6	4.8	5.1
1820–1830	1850–1860	1880–1890	1900–1910	1920–1930	1940–1950	1980–1990	2000–2010

Source: Pew Research Center, 2008.

The United States was concerned about risks in naturalizing immigrants from unfriendly nations too quickly in the 1790s, but until the 1870s, we encouraged immigration as helpful to build society. Then, in 1875, we barred immigration by convicts and prostitutes, adding paupers and "mentally defectives" to the immigrant ban in 1882, when we also halted Chinese immigration for ten years, extending that ban until 1943. Congress passed laws for two decades to require a literacy test of immigrants, but these laws were vetoed by three presidents before Woodrow Wilson's second veto was overridden in 1917 and all adult immigrants had to be able to read in some language. Immigration laws in the 1920s limited annual streams to 150,000, plus immediate families, and imposed a quota system favoring immigrants from northern and western Europe.

These quotas were eliminated in 1965, and later modifications increased the total annual immigrant limits. Immigration reform laws in 1986 tried to restrict illegal immigration by penalizing employers and offering amnesty to some illegals who came forward. Enforcement has been very uneven, even nonexistent, and illegal immigration expanded to our current estimates of 12 million to 23 million, but no exact figures exist. Legislation in the 1990s increased the annual number of legal immigrants from 270,000 to 675,000 and doubled the number of visas for economic and employment purposes to 140,000 (Meilander, 2001; Cornelius et al., 2004; Morris and McGann, 2007; Leonhardt, 2008), and we now have record numbers.

America's Great Peril

The peril to America is not from the idea of immigration. We have an immigrant tradition, but that occurred over a long time and a smaller scale. One aspect of the peril is simply the relative size of immigrant groups. Buchanan (2006) points out that there are 36 million foreign born now in the United States—three times the number that immigrated in the so-called Great Wave of 1910—and that "the Border Patrol catches as many illegal aliens every month as all the legal immigrants who came to America in the 1920s" (p. 10). Such large numbers produce dislocations, suspicions, economic uncertainty, and fear among existing citizens. The size of immigrant groups creates difficult assimilation conditions, taxes social services, and undermines local employment arrangements and social conditions.

A second important aspect of the peril to America is the disorderly, disruptive, and potentially dangerous illegal acts of people who come into America without proper authorization or who stay longer than their visas permit. The main threats of unfettered and uncontrolled immigration include the obvious: crime, disease, national security, undercutting American workers, dislocation in low-income communities, and overloading social services like health and education. One-third of all patients treated in the Los Angeles health system each year are illegal aliens (FAIR, 2008).

Between 2000 and 2005, about 4.5 million illegals were caught trying to break in to the United States, and more than 300,000 of them had criminal records (Buchanan, 2006). That is one criminal in every twelve immigrants, and that is only among illegals who were caught. The current immigration issue differs significantly from those in the past in that a large number of immigrants have come illegally or overstayed their visas and have become illegal. We have done little to fully identify these illegal immigrants or to enforce the laws that they have broken. Simply coming over our borders without official permission or overstaying an authorized visa is a crime. Those who intentionally engage in these activities are criminals. It is illegal for good reason. Open access to public schools should not be a reward for illegal activity.

A third aspect of the peril for America by uncontrolled immigration is more esoteric but important: challenges to American values, national unity, social relations, and commonalities of spirit that define the United States. Finding and nurturing common grounds for social life is a long and often grueling process; it can easily be fractured by competing ideologies from immigrant groups.

Our national security, national integrity, and economy depend on controlling our borders and developing clear and reasoned policies to limit immigration. We welcome immigrants who follow the rules. Most of our immigrant ancestors endured long and difficult journeys to come here. They applied for permission to enter, and those who desired citizenship fulfilled requirements that included good health, a law-abiding history, learning English, and passing a test of American history and government. They understood the needs for national security and border integrity that require laws, rules, and regulations regarding immigration. They desired opportunities and rights that American citizenship provides, and they used their time, energy, intelligence, and commitment to fulfill those requirements. They were often leaving places where those opportunities and rights did not exist.

True, some legal immigrants also have criminal records, serious health problems, or antipathy to American ideals, but they were often weeded out through the application, waiting, educational, and testing process for citizenship. And we had records for them. Rules and regulations worked in these cases to protect America. Orderly immigration and legitimate educational requirements well serve those who have properly immigrated.

Needed Basic Immigration Policies: Immigration Policy in the National Interest

America needs a thorough and vigilant border protection system as a beginning point. In an age of terrorist threats, fast transportation, and massive population shifts, a sound immigration policy has to start with full control of our borders

(Auster, 2003). That can mean fences, electronic monitoring, active and frequent land and air patrols, night-vision imaging, lighting, and similar screening devices. They work (Von Drehle, 2008). It can also mean personal identification that cannot be compromised, coordinated international verification and tracking systems, and speedy deportation arrangements.

We also need improved control over legal entry as visitors, workers, and scholars. This requires complete and verifiable application data, with continuing full information on travel and contact locations for all entrants to improve our ability to find them when their authorized visitation time is nearing completion. Our visa limits must be stringently enforced, with severe and enforced penalties for overstaying without permission.

We need clear and simple federal procedures for immigration and for illegals. Employers and sponsors should be legally responsible for checking positive identification for legality, with verification from government agencies, before employment. We should strengthen all bans on the hiring of illegal immigrants, with serious penalties that increase if the offense is repeated. In the meantime, we should do better enforcement of existing laws governing immigrant employment, identification, and supervision. The European Union recently passed tougher laws on immigration, with longer detention and easier expulsion (Brothers, 2008).

Our immigration system should be tuned primarily to improving our nation, with humanitarian and other purposes next in order. More intelligent and limited immigration policies are necessary to coordinate our national needs for well-educated people in particular fields. We must cut the sheer numbers of immigrants to ensure the continuation of American values and traditions, and we must encourage the best and brightest of those who want to come to the United States and who have skills complementary to our national interests. At a minimum, we should require at least high school graduation for all adult immigrants.

We must require demonstrated fluency in English as basic to permanent residency or citizenship, and we should provide government information, except for tourist purposes, only in English. A knowledge of American history, government, and economics and agreement with values should also be required of anyone applying for naturalization. Schools have responsibilities for this education; smaller numbers of and mandated minimal education requirements for immigrants can mitigate the costs and problems.

Summary

American immigration policies and practices continue as divisive and controversial social issues. A history of mostly dysfunctional approaches to immigration purposes, control, balance, and enforcement haunts us. Since before our nation's founding, we have argued about immigration and the relation of education to that process. Benjamin Franklin, in 1753, noted that bad immigration policies may create "great disorders" among us. He concluded that if the new German immigrants were distributed equally and mixed well with the English, *with English schools established in immigrant neighborhoods,* then there could be some benefit (Abbott, cited in Borjas, 1999, emphasis added).

Some immigrants have made major contributions to American education and to our culture. Many have used our open educational system as a springboard to a better life. Escaping oppression and finding freedom are educational, and so is trying to better oneself financially. But those may not be sufficient grounds for a national policy that only limits legal immigration by numbers and weak immigration practices that have allowed 12 million to 23 million illegal immigrants to remain—and to remain unidentified.

It is only with intelligent immigration reform and consistent enforcement practices that we can hope to deal with the educational problems that flow from the current immigration situation.

Immigration and education are linked. Lack of control and coordination of immigration creates problems for schools and society. Mass immigration threatens the basic fiber of the nation and overloads the schools. Illegal immigration has exploded, is hidden, and is a peril to our country. Immigration reform is necessary not only for national security and to promote our national interest but also to help schools refocus on their primary purposes for American citizens.

For Discussion

1. A Pew Research Center report (Passel and Cohn, 2008), covering U.S. population projections until 2050, contains the following key points:
   - Almost 20 percent of the U.S. population in 2050 will be immigrants.
   - The elderly population will increase by more than double, and the working-age group will decline as a percentage of population.
   - Hispanics, currently the largest minority group, will triple in size, becoming about 29 percent of the population.

   If this develops,
   a. What would you identify as the most important positive and negative consequences from this?
   b. What are the likely impacts of each point on schooling by 2050?
   c. What recommendations would you make to help the schools prepare for each of those potential impacts?
   d. What social, cultural, and economic impacts would you expect from this change?

   If you think this projection is negative for the United States,
   a. What would you propose for changing immigration policies and practices?
   b. How would your proposals affect schools?
   c. How would your proposals affect social and economic conditions in the United States and in the world?

2. Some experts maintain the thesis that the United States needs an expanding younger population to support economic growth and social services in addition to extending cultural development. The national birthrate is not at a level to do that and is unlikely to change, so immigration is needed whether legal or illegal.
   a. What evidence exists that confirms or contests this?
   b. What is a reasonable antithesis to this approach?

   c. Identify the main positive and negative consequences for the United States if either the thesis or the antithesis becomes public policy.

   d. Describe a viable synthesis of this issue.

   e. How would your proposed synthesis influence education in the United States?

3. Drachman and Langran (2008) state, "Language has become one of the most important and contentious problems in the United States. A major reason is that it is interlaced with a number of other highly controversial issues such as politics, immigration, civil rights, citizenship, equality of educational opportunity, and American culture and national identity. . . . Historically, the public schools have been the great Americanizing force, with the teaching of English their major tool" (p. 65).

   a. What evidence supports and what evidence is in opposition to their view about the level of controversy about language in the United States?

   b. Identify and evaluate some examples of how language is or is not interlaced with the list of other factors (e.g., politics, immigration, and civil rights) noted in the quote above. Pay special attention to examples involving immigration.

   c. If the authors are correct about language as one of the most problematic current issues, what does that say about the effectiveness of the public schools in its Americanizing role over history?

   d. Discuss how schools have attempted to meet their role in Americanizing and how English language instruction is related to that role.

   e. Develop a proposal for how schools could better address any language issues, with a focus on new immigrants.

4. Over 550,000 foreign students come to study each year in colleges and universities in the United States, but only a small proportion (65,000 in 2009) are able to obtain special visas, known as H-1B visas, to stay on for work in the United States. And these visas are awarded in a lottery system that is oversubscribed each year. The United Kingdom's immigration policy, however, is to welcome those it identifies as most likely to make contributions to the British nations, with no lottery.

   a. What are the main arguments for and against the policies in the United States and the United Kingdom?

   b. Whose interests are served under each policy?

   c. What would you expect to be the long-term results of both policies?

   d. If one policy is seen as a thesis and the other an antithesis, what would be a suitable synthesis?

References

ADAMS, L. D., AND KIROVA, A. eds. (2007). *Global Migration and Education*. Mahwah, NJ: Lawrence Erlbaum Associates.

ADESCOPE, O. O., ET AL. (2010). "A Systematic Review and Meta-Analysis of the Cognitive Correlates of Bilingualism." *Review of Educational Research* 80(2):207–245.

AKRESH, R., AND AKRESH, I. R. (2011). "Using Achievement Tests to Measure Language Assimilation and Language Bias among the Children of Immigrants." *Journal of Human Resources* 46(3):647–667.

ALLEN, J. T. (2010). "How a Different American Responded to the Great Depression." www.pewresearch.org/pubs/1810.

ARONSON, R. (2010). "Letter to the Honorable Tom Harkins and the Honorable Mike Enzi, United States Senate." May 4, http: www.tesol.org.

AUSTER, L. (2003). "Erasing America: Politics of the Borderless Nation." www.aic foundation.org

Bank Street. (2008). *Literacy Guide.* http://bnkst.edu/literacyguide.

BARCLAY, E. (2009). "Language Barriers Complicate Immigrants' Medical Problems." *Washington Post* and *Kaiser Health News.* April 21.

BRIMELOW, P. (2008). "Mass Immigration and Education." www.commonsenseonmass immigration.us?articles/art-brimelow.

BORJAS, G. J. (1999). *Heaven's Door: Immigration Policy and the American Economy.* Princeton, NJ: Princeton University Press.

BROTHERS, C. (2008). "EU Passes Tough Migrant Measures." *New York Times.* June 19. www.nytimes.com.

BUCHANAN, P. J. (2006). *State of Emergency.* New York: St. Martin's Press.

CAMAROTA, S. A. (2009). "Immigration's Impact on Public Coffers." www.cis.org/ articles/2009.

Castaneda v. Picard. (1981). 448 F.2d 989; U.S. APP Lexis 12063, June 23. http://stanford .edu/~kenro/LAU/IAPolicy/IA1bCastaneda.

Center for Immigration Studies. (2008). "The High Cost of Cheap Labor." April 15. www .cis.org.

COLLINS, D. (2008). "Failing to Reform Immigration Threatens Education." *Pittsburgh Tribune-Review*, September 8, 1.

CORNELIUS, W. A., ET AL., eds. (2004). *Controlling Immigration.* Stanford, CA: Stanford University Press.

CRAWFORD, J. (2007). "Hard Sell: Why Is Bilingual Education So Unpopular with the American Public?" In *Bilingual Education*, ed. O. Garcia and C. Baker. Clevedon: Multilingual Matters.

DARLING-HAMMOND, L. (2008). "Improving High Schools and the Role of NCLB." In *Holding NCLB Accountable: Achieving Accountability, Equity and School Reform*, ed. G. L. Sunderman. Thousand Oaks, CA: Corwin.

DRACHMAN, E. R., AND LANGRAN, R. (2008). Your Decide. 2d Ed., Lanham: Rowman and Littlefield.

Dream Act Portal. (2011). http://dreamact.info.

ESPINOSA, L. M. (2008). *Challenging Common Myth about English Language Learners.* New York: Foundation for Child Development. www.fcd-us.org/resources.

FactCheck. (2009). "Cost of Illegal Immigration." www.factcheck.org/2009/04/ cost-of-illegal-immigration.

FALTIS, C. J., AND COULTER, C. A. (2008). *Teaching English Learners and Immigrant Students in Secondary Schools.* Boston: Allyn and Bacon.

Federation for American Immigration Reform. (2002). "Immigration and School Over-crowding." www.fairus.org.

———. (2005). "What's Wrong with Illegal Immigration." March. www.fairus.org.

———. (2011). "Illegal Immigration a $113 Billion a Year Drain on US Taxpayers." July 6. www.fairus.org.

FRANKLIN, B. (1749). *Proposals Relating to the Education of Youth In Pennsylvania, 1749.* www.archives.upenn.edu/primdocs/1749proposals.

GAYTAN, F. X., ET AL. (2007). "Understanding and Responding to the Needs of Newcomer Immigrant Youth and Families." *The Prevention Researcher* 14:10–13.

GINGRICH, N. (2008). *Real Change.* Washington, DC: Regnery.

HANDLIN, O., ed. (1966). *Children of the Uprooted.* New York: George Braziller.

HANSON, G. H. (2007). "The Economic Logic of Illegal Immigration." www.Cfr.org/ content/publications.

HERNANDEZ, D. J., DENTON, N. A., AND MACARTNEY, S. E. (2007). "Children in Immigrant Families—The U.S. and 50 States: National Origins, Language, and Early Education." April. www.childtrends.org.

Immigration Counters. (2011). "Real Time Data." www.immigrationcounters.com.

JARZEN, M. (2009). "Language Barriers Limit Ability of Immigrants." March 12. www .unlvrebelyell.com.

KAESTLE, C. (1983). *Pillars of the Republic: Common Schools and American Society, 1780–1860.* New York: Hill and Wang.

KIEFFER, M. ET AL. (2009). "Accommodations for English Language Learners Taking Large-Scale Assessments. A Meta-Analysis on Effectiveness and Validity." *Review of Educational Research.* 79: 1168–1201.

LACEY, M. (2011). "Birthright Citizenship Looms as Next Immigration Battle." *New York Times,* January 5, A1.

Lau v. Nichols. (1974). 414 U.S. 563. http://supreme.justia.com/us/414/563/case.

LEONHARDT, D. (2008). "The Border and the Ballot Box." March 2. www.nytimes.com.

LOPEZ, M. P., AND LOPEZ, G. R. (2010). *Persistent Inequality: Contemporary Realities in the Education of Undocumented Latina/o Students.* New York: Routledge.

"Man in the Street." (1905). *New York Times.* January 15. www.nytimes.com/archive.

MEILANDER, P. C. (2001). *Toward a Theory of Immigration.* New York: Palgrave.

Migration Policy Institute. (2006). "Annual Immigration to the United States: The Real Numbers." www.migrationinformation.org.

———. (2008). "2006 American Community Survey and Census Data on the Foreign Born by State." www.migrationinformation.org.

MORRIS, D., AND MCGANN, E. (2007). *Outrage.* New York: HarperCollins.

National Association for Bilingual Education. (2007). *NABE Principles on the Reauthorization of NCLB.* Washington, DC: National Association for Bilingual Education. www .nabe.org/advocacy/nclb.

National Council of Teachers of English ELL Task Force. (2006). *NCTE Position Paper on the Role of English Teachers in Educating English Language Learners (ELLs).* National Council of Teachers of English. www.ncte.org.

PASSEL, J. S., AND COHN, D. (2008). *U.S. Population Projections 2005–2050,* Washington, DC: Pew Research Center. http//pewhispanic.org/files.reports/85.

———. (2011). "Unauthorized Immigrant Population: National and State Trends, 2010." February 1. www.pewhispanic.org/reports.

Pew Research Center. (2008). "U.S. Population Projections: 2005–2050." February 11. http://pewsocialtrends.org.

———. (2010). "Unauthorized Immigrants and Their US-Born Children." August 11. www.pewresearch.org.

———. (2011). "The Mexican-American Boom: Births Overtake Immigration." July 14. www.pewresearch.org.

Plyler v. Doe. (1982). 457 U.S. 202. http://supreme.justia.com/us/457/202/case.

PORTES, A., AND RUMBAUT, R. G. (2006). *Immigrant America: A Portrait.* Berkeley: University of California Press.

RABIN, N., COMBS, C., AND GONZALEZ, N. (2008). "Understanding Plyler's Legacy: Voices from Border Schools." *Journal of Law and Education* 37:15–82.

ROBERTS, S. (2004). *Who We Are Now.* New York: Henry Holt.

SALOMONE, R. C. (2010). *True American: Language, Identity, and the Education of Immigrant Children.* Cambridge, MA: Harvard University Press.

SEMPLE, R. (2011). "In New York, Mexicans Lag in Education." *New York Times,* November 25, A1.

SMITH, J. P., AND EDMONSTON, B., eds. (1997). *The New Americans: Economic, Demographic, and Fiscal Effects of Immigration.* Washington, DC: National Academy Press.

SOLORZANO, R. W. (2008). "High Stakes Testing: Issues, Implications, and Remedies for English Language Learners." *Review of Educational Research* 78:260–329.

Southern Poverty Law Center. (2009). "Language Barrier." April. www.splcenter.org.

SPRING, J. (2001). *The American School: 1642–2000.* 5th Ed. New York: McGraw-Hill.

STEWNER-MANZANARES, G. (1988). *The Bilingual Education Act: Twenty Years Later.* Washington, DC: National Clearinghouse for Bilingual Education. www.nclea.gwu/pubs/classics.

SUAREZ-OROZCO, C. ET AL. (2011). "Growing up in the Shadows: The Developmental Implications of Unauthorized Status." *Harvard Educational Review* 81: 438–472.

SUAREZ-OROZCO, M., AND GARDNER, H. (2003). "Educating Billy Wang for the World of Tomorrow." *Education Week* 8(October 22):43, 34.

SUAREZ-OROZCO, M., AND QIN-HILLIARD, D. B. (2004). *Globalization: Culture and Education in the New Millennium.* Berkeley: University of California Press.

SUAREZ-OROZCO, M., AND SUAREZ-OROZCO, C. (2001). *Children of Immigration.* Cambridge, MA: Harvard University Press.

SUAREZ-OROZCO, C., AND TODOROVA, I. L. G. eds. (2003). *Understanding the Social Worlds of Immigrant Youth.* San Francisco, CA: Jossey-Bass.

SUAREZ-OROZCO, C., SUAREZ-OROZCO, M., AND TODOROVA, I. (2008). *Learning a New Land: Immigrant Students in American Society.* Cambridge, MA: Belknap Press.

The Economist. (2011). "Amending the Amendment." August 19.

VON DREHLE, R.O. (2008). "A New Line in the Sand." *Time* 17:28–35.

WHITE, M. J., AND GLICK, J. E. (2009). *Achieving Anew; How Immigrants Do In American Schools, Jobs, and Neighborhoods.* New York: Russell Sage. Foundation.

WILEY, T. G. (2007). "Accessing Language Rights in Education: A Brief History of the U.S. Context." In *Bilingual Education*, ed. O. Garcia and C. Baker. Clevedon: Multilingual Matters.

What Should Be Taught?

Knowledge and Literacy

About Part Two: School curriculum battles are the outward sign of competing social forces. Decisions on what should be taught are political decisions, involving the definitions of knowledge, intelligence, literacy, and learning. These terms are complementary concepts—but they often have differing definitions and interpretations (Coiro et al., 2008). Schools are necessarily involved with definitions of these four terms and with disputes over them. Topics covered in Part Two include disparities in academic achievement, values and character development, multicultural education, technology, and testing. Each issue involves both theoretical and practical concerns: what does it mean to know something, and how should schools undertake that activity? Curriculum control is the result of power and politics (Au, 2012; Heller, 2012).

INTRODUCTION

You will not be surprised to hear that what is taught and what is learned are often different things. We are taught many things in many settings; we may or may not learn those things—but we learn.

What is learned can't be examined directly. We have to infer it from some observable demonstration, such as test results, oral statements, or performing some skill or activity. We can, however, directly structure what we think should be taught on the premise that it causes related learning. That is the great hope of education, and there is some evidence that it works in general. Structuring what should be taught—how schools organize information considered to be worth knowing—describes a curriculum. The traditional core material that society considers worth knowing includes English, math, science, history and social studies, the arts and applied arts, foreign languages, and physical education. Within these fields are many disputes about the nature of knowledge (academic arguments) and about what should be included in schools (curricular arguments). Academic arguments are usually among specialists in that field, such as the literary contributions of science fiction, Keynesian economics in policy development, and string theory in mathematics. Curricular arguments include applied and professional judgments about when certain subjects should be introduced in schools and what sequence of study should follow, but those are not all the curricular controversies.

More public and pervasive curricular issues arise as a result of political or ideological disputes. These arguments involve more than subject specialists debating academic points or school staff debating the curricular placement of subjects. The public debates exist in the context of larger questions: the social purposes and consequences of that knowledge, the cultural and political implications for teaching or limiting it in schools, and how to know if the socially acceptable knowledge is actually learned. The school curriculum is controversial (Rubio and Baert, 2012). Raskin (2004) points out,

> Throughout the twentieth century, brutal fights were waged about the content in education, what educators thought it proper to teach, analyze, and question. Hidden behind these struggles were issues of class, cultural homogenization, propaganda as knowledge, the abstract versus the concrete, and, of course, race, sex, and leisure. (p. 103)

From the testing of selected knowledge as mandated under federal and state law to school board arguments over evolution or intelligent design in science classes, curriculum debates abound. Should all students be held to the same academic standards? What standards should be used and for what purposes? What role should schools undertake in developing student character? What is the best use of technology in schools?

Teaching is, of course, more than telling or testing. And learning is more than listening and recalling. Good education requires more thought about what should be taught, how, and why. We may all think we are well educated, so it is easy to assume that what should be taught is what we were taught—and learned as we did. That self-congratulatory response answers a question about the central purpose for schools—what should be taught?—but not satisfactorily (Ippolito, Steele, and Samson, 2008).

If the best education is simply what we learned and recall, then teaching could be only telling and testing of what we already think we know. Education would be static and for some, it seems to be. What we were taught or what our parents and grandparents were taught represent ideas of important school knowledge in those times. But knowledge changes—and so do our conceptions of intelligence, literacy, and learning (Dzisah and Etzkowitz, 2012). Noble (2004) comments,

> As fashionable as it is to decry the woeful state of American schooling, and to mock students who can't locate one or another country on a map, the great mass of American citizens are probably better informed than they were

one hundred or even fifty years ago, when formal school stopped for most people at or before high school, and the curriculum was designed to teach the children of farmers and factory workers how to keep still and take orders. (p. 157)

Schools, from day care to graduate school, exist to determine, examine, convey, question, and modify knowledge. That responsibility is the root of issues surrounding what should be taught. Communicating knowledge, most people agree, is the core purpose of schools. That interactive communication depends upon our definitions (Coiro et al., 2008).

Issues arise because of major disagreements over how knowledge is to be defined, whose ideas of knowledge should prevail in the schools, how to package that knowledge, and how to organize and teach knowledge (Rosenberg, 2002; Rose, 2008). In addition to disputes about the nature, value, and expression of knowledge are disagreements about how to stimulate and measure it. Disputes that are this complex are often at the center of various school wars since the control of knowledge is the control of society.

The struggle to control what is accepted as valued knowledge is inevitably a struggle for power (Cherryholmes, 1978; Popkewitz, 1987; Sizer, 2004; Moran, 2005). Control of people's minds is control of their expectations, behavior, and allegiance. Deciding which students get access to which knowledge has a powerful impact on social policy and politics. Results can lead in opposite directions: more social egalitarianism or more elitism,

more social-class separation or more social integration (Rose, 2008).

INTELLIGENCE AND LEARNING

Knowledge, of course, depends on intelligence since it is only through intelligence that we gain, interpret, and use knowledge. Yet there are as many disputes about intelligence as there are about knowledge. As Ken Richardson (2000) notes,

> There has probably been a concept of intelligence, and a word for it, since people first started to compare themselves with other animals and with one another. We know this at least since thinkers first began to theorize about the nature of the mind . . . the existing ground does not offer a firm foundation for anyone seeking to answer the question: "What is intelligence?" Indeed, it is a complex confusion. (pp. 1, 20)

Psychologist Howard Gardner (1993, 1999, 2000, 2003) argues that we really have multiple intelligences, not just a single form. He suggests that intelligences are actually potentials for people to develop processes to solve problems or create things; they are not completed events, nor are they clearly observable or testable, and they are relatively independent of each other. Some kinds of intelligence (such as logical-mathematical and linguistic) are especially useful in satisfying school academic requirements, and others (such as intra- and interpersonal, musical, and bodily-kinesthetic) are more useful in other settings in and out of school. This level of complexity makes "intelligence" testing and other efforts to standardize and measure schooling more difficult, if not impossible. As Gardner (1999) puts it, "intelligence is too important to be left to the intelligence testers" (p. 3).

Similarly, we have multiple literacies and multiple learning processes (Hull and Schultz, 2002; Coiro et al., 2008). Literacy can be defined in many ways: as basic reading/writing skills, as computer skills, as economic ability, as cultural capabilities, as historical cognizance, or as artistic or critical literacy (Gee, 1996, 2000; Jetton and Shanahan, 2012). Critical literacy provides a way to use basic school knowledge to identify and correct significant power disparities between haves and have-nots (Freire, 1970; Freire and Macedo, 1987; Comber and Simpson, 2001).

Multiple learning processes are obvious to anyone who observes children acquire walking, speaking, reading, creative, and interpretive abilities. This sophisticated concept of multiple intelligences, literacies, and learning processes not only makes definitions of knowledge, intelligence, literacy, and learning very problematic but also raises important questions about school curriculum, national and state standardized testing, and teaching.

THE SCHOOL CURRICULUM: KNOWLEDGE AND POLITICS

The school curriculum of each society reflects the definitions of formal knowledge and literacy prevalent in that society and in that time—and they reflect political decisions. These definitions often conflict—arts versus sciences, practical versus theoretical, and socialization versus individual independence. In an age of witchery, a literate, intelligent person is one who shares the language and values of the sorcerer's form of knowledge. In an age of technology, a literate and intelligent person may be defined as one who shares the language and values of technological knowledge. Thus, the term *literate* may be thought of as a verbal badge given to those who possess knowledge considered socially valuable. Schools provide literacy credentials in the form of diplomas, degrees, and various types of professional certificates. When magic and witchcraft were socially credible, sorcerers enjoyed great power and status. Their pronouncements often became laws and policies. Only a select few had the opportunity to learn their secret rites. When knowledge of witchcraft came to be viewed as evil, sorcerers were burned. In modern societies where scientific knowledge is prized, "sorcerers" are considered interesting eccentrics. The postmodern society suggests new definitions and a new school curriculum for meeting the needs of the twenty-first century (Stanley, 1992; Greene, 1994; Ippolito et al., 2008; Au, 2012).

Typically, traditional school subjects coexist in the curriculum until new topics or arguments arise challenging that emphasis. In our seventeenth-century secondary schools, classes were taught in Latin, and Greek was required along with moral philosophy. In the last decades of the twentieth century, when test scores revealed deficiencies in the basic skills of reading, writing, and arithmetic, most elementary schools decreased the curriculum time spent on science, social studies, the arts, and applied arts and shifted it to reading and arithmetic. When computers became more socially valuable, schools made space to fit computer study into a crowded school curriculum. Other additions, such as driver's education, physical education, drug education, and character education, illustrate curriculum changes based on redefinitions of knowledge and the politics of schools. The specific mix of courses and emphasis within the curriculum depend on prevailing visions of the "good" individual and the "good" society. In every age, people hold disparate views on what kinds of individuals and society are most desirable. Some want individuals to be free, independent, and critical; others advocate behavior modification to control deviation and ensure social conformity. Some demand prescribed moral values and beliefs; others demand release from moralisms and prescriptions. Some desire respect for authority; others prefer challenges to authority.

PRACTICAL, THEORETICAL, AND MORAL SCHOOLING

The literature is filled with disputes over how school should develop the good individual and the good society. Aristotle considered the state the fulfillment of our social drives and saw education as a state activity designed to provide social unity. He said that "education is therefore the means of making it [the society] a community and giving it unity" (Aristotle, 1962, p. 51). In *The*

Politics, Aristotle discussed the controversy over whether schools should teach practical knowledge, moral character, or esoteric ideas. Contemporary curriculum debate continues to focus on the relative emphasis that schools should give to practical, theoretical, and moral schooling.

Comprehensive public schools offer some useful applied educational programs, such as reading, music, wood shop, home economics, computer operation, physical education, and vocational training. They also offer the study of theoretical concepts in English, math, social studies, the arts, and science. And schools provide various forms of moral education; students study materials conveying ideas of the good person and the good society and learn from school rules and teachers to be respectful, patriotic, loyal, and honest. The exact mix of these forms of education varies as different reforms become popular and as local communities make changes.

Curricular reforms between 1980 and 2010 are seen by many as essentially mechanistic and "top down." The president, governors, legislators, and national commissions tell the schools what and how to teach to correct educational ills. Their prescriptions— for increased course requirements, longer schooldays and school years, more homework, more testing, and force-feeding knowledge to students in factory-like schools—do not prove curative abilities.

Most schools teach a relatively standard curriculum. States mandate certain courses, such as English, American history, and drug and alcohol education. Accrediting agencies examine schools periodically and review the curriculum for conformity. Publishers, aiming at a national market, produce teaching materials for a national curriculum. And school district curriculum coordinators and department heads attend national conferences and read journals that stress standard curricular structures. Thus, a broad outline exists for a general national curriculum based on common practices, even though specific curricula in each state differ.

In the second decade of the twenty-first century, external forces still largely determine the formal curriculum in American schools. We have national and state standards, increasing external accountability for student learning, and more complex ideas of socially expected literacy. Since colonial times, the curriculum has evolved from a narrow interest in teaching religious ideals to multiple and often conflicting interests in providing broad knowledge, skills, and values relevant to nearly every aspect of social life. In U.S. schools, the medieval curriculum of "seven liberal arts"—rhetoric, grammar, logic, arithmetic, astronomy, geometry, and music—has given way to a long list of subjects. And the formal curriculum is certainly not all that students are expected to learn in school.

THE HIDDEN CURRICULUM

The hidden curriculum of unexpressed and usually unexamined ideas, values, and behaviors conveys subtle, often unintended things to students (and teachers). A few brief examples illustrate the hidden curriculum at its simplest level. Teachers tell students to be independent and express their own ideas, but they often chastise or punish the student who actually exhibits independence and expresses ideas the teacher doesn't like. In history courses, students hear that justice and equality are basic American rights, yet they see that compliant and well-dressed students earn favored treatment. In school, students are told that plagiarism is an academic sin, then the news shows prominent and award-winning historians (probably quoted in the high school history textbook) who plagiarized from others. Students are told to not smoke by teachers who do. The hidden curriculum is a vast, relatively uncharted domain often much more effective than the formal curriculum in shaping student learning and knowledge.

At a deeper level, discrepancies between what schools say and what schools do may raise a more significant concern about competing ideologies. The hidden curriculum conflicts with the stated purposes of the visible curriculum. The stated curriculum may value diversity; the hidden curriculum expects conformity. The stated curriculum advocates critical thinking; the hidden curriculum supports docility. The visible curriculum emphasizes equal opportunity; the hidden curriculum separates students according to social-class background, gender, race, or other factors.

Critical literature examines the hidden curriculum and its ideological bases (see Young, 1970; Cherryholmes,

1978, 1988; Anyon, 1979, 1980; Giroux and Purpel, 1983; Popkewitz, 1987; Giroux, 1988; Apple, 2000; Aronowitz, 2008; Stanley, 1992). From this critical view, the "great debates" about schooling extensively covered in the media and mainstream educational literature are actually narrowly constructed differences between liberals and conservatives. At bottom, public debates do not raise ideological concerns about the control of knowledge and its social consequences. Tinkering with the stated curriculum leaves the powerful hidden curriculum intact. Superficial school reforms do very little to change schooling, and neither mainstream liberals nor conservatives really want much change.

At the surface level, where much school reform debate occurs, a discussion about whether to spend more school time on computers, math, and English and less on the arts and social studies is a comparatively trivial matter; it hides more fundamental disputes about whose interests are served and whose are maligned. Shallow arguments about whether the curriculum should stress the basics, provide vocational courses, allow electives, or emphasize American values should lead to deeper, more critical examinations of who controls the school curriculum and consequences of that control. In mainstream discourse, those basic issues are hidden.

A central issue in the struggle for control of knowledge is whether traditional knowledge provides enduring wisdom or promotes social oppression. In opposition to the traditional use of literacy as a tool of the dominant class to separate and control the masses is the idea of literacy as a tool for liberation, Paulo Freire's revolutionary concept (Freire and Berthoff, 1987). Freire, born in one of the most impoverished areas of Brazil, came to know the plight of the poor. He vowed to dedicate his life to the struggle against misery and suffering, and his work led him to define the "culture of silence" that he saw among the disadvantaged.

Freire realized the power of knowledge and recognized that the dominant class used education to keep the culture of silence among the victims—the poor and illiterate. He taught adults to read in order to liberate them from their imposed silence. As a professor of education in Brazil, he experimented to erase illiteracy, and his ideas became widely used in private literacy campaigns there. Freire became a threat to the government and was jailed after a military coup in 1964. Forced to leave his native country, he went to Chile to work with UNESCO, came to the United States, and then joined the World Council of Churches in Geneva as head of its educational division. Freire's program involves the development of critical consciousness, using communication to expose oppression. Teacher and student are "co-intentional," sharing equally in dialogues on social reality and developing a critical understanding that can liberate them from the culture of silence.

Henry Giroux, citing Freire, argues that we need a redefinition of literacy to focus on its critical dimensions. Mass culture via television and other electronic media is under the control of dominant economic interests and offers only immediate images and unthoughtful information. This creates a "technocratic" illiteracy that is a threat to self-perception, critical thought, and democracy. Giroux (1988) states,

> Instead of formulating literacy in terms of the mastery of techniques, we must broaden its meaning to include the ability to read critically, both inside and outside one's experiences, and with conceptual power. This means that literacy would enable people to decode critically their personal and social worlds and thereby further their ability to challenge the myths and beliefs that structure their perceptions and experiences. (p. 84)

CURRICULUM CONTROL

Control of knowledge and the school curriculum is a product of both prevailing social goals and prevailing social structures. During the formative years of the United States, religion was the basis. Differences existed among the colonies, but most people expected all young children to be taught religious precepts at home or at dame or writing schools. The purpose was to thwart the efforts of "that ould deluder, Satan," who sought to keep human beings from knowledge of the scriptures. After learning to read and write, however, most girls were not permitted further education. They returned home to learn the art of homemaking, while boys from more affluent homes continued their schooling at Latin grammar schools. African Americans and Native Americans were virtually excluded from schools.

Historically, the struggle for the control of knowledge has paralleled social-class differences (Anyon, 1980, 2005; Spring, 1998). The assumption was that workers needed practical knowledge, the privileged class needed higher knowledge, and both needed moral knowledge but with great disparity in the kinds of moral knowledge they required. Craft apprenticeships to acquire practical knowledge were for the masses. Formal schooling to learn critical thinking and study philosophy, science, and the arts was for the aristocratic class. In terms of moral instruction, the masses were to gain the moral character to obey, respect authority, work hard and be frugal, and suffer with little complaint. Members of the privileged class were supposed to gain the moral character to rule wisely, justly, and with civility.

One of the central purposes of schooling is to prepare future leaders of society. When the powerful class controls education and decides what is to be taught, the essential curricular question is, what should members of the ruling class know? In more democratic societies, involved in mass education, the curricular questions revolve around what all members of the society need to know to participate fully and actively.

Even in democratic societies, however, curricular needs of those identified as potential leaders receive special attention. We can see this in the higher academic tracks and honors programs characterizing many modern high schools. The correlation between social expectations, social-class structure, and what schools teach deserves ongoing examination.

R. H. Tawney (1964) criticized the elite "public boarding-school" tradition of the wealthy in England and advocated improvements in the developing system of free schools for the working classes. The very nature of the elite system was a part of the hidden curriculum, teaching the sons of the wealthy "not in words or of set purpose, but by the mere facts of their environment, that they are members . . . of a privileged group, whose function it will be, on however humble a scale, to direct and command, and to which leadership, influence, and the other prizes of life properly belong" (p. 83).

Social class is not the only major factor lying behind curricular decisions. Race, gender, national origin, and religion are other conditions that influence decisions about which people receive what knowledge in a society. The concept of privilege and the education that privilege brings have been linked to racism and sexism in American and other national histories. Educational discrimination against racial minorities, women, Jews, Catholics, Native Americans, Eskimos, and others is a sorry tradition in a democratic society.

About half a century ago, psychologist Kenneth Clark, whose studies were a significant factor in the Supreme Court decision that found segregated schools unconstitutional (*Brown v. Board of Education*, 1954), put the case clearly:

> The public schools in America's urban ghettos also reflect the oppressive damage of racial exclusion. . . . Segregation and inferior education reinforce each other. . . . Children themselves are not fooled by the various euphemisms educators use to disguise educational snobbery. From the earliest grades a child knows when he has been assigned to a level that is considered less than adequate. . . . "The clash of cultures in the classroom" is essentially a class war, a socioeconomic and racial warfare being waged on the battleground of our schools, with middle-class and middle-class-aspiring teachers provided with a powerful arsenal of half-truths, prejudices, and rationalizations, arrayed against the hopelessly outclassed working-class youngsters. (Clark, 1965, pp. 111–117)

Similar condemnations of educational discrimination based on religion, nationality, and gender are common in the critical literature (Hofstadter, 1944; Clark, 1965; Katz, 1971; Feldman, 1974; Spring, 1976, 1998; Apple, 1990, 2004; Sadker and Sadker, 1982; Walker and Barton, 1983; Grimshaw, 1986; Giroux, 1991; Lather, 1991; Weiler, 1991). As Rosemary Deem (1983) comments, "Women have had to struggle hard against dominant patriarchal power relations, which try to confine women to the private sphere of the home and family, away from the public sphere of production and political power" (p. 107). Weiler (1991) essentially agrees in a critique of the Western system of knowledge, arguing that feminist pedagogy is rooted in a critical, oppositional, and activist vision of social change. Schooling that provides different types of knowledge and skills to students who differ only in race, gender, class, religion, or nationality contributes to continued inequality of treatment and stereotypes.

SOCIAL EXPECTATIONS

Should schools concentrate on subject knowledge of historic and socially approved value or on material encouraging critical thinking and student interest? If individual students are expected to develop independent and critical judgment so that they can participate actively in improving the democratic society, we should expect schooling that leads to that goal and can expect educated individuals to have an impact on society. If society values a structure where only a few people have power and most people are expected to be docile and conform to social norms, we should expect schooling that leads to that end and the resulting society.

Those two hypothetical statements seem to suggest the choice is simple; it is not. There are complex and changing relationships between the kinds of individuals we desire, the society we want to develop, and schooling we provide. These relationships often send conflicting signals to schools, and the conflicts become enshrined in the school curriculum. Society wants students to become self-sufficient individuals—but not too self-sufficient too early so that students have little latitude in deciding what to study until they reach college. We desire a society that is democratic and inspires voluntary loyalty, but we do not trust open inquiry, so we require courses stressing nationalistic patriotism.

Prior to the American Revolution, religion was waning as the primary social glue. National political interests emerged. After the Revolution and into the nineteenth century, nationalism replaced religion as an educational force. Literacy became important not for religious salvation but for patriotism, preservation of liberty, and participation in democracy. The political-nationalistic tradition remains strong in U.S. schools, with a call for renewed emphasis each time social values seem threatened (Westheimer, 2007). The War on Terrorism is a prime contemporary example; there is a redoubled effort to require allegiance pledges, patriotic exercises, and U.S. history.

There are many other examples of political uses of schools. During the period of overt racism in the United States and as a reaction to the abolition of slavery, some regions used literacy tests to restrict voting rights. Since slaves had been prohibited (by law in some states) from receiving an education, these tests were intended to keep former slaves and the poor from voting. Their proponents also used them to limit participation of immigrants. David Tyack (1967) quotes an imperial wizard of the Ku Klux Klan as saying, "Ominous statistics proclaim the persistent development of a parasitic mass within our domain. . . . We have taken unto ourselves a Trojan horse crowded with ignorance, illiteracy, and envy" (p. 233).

The "Red Scare" of the 1920s, McCarthyism in the 1950s, and anticommunist political rhetoric in the 1980s were also periods when people perceived social threats; the effect was to strengthen a nationalist viewpoint in history, government, literature, and economics curricula. International competition in technology and trade threatens Americans today and translates into an increased curricular emphasis on mathematics, science, technological subjects such as computers, and foreign languages.

The formal curriculum is one of the most visible parts of a school, indicating the relative value that schools put on various forms of knowledge and definitions of intelligence and literacy. There is far more to knowledge and literacy than what schools organize and teach, but schools provide legitimacy to the knowledge they select and teach and credentials to those students who are successful in school.

Some people enjoy mathematics. For others, reading history or literature is a great joy. Some like to dissect white rats in biology class, saw wood in shop, or exercise in gym. Others are completely baffled or utterly bored by textbooks and teachers. Different strokes, as they say, for different folks. But aren't there some things that everyone should know, whether they enjoy it or not? Is there a set of skills that all should master? Should we require that anyone who graduates from high school be literate? Who should decide the criteria for literacy? What does it take to be educated in the twenty-first century?

The chapters of Part Two examine some of the current curriculum disputes that have emerged as part of reform movements in education. These disputes illustrate the question of what knowledge is most valuable in our society, a question that, in turn, relates to our differing visions of what constitutes the good individual and the good society.

References

Anyon, J. (1979). "Ideology and U.S. History Textbooks." *Harvard Educational Review* 7:49–60.

———. (1980). "Social Class and the Hidden Curriculum of Work." *Journal of Education* 162:67–92.

———. (2005). *Radical Possibilities.* New York: Routledge.

Apple, M. (2004). *Ideology and Curriculum.* 3rd Ed. New York: Routledge.

———. (2000). *Official Knowledge.* London: Routledge.

Aristotle. (1962). *The Politics of Aristotle.* Translated by E. Barker. Oxford: Oxford University Press.

Aronowitz, S. (2008). *Against Schooling: Toward an Education That Matters.* Boulder, CO: Paradigm Publishing.

Au, W. (2012). Critical Curriculum Studies. New York: Routledge.

Brown v. Board of Education of Topeka, Shawnee County, Kansas, et al. (1954). 74 Sup. Ct. 686.

Cherryholmes, C. (1978). "Curriculum Design as a Political Act." *Curriculum Inquiry* 10:115–141.

———. (1988). *Power and Criticism: Poststructural Investigations in Education.* New York: Teachers College Press.

Clark, K. (1965). *Dark Ghetto.* New York: Harper and Row.

Coiro, J., et al., (2008). *The Handbook of Research in New Literacies.* Mahwah, NJ: Lawrence Erlbaum Associates.

Comber, B., and Simpson A. (2001). *Negotiating Critical Literacies in Classrooms.* Mahwah NJ: Lawrence Erlbaum Associates.

Deem, R. (1983). "Gender, Patriarchy and Class in the Popular Education of Women." In *Gender, Class and Education*, ed. S. Walker and L. Barton. London: Falmer Press.

Dzisah, J. and Etzkowitz, H. (2012). The Age of Knowledge. Studies in Critical Social Sciences, Vol. 37. Boston: Brill.

Feldman, S. (1974). *The Rights of Women.* Rochelle Park, NJ: Hayden.

Freire, P. (1970). *Pedagogy of the Oppressed.* Translated by M. B. Ramos. New York: Herder and Herder.

Freire, P., and Berthoff, D. (1987). *Literacy: Reading and the World.* South Hadley, MA: Bergin and Garvey.

Freire, P., and Macedo, D. (1987). *Literacy.* South Hadley, MA: Bergin and Garvey.

Gardner, H. (1993). *Frames of Mind.* New York: Basic Books.

———. (1999). *Intelligence Reframed: Multiple Intelligences for the 21st Century.* New York: Basic Books.

———. (2000). *The Disciplined Mind.* New York: Penguin.

———. (2003). "Multiple Intelligences After Twenty Years." Paper presented at the American Educational Research Association meeting, April 23.

GEE, J. P. (1996). *Social Linguistics and Literacies.* 2nd Ed. London: Falmer Press.

———. (2000). "The New Literacy Studies." In *Situated Literacies,* ed. D. Barton et al. London: Routledge.

GIROUX, H. (1988). *The Teacher as Intellectual.* South Hadley, MA: Bergin and Garvey.

———, ed. (1991). *Postmodernism, Feminism and Cultural Politics.* Albany: State University of New York Press.

GIROUX, H., AND PURPEL, D. (1983). *The Hidden Curriculum and Moral Education.* Berkeley, CA: McCutchan.

GREENE, M. (1994). "Postmodernism and the Crisis of Representation." *English Education* 26:206–219.

GRIMSHAW, J. (1986). *Philosophy and Feminist Thinking.* Minneapolis: University of Minnesota Press.

HELLER, D. (2012). Curriculum on the Edge of Survival. Lanham, MD: Rowman and Littlefield.

HOFSTADTER, R. (1944). *Social Darwinism in American Thought.* Philadelphia: University of Pennsylvania Press.

HULL, G., AND SCHULTZ, K. (2002). *School's Out: Bridging Out-of-School Literacies with Classroom Practice.* New York: Teachers College Press.

IPPOLITO, J., STEELE, J., AND SAMSON, J. (2008). "Introduction: Why Adolescent Literacy Matters Now." *Harvard Education Review* 68(1):1–5.

JETTON, T. L. AND SHANAHAN, C., eds., (2012). Adolescent Literacy in the Academic Disciplines. New York: Guilford Press.

KATZ, M. B. (1971). *Class, Bureaucracy, and Schools.* New York: Praeger.

LATHER, P. (1991). *Getting Smart: Feminist Research and Pedagogy within the Postmodern.* New York: Routledge.

MORAN, B. T. (2005). *Distilling Knowledge.* Cambridge, MA: Harvard University Press.

NOBLE, C. (2004). *The Collapse of Liberalism.* Lanham, MD: Rowman & Littlefield.

POPKEWITZ, T. (1987). *The Formation of School Subjects.* New York: Falmer Press.

RASKIN, M. (2004). *Liberalism: The Genius of American Ideals.* Lanham, MD: Rowman & Littlefield.

RICHARDSON, K. (2000). *The Making of Intelligence.* New York: Columbia University Press.

ROSE, M. (2008). "Intelligence, Knowledge, and the Hand/Brain Divide." *Kappan* 89(9):632–639.

ROSENBERG, J. F. (2002). *Thinking about Knowing.* Oxford: Clarendon Press.

RUBIO, F. D. AND BAERT, P (2012). The Politics of Knowledge. New York: Routledge.

SADKER, P., AND SADKER, D. M. (1982). *Sex Equity Handbook for Schools.* New York: Longman.

SIZER, T. (2004). *The Red Pencil.* New Haven, CT: Yale University Press.

SPRING, J. (1976). *The Sorting Machine.* New York: McKay.

———. (1998). *American Education.* 8th Ed. New York: McGraw-Hill.

STANLEY, W. (1992). *Education for Utopia: Social Reconstructionism and Critical Pedagogy in the Postmodern Era.* Albany: State University of New York Press.

TAWNEY, R. H. (1964). *The Radical Tradition.* London: Allen and Unwin.

TYACK, D. (1967). *Turning Points in American Educational History.* Waltham, MA: Blaisdell.

WALKER, S., AND BARTON, L. (1983). *Gender, Class and Education.* London: Falmer Press.

WEILER, K. (1991). "Freire and a Feminist Pedagogy of Difference." *Harvard Educational Review* 61:449–474.

WESTHEIMER, J., ed. (2007). *Pledging Allegiance.* New York: Teachers College Press.

YOUNG, M. F. D., ed. (1970). *Knowledge and Control.* London: Collier-Macmillan.

CHAPTER 8

Standards-Based Reform: Real Change or Badly Flawed Policy

Will the standards-based reform movement improve education or sacrifice teachers' decisions and individual assessment to national standards and standardized testing?

POSITION 1: STANDARDS-BASED REFORM PROMISES QUALITY EDUCATION FOR ALL STUDENTS

Every child in America deserves a world-class education. . . . We will set a clear goal: Every student should graduate from high school ready for college and a career, regardless of their income, race, ethnic or language background, or disability status. Following the lead of the nation's governors, we're call- ing on all states to develop and adopt standards in English language arts and mathematics that build toward college- and career-readiness by the time stu- dents graduate from high school.

—President Barack Obama (U.S. Department of Education, 2010, pp. 1, 3)

Under the American system of government, legislative powers not expressly given to the federal government are reserved for the states or the people therein. The U.S. Constitution does not give the federal government any specific authority to regulate or control education, and therefore the United States has developed fifty state systems of education administered by 15,000 school districts. Local control of schooling is part of the American tradition of education. Nevertheless, the federal government has played an increasingly important role in education since the founding of the nation. Grants of federal land were used to create public schools, and the Morrill Act of 1862 helped support the development of over sixty land-grant colleges. Nowhere has the federal government's role in education been felt more powerfully than in the Supreme Court decision known as *Brown v. Board of Education* (1954), which held that segregated public schools were a violation of the Constitution. *Brown* was a significant assertion of federal authority in education, guaranteeing equal treatment before the law for all children in public schools. *Brown* addressed the issue of *equality* in schooling. Forty-seven years later, the No Child Left Behind (NCLB) legislation extended the role of the federal government to the related issue of *quality* in schooling for all children. As Chubb (2005, p. 29) argues, in addition to shouldering more of the costs of public schooling, the federal government has expanded its role and taken the high moral ground, "becoming the leading advocate for equality—for racial minorities, special education students, English language learners, and girls."

Standards-Based Reform and America's Underachieving Schools

The 1983 publication of *A Nation at Risk* was the catalyst for NCLB, today's standards-based reform movement. A short sixty-three-page book, written in direct, simple language without academic jargon or confusing statistics and tables, it called public attention to serious deficiencies in schools. "Our nation is at risk," the report begins. "Our once unchallenged preeminence in commerce, industry, science, and technological innovation is being overtaken by competitors throughout the world. . . . What was unimaginable a generation ago has begun to occur—others are matching and surpassing our educational attainments. If an unfriendly foreign power had attempted to impose on America the mediocre educational performance that exists today, we might have viewed it as an act of war" (National Commission on Excellence in Education, 1983, p. 5).

A sobersided panel of educators, which included college presidents and public school administrators, brought together by the secretary of education, used intentionally alarming language to describe the state of K–12 education and shake Americans from their quiescence and self-satisfaction. The panel found a host of problems in schools. Among other things, achievement scores on standardized tests were down, and international comparisons were embarrassing. Thirteen percent of all seventeen-year-olds were functionally illiterate, and many of their literate peers could not "draw an inference from written material, write a persuasive essay, or solve a math problem that required more than one or two steps." The report's directness attracted attention of parents, educators, and elected officials. Recommendations for public education were straightforward: (1) improve education for all students and (2) develop higher standards. The report urged those in charge of the nation's schools to chart a more rigorous course and measure student progress more systematically.

In the 1980s, President George H. W. Bush recognized that states by themselves were not able to bring about necessary national changes. President Bush believed that the nation needed to establish world-class national standards in core subject areas, and to make sure that students were meeting these standards, his administration called for voluntary testing in grades 4, 8, and 12. In 1989, at a conference in Charlottesville, Virginia, President Bush and the nation's governors agreed to six national goals for education. "America 2000," as the goals became known, stipulated that the following would be accomplished by the year 2000:

1. All children will start school ready to learn.
2. The high school graduation rate will increase to at least 90 percent.
3. All students in grades 4, 8, and 12 will demonstrate competency in English, math, science, civics, foreign language, economics, arts, history, and geography.
4. U.S. students will be first in math and science achievement.
5. Every adult will be literate.
6. Every school in the United States will be free of drugs and violence and the unauthorized presence of firearms and alcohol (Jennings, 1998, p. 14).

In 1994, Congress added additional goals designed to improve the quality of teacher education and increase parental involvement in schools. These proposals would take standards-based reform in a new direction. America 2000 encouraged high standards and high national expectations for all students. The federal government would not intrude on the states' control of education, but it could urge them to raise the academic bar. The standards proposed by President Bush were not designed to serve as a national curriculum. Instead, they were to be academic models that state and local school districts could adopt to raise expectations for teachers and students. Improved state standards promised national reform. Variations would continue to be found across state lines, but students, parents, and teachers in every state would know what was expected of them. Schools of education were asked to equip prospective and in-service teachers with the skills needed to help students meet the new standards. Test makers were asked to develop examinations keyed to the standards. By design, all students were to benefit.

Although the timetable proved to be overly optimistic, President Bush's call for high national standards and assessment of student performance set the stage for substantive reform in the quality of education. In 1992, Bill Clinton was elected president. Clinton, as governor, had been active in the 1989 education conference. A year later, President Clinton proposed "Goals 2000," a legislative package that, if it had been enacted, would have set into law the six national goals for education agreed to by George Bush and the nation's governors. Under President Bush, the Department of Education provided grants to national organizations of scholars and teachers to develop voluntary national standards in important school subjects. President Clinton's administration provided funds for states to develop standards of their own at about the same time that national standards were being released. The issue grew murky with both states and national organizations developing academic standards simultaneously. President Clinton tried to help by agreeing to support state standards as long as states volunteered to go along with national testing. However, the ensuing confusion between state and national standards and difficulty of assessing fifty state systems through one national test hindered the progress of school reform until 2001.

No Child Left Behind Act (2001)

The NCLB legislation, supported by large majorities of Democrats and Republicans in both houses of Congress and signed by President George W. Bush, is designed to create a stronger, more accountable education system. It does not call for national standards or national tests, as Presidents Bush and Clinton had advocated. NCLB legislation shifts the action back to the states. Under the new law, states are required to develop their own standards for what students should know at every grade level in math, English/language arts, and science. When the specific standards were put in place—stipulating the level at which a child should be reading by the end of third grade, for example—the states began to assess every student's progress with exams aligned with state standards. All states must administer academic assessments in reading and mathematics to students in grades 3 through 8 and once more in high school. Beginning in 2007–2008, NCLB required states to conduct assessments in science at least once in grades 3 to 5, 6 to 9, and 10 to 12.

States are required to develop a "single statewide accountability system" to ensure that schools and school districts—not individual students—are making "adequate yearly progress" in math, English/language arts, and science. Progress is to be demonstrated for all students, with "separate measurable annual objectives" for (1) economically disadvantaged students, (2) students from major racial and ethnic groups, (3) students with disabilities, and (4) students with limited English proficiency. By 2014, twelve years from the enactment of the legislation, "all students were to meet the proficient level on state tests." The legislation requires each school, school district, and state to make "adequate yearly progress"[1] toward meeting state standards. Parents with children in failing schools are given the right to have them transferred to better-performing schools. Students who have been victims of violent crimes and those who attend persistently unsafe schools also are allowed to transfer schools (No Child Left Behind, 2008). NCLB legislation focuses on all children, from all races and social classes. The legislation recognizes that the nation increasingly depends on the academic success of minority children and that their poor academic performance—the achievement gap between white and black and Hispanic students—is not only an affront to American values but also a threat to the nation's economic future (Reyna, 2005). For education to function as the great equalizer in American society, it must serve minority children, the children of low-income families, English language learners, and other disadvantaged children as well as it serves wealthier white Americans. NCLB is a step in that direction, and its high standards demand an end to the "soft bigotry of low expectations" for those on the margins of society (Hickok, 2010; Manna, 2011).

---

[1]As defined on the NCLB website (2008), adequate yearly progress is "an individual state's measure of progress toward the goal of 100 percent of students achieving state academic standards in at least reading/language arts and math. It sets the minimum level of proficiency that the state, its school districts, and schools must achieve each year on annual tests and related academic indicators." In late 2011, Secretary of Education Arne Duncan announced that states could request waivers of specific NCLB requirements, including adequate yearly progress and the 2013–2014 deadline.

Three presidents, two Republicans and one Democrat, established the priorities for the school reform agenda in the early twenty-first century. They agreed that to improve the nation's schools, the United States should develop a system of high state standards and rigorous state testing. The standards movement will help *all* students. This is a significant policy shift in itself. Currently, U.S. schools sort students into various categories by academic ability and treat different groups of students differently. The most able students are provided college-preparatory curricula of reasonably high quality. For all other students—in many cases, the vast majority of students—the curriculum is watered down, ineffective, and unlikely to equip them with the skills and knowledge needed for economic success and the common store of knowledge necessary for informed civic participation. The standards movement is designed to bring all students up to higher levels of academic performance no matter where they begin (Tucker and Codding, 1998). An education built around academic standards serves students from poor as well as wealthy homes, and it will be especially valuable to students who, in the course of their education, move from school to school or district to district. It should be self-evident that students are likely to learn more when there is common agreement about what they are supposed to learn and high expectations for their achievement. In fact, the logic of standards-based school reform is so obvious and compelling that one may wonder why it is referred to as a *reform movement* (Bennett, Finn, and Cribb, 1999, p. 586). Opinion polls indicate popular support for high academic standards and regular assessments of learning as well compensation plans that link teacher pay to student performance on standardized tests (Howell, Peterson, and West, 2011; Moe, 2011).

Support for the standards movement rests on the assumption that the subject matter that students learn in school is important: content counts. The store of knowledge possessed by individuals operates to determine success or failure in school and, to a large measure, success or failure in life (Hirsch, 1996). That is, individuals who know more—those who have a greater store of knowledge—are more successful in school and tend to be more successful in getting into college, securing employment, and earning higher-than-average salaries. Subject-matter knowledge is the very essence of education. It is important to be able to read, but it is more important what is read. Students who study and understand Dickens, Shakespeare, and Virginia Woolf are more likely to succeed than students who read less important, less challenging works. It is not enough for schools to pass students along from grade to grade simply because they attend regularly and are taught so many hours of reading and mathematics. States must establish content standards appropriate for success, and students must demonstrate command of subject matter and academic skills at the level described in the standards. Schools should not focus on "library skills" and "keyboarding" or other warm-and-fuzzy objectives. It is the content of education that matters.

When schools focus on content-free goals—for example, self-esteem exercises, discovery techniques, and cooperative learning strategies—all students suffer because they learn less subject-matter content (Hirsch, 1996; Bennett et al., 1999). Any approach to learning that emphasizes a process approach limits the futures of children by denying them access to intellectual capital—that is, the

FIGURE 8.1 Four Pillars of NCLB

Accountability: States must describe how they will close the achievement gap among all children and make sure all students achieve academic proficiency. States must produce annual report cards that inform parents of the academic progress made by the state and the various school districts within the state.

More local freedom: States and school districts have unprecedented flexibility in how they use federal education funds. Districts can use these funds for their particular needs, such as hiring new teachers, increasing teacher pay, and improving teacher training and professional development.

Encouraging proven methods: Federal funding is targeted to support programs that have been proven effective in increasing student learning and achievement. Reading programs are an example. NCLB supports scientifically based instruction in the early grades under the new Reading First Program and in preschool under the Early Reading First Program.

Choices for parents: NCLB allows parents to choose other public schools or take advantage of free tutoring if their child attends a school that needs improvement. Also, parents can choose another public school if the school their child attends is unsafe.

Source: No Child Left Behind (2008).

store of knowledge needed to do well in school and life. All children are harmed by a content-light approach, but children of the poor will be affected the most. Children from middle-class homes can count on their parents to compensate for schools' inattention to subject matter. They are likely to benefit from the company of literate adults, family trips, and private tutors to help them with foreign language acquisition, music and art, and mathematics. The negative effects of watered-down content, low standards, and low expectations fall hardest on the poor and students from less well educated families. For these students, standards reform can produce dramatic improvements (See Figure 8.1 Four Pillars of NCLB.).

Standardized Tests and Standards-Based Reform

Although standardized testing provides the scientific base necessary to support the art of teaching, standardized testing sometimes has a negative connotation. No doubt you have heard that standardized tests are biased or unfair or worse. This is a common but an unsupported piece of education folklore. The truth is that standardized tests are designed to provide fair evaluations and a level playing field for all test takers. *Standardized* refers to the fact that the test content and the conditions for test takers are always and everywhere the same and that students taking the tests are protected from an evaluator's personal preferences or prejudice. When students take the ACT or the SAT, for example, they are all taking the same tests under the same testing conditions, and they will be compared objectively with students of their age with similar years of schooling.

Standardized testing programs were introduced to counter charges of examiner bias and subjectivity. Nineteenth-century Britain, in the throes of an expanding economy and of becoming an empire, found that it could not satisfy the demand for large numbers of managers through traditional patronage appointments. There were simply not enough privileged males—the sons of civil servants, members of Parliament, and others of wealth and connections—to fill vacancies worldwide. Competitive exams were introduced to open the civil service to a broader range of male applicants. The United States also used testing to democratize the selection of government workers. Political abuse, through patronage, was rampant in the nineteenth century. Civil service reform began with the Pendleton Act of 1883, which established competitive exams for prospective government workers.

Today, standardized testing programs provide the yardstick needed to chart the progress and shortcomings of education, and test results allow schools to report the status of education to parents, public officials, and prospective employers. Previous generations of education reformers concerned themselves with making schooling available to children of all classes and races, and to a large extent they were successful. Today, a higher percentage of students are completing high school than ever before. The issue for reformers is no longer *availability*; the current generation of reformers now is obligated to consider the *quality* of schooling. As Mortimer Adler (1982) argues, we cannot satisfy the legal mandates for education simply by guaranteeing all children access to education. In order to satisfy the educational responsibilities of a democratic society, public education must demonstrate the extent to which each student is acquiring requisite skills and knowledge.

Standardized testing is an essential element of standards-based reform. By using standardized tests, schools can determine one student's command of content and compare that student to others in an objective and fair manner. Schools can also measure an individual teacher's contributions to student learning. Modern information technology enables school officials to assemble good data over time about student achievement and teacher abilities. By examining student performance on standardized tests, schools can determine which teachers add the most to student learning and the magnitude of a teacher's contributions. As Terry Moe (2011) writes, "Nothing could be more basic to school improvement than good information . . . modern data systems can readily be designed to *link* teachers to the students in their classes and thus to provide objective and continually updated measures of teacher performance" (p. 318).

Effective change does not occur by chance. Educational planners need to have appropriate measures of student progress and teacher effectiveness to move schools forward. Impressionistic data are not sufficient; anecdotal evidence is not scientific. It is not enough to say that a student "seems to be learning" or that this teacher "appears to be work well with hard-to-teach students." Schools need data-driven answers to direct questions about curriculum, student learning, and teacher effectiveness. At what grade level is a student reading? How much of the required curriculum has each student mastered compared to others students of the same age? How much mathematics learning has occurred in one teacher's class compared with the mathematics learning in the classes of other teachers? Data to answer these questions are available from standardized testing programs, and the data should be collected and analyzed. Standardized testing programs enable educators to measure the extent to which schools are meeting their responsibility to deliver quality education to all children.

Standards-Based Reform is Working

NCLB has brought new focus to minority student achievement by "disaggregating" data, that is, reporting student performance on tests by socioeconomic criteria, not only by the mean scores of all test takers. As President George W. Bush said in his advocacy of NCLB, "If you don't disaggregate, the achievement gap gets hidden in the averages" (quoted in Hickok, 2010, p. 12). Schools with above-average mean scores on standardized tests can hide the achievement gap experienced by low-performing groups. Standards-based school reformers embrace high academic standards for all students. As Finn and Petrilli (2011) write, education reformers "believe America's achievement gaps are morally unacceptable, socially divisive, and politically unstable, and we recognize that for the United States to remain secure and prosperous in a dangerous but shrinking and flattening world, our education system must be far more effective and productive than it is today" (p. 6).

Standards-based reform is beginning to show positive results. Since 1969, the federal government has financed an assessment program known as the National Assessment of Educational Progress (NAEP). Now administered by the Educational Testing Service of Princeton, New Jersey, NAEP's website (www.nces.ed.gov/nationsreportcard) describes the organization as the "only nationally representative and continuing assessment of what America's students need to know and can do in various subject areas"—mathematics, reading, science, writing, the arts, civics, economics, geography, and U.S. history. NAEP data from the national assessments are reported for individual state with attention to the national averages for specific subsets of the student population. Test results are disaggregated and reported by race, ethnicity, and gender.

In late 2011, NAEP released data on *The Nation's Report Card* (NCES, 2011). Much of what NAEP found is very positive and reflects solid academic progress:

- Fourth and eighth graders scored higher across a wide range of mathematics skills in 2011 than in previous assessment years.
- The white-black achievement score gaps have narrowed from 1992 to 2011 in 16 of 35 states with samples large enough to report results for black students.
- The white-Hispanic achievement score gaps have narrowed in four participating states with samples large enough to report results for Hispanic students.

Some of the data from the 2011 mathematics assessment are troubling:

- Despite long-term gains, there were no significant changes in white-black or white-Hispanic scores from 2009 to 2011.
- For grade 4, mathematics scores were not higher than they were in 2009 for the lowest-achieving students.
- Among fourth graders who scored below the 25th percentile, 31 percent were white, 28 percent were black, 34 percent were Hispanic, and 74 percent were eligible for free/reduced price school lunch.
- Private school students scored higher than students in public schools.

President Obama and the Prospects for Standards-Based Reform

In 2010, President Obama urged Congress to reauthorize the Elementary and Secondary Education Act. The U.S. Department of Education issued the "Blueprint for Reform," which describes, in the president's words, his commitment to high standards and the rigorous assessment of student learning: "We will support the development and use of a new generation of assessments that are aligned with college- and career-ready standards, to better determine whether students have acquired the skills they need for success" (U.S. Department of Education, 2010, pp. 3–4). The blueprint calls on states to develop standards in English/language arts and mathematics and high-quality assessments that measure the extent to which students have met standards of learning necessary for success. States may also develop standards and assessments in other subject areas, such as science and history and technical areas, if they choose, but the emphasis is on the core subjects needed for academic and career success after high school. Federal funding will be awarded to states to help them develop and implement assessments that are aligned with the new standards.

Standards-based reform is moving forward at the state level. The website of the Common Core State Standards Initiative (www.corestandards.org) reports the work begun by the National Governors' Association to develop rigorous, scientifically based standards for all students that are aligned with college and work expectations. The Common Core Standards were developed in collaboration with teachers, school administrators, and college faculty members to provide a framework of standards that will help all students succeed. By late 2011, all but six states had adopted the Common Core Standards. Popular enthusiasm for standards-based teaching and learning has increased since the passage of NCLB legislation in 2001. The reform movement has enjoyed support from every U.S. president, Republican and Democrat, since George W. Bush signed the NCLB amendment to the Elementary and Secondary Education Act. Standards-based reform will no doubt change shape and focus, but the reasoning that undergirds this approach to educational reform is compelling.

The Logic Behind Standards-Based Reform

Advocates of standards-based reform in education offer several arguments to support their position, and they encourage you to think about the issue with these points in mind:

- Although the U.S. Constitution makes no reference to the federal government's role in education, citizens expect a national effort to urge states along the path to better schooling, more rigorous outcomes, and scientifically validated instruction and assessment.
- Schools are not as good as they should be. The current patchwork of state standards and tests has produced a system of education of uneven quality and questionable academic rigor that does not serve all students or prepare them for success in a competitive global economy.

- The Common Core Standards, designed by the states with coordination by the federal government, will improve learning for all students and align K–12 education with college and work expectations.
- Standards-based reform places appropriate emphasis on "gateway disciplines," those subject areas, English/language arts and mathematics, that prepare students for success in higher education and the workplace.
- Content matters in education. For academic and career advancement and for the civic well-being of the nation, all students should command reasonable store of common knowledge in key academic disciplines.
- Schools are expected to be accountable for learning. The public deserves objective, measurable data on student performance as well as the learning outcomes produced by individual teachers.
- Standardized testing is an essential component of standards-based reform necessary to gauge the extent to which standards have or have not been met.
- Standardized testing has a long and distinguished history of objectivity and fairness around the world and in the United States.
- Standards-based reform is more than improving test scores. It is designed to ensure the academic and personal success for all students and to reduce the achievement gap experienced by economically disadvantaged students.

Standards-based reform and standardized assessments will alter for the better what is taught in American schools, what students learn, and how teaching and learning are assessed. NCLB is the most far-reaching reform of public education ever enacted in the United States. NCLB reflects a renewed commitment to the goal that no child will be ignored and left behind by the nation's schools. Standards-based reform was long overdue; it has begun to work now; and it holds every promise for continued success.

POSITION 2: STANDARDS-BASED REFORM IS FLAWED POLICY AND MISDIRECTED REFORM

NCLB was a punitive law based on erroneous assumption about how to improve schools. It assumed that reporting test scores to the public would be an effective lever for school reform. It assumed that shaming schools that were unable to lift test scores every year—and the people who work in them—would lead to higher test scores. It assumed that low test scores are caused by lazy teachers and lazy principals, who needed to be threatened with the loss of their jobs. Perhaps most naively, it assumed that higher test scores on standardized tests are synonymous with good education. Its assumption were wrong.

—Diane Ravitch (2010, pp. 110–111)

Advocates of the standards movement argue that they are responding responsibly to a crisis in education. *A Nation at Risk* (National Commission on Excellence in Education, 1983), the much-cited instigator of standards-based reform, describes a national danger brought about by anemic academic standards and poor student performance. The report argues that teachers are not teaching well and that students are not learning very much of value in schools. International comparisons of student achievement reflect so poorly on U.S. students that the result is considered a potential tragedy for all Americans. The authors of the report argue that Americans face a crisis both economically and politically. They claim that schools have let the nation down and that the nation is now in peril. If this were all true, an academic call to arms would be in order. The data and arguments of the report, however, defy common sense and do not stand up to even modest scrutiny. It's been thirty years since the publication of *A Nation at Risk*. In that time and despite terrorist attacks and natural disasters, the United States continues to experience prosperity and economic growth. American achievements in science, technology, and medicine are the envy of the world. When Nobel Prize winners are announced, you can bet half your SAT score that Americans will figure prominently among the winners. There is also solid evidence to indicate that the American students do quite well in international comparisons. Reviewing the results of six international achievement assessments conducted over a ten-year period, two researchers conclude that "U.S. students have generally performed *above average* in comparisons with students in other industrialized nations" (Boe and Shin, 2005, p. 694).

Everything is not perfect in education, but it is not crumbling and certainly not in crisis. The jeremiads are not to be believed. *A Nation at Risk* helped promote the myth of a failing public school system, and it is used for political purposes with little if anything to do with academic quality. Berliner and Biddle (1995) argue that the authors of the report distorted the picture of American schools. While there are still too many poor and failing schools, there is no evidence of systemic collapse, and overheated rhetoric and questionable comparisons do not match the facts. The charges, the authors say, are "errant nonsense":

> If we go by the evidence, despite greatly expanded student enrollment, the average American high school and college student is now doing as well as, or perhaps slightly better than, that student did in previous years. Indeed, not only is student achievement remaining steady or rising slowly across the land, but so also is student intelligence. (Berliner and Biddle, 1995, p. 64)

Errant nonsense or not, *A Nation at Risk* focused attention on school reform for the first time in a generation. The report, widely publicized by journalists, made Americans suspicious of their schools. While some politicians and school reformers saw this as an honest opportunity to create sounder academic standards, others seized the report and used it to attack schools and advance their own agendas. Those on the far right in religion and politics used the "manufactured crisis" as an opportunity to take control of schools and ban ideas they found ideologically distasteful. Only with national testing and statewide curricula could ultraconservatives be assured that disquieting local voices—advocates of gay rights, abortion rights, and birth control, for example—could be kept out of schools. Other, more centrist conservatives wanted schools to return to the "good old days," before they had been captured by "social experimentalists," advocates of whole language, new math, and sex education in schools (Berliner and Biddle, 1995). The report also serves the political agenda of homeschoolers, charter school supporters, and other advocates of alternatives to public schools (Gardner, 2002; Bracey, 2003). The publication of *A Nation at Risk* fueled the myth of failing schools and paved the way for NCLB and a conservative school agenda that has little to do with real reform.

Privatization and Other Risks of a Business Rationale in Education

Advocates of standards-based reform argue that schools will be improved if those in charge of schools apply business principles to education and use testing data to provide incentives and punishments for classroom teachers and school administrators. They assume that school personnel can be alternately rewarded and flogged into excellence (Darling-Hammond, 2010; Ravitch, 2010).

McNeil (2000) and Horn and Kincheloe (2001) provide instructive histories of the Texas standards movement, a statewide effort and a national model for standards-based reform influenced by Ross Perot, the highly successful businessman and unsuccessful presidential candidate in 1992 and 1996. Perot, appointed head of a state commission on education reform, argues that if something is proved to be effective in business management, it must be good for education. Many in Texas were persuaded by this argument as well as by Perot's record of business success and his folksy straight-talking personal style. Perot distrusts middle management—a lesson he learned from business. He likes to control things from the top, and he had found midlevel managers an obstacle to change and champions of the status quo. Middle managers in business like things the way they are, he argues, and he believes this also is true in education. Perot places the blame for Texas's education problems at the doorsteps of school administrators (education's middle managers) and is convinced that they are opponents of reform and incompetent.

The consequences of Perot's standards-based reforms have been profound and largely negative. Perot and the school reform committee that he chaired advocate top-down management and a centralized system designed to bypass Texas school administrators. Schools have to be changed quickly and all at once. Following Perot's advice, the Texas legislature tried to manage schools as if they were a large, foundering business. Linda McNeil (2000) argues that school reform failed in Texas because what works for a business does not necessarily work in education. Texas legislators, she writes, tried to simplify and standardize everything about classroom processes: planning, teaching, and assessment. They attempted to "teacherproof" the curriculum with a checklist for teacher behaviors and tests of students' minimum skills. This might be an effective way to change a production-line industry, but it is the wrong approach for education and is particularly damaging to the brightest and most thoughtful teachers.

By mandating certain forms of instruction and curriculum, Texas school officials made schools exceedingly comfortable for mediocre teachers who like to teach routine lessons according to a standard sequence and format and who like working as deskilled laborers not having to think about their work. They made being a Texas public school teacher extremely uncomfortable for those who know their subjects well, who teach in ways that engage their students, and who match their teaching to reflect their own continued learning (McNeil, 2000).

A business focus on schools distorts an understanding of teachers' work and the critical role that teachers play in education. It fails to take into account teachers' ability to encourage or discourage students, to bring out their potential or thwart it, to open students to new worlds of understanding, or to close them off. Business solutions are overly simple, with an emphasis on uniformity of outcomes and achievement measured along a single plane. Success in business is determined by profits and growth. According to a business model, school success could be measured by test scores and increases in the number of test takers who improve. The emphasis on scores and statewide achievement measures is too narrow a measure for schools. It is, McNeil (2000) writes, as if the multiple dimensions of a well-rounded, well-educated child had been reduced to a "stick figure." The narrowness of statewide testing fails to capture important dimensions of learning. While testing may indicate whether children can indent paragraphs or reduce fractions, it does not begin to capture a student's social awareness, civic responsibility, creativity and imagination, and emotional development. Learning reduced to the measurable leaves out more than it can report.

Education's embrace of business models is unwarranted, but it is not surprising. *A Nation at Risk* (National Commission on Excellence in Education, 1983) tied education and business together and frightened readers with threats to their economic comfort. Schooling must attend to the "new basics" or the American system was at risk. According to the report,

> The risk is not only that the Japanese make automobiles more efficiently than Americans and have government subsidies for development and export. It is not just that the South Koreans recently built the world's most efficient steel mill, or that American machine tools, once the pride of the world, are being displaced by German products. It is also that these developments signify a redistribution of trained capability throughout the globe. Knowledge, learning, information, and skilled intelligence are the new raw materials of international commerce. (pp. 6–7)

Think about the best teachers you have had in school. It is quite likely they all had high standards for your work, but did they simply take someone else's standards off the shelf and apply them? Did they use prepackaged lessons, or did they craft standards based on what they knew about you and your classmates and what they imagined you would like to read, explore, and think about? Were your best teachers the efficient managers of someone else's plan for your education, or were they the personal planners and evaluators for you and others in your class? How would you describe your best teachers? Jonathan Kozol says that the best teachers he knows are poets at heart who love the unpredictable aspects of teaching and uniqueness of every child in their classes. That's why, he argues, they are drawn to teaching children and not to business school. Teaching to standards that are not their own will make teachers technicians, and the classroom will lose its best teachers. Kozol writes, "If we force them to be a little more than the obedient floor managers for industry, they won't remain in public schools. The price will be too high. The poetry will have turned to prose: the worst kind too, the prose of experts who know every single thing there is to know except their own destructiveness" (quoted in Cohen and Rogers, 2000, p. xii).

Costs of High-Stakes Testing

In a witty attack on standardized testing, Banesh Hoffmann (1962) recounted a debate played out on the pages of the *Times* of London. A letter to the newspaper's editor asked for help in solving a multiple-choice problem from a battery of school tests the letter writer's son had taken. At first glance, the question seemed to be straightforward and not surprising to anyone who has taken school tests. It asked, "Which is the odd one out among cricket, football, billiards, and hockey?"

The letter writer believed the answer must be billiards because it is the only one of the four games played indoors. He admitted to being less than sure of his answer and reported that there was no agreement among his acquaintances. One of his neighbors argued that the correct choice was cricket because in all the other games, the object was to put a ball in a net. The writer's son had selected hockey because it was the only one that was a "girls' game." The letter writer asked readers of the *Times* for help. Ensuing letters and arguments succeeded only in muddying the waters since the logic supporting one choice was no more compelling than the logic supporting any other. For example, billiards could be considered the odd one out because it is the only one of the four games listed that is not ordinarily a team game. It is the only one in which the color of the ball matters. It is the only one in which more than one ball is in play, and it is the only one played on a green cloth rather than a grass field. Unfortunately, equally convincing briefs could be submitted in behalf of the other choices.

Hoffmann fumed about the inherent bias in the question. He assumed the test was designed to measure reasoning ability and not sports knowledge, but he argued that the test taker might be disadvantaged by too little experience with athletics; for example, not all students with good reasoning skills may know how cricket is played. Test takers who know too much about sports also might be disadvantaged; they might choose hockey as the odd one out because it is really two different games that share the same name—in England and in several other countries, hockey is a game typically played on grass by players who receive no salary; elsewhere, it is a game played on ice, often by professional athletes.

The language of this test item also may trip up students, preventing it from measuring reasoning ability. For example, many working-class students may not be familiar with either cricket or billiards. Items of this sort favor the language and culture of the middle and upper-middle classes, and low scores may reflect measures of social standing more than achievement. Americans also could be disadvantaged by the test item wording, which asks test takers to select the "odd one out." A similar test item in the United States probably would read, "Which of the following does not belong?"

Test questions of this sort seem silly. There is no readily discernible "right" answer, and test takers have no opportunity to demonstrate the thought processes that led to their decisions. As Hoffmann (1962) noted, "What sense is there in giving tests in which the candidate just picks answers, and is not allowed to give the reasons for his choice?" (p. 20). Multiple-choice questions are an unnatural problem-solving format incongruous with solving real-life problems. Rarely are life's dilemmas delineated by four answers, one of which is guaranteed to be correct. Good problem solvers in the real world seldom are locked away, deprived of books, computers, and human contact; they seldom are told to respond to a set of timed, multiple-choice questions with no practical meaning.

In the 1980s, the nation was deluged with reports critical of public education. (For examples written during the same period that were equally critical of public education, see Adler, 1982; Boyer, 1983; Twentieth Century Fund, 1983; Goodlad, 1984; and Sizer, 1984.) The standards movement recommended testing as a quick-fix solution, and like all quick fixes, it is overly simplistic and accompanied by problems. State accountability systems tied to common standards place students and school personnel in thralldom to testing companies. Multiple-choice tests have become the assessment tool of choice for most states, and they involve high stakes. Students who do poorly on state tests may not be promoted or graduate. Advocates of standards-based reforms want to tie teacher salaries to their students' performance on standardized tests. Art and music, typically not part of standards assessments, tend to disappear from many schools, and upper-level science electives, such as marine biology or biochemistry, also may fall victim to the standards movement because they are not tested. In many school districts, a good part of the school year is now given over to test preparation. When teachers take weeks and months from the regular curriculum to teach students test preparation skills, it cannot be known for certain if subsequent gains in test scores result from real advances in learning and improvements in the quality of education or if higher scores reflect the impact of drill and repetition and an improvement mainly in test-taking skills (McKeon, Dianda, and McLaren, 2001).

High-stakes multiple-choice tests have few fans in the education community. Practitioners and researchers in education believe that to capture the full range of a student's skill and knowledge, it is necessary to use an array of techniques, designed by classroom teachers, and administered over time. In addition to standardized tests, assessments should use classroom-based student assessments, portfolio reviews, and essay exams that measure academic subtleties and the complexities of thinking (Janesick, 2001; Neil, 2009). The education research community has opposed single "high-stakes" measures. Consider Figure 8.2, the position statement on high-stakes testing of the American Educational Research Association, the nation's largest organization dedicated to the scientific study of education. The NCLB's reliance on high-stakes testing ignores the experience and recommendations of testing researchers and other experts.

FIGURE 8.2 High-Stakes Testing in Pre-K–12 Education Position Statement of the American Educational Research Association (excerpted). Adopted July 2000.

---

1. **Protection Against High-Stakes Decisions Based on a Single Test**
   Decisions that affect individual students' life chances or educational opportunities should not be made on the basis of test scores alone. . . . [W]hen there is credible evidence that a test score may not adequately reflect a student's true proficiency, alternative acceptable means should be provided by which to demonstrate attainment of the tested standards.

2. **Adequate Resources and Opportunity to Learn**
   [I]t must be shown that the tested content has been incorporated into the curriculum, materials, and instruction students are provided before high-stakes consequences are imposed for failing examinations.

3. **Validation for Each Separate Intended Use**
   Test valid for one use may be invalid for another.

4. **Full Disclosure of Likely Negative Consequences of High-Stakes Testing Programs**
   Where credible scientific evidence suggests that a given type of testing program is likely to have negative effects, test developers and users should make a serious effort to explain these possible effects to policy makers.

5. **Alignment Between the Test and the Curriculum**
   Both the content of the test and the cognitive process engaged in taking the test should adequately represent the curriculum. High-stakes tests should not be limited to that portion of the relevant curriculum that is easiest to measure.

6. **Careful Adherence to Explicit Rules Determining Which Students Are to Be Tested**
   When schools, districts, or other administrative units are compared to one another or when changes in scores are tracked over time, there must be explicit policies specifying which students are to be tested. . . .

7. **Sufficient Reliability for Each Intended Use**
   Reliability refers to the accuracy or precision of test scores. It must be shown that scores reported for individuals or for schools are sufficiently accurate to support each intended interpretation.

8. **Ongoing Evaluation of Intended and Unintended Effects of High-Stakes Testing**

Source: www.aera.net/about/policyandprograms, 2011.

Equity

Low-income students, who are disproportionately children of color, go to under-resourced schools that serve up a thin gruel of test preparation (Neil, 2009, p. 31).

Because it is unrealistic to expect improvements in the educational system to fully offset the disadvantages faced by historically lower performing groups of students, we need to complement these programmatic and systemic reforms with out-of-school interventions, such as high quality preschool services, and programs that address nonschool conditions such as housing, poverty, health care and safety (Sunderman, 2008, p. 225).

Students come to school with various backgrounds and differing sets of academic advantages and disadvantages. More than 10 percent of children come from homes where English is not the primary language. One in five children lives in poverty. These children typically test poorly and have trouble with math, science, and language arts (Janesick, 2001; McKeon, Dianda, and McLaren, 2001). The nation may well be in crisis, Deborah Meier argues, but it's not the crisis described by the authors of *A Nation at Risk*. The real crisis, she says, is one of equity and justice for our most vulnerable citizens: the children of the poor. The United States spends "less on child welfare—baby care, medical care, family leave—than almost every foreign counterpart," and in the United States, the gap between rich and poor is greater than in other advanced industrial countries, while "our high rate of and investment in incarceration places us in a class by ourselves" (Meier, 2000, pp. 12–13). The size and costs of America's prison system have soared. In 2008, the Pew Center on the States (2008) reported that, for the first time in American history, more than 1 in every 100 adults was in prison, at a cost to the states of more than $49 billion a year. The incarceration rate for black men ages twenty to thirty-four was 1 in 9. The rate for all black men was 1 in 41; the rate for all white men was 1 in 245.

The real crisis facing the United States is social, not academic. Children who come to school hungry and poor are not likely to be helped by more rigorous standards. Children with children of their own and children from abusive homes are unlikely to see their lives improve through statewide accountability plans. The real national risk is more appropriately measured not by test scores but by dropout rates, unemployment statistics, and the juvenile incarceration rate. By itself, the standards-based reform movement will not affect deeper social problems. The standards movement can be thought of as a new kind of discrimination. Under the guise of fairness, offering all students the same curriculum, same forms of instruction, and same objective assessments, students from less wealthy homes with less well educated parents are denied the education they need. With its emphasis on drill and repetitive practice for the exams, the standards movement has increased classroom tedium and time spent on numbing routine. High-stakes testing has added stress and the threat of failure. The negative impact of standards reform has fallen hardest on poor and minority students. In Texas, the graduation rate for minority students has decreased since the beginning of the standards movement (McNeil, 2000). Increasing numbers of poor-performing students have been pushed out of schools made less pleasant by the changes brought by standards reform.

This is not a new phenomenon. Variables of class and race have always had high correlations with the dropout rate. SAT scores, for example, of both white and black students are influenced by social class. Low parental income predicts low SAT scores, and the higher the family income, the higher the scores for both races. The black-white test gap narrows at the highest income levels. It helps to have wealthy parents if you want to score well on standardized tests (Lemann, 1999). The relationship between achievement and social factors should not be a surprise in a society where race and class weigh so heavily in so much of life. Supporters of the standards movement pretend that academic achievement is more important than anything else in securing a job. However, educational attainment is less likely to predict who will get into college or land a good job than race and class (Bowles, Gintis, and Groves, 2005; Douthat, 2005). The standards movement is a smoke screen. Under competitive economic systems, not everyone is expected to prosper equally. Supporters of standards pretend to sort winners and losers by academic achievement, as if academic achievement were not proxies for race and class, the real variables that determine who will succeed and who will fail in life.

Standards Alone Cannot Solve the Problems of Schooling

Everyone wants to improve schools and raise the levels of learning. No one is opposed to standards, even though teachers know that high standards alone cannot solve the social problems that spill over into schools. The National Education Association (NEA) and the American Federation of Teachers, organizations representing the majority of America's classroom teachers, endorse high standards and advocate closing the achievement gap between rich and poor students. The NEA supports the Common Core Standards, released in 2010, and enthuses about their implications for classroom practice: "Gone are the days of summary book reports—students will have to analyze the story rather than rehash the plot—and no more teaching kindergartners to memorize the hands on the clock to tell time. Now they'll learn numeracy—the relationship between the numbers, so they're prepared to learn more complex relationships with higher numbers in first and second grade and beyond" (NEA, 2011).

The problem is not with standards. However, teachers and teacher organizations know that high standards cannot paper over the social problems students bring to school, and they also know that the accurate assessment of student learning demands more than standardized tests. Look carefully at these and other issues before you jump on the standards bandwagon.

Unresolved Issues of Standards-Based Reform

- *Standardized tests undermine standards-based reform.* Tests can play only a limited role in measuring what students learn and assessing what teachers and administrators contribute to student achievement. The narrow numerical measures of NCLB leads to a system of test-label-punish process that benefits no one, least of all the children it was supposed to help (Weingarten, 2008).
- *One standard fits none.* Outside of a very few core standards, there is no compelling reason that all students of a state should be held to the same standards. Such uniformity penalizes the highest-achieving students as well as those who have the most difficulty in school.
- *Classroom teachers have an important role to play in assessment.* Standardized tests cannot capture the full range of classroom learning, including processing skills, affective learning, and individual academic progress. Good assessment of student learning must include the professional judgment of teachers, not only a list of test scores (Ravitch, 2010).

- *Attend to social measures of poor performance.* The United States trails other industrialized nations in its ability to limit the percentage of citizens living in poverty and reduce the infant mortality rate, measures directly related to educational achievement. It is not likely educational achievement will rise until these statistics decline.
- *Who should be held accountable?* As Jonathan Kozol (2005) writes, "There is something deeply hypocritical about a society that holds an inner-city child only eight years old 'accountable' for her performance on a high-stakes standardized exam but does not hold the high officials of our government accountable for robbing her of what they gave their own kids" (pp. 53–54).
- *Don't shortchange the poor.* Students with good test scores in well-funded schools will continue to benefit from a full range of curriculum options, such as art and music, and elective courses and programs. Students from poor neighborhoods will have fewer options, more drill, and a leaner diet of basic skills (McKenzie, 2003, p. 2).
- *Emphasis on English/language arts and math hurts other subjects.* Standards-based reform has many worthwhile goals but it has served to narrow the curriculum, caused schools to discontinue successful programs, de-emphasized subjects not included on standardized tests, and forced low-achieving students out of school (Darling-Hammond, 2010).
- *Teaching to the test.* As one classroom teacher writes, despite its lofty goals, NCLB encourages teaching to the test, and "it was accompanied by a loss of freedom to teach and to learn. It forced teachers to focus instruction on test taking rather than learning" (Behrent, 2009).

Reform movements with so many problems and so many unresolved issues should be greeted with suspicion. Who will be served by standards-based reform? Who will be disadvantaged? Is this real reform, or is it the smoke and mirrors of sham reform? Standards-based reform is ignoring the real problems. It seems likely to discourage teachers and administrators while doing little to improve education for most students. We are puzzled how NCLB can be referred to as "reform."

For Discussion

1. The Tenth Amendment to the U.S. Constitution states, "The powers not delegated to the United States by the Constitution, nor prohibited by it to the States, are reserved to the States respectively, or to the people." As a result of this division of legislative authority, the United States has developed a system of local rather than national control of education. By contrast, Great Britain has moved toward national control, and France has long had a national system of education. Leaving aside constitutional issues, do you think that education in the United States would benefit if it were to move in the direction of national standards and national examinations? What, if anything, would be lost?

2. Charles Murray (2007) of the American Enterprise Institute writes, "For most high school students who want to attend an elite college, the SAT is more than a test. It is one of life's landmarks" (p. 1). Once a supporter of the exam, Murray now believes

that the exam should be abolished. Citing research evidence, he argues that the SAT does not predict college success any better than high school grades and that it has become a negative force in American life. FairTest (2008) reported that 755 four-year colleges did not use the SAT-1 or the ACT to admit a substantial number of undergraduates.

If you were designing the admission process for your college or university, what standardized tests, if any, would you use? In place of, or in addition to, standardized tests, how would you decide which students get the opportunity to attend your school? Would you use class rank, high school grades, interviews, records of extra-curricular activities, or the academic rigor of the student's high school classes? Would you include the applicant's history of service or athletics, whether the applicant was first-generation college, or the socioeconomic status of the applicant's family?

3. In 2011, cheating scandals came to light in several school districts in New Jersey and Pennsylvania and in the cities of Atlanta, New York, and Washington, D.C. Class-room teachers and school administrators were found to have given direct assistance to students taking standardized tests, and in some cases they erased incorrect test responses and bubbled in correct answers. The actions may have been prompted by the desire to help a struggling student graduate or make a school look better, but a newspaper article describes the teachers as "stressed educators who take inap-propriate risks—and brash ones who appear to believe they can flout the rules with impunity" (Otterman, 2011). Test tampering and providing assistance to test takers violates the integrity of the assessment process, and such actions are clearly prohib-ited by law. Teachers and administrators, guilty of these violations, are subject to a range of discipline ranging from suspension without pay to dismissal.

Is it ever possible to defend the actions of the teachers and administrators who give assistance to students taking exams? If teachers believe that the results of standardized tests will be damaging to their students, is it excusable for them to offer help with difficult questions or change student answers to some questions? What actions should be taken against teachers and administrators found guilty of violating the rules of test administration?

References

ADLER, M. J. (1982). *The Paideia Proposal: An Educational Manifesto.* New York: Macmillan.

BEHRENT, M. (2009). "Reclaiming Our Freedom to Teach." *Harvard Educational Review* 79:240–246.

BENNETT, W. J., FINN, C. E., AND CRIBB, J. T. E. (1999). *The Educated Child: A Parent's Guide from Preschool through Eighth Grade.* New York: Free Press.

BERLINER, D. C., AND BIDDLE, B. J. (1995). *The Manufactured Crisis: Myths, Fraud, and the Attack on America's Public Schools.* Reading, MA: Addison-Wesley.

BOE, E. E., AND SHIN, S. (2005). "Is the United States Really Losing the International Horse Race in Academic Achievement?" *Kappan* 86:688–695.

BOWLES, S., GINTIS, H, AND GROVES, M. O., eds. (2005). *Unequal Chances: Family Back-ground and Economic Success.* Princeton, NJ: Princeton University Press.

BOYER, E. L. (1983). *High School: A Report on Secondary Education in America.* NY: Harper & Row.

BRACEY, G. W. (2003). *What You Should Know about the War against America's Public Schools.* Boston: Allyn and Bacon.

Brown v. Board of Education. (1954). 347 U.S. 483.

CHUBB, J. E., ed. (2005). *Within Our Reach: How America Can Educate Every Child.* Lanham, MD: Rowman & Littlefield.

COHEN, J., AND ROGERS, J., eds. (2000). *Will Standards Save Public Education?* Boston: Beacon.

DARLING-HAMMOND, L. (2010). *The Flat World and Education; How America's Commitment to Equity Will Determine Our Future.* New York: Teachers College Press.

DOUTHAT, R. (2005). "Does Meritocracy Work?" *The Atlantic* 296(November):120–126.

FairTest. (2002). "Initial FairTest Analysis of ESEA as passed by Congress, Dec. 2001." www.fairtest.org/nattest/ESEA.html.

———. (2008). www.fairtest.org/NCLB-After-Six-Years.

FINN, C. E., AND PETRILLI, M. J. (2011). *ESEA Briefing Book.* Washington, DC: Thomas B. Fordham Institute. www.edexcellence.net.

GARDNER, H. (2002). "Too Many Choices?" *New York Review of Books*, April 11, 51–54.

GOODLAD, J. L. (1984). *A Place Called School: Prospects for the Future.* NY: McGraw-Hill.

HICKOK, E. W. (2010). *Schoolhouse of Cards; An Inside Story of No Child Left Behind and Why America Needs a Real Education Revolution.* Lanham, MD: Rowman & Littlefield.

HIRSCH, E. D. (1996). *The Schools We Need and Why We Don't Have Them.* New York: Doubleday.

HOFFMANN, B. (1962). *The Tyranny of Testing.* New York: Cowell-Collier.

HORN, R. A., AND KINCHELOE, J. L., eds. (2001). *American Standards: Quality Education in a Complex World.* New York: Peter Lang.

HOWELL, W., PETERSON, P. E., AND WEST, M. (2011). "The Public Weighs in on School Reform." *Education Next.* Fall 2011. www.educationnext.org.

JANESICK, V. J. (2001). *The Assessment Debate: A Reference Handbook.* Santa Barbara, CA: ABC-CLIO.

JENNINGS, J. F. (1998). *Why National Standards and Tests? Politics and the Quest for Better Schools.* Thousand Oaks, CA: Sage.

———. (2004). "Test Today, Privatize Tomorrow: Using Accountability to 'Reform' Public Schools to Death." *Kappan* 85:569–577.

KOZOL, J. (2005). *The Shame of the Nation; The Restoration of Apartheid Schooling in America.* New York: Crown.

LEMANN, N. (1999). *The Big Test: The Secret History of the American Meritocracy.* New York: Farrar, Straus and Giroux.

MANNA, P. L. (2011). *Collision Course: Federal Education Policy Meets State and Local Realities.* Washington, DC: CQ Press.

MCKENZIE, J. (2003). "Gambling with Children." www.nochildleft.com.

MCKEON, D., DIANDA, M., AND MCLAREN, A. (2001). "A National Call for Midcourse Corrections and Next Steps." www.nea.org/accountability/advancing.html.

MCNEIL, L. M. (2000). *Contradictions of Reform: The Educational Costs of Standardized Testing.* New York: Routledge.

MEIER, D. (2000). "Educating a Democracy." In *Will Standards Save Public Education?*, ed. J. Cohen and J. Rogers Boston: Beacon.

MOE, T. M. (2011). *Special Interest: Teacher Unions and America's Public Schools.* Washington, DC: Brookings Institution.

MURRAY, C. (2007). "Abolish the SAT." *The American.* www.american.com/archive/2007/july-august.

National Center for Educational Statistics. (2011). "The Nation's Report Card. Mathematics 2011. National Assessment of Educational Progress at Grades 4 and 8." www.nces.ed.gov/nationsreportcard.

National Commission on Excellence in Education. (1983). *A Nation at Risk: The Imperative for Educational Reform*. Washington, DC: U.S. Department of Education.

National Education Association. (2011). "Here Come Common Core Standards." http://NEAToday.org/2011/05/07.

NEIL, M. (2009). "A Child Is Not a Test Score." *Roots & Branches* 2:28–65.

No Child Left Behind. (2008). www.ed.gov/nclb.

OTTERMAN, S. (2011). "In Cheating Cases, Teachers Who Took Risks or Flouted Rules." *New York Times*. October 17. www.nytimes.com.

Pew Center on the States. (2008). *One in 100: Behind Bars in America*. www.pewcenter onthestates.org.

RAVITCH, D. (2010). *The Death and Life of the Great American School System: How Testing and Choice are Undermining Education*. New York: Basic Books.

REYNA, V. F. (2005). "The No Child Left Behind Act and Scientific Research: A View from Washington, DC." In *The No Child Left Behind Legislation: Educational Research and Federal Funding*, ed. J. S. Carlson and J. R. Levin. Greenwich, CT: IAP.

SIZER, T. R. (1984). *Horace's Compromise: The Dilemma of the American High School*. Boston: Houghton Mifflin.

SUNDERMAN, G. L., ed. (2008). *Holding NCLB Accountable; Achieving Accountability, Equity and School Reform*. Thousand Oaks, CA: Corwin.

TUCKER, M. S., AND CODDING, J. B. (1998). *Standards for Our Schools: How to Set Them, Measure Them, and Reach Them*. San Francisco: Jossey-Bass.

Twentieth Century Fund. (1983). *Making the Grade: Report of the Twentieth Century Fund Task Force in Federal Elementary and Secondary Education*. NY: The Twentieth Century Fund.

U.S. Department of Education. (2010). "A Blueprint for Reform; The Reauthorization of the Elementary and Secondary Education Act." March 2010. www2.ed.gov/policy/elsec/leg/blueprint.

WEINGARTEN, R. (2008). "Student Testing." www.aft.org/pdfs.

CHAPTER 9

The Academic Achievement Gap: Old Remedies or New

Do current policies sufficiently address the academic achievement gap or are new measures needed?

POSITION 1: CURRENT PROGRAMS HAVE BEEN SUCCESSFUL AND SHOULD BE MAINTAINED

The Academic Achievement Gap

If you were an African American or Latino teenager in the early 1960s, you probably were prevented from attending an integrated high school (Weinberg, 1977). The laws of your state might have specifically mandated separate schools for black and white students. In other areas, school districts enforced regulations prohibiting students from enrolling in schools outside their neighborhoods—and those neighborhoods were segregated by race. There was only a fifty-fifty chance you would graduate from high school. Your chances of finishing college were about 4 in 100 (Orfield and Eaton, 1996).

Tests designed to measure academic achievement also documented the gap between students of color and their white counterparts. The National Assessment of Educational Progress (NAEP) testing program was established in 1969 "to monitor the academic achievement of nine-, thirteen-, and seventeen-year-olds currently enrolled in school" (Jencks and Phillips, 1998, p. 152). NAEP annually tests 70,000 to 100,000 students in reading, math, science, and writing. It is influential and credible enough to be called "The Nation's Report Card." In the early 1970s, the NAEP demonstrated dramatic differences between white students and those of color. In all subjects, across all grade levels, white students outperformed African American and Latino students by 12 to 20 percent (Campbell, Hombo, and Mazzeo, 2000).

In the first half of the twentieth century, the common wisdom was that some students simply were incapable of mastering the standard curriculum. If most were students of color, that was to be expected; they simply were genetically or culturally inferior. Southerners justified segregated schools on that basis (Tyack, 1974). In the North, school districts created vocational and industrial educational programs. Many students of color were automatically assigned to them—and not to schools with college preparatory courses (Tyack, 1974; Angus and Mirel, 1999). Education reflected the reality that America was a racially segregated society. In housing, employment, and social relations, people of color and whites lived separate and definitely not equal lives. For the most part, those racial arrangements were not challenged in American public schools (Tyack, 1974; Anyon, 1997; Taylor, 1998; Angus and Mirel, 1999). Faint rumblings, however, could be heard heralding a revolution in American life (Tushnet, 1987).

After World War II, racial attitudes in America began at long last to change. Soldiers of African American and Latino descent had risked their lives for the United States and were unwilling to continue to accept second-class citizenship. Civil rights organizations such as the NAACP and LULAC began to challenge segregation and inequality in the courts. Inevitably, attention turned toward schools (Kluger, 1975; Tushnet, 1987; Taylor, 1998; Wilson, 2003). Members of these groups "rejected earlier diagnoses of the problem of poor [school] performers, especially those that located the trouble in the defects of individuals (whether of character or chromosomes)" (Deschenes, Cuban, and Tyack, 2001, p. 533). Instead, they believed that discrimination prevented students of color from having access to the kind of schools, instructions, and resources that white students had. And they had every intention of changing that situation.

Thanks to pressure from members of marginalized communities and their white allies, changes began that were nothing short of revolutionary. Over the last fifty years, we developed laws and programs designed to make equal educational opportunity a reality. The courts declared that laws mandating segregation in schools are illegal. Congress enacted legislation creating Head Start and Title I, which allocates funds to schools with high concentrations of low-performing students. The executive branch of government established affirmative action programs to remedy historic discrimination against people of color. Some of these programs faced tremendous opposition. It took many legal, political, and social struggles to put them into place. It was a fight well worth having; the combined consequences of these policies and programs have been revolutionary.

While estimates vary, approximately 92 percent of African American and 78 percent of Latino students receive "regular" high school diplomas (Aud, Fox, and KewalRamani, 2010). Twice as many African Americans and three times as many Latinos take the SAT as did in 1996 (College Entrance Examination Board, 1996, 2011). In the last thirty years, the percentage of African American students ages eighteen to twenty-four attending college has almost tripled. In the same period, the number of Latino American students attending college has increased sixfold. The gap between the scores of white and African American children on the NAEP in reading has decreased by almost half; the gap between white and Latino American students, by more than a third. The gap in NAEP scores in math has decreased approximately 45 percent for African Americans and by 40 percent for Latino Americans (Aud et al., 2010) (see Figures 9.1 and 9.2).

FIGURE 9.1 Long-Term Trend, NAEP Reading, Differences between Average Test Scores of Whites, Blacks, and Hispanics (ages 17, 13, and 9)

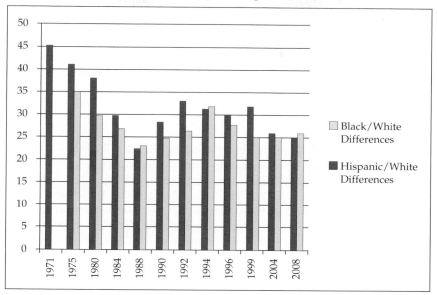

Source: Rampey, Dion, and Donahue, 2009.

FIGURE 9.2 Long-Term Trend, NAEP Mathematics, Differences between Average Test Scores of Whites, Blacks, and Hispanics (ages, 17, 13, and 9)

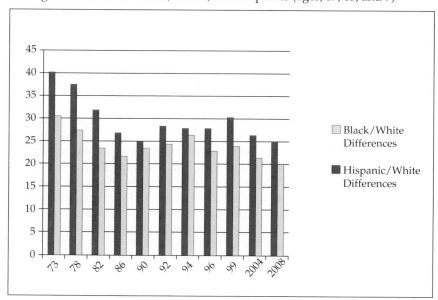

Source: Rampey, Dion, and Donahue, 2009.

If we want to eliminate poverty and the "underclass" in American society, we need to ensure that every child has equal educational opportunity. The academic achievement gap is the most important civil rights issue of the new century. Integration, affirmative action, Title I, and Head Start are legacies from those who knew school achievement was key to creating a more just society. Maintaining, extending, and even expanding these programs and policies is the best way to close the gap that prevents people of color from taking their rightful place in the United States.

Integration

The Supreme Court ruled in the landmark case *Brown v. Board of Education of Topeka, Kansas* (1954) that laws assigning students to school based on their race were unconstitutional. Segregated schools could never be equal, the Court declared in its unanimous ruling. The laws violated the Fourteenth Amendment's guarantee that the rights of all Americans deserved equal protection. Being separated from white students engendered feelings of inferiority in students of color and jeopardized their futures. The desegregation struggle for Hispanic Americans began differently. In many parts of the country, their segregation from Anglo students was not based on their "race," for the courts had declared them "white." States passed laws requiring that all instruction be conducted in English. Children of Spanish heritage were presumed to be "deficient" in English. So, without being evaluated, they were placed in separate classes or schools. There were twenty-eight lawsuits brought by Mexican Americans between 1925 and 1985. One of them, *Mendez v. Westminster School District of Orange County* (1946), used a framework that would later be articulated in *Brown* (Wilson, 2003). Mexican American lawyers came to understand that the power of *Brown* could be utilized for their own struggle. In *Cisneros v. Corpus Christi ISD* (1970) and in *Keyes v. School District No. 1, Denver, Colorado* (1973), the courts ruled that Hispanics could suffer the same kind of discrimination as blacks and were, therefore, eligible to receive the same kind of remedies—namely, desegregated schools (Wilson, 2003).

The struggle to carry out the Court's ruling was difficult—at times even violent. Two centuries of belief in white superiority did not disappear overnight and could not be "court-ordered" away. In the South, governors turned students away from schools they attempted to integrate. State troopers protected crowds of angry whites while leaving black schoolchildren vulnerable to expressions of hatred. School districts closed down rather than integrate. Many whites attended newly created private schools exempt from desegregation orders. Children of color were completely shut out. It took almost two decades for every state in the South to begin to comply with court orders to desegregate. In the North, the problem was different but equally difficult. There, most metropolitan areas were segregated by economics. Schools reflected housing patterns of communities and de facto segregation developed. Courts began to order school districts to assign students to schools outside their neighborhoods to desegregate them and transport them to their new schools. Many urban whites already felt "left behind" in the movement to the suburbs their wealthier neighbors began in the 1930s and 1940s. Taking away their neighborhood schools was the last straw. In the 1970s, the "busing" issue heated up and sometimes violent protests took place in large cities outside the South. The federal courts' uncompromising commitment in the early desegregation period meant, however, that there was no turning back. All across the country, school districts attempted to comply with desegregation orders. Creative opportunities for all students resulted including magnet schools whose innovative programs were designed to attract white students to attend integrated schools (Lewis, 1965; Sarratt, 1966; Cecelski, 1994; Taylor, 1998; Orfield, 2001).

Even though it was a tremendous struggle, desegregation was worth the effort. The integration era was a period of dramatic changes in the academic achievement gap. The difference in standardized tests scores between students of color and whites decreased dramatically in the years when integration plans were being implemented (Perie and Moran, 2005). Students of color who attended desegregated schools, especially if they began to do so in the early grades, had educational achievement levels one grade higher than they would have attained in a segregated school (Mahard and Crain, 1984). African American and Latino students who attended desegregated schools were less likely to become teenage parents or delinquents. They also were more likely to graduate from high school and to enroll in and be successful in college (Liebman, 1990; Orfield and Eaton, 1996; Orfield, 2001). "Racially integrated schools prepare students to be effective citizens in our pluralistic society, further social cohesion, and reinforce democratic values. They promote cross-racial understanding, reduce prejudice, improve critical thinking skills and academic achievement, and enhance life opportunities for students of all races. These benefits are maximized when schools are structured in ways that optimize intergroup contact. Communities also benefit from a potential work-force that is better prepared for a global economy, reduced residential segregation, and increased parental involvement in schools—all of which increase the stability of communities" (Orfield, Frankenburg, and Garces, 2008).

Despite its success, integration has become increasingly difficult to maintain. City and suburban schools have become increasingly resegregated. Students from the three largest racial groups (Latinos, Blacks, and Whites) typically attend schools where most of the students are from the same racial groups as themselves. On average, white youth attend schools where only 20 percent of the students are members of other racial groups. Blacks attend schools that are less integrated than they were before *Brown v. Board of Education*. Almost 40 percent of black and Latino students attend schools where only 10 percent of the student body is white (Tefera, Frankenberg, Siegel-Hawley, and Chirichingo, 2011).

The Supreme Court has narrowly defined the role of the judicial branch in creating desegregated schools. The courts can intervene only in cases where segregation results from previous governmental policies. If, for example, a school district constructed schools in racially isolated neighborhoods, then it can be held responsible for the resulting segregation. In such a case, the courts can order integration (*Keyes v. School District No. 1, Denver, Colorado*, 1973). If, however, the segregation is the result of individuals' choices—such as living in a more expensive suburb rather than the city—school districts cannot be forced to remedy the resulting segregation (*Milliken v. Bradley*, 1974). In addition to these understandings of when the courts can order integration, the increasing absence of whites in urban public schools also has caused a decrease in integration efforts. Once a school district has demonstrated it has done everything to desegregate schools and programs, it can be declared "unitary" and released from desegregation orders. School districts then can return to neighborhood school policies, even if they result in resegregation. The Supreme Court has even ruled that municipalities cannot protect the gains of the desegregation era by student assignment polices that maintain a racial balance comparable to that of the community—even when the voters and their elected officials deem those policies to be absolutely necessary to providing equal opportunity for every child in their school district (*Meredith v. Jefferson County (Ky.) Board of Education*, 2007; *Parents Involved in Community Schools Inc. v. Seattle School District*, 2007). In these rulings, they declined to see racial balance as a compelling state interest. Court-ordered integration of schools is possible only when it is a "remedy" for prior governmental "bad acts." Even in cases where such misconduct has been established, some locales fail to comply with orders to desegregate schools. For example, schools in Jefferson Parish, Louisiana, have remained under federal court supervision since 1964. Officials have petitioned to have the order lifted. However, the lawyer who represented the families who filed the original complaint prepared a report for the court that detailed methods by which the Parish continued to create and sustain a segregated school system. In particular, he cited failure to recruit Black students to newly opened "academies of excellence," failure to diversify the teacher staff, continued disproportionate disciplinary actions against black students, and an unwillingness to adopt student transfer policies that would result in integrated schools (Waller, 2011). The academic achievement gap is alive and well in the district as well. Schools that serve African American students have achievement rates that are lower than the state average on almost all performance measures (Jefferson Parish School Board, 2011).

The combination of court rulings, school district decisions, and white flight does not mean that the effort to integrate American schools has been lost. It does mean that a renewed commitment at the local level to create schools with diverse student populations is required. States could provide extra funds to urban and suburban municipalities that create consolidated, metropolitan school districts. Such systems could create extraordinary magnet schools that students of all races and ethnicities would be eager to attend. If communities became convinced once again of the value of integrated schools for all children, they could pressure legislatures to authorize and fund such efforts. They could use the political process and create constitutionally viable policies and practices that would support a new mandate for integration. Some districts have begun such pioneering efforts. The Memphis School Board surrendered the charter for the district, whose population is predominantly poor and African American district, to force a consolidation with the wealthier districts of the surrounding county, create more integrated schools, and avoid losses of funding. The fact that the change was able to take place only because of court decisions affirming its legality proves once again that governmental support of integration efforts is crucial (Dillon, 2011).

Head Start

In 1965, Congress funded an innovative program for preschoolers based on the belief that children born to poor families faced disadvantages that translated into school difficulties. Head Start goes far beyond traditional preschool programs. It attempts to address a multitude of factors affecting poor children and their families. It offers opportunities for three- and four-year-old children to become "school ready" through a variety of programs (U.S. Department of Health and Human Services, 2008). The bill authorizing the program stated, "It is the purpose of this subchapter to promote school readiness by enhancing the social and cognitive development of low-income children through the provision, to low-income children and their families, of health, educational, nutritional, social, and other services that are determined, based on family needs assessments, to be necessary" (Head Start Act, 2007). Over time, studies have shown that Head Start provides better preschool experiences for children than other options available to low-income families. Head Start also makes them more ready for school especially in the area of language and literacy development. In addition, children who attend Head Start programs are more likely to have health insurance and received dental care. The program is particularly effective for children with special needs and those who are dual language learners. Children with special needs showed benefits in math and social interactions, and children who were dual language learners showed benefits in language, literacy, and math (U.S. Department of Health and Human Services, 2010). The evidence also shows that, overall, the gains children make during their Head Start experience do not last beyond kindergarten. Critics want to use that evidence to end support for Head Start. However, their objections are more political than scientific. To date, researchers who have looked at Head Start's impact on later learning do not have access to information about the quality of the instruction children received in their kindergarten and first-grade classrooms. In addition, even the most recent studies look at experiences in Head Start that took place almost 10 years ago and cannot take into consideration recent improvements in Head Start programs—such as the implementation of rigorous teacher evaluation protocols and increased emphasis on school readiness skills required by the 2007 reauthorization of the Head Start Act (Guernsey, 2010). In short, there is just too much evidence that Head Start works for children and families while they are participating to discard the program. Recent reforms that hold Head Start programs accountable for providing high-quality preschool education should ensure critics that taxpayer dollars are being well spent. Head Start programs now have to show that they are meeting quality standards in the type of emotional climate, classroom organization, and instructional support. They will be evaluated by professionals using CLASS, a tool that has been developed and researched carefully. Failure to meet those standards will result in a loss of funding for individual Head Start programs (Landler, 2011). Such accountability provides an opportunity to weed out those settings in which the ideal is not being met rather than dismantling the whole system.

Accountability is important, but it cannot be achieved without adequate financial support. For more than forty years, Head Start has been underfunded in relation to its mandate. Only about half the children whose families meet the eligibility guidelines have been enrolled. In 2003, when the Head Start Act was reauthorized, legislators who support the privatization of public education made sure that the legislation contained provisions for transferring funding from publicly controlled programs to private ones. Despite the research showing that young children become school ready through playful exploration of the world around them, the bill emphasized formal academic instruction—and even testing similar to that being done in elementary schools. The legislation was not passed until 2007. In that time, funding had been frozen for six years, and hours of operation, transportation services, and staff were cut in centers across the country. When the bill was finally passed in 2007, the program was cut by $10 million, and no catch-up monies were allocated (National Head Start Association, 2008). Some additional funding was provided in the following years, but they were short-term increases as a result of funding tied to the Race to the Top initiative—a temporary infusion of funds, vulnerable to future budget cutting (U.S. Department of Health and Human Services, 2011b). The lack of stability in the program's resources jeopardizes this program whose value has been proven over time. Political smoke and mirrors about funding do not replace good public policy, and using taxpayer dollars to improve the life chances of poor children is good public policy.

Title I

In 1965, as a follow up to the Civil Rights Act, Congress passed the Elementary and Secondary Education Act (ESEA). Title I of that law provided financial assistance to school districts that service large numbers of low-income families. It provided money for library improvement, instructional materials, and educational innovations. Over time, Title I has evolved to include funding for school-wide programs to improve the instructional program for the whole school. The money can also be used to provide targeted assistance programs that address the needs of students who are failing or in danger of failing. The instructional programs are designed to help student meet state standards and demonstrate proficiency on state tests.

In the 2010s, more than 56,000 public schools used Title I funds to close academic achievement gaps. Programs served more than 21 million children in preschools and elementary and secondary schools (U.S. Department of Health and Human Services, 2011a). Title I has been enormously successful. In the 1980s, when funding increased, test scores of children of color improved—especially in schools where the funding was applied to targeted assistance programs. The differences between the average national test scores of white students and their Latino and black peers narrowed steadily.

However, funding for Title I has not kept pace with the demands made on schools under No Child Left Behind. In 2004, Congress appropriated only 67 percent of the money needed to serve all eligible children (Center on Educational Policy, 2005). Over time, the difference between authorized funds (the maximum set by Congress) and appropriated funds (the amount states actually receive) has increased. Now, states receive only a little more than half the authorized money. "In Ohio, for example, a study estimated that the state would have to spend about $1.5 billion more on education each year to meet NCLB's additional accountability requirements and achievement goals. In fiscal year 2006, Ohio received $634 million from the federal government for NCLB programs" (New America Foundation, 2011). Title I works to close the achievement gap. It deserves to be fully funded.

Affirmative Action

Closing the academic achievement gap also requires a commitment to remedying past discriminatory practices through affirmative action policies. They are the most controversial of all the political legacies of the civil rights era—perhaps because they have been so effective at disturbing structures of racial and ethnic privilege. They have not always been implemented perfectly and certainly have not ended prejudice and discrimination.

For forty years, Americans have attempted to deal with the effects of discrimination—for almost two centuries, people of color were denied employment and educational opportunities because of race or ethnicity while white males received preferential treatment. Before affirmative action, for example, it once was legal to pay white workers more than people of color for doing the same job and to have separate sections in the "want ads" for each group. Employers could refuse to hire people because of the color of their skin or the place they or their parents were born. Even private schools, colleges, and universities could refuse to admit students on the basis of race or ethnicity. Schools could set "quotas" limiting their number of nonwhite students. Colleges and universities insisted students abide by segregated housing policies or would transfer a roommate simply because of race or ethnicity. White Americans didn't wake up one morning and decide that such practices were unfair and had to be eliminated. It took a long, slow process in which people of color and their allies demanded everyone be given the equal protection the Fourteenth Amendment guaranteed.

Even when it became illegal to continue such practices, their consequences lingered and adversely affected people of color. "The disadvantages to people of color and the benefits to white people are passed on to each succeeding generation unless remedial action is taken" (Kivel, 1996, p. 2). Discrimination people's ancestors faced continues to affect them generations later. Because one family faced little prejudice, its members may have, through contacts with their friends, obtained well-paying jobs, purchased a home in a neighborhood with good schools, learned about cultural events and institutions, and gone to college. A family that faced more discrimination would have few of those advantages. Their friends would have been as shut out from information about jobs, culture, and education as they were. The cycle would perpetuate itself for many years.

Affirmative action is meant to break this cycle by outlawing prejudice in favor of whites in hiring and admission policies and starting a larger process of creating equal opportunity. If a person of color is qualified for a job or a school, neither an employer nor an admissions officer can turn them down simply because of race or ethnicity. If two equally qualified people seek the same benefit, affirmative action requires that the job or college placement be offered first to the person of color. The law also allows employers or schools to choose a person of color whose qualifications are roughly comparable but not exactly equal to those of a white person. By providing such opportunities for members of groups who experienced previous discrimination, we started to end the cycle described before. Now people of color have access to jobs or education, can begin to accumulate both material and cultural "wealth" to pass on to their descendants, and have a chance to experience the "rising tide that lifts all boats" in America.

Opponents of affirmative action protest that it's not fair. The question is, not fair to whom? There are few, if any, complaints about higher-education policies that are equally "unfair." Colleges have preferential recruiting and admission policies for veterans, children of alumni, athletes, and students whose families are wealthy enough to afford the tuition with no financial help from the school. Members of these groups do not have to have exactly the same test scores as other applicants to be admitted. These policies represent honest attempts by colleges and universities to create winning teams, balance budgets, and reward school loyalty and patriotism. Many people would argue that the attempt to create racial diversity is of greater moral importance that those goals.

A compelling case can be made that affirmative action in educational settings has benefits for all students, not just those of color. There is a growing body of evidence that students educated in universities, colleges, and graduate programs where there is a diverse population actually experience academic gains. They learn to think in more complex ways. Diversity on a college campus directly increases the numbers of interactions among members of racial and ethnic groups typically isolated from one another. These interactions indirectly lead to greater understanding of people whose backgrounds are different from students' own (Pike, Kuh, and Gonyea, 2007). A recent survey of 1990–1994 graduates of the University of Michigan showed that more than a decade after graduation, they still believed being a member of a diverse undergraduate student body had helped them professionally and personally. Researchers found that alumni identified specific benefits, such as being able to relate to diverse groups of patients, clients, and students as a result of being part of a heterogeneous student body (Pluviose, 2008). The Supreme Court recognized the need for leaders who, through their educational experiences, are prepared to understand the ideas and cultures of those whose backgrounds differ from their own. This interest is serious enough to justify the use of race as one of a range of factors that a college or university can consider in admissions decisions as long as the institution does not establish a quota system and does not make an applicant's race or ethnicity the defining factor in the acceptance (*Grutter v. Bollinger*, 2003).

Those who attack affirmative action sometimes call it "reverse discrimination." Quite often, what they describe is not discrimination but a loss of privilege. Recent research shows that white Americans see racism as a "zero-sum" game; that is, they believe that there is a limited amount of racial respect or privilege in American society. Therefore, they think that gains made by African American are harming them. "Whites think more progress has been made toward equality than do Blacks, but Whites also now believe that this progress is linked to a new inequality—at their expense" (Norton and Sommers, 2011). However, it is not racism that is a zero-sum game; rather, it is competition for scarce resources. "This includes jobs that pay well and a quality education. When white people perceive that they are disadvantaged by a level playing field, they are correct" (Butler, 2011).

We must continue to work to eliminate the last effects of discrimination in elementary and high schools so that race is no longer a factor in a young person's opportunity to become prepared for higher education. As we engage in that long struggle for a better future, however, we must keep faith in the present and maintain our commitment to providing short-term remedies through affirmative action policies.

Social change takes place slowly, and closing the academic achievement gap between students of color and their white counterparts constitutes a dramatic change in American society. Some advocates for reform argue that minimizing government's role in schooling will produce better results than the programs described in this chapter. However, the results of their experiments are not convincing. Students of color are isolated in schools with the least experienced and qualified teachers—and with the lowest test scores. Charter schools have been successful at controlling students but not in raising their academic achievement. The elimination of affirmative action programs has decreased the numbers of students of color in colleges and universities. Hesitancy about enforcing those programs has also resulted in fewer African American and Latino American faculty members. Linking Title I funds to results of high-stakes tests has caused large numbers of public schools to be ranked as "failing"—even though the funds needed to produce the required results have been absent. Making the reauthorization of Head Start into an ideological battle has caused the loss of staff and limited the number of children who can be served. Arguing that programs are not effective when they have been starved for funds, misrepresented in the media, or handcuffed by decisions made by right-wing activist district judges and Supreme Court justices is disingenuous and deprives millions of American children of equal opportunity for academic achievement. Knowingly or unknowingly, these policies weaken Head Start, racial integration, Title I, and affirmative action and secure advantages for already privileged white children while limiting the prospects of students of color. The consequences of abandoning the remedies of the past will fall on all of us. Knowing that the possibilities for success are extremely limited, young people lose faith in education. Such hopelessness is a breeding ground for social alienation. Without a stake in society, people have no reason to obey its laws or support it against its enemies. The nation's security demands we maintain our commitment to providing programs that promote educational equality. Fully funding and supporting Head Start, Title I, desegregation, and affirmative action are the best ways to fulfill that obligation.

POSITION 2: NEW PROGRAMS ARE NEEDED

In a word, America's schools need innovation. Educational innovation should not be confused with just generating more great ideas or unique inventions. Instead we need new solutions that improve outcomes—and that can, and will, be used to serve hundreds of thousands of teachers and millions of students.

—Duncan (2009)

Reconsidering the Academic Achievement Gap

A decade of differences in academic achievement between young white Americans and their African American and Latino counterparts was a nagging, persistent reminder of just how ineffective large, bureaucratic governmental programs actually are. On the NAEP—"The Nation's Report Card"—students of color made progress in closing the gap between them and their white counterparts during the 1970s and 1980s. Then, for almost a decade, progress stalled. At all ages and in all subjects, the gap was larger in 2000 than it was in 1988—in some cases by as much as 50 percent (Campbell, Hombo, and Mazzeo, 2000). The average SAT scores of African Americans were 195 points lower than the average scores of white test takers; for Latinos, the difference was 100 points less. Although the gap narrowed, African American and Latino students still had lower rates of college entrance and completion and lower grades than did white students (Campbell et al., 2000; Haycock, 2001).

These statistics painted a gloomy picture. Some gains made through older strategies were lost and others too small to be meaningful. The remedies applied in the 1970s and 1980s suited the causes of the achievement gap as we then understood them; our national culture and the political climate has changed. There is great pessimism about government's ability to solve problems and more irritation with the ways it interferes with individual freedom. These attitudes are dramatically different from those of the 1960s and 1970s when a liberal optimism pervaded the country, promising that with enough regulation and tax dollars, we could fix anything that was wrong with America.

Blaming the Victims

Clearly, there is no one easy answer to the question of why African American and Latino children continue to have lower scores on standardized tests and generally experience less academic success than white students. The reasons are complex and fluid and probably interact with one another in ways we have yet to understand. We can, however, think of them in two categories: sociocultural and school related.

For most of the last thirty years, we emphasized sociocultural causes, believing that segregation, discrimination, and effects of poverty were mostly to blame for the low levels of achievement among students of color. Our thinking about these causes resulted in national soul-searching and in making necessary corrections to laws and policies—for example, putting an end to racially separate and unequal schools.

We also focused on what we perceived to be "lacks" in the children and families we hoped to serve. We believed that parents' low level of educational achievement, lack of financial resources, and child-rearing practices all contributed to their children's low levels of academic achievement. We thought that by creating antipoverty programs such as Head Start, food stamps, job training, and Medicaid and finding ways of connecting poor people to them, we'd improve children's chances of succeeding in schools.

We thought children of color were themselves partly to blame for their educational difficulties. Linguistic differences between them and the school communities created problems, but the young people were unwilling to give up their unique ways of speaking. They used drugs, became parents themselves in their teens, and appeared to prefer the culture of the streets to the promise of entrance into mainstream America. So we introduced drug and sex education into school curricula, introduced bilingual education, and attempted to teach the values of hard work and perseverance.

The solutions we created in response to our understandings, however, were only partially effective and, in some cases, actually have worsened the problems they were intended to correct. For example, thirty years ago, we believed that the academic achievement gap was caused by segregation and discriminatory practices. Segregation isolated children of color and convinced them that they were inferior to whites (*Brown v. Board of Education of Topeka, Kansas*, 1954). If we could only get them into integrated schools, then their success rates would soar. So the government mandated desegregation programs all across the country. Most of the policies involved busing children around cities, increasing their time away from home and their studies, and removing many urban children from their neighborhoods. In many cases, such policies destroyed the work of generations of city dwellers who had painstakingly built up connections between their schools and communities (Cecelski, 1994; Taylor, 1998). Parent involvement became more difficult and involved long treks to schools in unfamiliar areas of the city. Eventually, those who could—admittedly, most often whites—voted with their feet and left the cities and "integrated" public schools. As a result, in most cities the majority of the population overwhelmingly consists of people of color. Suburbs are equally segregated; it's just that whites are the majority there.

Consequently, schools are becoming increasingly racially isolated (Orfield et al., 2008; Tefera Frankenbreg et al., 2011). There are many reasons for these changes in school populations. Some are relatively benign, such as people seeking the more relaxed lifestyle of the suburbs. Some are more troubling. Forced integration did not change people's minds and hearts; racial prejudice still exists, and some whites have expressed their preferences by moving away from neighborhoods with diverse populations. Court-ordered desegregation of schools did not prevent the continued residential isolation between white people and those of color.

The end of court-mandated integration actually may be a good thing. There was a kind of racial superiority implicit in the frantic efforts to get children of color into "good" schools—schools whose populations historically had been white (*Parents Involved in Community Schools Inc. v. Seattle School District*, 2007). The same sense permeated attitudes toward African American and Latino American parents; middle-class European American practices were set as the norm, and the cultural differences among parenting styles were deemed "deficits" that had to be corrected (Manadara, 2006; Gosa and Alexander, 2007; Guilamo-Ramos et al., 2007). Similarly, affirmative action programs also contained a hidden belief in the inferiority of some groups of people: they are simply less able and, without special treatment, cannot compete with those who are more competent (Townes, 2008). Even the way young people of color dressed and talked, the music they liked, the foods they ate, and the recreational activities they enjoyed were seen as "improper" and as hindrances to their future success. They were placed on notice that were obliged to "act white" in order to be successful, and, forced to choose between their identity and academic success, they often chose membership in their primary community over acceptance by teachers (Fryer and Torelli, 2005; Ford, Grantham, and Whiting, 2008).

Analyses of the academic achievement gap between children of color and their white counterparts that focus on cultural differences between the groups but ignore socioeconomic ones are incomplete. Nearly 2 million of the 5.6 million American children living in extreme poverty are black; 1.6 million are Latino. In the first decade of the twenty-first century, government funding decreased for housing, health, and nutrition programs, while the number of children living in poverty rose dramatically (Children's Defense Fund, 2008). These social factors place young people at risk of attending schools that, quite simply, have failed children.

School-Related Causes of the Academic Achievement Gap

In the past decade, researchers have identified several school-related causes of the academic achievement gap. In many public schools, children of color encountered teachers who had low expectations of them and viewed them through a lens of prejudice. Teachers did not search aggressively for instructional strategies to help African American or Latino American students who were having difficulty, having already concluded that those children had limited potential. In turn, students of color internalized these low expectations and did not see themselves as capable of succeeding in school (Diamond, Randolph, and Spillane, 2004). Children of color were less likely than their white counterparts to attend schools with experienced teachers, more likely to have teachers without college preparation in subjects they were teaching, and twice as likely to have teachers without state certification (Peske and Haycock, 2006; Clotfelter, Ladd, Vigdor, and Wheeler, 2007). All these factors negatively affected student performance.

In schools that served these students, policies and practices too often accepted and contributed to the achievement gap. Students of color were more likely than their white peers to attend schools that prepared them for industrial jobs that no longer existed (Haycock, 2003). Students of color were less likely than their white peers to attend schools that offered advanced math and science or be prepared to take advantage of them if such opportunities were presented. They too often had been tracked into "general" or "basic" courses where the curriculum was simplified and teachers covered less material, gave less homework, and rewarded low-level performance with high grades. This failure to take high-level course work resulted in lower scores on standardized tests and lower likelihood of college enrollment—and so contributed greatly to the achievement gap (Tyson, Lee, Borman, and Hanson, 2007). By opting out or being forced out of the most challenging curriculum, the futures of students of color were being limited.

Teachers and administrators complained that African American and Latino American parents were not involved enough in schools. Yet most research showed that African American and Latino parents wanted to be involved in their children's schooling but were often prevented from doing so by school policies and practices. School personnel often failed to take the most elementary steps to increase parent involvement. For example, when Latino parents came to school, they often encountered a staff that spoke only English, and interpreters were rare (Wong and Hughes, 2006).

School districts that serve students of color have high mobility rates. Children routinely move from one to school to another in the district *within* a school year. Yet urban districts did little to respond to that reality. They did not standardize curriculum, textbooks, or instruction. Students who moved found themselves repeating material they already had learned or being challenged to do work for which they had not been prepared. They often lost heart and stopped trying (Smith, Fien, and Paine, 2008).

Policies and practices that ignored or disparaged children's cultural lives also contributed to low academic achievement. Students who believed their teachers did not value their communities or background felt alienated from school. They found it difficult to respect the requests or suggestions of such adults—even when they were well intentioned and, if taken, might have led to improvements in the students' life chances. Instead, the students resisted and rebelled and were often disciplined and suspended. Their performance on high-stakes tests suffered and perpetuated the academic achievement gap (Fenning and Rose, 2007).

Closing the Academic Achievement Gap: New Solutions

Studying and coming to understand the socioeconomic and school-related causes of the academic achievement gap and the intersection between them has resulted in new solutions. However, rather than attempting to change society, these new remedies attempt to change schools and teachers through pragmatic and flexible efforts that are routinely and regularly evaluated. Effective approaches are continued, and unsuccessful ones are modified or abandoned.

In 2002, Congress reauthorized federal assistance to elementary and secondary schools in the No Child Left Behind (NCLB) Act. The descendant of the original ESEA passed in 1965 during the heyday of the War of Poverty, NCLB has a dramatically different approach to the academic achievement gap. It is true that some teachers and administrators accomplished a great deal with the funding ESEA provided. The drill and practice approach to remediation most often subsidized by the legislation did improve basic skills of many students of color. Test scores rose in the 1970s and 1980s but then stalled as the solutions of the 1960s proved insufficient to help students master higher-level skills, such as analyzing, not merely decoding, what they were reading and using critical thinking skills to solve complex mathematical problems. NCLB was an attempt to use the influence of the federal government to help all students meet the more challenging standards of a new century.

One of the most significant aspects of NCLB with regard to closing the achievement gap is the emphasis on state and local accountability for the progress of all students. Each state must specify what children are to learn, when they are to learn it, and how their learning will be assessed. Teachers, administrators, and school districts are held accountable for their students' progress through an in-depth, appropriate, and ongoing testing system developed by each state for students in grades 3 to 8. In addition, a group of fourth and eighth graders in each state must participate in the NAEP each year. In reporting the results of both the state tests and the NAEP, states must disaggregate the scores. That is, they must be reported by students' race, ethnicity, and poverty status. If a school fails to make adequate yearly progress (AYP) toward the goal of having 100 percent of students meet state standards in literacy and math by 2014, it suffers serious consequences. Students immediately must be allowed to transfer to a school within the district that *has made* progress; after three years without satisfactory improvement, districts must provide supplementary tutoring options for all students; if in five years the goals are not met, the school can be closed, reorganized, and reopened with new administrators, faculty, and staff (U.S. Department of Education, 2002).

The accountability provisions in NCLB were accompanied by greater freedom for innovation. The bill has promoted the creation of educational settings where students can receive the instruction, attention, and support they need to meet high standards, score well on standardized tests, and graduate from high school prepared to attend college. These include "small schools" and "charter schools." Both types of schools serve around 400 students, allowing a personal setting where every student is known by several adults who serve as advisers and confidants. Families are seen as members of the school community—teachers, administrators, and family members work together to ensure student success. They are relatively autonomous, even though they are still part of the school district; the school community is able to make decisions about its direction. They have a distinctive and focused curriculum and use multiple types of assessments (Center for Education Reform, 2008; Small Schools Project, 2008).

NCLB also requires that each child has a "highly qualified" teacher in every class and every grade, one who has a bachelor's degree, state certification, and knowledge of the discipline in which he or she teaches. Recruiting and retaining such teachers in urban and rural areas has been historically difficult. Now, states have been forced to utilize every effective strategy to attract good teachers in order to meet NCLB requirements. Teacher education programs have been strengthened and streamlined. Alternative routes to teacher certification have been established. Notable among these are "fellows" programs in major cities that have in the past had chronic shortages of qualified teachers (Chicago Teaching Fellows, 2008; D.C. Teaching Fellows, 2008; New York Teaching Fellows, 2008). These programs recruit people with experience in business, research, engineering, and other professions to become teachers. In addition, privately funded programs such as Teach For America (TFA) have enticed graduates from elite colleges and universities to work for several years in high needs schools. TFA "corps members" and fellows receive a seven-week-long summer training before becoming classroom teachers. Generally, they make a two-year commitment, during which time they receive the same salary as other beginning teachers in the district and complete a certification or graduate degree program at a deeply discounted price. Although most TFA corps members generally leave teaching after two years, some continue to work for educational equity in other ways. Districts tend to have somewhat better retention with teaching fellows.

The connection between families and schools is another area in which new responses to the academic achievement gap have been developed. NCLB allows federal funds to be used to improve communications with parents, make child care available at school events, and provide literacy instruction to family members. It even respects parents' rights to use funds designated for supplemental tutoring services in faith-based and other community organizations whose values and cultures match the family's own. Instead of viewing parents as impediments to improving student performance, this new generation of remedies sees parents as full partners in the reform effort (Center for Education Reform, 2008; Small Schools Project, 2008).

These new approaches to closing the academic achievement gap are producing promising results. More students in low-poverty schools are being taught by highly qualified teachers (U.S. Department of Education, 2008b). Parents are reporting high levels of satisfaction with their children's schooling even in urban areas where problems were rampant in the past (New York City Department of Education, 2008). Graduation rates are improving (U.S. Department of Education, 2008a).

The achievement gap, as measured on the long-term trend NAEP, is closing, although not quickly or significantly enough. In 2004, the results provided evidence that NCLB reforms were making a difference (U.S. Department of Education, 2008a, Indicators 16 and 17). In 2009, while the test scores of black, Latino and poor students continued to improve, the difference between their scores and those of white students had not decreased. Performance improved or held steady across all groups. So, while the reforms mandated by NCLB have helped somewhat, additional steps must be taken.

The federal government's ability to influence the direction of those changes is limited. In the past, that influence was exercised through the courts. Now, the power of the purse provides a more effective weapon. For example, in the past, student performance had little effect on the amount of Title I funding a school received. In contrast, the funds provided through the stimulus package known as "Race to the Top" required that states comply with reform mandates in order to receive the money. Changes in teacher evaluations, opportunities for increasing the number of charter schools, and adoption of the Common Core Standards were long overdue. Competition for funding proved the level to make them happen. As a result, "44 States and the District of Columbia have adopted a common set of States-developed college- and career-ready standards; 46 States and the District of Columbia are developing high-quality assessments aligned with college- and career-ready standards. More than 40 States are developing next-generation accountability and support systems, guided by principles developed by the Council of Chief State School Officers. Many States are implementing reforms in teacher and principal evaluation and support, turning around low-performing schools" (U.S. Department of Education, 2011b). In addition, relief from AYP regulations authorized by President Obama in 2011 has provided additional flexibility in the use of Title I funding. As a result, school districts have access to the $2.7 billion mandated to be set aside for supplementary educational services and transportation expenses related to school transfers and are able to use them for academic interventions targeted to their students' needs. States can take a systemic approach to remediation and expand their school transformation activities to all schools, not just those that fall in the lowest 5 percent (Hyslop, 2011). However, to receive the waiver, states had to adopt college- and career-ready standards in reading/language arts and mathematics designed to raise the achievement of all students, including English language learners and students with disabilities; establish systems of differentiated recognition, accountability, and support; and establish principal and teacher evaluation system that include student performance on standardized tests (U.S. Department of Education, 2011b). The attractiveness of the waivers incentivized adoption of reforms by states that had not received Race to the Top money.

Other reforms remain necessary if we are serious about closing the achievement gap. These include changing working conditions for teachers by limiting or eliminating teacher tenure, the lifetime job protection that has been exploited by unions to protect noneffective teachers. In addition, districts must be able to offer differential salary scales for teachers depending on the discipline they teach, extend the length of their workday, and offer pay increases earlier in teachers' careers in exchange for reducing pension and health benefit contributions by the state. Understanding the advantages provided to them under these reforms will help achieve another reform—attracting brighter, more able people to the profession.

For Discussion

1. We might assume that Latino children would many academic challenges because of limited English language proficiency. However, the gap between their test scores and those of white students usually is less than the difference between black students' scores and those of whites (see Figures 9.1 and 9.2). How would you account for these findings? What factors might account for the differences?
2. Talk to an admissions counselor in your college or university about the institution's policy regarding affirmative action and admissions. Critique the policy from the point of view of its effectiveness in closing the academic achievement gap.
3. Using the NAEP database (http://nces.ed.gov/nationsreportcard/naepdata/search.asp), research the achievement gap in your state. Speculate on factors that may influence conditions in your state. Using databases and other sources of information, research and evaluate your state's efforts to close the gap.

References

ANGUS, D., AND MIREL, J. (1999). *The Failed Promise of the American High School 1890–1995.* New York: Teachers College Press.

ANYON, J. (1997). *Ghetto Schooling.* New York: Teachers College Press.

AUD, S., FOX, M., AND KEWALRAMANI, A. (2010). *Status and Trends in the Education of Racial and Ethnic Groups* (NCES 2010–015). Washington, DC: National Center for Education Statistics.

Brown v. Board of Education of Topeka, Kansas. (1954). 347 U.S. 483.

BUTLER, P. (2011). "White Folks Shouldn't Worry." *New York Times Room for Debate.* May 22. www.nytimes.com/roomfordebate/2011/05/22/is-anti-white-bias-a-problem/white-folks-shouldnt-worry.

CAMPBELL, J., HOMBO, C. AND MAZZEO. (2000). NAEP 1999 Trends in Academic Progress: Three Decades of Student Performance. National Assessment of Educational Progress. http://nces.ed.gov/nationsreportcard/pubs/main1999/2000469.asp

CECELSKI, D. (1994). *Along Freedom Road.* Chapel Hill: University of North Carolina Press.

Center for Education Reform. (2008). "Charter School Laws." www.edreform.com/index.cfm?fuseAction=document&documentID=60.

Center on Educational Policy. (2005). "Title I Funds: Who's Gaining, Who's Losing and Why?" www.cepdc.org/index.cfm?fuseaction=document.showDocumentByID&DocumentID=84&varuniqueuserid=00302986781.

Chicago Teaching Fellows. (2008). "Chicago Teaching Fellows." www.chicagoteachingfellows.org.

Children's Defense Fund. (2008). "Trends in Child Poverty and Extreme Child Poverty." www.childrensdefense.org/site/PageServer?pagename=research_family_income_2006childpovertytrends.

Cisneros v. Corpus Christi School District. (1970). 324 F.Supp. 599.

CLOTFELTER, C., LADD, H., VIGDOR, J. (2007). "Teacher Credentials and Student Achievement." *Economics of Education Review* 26(6): 673–682.

Coalition to Defend Affirmative Action, et al. v. Regents of the Univ. of Mich. (2011). U.S. App. LEXIS 18875.

College Entrance Examination Board. (1996). "2007 Profile of College-Bound Seniors." www.collegeboard.com/prod_downloads/about/news_info/cbsenior/yr2007/national-report.pdf.

———. (2011). "2011 Profile of College-Bound Seniors." http://professionals.college board.com/profdownload/cbs2011_total_group_report.pdf.

D.C. Teaching Fellows. (2008). "D.C. Teaching Fellows." www.dcteachingfellows.org.

DESCHENES, S., CUBAN, L., AND TYACK, D. (2001). "Mismatch: Historical Perspectives on Schools and Students Who Don't Fit Them." *Teachers College Record* 103(4):525–547.

DIAMOND, J., RANDOLPH, A., and SPILLANE, J. (2004). "Teachers' Expectations and Sense of Responsibility for Student Learning: The Implications of School Race, Class, and Organizational Habitus." *Anthropology and Education Quarterly* 35(1):75–98.

DILLON, S. (2011). "Merger of Memphis and County School Districts Revives Race and Class Challenges. *New York Times*, November 5, A18.

DUNCAN, A. (2009). "From Compliance to Innovation: Remarks of Arne Duncan to America's Choice Superintendent's Symposium." www.ed.gov/news/speeches/compliance-innovation.

FENNING, P., AND ROSE, J. (2007). "Overrepresentation of African American Students in Exclusionary Discipline: The Role of School Policy." *Urban Education* 42(6):536–559.

FORD, D., GRANTHAM, T., AND WHITING, G. (2008). "Another Look at the Achievement Gap." *Urban Education* 43(2):216–239.

FRYER, R., AND TORELLI, P. (2005). "An Empirical Analysis of 'Acting White.'" National Bureau of Economic Research Working Paper no. 11334. http://post.economics.harvard.edu/faculty/fryer/papers/fryer_torelli.pdf.

GOSA, T., AND ALEXANDER, K. (2007). "Family (Dis)Advantage and the Educational Prospects of Better Off African American Youth: How Race Still Matters." *Teachers College Record* 109(2):285–321.

Grutter v. Bollinger. (2003). 539 U.S. 982.

GUERNSEY, L. (2010). "Thoughts on Today's Release of the Head Start Impact Study." http://earlyed.newamerica.net/blogposts/2010/thoughts_on_todays_release_of_the_head_start_impact_study-26270.

GUILAMO-RAMOS, V., ET AL. (2007). "Parenting Practices among Dominican and Puerto Rican Mothers." *Social Work* 52(1):17–30.

HAYCOCK, K. (2001). "Closing the Achievement Gap." *Education Leadership* 58(60). www.ascd.org/readingroom/edlead/0103/haycock.html.

———. (2003). "A New Core Curriculum for All: Aiming High for Other People's Children." *Thinking K-16* 7(1):1–2.

Head Start Act. (2007). Sec. 636. [42 U.S.C. 9801]. http://eclkc.ohs.acf.hhs.gov/hslc/Program%20Design%20and%20Management/Head%20Start%20Requirements/Head%20Start%20Act/HS_Act_2007.pdf.

HYSLOP, A. (2011). "The Waiver Wire: Deal or No Deal?" *The Quick and the Dead Blog.* September 22. www.quickanded.com/2011/09/the-waiver-wire-deal-or-no-deal.html.

Jefferson Parish School Board. (2011). "District Reorganization Plan." www.jppss.k12.la.us/district/superintendent/SuperintendentBaseTemplate.aspx?id=2147504642.

JENCKS, C., AND PHILLIPS, M., eds. (1998). *The Black-White Test Score Gap.* Washington, DC: Brookings Institution.

Keyes v. School District No. 1, Denver, Colorado. (1973). 413 U.S. 189.

KIVEL, P. (1996). "Affirmative Actions Works!" *In Motion Magazine.* http://inmotion magazine.com/pkivel.html

KLUGER, R. (1975). *Simple Justice: The History of Brown v. Board of Education and Black America's Struggle for Equality.* New York: Knopf.

LANDLER, M. (2011). "Head Start Is Given New Rules for Grants." *New York Times.* November 8.

LEWIS, A. (1965). *Portrait of a Decade.* New York: Bantam Books.

LIEBMAN, J. (1990). "Desegregating Politics: All-Out School Desegregation Explained." *Columbia Law Review* 90:1463.

MAHARD, R., AND CRAIN, R. (1984). "Research on Minority Achievement in Desegregated Schools." In *The Consequences of School Desegregation,* ed. C. Rossell and W. Hawley. Philadelphia: Temple University Press.

MANDARA, J. (2006). "The Impact of Family Functioning on African American Males' Academic Achievement: A Review and Clarification of the Empirical Literature." *Teachers College Record* 108(2):206–223.

Mendez v. Westminister School District of Orange County. (1946). 64 F. Supp. 544 (D.C.CAL.).

Meredith v. Jefferson County (Ky.) Board of Education. (2007). 127 U.S. 575.

Milliken v. Bradley. (1974). 419 U.S. 815.

National Head Start Association. (2008). "Head Start Leaders Have High Hopes for New President and Congress." www.nhsa.org/press/News_Archived/index_news_061908.htm.

New America Foundation. (2011). "Background and Analysis: No Child Left Behind Funding." http://febp.newamerica.net/background-analysis/no-child-left-behind-funding.

New York City Department of Education. (2008). "Learning Environment Survey 2007–2008." http://schools.nyc.gov/NR/rdonlyres/F3D9A118-C51E-4E23-841C-3DB5B 24C87DC/40757/les2008citywide.pdf.

New York City Teaching Fellows. (2008). "New York City Teaching Fellows." www .nycteachingfellows.org.

NORTON, M., AND SOMMERS, S. (2011). "Whites See Racism as a Zero-Sum Game That They Are Now Losing." *Perspectives on Psychological Science* 6(3):215–218.

ORFIELD, G. (2001). "Schools More Separate: Consequences of a Decade of Resegregation." www.civilrightsproject.ucla.edu/research/deseg/separate_schools01.php.

ORFIELD, G., AND EATON, S. (1996). *Dismantling Desegregation.* New York: New Press.

ORFIELD, G., FRANKENBURG, E., AND GARCES, L. (2008). "Statement of American Social Scientists of Research on School Desegregation to the U.S. Supreme Court in Parents v. Seattle School District and Meredith v. Jefferson County." *Urban Review* 40:96–136.

Parents Involved in Community Schools Inc. v. Seattle School District. (2007). 127 US 2738.

PERIE, M., AND MORAN, R. (2005). NAEP 2004 Trends in Academic Progress: Three Decades of Student Performance in Reading and Mathematics (NCES 2005-464). U.S. Department of Education, Institute of Education Sciences, National Center for Education Statistics. Washington, DC: Government Printing Office.

PESKE, H., AND HAYCOCK, K. (2006). "Teaching Inequality." www2.edtrust.org/NR/rdonlyres/010DBD9F-CED8-4D2B-9E0D-91B446746ED3/0/TQReportJune2006 .pdf.

PIKE, G., KUH, G., AND GONYEA, R. (2007). "Evaluating the Rationale for Affirmative Action in College Admissions: Direct and Indirect Relationships between Campus Diversity and Gains in Understanding Diverse Groups." *Journal of College Student Development* 48(2):166–182.

PLUVIOSE, D. (2008). "American Association for Affirmation Action Conference Highlights Policy Action Themes." *Diverse: Issues in Higher Education* 22:28.

RAMPEY, B.D., DION, G.S., AND DONAHUE, P.L. (2009). NAEP 2008 Trends in Academic Progress (NCES 2009–479). National Center for Education Statistics, Institute of Education Sciences, U.S. Department of Education, Washington, D.C.

SARRATT, R. (1966). *The Ordeal of Desegregation.* New York: Harper & Row.

Small Schools Project. (2008). "What Are Small Schools?" www.smallschoolsproject.org/index.asp?siteloc=whysmall&section=whatss.

SMITH, J., FIEN, H., AND PAINE, S. (2008). "When *Mobility* Disrupts Learning." *Educational Leadership* 65(7):59–63.

TAYLOR, S. (1998). *Desegregation in Boston and Buffalo.* Albany: State University of New York Press.

TEFERA, A., FRANKENBERG, E., SIEGEL-HAWLEY, G., AND CHIRICHINGO, G. (2011). *Integrating Suburban Schools.* Los Angeles: The Civil Rights Project of UCLA.

TOWNES, G. (2008). "Affirmative Action a Hot Issue in 2008 Election," *The Amsterdam News.* April 17.

TUSHNET, M. (1987). *Segregated Education, 1925–1950.* Chapel Hill: University of North Carolina Press.

TYACK, D. (1974). *The One Best System: A History of American Urban Education.* Cambridge, MA: Harvard University Press.

TYSON, W., LEE, R., BORMAN, K., AND HANSON, M. (2007). "Science, Technology, Engineering, and Mathematics (STEM) Pathways: High School Science and Math Coursework and Postsecondary Degree Attainment." *Journal of Education for Students Placed at Risk* 12(3):243–270.

U.S. Department of Education. (2002). "No Child Left Behind Act." www.ed.gov/policy/elsec/leg/esea02/index.html.

———. (2008a). *The Conditions of Education, 2008.* Washington DC: National Center for Education Statistics. http://nces.ed.gov/pubsearch/pubsinfo.asp?pubid=2008031.

———. (2008b). "Mapping Educational Progress, 2008." www.ed.gov/nclb/accountability/results/progress/index.html.

———. (2011a). "Improving Basic Programs Operated by Local Educational Agencies (Title I, Part A)." www2.ed.gov/programs/titleiparta/index.html.

———. (2011b). "Obama Administration Sets High Bar for Flexibility from No Child Left Behind in Order to Advance Equity and Support Reform." www.ed.gov/news/press-releases/obama-administration-sets-high-bar-flexibility-no-child-left-behind-order-advanc.

U.S. Department of Health and Human Services. (2008). "About Head Start." http://eclkc.ohs.acf.hhs.gov/hslc/About%20Head%20Start.

———. (2011a). "About the Office of Head Start: Mission." www.acf.hhs.gov/programs/ohs/about/index.html#factsheet.

———. (2011b). "Fiscal Year 2011 Head Start Funding Guidance." http://eclkc.ohs.acf.hhs.gov/hslc/Head%20Start%20Program/Program%20Design%20and%20Management/Head%20Start%20Requirements/PIs/2011/resour_pri_002_042111.html.

U.S. Department of Health and Human Services, Administration for Children and Families. (2010). *Head Start Impact Study.* Final Report. Washington, DC: U.S. Department of Health and Human Services. www.acf.hhs.gov/programs/opre/hs/impact_study.

WALLER, M. (2011). "Jefferson Parish School Desegregation Case Nears Conclusion, but New Allegations of Inequity Emerge." *Times Picayune.* July 11. www.nola.com/education/index.ssf/2011/07/jefferson_parish_school_desegr.html.

WEINBERG, M. (1977). *A Chance to Learn.* Cambridge: Cambridge University Press.

WILSON, S. (2003). "*Brown* over 'Other White': Mexican Americans' Legal Arguments and Litigation Strategy in School Desegregation Lawsuits." *Law and History Review* 21(1):145–194.

WONG, S., AND HUGHES, J. (2006). "Ethnicity and Language Contributions to Dimensions of Parent Involvement." *School Psychology Review* 35(4):645–662.

CHAPTER 10

Values/Character Education: Traditional or Liberational

Which and whose values should public schools embrace and teach

POSITION 1: TEACH TRADITIONAL VALUES

The results . . . should be a warning sign to liberal activists that wish to inject controversial issues into the classroom. Parents are simply against social engineering in the classroom.

—Rev. Louis Sheldon (2011, p. 1)

Throughout history, and in cultures around the world, education rightly conceived has had two great goals: to help students become smart and to help them become good.

—Character Education Partnership (2008, p. 8)

Traditional Values Can Be Restored to Schools

There is a tight relationship between good families and good schools in a society based on common values. Efforts to bring schools and society back to their moral base can yield positive results (Institute of Education Sciences, 2007). Although we can differentiate among definitions of values, ethics, morals, and character, school programs bearing labels such as "values education," "ethics education," "moral education," and "character education" often use the same principles, purposes, and general practices. We will treat them equally unless the terms are used as covers for value-free or value-neutral programs. The best of the good programs restore traditional values to schools and students, and these good programs work. The Center for the 4th and 5th Rs (respect and responsibility) shows much promise in restoring "good" character to its historic place at the center of schooling. Leming and Silva (2001) report excellent results from a five-year study on teaching a special Heartwood Foundation ethics curriculum to fifth graders; the program produced more caring and respectful actions and fewer disciplinary referrals, and the teachers' approach to ethics teaching changed in a positive way. Others agree (www.character.org 2012; charactered.net 2012).

Other indicators of success include the increasing number and quality of educational materials available for teachers and parents. Teaching materials are aimed at instilling universal values in students: honor, honesty, truthfulness, kindness, generosity, helpfulness, courage, convictions, justice, respect, freedom, and equality.

Internet sites offer assistance (see www.goodcharacter.com, www.traditional valuescoalition.org, and www.charactercounts.org). The Character Education Partnership developed and maintains a database at www.character.org that includes ideas, materials, and descriptions and analyses of various instruments that can be used to assess character education. Among the agenda items in the new movement for family values is the restoration of religion and patriotism to U.S. schools (see www.freedomalliance.com).

Model centers and special programs for character education are under way in a number of states, including North Carolina, California, Iowa, New Mexico, Utah, Connecticut, Maryland, Washington, Missouri, Kentucky, New Jersey, and South Carolina. The centers sponsor such activities as programs devoted to creating safe and orderly school environments, encouraging students to take responsibility for their conduct and for others, preventing violence, and reinforcing efforts to curb drug abuse and weapons in school. Character education is developing quickly into one of the most important new projects in the schools (Thorkildsen and Wallberg, 2004; Nucci and Narvaez, 2008).

What Should Be Taught: Traditional Values as the Focus

Clearly, schools need to rediscover their proper role and function in a moral society. The United States was founded on Judeo-Christian ideals. They form the basis of our concepts of justice and democracy. Schools were established to transmit those values to the young to preserve values and society. Support for traditional values gave early American schools a clarity of purpose and a solid direction. Children did not receive mixed messages about morality and behavior and did not get the impression they could make up and change their values on a whim.

Renewing character education should include a prominent focus on traditional values at all levels. In elementary school, reading material should emphasize ideals (Anderson, 1994; O'Sullivan, 2002; Bennett, 2008). Stories of great heroes, personal integrity, resoluteness, loyalty, and productivity should dominate. The main emphasis should be on the positive aspects of U.S. history and literature, showing how individuals working together toward a suitable goal can succeed. Teachers should stress and expect ethical behavior, respect, and consideration (Lickona, 1991, 2004). Classes should study various religions with the purpose of understanding their common values and how those values apply to life. Providing time in school for children to reflect on personal religious beliefs would be appropriate.

Signs and symbols in school should reinforce American values. Pictures, displays, and assemblies on morality offer students a chance to see how important those values are to society and school. Inviting speakers into classes, showing films, and taking students to see significant monuments to American values are techniques that can help. Teachers can emphasize good values by providing direct instruction on moral precepts and rewarding students for good citizenship.

At the secondary level, emphasis on traditional values should continue with more sophisticated materials and concepts. There is no need for a special course on sex education if family values are covered in other courses and at home. A student honor roll, citing acts of outstanding school citizenship, might be as prominently displayed as athletic trophies. Libraries are good places for displays of books featuring the kinds of thoughts and behaviors we seek to encourage.

Literature classes should teach U.S. and foreign literature portraying rewards of moral behavior and negative consequences of immorality. American history classes should express ideals for which we stand and our extraordinary historical achievements. Science courses should feature stories of hard work and perseverance in making scientific discoveries as well as stories of how basic values and religious views have guided many scientists in their work.

The arts are a rich place to show values through study of paintings, compositions, sculptures, and other art forms that express the positive aspects of human life under a set of everlasting ideals. Religious music and art can be a part of the curriculum, as can nonreligious art idealizing such values as the golden rule and personal virtue. Vocational subjects afford numerous ways to present good attitudes toward work, family, responsibility, loyalty, decency, and respect. Sports are an especially important place in which to reaffirm these same values; numerous professional and college teams pray together before matches, and many players are leading figures in setting high standards of moral conduct.

We need teachers who demonstrate a strong personal commitment to traditional values and whose behaviors and lives exhibit that commitment. Obviously, determining a teacher's moral beliefs goes beyond examining his or her college transcripts since the subjects a person studies bear little relation to his or her moral conduct.

States have a right to require high moral standards from those who obtain state licenses to teach in public schools. Colleges preparing teachers should examine potential students' records and deny entry to those with criminal or morally objectionable backgrounds (e.g., a history of cheating, dishonesty, or sexual misconduct). Applicants for teaching credentials should be expected to submit references that speak to their moral character. Since we ask this of lawyers who take state bar exams, why shouldn't we expect it of people going into teaching? Schools should require applicants to prepare essays discussing their values. Clearly, student teaching and the first few years of full-time teaching provide opportunity to screen young teachers to ensure that they uphold moral standards. If these criteria are clearly and publicly stated, they have fair warning. Teachers found wanting should find employment in some other occupation. They should not be retained in positions where they can influence young people's ideals.

How Schools Destroy Values: Values Clarification and Moral Obfuscation

In many schools, children are taught that values they learn at home or church are a matter of choice. Through teachings such as "values clarification," children are led to believe that right and wrong are purely matters of individual opinion. There is no moral guideline for conduct or thought. In values clarification, teachers may ask children to publicly identify situations when their father or mother was wrong and to present their own view of what the parent should have done. Teachers ask children personal questions about their family lives and private thoughts. There are no criteria children can use to weigh right and wrong. Instead, teachers encourage children to determine their own set of values. Bennett (1992) describes values clarification:

> Schools were not to take part in their time-honored task of transmitting sound moral values; rather, they were to allow the child to "clarify" his own values (which adults, including parents, had no right to criticize). The "values clarification" movement didn't clarify values, it clarified wants and desires. This form of moral relativism said, in effect, that no set of values was right or wrong. (p. 56)

In class discussions on values, children who present their personal opinions with conviction can influence other children, and the teacher is not to intercede for fear of impeding the "clarification" of values. An entire class can agree that tying cans to a cat's tail, euthanizing people who are old or ill, or remaining seated during the salute to the flag may be acceptable behavior. Children also learn to report on their parents and to ridicule those who support traditional values concerning discretion and privacy. Obviously, without clear and consistent standards of acceptable behavior and belief, our society is doomed to ethical destruction. Can one argue seriously that a life of dishonesty and cheating is morally equal to a life of honesty and integrity? How can schools adopt a position of neutrality regarding values and character development? Yet that absurd view is behind values clarification and other relativistic approaches to dealing with values in schools.

American public schools, echoing the moral defects in American popular culture, commonly operate without an ethical compass. Schools should provide a firm education in ethical principles that help youth sort, analyze, and evaluate behaviors and values expressed in popular culture. This is character education, designed to instill and inspire good character—morally grounded behaviors and attitudes (Lockwood, 2009).

Unfortunately, schools are subject to the relativism that underlies much of life today. Relativism in schools reflects the ideas that (1) all values are relative, with none superior; (2) there is no enduring set of ethical standards; and (3) personal character is a matter of individual choice and particular situations.

It incorporates situational ethics and egotistical rationalization to justify any values or actions. Relativism keeps such schools and their students adrift in a sea of personal and social temptations.

Sommers (1998) demonstrates the link between a host of other school problems and the fact that Johnny can't read, write, or count; continuing, "It is also true that Johnny is having difficulty distinguishing right from wrong. . . . Along with illiteracy and innumeracy, we must add deep moral confusion to the list of educational problems" (p. 31). This is a very serious problem that will continue to haunt American society until it is adequately addressed. Hansen (2001) notes, "Studies suggest that teaching is inherently a moral endeavor" (p. 826). Morality cannot be escaped by pretending schools are outside its sphere.

We are not born with a set of values, they are all—good and bad—learned. Although we learn values in many places, from many people, and through many media, schools form a particularly significant institution for imparting values. Blackburn (2001) points out that Aristotle "emphasized that it takes education and practice in order to become virtuous" (p. 113). Former Secretary of Education William Bennett (1992) highlights the tradition of common schools as the basis of common values, with leaders of the common school movement coming mainly from people who "saw the schools as upholders of standards of individual morality and small incubators of civic and personal virtue; the founders of the public schools had faith that public education could teach good moral and civic character from a common ground of American values" (p. 58).

Yet, as Bennett documents, schools lost this central purpose in a contemporary welter of value-neutral, value-relative, and anything-goes approaches to values education. The former position of schools was to be stalwart conveyors of good values and sound character, with exemplary moral and ethical modeling by school teachers and administrators. That has been replaced by an institutional blind eye to values and educator disinterest in or fear of maintaining high standards of morality and ethics for themselves and their students. Far too many public schools lack a central core of fundamental morals and give students no ethical basis for guidance through life. Instead, secular domination of education mistakenly keeps religious values at bay, while self-absorption becomes a primary focus for students.

Education emphasizing selfishness, personal freedom, and permissiveness is a major contributor to the significant decline in social and family values (Sowell, 1992; Shapiro, 2005). Increased crime and abuse is a natural outcome of schooling that preaches self-indulgence. Where can one gain a deep respect for other people, property, and social traditions if schools assume the stance that these things do not matter?

Liberalism and Moral Decline

The liberal view of education—that traditional values don't matter and that students should decide basic value questions for themselves without guidance from educators, religious leaders, or parents—has an eroding effect on the cornerstones of American society. Liberalism itself is a culprit; in education, it does significant damage to American morality (Falwell, 1980; Bennett, 1993; Bork, 1996; Himmelfarb, 1999; Charen, 2004; Coulter, 2004, 2007; Hannity, 2004; Frank, 2005; Savage, 2005; Sowell, 2007). Common values undergirding civility, manners, and courtesies once dominant in the United States have given way to self-indulgent values of greed, destruction, consumption, and distrust of authority. This erosion has been the companion of permissive attitudes fostered in schools since progressive education concepts enveloped schools in the 1930s.

Family values have declined in the face of a long-term educational philosophy based on individualism and libertine lifestyles (Rafferty, 1968; Anderson, 1994; Roberts, 1994; Gallagher, 2005; Shapiro, 2005). Evidence of moral disaster surrounds us: extraordinarily high divorce rates, child and spouse abuse, lack of ethics in business and government, drug and alcohol addiction, out-of-control teenage pregnancy rates, excessive reliance on child care outside the home, acceptance of immorality on television and in the arts, cheating scandals, and bullying of explosive violence in schools (Colson, 1994; Bouza, 1996; Jacobs, 2004; Barter and Berridge, 2011; Hamburger, Basille, and Vivolo, 2011).

Schools have lost their moral focus and, thus, their ability to educate youth in the most important of areas—morality. Without a moral focus, other learnings are shallow.

Attacks on American family values have appeared under the banners of "diversity," "multiculturalism," and "sexual orientation." These banners share the root idea of moral relativism, the idea that all views are equally valid in the classroom—from killing by euthanasia or abortion to gay and lesbian advocacy (Biegel, 2010). As it destroys traditional values, moral relativism substitutes amorality or immorality as a guide to life. Even in this, there is rank logical inconsistency in the advocacy of value neutrality by many liberals. While claiming that no values are more important than any others, liberal advocates still propose a set of special interests that they claim deserve special treatment in classrooms and textbooks: minorities, women, disabled, gay, and lesbian (Charen, 2004; Gallagher, 2005; Savage, 2005). This special treatment constitutes a set of values they consider more important. Further, they accept mercy killings, abortions, and homosexuality as examples of perfectly acceptable topics of study and conduct, while praying in school is not. This is hypocrisy.

Lickona (1991, 1993, 2004) outlined the kinds of problems that demonstrate a decline in values among youth. He includes violence, vandalism, bad language, sexual promiscuity, peer cruelty, stealing, and cheating. He linked this decline to a series of factors, including the following:

> Darwinism and the relativistic view that springs from it

> A philosophy of pseudoscientific logical positivism that separates "facts" from "values"

> Personalism, emphasizing individual rights over social responsibilities and moral authority

Pluralism, suggesting multiple values and raising a question of which ones we should teach

Secularization, which falsely separates church and state and offers no religious guidance

Confusing Values in the Current Curriculum

School curriculum and textbooks currently present a wide array of relativistic values that only confuse children. Secular humanism, relativism, and liberalism are not defined as school subjects, and schools offer no courses with those titles. Instead, these insidious ideas filter into nearly all courses and often go unrecognized, even by teachers. Because no specific curriculum stresses traditional morals and values, teachers and courses easily present differing views, leading students to believe that there are no eternal or universal values, only personal ones. If courses and teachers do not attest to a common core of morality, students are left morally rudderless. This spawns confusion or self-indulgence at best and scorn for morality at worst.

Teaching materials children learn from often are either vapid, without any connection to moral thought and behavior, or confusing, displaying multiple values of supposedly equal weight. Current school reading materials include trash directing attention to the values of the worst elements of society and adult stories well beyond children's moral development. In civics and history, the focus is on political power, not virtue. Children are taught how to manipulate others and how interest groups get their way. History texts are bland and noncommittal concerning basic values and treat religion with disdain. Sex education instruction tends toward the belief that students will engage in promiscuity and sexual freedom, not exercise abstinence and responsibility (Shapiro, 2005). Science ignores religious views and substitutes the "value-free" ideas; any scientific experiment is okay. Instead of protecting and encouraging innocence, schools savage and debase it.

Results of this permissive and selfish education are apparent. We are subject to increasing abuse in contemporary life. We have seen a startling increase in child abuse, so prevalent that we now have twenty-four-hour telephone hotlines to report it. Spousal abuse is another item featured almost daily in newspapers.

Animal abuse is so common it no longer makes news. And sex and drug abuse have become epidemic. Bullying and antipatriotic actions in schools are among the signals that value-free morality has its consequences (Barter and Berridge, 2011; Hamburger et al., 2011).

Other abuses currently abound. We abuse our ideals, respect, heroes, national honor, and religious base. Political and business leaders abuse the public trust through cheating and corruption. Young people no longer understand why we fought wars to protect our liberties. Some children refuse to recite the Pledge of Allegiance or to sing the "Star-Spangled Banner." Graffiti covers many of our national monuments and our statues of heroes. Children no longer honor their parents or respect their elders.

An in-depth interview study of young adults across the United States shows the weak level of their moral thinking (Smith, 2011). David Brooks (2011), commenting on this study, noted, "The default position, which most of them came back to again and again, is that moral choices are just a matter of individual taste. 'It's personal,' the respondents typically said, 'It's up to the individual. Who am I to say? . . . Smith and company found an atmosphere of extreme moral individualism—or relativism and nonjudgmentalism" (pp. 1, 2). Another current study, surveying over 40,000 high school students in public and private schools, shows that well over half admitted to cheating on tests, about half admitted to lying, and almost one-fourth admit stealing (Character Counts, 2011). These examples illustrate the major reason we need a dramatic shift to traditional moral or ethical education, a school program and setting that gives a compass to young people for judging good and bad and acting to enhance the good.

Schools Are Rooted in Moral Values

Schools in America were founded to provide a moral foundation, and they were effective. Colonial schools had as their core a firm commitment to morality, ethics, and traditional values. The first school laws, passed in Massachusetts in 1642 and 1647, mandated that communities provide schooling for young people and that those schools preserve religious and social values. The *New England Primer*, the colonial schoolbook used to teach the alphabet and reading, incorporated moral virtues in its teaching of basic skills. All schoolbooks followed this pattern for many generations. Early Americans clearly recognized the link between a good society and solid religious, family, and school values. Religion continues to be a firm foundation for teaching traditional values and should not be kept out of public school classrooms.

From the *New England Primer* through the *McGuffey Readers*, the content studied in school was consistent with America's traditional values. We can learn much from the moral stories these old works present. Children learned that it was wrong to misbehave at home, in the community, and at school. They learned the consequences of affronting the common morality, reading about what happened to those who did. They gained respect for proper authority in families, churches, society, and school. We need to reject permissiveness and valuelessness of current schools and return to emphasizing moral precepts and proper behavior. The crisis in education has the same origin as the crisis in society: a decline in basic values. Correction in schools is the main avenue to correction in society.

Religion affords a good moral base for young people but isn't the only source of traditional values. Ethical personal behavior also derives from deep-rooted family and social values. The good society depends on citizens who have developed keen concern for others, awareness of personal responsibility, and habits of moderation. Etzioni (1998) argues that values education has broad and deep support among the American public, and he proposes that "we just teach the values that most Americans agree upon" (p. 448). Sommers (1998) presents a clear case for classical moral education for students, the "core of noncontroversial ethical issues that were settled long ago. . . . We need to bring back the great books and the great ideas" (pp. 33, 34).

The obvious decline in values among the young results from a number of factors. Foremost is that schools have forsaken the responsibility to teach solid values, instead substituting highly relativistic opinions that undermine parental and religious authority. Children are taught that all values are equal, so whatever they value is fine. We can't hold children responsible for this rejection of common morality because their natural tendency is to be selfish. Parents must teach children to share and to respect traditional social values. Historically, we relied on schools to reinforce and extend the basic ethical code families, churches, and other religious institutions teach. When parents are unable or refuse to teach children right from wrong, schools usually have supplied this important function. Those who now run the schools have forgotten their history, and people who forget will repeat mistakes of the past.

With current high divorce rates and parental lack of attention to their children's moral development, schools should play an even more significant role in conveying American values to children. In times of family and social stress, schools should exert expanded influence to ensure continuation of our heritage. Many of our young parents grew up during the 1960s and 1970s, when there was a sharp decline in religious participation and a significant increase in immorality. Without the value base provided by strong religious and national traditions, the United States will be in trouble. Schools must assume an increased responsibility for training students in traditional values.

We must restore basic American values to schools and to our young people, and it is possible. But a potential opportunity is not enough. It is crucial that we move quickly to reinvigorate our school leaders with the resolve to do it. We are facing a crisis of values in society, and the crisis is reflected in our schools. Our society is extremely vulnerable. Schools must reassume their original responsibility for moral teachings.

POSITION 2: LIBERATION THROUGH ACTIVE VALUE INQUIRY

The great majority of character education programs consist largely of exhortation and directed recitation. . . . Most character education programs also deliver homilies by way of posters, banners, and murals throughout the school. . . . The children are passive receptacles to be filled—objects to be manipulated rather than learners to be engaged.

—Kohn (1997, p. 158)

"Character" is an archaic, quasi-metaphysical term, more related to horoscopes than any scientific concept. It is a term with no agreed upon definition, even among proponents of character education . . . character education is part of an agenda to introduce conservative ideology, alone, into the minds of . . . students.

—Cornwall (2005, p. 1)

School is not a neutral activity. Decisions to provide and to participate in education are based on a set of values. Everything schools do and decide not to do reflects a set of values. We educate and are educated for some purpose we consider good (Purpel, 2003; Spring, 2008). We teach what we think is a valuable set of ideas. How else could we construct education? It would be absurd to have schools without goals, teaching without purpose, and curricula without objectives.

Schools, then, are heavily involved in a series of value-based decisions. Schools provide values and character education through a variety of forms, whether intended and thoughtful or not. Thoughtful education about values incorporates society's primary ideals expressed and examined by students in a rational, respectful approach. That requires teachers to encourage intelligent and critical examination that reflects the ethical dimensions of education (Giroux, 2004; Kohn, 2008). It respects student learning and maturity as well as disagreements. Rather than preach morality and goodness, it expects students to develop reasoned appreciation of core civilizing values and correlated ethical behavior.

Students come to school with a collection of values and opinions on good and bad; these have been acquired from family, television, friends, and other experiences (Aronowitz, 2008). Students do not come to school as empty moral vessels, waiting for proper values to be poured in. Even primary-grade children have a pretty clear sense of right and wrong; in fact, they are almost too clear in their determination of what is fair and what is not and who should get punished and for what infractions. There are few gray areas. Try playing a game with young children and see how rules are interpreted.

Nikki Stern (2011), a widow as a result of the September 2001 attacks on the World Trade Center, writes forcefully about the dangers inherent in moral authoritarianism: "My experience and observation suggest that people who believe themselves in possession of the truth tend to believe they're also in possession of the moral authority to act on it" (p. 17). She defines the dangers in national presumptions of moral authority and the troubling international actions that can follow, but similar dangers occur in attempting to impose morality on schoolchildren rather than have them gain a critical understanding of morals, values and ethical behavior. As Stout (2011) shows, "Emerging evidence suggests that cultural habits of unselfish prosocial behavior . . . are powerful engines for social stability and economic growth. . . . A healthy, productive society cannot rely solely on carrots and sticks" (p. 19). Maturity brings a more sophisticated sense of justice, morality, ethics, and values—much of which is honed among families, friends, media, and such institutions as formal religion and schools.

Good character is a work in progress, exhibited in actions in situations where morals, values, and ethics are tested. Values education should critically examine traditional and contemporary moral ideas and test and refine a set of personal beliefs about ethical conduct. Attempted indoctrination by slogans, moralisms, and dogmatic piety does not meet that high standard and can result in nonthinking knee-jerk reactions. Examples of unethical and immoral actions by some clergy and corporate executives over the recent past show that moral righteousness can be spoken by everyone, but moral action requires a higher level of principles and fortitude. There are no guarantees but more likely good results from value inquiry than from programs of moralisms and authoritarian pronouncements. Sociologist J. S. Victor (2002) points out, "It is much more useful to offer our children a path to follow than a battery of abstract values . . . a way of thinking rather than a code of rules to follow" (p. 31).

Liberation = Education

Education's primary purpose is liberation. Liberation from ignorance is the foundation beneath freedoms from slavery, dictatorship, and domination. Freedom to know underlies the freedom to participate fully in a democracy, enjoy and extend justice and equality, live a healthy and satisfying life, and provide the same opportunities to others. These are all solid values students can examine and relate to their own lives. But that inquiry requires freedom. Freedom to think and freedom to act are based on freedom to know. Any society intending to be free and democratic must recognize an elemental equation: liberation = education. Schools that restrict and contort the minds of the young oppose that principle, and democratic civilization is the victim. Since students learn a lot about values by observing the operation of values in the world about them, unreasonably authoritarian schools convey antidemocratic values inconsistent with many basic moral principles in addition to being disrespectful of student intelligence (Kessler, 2000; Kincheloe, 2008; DeLeon and Ross, 2010).

Clearly, this is not an essay in favor of abandoning the civilizing characteristics of human society, including decency, respect, responsibility, courage, and magnanimity. Indeed, it is the opposite—a plea in favor of values inquiry that offers to empower students to develop and enhance civilization without hypocrisy. We cannot impose traditional values on schoolchildren and not allow criticism of those values. Students, in traditional values indoctrination courses, learn conformity to authority, not thinking. Value inquiry into basic values of civilization will yield stronger, more realistic convictions among students than mere sloganeering and student conformity. Often, as a result of student passivity and obedience, such moral problems as social injustice and inequality are ignored. Instead of questioning and acting to improve society, students are expected to sponge up moralisms and be quiet. Greene (1990) argues that moral choice and ethical action should be products of careful and critical thought. That occurs when the community provides freedom and encouragement for individual students and teachers to engage in such thinking.

Limits and Conditions

There are, of course, reasonable limits and conditions to this concept of freedom, as there are to all freedoms. Very young children require guidance and direction in basic good habits. And the small number of people whose development has been arrested at an equivalent level of infancy or young childhood may require some caring control for their own safety and well-being over much of their lives. We should expect the vast majority of children and school students, however, to mature in terms of intellect and values, progressing beyond fixed habits and adopting a reasoned understanding and independent judgment of suitable values and ethical conduct.

That maturing requires the opportunity to question, challenge, and critically examine moral pronouncements within the context of a considered view of right and wrong. Does that support a school approach to values as anything goes? Absolutely not. It means that students need to fully comprehend social mores and values and recognize and take responsibility for the consequences of their actions. It also means they must understand and reason through moral principles undergirding adequate ethical conduct and values.

Such principles as humanity and human rights, justice, equality, freedom, and civilization deserve considerable rational deliberation in order to be used as standards against which to weigh ethical conduct and values in given situations. Confronted with a choice between rational deliberation and emotional outburst, few thinking students will pick emotion. They want to reason, even as emotion plays some role in their decisions (Smith, 2006; Harris, 2011). Given a choice between freedom and slavery, most will pick freedom—and for good reasons.

Value inquiry involves the thinking through of fundamental moral principles, testing those principles in the cauldron of value conflicts in society and daily life, providing opportunity to rationally criticize, and developing a more consistent set of values and operational ethics (Singer, 2002). This is not license to do whatever one wants, and it is clearly not blind obedience to authority. Ayn Rand, known for her right-wing libertarian positions, had ethical views, according to Smith (2006), that are grounded in rational decision making—the "fundamental means by which human beings can maintain and advance our lives" (p. 80). Sam Harris (2010), from a much more liberal view, argues that reason based on evidence, as in science, can provide a basis for morality.

Wolfe (2001) found in interviews across the United States that a concept of moral freedom is evolving. Moral freedom draws from ideas similar to those political, economic, and religious freedom ideas flowing from the revolutionary ideas in the founding of this society—a recognition that freedom and democracy are necessary cohabitants. Wolfe (2001) notes that previous ideas of character formation required unthinking obedience to institutional authoritarianism, based on the idea that individuals were basically evil and needed correction:

> Character formation involved the alchemist task of making something good (virtue) out of something bad (human nature) . . . the process of character formation, premised on individual weakness, always sits uncomfortably in a liberal democratic society. . . . Highly structured systems of moral authority require that we repress our instincts and needs for the sake of authority. But if we believe ourselves to be inherently good people—or at the least neither good nor bad—why can't we trust ourselves more and learn to trust institutions, which are capable of abusing the power they have, less? (pp. 179, 180)

We have certainly seen enough authoritarian institutions who have abused their power in the past decades. From churches to government to corporations, there are plenty of examples of abuse. Some who preach morality, ethics, and responsibility have been found to be wanting in exactly those areas. But this new moral freedom from such authoritarianism does not lead to personal anarchy or irresponsibility, with no central values. Many key traditional moral precepts remain, but, as Wolfe (2001) points out for those he interviewed, "In an age of moral freedom, moral authority has to justify its claims to special insight" (p. 226). Legitimacy and credibility are necessary conditions for sound moral authority. Wolfe found that respondents had strong feelings supporting such traditional values as loyalty, self-discipline, honesty, and forgiveness. They had consulted authorities and institutions but did not simply obey them in arriving at these values. They were struggling with how to apply them to everyday life in a variety of situations but felt free to do that and question them at the same time. This is a form of value inquiry based on the concept of liberation, consistent with the research of Coles (1997) and Piaget (1997) on how moral reasoning develops. Eisgruber (2002) comments,

> One of the defining characteristics of liberal democracy is that persons must give reasoned justification for the power they seek to exercise; they behave undemocratically insofar as they rely only on personal status or authority . . . the liberal democratic state teaches most powerfully by example, not by sermonizing. (pp. 72, 83)

Principles of liberation and education operate whether students are learning basic skills and knowledge or values, ethical conduct, morality, and character development. While it may be possible to develop basic skills and rote information in dogmatic and dictatorial schools, that denies the concept of independent thinking necessary to a democracy. It is, therefore, undemocratic to teach academic subjects in that system. Similarly, it is possible to indoctrinate students with values and ethical standards, but that approach is inconsistent with democracy and independent thinking. In addition to being undemocratic, teaching values and ethics in authoritarian settings also is counterproductive. The purpose of values education is to get students to understand, examine, derive, and thoughtfully adopt a set of socially positive values that can be translated into ethical behavior. Authoritarianism is in opposition to that purpose; it requires only obedience, blindly.

School Decisions about Values Education

The issue is not whether schools should be engaged in values education since all are by their very nature. Rather, the issues are what kinds of values should be central to schoolwork and how should they best be taught and learned. Teachers, textbooks, and schools in general all teach some set of values to young people. Schools can be organized and operate in ways that develop conformity, obedience to external authorities, and passive, docile behavior. Schools also can work to develop thoughtful critics of society's problems, students who are willing to challenge social norms and pursue continued improvement of humankind into the future (Kidder, 1994, 2010; Haydon, 1995; Kohn, 1997, 2008; Purpel, 2003; Anyon et al., 2008). There are many variations on these purposes of either socializing students to conform to social values or liberating them to engage in social improvement.

Unfortunately, for those who believe that schools have more significant social purposes, much contemporary school activity is devoted to producing docile, passive students who will be unlikely to challenge the status quo or raise questions even in the face of unreasoned authoritarianism. Current materials for teaching values and character in schools often are intended to protect the status quo, make students vessels for conformist behavior, and offer a noncritical perspective on religious views. Kohn (1998), for example, provides ample evidence that "conventional character education rests upon behaviorism, conservatism, and religious dogma" (p. 455). Even more unfortunately for students and society, schools often are successful in this purpose. School life focuses far too much on conformity, placing extreme pressure on all students to think, behave, and view life in the same way. Not only is this hypocritical, since many adult citizens and educators do not adhere to the moralistic standards prescribed, but it destroys our young people's creativity and energy. It also leads to passivity in civic life—a serious malady in a democracy.

John Stuart Mill (1956) defines the commonplace conformist education of his time:

> A general State education is a mere contrivance for moulding people to be exactly like one another; and as the mould in which it casts them is that which pleases the predominant power in the government—whether this be a monarch, a priesthood, an aristocracy, or the majority of the existing generation—in proportion as it is efficient and successful, it establishes a despotism over the mind, leading by natural tendency to one over the body. (p. 129)

Mill's comments still are appropriate today. Sadly, many schools aim to produce obedient citizens to ensure social control, not critical thinking to enhance the society.

In traditional schools, students are force-fed moralisms and value precepts inconsistent with what they see in society. Poorly paid teachers preach honesty while wealthy financiers, bankers, and politicians loot the public. Well-heeled or well-connected people who commit so-called white-collar crimes seldom are punished, although a few may be sent to luxurious detainment centers for brief stays. However, people from lower-social-class backgrounds who commit nonviolent crimes often receive long and debilitating sentences in standard prisons, where they learn more criminal behavior. Even recent U.S. presidents who engage in questionable ethical behavior are given credibility, as though the behavior is acceptable. These obvious disparities in our concept of justice and in our other values are evident to students. Similar examples of disparity in equality, justice, honesty, and citizenship abound in our national life. Students are well aware of these inequities. A moralistic slogan or required reading in school does not hide the defect.

Liberation Education and Critical Pedagogy: Values Inquiry

Liberation education offers an opportunity to examine social problems and conflicting values. It is linked well with ideas of critical pedagogy, a program to assist teachers to engage students in this examination (Shor, 1987; Burbules and Berk, 1999; Kincheloe, 2008; de Lissovoy, 2010). Liberation education is not a prescribed set of teacher techniques, a specific lesson plan, or a textbook series for schools to adopt. There is no mechanistic or teacherproof approach that will produce liberation. Critical pedagogy is anything but mechanical and teacherproof; it is dynamic and teacher oriented. Liberation is the emancipation of students and teachers from the blinders of class-dominated ignorance, conformity, and thought control (Shor, 1987; Clark, 1990; Ahlquist, 1991). Its dynamic quality views students and teachers as active participants in opposing oppression and improving democracy (Giroux, 1991, 2004, 2008). Applied to values, it proposes that students inquire into basic moral concepts, apply them to disparities in society's values, examine alternative views, and arrive at a valid and usable set of ethical guidelines. It is grounded in reason, based on well-examined beliefs. A very popular ethics course at Harvard appropriately includes work on liberation education (www.ethics.harvard.edu).

Liberation education is complex because the social forces it addresses are complex. The central purpose is to liberate the individual and society and to broadly distribute liberating power (Freire, 1970; Glass, 2001). It requires a set of values, including justice and equality, to serve as ideals in opposition to oppression and authoritarianism and a critical understanding of the many cultural crosscurrents in contemporary society and mechanisms of manipulation that hide ideological purposes. Liberation education and critical pedagogy uncover myths and injustices evident in the dominant culture. They also embrace the expectation that the powerless can, through education, develop power. This requires us to recognize that forms of knowledge and schooling are not neutral but are utilized by the dominant culture to secure its power.

Schools must become sites where we examine conflicts of humankind in increasing depth to understand ideological and cultural bases on which societies operate. The purpose is not merely to recognize those conflicts or ideologies but also to engage in actions that constrain oppression and expand personal power. This profound, revolutionary educational concept goes to the heart of what education should be. Schools themselves need to undergo this liberation, and we should take actions to make them more truly democratic. Other social institutions also merit examination and action. Obviously, liberation education, a redundant term, is controversial in contemporary society. Liberated people threaten the traditional docility and passivity that schools now impose.

What Should Be Taught

Liberation education for values inquiry requires us to blend curriculum content with critical pedagogy. We cannot separate what students study from how they study it. The basis of this approach to schooling is to engage students in critical study of the society and its institutions with the dual purpose of liberating themselves from blinders that simply reproduce old values that continue such ethical blights as greed, corruption, and inhumanity and liberating society from oppressive manipulation of people by government, corporate, and institutional propaganda (Baker and Heyning, 2004; Yu, 2004; Blau, 2005).

Critical study involves both method and content. It expects an open examination and critique of diverse ideas and sees the human condition as problematic. That places all human activity within the scope of potential curriculum content and makes all activity subject to critical scrutiny through a dynamic form of dialectic reasoning.

Obviously, students cannot examine all things at all times. Thus, selection of topics for study depends on several factors, including what students previously have studied and the depth of those investigations, which contemporary social issues are significant, students' interests and maturity level, and the teacher's knowledge. There is no neatly structured sequence of information that all students must pass through and then forget. Students should examine the nature of knowledge itself. That can lead to liberation. And liberation develops strong character.

Among topics of early and continuing study should be ideologies. Students need to learn how to strip away layers of propaganda and rationalization to examine root causes. Ideology, in its most literal sense, is the study of ideas. Those ideas may be phrased in a language intended for mystification or designed to persuade people. Racism and sexism are not considered acceptable public views in the United States, yet they often lie behind high-sounding pronouncements and policies. Test scores from culturally biased tests are rationalized to segregate students for favored treatment in neutral-sounding nonracist and nonsexist terms, but basic causes and consequences are still racist or sexist. Imperialism is not considered proper in current international relations, but powerful nations do attempt to control others through physical or political-economic means while labeling their actions defensive or even "freedom fighting." Ideological study can help students situate events in historic, economic, and political settings deeper and richer than surface explanations.

Mainstream Mystification

Too little in popular educational literature speaks to liberation, opposition to oppressive forces, and improvement of democracy. Most mainstream educational writing raises no questions about the context that schools sit within; the writers seem to accept the conservative purposes of schools and merely urge us to "fine-tune" them a bit. Standard educational writing does not examine our schooling system to the depth of its roots, ideologies, and complexities. Instead, teachers and teachers in training read articles on implementing teaching techniques and making slight modifications in curriculum. There is nothing critical in these pieces and no liberation of the mind from strictures of a narrow culture. The dominant concern is to make schools more efficient, mechanical, factory-like, and conformist.

Mainstream educational literature rests on a mainstream of thought in American society. This thought is bound by a narrow band between standard conservative and liberal ideas. Those who go outside this band are labeled radical or "un-American" and viewed with suspicion. Outside ideas and criticisms have no public credibility. Neither conservatives nor liberals are pleased to see schools critically examine American democracy.

Conservatives and liberals do seem to agree that U.S. schools should support democracy. Numerous platitudes about schools preparing citizens for democracy or about schools as a minidemocracy fill mainstream literature. This literature can be classified as mystification because it uses high-sounding phrases to cover its ideology, a continuation of the status quo, and the power of the already dominant class. It is not active democracy, with its liberation values, that this literature commends. The real purpose of this line of thought is to keep the masses content as uncritical workers who believe themselves to be free but actually are bound and powerless. The function of mainstream writing, in other words, is to mystify readers with a rhetoric of freedom while maintaining domination of the powerful.

Current educational terms, such as "excellence," "standards," "humanistic," and "progressive," fill mainstream periodicals. Although the terms may be useful in discussing education, they often serve as camouflage. Conservatives use the terms "excellence" and "standards" to mask the interests of the dominant classes in justifying their advantages and the interests of business in production of skilled but docile workers. Liberals use the terms "humanistic" and "progressive" to hide a soft, comfortable individualism that ignores society's basic problems and conflicts (Giroux, 2008). Together, the terms combine the business ideology dominating schools and society and narcissism preventing groups from recognizing defects in that ideology. That is *mystification*—an effort to mystify the public and hide the real school agenda.

That agenda is to maintain what Joel Spring (2008) calls a "sorting machine," sorting different social classes into various categories of citizenship. Raymond Callahan (1962) documents this agenda as a business orientation in schools, designed to prepare the masses to do efficient work and the elite to manage. Jean Anyon (1980) exposes the actual curriculum of docility and obedience taught to the lower classes. Henry Giroux (1988) describes the hidden curriculum imposing dominant class values, attitudes, and norms on all students. And Aronowitz and Giroux (1991) identify the need for a strong schooling in criticism to buttress students against crippling effects of traditional values that society imposes.

The mass media amplify conservative and liberal arguments about schooling, but, in fact, little separates them. Schools can and do, by making slight modifications every few years, accommodate each side for a while. The pendulum swings in a narrow arc from the center, but schools remain pretty much the same, with only cosmetic changes. When conservatives are in power, people express more concern about competition, grading, passing tests, and knowing specific bits of information. Liberals try to make students feel happy, allow more freedom in the curriculum, and offer more student activities.

With regard to democracy and schooling, differences between conservative and liberal views lie in how narrowly democracy is defined and at what age students are to begin practicing democracy. Conservative rhetoric calls for a narrower definition and inculcation of good habits and values among students at an early age. Liberals call for a somewhat broader definition and for establishment of schools as places where students pretend to practice a form of democracy.

Neither conservative nor liberal mainstream views raise questions about democracy's basic nature or the means we use to achieve it. Neither view is critical of existing class domination over knowledge and schools. Neither sees democracy as problematic, deserving continuing critical examination to improve it. Both views assume that there is a basic consensus on what democracy is and that schools are an agency for achieving it. As a result, conservative and liberal views about schooling in a democracy differ very little. The two groups express only shallow differences over what subjects schools should emphasize and how much freedom students should have. Those may sound like important differences, but debates over such matters as how tough grading practices should be or whether students need extra time for reading drill do not address serious, significant issues of democratic life. Ideologically, conservatives and liberals share basic beliefs. Their form of values education is devoted to the status quo to avoid confronting more serious social problems of injustice and inequality.

Reactionary Indoctrination and Cultural Reproduction

Right-wingers are open advocates of indoctrination and censorship. If you know the truth, why would you present other ideas? Dissent, of course, should be stifled because it confuses children of all ages, and deviation cannot be tolerated. This view has potentially disastrous consequences for any democracy and its schools (Noddings, 2003; Yu, 2004).

Interestingly, both conservatives and liberals expect indoctrination but are loath to tell anyone because it sounds undemocratic. Instead, since they control schools and society, they can impose their dominant views by more subtle means. Through state laws, this coalition controls school curriculum, textbook selection, school operation, and teacher licensing. State agencies monitor schools and prescribe limits. The news media, which also are dominated by mainstream conservative and liberal forces, persuade the public that democracy is working relatively well. Basic ideological disputes on social values are not confronted because no real disputes arise between standard conservative and liberal views (Chambers and Kymlicka, 2002; Giroux, 2008).

So schools are expected to indoctrinate students into mainstream culture, and the mainstream has the power to require conformity. "Cultural reproduction" means that each generation passes on to the next the dominant cultural ideology that was imposed on it. In the United States, this cultural reproduction takes two forms: (1) a set of positive beliefs that the United States is a chosen country, with justice and equality for all and the best of economic systems, and

(2) a set of negative beliefs that any views raising troubling questions about American values are automatically anti-American. This twofold reproduction ensures that teachers and students will not engage in serious critical thinking but will merely accept dominant ideologies. Thus, the very nature of democracy and the means for improving it are perceived as naturally existing and beyond the school's scope of inquiry.

In school, students read mainstream literature, hear mainstream views from teachers and peers, see mainstream films, listen to mainstream speakers, and engage in mainstream extracurricular activities. The school library carries only mainstream periodicals and books. Finding an examination of highly divergent ideas is virtually impossible. When students are not in school, they read the mainstream press, watch mainstream television, and live in families of people who were educated in the same manner. Teachers prepare in colleges where they study mainstream views of their subjects and the profession of teaching. No wonder schools are prime locations for cultural reproduction; they contain no other sources of ideas. To have mainstream ideas broadly represented in schools is certainly not improper, but to suppress critical examination of those ideas and limit students to such a narrow band of ideas is not liberating.

Students often are surprised to stumble on a radical journal or book legitimately challenging basic assumptions about capitalism and U.S. politics and their impact on justice and equality. Those students rightfully are concerned about an education that did not permit them to consider opposing values and ideologies. Unfortunately, the vast majority of students never come across radical materials, or they automatically and unthoughtfully reject any divergent views because schools have effectively sealed their minds—hardly character building.

Mainstream Control of Knowledge

Not only do schools sort and label students and limit the range of views that undergo examination, but they also provide class-biased knowledge to differing groups of students. Young (1971) a British sociologist, argues that the powerful try to define knowledge and to determine who gets what kinds.

Essentially, those in power in schools guard knowledge that they consider high status and use it to retain power and differentiate themselves from the masses. Although some auto mechanics, for example, must use complex skills and knowledge, it is not considered high-status knowledge. Law and medicine, which also utilize complex skills and knowledge, are considered high status. Apple (1990) notes a relationship between economic structure and high-status knowledge. A capitalist, industrial, technological society values knowledge that most contributes to its continuing development. Math, science, and computer study have demonstrably more financial support than do the arts and humanities. A master's degree in business administration, especially if from a "prestigious" institution, is more valuable than a degree in humanities. Technical subjects, such as math and the sciences, are more easily broken into discrete bits of information and are more easily testable than are the arts and humanities. This leads to easy stratification of students, often along social class lines. The idea of school achievement is to compete well in the "hard" technical subjects where differentiation is easiest to measure. Upper-class students, however, are not in the competition since they are protected and usually do not attend public schools. The upper middle class provides advantages for its children; the working-class child struggles to overcome disadvantage.

Separation of subjects in the discipline-centered curriculum serves to legitimize the high status of hard subjects and academic preparatory sequence. Few critically examine the organization of knowledge or understand it as class based or problematic. Instead, schools present information in segments and spurts, testing on detail and ranking students on how well they accept the school's definitions. We pretend that knowledge is neutral, that numerous subject categories and titles are merely logical structures to assist understanding. This separates school learning from social problems, reinforces the existing authority's domination over what is important to know, and maintains students as dependent and uncritical thinkers.

The Dynamic Dialectic

Liberation education requires teachers and students to engage in a dynamic form of dialectic reasoning to uncover ideological roots of significant values. A dynamic dialectic opens topics to examination. It does not impose a set of absolutes with a known truth but operates more like a spiral, digging deep into rationales. It examines the topic in its total social context, not in segments as in the discipline-centered curriculum. And it requires a vision of liberation allowing students to dig beneath the topic's surface to uncover its basic relationships to society's structure and to dominant interests. The purpose of the dialectic is to encourage students to transcend their traditional nonactive, sterile roles and accept active roles as knowledgeable participants in the improvement of civilization. In theory, the dialectic is never ending since civilization is in continual need of improvement. In practice in the schools, the dialectic is limited by time, energy, interest, and topics under study.

These divergent ideas must be examined in a setting where they can be fully developed and are perceived as legitimate rather than strange or quaint. Adequate time and resources must be available and censorship and authoritarianism kept at bay.

To ensure a truly liberated society, one cannot expect less of schools than education for liberation. Critical pedagogy offers a major opportunity to move in that direction. An emancipatory climate in schools will regenerate students and teachers to fully use their intellects and creativity. Those are fitting and proper goals for schools, unachievable under restricted mainstream forms of schooling our society now practices. This is values inquiry for liberation.

For Discussion

1. Values and character are two very important dimensions of education. If indoctrination is one view of how values should be imparted—a thesis—and relativistic open inquiry is another—an antithesis—what are some possible school approaches that could represent a synthesis view? How do you justify your proposal?

2. You have been asked to recommend 10 members to a local advisory council on values and character education. The council's charge is to identify how schools should approach teaching values and character development.
   a. What process would you go through to find the best people?
   b. What kinds of people would you select, and how many of each? Why?
   c. What educational background should be required?
   d. What occupations should be represented, and in what proportions?
   e. What groups or agencies should be represented, and in what proportions?
   f. What age, gender, or ethnic categories should be represented, and in what proportions?
   g. What other characteristics would you look for?
   h. What kinds of people would you want to exclude? Why?

3. Paulo Freire, a major advocate of liberation education, claims that traditional teaching is fundamentally "narrative," leaving the subject matter "lifeless and petrified." Freire (1970) writes, "The teacher talks about reality as if it were motionless, static, compartmentalized, and predictable. Or else he expounds on a topic completely alien to the existential experience of the students. His task is to fill the students with the contents of his narration—contents which are detached from reality. . . . The more completely he fills the receptacles, the better a teacher he is. The more meekly the receptacles permit themselves to be filled, the better students they are" (pp. 57, 58).

   Does this description fit your experience in schools? What evidence can you provide? Criticize Freire's view of this "banking" form of education. Has he properly characterized what happens in schools? Should it happen? What are the social costs of changing to liberation education? What are the costs of not changing? What would be an example of an antithetical position to Freire's?

4. Many agree we should teach values in school but disagree about which values and who makes that choice. Some propose everlasting universal values, others propose utilitarian short-term values, some propose general and vague social values, and still others propose values based on individual or immediate circumstances. What is a reasonable way to determine what kind of values education we should teach in U.S. schools? What possible social consequences can you foresee for the various forms of values education? Who should decide on which values should be taught?

References

AHLQUIST, R. (1991). "Critical Pedagogy for Social Studies Teachers." *Social Studies Review* 29:53–57.

ANDERSON, D. (1994). "The Great Tradition." *National Review* 46:56–58.

ANYON, J. (1980). "Social Class and the Hidden Curriculum of Work." *Journal of Education* 162:67–92.

ANYON, J., ET AL. (2008). *Theory and Educational Research: Toward Critical Social Explanation.* New York: Routledge.

APPLE, M. (1990). *Ideology and Curriculum.* 2nd Ed. London: Routledge and Kegan Paul.

ARONOWITZ, S. (2008). *Against Schooling.* Boulder, CO: Paradigm Publishers.

ARONOWITZ, S., AND GIROUX, H. A. (1991). *Postmodern Education: Culture, Politics, and Social Criticism.* Minneapolis: University of Minnesota Press.

BAKER, B. M., AND HEYNING, K. E. (2004). *Dangerous Coagulations? The Uses of Foucault in the Study of Education.* New York: Peter Lang.

BARTER, C., AND BERRIDGE, D. eds. (2011). *Children Behaving Badly.* Malden, MA: Wiley-Blackwell.

BENNETT, W. J. (1992). *The De-Valuing of America.* New York: Summit Books.

———. (1993). *The Book of Virtues.* New York: Simon and Schuster.

———. (1994). "America at Risk." *USA Today* 123:14–16.

———. (2008). *Book of Virtues for Boys and Girls.* New York: Aladdin Paperbacks.

BIEGEL, S. (2010). *The Right to Be Out.* Minneapolis: University of Minnesota Press.

BLACKBURN, S. (2001). *Being Good.* Oxford: Oxford University Press.

BLAU, J. R. (2005). *Human Rights: Beyond the Liberal Vision.* Lanham, MD: Rowman & Littlefield.

BORK, R. (1996). *Slouching toward Gomorrah: Modern Liberalism and American Decline.* New York: Regan Books.

BOUZA, A. V. (1996). *The Decline and Fall of the American Empire.* New York: Plenum Press.

BROOKS, D. (2011). "If It Feels Right . . ." *New York Times.* September 12. www.nytimes.com

BURBULES, N., AND BERK, R. (1999). "Critical Thinking and Critical Pedagogy." *In Critical Theories in Education,* ed. T. Popkewitz and L. Fendler. New York: Routledge.

CALLAHAN, R. (1962). *Education and the Cult of Efficiency.* Chicago: University of Chicago Press.

CHAMBERS, S., AND KYMLICKA, W., eds. (2002). *Alternative Conceptions of Civil Society.* Princeton, NJ: Princeton University Press.

Character Counts. (2011). "The Ethics of American Youth." September 28. www.character counts.org.

Character Education Partnership. (2008). "Performance Values." April. www.character.org.

CHAREN, M. (2004). *Do-Gooders: How Liberals Hurt Those They Claim to Help.* New York: Sentinel.

CLARK, M. A. (1990). "Some Cautionary Observations on Liberation Education." *Language Arts* 67:388–398.

COLES, R. (1997). *The Moral Intelligence of Children.* New York: Random House.

COLSON, C. (1994). "Begging for Tyranny." *Christianity Today* 38:80–81.

CORNWALL, W. (2005). "The Problem with Character Education." *Patriotism for All.* www.members.cox.net/patriotismforall/ April.

COULTER, A. (2004). *How to Talk to a Liberal (If You Must).* New York: Crown Forum.

———. (2007). *Godless: the Church of Liberalism.* New York: Three Rivers Press.

DeLEON, A.P. AND ROSS, E. W. (2010). Critical Theories, Radical Pedagogies, and Social Education. Rotterdam, Netherlands: Sense Publications.

DE LISSOVOY, N. (2010). "Rethinking Education and Emancipation. *Harvard Education Review* 80 (2) 203–220. summer.

EISGRUBER, C. L. (2002). "How Do Liberal Democracies Teach Values?" *In Moral and Political Education,* ed. S. Macedos and Y. Tamir. New York: New York University Press.

ETZIONI, A. (1998). "How Not to Discuss Character Education." *Kappan* 79:446–448.

FALWELL, J. (1980). *Listen, America!* Garden City, NJ: Doubleday.

FRANK, J. (2005). *Left Out! How Liberals Helped Reelect George W. Bush*. Monroe, ME: Common Courage Books.

FREIRE, P. (1970). *Pedagogy of the Oppressed*. New York: Herder and Herder.

GALLAGHER, M. (2005). *Surrounded by Idiots: Fighting Liberal Lunacy in America*. New York: William Morrow.

GIROUX, H. (1988). *Teachers as Intellectuals*. Granby, MA: Bergin and Garvey.

———. (1990). "Curriculum Theory, Textual Authority, and the Role of Teachers as Public Intellectuals." *Journal of Curriculum and Supervision* 4:361–383.

———. (1991). "Curriculum Planning, Public Schooling, and Democratic Struggle." *NASSP Bulletin* 75:12–25.

———. (2004). "Critical Pedagogy and the Postmodern/Modern Divide." *Teacher Education Quarterly* 31(1):31–47.

———. (2008). *Against the Terror of Neoliberalism*. Boulder, CO: Paradigm Publishers.

GLASS, R. D. (2001). "On Paulo Freire's Philosophy of Praxis and the Foundations of Liberation Education." *Harvard Education Review* 20(2):15–25.

GREENE, M. (1990). "The Passion of the Possible." *Journal of Moral Education* 19:67–76.

———. (1991). "Con: The Schools Should Presume that Parents Have the Primary Authority to Determine the Cultural Traditions to Be Transmitted to Pupils." *Curriculum Review* 31:6–10.

HAMBURGER, M., BASILLE, K, AND VIVOLO, A. (2011). *Measuring Bullying Victimization*. Washington, DC: U.S. Government Printing Office.

HANNITY, S. (2004). *Deliver Us from Evil: Defeating Terrorism, Despotism, and Liberalism*. New York: Regan Books.

HANSEN, D. T. (2001). "Teaching as a Moral Activity." In *Handbook of Research on Teaching*, 4th Ed., ed. V. Richardson. Washington, DC: American Educational Research Association.

HARRIS, S. (2011). *The Moral Landscape*. New York: Free Press.

HAYDON, G. (1995). "Thick or Thin: The Cognitive Content of Moral Education." *Journal of Moral Education* 24:53–64.

HIMMELFARB, G. (1999). *One Nation, Two Cultures*. New York: Knopf.

Institute of Education Sciences. (2007). "*What Works: Character Education*." Washington, DC: U.S. Department of Education. June 4. www.whatworks.ed.gov

JACOBS, J. (2004). *Dark Age Ahead*. New York: Random House.

KESSLER, R. (2000). *The Soul of Education*. Alexandria, VA: Association for Supervision and Curriculum Development.

KIDDER, R. (1994). "Universal Human Values." *The Futurist* 28:8–14.

———. (2010). *Good Kids, Tough Choices*. San Francisco: Jossey-Bass.

KINCHELOE, J. (2008). *Critical Pedagogy Primer*. New York: Peter Lang.

KOHN, A. (1997). "The Trouble with Character Education." In *The Construction of Children's Character*, ed. A. Molnar. Chicago: National Society for the Study of Education.

———. (1998). "Adventures in Ethics Behavioral Control." *Kappan* 79:455–460.

———. (2008). "Progressive Education: Why It's Hard to Beat, but Also Hard to Find." *Independent School*. Spring.

LEMING, J., AND SILVA, D. (2001). "A Five Year Follow-Up Evaluation of the Effects of the Heartwood Ethics Curriculum on the Development of Children's Character." www.character.org.

LICKONA, T. (1991). *Educating for Character*. New York: Bantam.

———. (1993). "The Return of Character Education." *Educational Leadership* 51(3):6–11.

———. (2004). *Character Matters*. New York: Simon and Schuster.

LOCKWOOD, A. (2009). *The Case for Character Education*. New York: Teachers College Press.

MILL, J. S. (1956). *On Liberty.* Edited by C. V. Shields. Indianapolis: Bobbs-Merrill.

NODDINGS, N. (2003). *Happiness and Education.* Cambridge: Cambridge University Press.

NUCCI, L., AND NARVAEZ, D. (2008). *Handbook of Moral and Character Education.* Mahwah, NJ: Lawrence Erlbaum Associates.

O'SULLIVAN, S. (2002). *Character Education through Children's Literature.* Bloomington, IN: Phi Delta Kappa Foundation.

PIAGET, J. (1997). *The Moral Judgment of the Child.* New York: Free Press Paperbacks.

PURPEL, D. (2003). "The Decontextualization of Moral Education." *American Journal of Education* 110(1):89–95.

RAFFERTY, M. (1968). *Max Rafferty on Education.* New York: Devon-Adair.

ROBERTS, S. V. (1994). "America's New Crusade." *U.S. News and World Report* 117:26–29.

SAVAGE, M. (2005). *Liberalism is a Mental Disorder.* Nashville: Nelson Current.

SHAPIRO, B. (2005). *Porn Generation: How Social Liberalism Is Corrupting our Future.* Washington, DC: Regnery.

SHELDON, L. (2011). "Traditional Values Coalition News Release." September 22. www .traditionalvaluescoalition.org.

SHOR, I. (1987). *Pedagogy for Liberation.* South Hadley, MA: Bergin and Garvey.

SINGER, M. G. (2002). *The Ideal of a Rational Morality.* Oxford: Oxford University Press.

———. (2000). *Writings on an Ethical Life.* New York: Ecco Press/HarperCollins.

SMITH, C. (2011). *Lost in Transition: The Dark Side of Emerging Adulthood.* Oxford: Oxford University Press.

SMITH, T. (2006). *Ayn Rand's Normative Ethics.* Cambridge: Cambridge University Press.

SOMMERS, C. H. (1998). "Are We Living in a Moral Stone Age?" *Current* 403:31–34.

SOWELL, T. (1992). "A Dirty War." *Forbes* 150:63.

———. (2007). *Conflict of Visions.* New York: Basic Books.

SPRING, J. (1976). *The Sorting Machine: National Educational Policy since 1945.* New York: McKay.

———. (2008). *American Education.* 13th Ed. Boston: McGraw-Hill.

STERN, N. (2011). "Because I Say So." *The Humanist* 71(5):13–17.

STOUT, L. (2011). *Cultivating Conscience: How Good Laws Make Good People.* Princeton, NJ: Princeton University Press.

THORKILDSEN, T. A., AND WALLBERG, H., eds. (2004). *Nurturing Morality.* New York: Kluwer Academic Press.

VICTOR, J. S. (2002). "Teaching Our Children About Evil." *The Humanist* 62(4):30–32.

WOLFE, A. (2001). *Moral Freedom: The Search for Virtue in a World of Choice.* New York: Norton.

YOUNG, M. F. D. (1971). *Knowledge and Control.* London: Collier-Macmillan.

YU, T. (2004). *In the Name of Morality: Character Education and Political Control.* New York: Peter Lang.

CHAPTER 11

Multicultural Education: Democratic or Divisive

Should schools emphasize America's cultural diversity or the shared aspects of American culture?

POSITION 1: MULTICULTURALISM: CENTRAL TO A DEMOCRATIC EDUCATION

Multiculturalism is a philosophical concept built on the ideas of freedom, justice, equality, equity, and human dignity as acknowledged in various documents, such as the United States Declaration of Independence, the constitutions of South Africa and the United States, and the Universal Declaration of Human Rights adopted by the United Nations.

—National Association for Multicultural Education (2011)

The population of the United States is expected to rise from 309 million in 2010 to 438 million by 2050, and most of the increase will come from new immigrants and their descendants. According to the Pew Research Center, nearly one in five Americans will be an immigrant in 2050, the Latino population will triple in size, the Asian population will continue to grow, and the non-Hispanic white population will increase more slowly than other groups, becoming a minority by 2050 (U.S. Census Bureau, 2010). The waves of "old immigrants" from Europe have been replaced by the arrival of "new immigrants" from Asia, India, Somalia, Mexico, and Central America.

Consider Figure 11.1. In 2010, 13 percent of the U.S. population was foreign born (U.S. Census Bureau, 2010). The foreign-born population of the United States is expected to swell every year, and the nation is becoming more racially and ethnically diverse. The census data paint a vivid picture of an increasingly multicultural nation. Not only will there be more Americans in the future, but they will differ from one another more than ever before in history. The United States already

FIGURE 11.1 Population, 1960–2050.
Percentages by Racial and Ethnic Groups

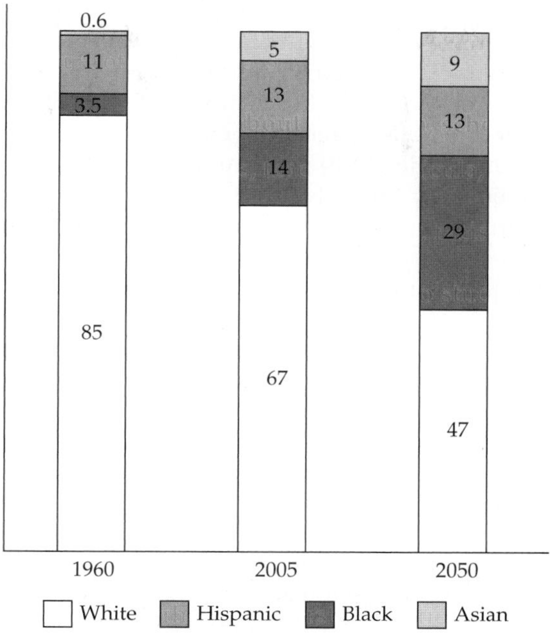

Source: Passel and Cohn (2008, p. 1).

is multicultural, and it will become even more so. Multicultural approaches to education are not an option.

Multicultural education can take many forms. Some scholars in the field, for example, believe that multicultural education should focus mainly on the concept of culture and problems resulting from the clash of cultures. They believe that students should examine the conflicting demands of home versus school culture as well as the conflict between cultures of the powerful and the powerless and unequal treatment afforded certain groups because of race, gender, and sexual preference (Spring, 2000). For other scholars, multiculturalism is less about the study of culture than a vehicle for change. It is the method for critiquing and reforming society that includes political and moral correctives to assist working-class and nonwhite students in attaining social and economic advancement (Sleeter, 1996; Giroux, 1997; Willett, 1998; Steinberg and Kincheloe, 2001; McLaren, 2006).

Some critical multiculturalists consider their approach as a way to challenge "Eurocentric" ways of thinking and as a means to question the taken-for-granted assumptions about "meritocracy, objectivity, knowledge construction and individualism" (Sleeter and Delgado-Bernal, 2004, p. 246). Other critical multiculturalists see multiculturalism as a remedy for the ills of "global capitalism" and "state repression" (McLaren and Farahmanpur, 2005, p. 117). The

National Association for Multicultural Education (2011) defined multicultural education as a "process that permeates all aspects of school practices, policies, and organizations. . . . It prepares all students to work actively toward structural equality in organizations and institutions by providing the knowledge, dispositions, and skills for the redistribution of power and income among diverse groups. Thus, school curriculum must directly address issues of racism, classism, linguicism, ablism, ageism, heteroism, religious intolerance, and xenophobia." Nieto and Bode (2008) view multiculturalism as a strategy to confront educational inequality and advance social justice. It is not enough, they argue, that multiculturalism seeks to help students get along, feel better about themselves, and to be more sensitive to one another. "If multicultural education does not tackle the far more thorny questions of [social] stratification and inequity . . . these goals can turn into superficial strategies that only scratch the surface of educational failure" (p. 10).

Taking a conservative approach to multiculturalism, Glazer (1997) argues that "we are all multiculturalists" because whether you may favor or oppose it, multiculturalism is here, necessary, and unavoidable. All groups—ethnic, religious, and racial—belong in any study of American culture because of their unique contributions and perspectives. Glazer argues that some groups have been denied appropriate recognition. "Multiculturalism is the price America is paying for its inability or unwillingness to incorporate into its society African Americans, in the same way and to the same degree it has incorporated so many groups" (p. 147). Multiculturalism is a complex field, with multiple definitions and varied teaching approaches reflecting the many definitions. As one educator notes, even "Crayola crayons offer what it calls a 'multicultural' crayon set purportedly with hues that represent various skin colors" (Ladson-Billings, 2004, p. 52).

Although there are many approaches to multicultural instruction in schools, this section draws on Banks and McGee-Banks, who write,

> [Multiculturalism is a] reform movement designed to change the total educational environment so that students from diverse racial and ethnic groups, both gender groups, exceptional students, and students from social-class groups will experience equal educational opportunities in schools, colleges, and universities. (Banks and McGee-Banks, 2007, p.474.)

Banks and McGee-Banks argue that the successful implementation of multicultural curricula requires schools to recognize the multiple dimensions of multicultural education (see Figure 11.2). Schools should not assume that multicultural education is the responsibility only of social studies and language arts teachers. Multiculturalism has to be defined broadly so that everyone in every school discipline can embrace it appropriately.

The Best That Is Thought and Known?

Multiculturalists agree that people construct knowledge from slightly different perspectives. Everyone brings understandings to events based on their personal and academic experiences and on other interpretive lenses

FIGURE 11.2 Dimensions of Multicultural Education

Content Integration:
Teachers use examples from many cultures and groups in their teaching.

Equity Pedagogy:
Teachers organize their teaching to encourage the academic success of students from diverse racial, cultural, and social-class groups.

The Knowledge Construction Process:
Teachers help students understand how knowledge is constructed as part of cultural processes.

Prejudice Reduction:
Teachers use materials and methods to modify students' racial attitudes.

An Empowering School Culture and Social Structure:
The school culture is examined and analyzed to empower students from diverse racial, ethnic, and cultural groups.

Source: Banks and McGee-Banks (2007, pp. 20–22).

through which they view the world. Women, minorities, and new immigrants, for example, may see the world from a different vantage point than men, majority-group members, and long-established American families. Everyone develops separate frames of reference and different perspectives for interpreting the social and political world. No one frame of reference is more "true" than others, and all deserve to be heard and understood. Multiculturalism may be considered as part of the struggle to incorporate a wider range of perspectives into the way we make meanings in school (Takaki, 1993; Gordon, 1995). As Banks (2002) notes, "Individuals who know the world only from their own cultural and ethnic perspectives are denied important parts of the human experience and are culturally and ethnically encapsulated" (p. 1).

Multicultural education provides appropriate representation in the school curriculum to groups previously marginalized or excluded because of gender, class, race, or sexual orientation. Public schools should be places where students hear the stories of many different groups. The curriculum should present the perspectives of women as well as men, the poor as well as rich, and should celebrate the heroism not only of conquering generals but also of those who are victorious in the struggles of everyday life. In a multiculturally reconfigured curriculum, the voices of all Americans would find legitimacy and academic consideration (Spring, 2000; Banks and McGee-Banks, 2007). Multiculturalism is not about pitting one group against others or claiming that any one perspective is more valid or more valued. Multicultural education is about fairness and justice. In the past, schools have done a disservice to students by assuming a single view of truth and ignoring students' need to create their knowledge of the world by considering multiple truths and multiple perspectives. A multicultural society will inevitably have competing views of truth and multiple sources of knowledge.

Different Voices

If you were to believe the critics of multiculturalism, you might conclude that multiculturalists are bent on destroying not only the schools but the whole of Western civilization. Samuel P. Huntington castigates multiculturalism as an immediate and dangerous challenge to America's sense of itself. Multiculturalists have "denied the existence of a common American culture and promoted racial, ethnic, and other subnational identities and groupings" (Huntington, 1996, p. 305).

Huntington is not alone. Other traditionalists see multiculturalism as a threat to national identity, one that will divide the nation. E. D. Hirsch (1987, 1996, 2006), for example, tried to convince his readers that the nation would disintegrate unless schools required all students to study a common unifying curriculum. Allan Bloom (1987) warned that multiculturalism poses the threat of cultural relativism, a disease, he says, that regards all values as equally valid and that would likely cause the decline of the West. Another critic of multiculturalism, Diane Ravitch, argues that multiculturalism would lead to the death of education and fragmentation of American society. Ravitch touts the elementary school curriculum of what she believes was a better time, the first decade of the twentieth century, when children were exposed to a common culture and high expectations:

> Most children read (or listened to) the Greek and Roman myths and folklore from the "oriental nations." . . . The third grade in the public schools of Philadelphia studied "heroes of legend and history," including "Joseph; Moses; David; Ulysses; Alexander; Roland; Alfred the Great; Richard the Lion Hearted; Robert Bruce; William Tell; Joan of Arc; Peter the Great; Florence Nightingale." (Ravitch, 1987, p. 8)

This represents a rich literature, to be sure, but, like the canon championed by Huntington, Hirsch, and Bloom, it is skewed toward a white, Western, male orientation. No people of other races were represented in classroom readings during the "good old days," and for women to find their way into the curriculum, they had to either be burned at the stake or pioneer as nurses. Multiculturalists find little that was good in the so-called good old days of schooling. Very few students experienced schools that had high standards and excellent teachers. The old days were good for only a privileged handful—the high-achieving children of English-speaking families of means. For most others, it was a time of alienation caused by a denial of their ethnic heritages. Henry Louis Gates Jr. (1992) refers to the nostalgic celebration of the good old days as the antebellum aesthetic position, "when men were men, and men were white . . . when women and persons of color were voiceless, faceless servants and laborers, pouring tea and filling brandy snifters in the boardrooms in the old boys' clubs" (p. 17).

Multicultural Perspectives

What do the multiculturalists want? Are they a threat to schools and the social cohesion of the country? Are they trying to impose political correctness on all Americans? Take a look at some of the multiculturalist arguments for curriculum change in the schools and decide for yourself.

As noted earlier, multiculturalists are a diverse group that includes feminists, Afrocentrists, social critics, and many people who defy labels but who simply want to transmit the variety of American culture more faithfully to their children. The charge that multiculturalists want to purge the school curriculum of Western culture is simply false. Multiculturalism, as the term is used here, does not require schools rid the curriculum of stories of white males and substitute the experiences of women, gays, African Americans, and other exploited and disadvantaged persons (Sobol, 1993). Multiculturalism is not a euphemism for white-male bashing or an anti-Western movement. Multiculturalists ask only for a fair share of curricular attention, an honest representation of the poor as well as the powerful, and reasonable treatment of minority as well as majority culture perspectives. Whatever the outcome of the current struggle over cultural representation in the curriculum, the world that American students know already is multicultural (Gates, 1992, p. xvi). The curriculum must change to reflect this society, or it becomes irrelevant to students' lives.

You might think of the multiculturalist reaction against the traditional curriculum as a "victims' revolution," a repudiation of the top-down approach to literature, art, music, and history. It demands change by those discounted and otherwise harmed by traditional approaches to schooling. Multiculturalists ask schools to tell the cultural tale in a way that weaves experiences of the disadvantaged and marginalized into the tapestry of the U.S. rise to prominence. Multiculturalism is a call for fairness and a better representation of the contributions of all Americans. Multiculturalists do not disparage the school's role in developing a cohesive, national identity. At the same time, however, they recognize that schools must ensure *all* students preserve, as well, their individual ethnic, cultural, and economic identities (Banks, 2004; Nieto, 2004; Pang, Kiang, and Pak, 2004).

Schools are obligated to teach multiple perspectives in the name of academic fairness and historical accuracy. Few events of significance can be understood considering only one perspective, and viewing any event from diverse, competing viewpoints leads to a fuller, more complete representation of truth. For example, school textbooks typically emphasize the role that nineteenth-century white abolitionists played and discuss how whites struggled to achieve integration in the twentieth century. This is, of course, appropriate; many whites have played and continue to play vital and significant roles in the struggle for social justice. But these same textbooks typically minimize the stories of African American resistance to slavery as well as their efforts to achieve integration and equality (Asante, 1991). These omissions alienate young African American students and present an inaccurate picture to their white peers. The story of slavery must be told from many sides, including the perspective of African Americans as agents in their own history and not simply as people who were colonized, enslaved, and freed by others (Asante, 1987, 1995). A multiculturally educated person would be able to see the slave trade from the view of the white slave trader as well as from the perspective of the enslaved people. The point is not to replace one group's story with another but rather to tell the whole story more fully. To include women, the poor, and minorities is simply a way to make history richer and more complete. Including reports of the powerless as well as the powerful allows students to examine the historic relationship among race, class, gender, and political power (Sleeter and Delgado-Bernal, 2004; Grant and Sleeter, 2007).

Multiculturalism Is Basic Education

> Critics of multicultural education . . . define the interests of dominant groups as the "public" interest and those of people of color such as African Americans and Latinos as "special" interests that endanger the polity. (Banks, 2008, p. 132)

Curriculum change may come from the top down or from the bottom up, but it never comes easily. The goal of multiculturalists is to bend education around the lives of students so that all students can experience a real chance at school success. Today's multiculturalism has been influenced by earlier ethnic studies and black studies movements (Banks, 2008), and the logic of those reforms continues to be convincing. Anyone familiar with schools knows that the most effective way to teach is to make the curriculum relevant to students. Curricula have more meaning when students find characters like themselves in the books they read, and instruction has a better chance of engaging students when the subject matter speaks to their experiences. Exclusion of particular groups of students and their history from the literature alienates students and diminishes academic achievement. Children who find themselves and their culture underrepresented in the school curriculum cannot help but feel lost and resentful (Asante, 1991; Au, 2006).

Everyone benefits from multicultural education. Descendants of immigrants from northern and western Europe need to read stories and listen to tales that resonate with their experiences. They also need to learn about the narrative experiences and cultural perspectives of children and families different from their own (Phillion, He, and Connelly, 2005; Banks and McGee-Banks, 2007). Children of new immigrants from Asia and Latin America need to learn about the lands they left, their new home, and varied neighbors. They must examine their cultural histories and perspectives so that they can better understand how they and their families fit into their new society. The stories told and read in schools must become richer and broader, reflecting the traditions of African Americans, Native Americans, as well as Europeans. Multicultural education reflects the multicultural realities of schoolchildren. Multicultural education is an essential component to a sound basic education, as indispensable as reading, arithmetic, writing, and computer literacy (Nieto and Bode, 2008). Students cannot be considered well educated unless they are able to consider broadly inclusive content and multiple interpretations of events.

A Responsible Multicultural Curriculum

Multicultural education reform has spread to every state. The experience of New York State is an interesting example because of the state's ethnic complexity and its combination of urban, suburban, and rural school districts. In the late

1980s, the New York State commissioner of education invited scholars and curriculum writers to review the appropriateness of the state's K–12 social studies curriculum and recommend any needed changes.[1]

The report, *A Curriculum of Inclusion, 1989*, recognized that New York's curriculum was not fairly representing minorities. Although the state had opened its doors to millions of new immigrants, their ways of life, foods, religions, and histories were not found in the curriculum. Instead, the new immigrants were socialized along an "Anglo-American model" (New York State Social Studies Syllabus Review and Development Committee, 1991). New York was asking new immigrants to exchange their families' habits and rituals for a homogenized American culture. The unstated curricular message asked new immigrants to abandon their forebears' cultures and learn to prize the literature, history, traditions, and holidays of the Anglo-American founding fathers.

This is a familiar model of cultural assimilation. Proponents of state-funded education in the nineteenth century encouraged schools to teach immigrants social behaviors and patriotic rituals designed to encourage "Americanization." Such assimilation worked reasonably well for white Europeans who came to this country in the nineteenth century, but it did not work for other immigrants. Now, in the face of new immigration patterns, it seems to be an untenable ideal. A significant demographic difference distinguishes today's immigrants from those of the past. In the nineteenth century, most of the nation's voluntary immigrants came from Europe, and socialization toward an Anglo-American model of behavior may not have been very discontinuous with their heritage. Now, the majority of immigrants are from Asia and South America. People newly arrived from Korea and Colombia are less likely to find resonance in the Anglo-American cultural ideal than those who came to the United States from Ireland, Germany, and Italy.

New York State curriculum planners and teachers debated the design and implementation of a multicultural approach for the better part of twenty years. The new curriculum acknowledges the importance of socialization and nation building for an increasingly diverse population but also fosters respect for cultural diversity. The New York State curriculum recognizes that teaching the nation's history appropriately requires teaching from multiple perspectives. Classroom attention must be focused on a wide range of people, their culture, and perspectives that make up the nation. The New York State Education Department (2009) describes "multiculturalism and multicultural perspectives" and recommends that

> students should understand diversity and the multicultural context of American society . . . The primary issue is the nature and extent of inclusion of histories and cultural experiences of diverse groups [but] students should understand that all members of a given group will not necessarily share the same view. (pp. 5–6)

[1]Task Force members were asked to examine the curriculum and address questions about its fairness and balance. Did this curriculum speak to the varied needs of female as well as male students, African Americans and Asian Americans as well as European Americans, and the disadvantaged as well as the advantaged? On the basis of the reviewers' recommendations, New York developed a new curriculum promising a fresh focus on the treatment of all students in the state. To compare New York's approach with that of a more rural state, see the "Nebraska Multicultural Education Bill" (Banks, 2002, pp. 128–130).

The multiculturalist argument is not that Eurocentric views are wrong or evil or that children of Asian or African descent should not learn about the European cultural legacy. Multiculturalism asks schools to subscribe to one simple educational truth: tolerance cannot come without respect, and respect cannot come without knowledge of others and their point of view (Gates, 1992, p. xv). Multiculturalism begins by recognizing the cultural diversity of the United States and asks that the school curriculum explore that diversity. Being well educated in a multicultural sense means learning about the histories, literature, and contributions of the varied people who have fashioned the complex tapestry of American life. All students should sample broadly from all the cultures and all the ideas that have contributed to the making of the United States.

POSITION 2: MULTICULTURALISM IS DIVISIVE AND DESTRUCTIVE

Multiculturalism is not just a recognition that different groups have different cultures. We all knew that before multiculturalism became a cult that has spawned mindless rhapsodies about "diversity" without a speck of evidence to substantiate its supposed benefits.

—Thomas Sowell (2010)

Schools and the Cultural Heritage

For the past 150 years, public schools have had three broad objectives: to educate individual citizens for democratic participation, to encourage individual achievement through academic competition, and to promote, encourage, and teach the values and traditions of the American cultural heritage. The United States has been enriched by every ethnic and racial group to land on these shores, and the immigrants, in turn, have been well served by the nation and the nation's schools. The public schools have their share of detractors, to be sure, but the multiculturalists' attack on the schools' curriculum seems misguided. Any fair assessment would find it difficult to fault the success that schools have had in passing the common culture of the United States to new generations of Americans—immigrants and native-born citizens alike. No mean accomplishment, the transmission of the cultural heritage requires an appreciation for the complex aspects of U.S. history, literature, and political traditions (Ravitch, 1990; Schlesinger, 1998; Ravitch and Viteritti, 2001). American culture is, after all, a hybrid—a mix of European, Asian, and African cultures—and the school's job is to transmit this cultural legacy faithfully in all its complexity. The school's role in cultural transmission has been one of brilliant success for well over a century.

Nineteenth-century proponents of public education recognized that the United States was a dynamic nation, with succeeding waves of immigrants changing and invigorating American culture. The new arrivals came from every corner of the world and brought energy, talent, and cultural variation never before gathered in one nation. When they arrived in the United States, they spoke different languages, were of many races, and practiced many religions. What they shared was an eagerness to succeed economically and politically and to learn how to become "American," to fit into a unique, unprecedented cultural amalgam.

Nineteenth-century common schools, influenced by Western ideas of philosophic rationalism and humanism, were an expression of optimism about human progress and democratic potential. Advocates of mass public education shared a common belief in education, "an education, moreover, which was neither a privilege of a fortunate few nor a crumb tossed to the poor and lowly, but one which was to be a right of every child in the land" (Meyer, 1957, p. 143). The common schools succeeded beyond anyone's expectations. Children of the poor as well as the rich received a public education, and children of immigrants read the same texts and learned the same lore as the children of native-born Americans. The mix of immigrants now coming to the United States is far richer and more diverse than the founders of the common schools could ever have envisioned. The need for schools to transmit the common culture has never been greater, and the preservation of democratic tradition has never been more difficult.

The United States always has been a haven for those seeking political freedom and political expression. In the nineteenth century, millions of immigrants came to this country, in large measure to enjoy the fruits and accept the burdens of participating in a democratic society. This still is true today, but unlike the immigrants of former times, today's new arrivals typically have had little or no direct experience with democratic traditions. For example, in the 1840s, after the collapse of the Frankfurt diet, immigrants from Germany flocked to America seeking the democratic political expression that they had been denied in their homeland. Today's immigrants may want democracy, but when they come from autocratic regimes in Asia and South America, they have had no experience with the responsibilities of democratic living. They are less prepared for assuming a role in a democratic society than any previous generation of immigrants. Clearly, it is up to schools to induct the children of the new immigrants into the complexities of a democratic society.

Although schools should expose children to the common culture, they need not pretend to a cultural homogeneity or deny individual students' ethnic experiences. Schools are obligated to represent the range of cultural voices—male and female, African American, Asian American, and European American—but these voices must be trained not for solo performances but to be part of a chorus. Schools must encourage individual identification with one central cultural tradition, or the United States might fall prey to the same ethnic tensions undermining the sovereignty of Afghanistan and the nations of eastern Europe and Africa. Students should learn about the common Western ideals that shaped the United States and bind us together as a nation: democracy, capitalism, and monotheism.

Particularism

> What happens when people of different ethnic origins, speaking different languages and professing different religions, settle in the same geographical locality and live under the same political sovereignty? Unless a common purpose binds them together, tribal hostilities will drive them apart. Ethnic and racial conflict, it seems evident, will now replace the conflict of ideologies as the explosive issues of our times. (Schlesinger, 1998, p. 10)

The United States stands to benefit—economically, politically, and socially—from the infusion of talent brought by new immigrants, as it has in the past. Assimilated new immigrants pose no threat to U.S. growth or nationhood. Instead, the United States faces a threat from those who deny that schools should teach a common American tradition or that a common culture even exists. Diane Ravitch calls these people particularists; they argue that teaching a common culture is a disservice to ethnic and racial minorities. "Particularism," writes Ravitch (1990), "is a bad idea whose time has come" (p. 346).

Particularists demand that public schools give up trying to teach the commonalities of cultural heritage in favor of teaching a curriculum centering on the specific ethnic mix represented in a given school or community. Students in predominantly white schools would have one focus, children in predominantly African American schools another, and so on. It is not at all clear where the particularists would stop in the balkanization of the curriculum. Would a school with a predominantly Asian population have an Asian-focused curriculum, or would they further divide the curriculum into separate strands of Korean, Chinese, Vietnamese, Filipino, and Cambodian culture (Fox-Genovese, 1991)?

The extreme arguments of the particularists do not lend support to the unifying and democratic ends that the founders of the common schools envisioned. Asante, for example, advocates an Afrocentrist curriculum that would teach young African American children about their African cultural roots at the expense of teaching them about Western traditions. He denounces those African Americans who prefer Bach and Beethoven to Ellington and Coltrane. African Americans, he believes, should center on their cultural experience; any other preference is an aberration. Asante argues that majority as well as minority students are disadvantaged by the "monoculturally diseased curriculum." He writes that few Americans of any color "have heard the names of Cheikh Anta Diop, Anna Julia Cooper, C. L. R. James, or J. A. Rogers," historians who contributed to an understanding of the African world (Asante, 1991, p. 175). He is probably right, but for better or worse, the most enduring mainstream white historians—for example, Spengler, Gibbon, Macaulay, Carlyle, and Trevelyan—are not likely to enjoy greater recognition.

The cultural focus of the curriculum is a serious matter, and although petty and irrational arguments exist on all sides, the real issue is the role schools must play in transmitting the common cultural heritage. Schools must teach children that regardless of race, gender, or ethnicity, one can achieve great feats. This is the record of the past and promise of the future. The public school curriculum should allow all children to believe that they are part of a society that welcomes their participation and encourages their achievements. As Ravitch (1990) writes, "In their curriculum, their hiring practices, and their general philosophy, the public schools must not discriminate against or give preference to any racial or ethnic group. . . . They should not be expected to teach children to view the world through an ethnocentric perspective that rejects or ignores the common culture" (p. 352).

Schools cannot fulfill their central mission to transmit the common culture if they cater to particularist demands for teaching the perspective of every minority group. Ravitch argues that in the past, generation after generation of minorities—Jews, Catholics, Greeks, Poles, and Japanese—have used private lessons, after school or on weekends, to instill ethnic pride and ethnic continuity in their children. These may be valuable goals, but they have never been the public schools' province, nor should they be. Public schools must develop a common culture, "a definition of citizenship and culture that is both expansive and *inclusive*," one that speaks to our commonalities and not our differences (Ravitch, 1990, p. 352). The public school curriculum must not succumb to particularists' demands to prize our differences rather than celebrate our common good.

Anticanonical Assaults

> When multiculturalism was first promoted as an educational philosophy, its stress seemed to be on the positive contributions of minority groups in this country and on a balanced portrayal of a variety of cultures around the world. But over the years, multiculturalism acquired an additional meaning. Instead of emphasizing the positive contributions of America's minority groups and a balanced range of social groups from around the world, the version of multiculturalism now promoted . . . posits an animus against what are perceived as Western values, particularly the value placed on acquiring knowledge, or analytical thinking, and on academic achievement itself. (Stotsky, 1999, p. xi)

Among the greatest absurdities the particularists have produced is their attack on the canon, denouncing it as racist, sexist, Eurocentric, logocentric, and politically incorrect. Before we put these distortions to rest, a few words about the nature of the canon. The term *canon* (from the Greek word *kanon*, meaning "measuring rod"), which originally referred to the books of the Hebrew and Christian Bibles, meant Holy Scripture as officially recognized by the ecclesiastic authority. Today, it has taken on secular and political meanings. The canon represents, first of all, the major monuments to Western civilization, great ideas embodied in books forming the foundation of our democratic traditions. The "great books" of the Western tradition (e.g., the writings of Plato, Aristotle, Machiavelli, and Marx, to name but a few) have shaped our political thinking, whether we trace our origins to Europe, Africa, or Asia; Homer, Sophocles,

George Eliot, and Virginia Woolf inform our sense of literature whether we are male or female. Every major university offers courses in the Western canon, and as the late Alan Bloom notes, generations of students have enjoyed these works. "Wherever the Great Books make up a central part of the curriculum, the students are excited and satisfied, feel they are doing something that is independent and fulfilling, getting something from the university they cannot get elsewhere. . . . Their gratitude at learning of Achilles or the categorical imperative is boundless" (Bloom, 1987, p. 344).

The particularists' attack on the canon is new and somewhat surprising. The value of the canon has long been taken for granted as the cornerstone of quality education. As the philosopher John Searle (1990) writes, educated circles accepted, almost to the point of cliché, that there is a certain Western intellectual tradition that goes from, say, Socrates to Wittgenstein in philosophy and from Homer to James Joyce in literature, and it is essential to the liberal education of young men and women in the United States that they receive some exposure to at least some of the great works in this intellectual tradition; they should, in Matthew Arnold's overquoted words, know the best that is thought and known in the world.

In the past, support for the canon was an article of faith, not belabored or examined at length. People considered these works and the ideas they contained to be of enduring worth, part of a timeless literary judgment—as Samuel Johnson spoke of it—and quite apart from the hurly-burly of politics. Canonical authors were acknowledged representatives of the evolution in the thought of ideas shaping Western civilization. No longer. Particularists and multiculturalists attack the canon at every turn. Searle (1990) writes that the cant of the anti-canonicals runs something like this:

> Western civilization is in large part a history of oppression. Internally, Western civilization oppressed women, various slave and serf populations, and ethnic and cultural minorities, generally. In foreign affairs, the history of Western civilization is one of imperialism and colonialism. The so-called canon of Western civilization consists of the official publications of the system of oppression, and it is no accident that the authors in the "canon" are almost exclusively Western white males. . . . [The canon] has to be abolished in favor of something that is "multicultural" and "nonhierarchical." (p. 35)

The particularists and multiculturalists are trying to do to the public school curriculum what they tried unsuccessfully to accomplish at universities: to politicize and bias the curriculum. In the name of justice and equity, they encouraged universities to broaden the curriculum and include non-Western as well as Western authors. This might not be so offensive if school *could teach everything*, but curriculum is a zero-sum game; that is, if a school adds something, it also must take something else out.

The case of Stanford University is instructive. In the late 1980s, Stanford proposed adding authors from developing countries and both women's and minority perspectives into the curriculum of the Western culture course. These changes would come at considerable cost. Plato's *Republic* and Machiavelli's

The Prince would be replaced by works such as *I, Rigoberta Menchu*, the story of the political coming-of-age of a Guatemalan peasant woman, and Franz Fanon's *Wretched of the Earth*, a book that encouraged violent and revolutionary acts among citizens of Third World countries (D'Souza, 1991). Although campus radicals demonstrated in support of the proposal, chanting, "Hey, hey, ho, ho, Western culture's got to go," cooler heads won the day. The required course in Western culture retained its reading list but added some optional assignments that provided a non-Western focus.

Stanford's approach to curriculum reform underestimated the value of Western literature, the ability of great books to capture the imaginations of majority as well as minority students, and the ability minority students have to appreciate Western classics. Sachs and Thiel (1995), Stanford students during the time of the "great curriculum wars," argue that Stanford multiculturalists rejected the universalism of Western culture and the power of ideas. They write,

> There exist truths that transcend the accidents of one's birth, and these objective truths are in principle available to everyone—whether young or old, rich or poor, male or female, white or black; individual (and humanity as a whole) are not trapped within a closed cultural space that predetermines what they may know. (p. 3)

Misguided Curriculum Change in the Name of Multicultural Reform

Stanford successfully resisted the multiculturalists' social engineering, as have most universities; public schools have been less successful. New York State barely survived an attempt to radicalize its schools. The curriculum was headed in a strident multicultural direction when reason prevailed and the radicals lost. New York State had plunged headlong into the maelstrom of multiculturalism in reaction to a report critical of the state's social studies curriculum. The New York proposal was filled with problems. Consider a few. One of the guiding principles of the report is that "the subject matter content should be *treated as socially constructed* and therefore tentative—as is all knowledge." The document had gone on to assert, "Knowledge is the product of human beings located in specific times and places; consequently, much of our subject matter must be understood as tentative" (New York State Social Studies Syllabus Review and Development Committee, 1991, p. 29). Supporters of this view believe that we should teach students that all knowledge is socially constructed—made up, fabricated—and that there is no overarching and agreed-on sense of truth or right moral action.

This is distressing. What are we passing on to succeeding generations if not the fruits of our culture's pursuit of truth? According to social constructionists, all concepts of "truth and falsehood," "right and wrong," and "good and bad" are products of the human mind, as varied as human experience, and equally valid. As Glazer (2001) notes, "As the absolute ground of truth and morality weaken, one will find students (and teachers) who will question the automatic disapproval of practices once considered abhorrent (human sacrifice among the Aztecs?) because they have been taught that every culture has its own standard, and that there are no absolute grounds for judgment" (p. 174). The New York State curriculum proposal (see New York State Social Studies Syllabus Review and Development Committee, 1991) would have taken the state in inappropriate directions. Its most extreme positions were beaten down by critics, and the current curriculum (New York State Education Department, 2008) contains less of the inflammatory language and ratiocinations of previous drafts. Many educators joined together and successfully denounced the earlier plan for its intellectual dishonesty and potential for divisiveness.

Multiculturalism lumps individuals together inappropriately and without their permission. One critic notes that "Americans now speak of the 'African American community,' 'the Asian American community,' the 'Latino community,' and the 'Native American community' as though these constitute a fully integrated, fully homogenous whole that are fully distinctive and unchangeable" (Welsh, 2008). Multicultural education serves to undermine the school's commitment to forging a single national identify. "Mexican children newly arrived in American public schools now frequently find themselves in classrooms where they are taught part of the day in Spanish, where they learn more about the achievements of Mayans and Aztecs than about the Puritans, where they are taught to revere Miguel Hidalgo and Emiliano Zapata on the same plane as George Washington or Thomas Jefferson, and to celebrate Cinco de Mayo with more fanfare than the Fourth of July" (Chavez, 2002, p. 387). The historian Arthur Schlesinger Jr. argues that the defining experience for Americans has not been ethnicity or sanctification of old cultures, "but the creation of a new national culture and a *new* national identity." It is foolish, he argues, to look backward in empty celebration of what we once were. Instead, schools need to look forward and blend the disparate experiences of immigrants into one American culture (New York State Social Studies Syllabus Review and Development Committee, 1991, p. 89). Schools should continue to serve the nation by passing on to children elements of the common culture that define the United States and bind its people together. This is not to say schools should be asked to portray the culture as unchangeable or force students to accept it without question. The culture of a nation changes as a reflection of its citizens; U.S. culture will continue to change. School curricula will of necessity expand and sample more broadly from the various influences that have shaped our culture. However, to turn the schools away from Western ideals of democracy, justice, freedom, equality, and opportunity is to renounce the greatest legacy one generation ever bequeathed to the next. No matter who sits in American classrooms—African Americans, Asian Americans, Latin Americans, or European Americans—and no matter what their religion or creed, those students and their nation have been shaped by democratic and intellectual traditions of the Western world, and they had better learn those traditions or risk losing them.

For Discussion

1. According to John Searle (1990), the following characteristics define a well-educated person:

   a. The person should know enough of his or her cultural traditions to know how they evolved.

   b. The person should know enough of the natural sciences that he or she is not a stranger in that world.

   c. The person should know enough of how society works to understand the trade cycle, interest, unemployment, and other elements of the political and economic world.

   d. The person should know at least one foreign language well enough to read the best literature that culture offers in the original language.

   e. The person needs to know enough philosophy to be able to use the tools of logical analysis.

   f. The person must be able to write and speak clearly and with candor and rigor.

   Do you agree or disagree with Searle's characteristics of a well-educated person? Do you like Searle's approach to defining a well-educated person, or do you prefer the approach of those who assemble long lists of supposedly significant dates, names, and events, such as *Cultural Literacy: What Every American Needs to Know* (Hirsch, 1987) or *Critical Literacy: What Literate Americans Ought to Know* (Provenzo, 2005)? Are there other ways to define a well-educated person?

2. Steinberg and Kincheloe (2001, pp. 3–5) identify five positions in the public discourse about multicultural education. From the following excerpts, do you find yourself more comfortable with one or more of these positions than others? Does your teacher education program adhere more closely to one or more of them?

   a. *Conservative multiculturalism or monoculturalism position:*
   Believes in the superiority of Western patriarchal culture
   Promotes the Western canon as a universal civilizing influence
   Targets multiculturalism as the enemy of Western progress

   b. *Liberal multiculturalism position:*
   Emphasizes the natural equality and common humanity of individuals from diverse race, class, and gender groups
   Argues that inequality results from lack of opportunity
   Maintains that problems that individuals from divergent backgrounds face are individual difficulties, not socially structured adversities

   c. *Pluralist multiculturalism position:*
   Exoticizes difference and positions it as necessary knowledge for those who compete in a globalized economy
   Contends that the curriculum should consist of studies of various divergent groups
   Avoids the concept of oppression

   d. *Leftist-essential multiculturalism position:*
   Maintains that race, class, and gender categories consist of a set of unchanging priorities (essences)
   Assumes that only authentically oppressed people can speak about particular issues concerning a specific group

   e. *Critical multiculturalism position:*

Grounds a critical pedagogy that promotes an understanding of how schools/ education work by the exposé of student sorting processes and power's complicity with the curriculum

Makes no pretense of neutrality, as it honors the notion of egalitarianism and elimination of human suffering

Analyzes the way that power shapes consciousness

3. Diane Ravitch argues that pressure groups from both the left and the right have persuaded textbook publishers to censor the words and ideas children are allowed to read. Ravitch (2003) compiled "A Glossary of Banned Words, Usages, Stereotypes, and Topics" to illustrate some of the "words, usages, stereotypes, and topics banned by major publishers of educational materials and state agencies."

Consider some examples of banned terms that Ravitch uncovered. Does the conscious omission of these terms from textbooks constitute a reasonable or an unreasonable censorship of ideas? Are the terms so offensive that students should be protected from reading them, or is this, as Ravitch claims, a form of censorship and little more than an exercise in "political correctness"?

Able-bodied (banned as offensive; replace with *person who is nondisabled*)

Black (banned as adjective meaning "evil")

Cowboy, cowgirl (banned as sexist; replace with *cowhand*)

Dwarf (banned as offensive; replace with *person of short stature*)

Eskimo (banned as inauthentic; replace with Inupiat, Inuit, Yupik, Yuit, or Native Arctic peoples or Innuvialuit; note: *Yupik* and *Yuit* are "not interchangeable."

Fat (banned; replace with *heavy, obese*)

Indian giver (banned as offensive)

Slave (replace whenever possible with *enslaved person, worker,* or *laborer*)

West, Western (banned as Eurocentric when discussing world geography; replace with reference to specific continent or region)

White (banned as adjective meaning "pure")

References

ASANTE, M. K. (1987). *The Afrocentric Idea.* Philadelphia: Temple University Press.

———. (1991). "The Afrocentric Idea in Education." *Journal of Negro Education* 60:170–180.

———. (1995). *African American History: A Journey of Liberation.* Maywood, NJ: The Peoples Publishing Group.

AU, K. (2006). *Multicultural Issues and Literacy Attainment.* Mahwah, NJ: Lawrence Erlbaum Associates.

BANKS, J. A. (2002). *An Introduction to Multicultural Education.* 3rd Ed. Boston: Allyn and Bacon.

———. (2004). "Multicultural Education: Historical Development, Dimensions, and Practice." In *Handbook of Research on Multicultural Education,* 2nd Ed., ed. J. A. Banks and C. A. McGee-Banks. San Francisco: Wiley.

———. (2008). "Diversity, Group Identity, and Citizenship Education in a Global Age." *Educational Researcher* 37:129–139.

BANKS, J.A. AND C.A. McGEE-BANKS, eds. (2007), *Multicultural Education: Issues and Perspectives,* 6th Ed.: Hoboken, NJ: John Wiley and Sons.

BLOOM, A. (1987). *The Closing of the American Mind.* New York: Simon and Schuster.

CHAVEZ, L. (2002). "The New Politics of Hispanic Assimilation." In *Beyond the Color Line: New Perspectives on Race and Ethnicity in America*, ed. A. Thernstrom and S. Thernstrom. Stanford, CA: Hoover Institution.

D'SOUZA, D. (1991). "Illiberal Education." *Atlantic Monthly*, March, 51–79.

FOX-GENOVESE, E. (1991). "The Self-Interest of Multiculturalism." *Tikkun* 6(4):47–49.

GATES, H. L., Jr. (1992). *Loose Canons: Notes on the Cultural Wars*. New York: Oxford University Press.

GIROUX, H. A. (1997). "Rewriting the Discourse of Racial Identity: Towards a Pedagogy and Politics of Whiteness." *Harvard Educational Review* 67:169–187.

GLAZER, N. (1997). *We Are All Multiculturalists Now*. Cambridge, MA: Harvard University Press.

———. (2001). "Problems in Acknowledging Diversity." In *Making Good Citizens: Education and Civil Society*, ed. D. Ravitch and J. P. Viteritti. New Haven, CT: Yale University Press.

GORDON, B. M. (1995). "Knowledge Construction, Competing Critical Theories, and Education." In *Handbook of Research on Multicultural Education*, ed. J. A. Banks and C. A. McGee-Banks. New York: Macmillan.

GRANT, C. A., AND SLEETER, C. E. (2007). *Doing Multicultural Education for Achievement and Equity*. New York: Routledge.

HIRSCH, E. D., JR. (1987). *Cultural Literacy: What Every American Needs to Know*. Boston: Houghton Mifflin.

———. (1996). *The Schools We Need, and Why We Don't Have Them*. New York: Doubleday.

———. (2006). *The Knowledge Deficit: Closing the Shocking Education Gap for American Children*. Boston: Houghton Mifflin.

HUNTINGTON, S. P. (1996). *The Clash of Civilizations: Remaking of the World Order*. New York: Touchstone.

LADSON-BILLINGS, G. (2004). "New Directions in Multicultural Education: Complexities, Boundaries and Critical Race Theory." In *Handbook of Research on Multicultural Education*, 2nd Ed., ed. J. A. Banks and C. A. McGee-Banks. San Francisco: Wiley.

McLAREN, P., ed. (2006). *Rage and Hope*. New York: Peter Lang.

McLAREN, P., AND FARAHMANPUR, R. (2005). *Teaching against Global Capitalism and the New Imperialism: A Critical Pedagogy*. Lanham, MD: Rowman & Littlefield.

National Association for Multicultural Education. (2008). "Resolutions and Position Papers." www.nameorg.org.

New York State Education Department. (2008). *Social Studies: Resource Guide with Core Curriculum*. www.emsc.nysed/gov/ciai/socst/pub.

———. (2009). *Social Studies Overview*. www.p12.nysed.gov/socst/pub.

New York State Social Studies Syllabus Review and Development Committee. (1991). *One Nation, Many Peoples: A Declaration of Cultural Independence*. Albany: State Education Department, State University of New York.

NIETO, S. (2004). "Puerto Rican Students in US Schools: A Troubled Past and the Search for a Hopeful Future." In *Handbook of Research on Multicultural Education*, 2nd Ed., ed. J. A. Banks and C. A. McGee-Banks. San Francisco: Wiley.

NIETO, S., AND BODE, P. (2008). *Affirming Diversity; The Sociopolitical Context of Multicultural Education*. 5th Ed. Boston: Pearson.

PANG, V. O., KIANG, P. N., AND PAK, Y. K. (2004). "Asian Pacific American Students: Challenging a Biased Educational System." In *Handbook of Research on Multicultural Education*, 2nd Ed., ed. J. A. Banks and C. A. McGee-Banks. San Francisco: Wiley.

PASSEL, J., AND COHN, D. (2008). *"Immigration to Play Lead Role in Future U.S. Growth."* http://pewresearch.org/pubs/729/united- states-population-projections.

PHILLION, J., HE, M. F., AND CONNELLY, F. M., eds. (2005). *Narrative and Experience in Multicultural Education*. Thousand Oaks, CA: Sage.

PROVENZO, E. F. (2005). *Critical Literacy: What Every American Ought to Know*. Boulder, CO: Paradigm

RAVITCH, D. (1987). "Tot Sociology, Grade School History." *Current*, December, 4–10.

————. (1990). "Multiculturalism, E Pluribus Plures." *American Scholar*, Summer, 337–354.

————. (2003). *The Language Police: How Pressure Groups Restrict What Students Learn*. New York: Alfred A. Knopf.

RAVITCH, D., AND VITERITTI, J. P. (2001). *Making Good Citizens: Education and Civil Society*. New Haven, CT: Yale University Press.

SACHS, D. O., AND THIEL, P. A. (1995). *The Diversity Myth, "Multiculturalism" and the Politics of Intolerance at Stanford*. Oakland, CA: The Independent Institute.

SCHLESINGER, A. M. (1998). *The Disuniting of America*. New York: Norton.

SEARLE, J. (1990). "The Storm over the University." *New York Review of Books*, December 6, 34–41.

SLEETER, C. E. (1996). *Multicultural Education as Social Activism*. Albany: State University of New York Press.

SLEETER, C. E., AND DELGADO-BERNAL, D. (2004). "Critical Pedagogy, Critical Race Theory, and Antiracist Education: Implications for Multicultural Education." In *Handbook of Research on Multicultural Education*, 2nd Ed., ed. J. A. Banks and C. A. McGee-Banks. San Francisco: Wiley.

SOBOL, T. (1993). "Revising the New York State Social Studies Curriculum." *Teachers College Record*, Winter, 258–272.

SOWELL, T. (2010). "The Cult of Multiculturalism." October 19. www.nationalreview.com/articles.

SPRING, J. (2000). *The Intersection of Cultures: Multicultural Education in the United States and the Global Economy*. 2nd. Ed. New York: McGraw-Hill.

STEINBERG, S. R., AND KINCHELOE, J. L. (2001). "Setting the Context for Critical Multi/Interculturalism: The Power Blocs of Class Elitism, White Supremacy, and Patriarchy." In *Multi/Intercultural Conversations*, ed. S. R. Steinberg. New York: Peter Lang.

STOTSKY, S. (1999). *Losing Our Language: How Multicultural Classroom Instruction Is Undermining Our Children's Ability to Read, Write, and Reason*. New York: Free Press.

TAKAKI, R. (1993). *A Different Mirror: A History of Multicultural America*. Boston: Little, Brown.

U.S. Census Bureau. (2010). *American Community Survey*. www.census.gov/population.

WELSH, J. F. (2008). *After Multiculturalism: The Politics of Race and the Dialectics of Liberty*. Lanham, MD: Rowman & Littlefield.

WILLETT, C., ed. (1998). *Theorizing Multiculturalism: A Guide to the Current Debate*. Malden, MA: Blackwell.

CHAPTER 12

Technology and Learning: Enabling or Subverting

What technology deserves significant school attention, and who should decide?

POSITION 1: TECHNOLOGY ENABLES LEARNING

Digital literacy is less about tools and more about thinking.

—New Media Consortium (2011)

When computers are integrated into the flow of classroom action, a qualitative transformation occurs regarding the ways teachers teach and students learn.

—Angeli (2008)

Technology is transformative. It changes as it is used, and it changes those who use it. Ideas to improve technology arise from its use—and new technology leads farther, spiraling in speed and complexity. As we employ new tools, like laser surgery or satellite communications, we alter our perceptions of technology and our environments—and we are changed. Changes occur in other areas of life with the advances in such areas as solar energy, radio, television, microwave, medical imaging, satellite and telecommunication, and other modern conveniences. Romano (2003) writes, "At the beginning of the twenty-first century, how we live, work and recreate are being transformed by a powerful, pervasive, global force—technology" (p. 2).

Teaching and learning are also changing as a result of technology (International Society for Teaching in Education [ISTE], 2008b; Baker, 2012). Spiro (2006) argues that a revolution is happening but that the pace in schools is too slow, that incremental school thinking should be replaced by "principled leaps" (p. 4). He identifies several themes emerging:

Increasing complexity with cognitive understanding

Speeding up the acquisition of experiences

Newer ways to comprehend knowledge structures without traditional pedagogy

Changing the way people think and getting them to think for themselves

Technology in schools is changing from relatively simple devices to more complicated, sophisticated, and engaging environments. Technology has moved from chalkboards and textbooks to complex interactive media, complete systems of distance learning, e-learning, and virtual schools with customized pacing for individual students (Rotherham, 2006; Livingston, 2008; Reigeluth, 2011; Villinger, 2012). Technology demonstrates daily its practical value in classroom instruction, teacher and student research, improved school design and operation, increasing student interest and teacher scope, and interlinking the school and the globe. Inherent in these illustrations is technology's obvious importance to education and to society. In education, technology has the potential to completely reconstruct what we normally think of as schooling, learning, and teaching.

Current teenagers have a unique relation with technology, are immersed in media and gadgets, adapt easily to highly mobile technology, have become multitaskers, and are unknowing of or indifferent to the consequences of their use of technology for recording, altering, and sharing music, videos, and various forms of entertainment. Pew data show that 99 percent of teenagers have a television in the home and that 98 percent have CD or tape players. Compared with older generations, teenagers are "digital natives in a land of digital immigrants" (Rainie, 2006, p. 3).

"Screenagers" is a term used to describe teenagers who engage with screens, as on televisions, cell phones, computers, and so on, as their natural habitat and use these devices to comprehend and shape their environments, and with those younger than teenagers now, "technology is deeply embedded in their lives" (Watson, 2010, p. 29). Researchers at the Pew Research Center (2011; 2012) surveyed teenagers in 2006 and 2009, finding that 93 percent now use the Internet, including 88 percent of those ages twelve to thirteen and 95 percent of those ages fourteen to seventeen. It is used primarily by them for online social networking and keeping up with current events but also for purchases and finding information. Smith (2011) finds that cell phone owners under age twenty-four exchange an average of 109.5 text messages per day. Robotics, nanotechnology, genetics, Internet development, and myriad emerging technologies are or will be an integral part of life for youth of school age (Brockman, 2010; Allenby and Sarewitz, 2011; *Technology Review*, 2011). The implications for schools are enormous, as "learning and research tasks will be shaped by their new techno-world" (Rainie, 2006, p. 15).

More than Just Teacher Gimmicks

We can no longer treat technology in school as just a collection of devices occasionally used by teachers to illustrate a lesson. Educational technology and technological education are no longer merely peripheral to the basic knowledge that students must have to survive and thrive in our society. Technological knowledge itself is fundamental and should be deeply incorporated into the main courses of study in schools (Smith and Throne, 2007; Edutopia, 2011, 2012). Technology has become so important that we must fully integrate it into the central purposes of schooling. The teacher's role changes from "sage on the stage" to "guide on the side," designing and organizing instructional material, facilitating learning, and acting as a knowledgeable and supportive mentor, using technology for actual instruction and assessment as well as record keeping (Reigeluth, 2011). This requires teachers to be well prepared and practiced in technology as well as subjects. It also suggests a more comprehensive approach to teacher education. Collins and Weiner (2010) propose a new subdiscipline—education informatics—to develop and improve practice, conduct scholarship, and communicate about digital technologies in education.

Technology is knowledge, but it is also a major means to learning and to developing improved knowledge. Technology is one of the knowledge products of human minds; it is useful in conveying that knowledge to others, and it is used in conducting research to improve knowledge. Learning, as well as teaching, is enabled by technology. Integrating technology into instruction seamlessly is an important teacher task, transforming classrooms and education (King, 2011).

New Media Consortium (NMC), a group of major corporations, over 200 colleges, museums, and other organizations, is "transforming the way people teach, learn, and create" (http://nmc.org). The NMC's (2011) *Horizon Project* is a research effort to identify emerging technologies likely to have a large impact on teaching, learning, and creative expression. NMC advocates developmental work on six emerging technologies:

User-created content

Social networking

Mobile phones

Virtual worlds

New scholarship and forms of publication

Multiplayer educational games

Many elementary and secondary schools are engaged in similar frontier efforts using technology to change learning and teaching, like the Virtual Learning Resources Center and 21st Century Connections (www.virtuallrc.com; see also McCain, 2000; McKenzie, 2000, 2001; Kirsner, 2002; O'Neil and Perez, 2003; Borja, 2005; Livingston, 2008; Dillon and Tucker, 2011; Schorr and McGriff, 2011).

Evidence That Learning from and with Technology Is Beneficial

Reeves (1998) finds that "50 years of educational research indicates that media and technology are effective in schools as phenomena to learn *from* and *with*" (p. 1; emphasis in the original). Others are consistent in demonstrating the educational value of technology in schools and of students learning from and with it (Prensky, 2006). Johnson and Barker (2002), examining studies of about 100 government-funded educational technology projects, show the positive results from using technology, including improved student outcomes in cognitive knowledge and information access and improved teaching. Ringstaff and Kelly (2002) analyzed findings from a large variety of research studies on the use of technology in learning and teaching, finding substantial improvements in most subjects.

Tamin (2011) conducted a meta-analysis of many studies of the impact of technology on learning conducted over a forty-year period and found that using technology in instruction produced gains in student learning over instruction that does not include technology. Gains were better for when technology is used to support the teacher than when technology is used alone. And blended, face-to-face, and online learning environments produced the best results in student learning. Projects involving blended instruction are under way in several large city schools, an applied test of this research work (Schorr and McGriff, 2011). A summary of research findings shows that there are many positive outcomes for technology use in schools (Strawn, 2011).

K[12] is the largest provider of online education for grades K–12 grades. They offer online courses and programs for public schools, for private schools, and as individual courses for students. They also operate virtual schools under charterlike arrangements with states and school districts. Their efforts have won awards from the Association of Educational Publishers, the U.S. Distance Learning Association, and *Business Week* magazine, among others (www.k12.com). These honors—and many individual compliments from parent, school administrators, and student clients—attest to the effectiveness of online instruction.

The Importance of Technology in Schools

The relation between technology and learning is not lost on policymakers. Lemke (2005) writes,

> Today's education policymakers are seeing technology through the lens of the No Child left Behind (NCLB) Act, which is creating expectations for a "learning return" on all technology investments. (p. 1)

Local, state, and federal governments spend billions to place new technology in schools, and private support adds considerable amounts. The results are remarkable. In 1994, about 35 percent of public schools had Internet access; by 2005, at least 99 percent of public schools had access. And the ratio of students to computer has decreased, from twelve to one in 1998 to five to one (U.S. Department of Education, 2004, 2005, 2012).

Gallup's national surveys for the International Society for Technology in Education find that 98 percent of respondents stated that technology should be in the school curriculum and identified topics for inclusion, as shown in Table 12.1.

Not only is study from and with technology of great benefit to students, teachers, and the school curriculum, it also has benefits for the society. The economics and politics of international competition demand that the United States

Table 12.1 Gallup Survey on Important Technology Topics for Schools to Teach			
Topic	Not Important	Important	Very Important
Relation among math, science, technology	2%	19%	79%
Skills for using technologies	1%	22%	76%
Effects of technology on society	2%	27%	71%
Technology and the environment	2%	29%	68%
Pros and cons of each technology	2%	29%	58%
How technology products are designed	12%	45%	41%

Source: Rose et al. (2004).

remain in the forefront of technological innovation and development. Through technological innovation, we can put the best schooling in the hands of all children—rural, suburban, or urban. Children can have access to fine teachers, excellent culture, significant science, and interesting learning (U.S. Department of Education, 2005; Salpeter, 2008; Villinger, 2012).

Developing Technological Knowledge, Skills, and Attitudes

Technological *knowledge* involves a working understanding of technical and operational language, an understanding of common technological equipment and related software, a grasp of basic scientific and mathematical principles on which technology rests, and an understanding of the history of technology and its impacts on society. It also includes the use of technology to learn: to discover, analyze, test, and comprehend ideas.

Technological *skills* are the techniques useful in efficient and effective operation of various technical devices, from computers and telecommunication equipment to image reproduction and robotics, and the techniques useful in dealing with the results of that work. This incorporates skills used in learning, evaluating, reporting on, and correcting or repairing technological, academic, and creative material.

Technological *attitudes* include a curiosity about ideas and knowledge, an awareness of the need for continued technological innovation, an openness to change, a desire to improve technology, and an optimistic sense that recognizes the value of technology to social and individual lives. This functional set of knowledge, skills, and attitudes should be included in the basic education for all students.

The United States requires a populace well informed about new technologies, their use, and their social value (Braun, 2007). Technological literacy is the beginning point, and schools are the obvious place to start (Salpeter, 2008). No other institution in society has taken such broad responsibilities for the development of various literacies—the ability to read, write, speak, understand, and apply information—among the young. Schools have a long, proud tradition of providing a common curriculum in necessary and important learnings: language use, civic responsibility, computation skill, scientific and economic understanding, and appreciation of the arts. Each involves forms of literacy, with schools offering the means to student comprehension and use. Because of technology's obvious and increasing significance to human life and societal well-being, schools must ensure basic education from and with technology, providing digital citizenship, to use Edutopia's term (Edutopia, 2008, 2011; Prensky, 2008b; Allenby and Sarewitz, 2011).

In addition to Internet connections, schools with state-of-the-art equipment and teaching materials, a suitable technology curriculum, and teachers well prepared in the use and value of various technologies are a necessity. Schools play a particularly important role in diagnosis, delivery, and development of technological learning. Qualified teachers diagnose the students' technical knowledge and skill in reference to national standards, deliver appropriate learning to improve student mastery, and develop innovative and interesting teaching materials and techniques for continuing improvement. Further, schools must provide a supportive, sustaining environment for technology, assisting teachers and other staff to acquire and improve their skills.

Papert (2002) thinks technology can do the following:

1. Change the whole system of schooling to improve learning and teaching (e.g., show that knowledge is interdisciplinary with no need for separate, compartmentalized subjects and that the learning process has continuity without age segregation)
2. "Mobilize powerful ideas" (e.g., use virtual reality to try things out and offer immediate feedback from multiple sources)
3. Encourage "children to become a driving force for educational change instead of passive recipients" (e.g., students teach along with teachers, and children's curiosity stimulates innovative uses for technology)

Technological knowledge goes beyond basic operations and information to expand and engage students and teachers in redesigning the very nature of schooling and learning. It is transformative.

Setting Standards for Technological Learning

National education standards have a major impact on schools, providing focus for curriculum and instruction and offering accountability to society. Any subject not included in approved national standards is destined to be marginalized in schools.

The ISTE established the National Educational Technology Standards (NETS) for schools. These now provide the basis for nearly every state's standards documents (www.cnets.iste.org). General standards for technology education are to enable students to become capable users, information seekers, problem solvers, communicators, analyzers, evaluators, and decision makers—thus, informed, responsible, and productive citizens (NETS, 2002).

There are some problems. For many schools and teachers, after "50 years of costly trial and error, technology is still not an integral, routine part of what happens in the classroom . . . there is still no common, coherent vision of how technology is to be used in the classroom; there are only unrealized expectations" (Romano, 2003, pp. 2, 23).

And there is an unfortunate development in cyberbullying that must be addressed by school administrators, educators, and parental efforts to protect students from the use of technology for malicious attacks, destruction of reputations, and personal vendettas (Edutopia, 2011).

The U.S. Department of Education (2005) identifies the problem: "Over the past 10 years, 99 percent of our schools have been connected to the Internet with a 5:1 student to computer ratio. Yet, we have not realized the promise of technology in schools" (p. 5). The U.S. Department of Education (2010) is more optimistic moving toward "leveraging technology" to improve student learning and increase productivity in schools.

Obstacles to Technological Education

Some obstacles to adequate technological education are evident, including financing, adequate staffing, suitable curriculum, technological fear, and the traditional slow speed of educational change. Financing is an important issue but must be weighed against the social costs of not preparing students for twenty-first-century technical life. If funds are not provided, we expand the digital divide between the well-to-do and the poor. A ten-year national investment in wiring schools helps to close that divide and Internet access in public schools increases each year, moving from less than one-third of all schools in the mid-1990s to virtually all schools now. Community Tech Centers offer a national network of over 600 affiliates and more than 4,000 locations. The National Urban League, Boys and Girls Clubs, YMCA and YWCA groups, and others, with help from the Bill and Melinda Gates Foundation, will technologically link over 7,000 libraries (Edutopia, 2008, 2011).

Some teachers fear or are reluctant about technology and are not prepared to properly educate students. This fear can prevent them from exploring its uses and benefits as instructional tools. Some teachers disparage new computer or telecommunications devices as useful only for "entertainment" or "self-indulgence." A sizable number of teachers see laptop computers merely as a "presentation" tool and "marginalize every aspect of the laptop" in their classrooms (Windschitl and Sahl, 2002, p. 197). Teacher-imposed classroom rules often prohibit students from bringing in technological equipment; school rules may limit use of such equipment in the building. McKenzie (1999) points out that "except for a hardy group of pioneers who have shown what is possible, the bulk of our teachers lack the support, the resources, or the motivation to bring these intruders [new technologies] into the classroom core" (p. 1). McKenzie's (1999, 2000, 2001, 2009) books are designed to assist schools and teachers in overcoming this obstacle with practical ideas.

Some schools make it difficult for students to get access to various devices, and experimentation is not permitted. School computer rooms are often separated from class work areas, are limited to select students or times, are heavily controlled and monitored, and have too few computers that are often poorly maintained older models with creaky programs. Only certain students get special training on computers. Teachers and administrators often perceive technical equipment as expensive and separate from standard schoolwork. They don't trust the students, and they may be uncomfortable around the equipment themselves. Sometimes they suspect that students are using computers and other equipment inappropriately, as in "surfing" the Internet and finding something interesting. That hardly ties them into the ongoing educational activity in classrooms. This is not a setting that encourages learning from or with technology.

Academic Problems

We need constantly improving math, science, and technology education. This is not only for students who want to go into careers in math, science, and technology; technological knowledge is needed in virtually all contemporary occupations. Long-distance truck drivers, building contractors, salespeople, government employees, lawyers, doctors, travel agents, and farmers use and rely on technological equipment for their work. Home owners, renters, taxpayers, parents, and voters need technological knowledge.

Technological change happens faster and faster but not school change (Prensky, 2008a). The time gap between discoveries in science and their application in technology has been shortening at an increasing rate. While it took more than 100 years to transform scientific discoveries about light in the eighteenth century into technology for photography, it took only sixty-five years between the science behind electric motors and the technology that provided them. For radios, the gap between discovery and technology was about thirty-five years. From discoveries in atomic theory to technology for atomic weapons, the gap was only six years, and from science to technology on transistors it was only three years (Gleick, 1999).

But we have a continuing deficiency in U.S. scientific and technological education. Comparative tests of math and science achievement show American students well behind some European countries and Japan. Math, science, and technology are very significant subjects; the United States should not be behind in these areas. Friedman (2005) noted that one U.S. university tied for seventeenth place, the lowest ranking ever in the twenty-nine-year history of an international programming competition, and that no U.S. school had won since 1997. American colleges dominated this competition for years but have been falling behind. He attributes it to a serious lack in math and science education in precollegiate schools.

Developing Technological Proficiency

Education occurs in a variety of locations, under a number of circumstances, at any time, and through uncountable individual interests. Not only is technology a necessary subject to be taught, but it offers the means and variety to improve and expand all learning for twenty-first-century schools. Student research is incredibly enhanced via Internet, satellite telecommunications, laser, and other resources. Virtual situations and simulations approximate real life and provide extraordinary learning experiences not available from books and teachers. Distance learning programs allow students to stay at home, sit on a beach, wait in a line, sip some milk and eat cookies, or be anywhere and still connected for learning. Computer programs exist in all subjects: English literature and grammar, histories of all types, math beyond belief, philosophy, multiple combinations of sciences, any of the arts, foreign language and culture, homemaking and home construction, and any other topic deemed important or interesting. Appreciation for and participation in creative arts is stimulated through use of technologies. Health and physical education can be better designed to suit individual needs and monitored more effectively by teachers with technology.

Not only are available technological options for education more interesting and involving, but they are lower in cost and time than many equivalent educational activities. A trip to Italy to use Italian and see art can be simulated by computer at far less cost than by plane and guide. Designing a building or city is more efficient by computer. Reconstructing historical events is possible and educationally entertaining by computer. Obviously, technology can't fully substitute for real experience, but it is far better than the unreality that typifies standard schooling and is safer and more open to multiple tries and modification than real experience. It allows rapid rethinking with "what-if" possibilities, stretching student thinking and creativity.

Available technology in schooling also is intellectually stimulating, interactive, visually stunning, pleasing in sound, and engaging of mind. It is tuned to individual student interests, tastes, and levels of knowledge—it is customized education that can be reorganized and resorted to fit changes in interests or level of understanding. Such education can occur at various times in libraries, on laptops, in centers, at home, and by handheld device and multiple other means at various locations and times. In addition, there is evidence that introduction of technology into classrooms has many other educational benefits, including a significant increase in the potential for learning (Armstrong, 2008; Tamin, 2011). Students can gain understanding, via technology, of the most theoretical and most applied knowledge. And that knowledge can be rerun as often as students desire until it is mastered or revised.

Good examples of school-related programs aimed at improving technological knowledge and skills include FIRST (For Inspiration and Recognition of Science and Technology), a national championship robotics competition among school students. Over 1,130 teams made up of almost 30,000 students from North and South America and Europe compete. Students design, build, and operate robotic devices of all types (FIRST, 2006). Virtual schooling is a real possibility; some twenty-two states have established virtual schools now, and more are on the way. Thousands of students are in virtual education with good results and lower costs (Winograd, 2002; Borja, 2005; Rotherham, 2006; U.S. Department of Education, 2007, 2012). And online courses abound (see www.nrocnetwork.org).

Technological progress requires talented people, with solid educations, and substantial resources in funds, facilities, and encouragement. Schooling is the key to continuing scientific achievements. In the past century, expansion of public schooling, a shift toward science and technology, new attitudes among workers and management about technology in the workplace, government encouragement of research and development, improved patent systems, and incentives for innovation helped make America powerful. Bromley (2002) points out how we overtook European nations in new knowledge in science and technological innovation after World War II by effective use of technology, giving us a jump start on the emerging global economy.

There is no better way to assess the future development of American science and technology than by examining our educational system. The future of American enterprise exists in the schools. We can tinker with current technology for short-term improvements, but long-lasting development depends on new generations of scientists, inventors, business leaders, skilled workers, and knowledgeable consumers. If schools falter, we are likely to continue declining in society and in world leadership.

POSITION 2: TECHNOLOGY CAN SUBVERT LEARNING

without a broader vision of the social and civic role that schools perform in a democratic society, our current excessive focus on technology use in schools runs the danger of trivializing our nation's core ideals.

—Cuban (2011, p. 197)

We have to find a way to live with seductive technology and make it work to our purposes. This is hard and will take work . . . we have agreed to a series of experiments; robots for children and the elderly, technologies that denigrate and deny privacy, seductive simulations that propose themselves as places to live. . . . We deserve better.

—Turkle (2011, pp. 294, 296)

Technology is the application of science for some practical purpose. Decisions about suitable applications of science and the evaluation of practical purposes, however, require serious scrutiny. Some technologies seem to be just good sense. Safety goggles for welders, testing equipment used to ensure safe blood supplies, staplers, and gummed stamps are examples. But some technologies bring serious problems; technologies are also responsible for supplies of crack cocaine, torture machinery, surveillance systems that abrogate civil liberties, and pollution of air and water. We can use weapons technology to protect ourselves and maintain peace or to threaten others in belligerence. Lasers can be used to save lives or to take them.

Personal experiences in technology may also fuel belligerence. Fox (2004) states,

> One-third of computer users admit to physically attacking a computer. More than 70 percent confess they swear at them. Frustration, anger, and exasperation—minus the swearing and hitting—affect 67 percent. (p. ix)

Fox notes that this behavior is variously called tech rage, Web rage, or CRAP (computer rage, anxiety, and phobia). The commonly identified remedy is that "people must, in other words, adapt to the machine" (Fox, 2004, p. x). But that is not the only answer, probably not even the best answer. Neither is the extreme Luddite response, nor are head-in-the-sand attitudes about all new technology. Technology does not automatically or inevitably help learning. In some cases, it can be a detriment, including psychological problems (Rosen, 2012).

We need reasoned criteria, solid evidence, and critical skepticism to make adequate judgments about the relative value of technologies. Commercialism, politics, and ideology are commonly the pressures for or against certain technological uses—these forces are not consistent with the reasoned judgment needed. You don't have to be a knee-jerk advocate of technology to show you are modern, and you don't have to be Neanderthal in views against technology to show you resist being dragooned. Good critical judgment based on evidence and logic, along with some healthy skepticism, is pertinent. But that critical judgment is what is often lacking in discussions about technology in education.

Morozov (2011) makes an important point about the overzealous salesmanship and lack of critical thinking behind the advocacy of new technologies:

> After all, it's not the historians of technology but futurists—those who prefer to about the bright but unknowable future rather than confront the dark but knowable past—that make the most outrageous claims about the fundamental, world-transforming significance of any new technology. . . . As a result, excessive optimism about what technology has to offer, bordering at times on irrational exuberance, overwhelms even those with superior knowledge of history, society, and politics. (p. 313)

Some advocates of technology in schools want students trained to use and love the latest device and do not enjoy it when students or teachers use critical judgment to question the value or use. Bromley and Apple (1998) warned early that most writing in this area "implicitly assumes that technology is beneficient, sure to bring us a better tomorrow if we simply attend to a little fine-tuning now and then" (p. 3). Technology, in the form of more computer activity, is often treated as an inevitable happening in schools, a type of determinism that leads us to feel helpless to stop or modify expansion (Watson, 2010; Wu, 2010; Cuban, 2011).

Pflaum (2004) states,

> Test scores would soar, or tests would disappear altogether, as newly engaged, motivated students acquired skills, problem-solving abilities and a newfound thirst for knowledge. That was technology's promise. The reality, so far, has fallen short. (p. 4)

Jamie McKenzie (2008), editor of *From Now On*, the online journal of educational technology, makes the point:

> Technology vendors and cheerleaders would have you believe this is a digital age, but . . . shall we walk through a virtual rainforest or a real one? Hardly a choice unless you are addicted to the couch, the tube, and your headphones. . . . To accept the digital label uncritically is a form of surrender to cultural trends that should inspire dissent and apprehension. (p. 1)

Old and New Technologies: Teachers Find the Good Ones

Teachers have used technologies in schools for centuries, and schools are often the key location for inventing and developing new technologies. Elementary school teachers are well known for inventing creative ways to improve their classrooms and their practice, and technologies are often a key ingredient. Universities house research centers and individual faculty members devoted to innovations in technology. So education is already well suited to technologies that can improve schooling; education is also the most suitable location to raise questions and challenge the use and value of various technologies.

Teachers have a long history of using technologies that they find useful in their work and ignoring those that aren't. As Tyack and Cuban (2000) note,

> Many Americans relish technological solutions to the problems of learning. It has long been so . . . advocates of educational radio, film, television, and programmed learning predicted pedagogical Nirvanas that never materialized.
>
> Reformers have turned to machines when they were concerned about the competence of teachers, or the high cost of schooling, or some external threat to American security or prosperity that gave special urgency to education. . . . Teachers have regularly used technologies to enhance their regular instruction but rarely to transform their teaching. (pp. 247, 248)

Teachers use and alter technologies that show value in assisting learning—but there is no good reason to "transform" or "revolutionize" teaching by replacing solid teaching practices. Good teachers and not machines or devices are the key to good education. Students recognize the value of teacher-mitigated technology: "Teachers are vital to the learning process. Technology is good, but it is not a perfect substitute" (Oblinger and Oblinger, 2005).

Teachers already help students learn how to use writing instruments; printed material; graphics, arts-and-crafts, and physical education equipment; and myriad other technological means to help learning. Most of the pleas made for significant expansion of technology in schools are about computers—that computers improve the quality of learning, lower costs, and improve teaching—so those arguments should be addressed.

Raising Questions: Do Computers Improve Learning?

In terms of academic learning, there is little evidence that computers add much. Cuban (2001) studied classroom use of computers in the place most likely to be in the forefront of educational technology: Silicon Valley in northern California.

He found no strong, consistent evidence that students increased academic achievement by using information technologies. Computers did not become the classroom's central learning feature. An Alliance for Childhood (2004) analysis found that "there is scant evidence of long-term benefits—and growing indicators of harm—from the high tech lifestyle and education aggressively promoted by government and business" (p. 4).

MacDonald (2004) reports on a mammoth research project at the University of Munich, sampling computer usage among 175,000 fifteen-year-old students in thirty-one countries. Findings are that "performance in math and reading had suffered significantly," that students seemed to benefit from limited computer use at school, and that academic performance fell significantly among students who used computers several times a week. A lead researcher noted that if computers are overused and substituted for other types of teaching, it actually "harms the student." This large study controlled for variables of parental education and economic position.

Landry (2002) notes, "Yet, after hundreds of exhaustive studies, there remains no conclusive proof that technology in the classroom actually helps to teach students. In fact, in some cases it hinders learning" (pp. 37, 38). When students are distracted from schoolwork by machines or programs, their academic learning suffers. There is more to good education than mechanical presentation, even when that presentation uses all kinds of eye-and-ear-catching accompaniments.

Economists Angrist and Lavy (2002) studied computer use in Israeli schools: "There is no evidence, however, that increased educational use of computers actually raised pupil test scores" (p. 3). Indeed, there was surprising evidence of negative effects from computer use regarding math scores at the fourth- and eighth-grade levels, more surprising since the fourth grade was where the computers were reported to have the largest impact on teaching methods. An explanation offered was that computer-assisted instruction "may have consumed school resources or displaced educational activities, which, had they been maintained, would have prevented a decline in achievement" (p. 23). In contrast, the authors note that research has shown that reductions in class size and more teacher training do benefit student learning.

Gabriel and Richtel (2011) report that a U.S. Office of Education review of research conducted on major software products designed for teaching reading and math shows "no discernible effects" (p. A1) in student achievement outcomes for computer-based education in comparison with regular teaching. The Department of Education has long advocated increased technology and more computers in the classroom, but research shows that the available educational software, at an annual average cost of about $2.2 billion, is no more effective than teaching without the programs. The corporations that publish the software, however, continue to heavily promote it as educationally valuable, and teachers and school administrators are attracted by those promotions and the presumed ease of use and student interest in computers.

A profound and systematic analysis of multiple small-scale and mega-studies on the impact of online schooling on student achievement shows lackluster results (Glass and Welner, 2011) for online work. Online education has been sold to the public, policymakers, and schools as the future of educational improvements, but there is no research substantiation for this or a variety of other excessive claims for technology in schools. The main studies are in the most obvious areas of reading and math, but objective research shows no statistically significant difference in student achievement in those areas when compared with regular teaching. And there is a "vast lack of supportive research" on online education efforts. While the largest purveyor of online education, K[12] (www.k12.com), promotes partial or full-time virtual schooling, the review of research literature finds that there is no evidence that it is a "replacement for traditional face-to-face teaching and learning" (Glass and Welner, 2011, p. 5). Gail Collins (2011), in a *New York Times* op-ed column, explores some of the extraordinary claims of cyberschooling and the lobbying by some proponents to get special legislation to help private online contractors gain contracts, noting that there is essentially no research that supports it.

Reports of studies that seem to show there is some educational improvement by use of computers need to be examined carefully (McKenzie, 2007). Most are very short-term studies that rely heavily on specific test scores that don't represent comprehensive learning, many are sponsored by corporations with special interests in computer sales, and some are by government agencies previously committed to expanding computer usage. All studies should be analyzed to see if they are narrowly structured and controlled to show computer advantages without adequate study of comparable noncomputer settings (Wenglinsky, 1998; Cordes and Miller, 2000; Oppenheimer 2003; Alliance for Childhood, 2004; McKenzie, 2007; Tamin, 2011; Hiltzik, 2012).

Raising Questions: Do Computers Expand the Quality of Learning?

Broad integrative learning, beyond acquiring bits of information, can be even less satisfying via computer. Learning involves much more than test-item information easily presented in workbook form, but educational computer programs often follow that format, wherein students try to find answers to posed questions by using signals in the computer program. Visuals, narratives, and data may be impressive, but most students realize that the whole of the material is contained in the program, and their work is not to think outside that box. A curriculum based on computers suffers a decline in time for critical thinking, humanities, arts, health, and exercise.

Computer technology conveys information to students very quickly, develops skills of machine and program usage, and has excellent visual and auditory features. But it does not encourage questioning or critical examination—certainly not examination of the technology itself. Papert (1993) has reservations about noncritical true believers: "Across the world children have entered a passionate and enduring love affair with the computer. . . . In many cases their zeal has such force that it brings to mind the word *addiction* to the minds of concerned parents" (p. ix). Significant expansion of computers in schools often is accompanied by a blind and mistaken belief in technology and collateral decline in support for the academic work of schools (Cuban, 2011).

Students develop an inclination to get the quickest, most efficient right answer that they know is hidden in the program. Speed, not thought, becomes more important. This translates into a distaste for intellectual work that requires struggle or time, uses resources outside the classroom, and may have no right answer. They lose the richer context of human issues that are not mathematically computable. It becomes easy just to let machines take over, giving instant gratification and demanding little in response.

School computer use is usually individual and lacks social involvement or ethical considerations (Healy, 1998; Alliance for Childhood, 2004). So-called interactive educational programs are actually highly programmed and provide a limited set of responses to predictable keyboard or mouse entries, with an air of unreality and superficiality. Imagine learning to play tennis using only the computer and not going outdoors to swing a racket. The same occurs in learning chemistry, biology, physics, and many more subjects by computer without labs or outdoors for real experience. Learning by machine does not provide the quality of educational experience that a classroom or lab of live students offers in the various questions and interchanges and experiments.

Ironically, a Waldorf School in Silicon Valley to which many executives and experts from high-tech companies send their own children does not allow computers or other screens and has no tech-based classrooms. Three-fourths of the students have parents with high-tech connections. But the school also discourages computer and high-tech use at home. Starting in eighth grade, students can engage in limited gadget use. Waldorf stresses learning through participatory, creative activities and physical action. They claim that computers "inhibit creative thinking, movement and human interaction, and attention spans" (Richtel, 2011).

The accumulation of memorization and simplistic, often useless information is anti-intellectualism dressed up in technology and corporate language (Siegel, 2008). A school curriculum heavily dependent on technology is unlikely to offer questioning or critical evaluation. Having individual students at separate machines for long hours of lesson learning or surfing is not a prescription for an education in critical judgment. The educational needs of students and society are not met in such an environment. The strong commercial interest in having schools adopt a technology-heavy and noncritical school program is evident in corporate support for technology in schools (Bromley and Apple, 1998; Giroux, 2001; Oppenheimer, 2003; Gabriel, 2011).

Raising Questions: Do Computers Cut Costs?

Distance learning is one example of a claim that technology lowers educational costs. Would you want to be educated like that over the course of several years?

Where students live vast distances from schools, as in Australia's outback or sparsely settled parts of the United States, there is a good reason to provide the highest-quality television and computer courses that can be arranged. Similarly, continuing education for professionals and preliminary classes for students who just want to try out a subject for interest may be good places for electronic schooling. But for mass public education, it often is touted as a way to save money and standardize education. Neither of these is an adequate reason to limit our students by massive distance learning. School, of course, is more than a set of taped lectures, an interesting keyboard or mouse activity, some "interactive" homework, and answering questions on a keypad. This trade-off is not worth it.

Distance learning and other forms of technological replacement of schools will be shown, in the long run, to be neither efficient nor effective (Gabriel, 2011). Temple University started a prototype virtual college but closed it after determining that it would not make a profit (Ohman, 2002). At the precollegiate or collegiate level, well-done distance education takes more resources and money—not less. Large volume and cheaper distance learning may mean that only the rich can afford real schools and real teacher contact; the rest get terminals.

In their economic studies of computers placed in Israeli schools, Angrist and Lavy (2002) found that the cost of the computers was about $120,000 per school, equivalent to four teacher salaries. The annual depreciation rate of the computers and software was calculated at 25 percent; thus, Angrist and Lavy summarize, the flow cost of these computers is about one teacher per year. They conclude that "the question of future impacts remains open, but this significant and ongoing expenditure on education technology does not appear to be justified by pupil performance results to date" (p. 27).

Further problems occur in the corporatization of schooling, technology providing an easy means to make corporations more influential in education by control over machines, software, faculty, and intellectual property (Giroux, 2001; Werry, 2002). Corporate control is not likely to lead to critical education. Who benefits? Those already in power gain more, and the rest lose more. More than $5 billion per year is spent for computer technology in classrooms, providing great benefits to tech companies (Landry, 2002; Gabriel 2011). Expensive equipment, programs, and maintenance divert scarce resources from other educational activities. Corporate intrusions into education are abundant, but few have been so successful and so generally supported by government and school officials as the effort to computerize all schools (Leistnya, 2008). Sofia (2002) states, "The computer is an educational technology that did not arise within the classroom, but was imported into it as a result of vigorous corporate and government efforts to commercialize and eventually domesticate a tool initially developed within military-industrial complexes" (p. 29).

Raising Questions: Do Computers Improve Teaching?

A significant problem resulting from the overselling of technology in schools is the deprofessionalization of teachers and a decline in respect for teachers, teaching skill, and the value of academic/professional judgment. This problem is exacerbated by the too-easy manipulation of students, teachers, and curriculum as a result of corporate pressures and institutional control of electronic educational sources and testing. If the operation of a machine is all there is to good education, where does that leave teachers at any level? Academic knowledge, teaching experience, instructional theory, and practice will come to mean less, leading to no need for credentialed teachers, no respect for the position, no tenure to protect academic freedom, and no security (Bromley and Apple, 1998; Oppenheimer, 2003).

Erosion of intellectual freedom for teachers and students is a very serious possibility, denying the open pursuit of knowledge because technology substitutes sterilized and canned material that is easily controlled and censorable. A related problem is the question of intellectual property: who has economic and editorial rights to material produced for technology, and who can change it? With increasing technological incursions into schools, administrators are more likely to become like corporate vendors, and teachers will be less likely to make academic decisions about their courses or their students. Teachers will lose instructional freedom and responsibilities for actual education but are likely to remain accountable for any test results and school failures.

Are teachers the problem? Technology advocates in earlier times proposed to "revolutionize" classrooms and eliminate teachers by the use of such new technologies as (1) printed textbooks, (2) educational films and filmstrips, (3) school-based radio, (4) classroom television, (5) programmed learning, and (6) computers and online learning. (Tyack and Cuban, 2000; Monke, 2001; Oppenheimer, 2003). Thomas Edison predicted in 1922 that "the motion picture is destined to revolutionize our educational system and that in a few years it will supplant largely, if not entirely, the use of textbooks" (Lee, 2000, p. 48). Movies have changed much of American life and influenced teaching, but they have not replaced books, libraries, or reading. Other "seers" have predicted at one time or another that radios, phonographs, audiotapes, television, video courses, programmed textbooks, teaching machines, and/or computers would each replace teachers and classrooms (Cuban, 1986; Light, 2001; Oppenheimer, 2003).

These devices help schools and teachers in their work but have not replaced them. It is presumed that technological devices offer more variety and consistent quality and are more efficient, cheaper, controllable, and generally better than teachers. Had those characteristics actually been demonstrated in use, teacher replacement would have occurred long ago with movies, radio, or television. Most of these innovations have evolved into forms of entertainment, useful in but not central to education. Many of these former wonder devices now sit unused in school storage closets or have been tossed onto trash dumps.

Oppenheimer (2003) states,

> The message here is pretty plain. Education's opportunities lie primarily in the teacher's hands, not in technology. . . . It's a lethal combination, this alliance between education and technology, because it joins two domains in which people are particularly gullible. . . . American people are especially susceptible to idealistic pitches. (pp. 399, 402)

There is another, perhaps more important toll on the teaching profession and on educational policy when public perception of good schools focuses more on technology than learning. Even some supporters of technology in education agree that the focus should not be on technology; as McKenzie (2001) notes, "It is wrong-minded and shortsighted to make technology, networking, and connectivity the goal" (p. i). This problem is illustrated by the current craze to get more computers into schools, without providing the well-prepared teachers, effective educational programs, and critical literacy elements that McKenzie and others advocate (Leistnya, 2008; McKenzie, 2009).

Technology and the Schools: The Digital Divide

Uncritical expansion of computer technology in schools spawns social and personal problems. One widely held assumption is that more computers means more democratic technological development. The digital divide, however, has not diminished. It separates high-income people from low, those living in urban or suburban locations from the rural, the young from the old, and the otherwise privileged from those who are not. It is sometimes hidden by the veneer of corporate advertising that implies that their products are necessary for all people for a better life. Bill Gates predicted in 1995 that the Internet would assist rural people to stay in small communities since they would have equal advantage with city dwellers in terms of their access; his foundation provided substantial support to wire and equip many small-town libraries. But evidence suggests new computers may aid the exodus from rural areas as people go online to find jobs in other locations (Egan, 2002).

Schools that can afford it add more technology and frills, and those that can't are separated even further. Another divide in the technological workforce also has an educational component. Most jobs created by technology actually will be low-paid and boring work in such areas as maintenance; fewer jobs will occur in well-paid high-tech positions, and these will require more advanced education. Should schools be responsible for training workers for low-paid, boring corporate jobs and not provide all students with critical thinking skills challenging that system? Education should work to provide equity by enhancing equality of opportunity. The digital divide seems to move schools in the opposite direction. It separates races and classes even more—producing a new class of poor, the technologically illiterate, with increased disparity between managers and workers.

Personal and Social Costs of Excessive Reliance on Technology

Schools are social institutions; they cannot ignore how technologies influence personal and social life. A dependence on technology contains the seeds of narcissism, with individuals losing connections to others' political, economic, social, and personal problems. Social responsibility is ignored in the rush for self-satisfaction. Technology can separate people and soften the reality of human suffering (Turkle, 2011).

Technologies can threaten society and human decency and contain threats to individual freedoms and privacy. Secret surveillance and invisible recording of personal information, buying habits, interests, and contacts with others now are easily possible. This capacity is more than just annoying; it abrogates basic rights to personal privacy and against illegal search and places an unnecessary caution on your exercise of rights to free speech, assembly, and association. Technology is used to steal your personal identity, alter your records, confound your credit, and cause you substantial misery and trouble. Further, censorship by electronic screening of material restricts your access to ideas. Whether by commercial, criminal, or governmental action, technological intervention has multiple implications for personal and, thus, school life (Wu, 2010).

In addition to the costs of technology in personal loss of independence, ingenuity, and intellectual stimulation, there are various social costs. When individualism overcomes social responsibility, we lose the contribution many people could have made to improve society. Much new technology fragments people's lives and adds to isolation and alienation. We expect increased speed in everyday life, have lost the patience and focused attention that thoughtful reflection or social interaction require, and have seen dissolution of the family and home setting for maintaining social values and attitudes. Social bonds have deteriorated, and there are increases in violent and technology-based crime, technologically produced drug abuse, and noninvolvement in community affairs. Technology saps the core of culture, too great a loss for the limited benefits (Postman, 1992).

Technology has been used to monitor and help clean the environment but has also created significant threats to the environment and ecosystem, including ozone depletion, various pollutions, and health hazards. Other threats include the possibility of inappropriate cloning and inadequate ethics for technological medical research; insufficient regulation of gene research; racist, sexist, or humanly degrading content on the Internet; and military development of laser, nuclear, or biological weapons, making mass destruction simple and distant (Talbott, 2008). Other social costs from technology include the multiple health problems associated with it and related costs in life quality, time, energy, and money. For the users of computers and other equipment, we now have unusual muscle and eyestrain problems, headache, fatigue, crippling hand and arm pain, and the potential of other long-term problems from monitor radiation. Cell phones are being investigated for causing some new health problems. Workers in high-tech manufacturing are subject to safety problems from chemical and radiological materials along with many ailments related to that work. In many industries, workers must have protective gear—but we don't know the longer-term results of that protection. Gleick (1999) points out, "Modern times have brought certain maladies that might be thought of as diseases of technology: radiation poisoning (Marie Curie's truest legacy); carpal tunnel syndrome (descendant of Scrivener's palsy)" (p. 102). Beyond the examples suggested, there are many other personal and social costs to technology; school offers opportunity to consider them in critical examination of technology in society.

The Need for Critical Technological Education

We need *critical* technological education, where serious questions are raised about technologies and their multiple impacts on individuals, society, and schools. The addition of the word *critical* to the idea of technological education changes the concept in basic ways. This phrase connotes an analysis of technology that does not varnish over or ignore important negative implications. It does not simply accept excessive claims made for technical improvements as though there were only benefits and no social, human, or educational costs. Critical technological education is the full examination of issues involving the use and value of technology in schools and the many issues that arise in considering technology in the larger society. Critical technological education expects students to fully examine claims and evidence provided by advocates and opponents of more technology, measured in terms of supportable criteria derived from civilizing individual and social values (Leistnya, 2008).

A good life is far more than the ability to read manuals and operate new devices, and technological education is more than just recreational or vocational training to use machines. Education is rich and intellectually rewarding, entailing the posing of questions, examination of issues, and search for adequate evidence (Dewey, 1933). These are elements of critical thinking, needed in the study of technology in society and school. Technological issues, both social and educational, are suited to examination in classes because schools exist to help students comprehend and deal with aspects of their environment, and technology has certainly become a major player in all our environments.

This position does not oppose all technologies; it is against the overselling of certain technologies with little critical examination. It also is against development of a school curriculum or school system where technology supplants teachers as a main ingredient. The headlong and uncritical plunge into electronic technology over the past decades has had mixed results. The deprofessionalizing of teachers and runaway computer budgets are examples in schools (Bromley and Apple, 1998; McKenzie, 2005). Has the wonder of technology caused our enchantment with it, or is it just extraordinarily good salesmanship?

Schools should be the best places for students to evaluate these kinds of questions without commercial or ideological interference or influence. The mass media, corporations, and those with strong linkages to technological development cannot be expected to provide both sides of this argument fairly; forces related to the marketplace and ideology limit media and business presentations of negative ideas about the technology they like or in which they have huge investments. The current and future social impact of technology is directly related to the kind of instruction and questioning that goes on in technological education.

Good educators want good schools with students evaluating important ideas. Such teachers also want students to learn, use, and improve their critical thinking. Whether working with students on the study of technology or using technologies in the classroom to explore another topic, responsible teachers recognize the importance of critical thinking on significant ideas and issues. Where technological innovation serves those ends in classrooms, teachers will pursue technologies with relish. But educators realize that educational technologies are not a panacea and do not exist in a social vacuum. There are large-scale issues beyond the classroom use of machines, issues involving the use, value, and impact of technologies in society. Critical examination of the social context of technological innovation and the instructional use of technologies are both topics of importance to educators.

We should subject technologies to critical examination in terms of education and society. The essential question is this: does a new technology improve or diminish the quality of life for most people? If it does, then we need to ask whether the technology is worth its various costs. Answering those questions involves dealing with many other questions about technology, history, social values, and making choices. We cannot expect students to use and improve their critical thinking if teachers don't think critically themselves about such issues as the role and impact of technologies.

The overpromise and underachievement of computer technology in schools represents a major concern for education, one that goes far beyond financing problems. It includes questions about the nature and quality of learning that results, unfortunate alterations in the culture of schools that deprofessionalize teachers and restrict intellectual freedom, and the corporatization of schools and increases in the digital divide. Critical technological education also provides for full study of multiple personal and social costs of technology.

For Discussion

1. Millard Smedley, in 1831, argued that "new technologies now available in chalkboards" will "replace teachers and make schools more efficient." You can judge whether Smedley was as good as weather or horse race predictors. Teachers may not have been replaced, but nearly all classrooms have chalkboards, most of them well used. Identify two current (post-1970) technologies used in some classrooms and discuss their longer-term impact on teachers and schools. Provide supporting evidence for your view from your personal experience, information from others, and publications.

2. Dialectic Analysis: A common definition of technology is science applied to a specific purpose. W. Brian Arthur (2009) notes that it not only serves human purposes but can also direct and control our lives—including, presumably, addictive tendencies and controlling our behaviors. That tension, a servant or a master, gives pause to many who criticize technology in schools.

   Prepare a reasoned position for each side—technology as human directed and technology as directing humans. Using one as a thesis and the other as antithesis, construct a possible synthesis of these positions.

3. Dialogue Ideas: The essays in this chapter propose distinctly different projections about the possible social and educational consequences of a school curriculum heavily weighted toward technology. Select some examples of technology in schools, either from the essays or from your own experience, and present a discussion of

your views of the projections. How likely are any of them to occur? Are the potential consequences mostly positive or negative? On what grounds do you determine that they are positive or negative? Do you have some suggestions for enhancing the positives and diminishing negatives?

4. Technology, some argue, is neutral—it simply exists. The real question revolves around how the technology is used. From that perspective, draft a short statement that addresses these questions:

   a. How should schools organize their use of technology?

   b. What are the best criteria for judging the most educational use of technology?

   c. Should technological innovators be free to develop any technology?

   d. Should technology advertising be regulated to prohibit misleading or incomplete information?

   e. Should education about technology be changed? How?

   Now draft a short statement of opposite positions based on the perspective that technology is not neutral. This view would hold that every technology has some value orientation, from potato peelers to hydrogen bombs. For example, hydrogen bombs have a political purpose; new potato peelers involve value assumptions about the market, the users, and how time should be used. Contrast the two statements to see if you can find a workable synthesis.

5. Is there a digital divide? What evidence can you find that supports your contention? How do you define it?

   If you find a divide, consider these questions:

   a. What are its characteristics—those identifying elements like social class, race, gender, and age?

   b. What would you propose doing about a divide?

      If you do not find a digital divide, consider these questions:

   c. What criteria and what resources did you use to get evidence?

   d. What policies would you propose to prevent a divide?

6. What would you think if a local school offered programs for students to do the following?

   Stay away from school for all courses and all years, with school-provided technology

   Have an implant to permit instant information transfer to the brain

   Get full school credit for Internet game scores

   Graduate only if they invent one important technological innovation

   Using your sense of the development of technological education over the next thirty to fifty years, present your view of a school of the future. Include physical features and curriculum.

References

ALLENBY, B. R., AND SAREWITZ, D. (2011). "The Accelerating Techno-Human Future." *The Futurist* 45(5).

Alliance for Childhood. (2004). *Tech Tonic: Toward a New Literacy of Technology*. College Park, MD: Author. www.allianceforchildhood.org.

ANGELI, C. (2008). "Distributed Cognition." *Journal of Research on Technology in Education* 40(3):271–297.

ANGRIST, J., AND LAVY, V. (2002). "New Evidence on Classroom Computers and Pupil Learning." *The Economic Journal* 112:1–31.

ARMSTRONG, S. (2008). "Virtual Learning 2.0." *Technology and Learning*. November. www .techlearning.com.

ARTHUR, W. B. (2009). *The Nature of Technology*. New York: Free Press.

BAKER, F. W. (2012). "Media Literacy in the K-12 Classroom." *International Society for Technology in Education*. www.iste.org.

BORJA, R. R. (2005). "Cyber Schools' Status." *EdWeek*. May 5. www.edweek.org.

BRAUN, L. W. (2007). *Teens, Technology, and Literacy*. Westport, CT: Libraries Unlimited.

BROCKMAN, J. (2010). *Future Minds*. Boston: Nicholas Brealey Publishing.

BROMLEY, H. (2002). "Science, Technology, and Politics." *Technology in Society* 24(1–2):9–26.

BROMLEY, H., AND APPLE, M., eds. (1998). *Education/Technology/Power: Computing as a Social Practice*. Albany: State University of New York Press.

COLLINS, G. (2011). "Virtually Educated." *New York Times*. December 2. www.nytimes.com.

COLLINS, G., AND WEINER, S. A. (2010). "Proposal for Creation of a Subdiscipline." *Teachers College Record* 112(10):2523–2536.

CORDES, C., AND MILLER, E. (2000). *Fool's Gold: A Critical Look at Computers in Childhood*. College Park, MD: Alliance for Childhood.

CUBAN, L. (1986). *Teachers and Machines*. New York: Teachers College Press.

———. (2001). *Oversold and Underused: Computers in the Classroom*. Cambridge, MA: Harvard University Press.

———. (2011). "Critique of Celebratory Accounts of School Digital Technology." Book review of Neil Selwyn, *Schools and Schooling in the Digital Age*. *Educational Technology* 51(4):49–51.

DEWEY, J. (1933). *How We Think*. Lexington, MA: D. C. Heath.

DILLON, E., AND TUCKER, B. (2011). "Lessons for Online Learning." *Education Next* 11(2):50–57.

EDUTOPIA. (2008). "Why Integrate Technology into the Curriculum?" March 16. www .edutopia.org.

———. (2011). "Digital Citizenship and Cyber-Bullying." www.edutopia.org.

EGAN, T. (2002). "Bill Gates Views What He's Sown in Libraries." *New York Times*. November 6. www.nytimes.com.

FIRST. (2006). "9,600 Students Converge on Georgia Dome." April 5. www.usfirst.org.

FOX, N. (2004). *Against the Machine*. Washington, DC: Island Press.

FRIEDMAN, T. (2005). "Americans Are Falling Further Behind." *New York Times*. May 13.

GABRIEL, T. (2011). "More Pupils Are Learning Online, Fueling Debate on Quality." *New York Times*. April 5. www.nytimes.com.

GABRIEL T., AND RICHTEL, M. (2011). "Inflating the Report Card." *New York Times*, October 9, A1.

GIROUX, H. A. (2001). *Stealing Innocence: Corporate Culture's War on Children*. New York: St. Martin's Press.

GLASS, G. V., AND WELNER, K. G. (2011). "Online K-12 Schooling in the U.S." Report of the National Education Policy Center, University of Colorado. October. www.nepc.org.

GLEICK, J. (1999). *Faster: The Acceleration of Just about Everything*. New York: Pantheon.

HEALY, J. M. (1998). *Failure to Connect: How Computers Affect Our Children's Minds—For Better and Worse*. New York: Simon and Schuster.

HILTZIK, M. (2012). "Who Really Benefits from Putting High-Tech Gadgets in Classrooms?" *Los Angeles Times*. www.latimes.com. Feb. 4.

International Society for Technology in Education. (2008a). *National Educational Technology Standards for Teachers*. 2d Ed. www.iste.org.

———. (2008b). *Transforming Classroom Practice*. www.iste.org.

JOHNSON, J., AND BARKER, L. T. (2002). *Assessing the Impact of Technology in Teaching and Learning*. Ann Arbor: Institute for Social Research, University of Michigan. www.dlrn .org/star/sourcebook.html.

KING, K. P. (2011). "Teaching in an Age of Transformation." *Educational Technology* 51(2):4–10.

KIRSNER, S. (2002). "High Schools Vie to Build a Robotic Champ." *New York Times*. April 18.

LANDRY, J. (2002). "Is Our Children Learning?" *Red Herring* 116:37–41.

LEE, L. (2000). *Bad Predictions*. Rochester, MI: Elsewhere Press.

LEISTNYA, P. (2008). Introduction: Teaching about and with Alternative Media. *Radical Teacher*, no. 81. www.radicalteacher.org.

LEMKE, C. (2005). "Measuring Progress with Technology in Schools." Special report. *T.H.E. Journal*. April. www.thejournal.com.

LIGHT, J. (2001). "Rethinking the Digital Divide." *Harvard Educational Review* 71(4): 709–733.

LIVINGSTON, P. (2008). "E-Learning Gets Real." *Technology Learning*. May 22. www.tech learning.com.

MacDONALD, G. J. (2004). "Contrarian Finding: Computers Are a Drag on Learning." *Christian Science Monitor*. December 6.

McCAIN, T. (2000). *Windows on the Future: Education in the Age of Technology*. New York: Corwin Press.

McKENZIE, J. (1999). *How Teachers Learn Technology Best*. Bellingham, WA: FNO Press.

———. (2000). *Beyond Technology*. Bellingham, WA: FNO Press.

———. (2001). *Planning Good Change with Technology and Literacy*. Bellingham, WA: FNO Press.

———. (2005). "Singular Displeasure: Technology, Literacy, and Semantic Power Plays." *From Now On* 14(3). www.fno.org.

———. (2007). "Digital Nativism, Digital Delusions and Digital Depravation." *From Now On* 17(2). www.fno.com.

———. (2008). "What Digital Age?" *From Now On* 17(5). www.fno.com.

———. (2009). *Beyond Cut-and-Paste*. Bellingham, WA: FNO Press.

MONKE, L. (2001). *Breaking Down Digital Walls: Learning to Teach in a Post-Modern World*. Albany: State University of New York Press.

MOROZOV, E. (2011). *The Net Delusion*. New York: Public Affairs Press.

National Educational Technology Standards. (2002). *International Society for Technology in Education*. October/December. www.cnets.iste.org.

New Media Consortium. (2011). *The Horizon Project*. K–12 Ed. www.nmc.org.

OBLINGER, D. G., AND OBLINGER, J. L. (2005). *Educating the Net Generation*. www.edu cause.edu.

OHMAN, R. (2002). "Computers and Technology." *Radical Teacher* 63:206.

O'NEIL, H., AND PEREZ, R., EDS. (2003). *Technology Applications in Education*. Mahwah, NJ: Lawrence Erlbaum Associates.

OPPENHEIMER, T. (2003). *The Flickering Mind: The False Promise of Technology in the Classroom and How Learning Can Be Saved*. New York: Random House.

PAPERT, S. (1993). *The Children's Machine: Rethinking School in the Age of the Computer*. New York: Basic Books.

———. (2002). "Technology in Schools: To Support the System or Render It Obsolete." www.mff.org/edtech.

Pew Research Center. (2011, 2012). "Internet and American Life Project." www.pewresearch .org.

PFLAUM, W. D. (2004). *The Technology Fix*. Washington, DC: Association for Supervision and Curriculum Development.

POSTMAN, N. (1992). *Technopoly: The Surrender of Culture to Technology*. New York: Knopf.

PRENSKY, M. (2006). *Don't Bother Me Mom—I'm Learning*. St. Paul, MN: Paragon.

———. (2008a). "The True Twenty-first Century Literacy is Programming." *Edutopia Magazine*. February. www.edutopia.org.

———. (2008b). "Young Minds, Fast Times." *Edutopia Magazine*. June. www.edutopia.org.

RAINIE, L. (2006). "Life Online." Paper presented to the Public Libraries Association, Boston, March 23.

REEVES, T. C. (1998). *The Impact of Media and Technology in Schools*. Research report for the Bertelsmann Foundation. February 12. www.athenscademy.org.

REIGELUTH, C. M. (2011). "An Instructional Theory for the Post-Industrial Age." *Educational Technology* 51(5):25–29.

RICHTEL, M. (2011). "A Silicon Valley School That Doesn't Compute." *New York Times*, October 23, A1.

RINGSTAFF, C., AND KELLY, L. (2002). "The Learning Return on Our Educational Technology Investment: A Review of Findings from Research." #IR021079. www.ERICIT.org.

ROMANO, M. T. (2003). *Empowering Teachers with Technology*. Lanham, MD: Scarecrow Press.

ROSE, L., ET AL. (2004). "A Report on the Second Survey Conducted by the Gallup Organization for the International Technological Education Association." www.itea.org.

ROSEN, L. D. (2012). iDisorder. New York: Palgrave Macmillan.

ROTHERHAM, A. J. (2006). "Virtual Schools, Real Innovation." *New York Times*. April 7. www.nytimes.com.

SALPETER, J. (2008). "Make Students Info Literate." *Technology and Learning*. May 22. www.techlearning.com.

SCHORR, J., AND MCGRIFF, D. (2011). "Blended Face-to-Face and Online Learning." *Education Next* 11(3):11–17.

SIEGEL, L. (2008). *Against the Machine: Being Human in the Age of the Electronic Mob*. New York: Spiegel and Grau.

SMITH, A. (2011). "Americans and Text Messaging." September 19. www.pewresearch.org.

SMITH, G., AND THRONE, S. (2007). "Differentiating Instruction with Technology in K–5 Classrooms." www.iste.org.

SOFIA, Z. (2002). "The Mythic Machine." In *Education/Technology/Power*, ed. H. BROMLEY AND M. APPLE. Albany: State University of New York Press.

SPIRO, R. J. (2006). "The New Gutenberg Revolution." *Educational Technology*, January/February, 3–5.

STRAWN, C. (2011). Research Windows: What Does the Research Say?" *Learning and Leading* 39(2).

TALBOTT, S. (2008). *Beyond Biotechnology: The Barren Promise of Genetic Engineering*. Lexington: University Press of Kentucky.

TAMIN, R. M. (2011). What 40 Years of Research Says about the Impact of Technology on Learning." *Review of Educational Research* 81:4–28

Technology Review. (2011). "The Next Generation of Technology." 114(5).

TURKLE, S. (2011). *Alone Together: Why We Expect More from Technology and Less From Each Other*. New York: Basic Books.

TYACK, D., AND CUBAN, L. (2000). "Teaching by Machine." In *Jossey-Bass Reader on Technology and Learning*. San Francisco: Jossey-Bass.

U.S. Department of Education. (2004). "National Education Technology Plan." January 7. www.ed.gov.

———. (2005). *Toward a New Golden Age in American Education*. National Education Technology Plan. Washington, DC: U.S. Department of Education.

———. (2007). "Connecting Students to Advanced Courses Online." December. www.ed.gov.

———. (2010). *Transforming American Education: Learning Powered by Technology*. National Educational Technology Plan 2010. Washington, DC: U.S. Department of Education.

U.S. Department of Education. (2012). National Education Technology Plan. Washington, DC: March. www.ed.gov.net.

VILLINGER, S. (2012). "Get the Most our of School PCs". Education World. www.educationworld.com.

WATSON, R. (2010). *Future Minds*. Boston: Nicholas Brealey Publisher.

WENGLINSKY, H. (1998). *Does It Compute?* Princeton, NJ: Educational Testing Service.

WERRY, C. (2002). "The Rhetoric of Commercial Online Education." *Radical Teacher*, Spring, 63.

WINDSCHITL, M., AND SAHL, K. (2002). "Tracing Teachers' Use of Technology in a Laptop Computer School." *American Educational Research Journal* 39(1):165–205.

WINOGRAD, K. (2002). "ABCs of the Virtual High School." http://ts.mivu.org.

WU, T. (2010). *The Master Switch*. New York: Alfred A. Knopf.

PART THREE

The School Community

Individuals and Environments

About Part Three: In Chapter 1, we argue that educational issues can be fully understood only by examining them against a larger social backdrop. Schooling and school policy are part of the political and economic context of society, and while issues in education may at first glance seem to concern only matters of instruction and learning and assessment, we believe that schools are influenced by the social values of the communities in which they are located and the political systems that sustain them. Schools and society cannot be separated, and the influence flows in both directions. Schools influence society by how young children are educated and the values and content that are prized and passed on to them. Schools and society form a mutually sustaining environment with obvious tensions.

Discipline and justice, unions and school reform, academic freedom, inclusion and disability, and violence and bullying in schools are issues about the school environment you will be asked to consider here. The five chapters in this section focus on questions about the ways in which schools are organized and operated and their relationship to justice and the just society.

PUBLIC EDUCATION AND PUBLIC PURPOSE

The link between society and the kinds of schools necessary to support it was described by Plato (427–347 BCE). Although Plato often is referred to as the "first philosopher of education," he was less interested in schools than in their role in supporting the state. Plato's views of education came directly from his ideas about justice and the just society. For Plato, justice is so great a good that it is worth any cost, even the sacrifice of individual liberty. Plato believed that democracy was dangerous and unnecessary and beyond the intellectual grasp of most citizens. He argued that the great mass of people were not able to move beyond the enjoyment of bodily pleasure to the pleasure of honor and that only a few of the latter group were capable of enjoying the truest pleasure, that of the intellect (Curren, 2000). For Plato, justice is the harmony achieved by everyone doing the work for which they were best suited and trained. Farmers farm, craftsmen build, and philosophers rule. Democracy is dangerous to Plato's way of thinking; it could produce injustice and chaos by allowing people without good reasoning powers the freedom to choose their own direction in life as well as their own leaders.

Most contemporary definitions of justice involve the equal treatment of individuals and relationship among individuals within a fair and democratic system. That is, justice is related to the principle of each person getting what he or she is due—no more, no less—of all things, good and bad. Most modern writers try to situate justice in an individual context. They ask, what should the state do (or refrain from doing) to determine who should enjoy the benefits and shoulder the burdens of society when other citizens have equally good claims to them (Rawls, 1971; Nozick, 1974)? In America, we often think of justice both as a right of citizens and an obligation of the state. Justice demands certain actions by the state to ensure fairness. By law, American citizens are to be treated equally. Their

behavior, right or wrong, is to be judged independent of gender or race or social class. The just society treats everyone fairly. Of course, all of us can think of exceptions to this principle of justice. It is a safe bet there are always more paupers than millionaires on death row, and all of us can name individuals who have escaped minor infractions of the law because of who they are or who they know. Our notion of modern justice, however, is rooted in the principle of fair treatment by the state for all individuals, and we are taught to accept no less.

In Part One, we argue that school is both the source of public disputes and a logical place for their thoughtful resolution. We encourage you to consider the logic and evidence of competing views on five specific issues. We ask, whose interests should schools serve based on what is just and equitable? In Part Two, we ask you to consider what knowledge is of most value and what should be taught. The organization of this book reflects our belief that schools are social institutions, and any notion of schooling begins with questions focusing on the expectations society has for student achievement and behavior and social justice. Plato's view of schools is similarly linked to social ends, but because we might not share his view of justice, we might not share his vision of the ideal school.[1]

[1]Karl Popper, the late British philosopher (1902–1994), argues that Plato's sense of justice is not based on fairness for the individual or right action by the state to protect the individual but is instead a justification for what is good for the state and the ruling aristocracy. Plato's justice, according to Popper, is designed to protect the state from any change and to hold firm the rigid class structure of craftsmen, guardians, and rulers. Plato's justice is a property of the state necessary to ensure its own best functioning and ultimate survival. Citizens of Plato's state fall into social classes because of their natural talents and abilities, and all are expected to serve the state in different, fixed, and predetermined ways. Some men will naturally be weavers, others will be warriors, and a few will be selected to lead. Craftsmen will never become warriors, and leadership will be left to the leaders. Justice is the harmonious and selfless toil of individuals in support of the state (Popper, 1966).

Of particular interest in Part Three is the job of teaching. One set of questions running through Chapters 13 through 17 asks you to consider the role that teachers should play in schools. How is school discipline related to and affected by notions of justice? Should teachers be asked to prevent bullying and work with potentially violent students? Should most students receive a common education? When is a special education warranted? Are teachers unions beneficial for students as well as teachers? How free should teachers be to select and teaching methods?

Consider Plato's recommendations for teaching subject matter. In Book II of the *Republic*, Plato argues, "We must set up a censorship over the fable-makers, and approve any good fable they make, and disapprove the bad; those which are approved we will persuade the mothers and nurses to tell the children, and to mould the souls of the children by the fables even more carefully than the bodies by their hands. Most of those they tell now must be thrown away" (Plato, 1984, p. 174). Plato recognizes that stories have great influence on children's behaviors, and many childhood behaviors carry into adulthood. Plato advocates censorship of all stories that are either (1) false or (2) true if the truth of the story is not in harmony with the needs of the state. The poets and other storytellers, Plato tells us, are dangerous because their writing is so beautiful and engaging. The charm of their words, when false, could lead children to adopt the wrong attitudes, but even when they speak the truth, they could lead children astray (Copleston, 1993).

Plato argues that public education "is necessary to a just city because it is essential to good order, consensual rule and human virtue, happiness and rationality" (Curren, 2000, p. 53). For Plato, exercising censorship over what is taught helps to create a positive educational environment. It protects a vulnerable class of young citizens from dangerous effects of an inappropriate body of literature: stories that harm the individual and myths that undermine the state. Children are sheltered from stories in which the gods are portrayed as deceivers or dissemblers, changeable or fickle. In school, the gods always are represented as eternal simplicity and truth. To portray the gods in a bad light would harm the child and ultimately the state. It is nothing less than the duty of schools to prevent damage, as long as the methods of prevention are no more harmful than the evils they are to guard against (Copleston, 1993). Platonic education is to form character and judgments about good and evil in harmony with virtues of both the individual and the state. Education, according to Plato, is designed to "induce an admiration for what is admirable and hatred for what is shameful, and by means of this harmony with reason, as receptivity to reason which will mature into a capacity to grasp why some things are to be admired and others condemned" (Curren, 2000, p. 52).

Plato represents the authoritarian school tradition in which (1) society has an obligation to exclude from consideration in schools anything that may harm its interests and (2) teachers have no inherent right to teach; they are to be the obedient servants of the state. Plato prized tradition and recommended censorship of new ideas: "When the poet says that men care most for 'the newest air that hovers on the singer's lips,' they will be afraid lest he be taken not merely to mean new songs, but to commending a new style of music. Such innovation is not to be commended, nor should the poet be so understood. The introduction of novel fashions in music is a thing to beware of as endangering the whole fabric of society" (Cornford, 1968, p. 115).

Unlike Plato, most people today believe in the potential of progress and value of change. Few people would deny teachers the right to select appropriate teaching methods and be innovative in the classroom. Many believe, however, that control of the curriculum's subject matter remains the rightful province of the state or community and not the teacher. To empower teachers with authority over the curriculum is to disempower taxpayers, their elected community representatives (boards of education), and school administrators. Consider yourselves, for a moment, not as teachers or prospective teachers but as taxpayers with children in public schools. Would you be comfortable paying school taxes while having little or no say in the education of your children? Would you be willing to leave decisions about curriculum, textbooks, teaching methodology, and evaluation to teachers who are not directly accountable to you? Or would you prefer to have these policy matters rest in the hands of elected school boards who are responsible to you as a citizen and community resident? Clearly, a strong case can be made for community control of schools.

Others will argue with equal conviction that school reform has failed in the past largely because reformers have ignored the role teachers play. For today's schools to become more satisfying and more thought provoking for children, they must first become better workplaces for teachers. Teachers must be allowed to assume their rightful place as professionals with genuine authority in schools; they should control matters of curriculum, instruction, and policy. Teachers should be able to assume a responsible role in shaping the purposes of schooling (Aronowitz and Giroux, 1985). How many thoughtful, creative people would teach in a school district that refused to listen to them about matters of curriculum and instruction?

Arguments about the organization and management of schools lie along a continuum of political thought. The left, or liberal, end of the continuum includes those who tend to be sympathetic toward the rights of workers and toward teacher empowerment. It also includes those with positive views of unions and union involvement in school reform as well as those who champion academic freedom for public school teachers. The left also tends to be critical of discipline policies that fall most heavily on minorities and the poor. Instead of developing increasingly draconian punishments, they argue, schools should work to reduce the causes of disorder in schools. The right, or conservative, end of the continuum includes those more comfortable with the traditional exercise of authority in the schools. They tend to oppose any attempt to weaken community control of schools, such as granting greater power to teachers. Those on the right tend to be less sympathetic toward unions, often viewing them as the protectors of incompetent teachers and as unwise meddlers in local school management. Conservatives typically share a less than generous view toward extending academic freedom to public school teachers, regarding it as an overused shield for spreading ill-founded and even dangerous ideas in the classroom. Conservatives tend to support strict school disciplinary practices to maintain an orderly learning environment and zero-tolerance policies to punish those who cross the line from order to disobedience and dangerous behavior. Of course, we need to be cautious about painting with too broad a brush. Our goal is not to label school critics but to make you more aware of competing perspectives in education. As you think about what teaching should be, look to the arguments of both left and right. Where do you find yourself along the spectrum of opinion on each issue? What evidence do you find most convincing? Is there a middle ground between any or all of the issues?

THE ISSUES OF SCHOOL REFORM AND ACADEMIC FREEDOM

The public views teachers positively. A poll by Phi Delta Kappa and the Gallup Organization asked parents if they would like to see their child pursue a career as a teacher in the public schools. Sixty-seven percent of the respondents said yes. Another question asked, "Suppose the brightest person you know said he or she would like to become a teacher.

What would you most likely do?" Seventy-four percent said that they would "encourage that person," slightly higher than the response had been to the same question in 1996 (Bushaw and Lopez, 2011, pp. 10–11). This is not to say that all is well with the teaching profession. Teaching continues to be described as a "careerless profession," a good entry-level job that offers only limited opportunity for promotion or increases in authority and salary (Etzioni, 1969; Lortie, 1975). On graduation from college, most people pursue a series of work experiences and job-related career moves that bring them additional responsibilities and greater compensation. A few teachers—mainly those who move from classroom teaching through the principalship to central office administration—follow a similar ascent. However, most teachers typically do not have access to a promotion path that includes a series of increasingly rewarding positions.

Beginning in the 1980s, researchers uncovered a variety of problems with public schooling. Educational expenditures had never been higher, but scores on standardized achievement tests were hitting all-time lows. Restive teachers demanded higher salaries, while the popular press delighted in printing stories of increases in school violence, crime, and the numbers of poorly educated students. Studies criticized everything from student learning to teacher preparation (Boyer, 1983; National Commission on Excellence in Education, 1983; Goodlad, 1984, 1990; Sizer, 1984; Archibold, 1998; Levine, 2006). Schools were said to be in crisis, and the nation was declared at risk because of the poor quality of teaching and learning. Teachers were held up to public scrutiny, and their work was weighed, measured, and assessed. Everywhere, researchers found dull, lifeless teaching; an absence of academic focus; bored, unchallenged students; and teachers mired in routine and paperwork. An inescapable conclusion of the 1980s research was that teachers were not doing—or were not able to do—the job expected of them. While some advocates of change seized on standards-based reform and championed No Child Left Behind legislation, others focused on teachers and teaching. The conditions of teaching were revisited as objects of policy reform, and teachers' work has been reopened for debate (Ravitch, 2010; Brill, 2011). Teacher unions have come under new attacks. Once seen as the protector of underpaid and vulnerable employees, teacher unions find themselves cast in the role of villains who oppose school reform. The public is divided about the value of teacher unions. According to a recent Phi Delta Kappa Poll, 47 percent of the respondents believe that unionization has harmed the quality of public school education, 26 percent believe that it has helped, and 25 percent believe that unionization has made no difference. The poll also reported that in disputes between teacher unions and state governors over collective bargaining issues, 44 percent of the public sides with the governors, and 52 percent side with teacher unions. Among respondents who identify as Republicans, 71 percent side with governors; among respondents identifying as Democrats, 80 percent side with teacher unions. Independents were evenly divided in their support (Bushaw and Lopez, 2011).

Plato introduced the topic of censorship in education: modern democracies pay less attention to school censorship than they do to the other side of the coin—the right to inquire freely in schools. What place should academic freedom play in defining the teacher's role? If you view teachers as well educated and well trained, then you are likely to believe that they have a "right to teach," based on their special skills and knowledge and that this right should be supported and protected. If, instead, you see teachers as craftsmen or practitioners who merit little authority over the curriculum, then you may be less willing to grant them the same freedoms enjoyed by those who teach in colleges and universities. "Academic freedom," as commonly applied to higher education, is a contemporary term for the classical ideal of the right to teach and learn (Hofstadter and Metzger, 1955). Socrates, Plato's teacher, charged with impiety and the corruption of Athenian youth, defended himself by arguing that all wickedness is due to ignorance and that he and his students had the freedom to pursue truth. Socrates argued the freedom to teach and learn is essential to uncover knowledge and improve society. His fellow citizens were not persuaded and sentenced Socrates to death. Academic freedom has fared better; though regularly attacked and battered, it has survived. Academic freedom, as applied to American higher education today, typically refers to several related freedoms: (1) the freedom of professors to write, research, and teach in their field of special competence; (2) the freedom of universities to determine policies and practices unfettered by political restraints or other outside pressures; and (3) the freedom of students to learn.

Advocates argue that academic freedom ensures freedom of the mind for both students and scholars and therefore is essential to the pursuit of truth, the primary mission of higher education (Kirk, 1955; MacIver, 1955). The American Civil Liberties Union (ACLU) objects to limiting academic freedom to university settings. The ACLU claims academic freedom should extend to public schools, which they describe as the "authentic academic community" for young people. "If each new generation is to acquire a feeling for civil liberties," the ACLU argues, "it can do so only by having a chance to live in the midst of a community where the principles are continually exemplified" (ACLU, 1968, p. 4). The issue of academic freedom raises a series of difficult questions about the organization of the school environment: What is academic freedom and whom should it protect? Is it a right that can be extended to teachers at all grade levels? Does academic freedom clash with the community's right to determine what to teach its children? Can higher education continue to claim academic freedom as a special right reserved for university experts (Hook, 1953)? Or is this an essential right in all learning environments?

designed and organized to teach subject matter and may weed out or exclude those students who do not show sufficient compliance or the ability to learn. The other side counters that schools are student-centered institutions and therefore must bend subject matter and programs around all the students. The argument has been going on for over 100 years. It was central in the discussions about schools throughout the twentieth century and so far has resisted resolution in the early twenty-first century. In 1902, John Dewey characterized the dispute as argument between two "sects." The subject-matter sect wanted to organize schools by academic topics, subdivided into separate lessons, with each lesson having its own set of facts for students to learn. Children were to proceed step-by-step in the mastery of individual facts until they had covered the prescribed academic terrain. The other sect, Dewey argued, focused on the individual child as the starting point, middle, and end of education. The academic terrain was irrelevant compared to the needs and interests of individual learners (Loveless, 2001).

ORGANIZING SCHOOL ENVIRONMENTS FOR STUDENTS WHO ARE "HARD TO TEACH" AND MANAGE

Among the great debates about schooling is one that asks what schools should do with students who are hard to teach. Those on one side in the debate argue that schools are

Among other things, we ask that you consider how school should provide the most appropriate education for students who have "special needs." Children with particular mental or physical disabilities, who are emotionally disturbed, or who have other specific needs fall into this category. Sometimes the term *exceptional* is applied to this group of children in educational literature; usually, this term also includes children identified as gifted and talented. The main reason for trying to identify and evaluate children with special or exceptional needs is to provide them with appropriate educational assistance. For children with physical disabilities, that may mean special equipment such as magnification devices for the children with visual impairment. For children with learning disabilities, it may mean specially prepared teaching materials. For gifted and talented children, it may mean artistic tutoring or advanced academic work. The fundamental question is one of degree: How much should school environments be modified to accommodate learners? When schools try to meet the needs of all students, do they run the risk of serving no student very well?

In the twenty-first century, public schools are asked to do more with a wider range of students than ever before. In the heavy-handed state idealized by Plato, citizens received an education limited by social class. In the *Republic*, justice was served when every citizen and every class of citizens functioned harmoniously, each being educated and performing according to his or her abilities and inclinations for the harmonious good of the state. Athenian education was not to produce citizens who were "to go their own way," as Plato put it. American society and its schools, along with others in the West, have adopted a different understanding of justice and relationships between the individual and the state. Influenced by philosophers who followed Plato (in particular, his student Aristotle and later Immanuel Kant), justice has been identified less frequently as

something that exists in the state and more often as something that resides within the individual. Education in democracies requires that individuals make their own decisions about vocation and training and type of schooling to be received. Interests of the individual are considered paramount, and the state is thought to be just only when the majority of citizens are served well. Public schools are designed to serve all students. Clearly, problems arise at the margins. How should schools tend to children with special needs, the unusually disaffected, the gifted, as well as the troubled? We know that students are at a terrible disadvantage if they have not graduated from high school, but what should be done with students whose very presence in school works to the academic detriment of others? Chapter 14 will ask you to look at the issue of school violence.

As you are no doubt aware, bullying and violence have become one of the most troubling problems facing American educators. Schools, once safe havens from the outside world, now must contend with acts of bullying and violence at every grade level. With school violence on the increase, experts continue to debate its causes and how schools should handle violent students. Many teachers and criminologists argue that the time has come to crack down on the most violent offenders and expel them from school. They argue that the school's job is to teach academic subject matter to those who are at least minimally willing to cooperate. Others argue that educators are responsible for helping students with whatever problems they bring to school, even if this means expanding the role of schools into nonacademic areas.

Although this book is divided into three parts, we believe that the parts are related to one another in important ways and also believe you are better able to understand schools and issues surrounding education by considering the interrelationships. Part One focuses on the interests that schools should serve; the chapters ask you to consider the nature of justice and equity and what they mean for people interested in public education. Justice is one of the oldest of the social virtues. If justice is about social fairness, with each getting what he or she is due, how is this related to the practical matters of education? The chapters in Part One ask you to examine competing perspectives about the interests schools should serve and ask you to decide which positions seem to you to be the more just and offer greater equity.

Part Two asks what knowledge schools should teach. Those on one side of the debate argue that knowledge is neutral and that American society in the early twenty-first century has an agreed-on body of knowledge important for all citizens and should be taught in all schools. Not everyone believes that there is or should be one uniform body of knowledge. Picking up a philosophic argument as old as Heraclitus, a pre-Socratic philosopher, and amplified by Friedrich Nietzsche and more contemporary philosophers, those on the other side of the argument claim that all truth is perspectival. For them, a single or absolute truth does not exist; what we call knowledge

is the perspective or interpretations made by various groups and classes of people. There is no single truth but many truths based on individual factors, such as age, race, nationality, religion, and gender. Men and women see the world differently; the young and the old rarely agree. No one perspective is considered to be more true than others. All have an equal right to be heard. Schools, for those who subscribe to this view, should not pretend to teach knowledge as if it were an agreed-on, objective, and neutral representation of reality. There are many competing realities, and schools must teach multiple perspectives of what is true. Joel Spring (2002a, 2002b), for one, argues that schools will always be places of conflict among those who hold competing notions of justice, equity, and forms of knowledge flowing from varied perspectives.

Part Three asks you to consider the human environment of schools, specifically the rights and roles of teachers and whether we can teach all students in public schools. These issues are likely to be related to your positions on the nature of knowledge, the content you believe schools should teach, and ultimately your views of justice and equity. We hope you will find the arguments on both sides convincing and engaging and encourage your thoughtful deliberations and disagreements. Our goal is to present for your consideration competing perspectives on important issues. We again invite your understanding and encourage well-reasoned dialogues. As we wrote in Chapter 1, if you like arguments, you'll love the study of education.

References

American Civil Liberties Union. (1968). *Academic Freedom in the Secondary Schools.* New York: American Civil Liberties Union.

ARCHIBOLD, R. C. (1998). "Getting Tough on Teachers." *New York Times.* November 1.

ARONOWITZ, S., AND GIROUX, H. A. (1985). *Education under Siege: The Conservative, Liberal, and Radical Debate over Schooling.* South Hadley, MA: Bergin and Garvey.

BOYER, E. L. (1983). *High School: A Report on Secondary Education in America.* New York: Harper and Row.

BRILL, S. (2011). *Class Warfare: Inside the Fight to Fix America's Schools.* New York: Simon and Schuster.

BUSHAW, W. J., AND LOPEZ, S. J. (2011). "The 43rd Annual Phi Delta Kappa/ Gallup Poll of the Public's Attitudes toward the Public Schools." October. www.pdkint.org/poll.

COPLESTON, F. (1993). *A History of Philosophy, Vol. I: Greece and Rome.* New York: Doubleday.

CORNFORD, F. M., ed. and trans. (1968). *The Republic of Plato.* New York: Oxford University Press.

CURREN, R. R. (2000). *Aristotle on the Necessity of Public Education.* Lanham, MD: Rowman & Littlefield.

ETZIONI, A., ed. (1969). *The Semi-Professions and Their Organization: Teachers, Nurses, Social Workers.* New York: Free Press.

GOODLAD, J. I. (1984). *A Place Called School: Prospects for the Future.* New York: McGraw-Hill.

———. (1990). *Teachers for Our Nation's Schools.* San Francisco: Jossey-Bass.

HOFSTADTER, R., AND METZGER, W. P. (1955). *The Development of Academic Freedom in the United States.* New York: Columbia University Press.

HOOK, S. (1953). *Heresy, Yes—Conspiracy, No.* New York: John Day.

KIRK, R. (1955). *Academic Freedom: An Essay in Definition.* Chicago: Henry Regnery.

LEVINE, A. (2006). "Educating School Teachers." www.edschools.org/pdf/ Educating_Teachers_Report.

LORTIE, D. (1975). *Schoolteacher.* Chicago: University of Chicago Press.

LOVELESS, T., ed. (2001). *The Great Curriculum Debate: How Should We Teach Reading and Math?* Washington, DC: Brookings Institution.

MacIVER, R. M. (1955). *Academic Freedom in Our Time.* New York: Columbia University Press.

National Commission on Excellence in Education. (1983). *A Nation at Risk: The Imperative for Educational Reform.* Washington, DC: U.S. Government Printing Office.

NOZICK, R. (1974). *Anarchy, State, State and Utopia.* New York: Basic Books.

PLATO. (1984). *Great Dialogues of Plato.* Translated by W. H. D. Rouse and edited by E. H. Warmington and P. G. Rouse. New York: Mentor.

POPPER, K. (1966). *The Open Society and Its Enemies.* Princeton, NJ: Princeton University Press.

RAVITCH, D. (2010). *The Death and Life of the Great American School System: How Testing and Choice Are Undermining Education.* New York: Basic Books.

RAWLS, J. (1971). *A Theory of Justice.* Cambridge, MA: Harvard University Press.

SIZER, T. R. (1984). *Horace's Compromise: The Dilemma of the American High School.* Boston: Houghton Mifflin.

SPRING, J. (2002a). *Conflict of Interests: The Politics of American Education.* Boston: McGraw-Hill.

———. (2002b). *Political Agenda for Education: From the Religious Right to the Green Party.* 2nd Ed. Mahwah, NJ: Lawrence Erlbaum Associates.

CHAPTER 13

Discipline and Justice: Zero Tolerance or Discretionary Practices

What concept of justice should govern school and classroom discipline?

POSITION 1: ZERO TOLERANCE POLICIES PROVIDE JUSTICE IN PUBLIC SCHOOLS

In the end, those kids who receive less than firm, fair, and consistent discipline end up being taught that there are no consequences for inappropriate—and sometimes illegal—behavior as long as it occurs within the grounds of those schools having administrators who are often more worried about keeping their disciplinary and criminal incident reports down for the sake of their own career advancement.

—National School Safety and Security Services (2011)

Why We Need Zero-Tolerance Policies

Every day in American public schools, students and adults face disrespect, disruption, and disorder. Countless minutes and hours that could be used for teaching and learning are lost in classrooms each year as teachers struggle to control unruly students. Zero-tolerance policies ensure that such students can and will be removed from the school setting. They protect the educational rights of the majority of students from being violated by undisciplined classmates. While these policies may at first appear harsh, in fact, they are an important tool for school personnel who seek to carry out their mandate to educate the next generation of responsible American citizens.

Discipline problems in public schools receive substantial attention when the rare but devastating acts of violence take place. However, once the media spotlight dims, the significant but less dramatic difficulties faced by teachers and students in thousands of schools continue. In the most recent government reports about school disruption, 6 percent of students reported that verbal abuse of teachers happens at least once a week, and 11 percent reported that other acts of disrespect for teachers take place as often. In urban schools, the percentages are higher. Twelve percent of students in those schools reported that verbal abuse took place once a week, and 18 percent said that they saw other acts of disrespect that often. Four percent of students nationally and 8 percent in urban schools reported that widespread disorder in their classrooms happened at least once a week as well. In schools where more than 50 percent of the students were black, Hispanic, Asian, and/or Native American or where more than 75 percent received free or reduced lunch, almost twice as many students reported those behaviors and conditions (Roberts, Zhang, and Truman, 2010).

Removing disruptive students from class has become a Herculean task in some school districts. For example the discipline code for New York City schools is over twenty-seven pages long. It includes a "range of possible disciplinary options" that leaves students and, to a large extent, teachers and administrators confused about what happens when a child or adolescent violates an element of the code. The infractions are categorized in five levels, with a set of possible consequences for each level (see Table 13.1).

There are thirteen possible consequences running the gamut from admonishment by school staff to expulsion. Each consequence can be meted out only by the appropriate bureaucrat. As the severity of the infraction increases, the authority to apply any consequence is reserved for personnel farther and farther removed from the student's action—and its impact on the learning environment. For example, a teacher can remove a student from her classroom for disruptive behavior, but only a regional superintendent can suspend a student for longer than five days. Principals who want to suspend a disruptive general education student must follow most of the following steps *every* time:

- Confirm that the teacher who originally removed the student from class has followed the applicable regulations.
- Determine that the student's behavior is so disruptive as to prevent the orderly operation of the school or represents a clear and present danger to the student, other students, or school personnel.
- Inform the student of the charges and evidence against him or her and listen to student's side of the story.
- Inform the student that he or she is suspended and for how long.
- Notify the parent or guardian to come and pick up the child.
- Reach the parent within twenty-four hours with a written notice that describes the event and the time and place of the suspension conference (which must be held within five days of the written notice).
- Write a second letter to parents explaining that the student is going to have a suspension conference, describing the alternative instruction arrangements and the hearing process, notifying them that they may bring a translator, and listing the parents' and student's rights to question witnesses at the hearing, be accompanied by advisers (including a lawyer), be returned to school at the end of the suspension, and appeal the process.
- Hold the suspension conference at a time convenient for the parents.

Table 13.1 Levels of Infractions and Range of Consequences—New York City Schools

Level	Infraction	Examples	Range of Consequences
1	Insubordinate behavior	Failing to wear uniform Being late to school Bringing cell phone to school Making excessive noise Wearing clothing that disrupts the learning process	Admonition by school staff to removal from classroom to principal suspension
2	Disorderly disruptive behavior	Smoking and gambling Using profane or obscene language Lying to school personnel Leaving school premises Causing school bus disruptions Cheating, plagiarizing Persistent level 1 behavior	Admonition by school staff to removal from classroom to principal suspension
3	Seriously disruptive or dangerous behavior	Being insubordinate or disobedient Using hate speech Fighting Stealing Tampering with school records Committing vandalism Making false fire alarms or bomb threats Persistent level 2 behavior	Admonition by school staff to removal from classroom to thirty-day regional superintendent's suspension
4	Dangerous or violent behavior	Engaging in intimidation, threats, extortion Engaging in risky, intimidating, bullying, gang-related or sexually harassing behavior Possessing illegal drugs or alcohol Participating in an act of group violence Committing arson Persistent level 3 behavior	Parent conference to one-year regional superintendent's suspension
5	Seriously dangerous or violent behavior	Using force against school personnel or students Selling drugs Possessing or using a weapon	Regional Superintendent's suspension or expulsion

- Reschedule the conference if the parents cancel.
- Prepare and maintain a record of the conference.
- Notify the parents within ten days whether the suspension was ruled justifiable.
- Notify the parents within ten days of additional recommendations.
- Respond to the regional superintendent in writing within five days if student appeals the suspension.
- Respond to the chancellor if the student appeals to him (Common Good, 2008).

Disciplining a student with disabilities is even more complicated and time consuming. In that case, a hearing must be held to determine whether the behavior is a "manifestation of the student's disabilities" and if the school somehow failed to provide "appropriate" (and usually very costly) services. If such a determination is made, the administrator's options become even more limited.

Regulations like these limit administrators' effectiveness in almost every school district in the United States. Given these cumbersome processes, many principals simply do not have the time to suspend disruptive students. Instead, the youngsters are returned to classrooms, and the cycle of disrespect and disorder continues. Without zero-tolerance policies that clearly spell out the inevitable consequences for inappropriate school behaviors and give administrators the freedom they need to apply them swiftly and consistently, students who wish to learn and teachers who want to teach are the ones being punished.

Emergence of Zero-Tolerance Policies

Zero tolerance in law enforcement and in school discipline "relies upon the motivation of deterrence to insure that people will make positive decisions.... Anti-social behavior, according to this approach, is not tolerated, and both major and minor infractions are punished severely" (Livermore, 2008). In the late 1980s, school districts across the country enacted disciplinary policies that promised "zero tolerance" for the possession of weapons in schools. At the federal level, the concept inspired the 1994 Gun-Free Schools Act (PL 103-227), which mandated a minimum one-year expulsion for a student who brought a gun (and later other weapons) to school. An amendment to the Elementary and Secondary School Act required that school districts or states develop disciplinary policies that conformed to the law or else lose federal funding. Over time, the term has come to be applied not only to those infractions for which the consequence is expulsion or suspension. In practice as a school disciplinary method, the zero-tolerance method manifests itself in mandatory suspension and/or expulsion rules for incidences involving weapons, drugs, alcohol, and violence, without investigation into context or intent (Livermore, 2008).

States have taken advantage of the opportunity to create clear and definitive behavioral codes and initiated expulsion for possessing, selling, or using drugs or alcohol and for fighting and threatening students or staff (Skiba, 2000; Casella, 2003a; Brownstein, 2010). They also created zero-tolerance policies to actions that, while ostensibly less dangerous, create an atmosphere that is not conducive to learning. These actions include open defiance of authority, disruptive or disorderly behavior, deliberate disobedience, sexual harassment, theft, threats, extortion, membership in a gang, the use of profane language, and defacing school property (Brady, Balmer, and Phenix, 2007; Evenson, Justinger, Pelischek, and Schulz, 2009).

There is a clear and present danger in America's schools; children live in a society where the media creates "heroes" who are disdainful of legitimate authority and pursue their own interests at the expense of other people's safety. For those characters, revenge and retaliation for real or imagined injuries are justified. When young people accept the values of such role models, there are several results. At worst, they put the lives of others at risk. In less severe cases, they jeopardize the learning process. Since education leads to individual success and provides society with competent citizens and leaders, anything that interferes with schooling puts all of us at risk. Zero-tolerance policies are efficient responses to this crisis, and, by definition, they are fair—applied in the same way to each student.

Zero Tolerance and Rational Choice

Zero-tolerance policies do allow schools to remove students who endanger the safety and well-being of others, but they are even more important as deterrents. They are designed to persuade young people not to engage in dangerous, disruptive, or disrespectful behaviors. Like other crime prevention policies, they are meant to "head off trouble" before it begins (Casella, 2003a, p. 875). These policies are based on the theory of "rational choice," which is rooted in understandings of human behavior developed by classical economists, including Jeremy Bentham. These theorists assume that humans act in their own best interests based on calculations they make about the costs and benefits inherent in a particular choice. People always choose the action that they believe will maximize their pleasure—and minimize their pain. Since punishment will result in increased pain, the perception that swift, severe consequences are inevitable deter individuals from choosing to behave in ways that violate the common good. If people do not fear being caught or punished for an act, there is little to deter them from engaging in whatever behavior enhances their own pleasure.

Zero-tolerance policies provide exactly the kind of punishment that acts as a deterrent. Young people are impetuous and often ill equipped to judge the potential of their actions to cause serious harm to themselves or others. Indeed, if causing such injury interferes with the pursuit of their own pleasure, it may not even reach their "radar screen." They need the external, counterbalancing forces of swift, severe, and certain punishment to rein in their impulsiveness. Zero-tolerance policies provide that counterweight. They "heighten the consequence side of the crime and punishment balance, attempting to convince individuals that the consequences are not worth the risks" (Casella, 2003a, p. 877). When the policies are followed consistently, students calculate their choices differently. When they perceive school authorities as serious about discipline—and when they understand that no one is exempt from taking responsibility for their actions—they make choices that better contribute to the order of the schools and ultimately to their own education.

The key component of zero-tolerance policies *is* the consistency with which the consequences are applied. Young people recognize that the only rules that really count are ones that apply equally to everyone. Many students regularly experience this kind of discipline outside of school. Children who play Little League baseball, for example, recognize that batters who swing and miss the ball three times are "out"—no matter whether they are the best or the worst player on the team. The "punishment" is immediate, can have serious implications for the outcome of the game, and is absolute. Consequently, players practice batting for hours, learning how to make good choices about when to swing and when not to do so. Although parents and coaches may protest a strikeout call, they never bring lawyers into the argument and rarely hold up the game for very long. The rules are the rules, the umpire is the interpreter of the rules, and, if you want to play baseball, you abide by them.

Similar consistency in schools provides students with the "certainty" that they will not be able to escape punishment for inappropriate behavior. Giving administrators or school boards discretion in applying consequences dilutes the power of zero-tolerance policies. "Many educators tend to bend over backwards to give students more breaks than they will ever receive out on the streets of our society and in the workplace where we are supposed to be preparing them to function" (Trump, 2011). Punishment is no longer "swift, severe, and certain," and, therefore, it loses its efficacy in controlling students' choices. Such an atmosphere does not encourage young people to set aside their own interests. The consistent application of consequences for actions that jeopardize the safety and freedom of others does.

Benefits of Zero-Tolerance Policies

Zero-tolerance school disciplinary policies are beneficial to students, teachers, parents, administrators, and taxpayers in several important ways. They are fair, position public schools to compete effectively with private schools, turn the job of law enforcement over to professionals, minimize time spent on discipline, and—most important—are effective at creating and maintaining orderly learning environments.

The orderliness of a school has a tremendous impact on whether parents allow their children to attend it. In the past, parents believed that they were faced with choices between public schools that tolerate disruptive or disrespectful behavior and private schools that remove students whose actions endangers others' ability to learn. The ability of private school administrators to expel misbehaving students has been seen as one of their primary strengths (Casella, 2003b). Zero-tolerance policies provide administrators of public schools with that same freedom and reassure taxpayers that their money is being well spent. The fact that disciplinary policies of charter schools more closely resemble those of private schools is a factor that parents cite as a reason for choosing those schools and for their high degree of satisfaction with them (Gleason, Clark, Tuttle, and Dwoyer, 2010).

For example, the no-excuses policy and rigorous discipline at KIPP (Knowledge Is Power Program) schools provides evidence of what a zero-tolerance for inappropriate behaviors can do to provide schools that work for children who face significant challenges. At KIPP schools, the "broken-windows" theory, on which zero-tolerance policies are based, means that no sign of disorder and not one rule violation is ignored—whether it be a piece of trash on the floor, a uniform violation, or the use of foul language (Livermore, 2008). Every unacceptable action has a highly structured and swift consequence (Matthews, 2009). Uncommon Schools, another group of highly successful charter schools, also have zero tolerance for small infractions and, in doing so, ensure that more serious behaviors do not happen. The Code of Conduct at one Uncommon School, Leadership Prep in Brownsville, New York, is typical. It states, "Without a firm and consistent discipline policy, none of what we envision for the School can happen. We cannot overemphasize the importance of providing a strong discipline policy that every student and family knows and understands. Students and families have a right to attend a safe and orderly school. Therefore, for every infraction, there will be a consequence. This is the basis of our student Code of Conduct" (Leadership Prep Brownsville, 2011).

In most states, zero-tolerance policies have resulted in the increased presence of law enforcement officers in school. The COPS in Schools program has awarded grants to provide funding for over 6,500 "school resource officers" (SROs)—trained, sworn in law enforcement officers (U.S. Department of Justice, 2001; Weiler and Cray, 2011). Generally, when a student's behavior requires arrest, the on-site SRO is able to act quickly. Because they are known to students, their presence as the arresting officer minimizes any danger or disruption inherent to the process. The presence of SROs is also a strong deterrent to inappropriate or dangerous student behaviors. A great deal of their time is spent on preventive duties, such as one-on-one counseling with students and coordinating extracurricular activities. They teach crime prevention in classes, help students deal with the presence of gangs in schools and neighborhoods, and help administrators develop policies and procedures that increase school safety.

Civil Rights Protections under Zero-Tolerance Policies

Critics of zero-tolerance policies are quick to point out applications of the policy that they believe are fundamentally unfair. They argue that discipline codes conforming to the Gun-Free Schools Act and No Child Left Behind result in punishment of "good" kids who made one "mistake." They also suggest that students with disabilities forfeit some of their rights, as protected by the Individuals with Disabilities Acts (IDEA). However, such claims ignore the law's language: "The provisions of this bill shall be construed in a manner consistent with the Individuals with Disabilities Acts" and "State law shall allow the chief administering officer of a local educational agency to modify such expulsion requirement for a student on a case-by-case basis if such modification is in writing" (U.S. Department of Education, 2001, sec. 4141b, c). The Department of Education reports that such modifications have been utilized in an average of 35 percent of expulsions since the school year 1997–1998. Students with disabilities received almost 30 percent of those adaptations. In those rare instances where real miscarriages of justice have taken place, students have been successful in using the courts for recourse (*Seal v. Morgan*, 2000; *Butler v. Rio Rancho Public School Board*, 2002). Critics also argue that a disproportionate number of students of color are suspended or expelled under zero-tolerance policies. However, since the policies are designed to treat all students who misbehave without bias, the cause of the discrepancy between exclusionary discipline rates and racial or ethnic representation in a school community cannot be blamed on zero tolerance. In fact, such policies were designed to address earlier findings of discretionary applications of discipline policies that were skewed by the biases of those administering them (Billitteri, 2008). For example, a study in Texas showed that only 3 percent of suspensions were for offenses the punishment of which is mandated. Most suspensions were for violations of school conduct codes and made at the discretion of school administrators. "The great majority of African-American male students had at least one discretionary violation (83 percent), compared to 74 percent for Hispanic male students, and 59 percent for white male students. The same pattern was found, though at lower levels of involvement, for females—with 70 percent of African-American female pupils having at least one discretionary violation, compared to 58 percent of Hispanic female pupils and 37 percent of white female pupils. Whereas white, Hispanic, and African-American students experienced discretionary actions at significantly different rates, students in these racial groups were removed from school for mandatory violations at comparable rates" (Fabelo et al., 2011, p. x)

Providing protection with regard to the application of the most serious consequences makes good sense. Insisting on complex and time-consuming procedures that ostensibly protect students' rights to "due process" for minor infractions with less serious consequences do not. When justice is invoked only for those members of society who fail to carry out their obligations and the rights of the majority of students to attend safe and orderly schools are violated, something is seriously wrong. When making "exceptions" becomes discipline policy, rules become meaningless to students. Then learning does not happen, and taxpayers' hard-earned money is wasted. Justice for all demands the better solution offered by zero-tolerance policies.

POSITION 2: DISCRETIONARY DISCIPLINE POLICIES PROMOTE JUSTICE IN PUBLIC SCHOOLS

Zero-tolerance policies undermine the chances for a youth to earn a reward for "good" behavior. Metal detectors teach African American and Latino youth that we expect them to use violence and participate in criminal acts while zero-tolerance policies scream that second chances do not exist. Surveillance teaches youth that we need to watch them because we do not trust them . . . that we fear them and need the threat of weapons in order to manage them.

—Farmer (2010)

The Social Context of Zero-Tolerance Policies

Fear and love do strange things to people. When Americans became frightened by drug-related violent crime in the late 1980s, severe and nonnegotiable penalties for illegal acts seemed to make sense. The passage of the Violent Crime Control and Law Enforcement Act of 1994 was evidence of these concerns. The bill made it possible to invoke the death penalty for large-scale drug trafficking, provided new and stiffer penalties for gang members found guilty of violent or drug-related crimes, and imposed mandatory life sentences without possibility of parole for those convicted of a third federal felony. Since approximately 6 percent of criminals are responsible for 70 to 80 percent of the illegal acts in this country, the provision was meant to "provide a method for society to attempt to capture this highly active and dangerous group of career criminal, thus reducing crime level substantially" (Jones, Connelly, and Wagner, 2001, p. 1). Since 1993, thirty-seven states have adopted similar laws. Research about the effectiveness of the laws has produced surprising results. In California, for example, researchers found that there was no deterrent effect from the law and that counties that used the law most often actually had no lesser reductions in violent crimes than did counties that used the law the least (Males, 2011). Some reports even indicate that an unintended consequence of the laws is the increase of violence in the crimes being committed, especially by offenders with two strikes (Iyengar, 2008; Males, 2011). Mandatory sentencing policies—ostensibly "color blind"—also exacerbate racial disparities in the justice system. For example, African Americans account for 34 percent of arrests for drug-related crimes, while they constitute only 12 percent of the population. Disproportionality in arrests leads to disparity in sentencing, with the result that 65 percent of people in prison for drug-related crimes are African Americans or Latinos (Mauer, 2011). The laws take away the discretionary power of judges who are meant to weigh the circumstances of a case; the age, intellectual capabilities, and emotional state of the accused; and the impact of the crime when deciding guilt and imposing consequences (Simons, 2010).

Despite evidence that mandatory sentencing policies are ineffective deterrents to crime, are racially discriminatory, and limit the decision-making authority of those closest to a situation, they have been adopted in the disciplinary policies of almost all school districts in the United States. They found their way into schools for seemingly valid reasons. Although incidents of gun violence in schools were relatively small in number, they prompted a desire to protect young people. The original zero-tolerance policy, the Gun-Free Schools Act, was clear-cut—if you brought a *gun* to school, you were expelled. Over time, however, the concept was applied to more and more infractions that were less and less serious. Harsh discipline codes tied the hands of caring school professionals as surely as mandatory sentences limited options for judges and resulted in serious consequences for students who had no intention of causing harm to anyone. They have a disproportionate impact on students of color and those with disabilities. They are costly in terms of money and time, taking both away from more pressing educational issues. They provide little return in deterring disruptive, disorderly, or disrespectful behavior in schools. In addition, they violate a basic democratic norm—that punishment should fit the crime.

Disproportionate Impact on Students of Color

Mandatory sentencing policies have resulted in racial disparities in the justice system. Similarly, the expansion of zero-tolerance policies in schools to behavior that does not threaten the safety of students or staff has resulted in significant racial disparities in the rates of punishments for disciplinary infractions. For the last thirty years, researchers have consistently shown that students of color are suspended at significantly higher rates than their white counterparts (Gregory, Skiba, and Noguera, 2010). Black males are suspended three times as often as whites and black females four times more often (Losen and Skiba, 2010). In Michigan, black students constitute 33 percent of the school populations, yet they receive 52 percent of the suspensions (American Civil Liberties Union [ACLU] of Michigan, 2009). In Texas (Fabelo et al., 2011), Colorado (Hubbard, 2010), Minnesota, New Jersey, South Carolina (Billitteri, 2009), Florida (Florida ACLU, 2011), and most other states, the pattern is the same. African American and Latino students are suspended at rate disproportionate to their presence in the schools.

Children of color are also overrepresented in lesser school disciplinary practices, such as referrals to the principal and reprimands by the teacher. If such disparities could be explained because children from minority groups actually were more violent or had higher rates of misbehavior, then the zero-tolerance policies themselves could not be faulted. However, that is simply not the case. Students of color receive harsher penalties than their white counterparts for the same offense (Fenning and Rose, 2007; Losen and Skiba, 2010). In many schools, African American and Latino students are suspended most often for being "disrespectful," "defiant," or "loud" (Walsh, 2008). These terms are clearly subjective—and culturally specific. (Gregory, Skiba & Noguera, 2010). Teachers and administrators are as susceptible as the rest of the population to stereotypes about people of color. These stereotypes can affect educators' perceptions of students, causing them to see children of color as more threatening or dangerous than their white counterparts. When disruptive events occur in a classroom, for example, teachers become fearful that they will not be able to manage the event. When that fear intersects with racial stereotypes, that concern often results in a student of color being identified, removed from class, and suspended. Studies reveal that "those singled out tended to be the 'spokespersons' for the class, and these interactions occurred in the midst of the teacher perceiving lack of control rather than an actual violent offense occurring" (Fenning and Rose, 2007). Students of color report feeling as though they are expected to act badly (New York Civil Liberties Union, 2007; Farmer, 2010). So some young people respond by acting out in inappropriate ways, while teachers and administrators fail to reflect on their contributions to students' behaviors. Zero-tolerance policies do not require such introspection. In fact, they cloak racial bias and cultural misunderstanding with the mantle of impartiality and contribute to its perpetuation (Brady et al., 2007; Fenning and Rose, 2007).

Discipline and Students with Disabilities

Most students come to school able to understand the rules and how to follow them. For students with disabilities, however, especially students with "behavioral disorders," coming to understand and being able to conform to expectations is a much more difficult task. The result is that students with disabilities are more likely to be excluded from schools. Approximately 20 percent of students with disabilities are suspended or expelled each year, compared with only 10 percent of their nonclassified counterparts. In New York City, for example, students with disabilities are four times as likely to be suspended as their nonclassified peers (Miller, 2011). The rate is higher for students with particular disabilities. Forty-four percent of students with emotional or behavioral disorders and 21 percent of students with other health impairments (usually attention deficit disorder) are suspended each year (Achilles, McLaughlin, and Croninger, 2007). Students with conduct disorders "come into the classroom with perceptions and beliefs . . . that may leave them less capable of recognizing and responding to the typical social curriculum of schools" (Skiba and Peterson, 2003, p. 3). More recent studies confirm the effects of these conditions on disciplinary actions. In Texas, "Nearly three-quarters of the students who qualified for special education services . . . were suspended or expelled at least once. The level of school disciplinary involvement, however, varied significantly according to the specific type of disability. For example, students coded as having an "emotional disturbance" were especially likely to be suspended or expelled. In contrast, students with autism or mental retardation—where a host of other factors was controlled for—were considerably less likely than otherwise identical students without disabilities to experience a discretionary or mandatory school disciplinary action. "Approximately half (48.4%) of the students coded as having an emotional disturbance were suspended or expelled 11 or more times" (Fabelo et al., 2011, pp. x, 50). Some students whose disabilities make the academic tasks of school extremely difficult become disruptive or disorderly in order to avoid doing work that is too hard. All these behaviors make sense to children in light of what they "know" and feel about the world and their place within it. Since teachers and administrators do not perceive the world in the same way, the students are viewed as disrespectful, disorderly, disobedient, defiant, and disruptive. Their behaviors simply make no sense to adults who do not share their experiences and disabilities.

Students with disabilities often have trouble making sense of peer relationships as well. Interactions with their schoolmates become difficult. Disagreements break out over misunderstandings resulting from the "failure" (i.e., the inability) of students with disabilities to pick up on verbal and nonverbal cues. They continue talking when their classmates want to say something. They refuse to share toys, supplies, and materials they have taken without asking and are surprised by other children's anger. They fail to respect personal space and physically crowd, jostle, or bump others who resent the intrusion. Consequently, they are involved in more verbal and physical altercations with other students.

It is true that the original Individuals with Disabilities Act (1997) provided extensive procedure protection for students with disabilities with regard to school discipline. For example, if a student's actions were found to be the result of their disabilities, they could receive "lighter sentences" than nondisabled students would. Objections to these protections were so strong, however, that when the bill was amended in 2004, the number of available modifications were reduced. This change was particularly true for behavior that fell into the "zero-tolerance" category for students without disabilities. In the revised bill, students with disabilities may be removed to on interim alternative educational setting for up to forty-five school days not only for weapon- or drug-related violations but also if they have inflicted serious bodily injury on another person at school or at a school function. The revised bill also eliminates the right of students with disabilities to remain in their current educational placements while they appeal a disciplinary decision if their violation of the school code would usually result in removal for more than ten days. What is problematic about such provisions is that they undo decades of work to prevent students with disabilities from being excluded from schools. These policies allow school administrators to remove students with disabilities from classrooms—and even schools—for behavior that is a result of their disabling condition; that is, students are removed *because* they are disabled. A recent study revealed that, although administrators said that they were aware of their responsibility to protect the rights of students with disabilities, most were more likely to give priority to what they perceived as the safety of the larger school community. They argued that their primary responsibility was to preserve order for the good of the entire school, and "most, but not all, viewed their obligation to implement IDEA's disciplinary regulations as a deterrent to that goal" (McCarthy and Soodak, 2007, p. 463). Instead of providing students with disabilities with the needed supports to behave appropriately in the least restricted setting possible, it appears that the "safety" of some schools may be achieved through the sacrifice of those students' civil rights.

Effects of Zero-Tolerance Policies

We have increasing evidence that zero-tolerance policies have negative effects on students. Despite arguments that applying one-size-fits-all consequences is fair, the mandated consequences—especially those that exclude young people from classes or school—affect some students more than others. "For some, zero tolerance adds another risk factor to lives that are already overburdened with risk factors. Although some students may have the support and know-how to wrangle and maneuver their way back to success after an expulsion or suspension, other students cannot. Applying the policy consistently does not mean that all students receive the same punishment. For example, there are great differences in expulsions when one student is expelled but can afford tutoring and another is expelled but cannot afford to be tutored" (Casella, 2003a, p. 881).

Researchers demonstrate that out-of-school suspension, the most commonly applied zero-tolerance consequence, is linked to continued academic failure, grade retention, negative school attitudes, less participation in extracurricular activities, higher placement in special education programs, lower grades, poorer attendance, and continued disciplinary problems (Nichols, 2004; Losen and Skiba, 2010). Most serious of all, being involved with school disciplinary practices is a strong predictor of dropping out (Kim, Losen, and Hewitt, 2010; Fabelo et al., 2011).

These consequences should come as no surprise. When students are suspended, they obviously lose instructional time. They are usually at home, and most are provided with no access to their teachers or to the assignments on which their classmates are working. There are very few publicly funded alternatives to schools, and most places in those settings are reserved for students with disabilities. Delays in getting back into school are common even when students have "served their time" or been found "not guilty." In addition, they often feel ostracized and rejected by the adults to whom they had previously looked for help. They often believe—sometimes correctly—that they have been unfairly singled out and lose faith in the integrity of teachers and administrators. Excluded students often become "transients," moving in and out of various educational settings, never feeling quite at home and never being able to establish the kind of relationships with other students that lead to academic success (Brown, 2007; Losen, 2011).

In fact, the increase in dropouts that is connected to mandatory suspensions and expulsions may not be accidental at all. Students whose behavior is inappropriate are often young people who are struggling with academic tasks. They "act out" their frustration with schools' inability to meet their needs. In an era of high-stakes testing, poor performance on standardized assessments negatively impacts the school's "report card." It is plausible that administrators may use zero-tolerance policies to raise test scores by "pushing out" low-performing students. Certainly, that remedy is more affordable than providing students with small classes, tutoring, mentoring, and after-school programs that might actually help improve their academic performance and, in turn, decrease their inappropriate behavior.

In addition to increasing the number of students who drop out of school—or, perhaps more precisely, as a result of doing so—zero tolerance has also created a "school-to-prison pipeline." In large cities, the number of police officers in schools has increased dramatically. All so-called SROs are actually sworn members of the local police department and as such can overrule a school administrator in decisions about arresting students. Because not all their time is spent on law enforcement activities, SROs often provide mentoring or counseling services to students. However, those relationships can be dangerous to students who may not realize that the SRO is really a police officer. They may make statements to an SRO that they would not make to another police officer or underestimate the need to have a parent or attorney present when speaking to an SRO. More than 400,000 arrests are made in schools each year. Misbehaviors that would have been taken care of by school administrators in the past have been criminalized. The overpolicing of schools interferes with instructional time, subjects students to intrusive searches with sexual overtones, and singles out students of color. The hostile environment in schools and the injustices students see around them contribute to the dropout rate in the United States, especially in urban schools (Petteruti, 2011).

Changes in the juvenile justice system have been taking place simultaneously. "Since 1992, 45 states have passed laws making it easier to try juveniles as adults, 31 have stiffened sanctions against youths for a variety of offenses and 47 loosened confidentiality provisions for juveniles. Despite a precipitous drop in juvenile crime during the last half of the 1990s, the number of formally processed cases involving juveniles—mostly non-violent—increased, along with the number of youths held in secure facilities for non-violent offenses" (Wald and Losen, 2004, p. 3).

Statistics also provide insight into the connection between school failure and incarceration (National Association for the Advancement of Colored People [NAACP], 2011). "Drop-outs are eight times more likely to be in jail or in prison as are high school graduates" (Bridgeland, DiIulio, and Morison, 2006). "Approximately 68 percent of state prison inmates in 1997 had not completed high school. 75 percent of youths under age 18 who have been sentenced to adult prisons have not successfully passed tenth grade. An estimated 70 percent of the juvenile justice population suffers from learning disabilities and 33 percent read below the fourth grade level. The "single largest predictor" of later arrest among adolescent females is having been suspended, expelled, or held back during the middle school years" (Wald and Losen, 2004, p. 4). The school-to-prison pipeline is self-perpetuating. Zero-tolerance policies have a chilling affect on relationships between adults and young people. Those most in need of assistance, including the mentally ill, are discouraged by such policies from seeking it for fear that their concerns will be misinterpreted or misunderstood and will result in punishment in school or in prisons (Skiba et al., 2006). Consequently, they receive no assistance in changing or dealing with the underlying causes of their behaviors. The acting out continues, harsh school penalties follow, and suspension leads to referrals to the criminal justice system or to behavior "on the street" that results in arrest and time in jail. There are strong correlations between the number of graduates from neighborhood schools and the likelihood that young people from those areas will be incarcerated. "In Los Angeles, 69 of the 90 low-performing schools (67 percent) are in neighborhoods with the highest incarceration rates. In Philadelphia, 23 of the 35 low-performing schools (66 percent) are clustered in or very near neighborhoods with the highest rates of incarceration; and in Houston, 5 of the 6 low-performing schools (83 percent) are in neighborhoods with the highest rates of incarceration" (NAACP, 2011).

Democratic Discipline

Admittedly, it is challenging to create disciplinary policies that exemplify the American ideal—protection of both individual rights and the common good. It is also necessary if young people are to believe that democratic values like fairness and justice are more than mere words.

School disciplinary policies can be crafted to incorporate the best characteristics of the U.S. justice system. For example, schools could act under the assumption that students are presumed innocent until their guilt is proven. Administrators could have the right to consider the facts of each case—including the student's intent, the circumstances surrounding an incident—before applying consequences. School districts could establish disciplinary codes that clearly spell out due process procedures.

In addition, schools can create disciplinary practices that identify "teachable moments" and use them to prevent problems. Educative practice means that teachers and staff are "intentional about teaching students the appropriate behaviors that are expected in school and society.... Some students require an intensive program; others learn by simply being in the environment. In either case, we should not leave learning to chance" (Lashley and Tate, 2009). Ronnie Casella argues alternatives like "restorative justice"—community service that replaces suspension—do just that. Instead of sitting at home watching television or in an in-school suspension room doing meaningless busywork, students provide academic tutoring for younger children, work in community agencies, or even improve the school building or campus through physical work. Schools establish peer mediation teams that work to resolve conflicts among students and recommend consequences for inappropriate behaviors. Such teams involve victims of students' aggression in deciding what would constitute appropriate restitution. The offenders also are required to take responsibility for ways to restore order and to remedy any damage their actions have caused (Lashley and Tate, 2009; Losen, 2011).

Schools that balance students' need for structure and support can also model democratic discipline. They have clear rules that are enforced consistently— but the structure is less rigid than zero-tolerance disciplinary policies. In a high school that adopted that structure, for example, when a rule was broken, the teacher or administrator would be able to decide how serious the infraction was and consider the student's intentions and the circumstances of the situation. Students would see that they were respected as individuals, that their motivations and intentions were considered, and that consequences fit the seriousness of the act. Such practices would support students' sense of justice and fairness—and reinforce their belief that those values are respected and lived out in the school (Gregory and Cornell, 2009; Olley, Cohn, and Cowan, 2010).

These models not only address problems that have already taken place but also go a long way in preventing future ones. They also send students the message that public authority in the United States is fair and operates in the best interest of all its citizens. By creating and sustaining such beliefs, disciplinary policies that allow administrators discretion in determining consequences and that involve students, families, and communities in implementing them provide greater assurance than do policies that prescribe one-size-fits-all remedies.

With the evidence mounting that the benefits of zero-tolerance policies are negligible, why do we not to have the political will to demand that they be abandoned? Perhaps because the real purpose of such laws is actually not to help young people change their behaviors but to give adults reassurance that they are still "in charge." It turns out that the benefits of zero-tolerance policies are illusory and merely the stuff of good public relations campaigns.

For Discussion

1. Opponents of zero tolerance argue that it is particularly harmful to students of color and that by giving administrators more discretion in disciplinary matters, the effects of prejudice could be lessened. However, administrators, like teachers, have biases. How can a district's disciplinary procedures protect students of color from racial prejudice without resorting to mandated consequences?
2. Are there some situations where zero tolerance is the correct or the only option? Discuss what they might be and why you think discretion is inappropriate in those cases.
3. Felons are allowed "three strikes" before mandatory life sentences are imposed. Would it be appropriate for schools to allow a similar three-offense policy before suspension or expulsion were imposed?
4. Interview a school administrator about his or her experiences with disciplining students with disabilities. Ask about the hardest situation that he or she has faced. Ask whether the administrator believes that making allowances for students with disabilities is appropriate. Discuss your findings in class. Drawing on class discussions and interviews, write an essay arguing for or against IDEA regulations regarding discipline.

References

ACHILLES, G., MCLAUGHLIN, M., AND CRONINGER, R. (2007). "Sociocultural Correlates of Disciplinary Exclusion among Students with Emotional, Behavioral, and Learning Disabilities in the SEELS National Dataset." *Journal of Emotional and Behavioral Disorders* 15(1):33–45.

American Civil Liberties Union of Michigan. (2009). *Reclaiming Michigan's Throwaway Kids.* Detroit: American Civil Liberties Union of Michigan.

BILLITTERI, T. (2008). "Discipline in Schools." *Congressional Quarterly Researcher* 18(7):145–168.

BRADY, K., BALMER, S., AND PHENIX, D. (2007). "School-Police Partnerships Effectiveness in Urban Schools." *Education and Urban Society* 39(4):455–478.

BRIDGELAND, J., DiIULIO, J., AND MORISON, K. (2006). "The Silent Epidemic: Perspectives of High School Dropouts." Report prepared for the Bill and Melinda Gates Foundation. Washington, DC: Civic Enterprises.

BROWN, T. (2007). "Lost and Turned out: Academic, Social, and Emotional Experiences of Students Excluded from Schools." *Urban Education* 42(6): 536–559.

BROWNSTEIN, R. (2010). "Pushed Out." *Education Digest*, March, 23–27.

Butler v. Rio Rancho Public School Board. (2002). 245 F. Supp. 2d 1188 (U.S. Dist. LEXIS 26238).

CASELLA, R. (2003a). "Security, Schooling, and the Consumer's Choice to Segregate." *Urban Review* 35(2):129–148.

———. (2003b). "Zero Tolerance Policy in Schools: Rationale, Consequences, and Alternatives." *Teachers College Record* 105(5):872–892.

COMMON GOOD. (2008). "Overruled." http://commongood.org/burdenquestion-2.html.

EVENSON, A., JUSTINGER, B., PELISCHEK, E., AND SCHULZ, S. (2009). "Zero Tolerance Policies and the Public Schools." *Communique* 37(5):1, 6–7.

FABELO, T., ET AL. (2011). *Breaking School Rules.* New York: Council of State Governments Justice Center.

FARMER, S. (2010). "Criminality of Black Youth in Inner-City Schools: 'Moral Panic,' Moral Imagination, and Moral Formation." *Race Ethnicity and Education* 13(3):367–381.

FENNING, P., AND ROSE, J. (2007). "Overrepresentation of African American Students in Exclusionary Discipline: The Role of School Policy." *Urban Education* 42(6): 536–559.

Florida ACLU, Advancement Project and Florida State Conference of the NAACP. (2011). "Still Haven't Shut Off the School-to-Prison Pipeline." www.advancement project.org/digital-library/publications/still-haven%E2%80%99t-shut-off-the-school-to-prison-pipeline-evaluating-the-imp.

GLEASON, P., CLARK, M., TUTTLE, C. C., AND DWOYER, E. (2010). *The Evaluation of Charter School Impacts: Final Report* (NCEE2010-4029). Washington, DC: National Center for Education Evaluation and Regional Assistance, Institute of Education Sciences, U.S. Department of Education.

GREGORY, A., AND CORNELL, D. (2009). "'Tolerating' Adolescent Needs: Moving beyond Zero Tolerance Policies in High School." *Theory Into Practice* 48:106–113.

GREGORY, A., SKIBA, R., AND NOGUERA, P. (2010). "The Achievement Gap and the Discipline Gap: Two Sides of the Same Coin?" *Educational Researcher* 39(1):59–68.

HUBBARD, B. (2010). "Data Shows Racial Gaps in Colorado Public-School Suspensions." *Denver Post.* January 5. http://www.denverpost.com/ci_14122916#ixzz1sVO5K04g

IYENGAR, R. (2008). "I'd Rather Be Hanged for a Sheep Than a Lamb: The Unintended Consequences of 'Three-Strikes' Laws." NBER Working Paper No. 13784. Cambridge, MA: National Bureau of Economic Research.

JONES, G., CONNELLY, M., AND WAGNER, K. (2001). "Three Strikes Law: Does It Really Work?" www.msccp.org/publication/strikes.html.

KIM, Y. K., LOSEN, D. J., AND HEWITT, D. T. (2010). *The School-to-Prison Pipeline: Structuring Legal Reform.* New York: New York University Press.

LASHLEY, C., AND TATE, A. (2009). "A Framework for Educative, Equitable, and Empowering Disciplinary Practice." *Journal of Special Education Leadership* 22(1):24–35.

Leadership Prep Brownsville. (2011). "Code of Conduct." http://leadershipprepbrowns ville.uncommonschools.org/lpbv/school-profile.

LIVERMORE, C. (2008). "Unrelenting Expectations: A More Nuanced Understanding of the Broken Windows Theory of Cultural Management in Urban Education." *Penn GSE Perspectives on Urban Education* 5(2). www.urbanedjournal.org/archive/Vol.%205%20 Iss.%202%20Order%20in%20Schools/Commentaries/Commentary_2_Broken%20 Windows%20Theory.html.

LOSEN, D., AND SKIBA, R. (2010). "Suspended Education: Urban Middle Schools in Crisis." http://civilrightsproject.ucla.edu/research/k-12-education/school-discipline/ suspended-education-urban-middle-schools-in-crisis/Suspended-Education_FINAL-2.pdf.

LOSEN, D. J. (2011). *Discipline Policies, Successful Schools, and Racial Justice.* Boulder, CO: National Education Policy Center. http://nepc.colorado.edu/publication/discipline-policies.

MALES, M. (2011). "Striking Out: California's "Three Strikes and You're Out" Law Has Not Reduced Violent Crime." www.cjcj.org/files/Striking_Out_Californias_Three_Strikes_And_Youre_Out_LawHas_Not_Reduced_Violent_Crime.pdf.

MATTHEWS, J. (2009). *Work Hard. Be Nice.* Chapel Hill, NC: Algonquin Books.

MAUER, M. (2011). "Addressing Racial Disparity in Incarceration." *The Prison Journal* 91(3, Supplement):87S–101S.

McCARTHY, M., AND SOODAK, L. (2007). "The Politics of Discipline: Balancing School Safety and Rights of Students with Disabilities." *Exceptional Children* 73(4):456–474.

MILLER, J. (2011). "Testimony before the New York City Department of Education on the 2011–2012 Discipline Code." June 21. www.nyclu.org/content/testimony-new-york-city-department-of-education-2011-2012-discipline-code.

National Association for the Advancement of Colored People. (2011). "Misplaced Priorities: Over Incarcerate, Under Education." http://civilrightsproject.ucla.edu/research/k-12-education/school-discipline/suspended-education-urban-middle-schools-in-crisis/Suspended-Education_FINAL-2.pdf.

National School Safety and Security Services. (2011). "Zero Tolerance: School Safety and Discipline Policies." www.schoolsecurity.org/trends/zero_tolerance.html.

New York Civil Liberties Union. (2007). *Criminalizing the Classroom.* New York: New York Civil Liberties Union. www.nyclu.org/policinginschools.

NICHOLS, J. (2004). "An Exploration of Discipline and Suspension Data." *Journal of Negro Education* 73(4):408–424.

OLLEY, R., COHN, A., AND COWAN, K. (2010). "Promoting Safe Schools and Academic Success: Moving Your School from Punitive Discipline to Positive Discipline." *Communique* 39(1):7–8.

PETTERUTI, A. (2011). "Education under Arrest: The Case against Police in Schools." www.justicepolicy.org/uploads/justicepolicy/documents/educationunderarrest_fullreport.pdf.

ROBERTS, S., ZHANG, J., AND TRUMAN, J. (2010). *Indicators of School Crime and Safety:* 2010 (NCES 2011-002/NCJ 230812). Washington, DC: National Center for Education Statistics, U.S. Department of Education, and Bureau of Justice Statistics, Office of Justice Programs, U.S. Department of Justice.

Seal v. Morgan. (2000). 229 F. 3rd 567 (6th Cir.)

SIMONS, M. (2010). "Symposium: Examining Modern Approaches to Prosecutorial Discretion: Prosecutorial Discretion in the Shadow of Advisory Guidelines and Mandatory Minimums." *Temple Political and Civil Rights Law Review* 19:377–389.

SKIBA, R. (2000). Zero Tolerance, Zero Evidence: An Analysis of School Disciplinary Practice." Bloomington, IN: Indiana Education Policy Center. Policy Research Report #SRS2. http://www.indiana.edu/~safeschl/ztze.pdf

SKIBA, R., AND PETERSON, R. (2003). "Teaching the Social Curriculum: School Discipline as Instruction." *Preventing School Failure* 47(2): 66–74.

SKIBA, R., ET AL. (2006). *Are Zero Tolerance Policies Effective in the Schools? An Evidentiary Review and Recommendations.* Washington, DC: American Psychological Association.

TRUMP, K. (2011). "Zero Tolerance and School Safety." www.schoolsecurity.org/trends/zero_tolerance.html.

U.S. Department of Education. (2001). No Child Left Behind Act. www.ed.gov/policy/elsec/leg/esea02/index.html.

WALD, J., AND LOSEN, D. (2004). "Defining and Redirecting a School to Prison Pipeline." Paper presented at the 2004 Midwest Conference on the Dropout Crisis: "Assessing the Problem and Confronting the Challenge." www.woodsfund.org/community/Folder_1036081004377.

WALSH, J. (2008). "Sent Home: The Suspension Gap." *Minneapolis Star Tribune*. May 18.

WEILER, C., AND CRAY, M. (2011). "Police at School: A Brief History and Current Status of School Resource Officers." *Clearing House* 84(4):160–163.

CHAPTER 14

Violence and Bullying in Schools: School Treatable or Beyond School Control

Can schools deal effectively with violent or potentially violent students?

POSITION 1: SCHOOLS CAN AND SHOULD CURB VIOLENCE AND BULLYING

I believe that school is primarily a social institution. Education being a social process, the school is simply that form of community life in which all of those agencies are concentrated that will be most effective in bringing the child to share in the inherited resources of the race, and to use his own powers for social ends. . . . I believe that education, therefore, is a process of living and not a preparation for future living.

> —Dewey, "My Pedagogic Creed" (1897), reprinted in Dworkin (1959, p. 22)

John Dewey helped define the relationship between Americans and their public schools. Schools are extensions of the community in this country, he argued. Schools share in the burden of caring for the community's children and for equipping them with skills and habits necessary to survive and succeed. Schools take the community's highest ideals and translate them into academic and social programs for all children. Everyone is responsible for the education of the community's children. As Dewey wrote, "What the best and wisest parent wants for his own child, that must the community want for all its children" (quoted in Dworkin, 1959, p. 54).

Dewey recognized that social conditions constantly change and that schools always have to adjust to new demands placed on communities. When social problems overwhelm community resources, schools are expected to lend strength and assistance. In a speech delivered in 1899, he said, "It is useless to bemoan the departure of the good old days of children's modesty, reverence, and implicit obedience, if we expect merely by bemoaning and by exhortation to bring them back. It is radical conditions which have changed, and only an equally radical change in education suffices" (quoted in Dworkin, 1959, p. 37).

In the late nineteenth century, the Industrial Revolution had upset the community's traditional structure and nature of work. Parents were working long hours, away from home, separated from their children. Many children also worked, at hard and often dangerous jobs. As a result, families had changed, and were not able to carry out the full range of their former functions. Schools were pressed to expand their role, to go beyond providing instruction in reading and arithmetic and help children adjust to the "radical conditions" of the day. Helping children adjust to the problems of a new industrial economy imposed a great burden on public education. Helping children understand and overcome the radical conditions of the twenty-first century may require even greater effort, but it is not a problem that schools can shirk. The community's problems are always the school's problems. We are concerned with violence here, a social problem with a long history and many causes.

The Violent Community

Violence is among the most "radical conditions" now confronting the nation and its school-age children. Violence increasingly affects the daily lives of children, and violence prevention and aggression management programs have become part of the common curriculum in schools. Society has changed in the past decades, and students' lives are filled with problems never before the concern of schools.

In some ways, school violence is a new American problem; in other ways, it is as old as the nation. American society is violent and has been so for a long time. You may recall that Andrew Jackson shot and killed a man who made insulting comments about his wife, and Aaron Burr killed political rival Alexander Hamilton in a New Jersey gun duel. The United States was born of revolution. It has made heroes of gunfighters and warriors. Americans have witnessed assassinations of national figures, racial lynchings, and riots by organized labor, farmers, and students. Violence is said to be as American as apple pie (Alvarez and Bachman, 2008). Until the 1930s, it was not possible to quantify the rate of violence, but since that time, the FBI's *Uniform Crime Reports* document a dramatic increase in violent crime, including murder, forcible rape, robbery, and aggravated assault over time. The U.S. murder rate is the highest in the industrialized world, and we remain a leader in school violence and bullying.

Violence and the Media

Violence currently presents unprecedented dangers to school-age children. American films, music videos, and television are the most violent in the world. Messages about aggressive behavior enter the world of children no matter how hard families work to screen them out. These messages flow not only from children's direct experiences but also from news reports, film, music, and advertising. War toys line store shelves, cartoon heroes destroy villains on television and in films, music videos play darkly on themes of anger and destruction, and computer games encourage interactive simulations of murder and mayhem. It's no wonder that many children suffer nightmares stemming from the violence in their lives (Jordan, 2002).

Television brings a steady volume of vicarious violence into living rooms. Over 97 percent of U.S. households have at least one television set, and young children watch about four hours of television daily. They likely watch passively— typically without adults present—acts of violence at unprecedented levels. The typical child in the United States views an estimated 8,000 murders and 100,000 acts of televised violence before the end of elementary school (Galezewski, 2005) and another 100,000 hours before the end of high school. Among other things, researchers have found that viewing portrayals of violence leads to aggressive behavior, and media violence is a significant correlate of real-world violence (Kunkel and Zwarun, 2006). Some researchers note the absence of a causal relationship between children viewing media violence and subsequent violent behavior (Trend, 2007; Grimes, Anderson, and Bergen, 2008). However, other researchers find that viewing media violence can desensitize viewers to real violence as well as make them excessively fearful of the potential for violence in their own lives (Galezewski, 2005).

Violence is an increasingly familiar aspect of students' lives (see Figure 14.1), and bullying has become an all-too-common experience for school-age children. In the most recent report of school crime and safety, 85 percent of schools report one or more incidents of violent crime during the previous school years. Students report incidents of bullying beginning as early as preschool. Almost half of all middle and high school students avoid school bathrooms for fear of being assaulted or harassed (Smith-Heavenrich, 2005). It may be naive for us to think we are not vulnerable to violence. Although violence is more prevalent in urban areas and among poor and minorities, no one in any neighborhood is immune. School violence affects the suburbs and rural areas as well as cities. In fact, the number of students reporting the presence of gangs, one indicator of school violence, increased more for rural and suburban students than it did for urban students (Robers, Zhang, and Truman, 2010).

Recent reports of school crime contain both bad and good news. The bad news is that in 2010, students between the ages and twelve and eighteen were victims of 1.2 million crimes in school. Ten percent of the male students and 8 percent of the female students were threatened or injured with a weapon. The good news is that the percentage of schools reporting crimes in 2008–2009 was lower than the previous years (Robers et al., 2010). The bad news may not be getting worse, but it is disturbing nonetheless. From the standpoint of any victim of school violence or the parents whose children have been victimized, there are no levels of acceptable violent behavior in schools.

Violence Prevention Curricula

The bad news is easy to tabulate. The statistics are alarming: Violence is common in schools, too many children feel unsafe in schools, and many schools

FIGURE 14.1 Percentage of Students Ages Twelve to Eighteen Who Reported Criminal Victimization at School during the Previous Six Months by Type of Victimization: Various, 1995–2007.

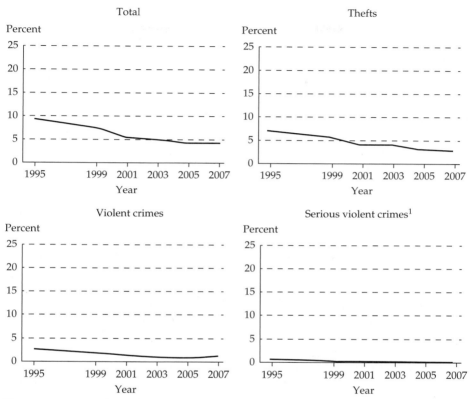

[1]Serious violent crimes are also included in violent crimes.

Note: Theft includes purse snatching, pickpocketing, all burglaries, attempted forcible entry, and all attempted and completed thefts except motor vehicle thefts. Theft does not include robbery in which threat or use of force is involved. Serious violent crimes include rape, sexual assault, robbery, and aggravated assault. Violent crimes include serious violent crimes and simple assault. Total crimes include violent crimes, and theft "at school" includes the school building, on school property, on a school bus, and, from 2001 on, going to and from school. Although indicators 2 and 3 present information on similar topics, the survey sources for these two indicators differ with respect to time coverage and administration.

Source: U.S. Department of Justice, 2010.

have to invest in metal detectors and guards instead of books and field trips. The good news is harder to quantify, but it should be reassuring: School programs can make a difference in preventing childhood aggressive behavior and future adult violence (Astor et al., 2002; Bowen et al., 2002; Zins, Elias, and Maher, 2007; Osher, Bear, Sprague, and Doyle, 2010). While schools alone cannot overcome the problem of violence, they are central in the struggle to protect children from violence and teach them that physical aggression is never the right answer. The problem of violence is complex, and there are no simple solutions. It is not the sort of problem, however, likely to be solved by applying zero-tolerance policies and simple punitive measures. To solve the problem of school violence, children must learn how to understand and control their anger. Schools can help students manage their aggression by teaching alternatives to violence through violence prevention curricula that address violence and bullying prevention in a schoolwide context. Violence prevention programs are necessarily complex. Reducing school violence entails social and cognitive training for students, counseling support, conflict resolution and management approaches, attention to diversity issues, programs to reduce isolation and alienation, drug and alcohol education, antigang and antibullying programs, suicide prevention, special training for staff, and parent outreach (International Association of Chiefs of Police, 2009). While some programs are heavy-handed and punitive, the best recognize that schools are places where mistakes can be opportunities to teach and that the disciplinary processes of schools are central to education (Fuentes, 2011).

Bullying and Cyberbullying

Although there is no consensus on how to define bullying, most people agree that students are bullied when they are exposed repeatedly and over time to negative actions at the hands of one of more other students and when the harassed have difficulty defending themselves against their harassers. Bullying always involves "asymmetric power relationships" in which the more physically or socially powerful bullies use their advantage to harm the less powerful victims (Olweus, 1993). Bullying takes many forms including overt bullying (verbal and physical attacks) and covert bullying (spreading rumors or purposely excluding someone from a group's activities). Bullying often varies by gender. Boys tend to be physically aggressive, while girls are "relationally aggressive," that is, intentionally harming others through gossip, spreading rumors, and excluding them from social contact (Leff et al., 2007). Students who identify as LGBTQ (lesbian, gay, bisexual, transgendered, or questioning) are at greater risk of all forms of bullying than straight-identified youth (Robinson and Espelage, 2011).

Bullying occurs everyday in our schools, and the majority of students have either been victims of bullying or witnessed bullying incidents. Bullying affects everyone. Bullies typically have social and academic difficulties. Victims and witnesses often suffer poor academic performance, low self-esteem, physical illness, and depression (Swearer et al., 2010). Researchers also find that the presence of a few disruptive and aggressive children in class can result in increased aggressiveness among other children (Cornell and Mayer, 2010). Schools cannot afford to ignore bullying. Inaction sends a message to bullies that they have a "right to hurt people," and it tells victims and witnesses that they are "not worth protecting" (Olweus, 2008).

Cyberbullying is a particularly insidious form of bullying in which harm is inflicted anonymously though the use of technology—emails, chat rooms, social networks, websites, and text messages. Traditional bullying is limited to places in or near the school; technology allows cyberbullies to harass students anywhere and anytime. Cyberbullying has been linked to the suicide of a fifteen-year-old Massachusetts student in 2010 and the suicide of thirteen-year-old Missouri student who was targeted on a social networking site in 2006. Cyberbullying shares many of the aspects of traditional bullying, such as repeated and intentional actions that cause harm, but it may be harder for schools to detect and stop because of the invisibility afforded cyberbullies. Compared with face-to-face bullying, cyberbullying may involve infinitely more witnesses to the bullying incidents, visiting widespread harm on the victims. Examples of cyberbullying include the following:

- Sending intentionally rude or mean text messages
- Spreading hurtful rumors or lies by email on social networks
- Creating websites, videos, or social media websites that are designed to embarrass, humiliate, or make fun of others (U.S. Department of Health and Human Services, 2011).

As of late fall 2011, forty-six states and the District of Columbia had enacted antibullying laws, and the laws of eight states specifically include the term "cyberbullying" (Handuja and Patchin, 2011). Guarding students against cyberbullying requires schools to extend a protective umbrella beyond the school grounds to include nonschool activities and the use of nonschool computers and electronic devices. The State of Connecticut, for example, has recognized the dangers of cyberbullying and the need for its schools to respond in new ways. According to Connecticut state law, "'Cyberbullying' means any act of bullying that uses the internet, interactive and digital technologies, cellular mobile telephone or other electronic devices or any electronic communications. . . . School policies must address provisions addressing bullying outside of the school setting if such bullying (A) creates a hostile environment at school for the victim, (B) infringes on the rights of the victim at school, or (C) substantially disrupts the education process or the orderly operation of a school" (Hinduja and Patchin, 2011, p. 3).

Most states have attempted to address bullying and cyberbullying, but state legislation is uneven, spanning the range from "effective to window dressing" (Davis, 2011, p. 29). The most effective programs are comprehensive schoolwide programs that involve students, parents, teachers, and staff (McQuade, Colt, and Meyer, 2009; Swearer et al., 2011). Schools can combat bullying and cyberbullying by developing a code of student conduct in which bullying of any sort is unacceptable and by establishing a school culture that ensures respect and tolerance for all students (U.S. Department of Health and Human Services, 2011).

School programs can help students find alternatives to violence. Nonviolence can be an important curriculum strand running through social studies, language arts, and other subject areas. Violence is a learned response, and because it is learned, it can be unlearned (Noguera, 1995). Schools, working with social service agencies and psychologists, can replace antisocial behaviors with prosocial behaviors and provide positive role models for children.

Violence prevention curricula are new, and their successes have not been carefully evaluated or scientifically assessed (Devine and Lawson, 2003). The evidence collected thus far, however, supports the effectiveness of conflict resolution programs and other violence prevention interventions (such as anger management and anger-coping programs and antibullying strategies) in teaching students to manage conflicts through nonviolent means (Bowen et al., 2002; Devine and Cohen, 2007). Even more convincing is the observable difference these curricula bring to schools. As one school administrator notes, "It makes a difference in my school, and I have a reduction of 10 percent in some problems. These materials are OK by me, and I don't need researchers to say it works" (Lawton, 1994, p. 10).

Viewed simply, violence is irrational destruction, an explosion of spontaneous rage. But violence doesn't just happen. It is not an act without cause or one that defies understanding. To prevent violence, schools and society should examine how history, economics, and culture find an outlet in violent behavior. Violent acts cannot be prevented unless schools and communities attend to social and political forces producing them. Violent behavior is one of the most frequently studied social phenomena of our day. The social and behavioral sciences have learned a lot about violence, and we have every reason to assume that schools can successfully stem the tide of violent behavior and protect children and society from the violent among us. We are ultimately very optimistic about schools and the ability of school personnel to make schools more just and more satisfying places for all students. Teachers and principals can extend the power of schooling into students' daily lives. Schools can help to reduce social conflicts and individual violence. The process likely will be slow and expensive, but if not begun in schools, future social and personal costs will be greater. Potentially violent children and their problems will not go away by themselves. To paraphrase John Dewey, what the best and wisest parents in the community want for their children should be made available to all children through the agency of the schools.

POSITION 2: THE PROBLEM OF SCHOOL VIOLENCE IS BEYOND SCHOOL CONTROL

Social scientists and educators have developed school-based antibullying programs in an effort to combat the perceived problem of school violence. These programs are unnecessary because, contrary to public belief, school violence is decreasing rather than increasing. They are also ineffective because they do not impart useful tools for responding to bullying but simply teach children how to identify and express their feelings. Several rigorous studies have failed to prove such programs actually reduce bullying. Antibullying programs may do more harm than good by leaving children even less prepared for the interpersonal conflicts that have always been a normal, albeit unpleasant, part of school life.

—Labash (2005, p. 13)

American schools began with modest academic goals: teach children to read and write. Over the years, schools expanded their curricula to include academic instruction in content as well as skills and subject matter from art to social studies. The argument in this section is simple, direct, and straightforward: schools should teach academic content in the most compelling and academically legitimate ways possible. This is the job that schools are entrusted with and is what teachers are trained to do. Without academic skills, students are at a disadvantage and will be unable to compete for places in the best colleges, earn scholarships, land good jobs, or launch satisfying careers. Schooling is primarily about teaching and learning academic subject matter and mastery of skills necessary for success in life. When society asks schools to engage in social engineering programs—such as preventing violence or solving the problems of crime and delinquency—it blurs the focus on cognitive learning and spreads their efforts across too many areas (Finn, 1993). Schools must teach about our history and literature and instill in students a sense of civic responsibility if we are to survive as a nation. School must equip students with intellectual skills necessary to understand science, math, the arts, and humanities if they are to succeed individually. School focus should be not on social reform but on academic achievement. A school's success is measured by the rigor and quality of teaching, not by the extent to which it confronts social problems (Ravitch, 2001).

We will further argue that (1) violence in schools is an overstated problem, (2) violence prevention curricula are of questionable value, and (3) schools should not try to do the job of welfare agencies, police, or social psychologists. Furthermore, we believe antibullying legislation is a prime example of an overly protective "nanny state" government that insinuates schools in areas beyond their responsibility.

Decline of Family Values

To spend much energy arguing that these are not normal times is to belabor the obvious. Everyone knows that the family is in disarray, and family values are all but lost to many Americans. Thirty percent of all children are born to single mothers, and the problem is even greater in some minority populations. Too many youngsters have no one to teach them basic skills, socially appropriate behavior, and other family values. Too many children show up at the doors of the nation's schools with only a vague sense of right and wrong, no self-discipline, and a limited ability to get along with other children. Increasing numbers of today's youth claim that the counterculture or gang life offers the sense of belonging, worth, and purpose that they fail to find within their families. Too many students refuse to accept responsibility for their actions.

Children do not show up for the first day of kindergarten as blank slates: the experiences of their early lives have etched on them many complex impressions, both good and bad. Most children are ready to begin school; their parents have invested tremendous amounts of time and energy in them. These children are self-controlled. They demonstrate mastery over their emotions, enthusiasm for learning, and respect for the teacher's authority. Others are not ready for school. Victims of poor parenting or no parenting at all, they come to school with insufficient preparation for the academic side of school and inadequate control over their own behavior to get along with classmates. Teachers spot these students quickly. They are overly impulsive, physically aggressive, and uncooperative. Psychologists have developed profiles of school bullies and other potentially violent youth. Among other things, they tend to be loners who lack empathy for others, frequently are victims of violence at home, and have a great deal of pent-up anger, a low frustration tolerance, a record of involvement in substance abuse and other risky behavior, and a lack of moral conscience (MacNeil, 2002). These troubled youth likely have average or above-average intelligence but are not likely to do well in school and threaten the educational quality and physical well-being of other children and themselves.

Only a small fraction of students, however, exhibit aggressive behaviors or other traits that predict violence. In fact, school violence is an overstated problem. Potentially violent students represent only 1 percent of children who enter school, and the rate of violence in school has not increased in twenty years. In 2010, the National Center for Education Statistics website (http://nces.ed.gov) reported data indicating a general decline in the victimization rate for violent crime between 1992 and 2008. The declining pattern holds true for the total crime rate reported by students ages twelve to eighteen (see Figure 14.2). In 2011, "lack of discipline" was ranked third among perceived school problems, identified by only 6 percent of survey respondents as the major problem faced by schools in their communities and trailing behind "lack of financial support" and "overcrowded schools" (Bushaw and Lopez, 2011, p. 17).

Despite widespread publicity depicting schools as dangerous places, rife with crime and violence, the conclusion drawn from reports of violence seems to say that school violence may be more of a media creation than a serious school problem. For the moment, at least, it seems fair to argue that schools are probably less dangerous for students than they have been in the past two decades. Every year since 1969, Phi Delta Kappa and the Gallup Organization conduct a poll of the public's attitude toward the public schools. For the first sixteen years of the poll, when asked to identify the biggest problem that the schools in their communities faced, most of those polled put "discipline" at the top of the list. "The use of drugs" replaced discipline in the top spot until 1991, when it was tied with "lack of financial support." Since 2000, "lack of financial support" has been unchallenged in the public's view as the major problem facing public schools. Researchers examining multiple data sources conclude that schools are generally safe places and that school safety has improved over the past decade (Mayer and Furlong, 2010).

Teaching is among the nation's safest professions. According to statistics compiled by the Department of Education and similar to the data for crimes against students, reported crimes against teachers continue to decline in both

FIGURE 14.2 Rate of Student-Reported Nonfatal Crimes Against Students Ages Twelve to Eighteen per 1,000 Students by Type of Crime and Location: 1992–2005 and 2007–2008.

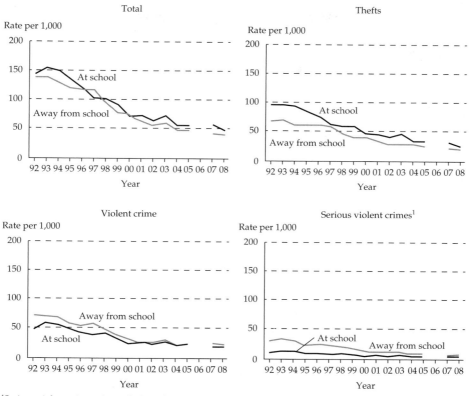

[1]Serious violent crimes also include violent crimes.

Note: Serious violent crimes include rape, sexual assault, robbery, and aggravated assault. Violent crimes include serious violent crimes and simple assault. Total crimes include violent crimes and theft.

Source: U.S. Department of Education (2010).

private and public schools. Compared with a decade earlier, 5 percent fewer teachers report being physically threatened by students. Male teachers are more likely than female teachers to be the victims of violent crimes. Secondary school teachers are at greater risk than elementary teachers, and urban teachers experience more violent crimes committed against them than reported by their rural and suburban colleagues, but the rate of crime committed against all categories of teachers is on the decline (Robers et al., 2010).

Schools are generally safe places, but disruptive students do exist. What responsibilities do schools have to teach the distracting handful of children who are unable to control their aggression? This is a difficult question. None of us wants to appear callous or indifferent to children, but schools are not social welfare agencies. Teachers are not social workers or psychiatrists. Educators are trained to teach children reading, math, social studies, and other important content and skills. We cannot reasonably expect schools and teachers to function as anger management therapists or antibullying specialists. Violence prevention curricula sound noble and high minded, but they are a diversion from the schools' academic mission and are of doubtful benefit. After reviewing seventy federally funded programs with a total of $2.4 billion in funds aimed at reducing school violence and substance abuse, the U.S. General Accounting Office (1997) concluded that these programs had not demonstrated their worth.

Similarly, a survey of nearly 400 schools in Ontario, Canada, indicated that "schools are investing significant resources into antibullying programs, despite scant evidence of program effectiveness. . . . Few schools evaluated their antibullying programs and the rigour of these evaluations was generally low" (Smith, Ryan, and Cousins, 2007, p. 120). Critical evaluations of antibullying programs in the United States cast similar doubts on their value (Swearer et al., 2010).

In other words, a great deal of money is being spent on a small minority of children with little to show for the expenditure. Today, a small group of problem students is attracting a disproportionate share of curriculum attention as well as federal and state dollars. The education of the majority of cooperative students is being held ransom by an unruly minority.

Antibullying Legislation and the "Nanny State"

No one likes bullies, and everyone wants bullying to stop, but recent legislation has increased the reach of the state into unwarranted areas and resulted in overly protective and unnecessary laws. Ordinary schoolyard issues are now treated as major crimes, and common bullies have become "public enemies." Antibullying cries have produced a cottage industry for consultants and companies selling programs and nostrums promising to curb this new school menace. Increasing numbers of states require schools to develop policies against harassment, intimidation, and bullying of every stripe, including cyberbullying. Schools have responded with policy documents that run for dozens of pages and include the appointment of school "antibullying specialists" and "school safety teams."

Bullying suggests physical threats and violent attacks, but for students ages twelve to eighteen, the most commonly reported categories of bullying were (1) being "made fun of, called names, or insulted" (21 percent), (2) "made subject of rumors" (18 percent), and (3) being "excluded from activities on purpose" (5 percent) (Robers et al., 2010, p. 43). Schools have expanded the definition of bullying to include acts, gestures, and speech directed by one student at another student that is motivated by characteristics such as race, religion, national origin, sexual orientation, mental or physical disability, and anything that makes him or her different. Such broad examples of actions and so many protected characteristics weaken the definition of bullying and fail to serve students. Most students experience occasional bad behavior from school peers with little or no lasting damage. On their own, students of every generation have learned to weather minor insults, name-calling, and being excluded from class parties without falling apart. Learning how to cope with insults and social slights as children steels students against life's inevitable false rumors, gossip, social snubs, and mishaps and makes them stronger more resilient adults. Schools should teach respect for others, and demonstrably dangerous and harmful behavior should be punished, but overly protective laws and policies are ultimately harmful examples of the nanny state run amok.

Who Are the Potentially Violent?

We know who is likely to commit crimes, the early experiences that lead to violent behavior, and the personal and family traits that tend to protect children from becoming violent adults. We know behaviors that alert teachers and administrators to the potentially troublesome (see Table 14.1). Unfortunately, beyond identifying troubled students, research has not yet developed a strong knowledge base about the causes of violent behavior or the ways it can be prevented. No one knows how to prevent potentially violent children from becoming violent adults. Schools now embracing one violence management curriculum or another are doing so without adequate evidence of its effectiveness. Many causes of violence are not within the schools' control. Violent children become violent adults, and if children have not learned to control their aggression by the time they come to school, it may not be possible for them to disentangle the patterns of violence that took shape in their early years.

In a perfect world, all children would come to school with no violent inclinations. All children would be raised in loving, drug-free, nurturing homes. All would bond with an adult who dispenses love freely and teaches them that they belong to someone and that someone belongs to them. Children's earliest experiences would have shown them that disagreements are part of life but that discord can be settled through calm discussions rather than rancor or violence. We would like all children to have high IQs and to have parents who are literate adults, who are free from alcohol and drug addiction, who study books about child rearing, who read stories to their children, and who place limits on television viewing. We would like all these things and more, but social policies cannot create them. Too many children are born to single mothers unprepared for the task or unable to give them what they need to be successful in life. Drug addiction, crime, and poverty are beyond school control. Schools cannot redistribute wealth or solve social problems. For better or worse, schools reflect society; they are not now—nor have they ever been—agents of social change. They have a mission to educate students and have little power and no authority to do anything else.

Table 14.1 Characteristics of Troubled Students
1. Has a history of tantrums and uncontrollable angry outbursts
2. Characteristically resorts to name-calling, cursing, or abusive language
3. Habitually makes violent threats when angry
4. Has previously brought a weapon to school
5. Has a background of serious disciplinary problems at school and in the community
6. Has a background of drug, alcohol, or substance abuse or dependency
7. Is on the fringe of his or her peer group with few or no close friends
8. Is preoccupied with weapons, explosives, or other incendiary devices
9. Has previously been truant, suspended, or expelled from school
10. Displays cruelty to animals
11. Has little or no supervision and support from parents or a caring adult
12. Has witnessed or been a victim of abuse or neglect in the home
13. Has been bullied and/or bullies or intimidates peers or younger children
14. Tends to blame others for difficulties and problems he or she causes him- or herself
15. Consistently prefers television shows, movies, or music expressing violent themes or acts
16. Prefers reading material dealing with violent themes, rituals, and abuse
17. Reflects anger, frustration, and the dark side of life in school essays or writing projects
18. Is involved with a gang or an antisocial group on the fringe of peer acceptance
19. Is often depressed and/or has significant mood swings
20. Has threatened or attempted suicide

Note: The National School Safety Center tracks school-associated violent deaths in the United States and has developed a checklist of behaviors to alert teachers and administrators to troubled students. *Source:* www.schoolsafety.us.

Although public schools must initially work with all students, they do not have to mix the disruptive and the potentially violent with the well behaved, nor do they have to encourage violent students to stay in school until graduation. Students who arrive at school ready to learn should be introduced to a rigorous, sound academic education. The academic side of school will matter to them in life. Children come to school to improve their academic skills and increase their store of intellectual capital—the knowledge needed for success in life. As Hirsch (1996) notes, "Sociologists have shown that intellectual capital (i.e., school knowledge) operates in almost every sphere of modern society to determine social class, success or failure in school, and even psychological and physical health" (p. 19). Students are disadvantaged by too small a share of intellectual capital and need to start early and move quickly in securing as much of it as they can. The vast majority of students do not need special curriculum treatments to teach them how to get along with others, settle disputes without violence, or manage aggression. They need academic content to succeed in life, and that's what schools should deliver.

Conflict resolution curricula distract students from academic pursuits and send students an undesirable, if unintended, message: "We expect school to be violent, so let's talk about it" (Devine, 1996, p. 165). Violence is not a way of life for most children. Directing conflict management programs to all students rather than at the violent minority sends a negative message that violence is a normal part of life and that everyone must learn to manage it or otherwise cope with it.

Schools and Violence

Let's look at what we know about potentially violent children and what schools can reasonably do about them. Overly aggressive children should be identified in kindergarten and trained to work on anger management. Although a school cannot replace the family, it can provide some supports found in homes of self-controlled, high-achieving students. For example, school discipline policies should incorporate the reward-and-punishment systems successfully used by middle-class parents. Students should learn that appropriate behavior earns teacher praise and special privileges, while inappropriate behavior results in loss of praise and privilege. This would be reasonable, inexpensive, and not too intrusive on the privacy rights of students or their parents. Working individually with counselors—and not consuming instructional time—violent and potentially violent students should be the focus of appropriate intervention and prevention strategies (Bemak and Keys, 2000).

Schools alone cannot solve problems of violence (Bowen et al., 2002; Osher et al., 2010). Influences of early family experiences and the greater society are pervasive. Research provides little encouragement that school interventions successfully prevent violence, and the research may simply be confirming public knowledge. Of course, schools should try to help all students but not impede the progress of the well behaved. Schools should try every measure to help young children adapt to school and school discipline. But some children never will adjust to academic demands and self-discipline required for success. According to one analysis of U.S. Justice Department statistics, about 6 percent of adolescents are responsible for two-thirds of violent crimes committed by juveniles (Bodine and Crawford, 1998). This tiny percentage of students should not be a major focus of school attention and a constant drain on school budgets. If these students have not learned to control themselves by early adolescence, schools should waste no more time or money on them.

Alternative Schools

When Cesar was in the ninth grade, his career ambition was to become an assassin. His credentials were impressive, urban gang member, hardened street fighter, handgun aficionado. . . . Three years later [as a student in a public alternative high school] he was a captivating poet with a scholarship to a private college. (Leiding, 2008, p. 29)

Educators have long recognized that alternatives in public education are sometimes necessary to serve special populations of students—teenage mothers, for example, or the physically disabled. The one-size-fits-all model of the comprehensive public high school does not serve everyone equally well, and some students rebel against the competition, perceived conformity, and order of traditional education. Many educators now acknowledge that the academic demands and social structure of traditional high schools may contribute to school violence. Students unaccustomed to impersonal rules governing school behavior and the emphasis that schools place on quiet compliance may lash out at teachers and other students (Epp and Watkinson, 1997; Brown and Beckett, 2007). By the time they reach middle school, students learn the focus of schooling is on academic achievement, and unfortunately students who do not achieve well often develop indifferent or hostile attitudes. As one supporter of alternative schools notes, "Their behavior is not irrational. Just as it is rational to embrace the repetition of successful experiences, it is equally rational to avoid repetitions of unsuccessful experiences" (Conrath, 2001, p. 587).

Alternative schools can siphon off the troubled, disaffected, potentially violent, and others for whom traditional schooling is not a good fit. Alternative schools often are better able to serve nonacademic students while allowing traditional schools to focus on the majority's academic needs. Sometimes housed within the regular school building and sometimes in separate facilities of their own, alternative schools are designed for students who, because of any number of problems—academic but more often behavioral or social—are not able to learn well in a traditional school environment. Today, all but three states have some form of alternative school program, sometimes as part of the school, other times as separate buildings with their own faculty and administrators. Alternative schools and programs serve students who are at risk of dropping out of school for any number of reasons. About 6 percent of elementary and secondary schools are alternative schools (Hoffman, 2010).

Alternative schools are likely to be less formal than traditional schools and typically offer a lower student-to-teacher ratio. The record indicates these schools can go a long way toward ameliorating the anonymity and isolation some students experience in traditional schools (Brown and Beckett, 2007; Easton and Soguero, 2011). Many formerly disruptive students behave better when they work in a small, supportive setting. They are able to find a niche that eluded them in traditional schools and teachers willing to focus on personal and social problems that they bring with them to school (Conchas and Rodriguez, 2008).

Alternative schools can be very effective and should be viewed as appropriate educational options for disruptive students who have not responded to special curricular treatment and counseling in regular schools and classes. Unfortunately, although alternative schools try to accommodate students with a wide range of problems, they do not work for everyone. In fact, they may not work well for many of the most disruptive students. The same students who caused problems in traditional schools often continue to present problems when they transfer to alternative schools. For these students, more dramatic action is likely to be in order.

Schools should embrace all students equally when they first begin school. Special curriculum interventions—the so-called conflict and dispute resolution curricula—should be reserved exclusively for students who demonstrate behaviors associated with violence in adults (e.g., physical aggression and lack of self-control). Schools should use every technique at their disposal to curb disruptive behavior and bring the unruly child back into the fold. However, by middle school, students who impede the learning process of their classmates or threaten the welfare of other children should be considered as candidates for alternative schools. Students who are not likely to succeed in one kind of school should be given another chance in a different kind of school. These alternative schools have amassed a sound though not perfect record for educating the disaffected. For the small handful of very disruptive students who are unable to cooperate in an alternative school, expulsion is a harsh but sensible last resort.

Will expelling problem students from the public school system be likely to increase their inclination toward further violence and criminality? Will these students inevitably wind up in the criminal justice system? It is hard to know. Research indicates future dropouts have high levels of criminal behavior while in school, but some evidence indicates that after these students drop out of school, they may have less trouble with the law (Herrnstein and Murray, 1994). Schools often add to the problems of young people. Many students who do not succeed academically feel frustrated. Others feel confined by alienating school rules and the abrasiveness of school crowding (Noguera, 1995; Neumann, 2003; Leiding, 2008; Fuentes, 2011). Some students may learn better in another environment, and schools should find places for such students. Schools are ultimately academic institutions designed to teach cognitive skills. Students who cannot learn to play by the rules of civilized behavior—to exercise self-discipline, order, and respect for others—ultimately have no place in school.

For Discussion

1. In 2011, several students brought suit against their suburban school district in Minnesota. They contend that the district had failed to stop anti-gay bullying because a district policy requiring teachers "to remain neutral on issues of sexual orientation" served to stigmatize homosexuality and protect bullies. The suit contends that anti-gay bullying is ignored, and, in some instances, the victims are blamed for bullies' abusive behavior. Advocates for gay students want the school district to teach tolerance for gay students and actively stop anti-gay bullying. Social conservatives, on the other hand, fear a "homosexual agenda" that teaches tolerance for an "abnormal and unhealthy lifestyle" (Eckholm, 2011).

   Do you support the district's neutrality policy on matters of sexual orientation? How should schools consider homosexuality and same-sex marriage, if at all? Should anti-gay bulling be treated differently than other forms of bullying behavior? Is there a possible middle ground or synthesis between the positions of the advocates for gay students and the social conservatives?

2. Researchers find that students and other youth express bullying in different ways according to gender. Boys tend to be physically aggressive, while girls are "relationally aggressive," that is, harming others through gossip, spreading rumors, and excluding them from social contact (Leff et al., 2007). Does this finding reflect your experiences with bullying and violence in elementary and secondary school?

In your experience, did the schools handle bullying appropriately for both victim and bully? Did the schools respond differently to incidents involving the physical violence of boys and the relational violence of girls? Should they?

3. In Scandinavian countries, corporal punishment is prohibited by law in schools and in homes. Minnesota is the only state in the United States to prohibit corporal punishment of any sort, even by parents (Smith, 2003). The 2006 Program Accreditation Criteria of the National Association for the Education of Young Children (2005) include the following statement about the interactions among teachers and children in preschools, kindergarten, and child care centers: "Teachers [should] abstain from corporal punishment or humiliating or frightening discipline techniques."

Is this a reasonable standard? Should parents have the right to determine whether corporal punishment can be used as a form of discipline on their own children at home or in the public schools they attend?

References

ALVAREZ, A., AND BACHMAN, R. (2008). *Violence: The Enduring Problem*. Los Angeles: Sage.

ASTOR, R. A., et al. (2002). "Public Concern and Focus on School Violence." In *Handbook of Violence*, ed. L. A. Rapp-Paglicci et al. New York: Wiley.

BEMAK, F., AND KEYS, S. (2000). *Violent and Aggressive Youth: Intervention and Prevention Strategies for Changing Times*. Thousand Oaks, CA: Corwin Press.

BODINE, R. J., AND CRAWFORD, D. K. (1998). *The Handbook of Conflict Resolution Education: A Guide to Building Quality Programs in Schools*. San Francisco: Jossey-Bass.

BOWEN, G. L., et al. (2002). "Reducing School Violence: A Social Capacity Framework." In *Handbook of Violence*, ed. L. A. Rapp-Paglicci et al. New York: Wiley.

BROWN, L. H., AND BECKETT, K. S. (2007). *Building Community in an Alternative School*. New York: Peter Lang.

BUSHAW, W. J., AND LOPEZ, S. J. (2011). "The 43rd Annual Phi Delta Kappa/Gallup Poll of the Public's Attitude toward the Public Schools." www.pdkint.org/poll.

CONCHAS, G. Q., AND RODRIGUEZ, F. F. (2008). *Small Schools and Urban Youth*. Thousand Oaks, CA: Sage.

CONRATH, J. (2001). "Changing the Odds for Young People: Next Steps for Alternative Education." *Kappan* 82:585–587.

CORNELL, D. G., AND MAYER, M. J. (2010). "Why Do School Order and Safety Matter?" *Educational Researcher* 39:7–15.

DAVIS, M. R. (2011). "Cyber Bullying." *Education Week Digital Directions*, Winter 2011, 28–33.

DEVINE, J. (1996). *Maximum Security*. Chicago: University of Chicago Press.

DEVINE, J., AND COHEN, J. (2007). *Making Your School Safe: Strategies to Protect Children and Promote Learning*. New York: Teachers College Press.

DEVINE, J., AND LAWSON, H. A. (2003). "The Complexity of School Violence: Commentary from US." In *Violence in Schools: The Response in Europe*, ed. P. K. Smith. New York: Routledge Falmer.

DWORKIN, M. S. (1959). *Dewey on Education*. New York: Teachers College Press.

EASTON, L. B., AND SOGUERO, M. (2011). "Challenging Assumptions: Helping Struggling Students Succeed." *Phi Delta Kappan* 92:27–33.

ECKHOLM, E. (2011). "In Suburb, Battle Goes Public on Bullying of Gay Students." September 13. www.nytimes.com/2011/09/13.

EPP, J. R., AND WATKINSON, A. M. (1997). *Systemic Violence in Education: Broken Promise*. Albany: State University of New York Press.

FINN, C. E., JR. (1993). "Whither Education Reform?" In *Making Schools Work*, ed. C. L. Fagnano and K. N. Hughes. Boulder, CO: Westview Press.

FUENTES, A. (2011). *Lockdown High: When the Schoolhouse Become a Jailhouse*. New York: Verso.

GALEZEWSKI, J. (2005). "Bullying and Aggression among Youth." In *Violence in Schools: Issues, Consequences, and Expressions*, ed. K. Sexton-Radek. Westport, CT: Praeger.

GRIMES, T., ANDERSON, J. A. AND BERGEN, L. (2008). *Media Violence and Aggression: Science and Ideology*. Los Angeles: Sage.

HERRNSTEIN, R. J., AND MURRAY, C. (1994). *The Bell Curve: Intelligence and Class Structure in American Life*. New York: Free Press.

HINDUJA, S., AND PATCHIN, J. W. (2011). "State Cyberbullying Laws." www.cyberbullying.us.

HIRSCH, E. D., JR. (1996). *The Schools We Need and Why We Don't Have Them*. New York: Doubleday.

HOFFMAN, L. (2010). *Numbers and Types of Public Elementary and Secondary Schools from Common Core Data: School Year 2007–2008*. Washington, DC: U.S. Department of Education.

International Association of Chiefs of Police, Bureau of Justice Assistance. (2009). *Guide for Preventing and Responding to School Violence*. 2nd Ed. Alexandria, VA: U.S. Department of Justice.

JORDAN, K. (2002). "School Violence among Culturally Diverse Populations." In *Handbook of Violence*, ed. L. A. Rapp-Paglicci et al. New York: Wiley.

KUNKEL, D., AND ZWARUN, L. (2006). "How Real Is the Problem of TV Violence?" In *Handbook of Children, Culture, Culture, and Violence*, ed. N. E. Dowd and R. F. Wilson. Thousand Oaks, CA: Sage.

LABASH, M. (2005). "Antibullying Programs Are Ineffective and Unnecessary." In *How Can School Violence Be Prevented?*, ed. S. Barbour. Detroit: Greenhaven.

LAWTON, M. (1994). "Violence-Prevention Curricula: What Works Best?" *Education Week*, November 9, 1, 10–11.

LEFF, S. S., et al. (2007). "Using a Participatory Action Research Model to Create a School-Based Intervention Program for Relationally Aggressive Girls—The Friend to Friend Program." In *Bullying, Victimization, and Peer Harassment*, ed. J. E. Zins, M. J. Elias, and C. A. Maher. New York: Haworth.

LEIDING, D. (2008). *The Hows and Whys of Alternative Education*. Lanham, MD: Rowman & Littlefield.

MACNEIL, G. (2002). "School Bullying: An Overview." In *Handbook of Violence*, ed. L. A. Rapp-Paglicci et al. New York: Wiley.

MAYER, M. J., AND FURLONG, M. J. (2010). "How Safe Are Our Schools?" *Educational Researcher* 39:16–26.

MCQUADE, S. C., COLT, J. P., AND MEYER, N. B. B. (2009). *Cyber-Bullying: Protecting Kids. and Adults from Online Bullies*. Westport, CT: Praeger.

National Association for the Education of Young Children. (2005). "Early Childhood Program Standards and Accreditation Criteria." www.naeyc.org/accreditation/criteria98.asp.

NEUMANN, R. (2003). *Sixties Legacy: A History of the Public Alternative Schools Movement, 1967–2001*. New York: Peter Lang.

NOGUERA, P. A. (1995). "Preventing and Producing Violence: A Critical Analysis of Responses to School Violence." *Harvard Educational Review* 65:189–212.

OLWEUS, D. (1993). *Bullying at School: What We Know and What We Can Do*. Cambridge, MA: Blackwell.

———. (2008). *Bullying Is Not a Fact of Life*. Rockville, MD: U.S. Department of Health and Human Services.

OSHER, D., BEAR, G. G., SPRAGUE, J. R., AND DOYLE, W. (2010). "How Can We Improve School Discipline?" *Educational Researcher* 39:48–58.

RAVITCH, D. (2001). "Education and Democracy." In *Making Good Citizens: Education and Civil Society*, ed. D. Ravitch and J. P. Viteritti. New Haven, CT: Yale University Press.

ROBERS, S., ZHANG, J., AND TRUMAN, J. (2010). *Indicators of School Crime and Safety.* Washington, DC: U.S. Department of Education.

ROBINSON, J. P., AND ESPELAGE, D. L. (2011). "Inequities in Educational and Psychological Outcomes between LGBTQ and Straight Students in Middle and High School." *Educational Researcher* 40:315–330.

SMITH, J. D., RYAN, W., AND COUSINS, J. B. (2007). "Antibullying Programs: A Survey of Evaluation Activities in Public Schools." *Studies in Educational Evaluation* 33:120–134.

SMITH, P. K., ed. (2003). *Violence in Schools: The Response in Europe.* New York: Routledge Falmer.

SMITH-HEAVENRICH, S. (2005). "Bullies in the Schoolyard," in *School Violence*, ed. K. Burns. Farmington Hills, MI: Greenhaven Press.

SWEARER, S. M., ET AL., (2010). "What Can Be Done about School Bullying? Linking Research to Educational Practice." *Educational Researcher* 39:38–47.

TREND, D. (2007). *The Myth of Media Violence: A Critical Introduction.* Malden, MA: Oxford University Press.

U.S. Department of Education. (2010). "Indicators of School Crime and Safety." December. http://nces.ed.gov/programs/crimeindicators2010.

U.S. Department of Health and Human Services. (2011). "StopBullying.Gov." www.stopbullying.gov.

U.S. Department of Justice. (2010). "Indicators of School Crime & Safety, December 2010." http://nces.ed.gov/programs/crimeindicators2010.

U.S. General Accounting Office. (1997). "Substance Abuse and Violence Prevention." Testimony before the Subcommittee on Oversight and Investigations, Committee on Education and the Workforce House of Representatives. Washington, DC: U.S. General Accounting Office.

ZINS, J. E., ELIAS, M. J., AND MAHER, C. A. (2007). *Bullying, Victimization, and Peer Harassment: A Handbook of Prevention and Intervention.* New York: Haworth.

CHAPTER 15

Inclusion and Disability: Common or Special Education

When and why should selected children be provided inclusive or special treatment in schools?

POSITION 1: FOR FULL INCLUSION

Implementing inclusion effectively requires schools to make adjustments in order to fully accommodate students with disabilities. Unfortunately, many schools failed to make these changes.

—Ferri and Connor (2005, p. 467)

The sad irony has been that minorities have been disproportionately perceived as needing to be served in separate programs that have increased their isolation from the educational mainstream and limited their access to the kind of education valued by that mainstream.

—Harry et al. (2008)

Full inclusion of all children into school life is a fundamental principle in a free, democratic society. Full inclusion means that students who were classified "special" or "exceptional" because of individual physical or mental characteristics would not be isolated into separate schools, separate classes, or pullout sessions. They would be full citizens and members of the school community in regular classes and also legitimate participants in schools' multiple activities. Inclusion is consistent with fundamental principles of our society and with the law (Vargas, 1999; Kluth et al., 2001; Ferri and Connor, 2005; Oakes, 2005; Smith, 2010; Salend, 2011). The United States should do no less than provide full inclusion (Grossman, 1998; Koenig and Bachman, 2004; Wolbrecht and Hero, 2005; Cameron, 2008). Shevin (2007) makes it plain: "Inclusion is good for—even essential—to a thriving democracy" (p. xiii).

As a matter of human concern and fairness, we should not separate those who differ from the rest. Inclusive schools recognize the richness in human diversity. Cushner, McClelland, and Safford (2000) offer a philosophic and historic case for the inclusion of exceptional children:

> From its inception, a fundamental characteristic of American schooling has been its intended inclusiveness, across social boundaries, of gender, class, and—belatedly—race. Today, the term inclusion refers to the practice of including another group of students in regular classrooms, those with problems of health and/or physical, developmental, and emotional problems. . . . Like societal inclusion, inclusive education implies fully shared participation of diverse individuals in common experiences. (pp. 161, 163)

Similarly, Danforth (2008) presents philosophic grounds based on John Dewey's classic works on democracy—and proposing the unification of individual and social interests in a "coherent democratic framework" (p. 61). That framework does not make individual rights and needs, as in traditional special education, necessarily the opposite of social interests and values; it suggests unifying them to achieve a higher level of society.

Not only is inclusion a matter of fundamental principles and law, but it is better educationally—for students and teachers. (Kids Together, Inc., 2012)

Inclusion Is More than Mere Addition

Full inclusion expects far more of good education than merely adding classified students to general classes or mandating all students to run, climb, read, write, draw, or compute in only one way and at the same speed. Full inclusion assumes that schools will provide high-quality, individualized instruction, with well-prepared teachers, suitable and varied teaching materials, and appropriate schedules to support the idea that all students are capable of success. The principle of full inclusion merely extends the democratic principle of quality education for all to include children with special needs (Skiba et al., 2008).

The 1994 policy guidelines of the U.S. Department of Education specify that schools may not use lack of resources or personnel as an excuse for not providing free and appropriate education—in the least restrictive environments—to students with disabilities. But school districts have been very slow to follow the law and the policies. In the two decades since 1986, the percentage of students with intellectual disabilities who were in general classrooms more than 80 percent of the school time grew only 3.2 percent to a low 11.6 percent (Smith, 2010). That is almost no change. The common excuses of schools simply do not meet the standards set by the law: "we don't provide inclusion," "this child is too disabled to be in a regular classroom," and "we give them special programs." The law and supporting court decisions require inclusion unless the severity of the disability precludes satisfactory education in regular classes. This high standard does not allow schools to ignore or dismiss the requirement to provide inclusion for the vast majority of students with disabilities (Kluth et al., 2001; Cigman, 2007).

The Department of Education has implemented strong programs to implement the primary purposes of quality education for children with disabilities under the Individuals with Disabilities Education Act (IDEA). Response To Intervention (RTI) is a tiered instructional process to identify struggling students early, to provide research-based instruction, and to closely monitor progress. The National Center for Learning Disabilities (www.ncld.org) supports the RTI Action Network (www.rtinetwork.org), which offers assistance to schools, teacher, parents, and officials in developing RTI in the schools. Success in this effort is dependent largely on effective implementation by well-prepared teachers in positive school settings, for which the research- and evidence-based approach offers grounded teacher practice and close monitoring (Case, Speece, and Molloy, 2003; Jimerson, Burns, and VanDerHeyden, 2007; Glover and Vaughn, 2010). RTI is an approach fully consistent with inclusive education.

Another area of interest to the Department of Education and to scholars in the area of disabilities education is the transition of disabled children into and through schools and from schools to postschool adult life in work, further education, integration into their communities, and related positive development of adult living skills. Positive behavior support is an ongoing theme for this work. One of the foci of federal interest is the Rehabilitation Services Administration (www.rsa.ed.gov), which oversees grants and activities to help individuals with physical and mental disabilities to gain employment, to live more independently, and to be successful in the community and in the labor market. The Rehabilitation Services Administration produces annual reviews and conducts state-by-state monitoring to judge progress, with agency report cards that rank states on several criteria related to success. This interest in the constructive, positive, and productive participation of disabled people is consistent with full inclusion approaches in schools.

Full inclusion does not mean that schools should bring in students with special needs only to insist on blind conformity to a single standard for all students, nor does it mean that nonconforming students should be ignored or mistreated in "regular" schools (Danforth and Smith, 2005). Rather, the concept of inclusion assumes that the individual needs of every student, whether classified "special" or not, seriously must be considered to provide a quality education. This assumption undergirds the idea of full inclusion for students who are "special" or "exceptional."

The Legal Basis for Full Inclusion

Over the past quarter of a century, the U.S. Congress has shown its intent that all children with disabilities be provided a free and appropriate education in public schools. A series of modifications in supportive legislation, from 1975 to the present, have improved the educational rights of children with disabilities and their families. Full inclusion is the next logical step. Turnbull and Turnbull (1998) defined this evolving policy as "Zero Reject" and noted that an important effect was "to redefine the doctrine of equal educational opportunity as it applies to children with disabilities and to establish different meanings of equality as it applies to people with and without disabilities" (p. 92). Earlier laws relied on a concept of equality that meant equal access to different resources; children attended separate special education classes and schools. The newer laws assume that equal access means full access to regular resources—regular classes and schools but with special support to help students.

The principle of inclusion goes well beyond the mainstreaming that developed since the 1975 landmark federal legislation, the Education of All Handicapped Children Act (Public Law 94-142). At the time Congress was considering this law, 1 million out of 8 million disabled children under age twenty-one were completely excluded from the U.S. public school system. They were "outcast children" (Dickman, 1985, p. 181). Mainstreaming grew out of an important clause of the law, offering the concept of the "least restrictive environment"— meaning that students with special needs who "demonstrate appropriate behavior and skills" should be in general classrooms rather than segregated programs. The law gave some children with special needs the educational, emotional, and social advantages offered to other students. It also gave parents the right to be advocates in fashioning an appropriate education for their differently abled children.

Important changes in the law led toward full inclusion. The IDEA law and its 2004 renewal require schools to offer a set of placement options to meet the needs of students with disabilities and that, to the maximum extent appropriate, children with disabilities are to be educated with other children. Further, the law expects schools to provide supplementary aids and services for disabled children when needed, and it requires that any separate schooling or other removal of children with disabilities from the regular environment occur only when the child cannot learn in regular classes even with supplementary aids and services. This sets a high standard for schools to meet in order to exclude disabled students from regular classes.

Laws and court decisions are more expansive in their recognition of individual and social benefits of inclusion. *Mills v. Board of Education of the District of Columbia* (1972) produced a judgment in class-action litigation based on the foundational arguments of equal opportunity and due process. The judge in the *Mills* case decreed that children with physical or mental disabilities had a right to a suitable and free public education and that lack of funds was not a defense for exclusion. Full inclusion draws support from the courts (*Oberti v. Board of Education of the Borough of Clementon (NJ) School District*, 1993).

Democratic Purposes for Inclusion

At the center of education in a democracy are the concepts of equal opportunity and justice. Democracy, by its very nature, requires all citizens to have the opportunity to be fully educated. Equal opportunity and fairness underscore the idea of inclusion. There are many other important reasons for inclusion of special students in regular school classes and activities, but the fundamental premise of democracy expects no less (Burrello et al., 2001).

Education is the primary means for realizing the goals of the Declaration of Independence and the Constitution. Isolating special education students not only labels and stigmatizes them but also limits their full interaction with others during their most formative years. This is detrimental to these students and also is detrimental to the perceptions of nonexceptional students about life in the full society.

In addition to the obvious educational value of allowing all students to participate fully in the schools, inclusion is also a civil rights issue. Discrimination against persons with disabilities has been legally outlawed in the United States. The 1990 Americans with Disabilities Act barred such discrimination, just as other laws barred discrimination based on race, gender, or age.

Some institutions meet the access requirements of the Americans with Disabilities Act on purely physical grounds, providing ramps and elevators as well as stairs and modifying doors and bathrooms. This minimal approach would be the equivalent of simply removing "White Only" signs after racial discrimination was ruled illegal and doing nothing more; it still would not deal with underlying, more pervasive instances of institutional discrimination restricting access and opportunity. In a larger context, education is a primary means of access to all of society's opportunities. Separate-but-equal education for African Americans was actually separate but not equal; similarly, separate special education is also separate but not equal.

Social Context of Disabilities

Disability studies is a developing, broad-based approach to understanding social, cultural, economic, political, and historic identification and treatment of people with disabilities. It is an interdisciplinary field involving scholars in the humanities, social sciences, education, and science, with a focus on the interrelationship between disabilities and society. Topics of examination include the core question of how disabilities are defined, measured, and treated and the corollary/opposite idea that there is no such thing since all individuals have some physical or mental difference from the norm so that the line of separation is necessarily arbitrary and probably misleading. Disability studies is not limited to educational issues but relates to all segments of society, from the arts to zeitgeist, the intellectual and cultural climate of a time period. Some of the most important works cover literature, aesthetics, history, bioethics, critical theory, and human rights (Goffman, 1961; Batson and Bergman, 2002; Scully, 2008; Siebers, 2008, 2010; Valle, 2009; Garland Thomson, 2010; Smith, 2010). The Society for Disability Studies (www.disstudies.org), about twenty-five years old, and its journal, *Disabilities Studies Quarterly*, provide thoughtful discussion of issues.

The traditional definitions of and treatment for disabilities rely on medical views of whether the person can function in particular settings. This often identifies the disabled as somehow deficient and less worthy. More recent examinations in the field of disability studies examine cultural and social environments as determinants of disability and criticize negative social responses. This critical approach looks at orientations like social class and status, privilege and power, and the individually and socially detrimental results from ideologically limited views of disability. A third approach, related to the second, looks at minority status and disability through consideration of such factors as race, gender, age, ethnicity, sexual orientation, religion, national derivation, and language facility.

Exclusion and Segregation: Racism and Ableism

The long and strong effort to exclude some special needs students from regular school classes and activities has remarkable parallels with the racial segregation efforts of times past, as Ferri and Connor (2005) suggest:

> As in the case of school desegregation, the movement from segregated placements toward more inclusive ones for students with disabilities has involved a long and often difficult struggle. . . . Yet even when school systems have shifted to more inclusive practices because of legal requirements, the results were often characterized as cosmetic or shallow.

There are many parallels between how our society has treated minority children and how it has treated disabled children in schools. One is a function of forms of racism, the other a function of forms of ableism. Where they coincide is corrosive of our democracy and social values. One of the striking things about school-based classification of children into special education classes, programs, or schools is that students placed in the special category come disproportionately from minority ethnic and social class groups of society (Educational Testing Service, 1980; Heller, Holtzman, and Messick, 1982; Anderson and Anderson, 1983; Brantlinger and Guskin, 1987; Ferri and Connor, 2005; Artiles and Bal, 2008; Valle, 2009). Obviously, this combination of class, race, and classification as disabled becomes a recipe for discrimination. This parallel discrimination should be addressed as a civil rights issue on principle and a political issue in practice. Class and ethnicity have been used politically to limit the full participation of groups without wealth and power. Children with special needs have been subject to a similar political agenda restricting access, opportunity, and fulfillment of the democratic ideal (Barton, 1988; Harry et al., 2008).

Meier (2005), studying school board actions and educational politics, argues,

> At the extremes this [grouping and sorting children] includes sorting students into a variety of special education classifications or into various honors or college prep options. . . . Studies consistently find that minorities are assigned in disproportionate numbers to special education, lower ability groups, and vocational tracks and advanced classes, advanced placement classes, gifted programs, and college prep tracks. (p. 239)

Oakes (2005), following up on her famous study of inequality in schools, notes, "Thus, through tracking, schools continue to replicate existing inequality along lines of race and social class and contribute to the intergenerational transmission of social and economic inequality" (p. xi).

Exceptionality among individuals is a constant in human history. This condition of "abnormality" has historically been the basis for a variety of destructive actions by those in power, from infanticide to institutionalization. Poore (2007), for example, documents how the German treatment of children with disabilities changed over the twentieth century, including hiding them as invalids, starving them to death in institutions, and reducing them to street beggars or freak-show status in the Weimar Republic; sterilizing them through eugenics during the Third Reich; and increasingly providing education and opportunities for independence and self-determination in later decades. In many ways, this parallels the experiences of the disabled in the United States and other parts of the world over the same time period. Winzer's (1993) comprehensive history of special education is based on a pertinent principle: "A society's treatment of those who are weak and dependent is one critical indicator of its social progress. Social attitudes concerning the education and care of exceptional individuals reflect general cultural attitudes concerning the obligations of a society to its individual citizens" (p. 3). This, in the United States and in the civilized world, is a civil rights issue based on the most fundamental documents and foundational moral principles (Rotatori Obiakor, and Bakken, 2011).

Social Policy Considerations

Beyond the obvious democratic and civil rights concerns raised by separating special needs children from their peers in schools, there are other defects in this policy. As a matter of social policy, separation is inconsistent with the larger-scale interests of the United States (Sailor, Gerry, and Wilson, 1991; Shevin, 2007; Danforth, 2008).

Broad social policy goals underlie the tenets of inclusion for special needs youth in all society's activities and institutions. Full participation in the society requires full inclusion in the schools. Denying those rights to the disabled denies society the skills, the economic productivity, and the social and political values inherent in full participation of individuals with disabilities.

In the period before 1910, the United States had a pattern of institutionalizing children with disabilities in isolation from society. Families of these children hid them, provided private care, or sent them to institutions where they would live out their lives away from public view or participation. Changing public attitudes regarding our social responsibility for persons with disabilities, as well as a recognition of the general economic and social value in providing training for disadvantaged people, led to a variety of alterations in social policies and educational practices. This occurred at the same time as public schooling expanded in the early twentieth century. For the disabled, this meant segregation in separate schools and/or separate classes, teachers, and programs. The intent may have been benign, but segregation is inadequate as a social policy.

Social and Psychological Arguments for Inclusion

In addition to persuasive arguments based on fundamental democratic principles and on fair social policy in favor of full inclusion, social and personal psychology offer other important arguments. Separation of exceptional children from the mainstream of children in schools has been recognized as traumatic for those separated, whether by race, gender, or abilities. In the landmark Supreme Court decision that declared racially segregated schools and the concept of "separate but equal" unconstitutional (*Brown v. Board of Education of Topeka, Kansas,* 1954), Chief Justice Earl Warren argued that separation in schools can cause children to "generate a feeling of inferiority as to . . . status in the community that may affect their hearts and minds in a way unlikely ever to be undone" (p. 493).

Obviously, perceptions of special needs children are strongly influenced by their separation. It goes beyond individual feelings of insecurity to the concept that society values them less and prefers them out of sight (Shevin, 2007; Valle, 2009; Alur and Bach, 2010; Smith, 2010).

Avoiding Foreseeable Failures in Inclusive Practices

Positive inclusion in schools depends on collaborative efforts by regular and special education teachers, parents, and administrators. Ill-prepared, poorly organized past efforts at mainstreaming must be avoided in inclusion. Teacher preparation and in-service programs should integrate the most useful knowledge from special education research and practice and should emphasize special methods for dealing with a wide range of students and for individualizing lessons (Cooley et al., 2008; see www.disabilitystudiesfor teachers.org).

Not only are there serious detrimental consequences for the individual exceptional children who are placed in isolated or separated situations, but "average" children are likewise deprived of realistic social interaction and a more compassionate understanding of others' lives. Additionally, the community as a whole suffers from the suspicion, distrust, and misunderstanding created by separation (Risko and Bromley, 2001; Siebers, 2008, 2010).

The "Exceptional" and the "Average"

Identification and measurement of exceptionality is a tradition in modern society, though it varies to some extent by nation and time period (Taylor, 2003). Currently, in the United States, exceptionality usually refers to observable or measurable differences in physical, mental, emotional, or other abilities. In school terms, exceptional children differ from nonexceptional ones based on school achievement, for example, in reading, writing, listening, sitting attentively, seeing and hearing, and so on. Exceptionality in the United States has included both extremes of mental ability—the severely mentally or learning impaired and the gifted and talented. Both get special treatment and school support. The category of exceptional children also includes those with a variety of measured physical differences from "average" children, including differences in sight, hearing, and use of limbs, but does not include those with extraordinary physical abilities. Similarly, only one end of the potential spectrum of emotional abilities is included in the exceptional category: only those labeled emotionally impaired. There are some problems, then, with consistency in the way we apply the definition of "exceptional."

Causes of exceptionality include genetics, at-birth disabilities, improper medical practice, disease, parental irresponsibility, accidents, and inadequate health care. These exceptionalities are not self-inflicted; they are often chance happenings, as in afflictions caused by accidents, birth defects, or childhood disease. Although exceptionality, in these terms, is relatively rare, it should not create a wall of separation from the rest of society; human variety is extraordinarily complex and incredibly wide ranging. We have improved our measures, but the extent of human variability remains unknown. Further, the classifications themselves reflect cultural norms and prejudices.

The category of "disabled," "exceptional," or "handicapped" depends on the society, time period, and societal norms. *Disability*, according to Dickman (1985), is a deficit that occurs at birth or through disease or some other event, while handicaps are the secondary problems that occur because of discrimination, mistreatment, or help that is denied or delayed. The term *handicapped*, by this definition, represents a social problem of bias and discrimination, while disability is an individual problem. For another example, the category of "learning disabled," used widely in U.S. schools, varies significantly in the measures used to define it. The term is not used in developing nations, where certain forms of technological literacy are not as important, nor is it used much in the corporate world to define categories of people (Cushner et al., 2000; Cameron, 2008; Rotatori et al., 2011). And technology can aid the disabled (Jaeger, 2012).

Much of the history of prejudice and discrimination against exceptional children has been based on a false sense of the meaning of "average" and on people's insecurities about their own abilities and talents. Those who differ often are labeled negatively to maintain the status of the favored. Although we often refer to an average, there may be no actual "average" person in genetic traits, social characteristics, or preferred individual behavior. Who among us come from a family of 2.3 children; are exactly average in height, weight, IQ, and shoe size; earn average grades or average test scores; and desire an average marriage when over 50 percent end in divorce? Each of us does many things far better or far worse than the average. Average also suggests dullness and conformity; richness comes from diversity. Average is suitable as a broad guide for making tentative comparative judgments about many conditions, such as income tax deductions or sleep time needed each day, but should not be mindlessly used as a criterion to rank human qualities against. Exceptional children are exceptional when compared with certain measures of average, but every child differs from average in some respect.

Meeting Potential Problems in Full Inclusion

Full inclusion of all children into the lives of schools is not an easy task. As is clear from the history of special education, many problems are associated with implementing full inclusion. Schools must address the fears of some parents, teachers, administrators, and community members by developing strong programs of information, discussion, preparation, and positive interaction. Special education teachers may fear losing their expert status and, perhaps, their jobs; regular teachers are concerned about their lack of preparation and about no longer being able to send annoying students to special education classes. Thousand and Villa (1995) identify frequently cited causes of school intractability as "(1) inadequate teacher preparation; (2) inappropriate organizational structures, policies, and procedures; (3) lack of attention to the cultural aspects of schooling; and (4) poor leadership" (p. 53).

Smith (2010) adds other impediments:

- The power of behaviorist scholars
- Outmoded models of curriculum
- Fear—of disruption, difficulty, and social attitudes
- Tradition
- Teacher attitudes
- Low expectations

These factors have a detrimental impact on efforts to develop full inclusion programs in schools. We need improved teacher education to better prepare teachers for educating diverse students and meeting individual student needs. Regular education teachers also need assistance in changing their teaching practices and working with special education teachers and parents on well-designed and well-implemented plans for individual students. We need to shake the lockstep curriculum, tracking, and teacher isolation common in the current school structure. We must seek involvement and support, provide high-quality assistance and incentives for improvement, and enlist school faculty and administrators in the process of full inclusion to implement the best forms.

We can learn from some of the mistakes made in trying to implement mainstreaming without thorough preparation. Mainstreaming has been a success in many schools and in the lives of many individual students who had previously been shunted to separate schools or classes. It also has been especially successful in alleviating the separation and isolation of special education students and in bringing their situation to light. The needs of these students and previous inadequacies of schools in meeting their needs now are part of the public discourse.

Mainstreaming failures in some schools usually occurred where students with special needs were dumped into existing classes without adequate support—without preparing school staff or community or considering students' individual needs. Some special needs students were unable to demonstrate "appropriate behavior and skills" under school guidelines, and these schools made little effort to change programs or personnel to ensure students' success (Lombardi and Ludlow, 1996; Low, 2007). Mainstreaming became popular in the 1980s, but many schools and teachers were unprepared to handle special needs and faltered or were unnecessarily limited in their vision and operation. The most severely disabled students still are mainstreamed in only a few classes each day, usually classes such as art and physical education.

The individualized education plan (IEP) increases participation of general education teachers in planning for special needs students through membership on IEP teams and the development of a student's IEP. In addition, schools must consider how the student's disability affects involvement and performance in the school's general curriculum.

Inclusion, beyond mainstreaming, offers children with special needs the opportunity to be educated to "the maximum extent appropriate" in "the school or classroom he or she would otherwise have attended if he or she did not have a disability" (Rogers, 1993). Inclusion offers a broad educational program even more consistent with a society based on democracy and ethics.

Global Needs for Inclusive Education

Full inclusion is not a topic limited to the United States. Moderate to severe disabilities affect about 5.2 percent of the world population. This figure includes 7.7 percent of populations of developed countries and 4.5 percent of populations of less developed regions. The total number of disabled persons is estimated to reach over 300 million in the early twenty-first century. Disparity between proportions of disabled persons in developed and less developed areas of the world reflects differences in the definitions of disabled, in health practices, and in governmental policies on reporting disabilities in different nations. Improvements in health practices throughout the world are expected to cause an increased proportion of disabled persons since children who previously might have died at birth or in infancy will survive but may have serious impairments (Mittler, Brouillette, and Harris, 1993; UNESCO, 2008).

In many nations, integration of children with special needs into regular schools is a contemporary movement (see inclusiveschools.org). For example, Italy has developed national policies for integration, the United Kingdom has established legislative policies encouraging local schools to integrate, and Austria provides model experimental projects to demonstrate the value of integration (Wedell, 1993; Sefa Dei et al., 2000; Gibson and Haynes, 2009). The United Nations has a history of concern for children, including children with disabilities; the 1959 Declaration of the Rights of the Child recognized the right of every child to develop to his or her full capacity. The United Nations Convention on the Rights of the Child (1989) affirmed the right to an education and, for disabled children, services that "shall be designed to ensure that the disabled child has effective access to and receives education, training, health care services, rehabilitation services, preparation for employment, and recreational opportunities in a manner conducive to the child's achieving the fullest possible social integration and individual development" (Article 23, 3). The United Nations Convention on the Rights of Persons with Disabilities (2007) is a current international document recognizing global dimensions of disability issues. UNESCO (2008) sponsors a major program, Education for All, having a focus on quality inclusive education. The United States has, over the past several decades, met or surpassed the legislative expectations of international human rights documents regarding disabled children.

A sense of justice in society requires that all citizens have equal opportunity to build fulfilling lives in the society and the economy. We don't need, as individuals or as a society, forced separation and the stigmatization that results. It is ethically and practically inconsistent to continue separating children with special needs from other children in our schools.

POSITION 2: SPECIAL PROGRAMS HELP SPECIAL STUDENTS

I have heard stories from high school friends of mine who used to go to regular schools about what it was like to be "mainstreamed." They didn't get all the attention they needed, which is why they made a change and came to my school."

—Charlotte Farber, in Buchman (2006, p. 194)

General-education teachers are the primary caregivers in these full-inclusion classrooms, but their load and the classroom responsibilities have already increased with the additional number of classified special education students, not to mention the additional crowding in already crowded regular-education classrooms!

—Callard-Szulgit (2005, p. xii)

A central point of IDEA is that "to the maximum extent appropriate," disabled children will be educated with those who are not. Claims that this requires schools to place all disabled children in regular classrooms are faulty. Full inclusion advocates ignore the significance of the term *maximum extent appropriate* in the law. Inclusion is not mandated by the law; the word is not even stated there.

For many disabled children, placement into regular classrooms is a physical, mental, and emotional challenge that should not be mandated and is not "appropriate." Inclusion as an idea can mislead regular teachers into inappropriate treatment of special students in their classes. Special needs of individual students come in many varieties and regular teachers are often unprepared for all of them. Teacher actions may be well intentioned but inappropriate. School conditions may also be inappropriate. Bakken (2010) explains why general education classrooms are not the best place for all disabled students. He argues that schools need a continuum of educational placements for learners of a variety of special and diverse needs. Students with disabilities need special, individualized instructional programs with time for special work. The current climate in general education schools and classrooms does not lend itself easily or well to inclusive practices.

Academic requirements of the No Child Left Behind Act, overcrowding, district curricular or testing requirements, and financing problems cause schools and teachers to standardize classroom work and limit individualization (Kabzems, 2003; Taylor, 2003; Koenig and Bachman, 2004). That is detrimental to students with special needs. Inclusion may not be the best choice for all (Cromwell, 2004). But full inclusion advocates seem to ignore significant distinctions among children and the pressures on teachers and schools. With misdiagnosis and inappropriate treatment, inadequate preparation of regular teachers, and the increasing standardization in regular classes, full inclusion means that special children are not treated specially (Kauffman et al., 2002; Buchman, 2006).

Disabled youngsters have a particularly difficult situation, one that requires special treatment by special people. There was a time when disabled children were considered less than human and were sacrificed, shunned, ignored, and institutionalized. Thankfully, that bleak period passed long ago. In the United States, recognition of the special educational and emotional needs of disabled children is one of our finest traditions over the last half a century. These children need more than what we provide in regular classrooms; they deserve special care. That special care does not include poor-quality education, improperly prepared teachers, misdiagnosis of disabilities, prejudiced classmates and school staff, unsuitable curriculums, or dumping in regular classrooms to satisfy the unthoughtful do-gooders. We need only read the papers and reports to recognize that regular schools leave much to be desired in the education of regular students; how can they be expected to educate special students?

Humane and thinking people would not require a truly disabled child to undergo even more traumatic experiences to satisfy a stark, inflexible, and ill-informed interpretation of a law. But that is the apparent position of those who press for full inclusion of children into standard classroom settings. Certainly, for some mildly disabled children, placement in regular classes, along with specially trained teachers, special programs, and appropriate instruction and standards, will help and should be provided. But inflexible interpretation of laws adds further to potential damage to children and to schools.

For Careful Inclusion of Individuals

Full inclusion is not necessary in schools. Thoughtfully involving certain children with special needs in regular school classes and activities, on an individual basis and in suitable situations, offers benefits to schools and to children. Careful inclusion of many students, offered by a well-prepared school district to parents of children whose academic work is likely to be enhanced and whose behavior is not likely to disrupt the education of others, is a positive step. But careful inclusion is not full inclusion. Some describe the difference as "hard versus soft" inclusion, the radical universalists versus the moderates (Low, 2007).

Obviously, we already have careful inclusion in many good schools. Expert diagnosis, classification, parental involvement, individually developed special education programs, close evaluation of progress, and, for some, graduated access to regular classes have provided inclusion for individual students in many schools. These schools provide disabled children and their families with excellent resources, fine-tuned to the child's specific needs and carefully crafted to support the child's development. A focus on the child's highly individual needs and development is fundamental to this process.

Fads and schools go hand in hand. The best place to find the newest fads in young people's language, music, dress, and manners is in schools. Not only are fads in popular culture highly noticeable, but schools are the birthplace of many other types of fads, often as a response to calls for school or social reform. Unfortunately, many of these educational fads are poorly thought out and counterproductive.

Full inclusion appears to be one of the latest examples of education's susceptibility to fads and slogans. The damage that full inclusion policies and practices may create for the very children they claim to help can be significant. Full inclusion carries negative implications for schools, teachers, parents, children, and the community. Worse, the "pro-inclusionists" hide the inherent defects of inclusion behind noble-sounding slogans; they label opponents who speak against full inclusion as insensitive, inhumane, or undemocratic (Petch-Hogan and Haggard, 1999; Cromwell, 2004).

The mainstreaming movement, which thrust many disabled children into regular classrooms without adequate preparation for them and their new teachers and with excessive expectations, elicited the same type of defensive rhetoric. Reasonable people who argued against large-scale mainstreaming have been chastised, pilloried, or ignored. Full inclusion has become another politically correct view, even though it would damage effective special assistance programs our schools have spent years to develop and improve. As many experts (Kauffman and Hallahan, 1995; Kauffman, 2002; Bakken, 2010) suggest, full inclusion is an illusion because general classrooms and schools will never be capable of meeting the needs of all special or exceptional students. These children require separate assistance and facilities to meet their needs. Children with special needs suffer most from full inclusion. Kennedy and Fisher (2001) point out, "After almost 20 years of specific federal support through the Individuals with Disabilities Education Act (IDEA) of 1990, Public Law 101-476, [and other legislation], fewer than half of the students who receive special education services graduate with a diploma."

The U.S. Census Bureau (2011) reports the following data on the disabled:

- 12 percent of the civilian population, some 36 million people
- 5 percent of children ages five to seventeen
- 10 percent of people ages eighteen to sixty-four
- 37 percent of people age sixty-five and beyond

Disabilities include difficulty with the following:

- Hearing: 10 million people
- Vision: 6.5 million people
- Concentration: 13.5 million people
- Walking: 19.5 million people

Currently, 72 percent of the disabled are not in the workforce, and 21 percent are below the poverty level. About 28 percent have less than high school graduation, and only 13 percent have bachelor's or higher degrees.

These data indicate that the most serious social problems are with older adults, not with school-age children. This small percentage should be getting special schooling to better prepare them to graduate and/or find appropriate employment. The variations among the types and severity of disabilities suggest how unlikely it is that any given school district will have general education teachers and courses that can accommodate and adequately fulfill the legal and social requirements to responsibly educate these children for productive lives.

Regular classrooms and schools are designed to have nearly all students move more or less in unison to complete a diploma; they are not appropriate places to have the necessary interest, capabilities, and support for the special needs child. It will not be long before the early blush of full inclusion wears off for those teachers, students, and school staff—leaving the special needs child and family without proper attention and education (Ledoux, Graves, and Burt, 2012). This is the fallout from the uncritical rush toward full inclusion.

Typical special education programs provide specially trained teachers and paraprofessionals, smaller class sizes, adjusted curricula, and fairer competition. Such programs allow parents and teachers to jointly fashion an individualized program that maximizes the child's strengths and remediates areas of need. They are also able to access experts outside the school to assist children with special needs in preparing for the transition from school to work life.

Full Inclusion and Common Classroom Limits

Full inclusion limits regular classroom teachers by requiring them to allot extra time, materials, and energy to children who need extra support as well as requiring them to prepare and monitor individual education plans for each of these children. Full inclusion also limits nondisabled children by diverting time and energy from teachers to meet the special needs of a few students and by sometimes disrupting their schoolwork when the behaviors of a child with special needs are inappropriate in a general classroom. Finally, full inclusion limits the school's ability to make educational decisions in the best interests of individual students. Full inclusion is a form of social engineering that cannot fulfill what it promises without serious repercussions for children and schools. Disruption and discipline problems can occur when some disabled students are mainstreamed or fully included in regular classes.

A study by the General Accounting Office ("Student Discipline: Individuals with Disabilities Act," 2001), noted that 81 percent of public middle and high schools surveyed responded that they had one or more incidents of "serious misconduct" during 1999–2000. Further, when the study accounted for the relatively small numbers of specially classified students in schools, the rate of serious misconduct for special education students in regular schooling was over three times as high as for regular students (15 per 1,000 regular students, and 50 per 1,000 of special students). Misconduct, of course, can be by regular or special students, but a situation of bullying, taunting, or disrespect against the special student in regular classes offers good reason for a special student's misbehavior. Such situations are not always controllable by teachers and school staff and clearly do not provide the proper setting and special treatment that special youngsters deserve.

Bullying, for example, is an area of particular concern in regular classrooms and schools. Nearly 85 percent of special needs children experience bullying. Consistent research studies over ten years show that students with disabilities are two to three times more likely than nondisabled students to be the victims of bullying and that the bullying of the disabled was more chronic (*Walk-a-Mile-in-Their-Shoes*, 2011). Special needs students were also left out of the main social networks in regular classroom by the actions of the other students (Carter and Spencer, 2006). Saylor and Leach (2009) examine this peer victimization issue in inclusion programs.

In addition, one in five principals reported that protective disciplinary procedures required for special students under the IDEA regulations are "burdensome and time consuming." Many students with behavioral problems are mistakenly classified as special for a number of reasons, including the additional school income from state and federal sources. As Navarrette (2002) indicates, "Thus the mischievous and the misdiagnosed are mixed with those who really need special education, those with mental retardation and other disabilities." Full inclusion needs full examination before implementation.

Full Inclusion and School Reality

Theoretically, inclusion could provide all the good things special education now provides—special teachers, individualization, and more self-esteem but with the added benefit of allowing exceptional children to participate fully in the school program. Long-term experience with school reforms suggests that any immediate, positive effects of inclusion are likely to be overcome by long-standing conformist standardization, bureaucracy, and funding requirements that make most schools dull and ineffective even for many regular students. The special needs child will be overlooked in these schools.

The focus will shift from giving special attention to individual children's strengths and disabilities toward conforming to group standards imposed by federal or state officials, meeting community expectations in test scores, or facing other accountability measures of group success. Large class size will make it difficult for regular teachers to provide special assistance to exceptional children. Schools will not be able to fully control other students' disparaging or hurtful comments, and exceptional children again will suffer. School funds will decrease to a common standard, without special funds for special children. Exceptional students require exceptional effort, but schools will be stretched and unable to provide it (Noonan, 2008).

In addition, advocates of full inclusion are wrong when they argue that interaction with regular students in a regular program will benefit those who are disabled. A sorry history of bullying, taunting, labeling, ridicule, and exclusion by regular students is not likely to disappear because of some legislated program of interaction. There is no evidence that nondisabled children will suddenly develop appropriate classroom behavior when full inclusion takes place. Lectures and admonitions by school officials, no matter how well intentioned, are not likely to make a dent in the problem. Even if the majority of children are well behaved and nonprejudiced, it takes only a few to spoil the school setting for children with disabilities who already have been subjected to frequent stares and slights. School is tough enough for many regular students who happen to be different from the group. Life in many schools is not pleasant for children from poor families and for children who stutter, are noticeably shorter or taller or more plump, are slower in speed or intellect, are from certain cultural backgrounds, or are not as gregarious or athletic or pretty as others. School subcultures create cauldrons of despair for many students who are not accepted because of minor differences (Palonsky, 1975); consider the problem that those with significant disabilities would face in regular schools. Buchman (2006) describes the benefits of a special education for her daughter; her daughter agrees and wishes that all children with learning disabilities could have that special treatment (Farber, 2006).

Laudable but Unrealistic Goals

The goal of inclusion may be laudable under some conditions and for some individuals. However, full inclusion for all students represents an ideal that does not mesh with day-to-day reality for large numbers of students. Many children now are participating successfully in effective special education classes and schools. Zigler and Hall (1986) noted a problem regarding excesses in the 1980s mainstreaming movement. This movement was based on the "normalization" principle, an idea that we should provide more "normal" school settings to socialize disabled children:

> Ironically, the very law that was designed to safeguard the options of handi-capped children and their parents (the 1975 Education for all Handicapped Chil-dren Act) may, in the end, act to constrict their choices and result in disservice to the very children the legislators sought to help, by forcing schools to place them in programs that are not equipped to meet their needs. The normalization prin-ciple and the practice of mainstreaming may have deleterious effects on some children by denying them their right to be different.... Underlying the very idea of normalization is a push toward homogeneity, which is unfair to those chil-dren whose special needs may come to be viewed as unacceptable. (p. 2)

Full inclusion goes well beyond mainstreaming (Ryndak and Alper, 2003). As a result, it runs even greater risks of homogenizing our educational approach and causing a decline in special care and attention for children with exceptional needs. The political support for special programs and funds, support that took years to develop, will atrophy. Special education budgets will diminish. School administrators, with declining special education budgets, will be unlikely to champion the needs of this small and expensive proportion of their student populations. Regular class teachers, already overworked in large classes, will be unable to extend themselves even further for children who need more indi-vidualized help. Parents of nondisabled children may be sympathetic but are unlikely to support the diversion of general education funds, resources, and teacher time from the education of their own children.

McKleskey and Waldron (2000) may advocate inclusive education, but they point out that studies have shown that regular school staff continue to hold several unfortunate assumptions that undermine inclusion practices in schools. These include the significant assumption that "inclusion" students should still be perceived as "irregular" even when they are in regular classes and the assumption that inclusion students require specialized material and support that "could not be provided by the classroom teacher," depending instead on a special educator (p. 70). These assumptions are understandable, but they portend major problems in large-scale inclusion practices in school districts. And Bakken (2010) points out that inclusion is a topic that has "caused much debate, stirred emotions, and has received great attention" (p. 129) but that "inclusion" has no universally accepted definition and has changed over time. Instead, he argues strongly for "access to a high quality, effective, individualized educational environment" that is far more useful to students and "socially significant than mere placement and proximity to typically developing peers" (p. 129).

We want as many disabled children as possible to be self-reliant, to be equipped for successful and productive lives, to participate constructively in the larger society, and to develop feelings of personal worth. We want no less for any child, but the child who is disabled needs special attention and support to reach these goals. One of the primary purposes of special education programs is to provide the setting and individualized attention these children need to develop self-reliance, success, productivity, and feelings of personal worth. These programs are jeopardized by the steamroller tactics of the full inclusionists.

Well-Deserved Special Treatment

It is easy to fling out high-sounding phrases about full inclusion and democracy but more difficult to critically examine potential consequences of the way we treat exceptional children in our schools. Inclusion of special needs children into regular schools and classes is an educational policy needing critical assessment. Waving the flag of democracy may stir the faddists in education but will not hide the serious problems inherent in full inclusion.

Over history, children with disabilities have suffered; they have been reviled, ostracized, ridiculed, ignored, and destroyed. Some became members of circuses, some were hidden by their families, and others were placed in ill-funded and ill-supervised institutions with no chance for improvement. The families of disabled children also suffered social maligning. And society lost the contributions that it could have had from the many talents of people with disabilities.

Fortunately, society has made dramatic changes in the way it views the disabled. We now recognize that the special needs of these children require special treatment. Exceptional children can find success and develop on their own terms in school and life. Special programs offer a ray of hope to children who were ostracized and ignored in the past. Many special education schools and programs have been successful in preparing students to contribute to society.

Extra funding for special education provides more individualistic education, better-prepared teachers, more appropriate teaching materials, superior facilities, and a setting better organized to help these children. Full inclusion could be used to control school budgets by decreasing current special funding for special education and gifted and talented programs. Of course, it is cheaper to educate children with special needs in regular classes, an unwise and, in the long run, economically foolish move. The actual proportion of exceptional children is very small, in the range of 5 percent nationally. That small number deserves special financing, special treatment, special teachers, and special programs to ensure that they will become productive members of society, with the necessary self-respect.

Special education and exceptional programs offer important benefits to the child: a low student-to-teacher ratio for increased individualized instruction and attention; teachers especially trained to educate and develop the skills of exceptional students; experts organized into study teams to provide diagnosis, treatment, and evaluation of student development; homogeneous grouping to permit the teacher to concentrate on common needs and characteristics; more opportunity for student success among peers and more realistic competition in academics and/or athletics; funds for facilities, special equipment, and specially designed student learning materials; and increased student self-esteem from individual attention and by limiting negative interaction with nondisabled students. In addition, special education programs offer opportunity for remedial education that could return mildly disabled children to the regular program. These benefits continue to accrue to special education programs; they will be reduced with the advent of inclusion. Regular schools are unprepared to offer them in addition to their usual efforts, and initial extra funding will dry up or be absorbed into the ongoing operation of the schools.

Treating Other Exceptional Children: The Gifted

Presumably, full inclusion would require schools to eliminate separate, special programs, forcing all exceptional students into regular classes in regular schools. Deviation from this would occur when parents and school agree that a child cannot be educated in a regular class. But special school programs for exceptional children come in many varieties. Among them are programs for gifted and talented children, honors programs, and tracking.

Gifted and talented programs, for example, often are separately organized, taught, and evaluated. As Clark (1996) notes in a comprehensive analysis of such programs, "Gifted and talented students have more complex needs than average and below average learners . . . if these needs are not met we now know that ability cannot be maintained; indeed, brain research tells us that ability will be lost. . . . When no programs are available to this group of learners a disservice is done, not only to these students but to all of society, as our finest minds not only lack nurture, they are wasted" (p. 60). This is special education also; should these students be fully included in regular classes and activities to meet the law as seen by inclusionists?

Political realities surround efforts to end special programs for gifted, honors, or high-achieving students. These programs usually include children from the more powerful families in a community, demonstrate how special treatment makes a difference in student achievement, and enhance the school's academic reputation. Under full inclusion, gifted and talented children would be moved back into regular classes. Similarly, honors and remedial classes and tracking would be doomed. One-size-fits-all schooling, as full inclusion ideology proposes, is a prescription for mediocrity.

Slogans and Myths: Equal Education

There are many slogans in our society: save the whales, do your duty, and be prepared. Each of these ideas is significantly more complicated than putting a bumper sticker on a car, boycotting, or voting. Unfortunately, the simplicity and moral righteousness of such slogans can be deceptive. Life's problems are complex; slogans ignore the complexity and offer a tantalizingly singular answer. Simplistic answers may make problems worse. Making education a cornerstone of democracy is an excellent idea, but to make it work requires more than unsubstantiated claims and moral posturing (Meier, 2005).

Free and open education, equally available to all with no differences in treatment or result, is an interesting utopian idea so far from reality that it is painful. Yet this basic concept underlies the current interest in inclusion. We don't yet have free and equal education, equal treatment, or equal results for the wide variety of students who attend "regular" public schools. It is unrealistic to believe that students who are shifted to meet inclusion goals actually will obtain equal access, treatment, or results. The "regular" classroom is a figment of ideological imagination; schools do not offer equality now.

Currently, even outside separate special education classes, access to education differs along several dimensions. Tracking or grouping students by ability on the basis of how they score on tests and how teachers evaluate them separates students for most of their school careers (Oakes, 1985, 2005; Urban and Waggoner, 1996; Spring, 1998; Meier, 2005). Schools in different communities offer differing advantages to their students as a result of funding differences that citizens vote on. High school athletes are more costly to a school district than humanities students, and only the best athletes are selected for team membership. In elementary school classes, good readers are placed in one group and poor readers in another. Not all students are admitted to college preparatory or honors classes. Advanced woodshop is limited to select students, as are advanced Latin and chemistry. Students who misbehave and disrupt others are separated in schools and may be denied access by suspension or expulsion. Special education costs are about 2.3 times the cost of regular classrooms, most of which is covered outside of district funds. This funding, even with recent sizable increases in numbers of students classified as special, remains a relatively small proportion of school expenditures (Moe, 2002).

Where students live is related to how well they will do in school and in gaining access to further education; higher-income communities have schools where students obtain higher standardized test scores and higher rates of college admission. Female students have less access to higher-level math and science classes than males. Generally, minority students have less access to highly ranked colleges than majority students. When viewed on the basis of equality, these circumstances may not be ideal or even always supportable but are the reality of schooling. Democracy does not require exact equality of condition. The economic ideas behind capitalism, which have made this nation so successful, are inconsistent with mandated egalitarianism; capitalism requires that we reward competition and entrepreneurship.

On the Fairness of Life

Life, as we know, is unfair. We see unfairness in human relations of all kinds, including those in schools. We can't fix all unfairness, but we need to limit inappropriate discrimination and prejudice. Discrimination is inappropriate if based on criteria that are illogical or unethical or that lack a scientific basis. Discrimination is appropriate if it means separating existing individual differences to treat, protect, or nurture them. We discriminate among people by granting academic awards, among people with certain illnesses by treating them and protecting the society, and among animals by determining which are endangered and therefore deserving special treatment. Prejudice means that we "prejudge" without knowledge, but making a judgment based on an understanding of available information is not prejudice. It is prejudice to claim, before ever tasting it, that broccoli tastes bad—but not to make the statement after tasting. Throughout life, we make judgments. Some may turn out to be wrong, but we can only try to use the best, most complete available information and reasoning to inform a judgment.

Fairness sometimes may mean providing different strokes for different folks if the criteria are sensible and consistent with social goals and individual interests. Putting all students into advanced Latin or into woodshop does not make sense, keeping disruptive or violent children in regular classes regardless of their behavior does not make sense, and admitting all students to any college they desire does not make sense. We use criteria to limit those who can drive cars, handle food, practice medicine, cut and style hair, be convicted of a crime, or run for president. These limits are unfair only if they are abused, prejudicially applied, or not sensible.

Affirmative action programs, when they use quota systems and remove merit considerations, have engendered strong criticism from all parts of the political spectrum. They are defended now mainly by a hard core of disciples. The main purpose of affirmative action, to ensure equal opportunity under the Constitution, has been subverted by legislative zealotry and bureaucratic manipulation. Reasonable people from all sides decry prejudice, bias, hate crimes, and discrimination based on stereotypes—but they do not want government to mandate actions on matters best left to individual choice. That is a difficult line to draw, but it is important to do so in a democracy.

Legislation, Courts, and Problems Caused by Full Inclusion

Full inclusion of children with disabilities into regular classes runs some of the same risks of arousing overzealous legislation and activist court interpretation. Legislated mainstreaming has created significant problems—for schools, for teachers, for communities, and for both disabled and nondisabled children. Court interpretations of laws threaten to leave mainstreaming in another social engineering predicament akin to those of affirmative action. Extending mainstreaming to full inclusion promises to cause even more complicated problems and more bureaucratic, bungling answers. A court case, *Oberti v. Board of Education of Clementon (NJ) School District* (1993), illustrates problems associated with mainstreaming, the laws governing it, and court interpretations.

The case involves an eight-year-old Down syndrome child with impaired intellectual functioning and ability to communicate. The school district, after testing and review by specialists, determined that his educational interests would best be served by placing him in a developmental kindergarten class in the morning to observe and socialize with peer children, but his academic work would be done in a separate special class in the afternoon. During the morning class, the child exhibited serious behavioral problems, including repeated toilet accidents, temper tantrums, crawling and hiding under furniture, and hitting and spitting on other children. Also, the child repeatedly hit the teacher and teacher's aide.

Obviously, he was disruptive, and the frustrated teacher sought help from the district Child Study Team. The individualized education plan required under the IDEA law and used for the original placement did not cover ways to handle his behavioral problems. Interestingly, the child did not exhibit disruptive behavior in the separate afternoon special education class. After study, the district wanted to place the child in a completely separate program, but the parents refused. After a hearing, there was an agreement that he would be placed in a separate program for one year. In that year, his behavior improved, and he made academic progress. When the parents found, however, that the district did not plan to place him back into "regular" classes the following year, they objected, and another hearing occurred before an administrative law judge. The judge agreed with the district that the separate special education class was the "least restrictive environment" under the IDEA law, the child's misbehavior in the developmental kindergarten class was extensive, and there was no meaningful educational benefit from that class. Unsatisfied, the parents went to court, getting an expert witness professor from Wisconsin who claimed the child could be in regular classes provided that there were supplementary aids and special support, such as the following:

1. Modifying the existing regular curriculum for this student
2. Modifying this child's program to provide for meeting a different set of criteria for performance
3. Using "parallel" instruction—the child would be in the classroom but would have separate activities
4. Removing the child for instruction in certain special areas

The district's expert witness claimed the child could not benefit from placement in a regular class, his behavior could not be managed, the teacher could not communicate with him because of his communication problems, and the curriculum could not be modified enough to meet this child's needs without compromising its integrity. Other witnesses, including people who had worked with the child in other public school and Catholic school settings, testified that he had very disruptive behavior, including hitting, throwing things, and running away. This judge, citing the IDEA law, held that the district had the burden of proof and had failed to meet the law's requirement for mainstreaming (*Oberti v. Board of Education of Clementon (NJ) School District*, 1993).

This case suggests a series of problems for schools, parents, communities, and children under full inclusion. The court directed that a disruptive and misbehaving child is to attend regular classes, where his actions are likely to be detrimental to other students' academic work and to the teacher's ongoing work. The disabled child's schoolwork, apparently satisfactory in separate special education classes, suffered significantly in the regular placement, even on a part-time basis, yet under the court's order, he now would be in regular classes full-time. The child's parents may feel better that their child is in regular classes, but how will he progress? Parents of the nondisabled children do not have the same right to refuse placement, require formal hearings on details they don't like, or protest in court when their children are subjected to a significantly modified curriculum or class disruption. School rules established for all children to provide order and safety are placed in jeopardy by a court order that makes the school ultrasensitive to the parents of a single student.

A number of classroom issues are raised by the suggestion of the expert witness from Wisconsin to mainstream with supplementary activities and support. Teachers work hard on a school curriculum and finding ways to teach it. How are they to modify that curriculum adequately for one severely disabled student without compromising the integrity of the curriculum as a whole? Is it equal and fair treatment if the teacher gives very special treatment to one disabled child, designing different activities and individual levels of performance, but does not do so for each of the other children? If the special needs child has "parallel" instruction provided in class and is removed from the class for certain special instruction, how does that differ in substance from a separate special education program? Although the child is in a regular class, he is to be separated for much of his work, and he may even become more of a target for other children because of his differential treatment.

Excessive mainstreaming caught schools unprepared, frustrated good teachers, diminished special services provided to individual children, and created confusion in schools. Well-prepared schools, specially trained teachers, clear guidelines for diagnosis and education, smaller classes, special materials to enhance learning, and a setting conducive to the best education now exist in many places: special education and gifted and talented programs offer these advantages. Full inclusion would overturn these in favor of a mandate for standardization and chaos beyond what occurred in excessive mainstreaming programs.

Schools vary significantly: it is impossible to define a "regular" school or classroom. Is a one-room school in rural Nevada "regular"? What about an urban school in Manhattan or a suburban school in Beverly Hills? Schools have some common patterns, but much schooling occurs with separate groups of students. The Bronx High School of Science, vocational-technical high schools, tracking programs, honors programs, remedial courses, basic and advanced courses, reading groups, and selection for music and athletic programs illustrate the common practice of educating certain students separately for particular reasons. Full inclusion threatens these efforts to provide the best individual education for different students.

For Discussion

1. Dialectic Exercise: Identify the best arguments for and against full inclusion. Do they provide a thesis and antithesis? Analyze the evidence presented for each. What kinds of research would be needed to provide that evidence? Where would you go to find that kind of research? What research is currently available on these matters? What is your current view, and what would be the most convincing evidence for you to change your mind on full inclusion? Is there a synthesis for this argument that serves social policy, educational interests, and individual students and parents?

2. Discussion: How should the movement toward full inclusion influence teacher education programs? What would you propose for teacher preparation in this area? What should teachers know about and be able to do for special students included in general classrooms?

3. Data from the U.S. Department of Education show that the annual growth rate in children ages three to twenty-one who receive special education (over 3 percent) continues to exceed the annual growth rate in the general population between ages three and twenty-one (about 1 percent). The proportion of children evaluated as gifted and talented is about 3 percent of the student population. What reasons would explain an increase in proportion of children needing special education? What difference should this annual increase mean for school decisions on full inclusion? To critically examine this topic, what evidence would you need, and where would you expect to find that evidence?

4. How should gifted and talented programs be treated in terms of full inclusion policies? Should they be abolished, separated, enhanced, or diminished? On what grounds do you argue? Who should decide and on what criteria? Are separate programs appropriate in public schools in a democracy? How is this issue similar to and different from treatment of special education students under IDEA law?

References

ALUR, M., AND BACH, M. (2010). *The Journey for Inclusive Education in the Indian Sub-Continent.* New York: Routledge.

ANDERSON, G. R., AND ANDERSON, S. K. (1983). "The Exceptional Native American." In *The Politics of Special Education*, ed. L. Barton. London: Falmer Press.

ARTILES, A. J., AND BAL, A. (2008). "The Next Generation of Disproportionality Research." *Journal of Special Education* 42(1):4–14.

BAKKEN, J. P. (2010). "The General Education Classroom: This Is Not Where Students with Disabilities Should Be Placed." In *Current Issues and Trends in Special Education,* vol. 19, ed. F. E. Obiakor J. P. Bakken, and A. F. Rotatori. Bingley: Emerald.

BARTON, L. (1988). *The Politics of Special Education Needs.* London: Falmer Press.

BATSON, T., AND BERGMAN, E., eds. (2002). *Angels and Outcasts.* Washington, DC: Gallaudet University Press.

BRANTLINGER, E. A., AND GUSKIN, S. L. (1987). "Ethnocultural and Social Psychological Effects on Learning Characteristics of Handicapped Children." In *Handbook of Special Education,* vol. 1, ed. M. C. Wang et al. Oxford: Pergamon.

Brown v. Board of Education of Topeka, Kansas. (1954). 347 U.S. 483.

BUCHMAN, D. (2006). *A Special Education.* Cambridge, MA: Da Capo Press.

BURRELLO, L. C., ET AL. (2001). *Educating All Students Together.* Thousand Oaks, CA: Corwin Press.

CALLARD-SZULGIT, R. (2005). *Teaching the Gifted in an Inclusive Classroom.* Lanham, MD: Scarecrow Press.

CAMERON, L. (2008). "The Maine Effect or How I Finally Embraced the Social Model of Disability." *Intellectual and Developmental Disabilities* 46(1):54–57.

CARTER, B. B., AND SPENCER, V. G. (2006). "The Fear Factor: Bullying and Students with Disabilities." *International Journal of Special Education.* 21(1):11–23.

CASE, L. P., SPEECE, D. L., AND MOLLOY, D. E. (2003). "The Validity of a Response-to-Intervention Paradigm to Identify Reading Disabilities." *School Psychology Review* 32:557–582.

CIGMAN, R. ed. (2007). *Included or Excluded?* New York: Routledge.

CLARK, B. (1996). "The Need for a Range of Program Options for Gifted and Talented Students." In *Controversial Issues Confronting Special Education,* 2nd Ed., ed. W. Stainback and S. Stainback. Boston: Allyn and Bacon.

COOLEY, S. M., ET AL. (2008). "A Field at Risk: The Teacher Shortage in Special Education." *Kappan* 89(8):597–600.

CROMWELL, S. (2004). "Inclusion: Has It Gone Too Far?" www.education-world.com.

CUSHNER, K., MCCLELLAND, A., AND SAFFORD, P. (2000). *Human Diversity in Education.* 3rd Ed. New York: McGraw-Hill.

DANFORTH, S. (2008). "John Dewey's Contributions to an Educational Philosophy of Intellectual Disability." *Educational Theory* 58(1):45–58.

DANFORTH, S., AND SMITH, T. J. (2005). *Engaging Troubled Students.* Thousand Oaks, CA: Corwin Press.

DICKMAN, I. (1985). *One Miracle at a Time.* New York: Simon and Schuster.

Educational Testing Service. (1980). "New Vistas in Special Education." *Focus* 8:1–20.

FARBER, C. (2006). "Afterword." In *A Special Education,* by D. BUCHMAN. Cambridge, MA: Da Capo Press.

FERRI, B. J., AND CONNOR, D. J. (2005). "Tools of Exclusion: Race, Disability, and (Re)segregated Education." *Teachers College Record* 107(3):453–474.

GARLAND THOMSON, R. (2010). "Roosevelt's Sister: Why We Need Disability Studies in the Humanities." *Disabilities Studies Quarterly* 30(3/4). www.dsq-sds.org.

GIBSON, S., AND HAYNES, J., eds. (2009). *Perspectives on Participation and Inclusion.* London: Continuum.

GLOVER, T. A., AND VAUGHN, S., eds. (2010). *The Promise of Response to Intervention.* New York: Guilford Press.

GOFFMAN, E. (1961). *Asylums.* Garden City, NY: Anchor Books.

GROSSMAN, H. (1998). *Ending Discrimination in Special Education.* Springfield, IL: Charles C. Thomas.

HARRY, B., ET AL. (2008). "Schooling and the Construction of Identity among Minority Students in Spain and the United States." *Journal of Special Education* 42(1):15–25.

HELLER, K. A., HOLTZMAN, W. H., AND MESSICK, S., eds. (1982). *Placing Children in Special Education: A Strategy for Equity.* Washington, DC: National Academy of Sciences Press.

JAEGER, P. T. (2012). Disability and the Internet. Boulder, CO: Lynne Rienner Publishers.

JIMERSON, S. R., BURNS, M. K., AND VANDERHEYDEN, A. M., eds. (2007). *Handbook of Response to Intervention.* New York: Springer.

KABZEMS, V. (2003). "Labeling in the Name of Equality." In *Rethinking Disability*, ed. P. Devliger. Philadelphia: Garant.

KAUFFMAN, J., AND HALLAHAN, D., eds. (1995). *The Illusion of Full Inclusion.* Austin, TX: PRO-ED.

KAUFFMAN, J., ET AL. (2002). "Separate and Better." *Exceptionality* 10(3):149–170.

KENNEDY, C. H., AND FISHER, D. (2001). *Inclusive Middle Schools.* Baltimore: Paul H. Brookes.

Kids Together, Inc. (2012). "Benefits of Inclusive Education." www.kidstogether.org. April.

KLUTH, P., ET AL. (2001). "'Our School Doesn't Offer Inclusion' and Other Legal Blunders." *Educational Leadership* 50(4):24–27.

KOENIG, J. A., AND BACHMAN, L. F., eds. (2004). *Keeping Score for All.* Washington, DC: National Academies Press.

KOZOL, J. (1991). *Savage Inequalities.* New York: Crown Publishers.

LEDOUX, C. GRAVES, S. L., AND BURT, W. (2012). "Meeting the Needs of Special Education Students in Inclusion Classrooms." *Journal of the American Academy of Special Education Professionals.* Winter. pp. 20–34.

LOMBARDI, T. P., AND LUDLOW, B. L. (1996). *Trends Shaping the Future of Special Education.* Bloomington, IN: Phi Delta Kappa Educational Foundation.

LOW, C. (2007). "A Defense of Moderate Inclusion and the End of Ideology." In *Included or Excluded?*, ed. R. Cigman New York: Routledge.

MCKLESKEY, J., AND WALDRON, N. (2000). *Inclusive Schools in Action.* Alexandria, VA: Association for Supervision and Curriculum Development.

MEIER, K. J. (2005). "School Boards and the Politics of Education Policy." In *Politics of Democratic Inclusion*, ed. C. WOLBRECHT AND R. E. HERO. Philadelphia: Temple University Press.

Mills v. Board of Education of the District of Columbia. (1972). 348 F. Supp. 866.

MITTLER, P., BROUILLETTE, R., AND HARRIS D., eds. (1993). *Special Needs Education: World Yearbook of Education.* London: Kogan Page.

MOE, T. M. (2002). *A Primer on America's Schools.* Stanford, CA: Hoover Institution Press.

NAVARRETTE, R. (2002). "The Special Ed Dumping Ground." *San Diego Union-Tribune.* April 17.

NOONAN, M. A. (2008). "When Special Education As We Know It Ends—What, if Anything Will Replace It?" *Educational Horizons* 86(3):139–141.

OAKES, J. (1985). *Keeping Track: How Schools Structure Inequality.* New Haven, CT: Yale University Press.

———. (2005). *Keeping Track: How Schools Structure Inequality.* 2nd Ed. New Haven, CT: Yale University Press.

Oberti v. Board of Education of the Borough of Clementon (NJ) School District. (1993). 995 F.2d 1204 (3rd Cir. 1993).

PALONSKY, S. (1975). "Hempies and Squeaks, Truckers and Cruisers: A Participant-Observer Investigation in a City High School." *Educational Administration Quarterly* 2:86–103.

PETCH-HOGAN, B., AND HAGGARD, D. (1999). "The Inclusion Debate Continues." *Educational Forum* 35(3):128–140.

POORE, C. (2007). *Disability in Twentieth Century German Culture.* Ann Arbor: University of Michigan Press.

RISKO, V., AND BROMLEY, K. (2001). *Collaboration for Diverse Learners.* Newark, DE: International Reading Association.

ROGERS, J. (1993). "The Inclusion Revolution." *Phi Delta Kappa Research Bulletin* 11:1–6.

ROTATORI, A. F., OBIAKOR, F. E., AND BAKKEN, J. P., eds. (2011). *History of Special Education.* Bingley: Emerald.

RYNDAK, D. L., AND ALPER, S., eds. (2003). *Curriculum and Instruction for Students with Significant Disabilities in Inclusive Settings.* 2nd Ed. Boston: Allyn and Bacon.

SAILOR, W., GERRY, M., AND WILSON, W. C. (1991). "Policy Implications of Emergent Full Inclusion Models." In *Handbook of Special Education: Research and Practice,* vol. 4., ed. M. C. Wang et al. Oxford: Pergamon.

SALEND, S. S. (2011). *Creating Inclusive Classrooms.* 7th Ed. Columbus, OH: Pearson.

SAYLOR, C. F., AND LEACH, J. B. (2009). "Perceived Peer Victimization and Social Support in Students Accessing Special Inclusion Programming," *Journal of Developmental and Physical Disabilities* 21:69–80.

SCULLY, J. L. (2008). *Disability Bioethics.* Lanham, MD: Rowman & Littlefield.

SEFA DEI, G., ET AL. (2000). *Removing the Margins.* Toronto: Canadian Scholars' Press.

SHEVIN, M. (2007). *Widening the Circle.* Boston: Beacon Press.

SIEBERS, T. (2008). *Disability Theory.* Ann Arbor: University of Michigan Press.

———. (2010). *Disability Ethics.* Ann Arbor: University of Michigan Press.

SKIBA, R. J., ET AL. (2008). "Achieving Equity in Special Education." *Exceptional Children* 74(3):264–288.

SMITH, P. ed. (2010). *Whatever Happened to Inclusion?* New York: Peter Lang.

SPRING, J. (1998). *American Education.* 8th Ed. New York: McGraw-Hill.

TAYLOR, R. E. (2003). *Assessment of Exceptional Students.* 6th Ed. Boston: Allyn and Bacon.

THOUSAND, J. S., AND VILLA, R. A. (1995). "Managing Complex Change toward Inclusive Schooling." In *Creating an Inclusive School,* ed. R. A. Villa and J. S. Thousand. Alexandria, VA: Association for Supervision and Curriculum Development.

TURNBULL, H. R., AND TURNBULL, A. P. (1998). *Free Appropriate Public Education: The Law and Children with Disabilities.* 5th Ed. Denver: Love Publishing.

UNESCO. (2008). "Inclusive Quality Education." April. www.portal.unesco.org.

United Nations Convention on the Rights of the Child. (1989). New York: United Nations.

URBAN, W., AND WAGGONER, J. (1996). *American Education: A History.* New York: McGraw-Hill.

United Nations Convention on the Rights of Persons with Diabilities. (2007). New York: United Nations.

U.S. Census Bureau. (2011). "Anniversary of Americans with Disabilities Act." *Facts for Features.* May 31. Washington, DC: U.S. Census Bureau.

VALLE, J. W. (2009). *What Mothers Say about Special Education.* New York: Palgrave.

VARGAS, S. R. L. (1999). "Democracy and Inclusion." *Maryland Law Review* 58(1):150–179.

Walk-a-Mile-in-Their-Shoes. (2011). www.abilitypath.org.

WEDELL, K. (1993). "Varieties of School Integration." In *Special Needs Education: World Yearbook of Education,* ed. P. Mittler et al. London: Kogan Page.

WINZER, M. A. (1993). *The History of Special Education: From Isolation to Integration.* Washington, DC: Gallaudet University Press.

WOLBRECHT, C., AND HERO, R. E. (2005). *The Politics of Democratic Inclusion.* Philadelphia: Temple University Press.

ZIGLER, E., AND HALL, N. (1986). "Mainstreaming and the Philosophy of Normalization." In *Mainstreaming Handicapped Children*, ed. C. J. Meisel. Hillsdale, NJ: Lawrence Erlbaum Associates.

CHAPTER 16

Teacher Unions and School Reform: Advocate or Adversary

Do teacher unions support or subvert the nation's school reform agenda

POSITION 1: TEACHER UNIONS ARE CHAMPIONS OF TEACHERS AND SCHOOL REFORM

The countries that are among the top ten in student performance have some of the strongest teacher unions in the world.

—Tucker (2011, p. 1)

Forcing Teachers to Unionize

In the early part of the twentieth century, teachers were trained to believe that sacrifice was the essence of their profession. Teachers worked long hours, their classes often numbered fifty or more students, their salaries were low, and schools were at times poorly heated, poorly ventilated, and unsanitary. Women teachers were not allowed to go out unescorted (except to attend church) or frequent places where liquor was served; and in many communities, when women teachers married, they were forced to resign from their jobs. In addition to living truncated social lives, teachers served at the whim of school boards, without any promise of tenure or health or retirement benefits. They were not considered worthy of participating in the book selection process and were excluded from the more substantive deliberations about curriculum. As school systems developed into large bureaucratic organizations, teacher powerlessness became institutionalized. School principals became part of management and separated themselves from the teachers. Once referred to as the "principal teacher" or the "main teacher," the head of a school stopped teaching and became a manager who shared few of the problems of teachers and little of their perspective.

During the nineteenth century, it was assumed that those who taught school would do so for only a short time. Women typically chose marriage and homemaking after a few years in the classroom. Ambitious men were expected to move from teaching to loftier, better-paying occupations. Classroom teaching was seldom the chosen lifetime work of the more able. Teaching was considered as employment for workers who were "passing through" on their way to more serious pursuits (Holmes Group, 1986). At best, teaching was seen as a good short-term job, but most people disparaged it as a career choice, and those who chose to stay in the classroom for more than a few years often encountered social derision. In 1932, the sociologist Willard Waller observed that teachers were not treated like other workers and certainly not like professionals. He noted that in small towns, unmarried teachers were expected to live in a teacherage—a special boardinghouse—apart from other single adults who held nonteaching jobs. Waller also noted the popular prejudice against teachers commonly held by wealthier and better-educated members of the community. "Teaching," he wrote, "is quite generally regarded as a failure belt . . . the refuge of unmarriageable women and unsaleable men" (Waller, 1932, p. 61).

Teachers have been joining together for well over 100 years, but their earliest organizations were not really unions. The National Education Association (NEA), for example, was established in 1857 to represent the views of "practical" classroom teachers and administrators. Annual NEA conventions were not union meetings but rather settings for the exchange of ideas about teaching. Members typically avoided discussing labor issues or how teachers could influence decisions about their work or wages. The NEA was less concerned with the personal welfare of classroom teachers than it was with advancing the profession of education. In its early years, the NEA was a male-dominated organization for teachers that was led by school superintendents, professors of education, and school principals (Wesley, 1957). As one critic of the old NEA notes, the role of classroom teachers, especially women teachers, was "limited to listening" (Eaton, 1975, p. 10).

Teacher unionism dates to the early twentieth century, when Chicago teachers organized to fight for better working conditions. In 1916, the American Federation of Teachers (AFT) was formed as an affiliate of the American Federation of Labor. Initially, the older NEA and the upstart AFT cooperated. The NEA focused on professional and practical sides of teaching; the AFT concentrated on improving economic aspects of teachers' lives (Engel, 1976). Over the years, local affiliates of the NEA and the AFT have become rivals in their efforts to become the teachers' bargaining agents. More than 80 percent of U.S. teachers belong to either the NEA or the AFT, and more than 60 percent work under a formal collective bargaining agreement.

Teachers were never eager to join unions; they were forced to because the culture of administrative managers was at odds with the culture of working teachers (Jessup, 1978; Urban, 1982; Murphy, 1990). Teachers urged their colleagues to use unions and collective bargaining to improve their working conditions and gain a voice in improving education. Today, teacher organizations often bear a greater resemblance to professional associations (the American Bar Association or the American Medical Association) than to labor organizations (the International Ladies Garment Workers Union or the United Automobile

Workers). Leaders of the old AFT, however, identified with unionized workers in other industries. They believed that problems common to all workers could be solved through cooperation and collective action. They wanted teacher organizations to provide economic benefits for their members and argued that teacher unions also could assist labor by improving the education offered to working-class children. Despite numerous efforts to organize teachers and revitalize education, including development of a workers' college and special public schools for workers' children, AFT membership declined in the 1920s and remained flat throughout most of the 1930s. Most school administrators were openly hostile to organized labor. In the 1920s, fearing worker radicalism and union activity, many school superintendents demanded teachers, as a condition of employment, sign "yellow-dog contracts," agreements that they would not join a union.

The National Labor Relations Act (NLRA) of 1935 changed the status of unions by recognizing that workers in private industry had the right to bargain collectively. Employees are at a disadvantage when they bargain singly with employers, working alone against the power and resources at management's hand. Under collective bargaining agreements, employees, as a group, and their employers negotiate about wages and employment conditions. Collective bargaining laws recognize that workers have the right to join together and elect a bargaining agent (a union) to negotiate with management on their behalf. The NLRA required employers and unions to "meet at reasonable times and confer in good faith with respect to wages, hours, and other terms and conditions of employment."

Questions about its constitutionality clouded the NLRA's early history. The Supreme Court eventually decided the issue, judging the act constitutional (*NLRB v. Jones and Laughlin Steel Company*, 1937). This was a major victory for organized labor and represented a great change in the thinking of the courts. In earlier cases, the courts had ruled that unions were illegal and that workers who joined unions were guilty of entering into an illegal "conspiracy" to improve their wages. By the mid-nineteenth century, courts no longer held that those who advocated collective bargaining were involved in criminal conspiracies (*Commonwealth v. Hunt*, 1842), but unions and collective negotiations did not earn full legitimacy until the Supreme Court's 1937 decision.

The NLRA affects only workers in the private sector. It does not cover employees of federal, state, or local government, so this law did not guarantee collective bargaining for public school teachers. Teachers could still be fired by school boards simply for joining a union (Kahlenberg, 2007). Public schools are considered extensions of the state. School boards are, in a sense, state employers, and thus they are excluded from federal labor legislation. It has been left up to the states to regulate employment relations in public education. Following Congress's lead, the majority of state legislatures have taken action to recognize the rights of workers to organize and negotiate with employers.

The organization of teachers in New York City in 1960 is considered a watershed for public school unions (Lieberman and Moscow, 1966). The United Federation of Teachers (UFT), a local affiliate of the AFT, was made up of several New York City teacher organizations. The UFT asked the board of education to recognize the teachers' rights to bargain collectively and conduct an election to determine which organization should represent them. The board was unsure how to implement collective bargaining, and it did not move swiftly. The unions accused the board of stalling, and on November 7, 1960, the UFT declared the first strike in the history of New York City education.

It was a brief but effective job action. The teachers were back in the classrooms the next day, and the board agreed to hold elections and not to take reprisals against striking teachers. Union estimates put pickets at about 7,500, and it was claimed that another 15,000 teachers stayed home (Eaton, 1975). The strike alerted the nation to the power of unions, and teachers began to recognize the advantages of collective negotiation as well as the power potential of the strike. Collective bargaining changed the relationship between classroom teachers and administrators. It promised teachers more pay, better job security, and an audible voice in education. As one labor historian puts it, "It essentially refined and broadened the concept of professionalism by assuring [teachers] more autonomy and less supervisory control" (Murphy, 1990, p. 209).

The New York City strike reverberated nationally. The results encouraged teachers and sent the two largest unions, the NEA and the AFT, scrambling for members. The NEA represents about 3.2 million teachers, more than twice the number represented by the AFT. These organizations differ on specific issues. (You can examine the views of the AFT at www.aft.org and the NEA's views at www.nea.org.)

The decision to join the labor movement no doubt came hard to many teachers. Teachers tended to be socially conservative, first-generation college graduates who identified with management more than with labor (Rosenthal, 1969). They belonged (and still belong) to a special category of white-collar employees called "knowledge workers." Paid for what they know and how they use their knowledge to produce value, these workers, as a group, are highly individualistic and difficult to unionize and organize into collective action (Kerchner, Koppich, and Weeres, 1997). Strikes are anathema to most members of teacher unions (Rauth, 1990). The fact that the union movement has succeeded in recruiting teachers speaks well for unions; teachers believe that unions are necessary and useful. Most teachers now belong to some sort of union despite a decline in union membership in other fields and continued middle-class antipathy toward unions. Today, surveys find teachers supportive of unions, professional organizations they regard as a necessary protective shield in a workplace too eager to ignore them (Galley, 2003).

Protecting Teachers' Rights and Opposing False Accountability

Unions keep experienced teachers in our schools by providing them with health insurance and negotiating reasonable wages and working conditions. They prevent a master teacher from getting fired solely for disagreeing with administrators.

—Illana Garon, New York City public school teacher
(Garon, 2011, p. 98)

Unions have been good for classroom teachers. The research literature indicates that unions have had a positive effect on teachers' working conditions. As a result of collective bargaining, teachers' salaries have increased,[1] and teachers have gained protection against unreasonable treatment. Unlike the preunion days, teachers cannot be dismissed simply because they consume alcohol, change their marital status, or express unpopular political views. The philosopher John Dewey, described as the "intellectual guru" of the AFT, believed that a union was necessary to protect teachers' intellectual and academic freedom (Kahlenberg, 2007). Unions also have been good for students. They have put the faculty squarely in the front ranks of the battle for better schools and better education for children. The nations with the highest student test scores also have some of the strongest teacher unions in the world. Finland, for example, embraces its teacher unions and works to make teaching "the highest status, most desirable job in the country" (Tucker, 2011, p. 8).

Teacher unions have always attracted some bad press. Some of it is traditional antilabor rhetoric, and some is simply misinformed. No doubt you have heard that unions are to blame for declining student performance and that unions have hurt education by protecting weak teachers who deserve to be fired. This is not the case. In fact, it is mystifying when unions are blamed for protecting weak teachers. Before teachers are awarded tenure, they must be graduated from state-approved teacher education programs, convince administrators to hire them, and survive an extended probationary period, typically from three to five years. Unions currently play virtually no part in any of these processes. Weak teachers may make it through this system, but they do so with no help from organized labor. Teacher unions are embarrassed by poor teachers, just as the American Bar Association and the American Medical Association are discomfited by ineffective, corrupt, or lazy members in their ranks. No responsible union wants to protect incompetent workers.

Unions' Stake in Education Reform

> It is as much the duty of the union to preserve public education as it is to negotiate a good contract.
>
> —Albert Shanker (AFT, 2011a)

Teachers unions support the evaluation of teachers, using academically appropriate assessment designs, but teachers and their unions recognize how difficult it is to measure teacher performance. As Albert Shanker, the late AFT president argued, a used car salesman who sells twenty cars a month is probably twice as good as a salesman in the same dealership who sells ten a month (Kahlenberg, 2007). This simple assessment formula cannot be applied to the evaluation of teachers, but it has not discouraged so-called education reformers from trying.

---

[1] In the 2006–2007 school year, the average teacher salary was $51,009, up 4.5 percent from the previous year, and the average beginning salary was $35,284. For the most current state-by-state listings, see the "Salary Survey" of the American Federation of Teachers at www.aft.org.

Advocates of performance pay for teachers argue that some teachers move their students forward at a greater rate than expected, yet teachers are not rewarded financially for how much their students learn. A teacher's skill in the classroom, as measured by student achievement on standardized tests, should be reflected in the teacher's salary and job security. Especially productive teachers should receive additional rewards, and unproductive teachers should be dismissed.

Linking the compensation of public school teachers to the performance of their students has been traced back to the early 1700s to certain parts of England where teachers' salaries were based on examination of student proficiency in reading, writing, and arithmetic. As England developed a national system of education, performance pay expanded, along with its abuses. Teachers and students, under pressure to demonstrate achievement, cheated on exams and falsified records to deceive school inspectors. England ended its experiment with performance pay in the 1890s following public outcry over academic dishonesty and the negative effects of exams on students and teachers (Gratz, 2009).

Performance pay advocates resurface from time to time, and the early twenty-first century seems to be one of those times. Its supporters claim that performance pay motivates all teachers, compensates good teachers, and weeds out weaker teachers. It will also attract the most able college graduates into teaching and "eliminate the achievement gap, improve the economy, prepare students for work in today's economy and heighten national competitiveness" (Gratz, 2009, p. 17), If this sounds too good to be true, it is. Teacher quality cannot be measured solely by changes in student test scores. If it were that simple, students could be tested at point A. Teachers would provide instruction. Students would be retested at point B. We could then subtract A scores from B scores and attribute the difference between A and B solely to the teacher's skill. Simple and neat, but nothing in education works that way. Too much transpires between points A and B to make valid conclusions about a teacher's effectiveness based on gain scores alone.

Teachers know that determining how well students perform reflects social factors and family environment at least as much as it indicates student learning or teacher skill. As one teacher notes, "Of the five students who failed my senior advanced-placement English class last term, one was pregnant, one had just moved to a shelter, and one was bouncing between foster homes" (Garon, 2011, p. 97). Standardized testing never can account for student performance in the ways that teachers can. Among their many shortcomings, standardized testing systems typically fail to consider personal issues, test anxiety, and test preparation, and they do not tease out the differences between real learning and mere memorization (Perlstein, 2007).

Performance pay is not the answer, either, and research bears this out. The National Center for Performance Incentives is charged by the federal government with examining the relationship between financial incentives and the quality of teaching and learning. Are teachers working hard enough? Can financial incentives serve to make teachers work harder and result in better test results for their students? Take a look at their website (www.performanceincentives.org), and you will find studies that show that performance pay alone is not sufficient to raise student test scores. Responding to one of the reports published by the National Center, Randi Weingarten (2010), president of the AFT, argues that performance pay is not the motivational carrot it is claimed to be. She writes, "It's time to end our love affair with simplistic strategies that don't get us where we need to be in order to provide a great education for all children. . . . The countries where students outperform our students, such as Finland, Singapore, and South Korea, do the hard work of focusing on teacher preparation, recruitment and retention, and by making all schools places where parents want to send their children and the best teachers want to work" (p. 1).

Pay for performance is a simple business solution to a multilayered education problem. It assumes that the motivational rewards and punishments successfully used in American business can be equally effective when applied to American schools. Diane Ravitch (2010) describes this as a "false analogy," She writes that putative school reformers, enamored of the private sector, "think they can fix education by applying the principles of business, organization, management, law, and marketing and by developing a good data collection system that provides the information necessary to incentivize the workforce— principals, teachers, and students—with appropriate rewards and sanctions" (p. 11). Ravitch and others recognize that pay for performance is an inappropriate reward model for education. Although most college graduates may be somewhat motivated by financial rewards, those graduates who go into teaching are not driven principally by money. Most teachers and prospective teachers are motivated by working with students and subject matter, by making a difference, and by living socially useful lives (Gratz, 2009).

Opposing Pay for Performance, Unions Support Valid Assessment of Teaching

Teacher unions recognize that teacher evaluation processes need to be changed. For too long, the evaluation of teaching performance lacked rigor and consistency. Too few of the truly outstanding teachers received recognition, too few of the struggling teachers were given appropriate support, and too little effort was made to identify those teachers who should not be in the classroom at all. Teaching is complex, and any evaluation of teaching and teachers must be sensitive to its complexity. As the AFT (2011b) notes, "Any valid approach to evaluation necessarily will consider both outputs (test data and student work) and inputs (school environment, resources, professional development). . . . Student test scores based on valid assessments should be one of the performance criteria, as should classroom observations, portfolio reviews, appraisal of lesson plans, and student work" (p. 1).

What Do Teacher Unions Really Want?

Parents, legislators, and unions agree: the ultimate goal of schools is to help every student succeed. Unions want to use their collective strength to improve schools through appropriate policies and practices. Unionized teachers would like to add their collective voice to the debates about accountability and school assessment programs, teacher education and development, school administration, and policy issues, such as No Child Left Behind legislation, merit pay, and the salaries and working conditions of teachers.

Nowhere is the union voice more necessary than in the support of teachers. What do classroom teachers need, and how can unions help? While salaries have always been a major issue for teachers, teachers typically indicate that a "lack of support" is their top concern (NEA, 2005). Teachers need real-world mentors who have mastered the practical skills necessary to help children learn. Teacher unions want a voice in recruiting and sustaining a high-quality teaching force. Unions want to play a significant role in everything to do with teaching, from participation in preservice teacher education to the development of strong induction programs and meaningful evaluation of teachers. The unions know that to improve schools, they have to support everything necessary and central to the preparation, recruitment, and work of good teachers.

Everyone supports good schools. Too many schools are failing, and most are not doing well enough. Unions are supportive of many school reform proposals and suspicious of others. Unions are particularly wary of policies and procedures that are imposed on schools without the consultation of teachers and that exclude the teaching staff from the decision-making process. Since it is largely up to the teachers to make schools successful, unions are eager to see the education emphasis move from its current obsession with test scores to a focus on teacher creativity and the development of teacher expertise.

POSITION 2: TEACHER UNIONS STAND IN THE WAY OF SCHOOL REFORM

Why is it, after decades and decades, that the nation has done almost nothing to get bad teachers out of the classroom? What possible excuse could there be for inaction on something so incredibly basic and obvious? There isn't any excuse. There is only a reason: the teachers unions are extraordinarily powerful, and they are in the business of protecting the jobs of their members.

—Moe (2011, p. 387)

A History of Self-Serving and Unsupported Union Claims

Teacher union officials say that when public monies are spent to improve working conditions for teachers, children are the ultimate beneficiaries. Their arguments are, no doubt, familiar. Public school students suffer because teachers are underpaid. Hardworking, devoted teachers deserve greater compensation. Unless teachers earn higher salaries, not only will the current crop of teachers become discouraged, but the most able college graduates will not consider a teaching career. Union leaders further argue that teachers need a stronger voice in school affairs. They claim that teachers will be more effective if allowed to join administrators in all areas of school leadership, including school improvement and supervision and evaluation of teaching.

The logic in these examples is simple: what is good for teachers is good for children. If the public wants better education for its children, the public should support union efforts to improve education through increased remuneration and greater authority for teachers. Collective bargaining practices, picket lines, work stoppages (strikes), and expansion of union control over schools should be considered beneficial to the community, parents, and students. Convincing? Not really. Making schools better places for teachers does not necessarily serve the public interest. The public's interest is measured not in teachers' job satisfaction but in the quality of learning provided to students. Despite the rhetoric of organized labor, teacher unions do not have a positive effect on student achievement. Researchers find negligible differences in achievement between public school students in union and nonunion schools. While research indicates evidence that collective bargaining improves teachers' salaries, benefits, and working conditions, it is more difficult to find a consistently positive influence of unions on student learning (Stone, 2000; Goldhaber, 2006). Unions cannot claim to make a difference where it counts most: students' academic performance. Despite failures of teacher unions to prove their worth in student achievement, the positive wage effect of unions—that is, their power to improve teachers' pay—clearly ensures that unions will remain players in education.

Although only about 15 percent of American workers belong to labor unions, most teachers in America's schools are unionized. Over 80 percent of teachers belong to an affiliate of the NEA or the AFT, and with millions of dues-paying members, unions have great resources and great power. Not only can teacher unions exert influence on the day-to-day workings of schools, but their political activities have given them unrivaled influence in the local, state, and federal governments as well. As Terry Moe (2001) points out, "The key to the unions' preeminence in American education is that they are able to combine collective bargaining and politics into an integrated strategy for promoting union objectives" (p. 166). Moe goes on to note, "On education issues, the teacher unions are the 500-pound gorillas of legislative politics, and especially in legislatures where the Democrats are in control, they are in a better position than any other interest group to get what they want from government" (p. 175).

Teacher unions work for the benefit of teachers. Do not be misled when unions call for more rigorous training of teachers or stricter licensing standards. While there is little evidence that such changes would result in better education or improved student learning, there is abundant evidence to indicate that these policies would make good economic sense for teachers. Stricter standards for teacher certification, whether academic (requiring all teachers to have master's degrees) or arbitrary (requiring all teachers to be over six feet five inches tall), would result in a diminished supply of teachers at a time when demand is increasing. Obviously, unions are hopeful that market forces will result in improved salaries. It is hard for the public to trust unions. Who can say with certainty whether union advocacy of smaller class size represents a desire to help children or whether it is simply a way to make teachers' work easier and, concurrently, increase the demand for teachers? Consider another union recommendation: mentorship programs through which experienced classroom teachers help new teachers learn the ropes. When teachers serve as mentors for other teachers, does it benefit students, or is this simply driving up the cost of education through featherbedding—the addition of unnecessary workers (Ballou and Podgursky, 2000)?

Encouraged by their ability to improve teachers' salaries—the union-wage effect is in the neighborhood of 5 to 10 percent—unions have extended their influence beyond bread-and-butter work issues. Past union efforts typically were limited to traditional labor concerns: wages and hours, working conditions, fringe benefits, grievance procedures, organization rights, and such specific work-related issues as extra pay for extra duty (e.g., athletic coaching or directing school plays). Over time, teacher unions began to demand a voice in policy issues, including curriculum reform, class size, disciplinary practices, textbook selection procedures, in-service training, teacher transfer policies, and personnel matters—including hiring and awarding tenure (Kerchner, 1986; Kerchner and Koppich, 1993). Today, affiliates of both the NEA and the AFT want teachers to expand their activities and participate in discussions about school improvement, staff development, and student assessment. These demands go well beyond the traditional bargaining issues of salaries and working conditions. Some union contracts give teachers the right to make decisions about how schools spend money, how teachers teach, and how students are to learn. In strongly unionized urban districts, union contracts can be hundreds of pages long (Moe, 2001). Under the familiar argument that collective negotiations will create a better education for children, union leaders now claim that increased teacher participation in all the decision-making and managerial aspects of education also will improve schools. The public has greeted the new union arguments with a healthy skepticism. Unions grew up on industrial principles. They have used organizing and negotiating techniques borrowed from industrial unions in mining and manufacturing—collective bargaining and the threat of strikes—to improve their members' working conditions. There is every reason to be suspicious that unions can use the same tactics to improve the quality of student learning.

Apologizing for Bad Teachers

Unions have become apologists for poor teaching and an obstacle to school reform. On the one hand, unions heap praise on the magical effect good teachers have on children's lives. On the other hand, they fail to admit that weak teachers may be a cause of many of education's problems. Everyone familiar with public schools knows that the quality of classroom instruction varies tremendously. Nestled among the great teachers, the good teachers, and the marginally adequate teachers are those who fail to convey enthusiasm for learning and, unfortunately, more than a few who have neither the personal qualities nor the skills and knowledge necessary to teach children. While the good teachers whet students' appetites for academic achievement, bad teachers kill interest, leave students with enormous gaps of information, and tarnish the reputation of the profession.

According to *Waiting for Superman*, the popular documentary film directed by Davis Guggenheim that focuses on school reform, about one in every fifty-one physicians in America loses his or her license to practice medicine. One in every ninety-seven lawyers loses the license necessary to practice law. Yet only one in every 1,000 teachers is dismissed for incompetence. You have had far fewer than 1,000 teachers, but it would be pretty safe to assume that you would recommend that more than one of your former teachers lose his or her job and teaching certificate for classroom incompetence or worse.

Joel Klein (2011), former chancellor of New York City's public schools, argues that in a school system with about 55,000 tenured teachers, "we were able to fire only a half dozen or so for incompetence in a given year" (p. 5). Tenure, lifetime job security unknown to most workers, is a privilege enjoyed by public school teachers, supported by unions, and destructive of education. In the United States, tenure is awarded to public school teachers following three to six years of teaching with satisfactory evaluations. The tenure hurdle is not a particularly high bar to clear, with almost all teachers earning this sinecure for life. In New York City, where 99 percent of all teachers win tenure, teachers are protected against dismissal as long as they provide "competent and efficient service" and demonstrate "good behavior." Tenure has outlived its usefulness. In the days of patronage appointment, tenure law protected teachers from wholesale dismissal every time there was a change in city or town mayor, and tenure offered some shelter against despotic administrators of the old school. Few people deny that at one time teachers needed union protection. "Everywhere teachers were subject to the whims of principals often as tyrannical as the worst stereotype of an old-time factory boss. They were able to fire and make life miserable for teachers who questioned the curriculum, didn't want an extracurricular assignment, or gave a low grade to a child of a favored parent" (Brill, 2011, p. 33).

Those days are long gone. Teacher unions strengthened tenure rights beyond their original protective design and now make it nearly impossible to dismiss even the least competent teachers. Steven Brill (2009), writing in *The New Yorker* magazine, describes the workings of New York's Temporary Reassignment Centers, commonly known as "Rubber Rooms," where teachers were sent after being "accused of misconduct, such as hitting or molesting a student, or, in some cases, of incompetence, in a system that rarely calls anyone incompetent" (p. 2). With union protection, teachers in the Rubber Rooms were guaranteed a hearing by an arbitrator, a process that typically took three to five years and rarely resulted in dismissal. All the while, teachers in the Rubber Rooms around the city drew full salaries and added to their eventual pensions. It was possible for teachers assigned to the Rubber Rooms for years to retire at age fifty-five, with an annual pension of $60,000 that was free from state taxes (Brill, 2009, 2011).

Clearly, the unions have gone too far. Teachers should not be dismissed for personality disputes with an administrator, and teaching should not be a patronage position with a wholesale changes of staff following every election, but teacher unions have made it all but impossible to remove even the least effective teachers from the classroom, and they now serve as a roadblock to school reform (Moe, 2011). The role of the union is to protect teachers; their role is not to educate children. As one school principal put it, the union president "would protect a dead body [teaching] in the classroom. That's her job" (Brill, 2009, p. 7).

The public is generally sympathetic to teachers but not to teacher unions, and it is not hard to understand why. The sad fact remains that too many schools have teachers who are not able to do the work expected of them. Unfortunately, because of unions and tenure laws, even the poorest teachers will probably stay on the job until retirement. In many states, union opposition has brought actions against ineffective teachers to an absolute halt.

Unions Fail to Support the Best Teachers

You have all had good teachers and know from experience that good teachers can make a startling difference in student learning. Academic research demonstrates this as well. One team of researchers, for example, found that when low-income students have good teachers for four years in a row, their learning increases, and the gap between low-income students and the average-income student is eliminated (Eric Hanushek and Steven Rivkin, quoted in Moe, 2011, p. 4). Other research suggests that if we were to remove the bottom 5 to 8 percent of teachers and replace them with "average teachers," the United States would move close to the top of international student achievement in math and science (Hanushek, 2010).

Every public school student and their parents know that some teachers are more effective than others, more able to promote academic achievement. Those teachers should be recognized and compensated for their superior results. Rewarding unusually high productivity is the cornerstone of the private sector, and it works to the benefit of the individual and the company, but this elegant compensation equation runs counter to the union-supported single-salary schedule. Today, the salaries of most teachers reflect their years of service and the graduate credits they earned, not their performance. In most school districts, all first-year teachers, with baccalaureate degrees and no experience, are paid the same whether they work with disadvantaged or relatively advantaged students and whether they teach in subject areas with a shortage of teachers, such as math and science, or in a subject field with an abundant supply of candidates. All second-year teachers are likely to receive the same salary increases independent of the achievements of their students and the teacher's contributions to student progress. One has to question if this is the best way to attract and reward high-quality teachers. Consider the following approach to personnel decisions based on merit and quantifiable data.

Most states require student testing in multiple grades every year. All students in a given grade level take the same standardized tests. Over the years, states have amassed lots of good achievement data, and it seems quite reasonable to use these data to measure how effective individual teachers are in promoting learning. Of course, to measure how much value a teacher has added, it is necessary to control for student demographics, class size, and teacher experience, but it can be done. Examining student gain scores on objective tests would provide useful data for making tenure decisions and awarding salary increases as well as considering teacher terminations. With objective data at hand, it would be possible to reward good results and penalize poor classroom performance.

Unfortunately, teacher unions object. As Joel Klein (2011) writes, "I proposed that the City [of New York] use value-added numbers only for the top and bottom 20 percent of teachers: The top 20 percent would get positive credit; the bottom would lose credit. And even then, principals would take value-added data into account only as part of a much larger comprehensive tenure review. Even with these limitations, the [teacher union] said 'No way'" (pp. 3–4).

In November 2010, after eight years on the job, Joel Klein resigned frustrated by union obstruction to school reform. On his last day on the job, Klein was told that he could withdraw the contributions he had made to the retirement system or leave the money in the system and receive a guaranteed annual rate of return of 8.25 percent. Klein was stunned and wondered how the system could be so generous at a time when banks were paying 1 percent interest. He was told that the union contract guaranteed the high rate and that if investments fell short, the city would make up the difference. "Who else," Klein asked rhetorically, "but Bernie Madoff guarantees 8.25 percent a year permanently?" (quoted in Brill, 2011, pp. 400–401).

Teacher Unions Have Outlived Their Usefulness

In the days when teachers had few rights and principals ran roughshod over them, unions helped to improve the working lives and benefits of teachers. But times have changed, and teacher unions have outlived their usefulness. The industrial age made unions attractive to teachers. In a postindustrial age, unions are an anachronism harmful to both teachers and students and an adversary of the school reform movement. Reformers believe that bad teachers should be fired and good teachers rewarded. Teacher unions oppose the reform agenda for schools. Union opposition to pay for performance, a teacher compensation model based on student achievement, and other forms of school accountability is harmful to the education of students. Unions work for those paying union dues instead of the students and the community. They use their considerable power and influence to support teachers when the focus of education should be on supporting the education of students. Unions have resisted school reform and become an obstacle to change. Once necessary to protect teachers, unions have grown into a behemoth that stands in the way of what is ultimately good for students. If school reform is to be effective and all students are able to profit from a sound and rigorous education under the guidance of a skillful teacher, the power of the unions must be opposed and reduced.

For Discussion

1. Since the twentieth century, American schools have used a single-salary schedule for all teachers. The schedule has vertical steps, rewarding teachers for longevity, and horizontal lanes reflecting earned postbaccalaureate credit. Pay-for-performance advocates argue that teachers' salaries should be based, in part, on the performance of their students on standardized tests, perhaps averaged over several years. They believe that enhancing the salaries of the most successful teachers will reward demonstrated success, attract more of the most promising college graduates to teaching, motivate current teachers, and weed out those who do not contribute to student learning.

   Teacher unions argue that standardized test scores measure only a narrow range of student work and that performance pay could pit one teacher against another and undermine cooperation among teachers.
   - Is performance pay attractive to you? How should performance be measured?
   - Do you think performance pay is the best way to motive teachers?
   - Think of someone you believe would be a good teacher who is not now in teaching or preparing to be a teacher. Would performance pay attract that person to education? If not, what would?

2. The next generation of teachers is likely to hold views about their work different from the views of the teachers they will replace. Susan Moore Johnson and colleagues (2004) argue that the new generation is "less accepting of top-down hierarchy and fixed channels of communication, less respectful of conventional organizations, and generally more entrepreneurial than their predecessors" (p. 252). Johnson also notes that the new teachers—whether they are first-career or mid-career entrants—do not seek uniform treatment, do not expect to or want to work alone, and do not want to be isolated in the classroom without feedback about their performance. They also expect their salaries to reflect their success as teachers.

   Do these values match your own? Do you enjoy teamwork over the autonomy of a single-teacher classroom? Do you enjoy risk-taking entrepreneurial opportunities that could affect your salary?

   Looking at Johnson's findings, another researcher argues that the values of previous generations of teachers—job security and single-teacher classes with little competition among teachers—are a better fit for collective bargaining and teacher unions than are the values of the new teachers (Koppich, 2005). Do you agree? Can teacher unions be attractive to a new generation of teachers?

3. Some education reformers believe that education for all children will improve if we allow teachers to increase their use of technology, for example, by delivering advanced placement courses online and by encouraging elementary school teachers to download tested lesson plans in difficult-to-teach subjects, such as math and science (Moe and Chubb, 2009; Willingham, 2010). Technology would allow teachers to spend less time in preparation and more time working with individual students. As one advocate puts it, "Teachers will become coaches who help students engage with material presented by others" (Peterson, 2010, p. 2).
   - What do you see as the advantages and disadvantages of changing a teacher's role from lesson designer to classroom coach?
   - Unions see this use of technology as undermining teacher autonomy and creativity. Do you agree?
   - What are the advantages of technology applied to classroom instruction? Can technology be considered a threat to teachers? To teacher unions?

References

American Federation of Teachers. (2011a). "AFT: A Union of Professionals" www.aft.org.
————. (2011b). "A Continuous Improvement Model for Teacher Development and Evaluation." www.aft.org.

BALLOU, D., AND PODGURSKY, M. (2000). "Gaining Control of Professional Licensing and Advancement." In *Conflicting Missions?*, ed. T. Loveless. Washington, DC: Brookings Institution.

BRILL, S. (2009). "The Rubber Room: Battle Over New York City's Worst Teachers." *The New Yorker*, August 31, pp. 1–15. www.newyorker.com.

————. (2011). *Class Warfare: Inside the Fight to Fix America's Schools*. New York: Simon & Schuster.

Commonwealth v. Hunt. (1842). 445 Mass (4 met.) 111, 38 Am. Dec 346.

EATON, W. E. (1975). *The American Federation of Teachers, 1916–1961: A History of the Movement*. Carbondale: Southern Illinois University Press.

ENGEL, R. A. (1976). "Teacher Negotiation: History and Comment." In *Education and Collective Bargaining*, ed. E. M. Cresswell and M. J. Murphy. Berkeley, CA: McCutchan.

GALLEY, M. (2003). "Survey Finds Teachers Supportive of Unions." *Education Week*, June 4, pp. 1–3. www.edweek.org/ew/articles/2003/06/04.

GARON, I. (2011). "Four Myths about Teachers." *Dissent* 58:97–98.

GOLDHABER, D. (2006). "Are Teachers Unions Good for Students?" In *Collective Bargaining in Education*, ed. J. Hannaway and A. J. Rotherman. Cambridge, MA: Harvard University Press.

GRATZ, D. B. (2009). *The Peril and Promise of Performance Pay*. New York: Rowman & Littlefield.

HANUSHEK, E. A. (2010). "The Economic Value of Higher Teacher Quality." www.nber.org/papers/w16606.

Holmes Group. (1986). *Tomorrow's Teachers: A Report on the Holmes Group*. East Lansing, MI: Holmes Group.

JESSUP, D. K. (1978). "Teacher Unionization: A Reassessment of Rank and File Education." *Sociology of Education* 51:44–55.

JOHNSON, S. M., ET AL. (2004). *Finders and Keepers; Helping New Teachers Survive and Thrive in Our Schools*. San Francisco: Jossey-Bass.

KAHLENBERG, R. (2007). *Tough Liberal: Albert Shanker and the Battles over Schools, Unions, Race, and Democracy*. New York: Columbia University Press.

KERCHNER, C. T. (1986). "Union-Made Teaching: Effects of Labor Relations." In *Review of Research in Education*, vol. 13, ed. E. Z. Rothkopf. Washington, DC: American Educational Research Association.

KERCHNER, C. T., AND KOPPICH, J. E. (1993). *A Union of Professionals: Labor Relations and Educational Reform*. New York: Teachers College Press.

KERCHNER, C. T., KOPPICH, J. E., AND WEERES, J. G. (1997). *United Mind Workers: Unions and Teaching in the Knowledge Society*. San Francisco: Jossey-Bass.

KLEIN, J. (2011). "The Failure of American Schools." *The Atlantic*, June, pp. 1–13.

KOPPICH, J. (2005). "Addressing Teacher Quality Through Induction, Professional Compensation and Evaluation: The Effects of Labor Management Relations." *Educational Policy* 19: 90–111.

LIEBERMAN, M., AND MOSCOW, M. H. (1966). *Collective Negotiations for Teachers: An Approach to School Administration*. Chicago: Rand McNally.

MOE, T. M. (2001). "Teachers Unions." In *A Primer on America's Schools*, ed. T. M. Moe. Stanford, CA: Hoover Institution.

————. (2011). *Special Interest: Teachers Unions and America's Public Schools*. Washington, DC: Brookings Institution.

MOE, T. M., AND CHUBB, J. E. (2009). *Liberating Learning: Technology, Politics, and the Future of American Education*. San Francisco: Jossey-Bass.

MURPHY, M. (1990). *Blackboard Unions: The AFT and the NEA, 1900–1980*. Ithaca, NY: Cornell University Press.

NEA. (2005). "NEA Committed to Improving Teacher Quality." www.nea-org/teacher-quality.

————. (2011). "Proposed Policy Statement on Teacher Evaluation and Accountability." May 7. www.nea-org.

NLRB v. Jones and Laughlin Steel Company. (1937). 301 U.S. 1, 57 S.Ct. 615.

PERLSTEIN, L. (2007). *Tested: One American School Struggles to Make the Grade*. New York: Henry Holt.

PETERSON, P. E. (2010). "Only If the Past Trends Persist Is the Future Dismal." In *American Education in 2030*, ed. C. E. Finn. Stanford, CA: Hoover Institution.

RAUTH, M. (1990). "Exploring Heresy in Collective Bargaining and School Restructuring." *Phi Delta Kappan* 71:781–784.

RAVITCH, D. (2010). *The Death and Life of the Great American School System*. New York: Basic Books.

ROSENTHAL, A. (1969). *Pedagogues and Power: Teacher Groups in School Politics*. Syracuse, NY: Syracuse University Press.

STONE, J. A. (2000). "Collective Bargaining and Public Schools." In *Conflicting Missions?* ed. T. LOVELESS. Washington, DC: Brookings Institution.

TUCKER, M. (2011). "Teachers, Their Unions and the American Education Reform Agenda." www.ncee.org.

URBAN, W. J. (1982). *Why Teachers Organized*. Detroit: Wayne State University Press.

WALLER, W. (1932). *The Sociology of Teaching*. New York: Wiley.

WEINGARTEN, R. (2010). "Study on Benefits of Performance Pay Without Reforms." www.aft.org.

WESLEY, E. B. (1957). *NEA: The First Hundred Years*. New York: Harper and Brothers.

WILLINGHAM, D. T. (2010). "Classroom Teaching in 2030." In American Education in 2030, ed. C. E. Finn. Stanford, CA: Hoover Institution.

CHAPTER 17

Academic Freedom and Censorship: Teacher Rights or Responsibilities

How should the proper balance between teacher freedom and responsibility be determined?

POSITION 1: FOR INCREASED ACADEMIC FREEDOM

In short, discussing controversy in the classroom is an imperative in a democracy.

—Misco and Patterson (2007)

Intellectual freedom is the belief in the fundamental dignity of individual inquiry and the right to exercise it.

—LaRue (2007)

Schools are often the center of community life, and the focus of local debates about morals, sex and sexual orientation, religion, politics, economics, racism, and a host of other social value controversies. Efforts to censor or severely restrict teachers and students arise in the context of these issues. Academic freedom, a protection for the legitimate examination of controversial topics in the pursuit of knowledge, suffers when censorship occurs or when political restrictions are imposed on schooling. Censorship denies, defeats, or diminishes academic freedom.

Sex, Politics, and Religion: A Few Cases

A parent in Olathe, Kansas, demanded that John Steinbeck's *Of Mice and Men* be banned from the school curriculum and classroom because the book is "worthless" and "profanity filled." Two school board members actually voted to have the classic banned, but the majority rejected the effort.

In Oakley, California, some parents wanted the same Steinbeck book banned for racial epithets.

School use of the popular Philip Pullman book *The Golden Compass* was protested by a group of parents and Christian leaders in Winchester, Kentucky, because Pullman was called "an atheist" and the book "anti-Christian."

A tenured teacher in Colorado was dismissed for showing the publicly available Bertold Bertolucci film *1900* as part of a class discussion about fascism. The teacher appealed, the teachers' association provided an attorney for a hearing, and the teacher was reinstated.

Some years earlier, a well-respected high school history teacher in the Denver Public Schools was dismissed because the city newspaper published his and other candidates' views as they ran for a congressional seat; the district thought his views were too controversial. He appealed and won reinstatement, but the district limited him to teaching basic English and forbade his teaching history.

A high school student paper in Bakersfield, California, was prohibited from publishing a story with interviews about gender identity, but a county judge ruled that students have the right to exercise freedom of speech and press without prior restraint.

In Metuchen, New Jersey, the high school principal threatened a student-financed and -edited paper that included some material from national news magazines (like *Time* and *Newsweek*), with the magazines' permission, because he considered it too controversial. The board refused to back the principal.

Words about puberty and homosexuality were cut by school administrators at the last minute from a New York high school production of *A Chorus Line*; one student danced a part in silence.

Field trips at a Pennsylvania high school to see *MacBeth* and *Schindler's List* were canceled after some citizen complaints.

Over the past two decades, the most frequently banned books include *Harry Potter, Diary of Anne Frank, Catch-22, Farewell to Arms, Deliverance, The Great Gatsby, Adventures of Huckleberry Finn, To Kill a Mockingbird, The Chocolate War*, and *Slaughterhouse Five*.

Even comic books suffer censorship. Trombetta (2010) examines the history of very popular "horror" comics and a U.S. Senate Committee hearing in the McCarthy Period that effectively suppressed them when the industry imposed a new Comics Code that "annihilated" that genre, on charges like "create disrespect for established authority" (p. 82). Now, a collection of those "banned" comics is available in the Young Adult section of public libraries.

Among the most censored authors are Judy Blume, Mark Twain, Maya Angelou, John Steinbeck, J. D. Salinger, Toni Morrison, R. L. Stine, Maurice Sendak, William Golding, and Robert Cormier.

Some important public figures comment on censorship:

Supreme Court Justice Potter Stewart: "Censorship reflects a society's lack of confidence in itself."

Historian Henry Steele Commager: "Censorship always defeats its own purpose, for it creates in the end the kind of society that is incapable of real discretion."

Actress, playwright, screen writer, and sex symbol Mae West: "I believe in censorship. I have made a fortune out of it."

Efforts to restrict or ban books, films, speakers, topics of study, magazines, speech, press, dress, art, drama, field trips, and other student and teacher activities have permeated and undercut school life for generations. Most of these efforts involve controversies surrounding sex, politics, or religion, though other issues, like race and economics, sometimes arise.

(Sources: *Newsletter on Intellectual Freedom*, 1996–2012; Sherrow, 1996; Foerstel, 2002; Huff and Phillips, 2010; Trombetta, 2010; Brainy Quote, 2011).

A Climate of Fear

The American Library Association's *Newsletter on Intellectual Freedom* reports that challenges to school and library books have been 400 to 500 per year over the past three decades and that these were mostly by individual parents—but there has been a recent uptick in organized efforts to restrict schoolbooks. Apparently, the organized attacks stem from such websites as Parents Against Bad Books in Schools (PABBIS) and www.safelibraries.org. The PABBIS website contains general statements like "You might be shocked at the sensitive, controversial and inappropriate material that can be found in books in K-12 schools" (PABBIS, 2011). It then offers, after a simple verification that you are at least 18 years old, a long list of books and authors that are suspicious—from Barbara Kingsolver and Toni Morrison to Leon Uris and Kurt Vonnegut—and includes major literary award winners and notable, widely read figures in literature. To avoid having to actually read the books to find unsavory content, the most "shocking and inappropriate" segments of each book are printed and available.

Many more incidents are recorded each year across the United States, and many do not get recorded. Restrictions on inquiry, knowledge, and education, unfortunately, are common. They are also responsible for a climate of fear in schools that causes cautious teachers to self-censor or severely limit controversial topics in order to avoid similar situations. School administrators often fear parental or citizen complaints and take preemptive action to try to limit teachers and students by cumbersome and sometimes illegal school policies and practices that encroach on the rights of teacher and student.

Teachers may think they have academic freedom, but they sometimes engage in self-censorship to avoid threats or uncomfortable situations. Administrators may impose questionable restrictions but encounter no protest by teachers who fear problems. Parents may threaten teachers and cause them to limit inquiry. In good school districts, however, the legitimate rights of teachers and students, as well as the rights of parents and the public to raise questions about what is taught and how, are protected by well-prepared policies and practices on academic freedom.

Although some stories about censorship and political restriction end in a positive result, where teacher and student academic freedom is protected, many incidents do not end so well. Teachers lose jobs, students are suspended, students and teachers avoid controversy, and education suffers. Furthermore, the long and continuing history of efforts to control, censor, and restrict teachers and students shows that the idea of academic freedom is not so well established in society that it is no longer an issue. There is a need for constant vigilance to retain the intellectual freedom that education in a democracy requires. That freedom, academic and intellectual, is the central purpose for education.

A Necessity, Not a Frill

A society cannot be free when its schools are not. The need to provide strong support to academic freedom for teachers and their students should seem obvious to anyone who supports a free society. Ideas are the primary ingredients of democracy and education, and the realm of ideas is protected by academic freedom. This simple, elegant concept is not well enough understood by some of the public and even by some teachers. Academic freedom requires diligent effort, exercise, and expansion in schools. It is under constant threat (Dewey, 1936; American Association of University Professors, 1986; Nelson, 1990, 2003, 2010; American Library Association, 1996, 2010, 2012; Menand, 1996; McNeil, 2002; Stone, 2004; Lindorff, 2005; LaRue, 2007; Wilson, 2008).

Michael Simpson, assistant general counsel for the National Education Association (2010), summarizes a series of recent court-decision setbacks for K–12 teachers on academic freedom issues, noting the historic pattern of increasing teacher and student freedom in the 1960s and 1970s from federal court decisions. He suggests, in light of "the harsh reality" of current decisions that appear to turn over the landmark Supreme Court decision of *Tinker v. Des Moines Independent School District* (1969) that supported student and, implicitly, teacher freedom. Current court decisions, following *Garcetti v. Ceballos* (2006), a case involving public employee speech while in performance of duties, have ruled that teacher speech can be determined and limited by the employer (*Mayer v. Monroe County Community School Corp.*, 2007). This denial of First Amendment speech protection for teachers is extraordinary in terms of academic history; Simpson makes some suggestions for teachers, including advocating for protective and clear "academic freedom" conditions in teacher contract language and school board regulations and being sure to know the school policies regarding dealing with controversial material and your rights of appeal. Current restrictions on teacher speech also show the significance of tenure protection for teachers, where firing can be only for due cause and requires due process. It is also increasingly important for teachers to become more active advocates for academic freedom in public discourse and in political arenas.

The continuing development of American democracy requires that academic freedom be further expanded in schools for both students and teachers. Noddings (1999) points out that democratic education requires debate and discourse—only with teacher freedom can this happen. The basic principles are clear—enlightened self-governance is basic to democracy and academic freedom is basic to enlightened self-governance. Freedom to teach and learn is basic to good education (Moshman, 2009).

Historic arguments against academic freedom for teachers were based on a mix of traditional ideas, such as teachers were not "scholars," they have a captive audience, they can influence impressionable minds, and they are public employees subject to the will of boards and administrators. These arguments falter against the more important necessity for teacher freedom to educate in a democracy. Teachers are now required to have scholarly qualities, students are expected to inquire and challenge rather than be captive receptacles, teachers' professional ethics do not countenance brainwashing, and to fulfill their professional and contractual responsibilities to educate, teachers must have the freedom to examine and present topics.

We are well beyond the period when teachers were prohibited from marrying, dancing, or participating in politics. In contemporary schools, teachers are expected to do more than force-feed students memorized material; we have come to expect education and critical thinking. Yet there remain strong efforts to censor and restrain educators in performance of their profession.

Some people and groups with strong moralistic or other narrow agendas have increased their efforts to restrict schools and impose censorship on students and teachers (Nakaya, 2005; Seesholtz, 2005; American Library Association, 2012). They hope to advance their own political, religious, or economic views and to deny the views of others. They see education as a way to indoctrinate the young to become noncritical believers or as a way to inoculate and insulate students from controversial ideas. They see evil or controversy in anything that differs from their own beliefs.

Mischief in Defining Academic Freedom

Words can sometimes be twisted to hide true agendas. "Patriot," for example, has taken on various shades of meaning fraught with symbolism—flag, pledge, eagle, anthem—and it can be used for opposing behaviors: true believer and dissenter. Academic freedom has become such a term, with historic orientations of open inquiry using evidence and scholarly examination of controversial topics while seeking knowledge and more recent use by some to try to impose an ideological position through stealth or deception or to confuse and confound.

Zealots on different sides of political, economic, and religious fences have tried to use schools as agents to impose their views and values on the young. They don't want schools to present opposing views or conflicting evidence and are against real critical thinking. That zealotry has increased the vulnerability of teachers who realize good education requires dealing with controversial issues (Thelin, 1997; Pipkin and Lent, 2002).

Now we are seeing efforts to change the argument against teacher freedom by changing the definition of academic freedom to suit a political agenda. The "Academic Bill of Rights" (Students for Academic Freedom, 2003; Dogan, 2006) is touted as a protection for academic freedom, demanding neutrality for institutions and requiring a "diverse" faculty along political lines. This proposed Bill of Rights is for colleges but has obvious implications for precollegiate schools. It claims support of academic freedom, but some think it is a cover to require the hiring of more conservative faculty members and to impose new restrictions on teachers in schools and colleges (American Association of University Professors, 2003; Wilson, 2006). While the neutrality of schools and the impartiality of teachers are good educational concepts, the proposed Academic Bill of Rights implies political litmus tests for teachers and contains the seeds of censorship and self-censorship to avoid controversial subjects.

A related attempt to use the "academic freedom" title to mislead is the "Academic Freedom Petition," a single-issue document that argues that academic institutions should ensure student and teacher freedom to "discuss the scientific strengths and weaknesses of Darwinian evolution" (Academic Freedom Petition, 2011). No other topic is identified in the petition for the protection of "academic freedom." This appears to be a project related to support for the teaching of creationism–intelligent design in explaining nature, a view that is theologically dogmatic and not subject to scientific inquiry itself. The theory of evolution is continually subjected to scientific examination using physical evidence, whereas the creationist view is not. This twisted use of academic freedom can cloud the more valuable condition needed for critical thinking in schools and colleges.

The good teacher, willing to examine controversial topics, runs risks far beyond those who are fearful, docile, and self-censoring. Teachers who fulfill the basic educational responsibility to provide intellectual freedom may encounter threats, ostracism, or ridicule. Ominous overt threats and subtle pressure from administrators, school boards, parents, special interest groups, and even peer teachers can cool a teacher's ardor for freedom of ideas. Teacher self-censorship—where fearful teachers screen ideas from classroom use in order to avoid controversy—is a common but hidden threat to academic freedom. Teachers hear about others being fired or threatened and often try to avoid any topic that could have similar repercussions for them. It is true that a few teachers have been fired for doing what our society should expect all good teachers to do. It is also true that many times these firings are reversed when the teacher is given due process and facts become known. Still, such events produce a chilling effect on other teachers, restricting academic freedom for themselves and their students. It takes courage to remain professional in the pursuit of education, but it is necessary. When the censors win, education and democracy lose (Sinclair, 1923; McNeil, 2002; Stone, 2004; Fuentes, 2005; Moshman, 2009; Nelson, 2010).

The Essential Relationship of Academic Freedom to Democracy

One inescapable premise in a democracy is that the people are capable of governing themselves. That premise assumes people can make knowledgeable decisions and select intelligently from among alternative proposals. Education and free exchange of ideas are fundamental to the premise. To think otherwise is to insult the essential condition of democracy.

Academic freedom is the freedom of teachers to teach, of schools to determine educational policies and practices unfettered by political restraints or censorship and the freedom of students to engage in study of ideas. It is essential to democracy. A society that professes freedom should demand no less freedom for its schools (Rorty, 1994; Wilson, 2008; American Library Association, 2010).

The U.S. Supreme Court demonstrated its commitment to the principle of academic freedom in a 1967 decision, finding that a state law that demanded teachers take a loyalty oath was unconstitutional. The Court noted that academic freedom is a "transcendent value":

> Our nation is deeply committed to safeguarding academic freedom, which is of transcendent value to all of us and not merely to the teachers concerned. That freedom is, therefore, a special concern of the First Amendment, which does not tolerate laws that cast a pall of orthodoxy over the classroom.... The classroom is peculiarly the "marketplace of ideas." (*Keyishian v. Board of Regents*, 1967)

Propaganda and public deceit are practiced in all countries, including democracies, but citizens of a democracy are expected to have the right and the ability to question and examine propaganda and expose those deceits. Dictatorial regimes do not need—and do not desire—the masses to have an education enabling them to question information the government presents. Totalitarian states maintain their existence by using raw power and threats, utilizing censorship and restriction, and keeping the public ignorant. Governments in democracies can attempt the same maneuvers, but they run the risk of exposure and replacement. The more totalitarian the government, the more it uses threats, censorship, and denial of freedom in education. The more democratic the society, the less it employs threats, censorship, and restriction of education. This litmus test of a democracy is also a significant measure of the level of academic freedom.

The Evolution and Expansion of Academic Freedom

Academic freedom has evolved and expanded from early American education when a narrow definition limited it to a few scholars in colleges, and even there it was not well practiced. It has since become a fundamental educational concept embracing both the general framework of schooling and the work of teachers at all levels. We are closer now to the historic dual German intellectual freedoms—*Lehrfreiheit* and *Lernfreiheit*—the freedom of teachers to teach and of learners to learn without institutional restriction (Hofstadter and Metzger, 1968). The American concept of academic freedom evolved from this dual and mutually supportive freedom for teachers and students (Daly, Schall, and Skeele, 2001). It still has not evolved sufficiently to assure educators and the public that schools are places of real and critical education, but it is significantly more embedded in the culture of schools and educated society than it was.

Socrates, charged with impiety and corruption of youth, defended himself by claiming that he and his students had the freedom to pursue truth. All wickedness, he argued, was due to ignorance; freedom to teach and learn would uncover knowledge, eliminate ignorance, and improve society. The judges did not agree, and Socrates was sentenced to death. Academic freedom, over time, has fared better. Although it is regularly battered, it has survived and expanded.

Unfortunately, differences in state laws and confusing court opinions have produced a mixed view of what specific actions are legally protected under the idea of academic freedom in the United States (O'Neil, 1981, 2008, 2010; Simpson, 2010; American Library Association, 2012). The broad concept of academic freedom is generally understood, but practical application of that freedom in classrooms and schools often is contested, and local and state court decisions often are murky. While some courts have supported school board discretion over curricular and student newspaper matters, in general, courts have exhibited an expanding awareness of the need for academic freedom in schools and have provided protection for teachers. If this good trend continues and educators remain vigilant, this foretells a proper expansion of the concept to cover the work of competent teachers across the nation.

Courts often have been highly supportive of academic freedom for public school teachers. Justices Frankfurter and Douglas (*Wieman v. Updegraff*, 1952) argued that all teachers from primary grades to the university share a special role in developing good citizens, and all teachers should have the academic freedom necessary to be exemplars of open-mindedness and free inquiry. In *Cary v. Board of Education* (quoted in Rubin and Greenhouse, 1983), the decision included the following:

> To restrict the opportunity for involvement in an open forum for the free exchange of ideas to higher education would not only foster an unacceptable elitism, it would fail to complete the development of those not going to college, contrary to our constitutional commitment to equal opportunity. Effective citizenship in a participatory democracy must not be dependent upon advancement toward college degrees. Consequently, it would be inappropriate to conclude that academic freedom is required only in colleges and universities. (p. 116)

At the global level, a statement adopted by the International Federation of Library Associations and Institutions (IFLA, 1999) holds, "Human beings have a fundamental right to access to expressions of knowledge, creative thought, and intellectual activity, and to express their views publicly." Academic freedom for all teachers is consistent with this position. It needs continual nurturing, expansion, and vigilance in support of global democratization.

Educational Grounds for Academic Freedom

Where, if not in schools, will new generations be able to explore and test divergent ideas, new concepts, and challenges to propaganda? Students should be able to pursue intriguing possibilities under the guidance of free and knowledgeable teachers. Students can test ideas in schools with less serious risks of social condemnation or ostracism. In a setting where critical thinking is prized and nurtured, students and teachers can engage more fully in intellectual development. This is in society's best interests for two fundamental reasons: (1) new ideas from new generations are the basis of social progress, and (2) students who are not permitted to explore divergent ideas in school can be blinded to society's defects and imperfections and will be ill equipped to participate as citizens in improving democracy (Puddington, Melia, and Kelly, 2008).

Although teaching can be conducted easily as simple indoctrination, with teachers presenting material and students memorizing it without thought or criticism, that leads to an incomplete and defective education. Teaching also can be chaotic, with no sense of organization or purpose—this, too, is incomplete and defective education. Neither of these approaches to teaching offers education. Education consists of ideas and challenges, increasingly sophisticated and complex. Indoctrination stunts the educational process, shrinking knowledge and constricting critical thinking. Chaotic schools confuse the educational process, mix important and trivial ideas, and muddle critical thinking. A sound education provides solid grounding in current knowledge and teaches students to challenge ideas as a part of the process of critical thinking.

The defining quality of academic freedom is freedom in the search for knowledge. This freedom extends to all students and teachers engaged in the quest for knowledge. The search for knowledge is not limited to experts but is the primary purpose of schooling. Learning best occurs as people test new ideas against their own experiences and knowledge—that testing requires academic freedom. This active learning does more than just help clear up student confusion. It offers intellectual involvement and ownership. In addition, it is often students who recognize flaws in existing knowledge or who find new ways to understand. When only experts control knowledge or when censors limit ideas, we risk conformity without challenges or conflicting opinions. We may not like challenges to ideas we find comfortable, but those challenges are the stuff of progress. Finocchio (personal communication with the author, 2011), professor of biology emeritus from St. Bonaventure University, wrote a strong plea for his retirement event: "Beware of those who interfere with the search for Truth, Beauty, Knowledge, and Wisdom. The road to freedom of inquiry must be free and clear." These words are equally applicable to elementary and secondary schools.

Most young people encounter radical ideas in conversations with friends or in films, television, and other media. In an educational setting, students can more fully consider controversial ideas, and they have the opportunity to criticize each view. The real threat to society is that students will not examine controversial material in schools and that students will come to distrust education and society as places for free exchange of ideas (Simmons, 1994; Evans, 2007). Daly and Roach (1990) call for a renewed commitment to academic freedom to pursue these social and educational ends (National Council for Social Studies, 1974).

The Center of the Profession

Academic freedom is at the heart of the teaching profession (Nelson, 1990, 2003, 2010). Professions are identified by the complex, purposeful nature of the work; educational requirements for admission; and commonly held ethics and values. Medical professionals, for example, work to protect and improve health, have a specialized education in medical practice, and share a commitment to life. Attorneys work in the realm of law, have specialized training in the practice of law, and are dedicated to the value of justice. Teachers work to educate children, have subject knowledge and specialized education in teaching practice, and share a devotion to enlightenment.

The nature of teachers' work and their shared devotion to enlightenment require a special freedom to explore new ideas in the quest for knowledge. This freedom deserves protection beyond that provided to all citizens under the constitutional guarantee of free speech. Unlike other citizens, teachers have a professional obligation to search for truth and assist students in their search for truth (Zirkel, 1993; Nelson, 2003). The National Science Teachers Association states. "As professionals, teachers must be free to examine controversial issues openly in the classroom" (www.nsta.org). The National Council for Social Studies (2012) policy supports freedoms of teachers to teach and of students to learn. Similar statements advocating academic freedom for classroom teachers appear in the major documents of most national teacher associations. The Foundation for Individual Rights in Education (2005) maintains a website that archives such academic freedom statements from all over the world (www.thefire.org). Teachers' jobs must not be at risk because they explore controversial material or consider ideas outside the mainstream.

A general misunderstanding of the central role schools play in a free society causes teachers and students to live a peripheral existence in the United States. Teaching has been viewed as less than professional; often, teachers are considered low-level employees, hired to do what managers ask. Excessive restrictions are sometimes imposed on what teachers can teach and methods of instruction they can use. School boards and administrators try to censor teachers and teaching materials. And students are virtually ignored, are treated as nonpersons, or are expected to exhibit blind obedience. There may have been some historic reason to treat teachers as mere functionaries, in some came as indentured servants and others had inadequate academic preparation. Now all states require undergraduate degrees and a majority of teachers have graduate degrees. Increasingly rigorous teacher credential regulations and improved professional study and practice offer no grounds for demeaning restrictions on a teacher's work. Academic freedom, the essence of the teaching profession, has been insufficiently developed as a necessary idea in our society and in teacher education. A dual educational effort would increase public awareness of the need for academic freedom and inform and inspire the people who go into teaching.

Academic Freedom and Teacher Competency: The Tenure Process

Provision of academic freedom for teachers is not, however, without limits or conditions. Not all persons certified to teach or every action they take deserve the protection of academic freedom. The basic condition for academic freedom is teacher competence. Incompetent teachers do not deserve and should not receive that extra protection; they should be dismissed if a fair and evidential evaluation finds them incompetent. A license to teach is not a license to practice incompetence (Bernard, 2008).

Teacher competence is a mix of knowledge, skill, and judgment. It includes knowledge of the material and of the students in class, professional skill in teaching, and considered professional judgment. Competence depends on more than just accumulation of college credits; it includes a practical demonstration that teachers can teach with knowledge, skill, and judgment. As in other professions, competence is measured by peers and supervisors and continues to be refined as teachers gain experience. In teaching, initial competence is expected as the new teacher completes the teaching credential program. That program of four or more years includes subject field and professional study and practice teaching under supervision. Then, according to the laws of various states, teachers serve full-time for several years under school supervision and are granted tenure only if they are successful. This long test of actual teaching should be sufficient to establish competence. Incompetent teachers should not get tenure.

The main legal protection for academic freedom in schools is state tenure law. Under tenure laws, teachers cannot be fired without due process and legitimate cause. The tenured teacher who is threatened with firing has a right to know specific allegations, a fair hearing, and an evidentially based decision. This protects tenured teachers from improper dismissal as a result of personality conflicts or local politics. Grounds for dismissal, identified in state law, usually include moral turpitude, professional misconduct, and incompetence. The allegation must be clearly demonstrated and documented for the dismissal to be upheld. There should be a high standard for becoming a teacher and for obtaining tenure; there also should be a high standard for dismissing a teacher. Teachers should not be dismissed on the basis of personal or political disagreements with administrators or others.

Nontenured probationary teachers also deserve the general protection of academic freedom because they, too, are expected to engage in enlightening education. However, they do not have the same legal claims as tenured teachers (Standler, 2000). Tenured teachers serve on "indefinite" contracts that schools need not renew formally each year. Dismissal or nonrenewal of the probationary teacher's one-year contract can occur at the end of any given school term, often without specifying cause for dismissal. Dismissal for dealing with controversial topics in a competent manner should, however, be prohibited by school policy as a condition for all teachers. Many excellent school districts honor this concept. Tenured faculty, protected from improper interference, need to ensure that nontenured teachers are not subjected to dismissal for performing their proper teaching function. It is a professional responsibility.

Obstacles to Academic Freedom

Notwithstanding the compelling reasons that support academic freedom, there are historical, political, and economic pressures that can be overwhelming (Wilson, 2008). Sadly, censorship, political restraint, anti-intellectualism, and illegitimate restrictions on teacher and student freedom have a long and sordid history in the United States. Early schools, under religious domination, imposed moralistic requirements on teachers, firing them for impiety, for not attending religious services, or for not exhibiting sufficient religious zeal. In the nineteenth century, many contracts required teachers to remain single, avoid drinking and smoking, attend church each Sunday, substitute for the minister on occasion, not associate with "bad elements," and avoid controversy. Communities required strict conformity to social norms, and teachers could be dismissed for dating, visiting pool halls, or simply disagreeing with local officials. Teachers whose political views differed from those with power in the community were summarily fired. No recourse was available to stop vigilante school boards or administrators.

In the first half of the twentieth century, political restraint and censorship replaced religious and moralistic restrictions on teachers (Pierce, 1933; Beale, 1936; Gellerman, 1938). College teachers often fared no better, and many suffered great indignities at the hands of college officials (Sinclair, 1922; Veblen, 1957; Hofstadter and Metzger, 1968). Academic freedom was an ideal, not a common practice. John Dewey and a few other widely known scholars founded the American Association of University Professors in 1915 for the primary purpose of organizing to protect the academic freedom of college teachers. Dewey recognized even then that all teachers, not just those in colleges, needed academic freedom.

In the twenty-first century, teachers clearly have gained much in professional preparation and stature, but they are not yet free. Significant threats to academic freedom continue to limit education and place blinders on students. Censorship attempts have been launched in virtually every state. Some states have numerous censorship attempts each year, and thousands of teachers and students are restricted by actions of vigilante groups, school boards, and school administrators (American Library Association, 2012; National Coalition Against Censorship, 2012).

Textbook publishers shy away from controversial content to avoid censors. Texas censors forced a major American history textbook by highly respected historians to be stricken from Texas high schools because of two paragraphs (out of 1,000 pages) suggesting that prostitution was rampant in the West in the late nineteenth century (Stille, 2002).

The Internet is the most recent focus of censors, with scare tactics used to block access to many legitimate Internet sites (O'Neil, 2008; Vandergrift, 2012). Websites that protest such censor intrusion into libraries include the Electronic Frontier Foundation (www.eff.org), the Foundation for Individual Rights in Education (www.thefire.org), and Peacefire (www.peacefire.org).

Topics that arouse the censors vary over time and across locations and span both ends of the political spectrum. Socialism and communism were visible targets in the 1920s and again in the 1960s, surfacing again in the Reagan administration. Sexual topics and profanity are constant targets of school censors. A more recent issue is the charge that schools teach secular humanism—teachers and materials are anti-God, immoral, antifamily, and anti-American. Among other current topics stimulating people who want to stifle academic freedom are drugs, evolution, values clarification, economics, environmental issues, social activism, and the use of African American, feminist, or other minority literature (Jenkinson, 1990; Japenga, 1994; Sipe, 1999; Horowitz, 2005; Lindorff, 2005; Seesholtz, 2005; American Library Association, 2012).

Publicized censorship and restraint activities have a chilling effect on school boards, administrators, and even many teachers (Whitson, 1993; Ross, 2004; Patterson, 2010). The possibility of complaints on a controversial topic leads to fear. Daly (1991) found that few school districts had policies to protect teacher and student rights to academic freedom. As a result, teacher self-censorship denies students and society the full exploration of ideas. Many teachers avoid significant topics, or they neutralize and sterilize them to the point of student boredom.

A statement by the American Association of University Professors (1986) in support of academic freedom for precollege-level teachers identified a variety of political restraints imposed on such teachers. The American Civil Liberties Union (www.aclu.org) has a long tradition of support for academic freedom for teachers and students and assists in court proceedings to redress censorship and political restriction. Since 1970, the frequency of reported censorship incidents has tripled. Moreover, estimates suggest that for each incident formally reported, about fifty other censoring activities go unreported (Jenkinson, 1985). The National Coalition Against Censorship (www.ncas.org), affiliated with dozens of professional and scholarly associations, formed because of this increase in censorship.

A Free Society Requires Academic Freedom

Despite the often weak protection of academic freedom and often powerful political pressures brought to bear to stifle it, attaining freedom for teachers and students is worth the strenuous effort it demands. There are compelling democratic, educational, and professional grounds for expanding the protection of academic freedom to competent teachers and all students. And there are important social reasons why the public should support academic freedom in public education. Academic freedom is more than a set of platitudes, state regulations, and court decisions. It should be a fundamental expectation of schools in a free society. Academic freedom is a central truth for the profession of teaching.

POSITION 2: FOR TEACHER RESPONSIBILITY

Freedom of speech does not imply a right to an audience.... Unfortunately, many of those who talk the loudest and longest about "freedom of speech" and "academic freedom" are in fact trying to justify the imposition of propaganda on a captive audience in our schools and colleges.

—Sowell (2005, p. 1)

The K–12 public school establishment has adopted a quasi-official pedagogy that encourages the classroom teacher to shape students' beliefs on contemporary issues like race, gender, sexual preference, and American foreign policy.

—Stern (2006a)

Freedom from Indoctrination

Academic freedom involves more than unbridled indoctrination to one view. Yet some college professors and the K–12 teachers unions have asserted a right to academic freedom of that type. Stern (2006c) notes that "leftist political indoctrination in the classroom is now even more pernicious in K–12 education than it is on the university campus" (p. 1). Kline (2008) reports on a survey showing that about 40 percent of Americans said professors often use their classroom for political platforms. This is not academic freedom and teachers at any level who engage in it should not be protected (Olson, 2011).

Academic freedom consists of the presentation of balanced views, with the teacher as a neutral to be sure there is fairness. This can't be done if schools continue to hire teachers who think indoctrination is their right and if teacher education programs continue to emphasize political goals like "teaching for social justice" or progressivism. We need a professional code of ethics for teachers that emphasizes the teaching of basic skills to help students do schoolwork, not to turn them into activists. "If educators won't do this voluntarily, then let the legislators do it for them" (Stern, 2006c, p. 1). Freedom for teachers is directly linked to their responsibilities; a suitable code of ethics makes that clear.

Power and Responsibility in Teaching

All rights and freedoms are connected to responsibilities. Teachers' freedoms must be tied to their responsibilities, and their rights and freedoms are conditioned on their acceptance of those responsibilities. Teachers' freedoms are supported and limited by their responsibilities to parents, to society, to the child, and to the profession.

Society gives teachers authority to develop sound knowledge and values in children; school is compulsory for that purpose. The child, weaned from parental influence, looks to teachers for guidance. This is a particularly important responsibility. Teachers bear duties to parents, society, and the child to provide a suitable education. They also have ethical duties to the profession of teaching. These multiple responsibilities require accountability from teachers and schools.

Teaching is among the most influential positions in society. Teaching is next to parenting in its power to carry values and ideas from generation to generation. In some respects, teachers exert more influence on children's views and values than do parents. Parents have great control over what their children see, hear, and do during the earliest years, but after the child starts school, parents relinquish increasing amounts of that influence to teachers. That should be a good thing, with children becoming more mature and independent while studying under responsible, committed teachers. Parents retain strong interests in what their children see, hear, and do long after primary school, and good schools and teachers give them nothing to fear. The influence of teachers goes well beyond the classroom doors, school grounds, and school term; teachers exert influence that can last for years, even lifetimes. This capacity to influence the young carries heavy responsibilities.

Parental Rights

Parents have general, moral, and legal rights and obligations to and for their children, rights and obligations that teachers and schools must not undermine. Parents are expected to provide for the child's safety and welfare—physical, emotional, spiritual, and moral. Provision of food, clothing, and shelter is a parental obligation given up only when parents are incapable. Parents have moral obligations and rights, including instructing their children in determining right from wrong, good from bad. Parents instruct their children in ethical conduct by providing them with a set of socially acceptable behaviors, including integrity, honesty, courtesy, and respect. Under the law, parents can be held accountable for lack of adequate and appropriate care of their children; they can even be held legally responsible for their children's acts.

Because parents are presumed to have the child's interests at heart, they are given great latitude in providing care and upbringing. Parents are even permitted to exercise appropriate corporal punishment, more than any other person would be permitted to inflict on a child, under the legal idea that the parent has broad responsibilities and rights. At the root of laws regarding parents' rights and obligations is the idea that they are responsible for their children's upbringing, morality, and behaviors. Teachers, however, act as surrogate parents only in certain situations, with a number of limitations, and should not deviate from the norms of the good parent in the good society.

Children are not put in schools as punishment or as a way to make up for family irresponsibility. Schools, therefore, must continue the cultural heritage by inculcating positive and supportive social and family values in the young.

The comparative youthfulness of students, influential role of teachers, and authoritative nature of instruction make schools and teachers even more responsible to social and parental values and interests. Especially in public schools, where attendance is mandatory, schools and teachers need a greater sensitivity to the role of positive parental surrogate. Thus, public school teachers are even more accountable than private ones to the community and to parents for what they teach and how.

Teacher Responsibilities to Parents

Schools, then, have a special obligation to be responsive to parents' concerns for their children. This reasoning lies behind the legal concept that teachers act in loco parentis, or in place of the parent. That concept, with deep social and legal roots, protects teachers in handling student discipline and evaluation. It also requires teachers to remain sensitive to parental interests.

Teachers, standing in place of the parents, take on similar responsibilities for children's development and protection. Teachers have responsibilities for providing a safe, healthy classroom environment, and they assume protective moral, ethical, and legal duties. In addition, they have educational responsibilities: they must teach children necessary knowledge and skills. Discharging these responsibilities demands responsiveness to parental concerns about the kinds of knowledge and values taught.

Teachers cannot have license to do anything to students, physically or mentally. No one today would argue that teachers should be permitted to abuse children physically. Teachers can require students to be attentive to lessons, be orderly, and be civil, but they are prohibited from abusive activities, such as striking students. Malevolent teacher behavior is outside the standards of professional conduct.

Mental abuse of students is equally abhorrent but is less easy to detect. Mental abuse is no less harmful, however, to students, parents, or society. It can consist of vicious verbal personal attacks, indoctrination in antisocial values or behaviors, or manipulation of children's minds against parents or morality (Sowell, 2005; Stern, 2006b). Parents have a right to insist teachers not subject their children to these tactics but often are unaware of them until after the damage has been done.

Parents have a right to monitor what schools are teaching their children, hold the school accountable for it, and limit potential for damage to their children. Beyond necessary limits on teachers, schools also must be subject to limits that conform to social mores. For example, book, video, and film purchases for school libraries should be continuously and vigilantly screened so that only proper material is made available to our children. A parent review committee can be used to determine which books are suitable, with opportunity for any parent to complain about library materials and have that complaint acted on effectively.

PABBIS is organized to help parents identify and monitor books available to their children in school settings. As PABBIS (2011) states on its website, "You might be shocked at the sensitive, controversial and inappropriate material that can be found in books in K-12 schools." This organization collects parental comments, reviews books, and maintains a list with examples of school books that parents should check on the basis that "bad is what you think is bad for your child." This takes the parent's rightful position and provides information to help them make rational judgments about this material. The website offers documentation with quotes from many of the identified books that show their shocking contents.

We need not only worry about what teaching materials are used in classrooms; we also must be vigilant about other areas of schools where underage students have access. In school media centers, there is an increasing problem with Internet access. The Internet can be a valuable resource for children. There are many excellent websites for adding educational quality in such areas as science, history, the arts, literature, math, and other subjects. The opportunity to observe geographic locations, ancient art and culture, current news, and scientific experiments and achievements and to engage in available educational work via the Internet is exceptional and otherwise not available. However, there exists a serious problem in Internet usage when websites containing inhumane, anti-American, racist, antiauthority, sexual, antireligious, or other inappropriate material are available in schools. Federal legislation in

2000 requires libraries to use computer filtering software to prevent obscenity, child pornography, or other harmful materials to be shown to children on computer screens. This was challenged by the American Library Association, but the Supreme Court upheld the law (*United States v. American Library Association, Inc.*, 2003). Over twenty-five states also have laws that limit Internet use by minors. But parents still need to monitor and control, including Internet use in schools. Parents can exert control in their children's computer use at home to screen out undesirable sites; schools have a greater responsibility in screening out any such sites from their computers since schools serve a broad cross section of children.

Teacher Responsibilities to Children

The paramount responsibility of teachers is to their students. Because students are immature and unformed, teachers must carefully exercise their influence and temper freedom with responsibility. Teachers hold great potential power over children's lives, and teacher authority needs to be weighed heavily in teacher decisions as to what to teach and how. Teachers derive power from maturity, physical size, and position. Children are vulnerable.

In forming and testing ideas, attitudes, and behaviors, children look to teachers for direction. Children naturally are curious and positive but cannot yet fully discern between good and bad, proper and improper. Teachers have a responsibility to continue the moral and ethical education that parents have begun.

Teacher Responsibilities to Society

Society, as well as parents, has a significant interest in children's education. Schools were established to pass on the cultural heritage; to provide the skills, attitudes, and knowledge needed to produce good citizens; and to prepare children to meet their responsibilities in family, work, and social roles. Schools are social institutions, financed and regulated to fulfill social purposes. Society has values, standards of behavior, and attitudes that schools must convey to children. These standards have evolved over a long period, and they represent our common culture. Society charges schools and teachers to ensure that social standards and the ideals that these standards represent are taught by example and by word.

Schools do not exist as entities separate from society, able to chart their own courses as though they had no social responsibilities. They were not intended to instruct students in antisocial, anti-American, or immoral ideas or behaviors, nor will society allow them to continue to do so. Society trusts teachers to develop the young into positive, productive citizens. Those few teachers who use their position to attempt to destroy social values or create social dissension are violating that trust. Those who sow the seeds of negativism, nihilism, or cynicism also are violating that trust. Society has the right to restrict, condemn, or exclude from teaching those who harm its interests.

Teacher Responsibilities to Their Profession

The teaching profession has an extensive and illustrious history. It is based on the idea of service to children and society. The teachers' code of ethics recognizes teacher responsibilities as singularly important. Teachers want to convey the cultural heritage to their students, along with a strong sense of social responsibility. Teachers can ask no less of themselves.

A basic responsibility of the teaching profession is to prepare young people for life in society. That includes teaching students social values and knowledge, and teachers' personal conduct should exemplify society's ideals. The teaching profession recognizes both children's needs and society's needs. Teachers have an obligation not to go beyond professional bounds and to reject those who would tarnish the profession's reputation.

Teachers are the key to good education. They are also the key to poor education. When teachers are excellent, a school is excellent. But, as is widely known, many schools are not excellent, and many teachers are weak and ineffective. In fact, much of the great problem in U.S. education is due to teachers who should not be in classrooms. These teachers should be weeded out, but tenure laws and teacher unions protect the weakest and ensure poor educations for many of our children. These protections not only burden students, parents, and citizens but also pose a more serious threat to decency, patriotism, and social values (Limbaugh, 2005; Sowell, 2005).

Zealotry and Teacher Irresponsibility

Pied Piper teachers are not weak in their beliefs and sales techniques but often are weak in their intellectual capabilities and acceptance of fundamental responsibility to society and its values. These teachers fail to recognize the proper role of a teacher. Not only does tenure cover up poor teaching, but it also protects socially dangerous teachers. They use the hollow claim of academic freedom to camouflage their attempts to distort the minds of the young. Weak teachers who actually believe that they have a special freedom to do as they wish in the classroom are a major threat to our culture.

Teachers can be captured by radical ideas and have a captive audience of immature minds. Often, the academically weak teacher misunderstands the threats of anarchism, atheism, satanism, socialism, communism, and other extreme positions. They often have a simplistic utopian view and want their students to adopt the same and so impose their radical views on vulnerable young people. They may advocate extreme views of politics, economics, religion, family relations, drug use, sexual preferences, and other controversial topics. Students are expected to recognize the teacher's authority and may not be in a position to challenge the teacher's opinions. This denies the concept of education and threatens society. Nevertheless, state laws and unions protect teachers no matter how radical and socially detrimental their concepts are. This protection, under tenure laws and the false cloak of academic freedom, allows miseducation in schools. Tenure laws make it almost impossible to rid schools of poor teachers or those who are zealots.

The false claim that academic freedom gives teachers the right to do what they wish does not take into account the real history of academic freedom. The historic idea of academic freedom protects scientists and university scholars in pursuing and publishing their research. Even in this restricted setting, there are some limits for researchers; they cannot do any research that they might want, certainly none that knowingly harms people. Academic freedom in its original conception has little to do with schoolteachers and their work. Nor does the historic sense of academic freedom reflect social responsibilities attendant on teaching in public elementary and high schools. Because young, impressionable children must attend school by law, we demand greater accountability from public school teachers than we do from teachers in colleges, where students may be old enough to resist brainwashing. Students are a captive audience of relatively unsophisticated children; they are the ones who need protection. The historic definition of academic freedom applies solely to the protection of university scholars as they research their specialties. It was not intended to cover schoolteachers and their students.

Where current applications of academic freedom involve schoolteachers and their students is in ensuring that no indoctrination or politicization takes place in classrooms of our schools (Stern, 2006b, 2006c). The National Academic Freedom Conference provided significant evidence of the problems created when teachers attempt to impose their views without challenge (Dogan, 2006). Students subjected to teacher rants against the president or in support of foreign governments or ideologies make sad stories in the report.

Academic Freedom as License

A license to teach is not a license to impose one's views on others. Corruption of the young is at the least a moral crime; it is ethically reprehensible. The majority of teachers accept this and discharge their duties with integrity and care. For them, teaching is a calling to instruct the young in society's knowledge and values. This represents the best in the profession and is a great support to the well-being of the community and nation. Unfortunately, some teachers do not subscribe to the values of their profession.

There are teachers who are caught in drug raids, who have cheated on their income tax returns, and who have committed robbery—but these are exceptions (O'Connor, 2005). Most teachers are not criminals. When teachers do engage in criminal conduct, they are subject to criminal penalties and possible loss of employment. They do not receive special treatment. However, there is another form of crime, intellectual crime, that teachers may engage in under the guise of academic freedom.

Intellectual crimes include ridiculing student or family values, advocating antisocial attitudes, indoctrinating children in secular humanism, and influencing students to think or act in opposition to parent and community norms. These crimes may have an even greater, more devastating effect on children and society than legal transgressions because they tear at the nation's moral fiber. Perpetrators should not have special protection. There is nothing academic about confusing and confounding children about their families and society; teachers who commit such crimes deserve no consideration under the rubric of academic freedom. Distorting the minds of the young is misteaching and should be penalized (Olson, 2011; Wall Street Journal, 2012).

A child brought up to revere the family, believe in traditional marriage, support the United States, and respect people in authority may find it traumatic when a teacher expresses approval of such activities as participating in homosexual acts, supporting abortion rights, espousing anti-Americanism, engaging in civil disobedience, or sexually using children. Teachers should not have the right to damage children in this manner. And state laws, like new ones in California, should not mandate indoctrination in schools toward a gay-friendly curriculum and textbooks or to identify a left-wing political or social agenda required of teachers (Ryan, 2011). Stretching the idea of academic freedom to protect such teachers is an affront to the true meaning of academic freedom.

Some schoolteachers and their unions want to open a large umbrella of academic freedom to cover anything a teacher does or says. Their claims to protection are not justified but make school administrators wary. Administrators do not want the American Civil Liberties Union or other local vigilante groups interfering in school affairs. Thus, radical teachers often get away with their preaching and mind bending for years because the administration is afraid to reprimand them. Instead, the problem is hidden. Parents who protest are allowed to have their children transferred to other classes, but unsuspecting parents fall prey to these unprofessional classroom Fagins. It takes a courageous, persistent parent to thwart such a teacher. Often, public disclosure of the teacher's actions will arouse the community and force school officials to take action.

Radical teachers also have misused state tenure laws, which typically place excessive impediments to obstruct efforts to dismiss a teacher. As a result, very few school districts find it worthwhile to try to fire even the most incompetent teachers, and radical teachers recognize this. Tenured teacher firings are very rare; the radical teacher merely has to sit tight until tenure, and then anything is permissible. Tenure laws create burdensome requirements that save teachers' jobs even when those teachers have demonstrated a lack of respect for parents, students, and community values. We need to make it easier to dismiss teachers who behave irresponsibly.

Teacher tenure, protected under state laws, is undergoing serious scrutiny. Most revisions have tightened requirements for tenure and altered the conditions for attaining it or the burdensome procedure for dismissing ineffective teachers who have tenure. At least eighteen states have modified tenure regulations; the Education Commission of the States website shows current state approaches (www.ecs.org). Idaho has completely eliminated teacher tenure, and other states are considering significant reform. A discussion on www.procon.org notes that teacher tenure creates complacency, makes it difficult to remove teachers who are ineffective, actually limits student freedom, makes seniority more important than good teaching, and is costly to enforce. New York City spends an average of $250,000 per case to attempt to dismiss tenured teachers who have been charged and spent about $30 million to pay teachers charged with incompetent behaviors because dismissal procedures take years to complete. Charged teachers were assigned to a "Rubber Room" at full pay during those long procedures to get them out of classrooms. Joel Klein, former chancellor of New York City Schools, reportedly said that death penalty cases can be resolved faster than teacher misconduct cases. Tenure simply protects jobs and sometimes protects bad teachers imposing their views on students; it does not protect teacher and student freedom to educate well.

Teachers may have views that differ from community norms, but the classroom is not the place in which to express them. Teachers should not have the freedom to preach radical ideas in schools. Schools are not meant to be forums for teachers whose viewpoints differ sharply from those of the community. Instead, schools are intended to express and affirm community values. Malleable students are a captive audience; teachers must not have the right to impose contrary views on the young (Sowell, 2005).

Academic Freedom and Teacher Freedom

We must bear two important considerations in mind in any discussion of academic and teacher freedom in the schools. First, academic freedom provides limited protection to university-level scholars who are experts in their specialized fields, and the concept is more limited when applied to teachers below the college level. Second, other freedom for teachers below the college level is not unlimited or unrestrained; it is necessarily related to traditional teacher responsibilities.

There is no doubt that, within the limits of responsibility, teachers deserve respect and some freedom to determine how to teach. That is, teacher freedom can be separated from academic freedom, which is intended to protect the rights of experts to present their research results. This separation does not denigrate teachers any more than it denigrates lawyers, doctors, and ministers as respected people with no claim to special freedom in their work. Teacher freedom is protected by community traditions and the constitutional protection of free speech. Teachers do not need additional protections.

The U.S. Constitution's protections of free speech for all citizens are more than sufficient for teachers. Under the Constitution, any of us can say what we wish to say about the government, our employers, or the state of the world provided that it is not slanderous, imminently dangerous, or obscene. Obviously, we cannot say false things about someone without risking a libel suit, and we cannot yell "Fire!" in a crowded theater or "Bomb!" in an airport without risking arrest. Although we have the freedom to say them, we also must accept the consequences for our statements (Standler, 2000).

Public expression of controversial views, as in letters to a newspaper editor, is a right of all people in the United States. Teachers, of course, have the same right. But that does not mean that teachers are any different from other citizens or more deserving of job security no matter how inane or anti-American their public statements (Harden, 2012). Teachers' jobs are not safe regardless any more than are jobs of those employed by private firms who make controversial public statements. Anyone who wishes to make public statements must recognize the risks involved. Teachers, more than most citizens, should be aware of the responsibilities surrounding public discourse. A teacher's inflammatory comments can lead to public outrage. For public school teachers, the public is the employer.

Schoolteachers should not expect job guarantees when they make negative comments about schools, the community, or the nation, or when they teach children by using propaganda or inaccurate or provocative material. Classroom statements by teachers are actually public statements, subject to the same conditions as letters to the editor or public speaking. There is no special privilege granted to teachers merely because they close the classroom door.

Private schools can expect their teachers to uphold school and parent values because private school administrators and boards have more latitude in dismissing teachers they consider unsatisfactory in teaching or in judgment. State tenure laws do not apply to them. Public school boards and administrators are under some constraints because of those tenure laws and active teacher unions, but they should be more aggressive in weeding out poor teachers and those who engage in controversial acts. Each board of education has a responsibility to provide children with information, skills, a set of social values, and a moral code that strengthen society. Teachers cannot abrogate that responsibility.

Academic Freedom as a Function of Academic Position

Academic freedom protects scholars who recognize the academic responsibilities inherent in it. Scholars who have developed expert knowledge in a subject field may conduct research challenging accepted views—this is how we continue to refine knowledge. Academic freedom allows such scholars to publish or present their research without fear of losing their positions but only in those areas in which they have demonstrated expert knowledge. They have no greater freedom than any other citizen in areas outside their own expertise. The Constitution protects everyone's speech but does not and should not protect a faculty job. There is a difference between academic freedom and license, and no academic freedom should exist for those who indoctrinate others. Buckley (1951), Hook (1953), and Kirk (1955) provide philosophic grounds for limiting teacher freedom to expert scholars engaged in publication of their research. They would deny scholars or any other educators the right to proselytize or indoctrinate students under special protection of academic freedom (Limbaugh, 2005).

Goldstein (1976) argues that academic freedom is unsuited to elementary and secondary schools because of the age and immaturity of the students, the teacher's position of authority, the necessarily more highly structured curriculum, and the dominant role of schools in imparting social values. These factors cannot be easily dismissed. Elementary and secondary school teachers are different from university scholars in their training, functions, employment status, and responsibilities. Elementary and secondary schools have broad responsibilities to parents, community, and state that do not permit license. Schools and teachers serve in capacities that require support for and advocacy of social and family values. Rhetoric about academic freedom does not diminish that significant responsibility.

Teachers deserve respect and appreciation for their contributions to society, decent salaries, and comfortable working conditions. They deserve the protection the Bill of Rights gives to all U.S. citizens: freedom of speech, association, and assembly. For all of us, including teachers, these freedoms entail responsibilities. Teacher responsibilities to students, parents, school officials, the teaching profession, and society make classroom teachers one of our most treasured resources. Teachers do not, however, merit special treatment in regard to their freedom. Tenure should not protect them from losing their jobs for subverting students, advocating radical ideas, insubordination, or proselytizing.

For Discussion

1. Dialectic Exercise: The idea that academic freedom is limited to university researchers in their field of study only can be considered a thesis. What would be an antithesis? What evidence exists on each side? What philosophic grounds and logic support each position? What would be a suitable synthesis? How would your synthesis affect the current situation for K–12 teachers in regard to the exercise of academic freedom?
2. If you were asked by a local school board to be on a committee to prepare school district policies related to the following, what policies would you recommend? Draft an example set of policies to govern how a school district should handle such matters.
   Teacher freedom
   Student freedom
   Dealing with controversial material, and handling parental or citizen complaints about teaching material, methods, or school curriculum
3. Dialogue Ideas: Should there be any restrictions on what a teacher can discuss in class? What set of principles should govern establishment of those limits? Should students have the same freedoms and limits? Is student age or teacher experience a significant factor in this determination? How should schools handle questions that arise about how a teacher handles controversy?
4. Which, if any, of these topics should be banned from schoolbooks or class discussion?
   Explicit sexual material   Violence
   Sexism   Anti-American views
   Racism   Antireligious ideas
   Fascism   Socialism
   Inhuman treatment of people   Animal, child, or spouse abuse
   What are the grounds for justifying censorship of any of these? Who should decide? What are some good examples of thesis and antithesis statements about censorship? How would you construct a dialect on this topic?
5. What role should teachers play in learning about and responding to efforts at censorship? Should censors be censored? How should a teacher be prepared to deal with censors and political restraint?

References

Academic Freedom Petition. (2011). Discovery Institute Center for Science and Culture. www.academicfreedompetition.com.

American Association of University Professors. (1986). *Liberty and Learning in the Schools.* Washington, DC: American Association of University Professors.

———. (2003). "Academic Bill of Rights." December. www.aaup.org.

American Civil Liberties Union. (1988). *The Rights of Students.* 3rd Ed. Washington, DC: American Civil Liberties Union.

American Library Association. (2010). *Intellectual Freedom Manual.* Chicago: American Library Association.

———. (2012). *Newsletter on Intellectual Freedom.* Chicago: American Library Association.

BEALE, H. (1936). *Are American Teachers Free?* New York: Scribner's.

BERNARD, S. (2008). "Should There Be Limits on Teachers' Freedom of Speech?" *Edutopia.* March. www.edutopia.org.

Brainy Quote. (2011). www.brainyquote.com.

BUCKLEY, W. F. (1951). *God and Man at Yale.* Chicago: Regnery.

DALY, J. K. (1991). "The Influence of Administrators on the Teaching of Social Studies." *Theory and Research in Social Education* 19:267–283.

DALY, J. K., AND ROACH, P. B. (1990). "Reaffirming a Commitment to Academic Freedom." *Social Education* 54:342–345.

DALY, J. K., SCHALL, P., AND SKEELE, R. (2001). *Protecting the Right to Teach and Learn.* New York: Teachers College Press.

DEWEY, J. (1936). "The Social Significance of Academic Freedom." *The Social Frontier* 2:136.

DOGAN, S. (2006). "A Rousing Success." April 11. www.frontpagemag.com.

EVANS, R. W. (2007). *This Happened in America: Harold Rugg and the Censure of Social Studies.* Charlotte, NC: Information Age Publishing.

FOERSTEL, H. N. (2002). *Banned in the USA.* Westport, CT: Greenwood Press.

Foundation for Individual Rights in Education. (2005). www.thefire.org.

FUENTES, C. (2005). *This I Believe.* New York: Random House.

Garcetti v. Ceballos. (2006). 547 US. 410.

GELLERMAN, W. (1938). *The American Legion as Educator.* New York: Teachers College Press.

GOLDSTEIN, S. (1976). "The Asserted Right of Teachers to Determine What They Teach." *University of Pennsylvania Law Review* 124(1):293.

HARDEN, N. (2012). "Academic Freedom, Terrorism, and the NYPD." *National Review Online.* www.nationalreview.com.

HOFSTADTER, R., AND METZGER, W. (1955, 1968). *The Development of Academic Freedom in the United States.* New York: Columbia University Press.

HOOK, S. (1953). *Heresy, Yes—Conspiracy, No.* New York: J. Day Co.

HOROWITZ, D. (2005). "Academic Freedom: David Horowitz vs. Russell Jacoby. July 29. www.frontpagemag.com.

HUFF, M., AND PHILLIPS, P. (2010). *Censored 2011.* New York: Seven Stories Press.

International Federation of Library Associations and Institutions. (1999). "Libraries and Intellectual Freedom." March 25.

JAPENGA, A. (1994). "A Teacher at War." *Mother Jones* 19:17.

JENKINSON, E. B. (1985). "Protecting Holden Caulfield and His Friends from the Censors." *English Journal* 74:26–33.

———. (1990). "Child Abuse in the Hate Factory." In *Academic Freedom to Teach and to Learn*, ed. A. Ochoa. Washington, DC: National Education Association.

Keyishian v. Board of Regents. (1967). 385 U.S. 589.

KIRK, R. (1955). *Academic Freedom.* Chicago: Regnery.

KLINE, M. A. (2008). "Cold War on Campus." *Campus Report* 23(4):1, 5. www.academic .org.

LA RUE, J. (2007). *The New Inquisition.* Westport CT: Libraries Unlimited.

LIMBAUGH, D. (2005). "False Promises of Academic Freedom." www.townhall.com/ columnists.

LINDORFF, D. (2005). "Academic Freedom? What Academic Freedom?" February 10. www.commondreams.org.

Mayer v. Monroe County Community School Corp. (2007). 474 F3rd 477,479-80 (7th Cir.), *cert. denied* 128 S. Ct. 160.

McNEIL, K. (2002). "The War on Academic Freedom." *The Nation.* November 25. www.thenation.com.

MENAND, L., ed. (1996). *The Future of Academic Freedom.* Chicago: University of Chicago Press.

MISCO, T., AND PATTERSON, N. C. (2007). "A Study of Pre-Service Teachers' Conceptualizations of Academic Freedom and Controversial Issues." *Theory and Research in Social Education* 35(4):520–550.

MOSHMAN, D. (2009). *Liberty and Learning.* Portsmouth, NH: Heinemann.

National Coalition Against Censorship. (2012). "Censorship Arizona Style." www.ncac .org. Feb 10.

National Council for the Social Studies. (1974). *The Freedom to Teach and the Freedom to Learn.* Washington, DC: National Council for the Social Studies.

———. (2012). "Academic Freedom and the Social Studies Teacher." www.ncss.org.

NAKAYA, A. C., ed. (2005). *Censorship: Opposing Viewpoints.* New York: Thomson Gale.

NELSON, J. (1990). "The Significance of and Rationale for Academic Freedom." In *Academic Freedom to Teach and to Learn*, ed. A. Ochoa. Washington, DC: National Education Association.

———. (2003). "Academic Freedom, Academic Integrity, and Teacher Education." *Teacher Education Quarterly* 30(1):65–72.

———. (2010). "The Need for Courage in American Schools" *Social Education* 74(6):298–303.

NOBLE, W. (1990). *Bookbanning in America.* Middlebury, VT: Paul Ericksson.

NODDINGS, N. (1999). "Renewing Democracy in Schools." *Kappan* 80(8):579–583.

O'CONNOR, E. (2005). "Academic Freedom Does Time." www.ericoconnor.org.

OLSON, K. Indoctrination. Bloomington, IN: Authorhouse publishers.

O'NEIL, R. M. (1981). *Classrooms in the Crossfire.* Bloomington: Indiana University Press.

———. (2008). *Academic Freedom in the Wired World.* Cambridge, MA: Harvard University Press.

———. (2010). "Legal Issues in the Protection of Student Freedoms." *Social Education.* 74(6), 322–325.

Parents Against Bad Books in Schools. (2011). www.pabbis.org.

PATTERSON, N. C. (2010). "What's Stopping You? Classroom Censorship for Better or Worse." *Social Education.* 74(6), 326-331.

PIERCE, B. (1933). *Citizens' Organizations and the Civic Training of Youth.* New York: Scribner's.

PIPKIN, G., AND LENT, R. C. (2002). *The Schoolhouse Gate: Lessons in Intellectual Freedom.* Portsmouth, NH: Heinemann.

PUDDINGTON, A., MELIA, R. O., AND KELLY, J. (2008). *Today's Americans: How Free?* Lanham, MD: Rowman & Littlefield.

RORTY, R. (1994). "Does Academic Freedom Have Philosophical Presuppositions?" *Academe* 80:52–63.

ROSS, S. J. (2004). "21st Century Book-Burning," *Los Angeles Times.* October 14. www .commondreams.org.

RUBIN, D., AND GREENHOUSE, S. (1983). *The Rights of Teachers: The Basic ACLU Guide to a Teacher's Constitutional Rights.* Rev. Ed. New York: Bantam.

RYAN, K. (2011). "Public School Indoctrination." www.thecrisismagazine.com.

SEESHOLTZ, M. (2005). "Diversity, Academic Freedom and Conservative T-Shirts." July 11. www.counterbias.org.

SHERROW, V. (1996). *Censorship in Schools.* Springfield, NJ: Enslow Publishers.

———. (1994). *Censorship: A Threat to Reading, Learning, Thinking.* Newark, DE: International Reading Association.

SIMPSON, M. D. (2010). "Defending Academic Freedom: Advice for Teachers." *Social Education* 74(6):310–315.

SINCLAIR, U. (1922). *The Goose-Step.* Pasadena, CA: Sinclair.

———. (1923). *The Goslings.* Pasadena, CA: Sinclair.

SIPE, R. B. (1999). "Don't Confront Censors, Prepare for Them." *Education Digest* 64(6):42–46.

SOWELL, T. (2005). "Academic Freedom?" February 15. www.townhall.com/columnists.

STANDLER, R. B. (2000). "Academic Freedom in the USA." www.rbs2.com/academic freedom.

STERN, S. (2006a). "High School Indoctrination." March 8. www.frontpagemagazine.com.

———. (2006b). "Pinko Teachers, Inc." March 12. www.nypost.com.

———. (2006c). "Social Justice and Other High School Indoctrinations." April 13. www .frontpagemag.com.

STILLE, A. (2002). "Textbook Publishers Learn to Avoid Messing with Texas." June 29. www.nytimes.com.

STONE, G. R. (2004). *Perilous Times: Free Speech in Wartime.* New York: Norton.

Students for Academic Freedom. (2003). "Academic Bill of Rights." www.studentsfor academicfreedom.org.

THELIN, J. (1997). "Zealotry and Academic Freedom." *History of Education Quarterly* 37(3):338–420.

Tinker v. Des Moines Independent School District. (1969). 393 U.S. 503, 510–11.

TROMBETTA, J. (2010). *The Horror, The Horror!: Comic Books the Government Didn't Want You to Read.* New York: Abrams Comic Arts.

United States v. American Library Association, Inc. (2003). 539 U.S. 194.

VANDERGRIFT, K. (2012). "Censorship, the Internet, Intellectual Freedom, and Youth." SCILS, Rutgers University. www.comminfo.edu. April.

VEBLEN, T. (1957). *The Higher Learning in America: Memorandum on the Conduct of Universities by Businessmen.* New York: Sagamore.

Wall Street Journal. (2012). "Tennessee Legislature Passes Landmark Academic Freedom on Evolution Bill." www.marketwatch.org. Mar. 26.

WHITSON, J. A. (1993). "After Hazelwood: The Role of School Officials in Conflicts over the Curriculum." *ALAN Review* 20:2–6.

Wieman v. Updegraff. (1952). 244 U.S. 183.

WILSON, J. K. (2006). "Interview with David Horowitz." March. www.collegefreedom.org.

———. (2008). *Patriotic Correctness: Academic Freedom and Its Enemies.* Boulder, CO: Paradigm Press.

ZIRKEL, P. (1993). "Academic Freedom: Professional or Legal Right?" *Educational Leadership* 50:42–43.

Index